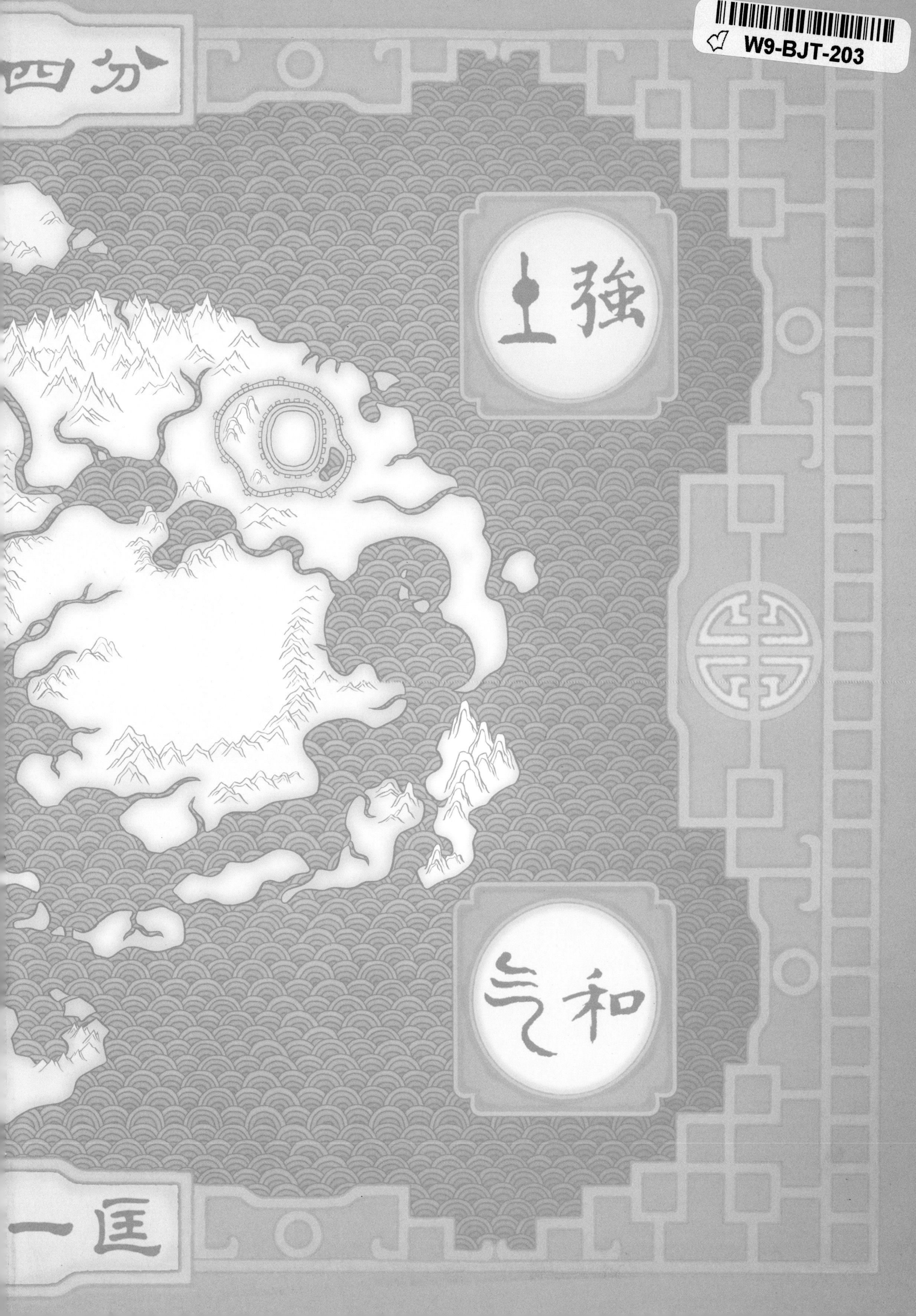
四分
強
和

AVATAR
THE LAST AIRBENDER

Created by

BRYAN KONIETZKO

MICHAEL DANTE
DiMARTINO

nickelodeon

降世神通

AVATAR

THE LAST AIRBENDER

NORTH AND SOUTH

GENE
LUEN YANG
Script

GURIHIRU
Art & Cover

MICHAEL
HEISLER
Lettering

DARK HORSE BOOKS

MIKE RICHARDSON
Publisher

DAVE MARSHALL
Editor

RACHEL ROBERTS
Assistant Editor

JUSTIN COUCH
Collection Designer

CHRISTIANNE GOUDREAU
Digital Art Technician

Translation by AKI YANAGI

Special thanks to LINDA LEE,
KAT VAN DAM, JAMES SALERNO, *and* JOAN HILTY
at Nickelodeon, and to BRYAN KONIETZKO *and*
MICHAEL DANTE DiMARTINO.

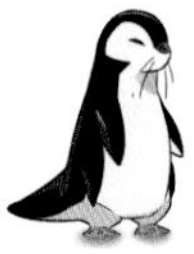

9 10 8

ISBN 978-1-50670-195-0 Nick.com DarkHorse.com First edition: October 2017

Published by **DARK HORSE BOOKS**, a division of Dark Horse Comics LLC, 10956 SE Main Street, Milwaukie, OR 97222

To find a comics shop in your area, visit comicshoplocator.com

This book collects *Avatar: The Last Airbender—North and South* Parts 1 through 3.

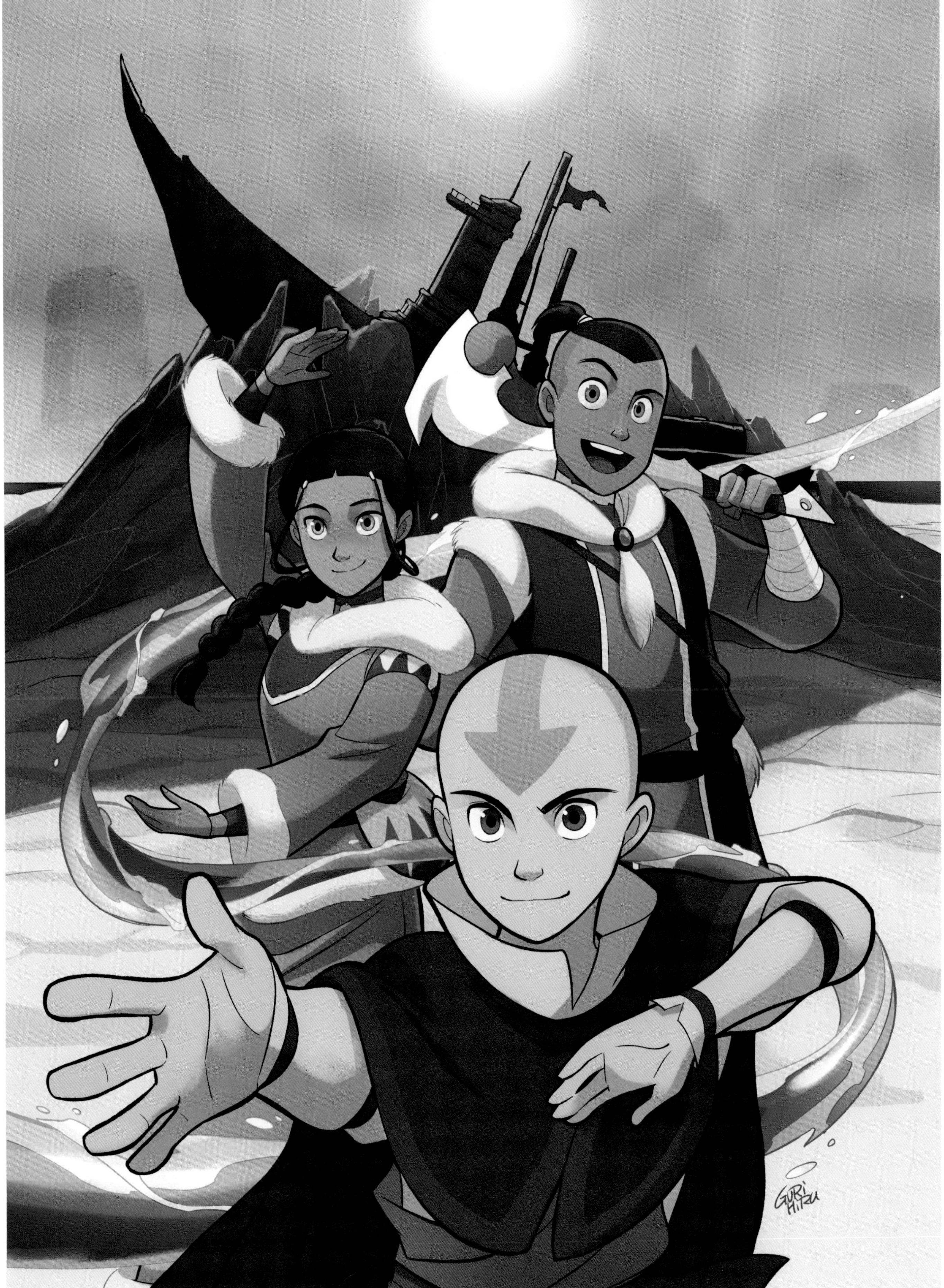
GURI HIRU

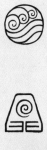

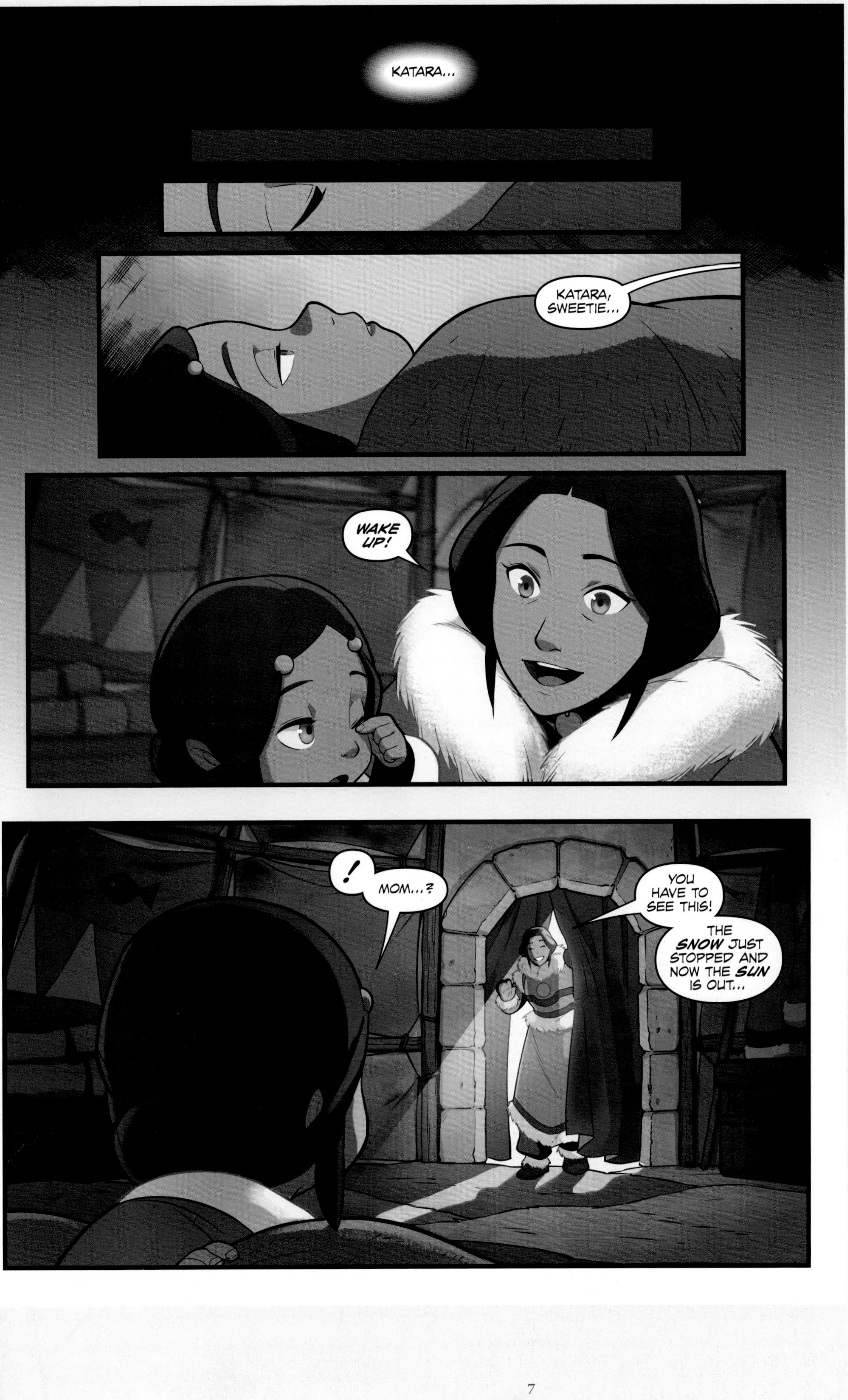
KATARA...
KATARA, SWEETIE...
WAKE UP!
!
MOM...?
YOU HAVE TO SEE THIS!
THE SNOW JUST STOPPED AND NOW THE SUN IS OUT...

GENE LUEN YANG: *I love the way Gurihiru draw little-kid Katara. So cute!*

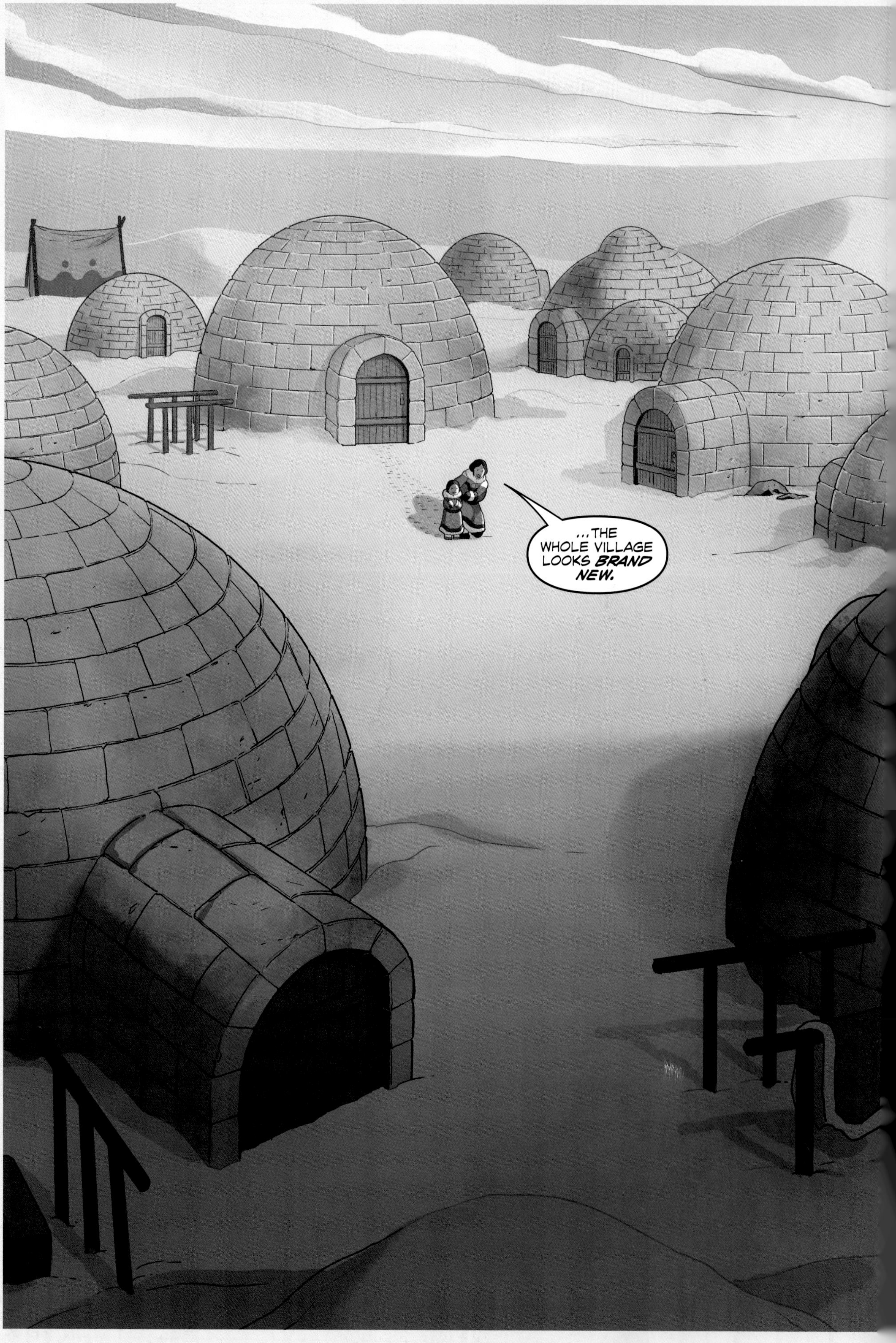
...THE WHOLE VILLAGE LOOKS BRAND NEW.

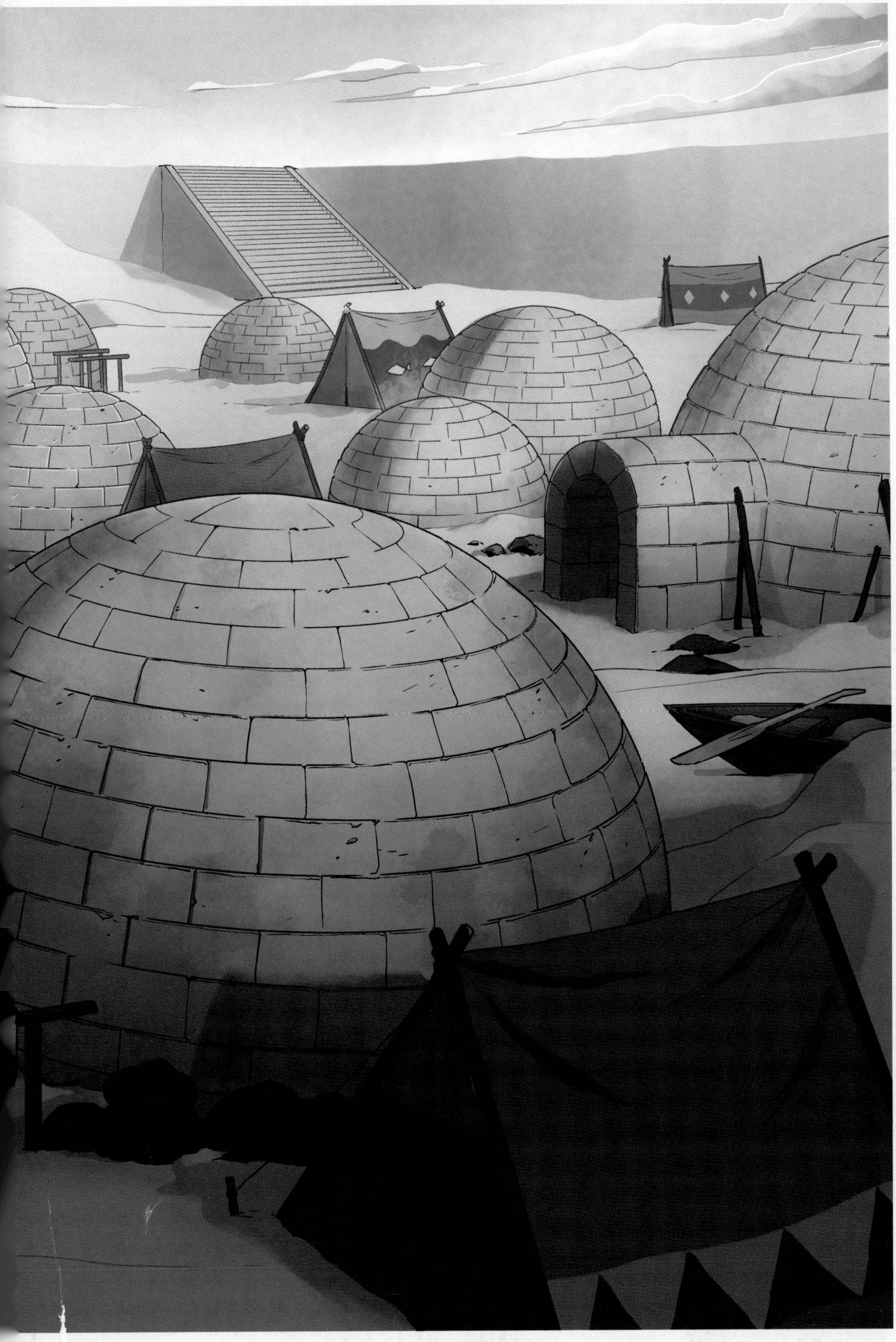

GURIHIRU: *Young Katara still has a bit of innocence, and we think we were able to make her adorable.*

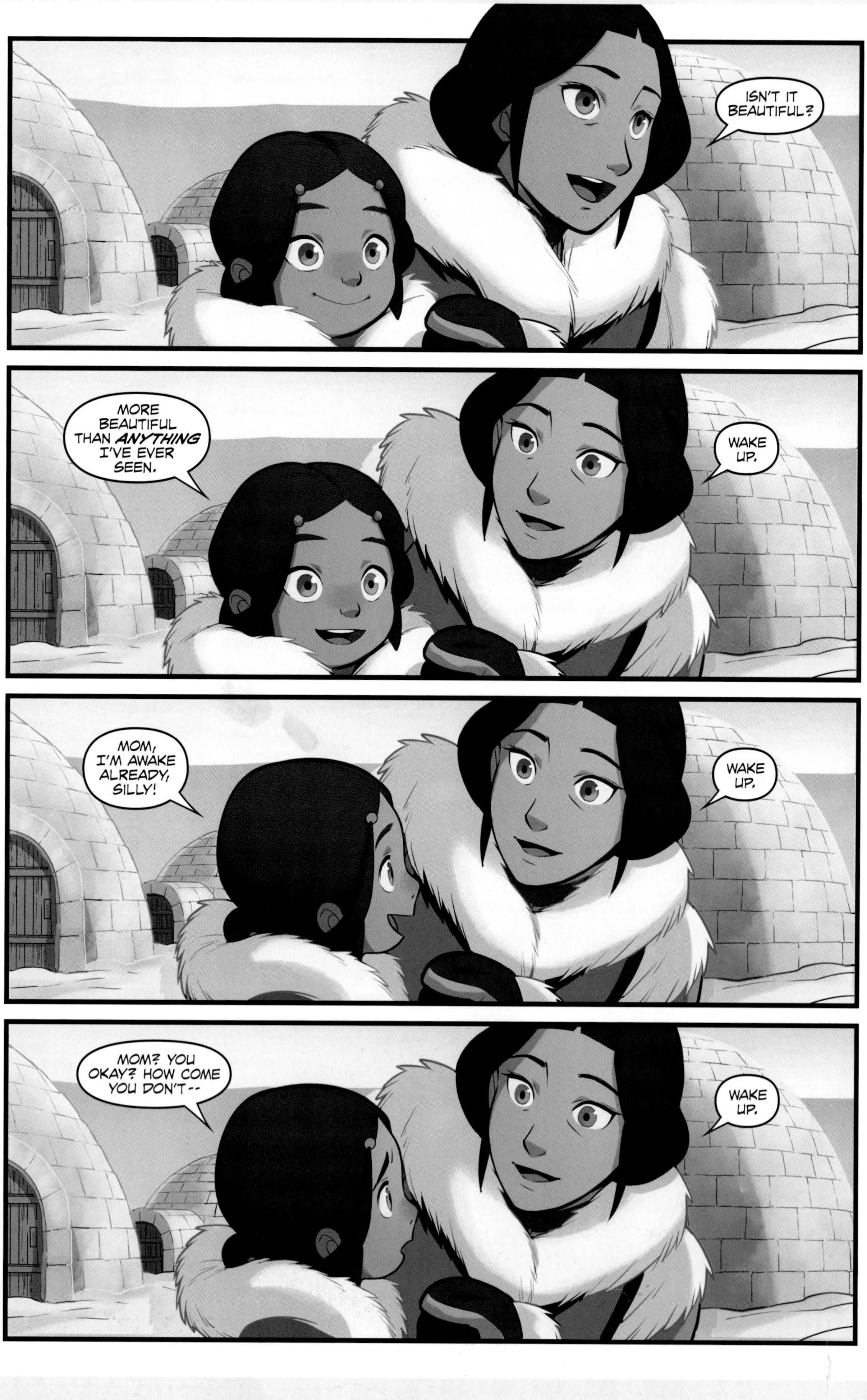
ISN'T IT BEAUTIFUL?
MORE BEAUTIFUL THAN ANYTHING I'VE EVER SEEN.
WAKE UP.
MOM, I'M AWAKE ALREADY, SILLY!
WAKE UP.
MOM? YOU OKAY? HOW COME YOU DON'T--
WAKE UP.

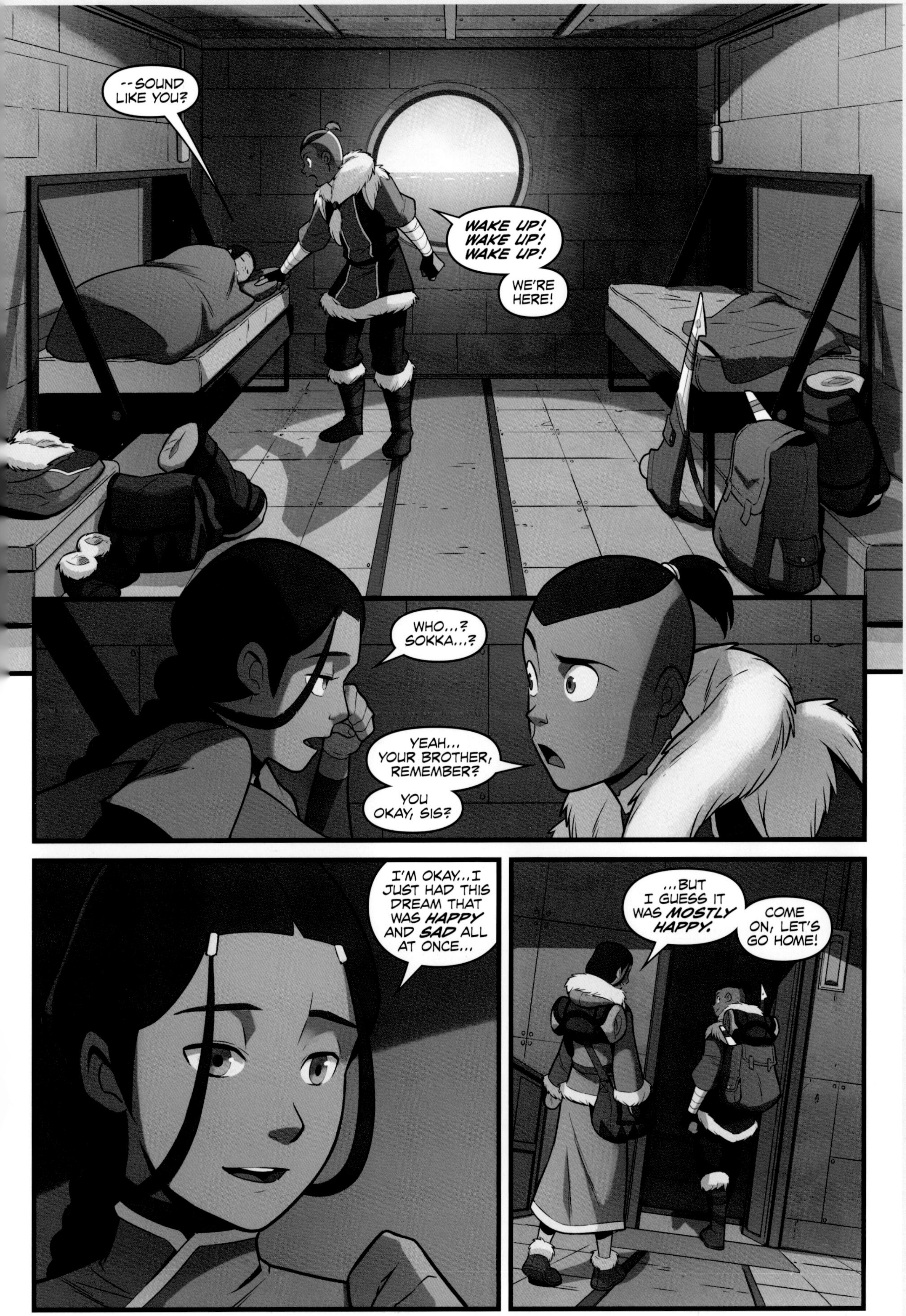
--SOUND LIKE YOU?
WAKE UP! WAKE UP! WAKE UP!
WE'RE HERE!
WHO...? SOKKA...?
YEAH... YOUR BROTHER, REMEMBER?
YOU OKAY, SIS?
I'M OKAY...I JUST HAD THIS DREAM THAT WAS HAPPY AND SAD ALL AT ONCE...
...BUT I GUESS IT WAS MOSTLY HAPPY.
COME ON, LET'S GO HOME!

GLY: *Before North and South, Gurihiru and I had done four volumes of Avatar: The Last Airbender comics. We'd focused on every member of Team Avatar except Katara and Sokka. We felt that it was time to give the two siblings from the South Pole their due.*

G: *For these books, we brought Katara back to her Water Tribe hairstyle.*

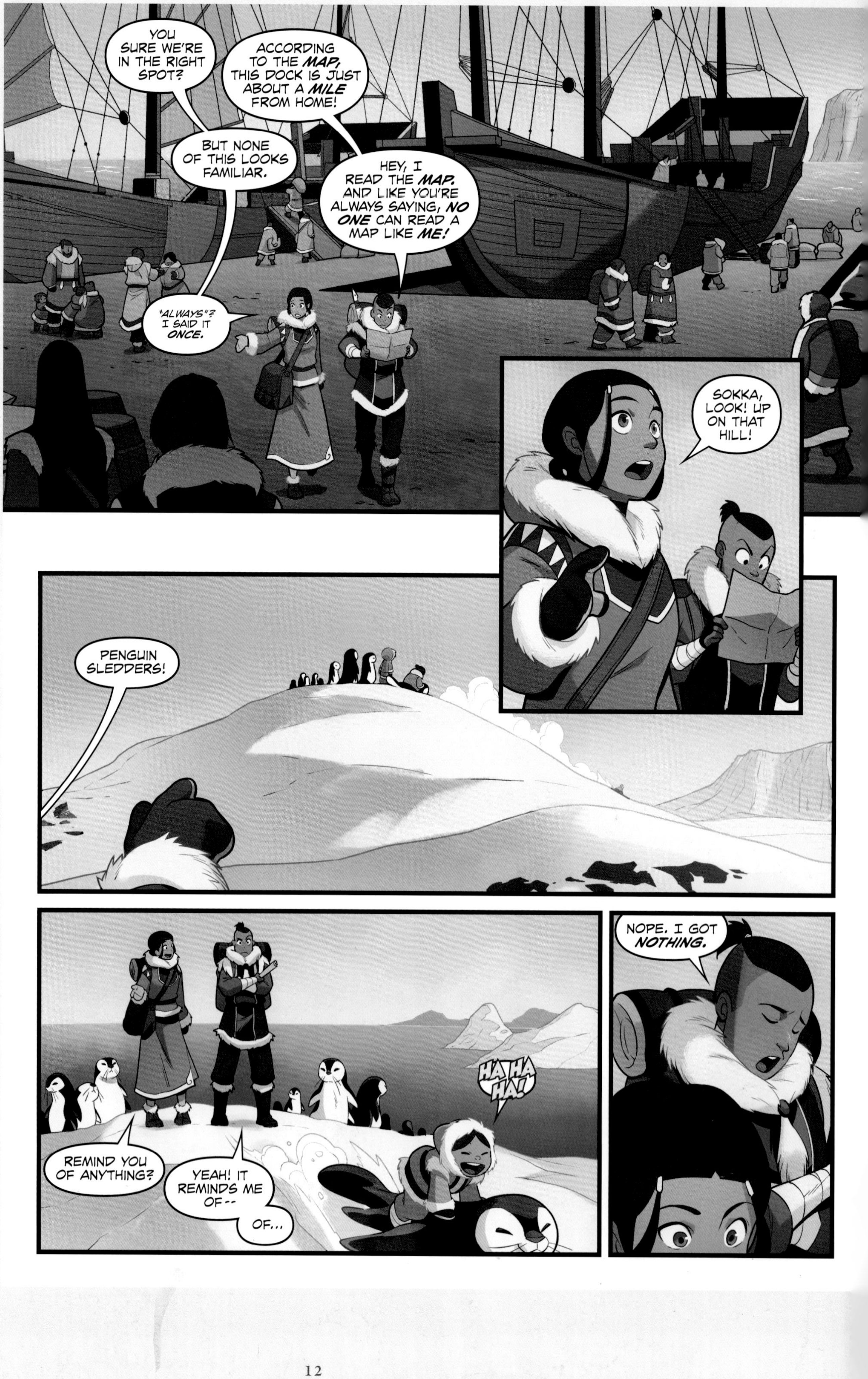
YOU SURE WE'RE IN THE RIGHT SPOT?
ACCORDING TO THE MAP, THIS DOCK IS JUST ABOUT A MILE FROM HOME!
BUT NONE OF THIS LOOKS FAMILIAR.
HEY, I READ THE MAP. AND LIKE YOU'RE ALWAYS SAYING, NO ONE CAN READ A MAP LIKE ME!
"ALWAYS"? I SAID IT ONCE.
SOKKA, LOOK! UP ON THAT HILL!
PENGUIN SLEDDERS!
HA HA HA!
REMIND YOU OF ANYTHING?
YEAH! IT REMINDS ME OF--
OF...
NOPE. I GOT NOTHING.

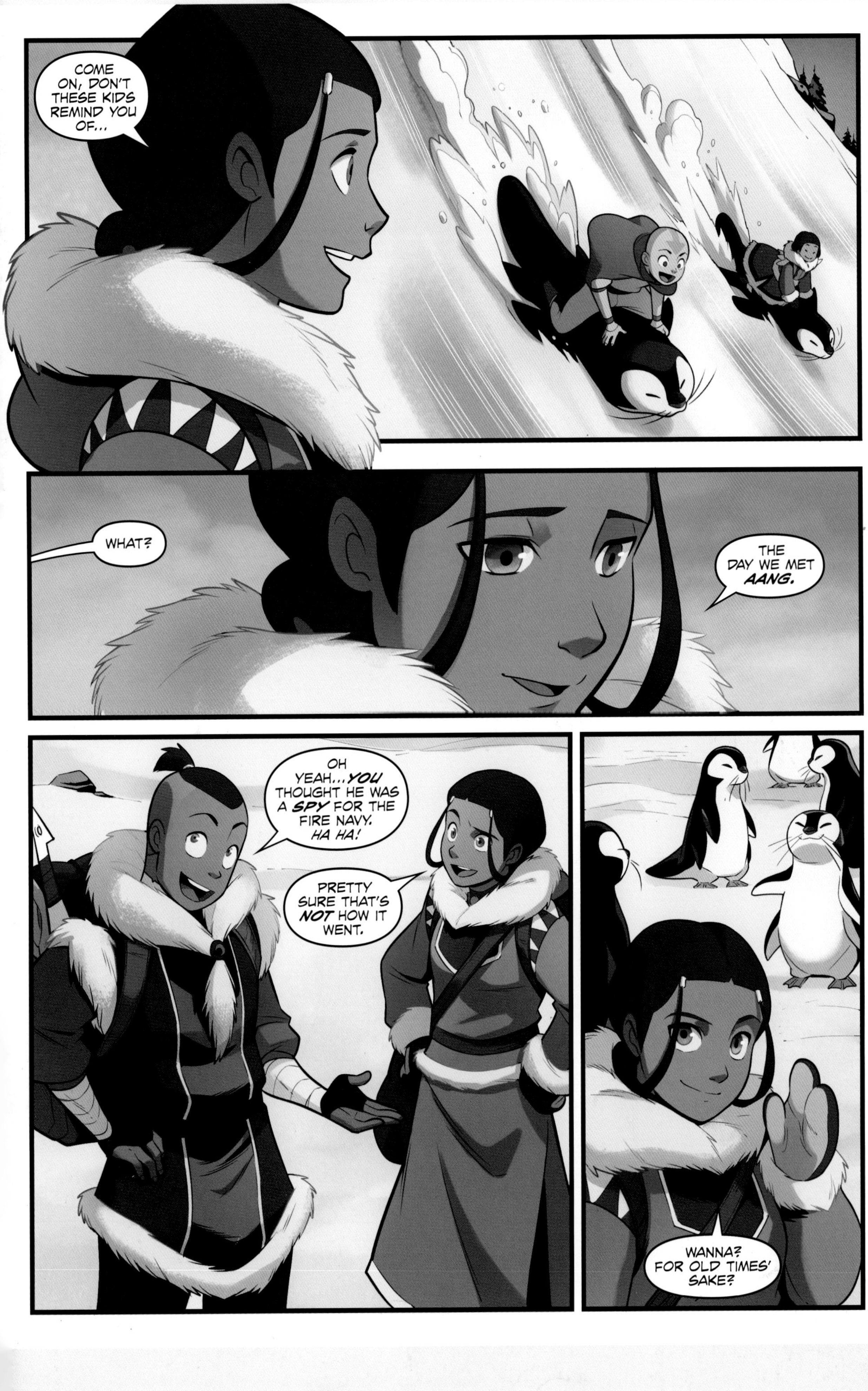
COME ON, DON'T THESE KIDS REMIND YOU OF...
WHAT?
THE DAY WE MET AANG.
OH YEAH...YOU THOUGHT HE WAS A SPY FOR THE FIRE NAVY. HA HA!
PRETTY SURE THAT'S NOT HOW IT WENT.
WANNA? FOR OLD TIMES' SAKE?

GLY: *This is a reference to "The Boy in the Iceberg," the very first episode of the Avatar: The Last Airbender television series. Within moments of waking up from his decades-long imprisonment, Aang invites Katara and Sokka to go penguin sledding. It's a brilliant scene that brings out the characters' personalities and accomplishes some slyly efficient world building.*

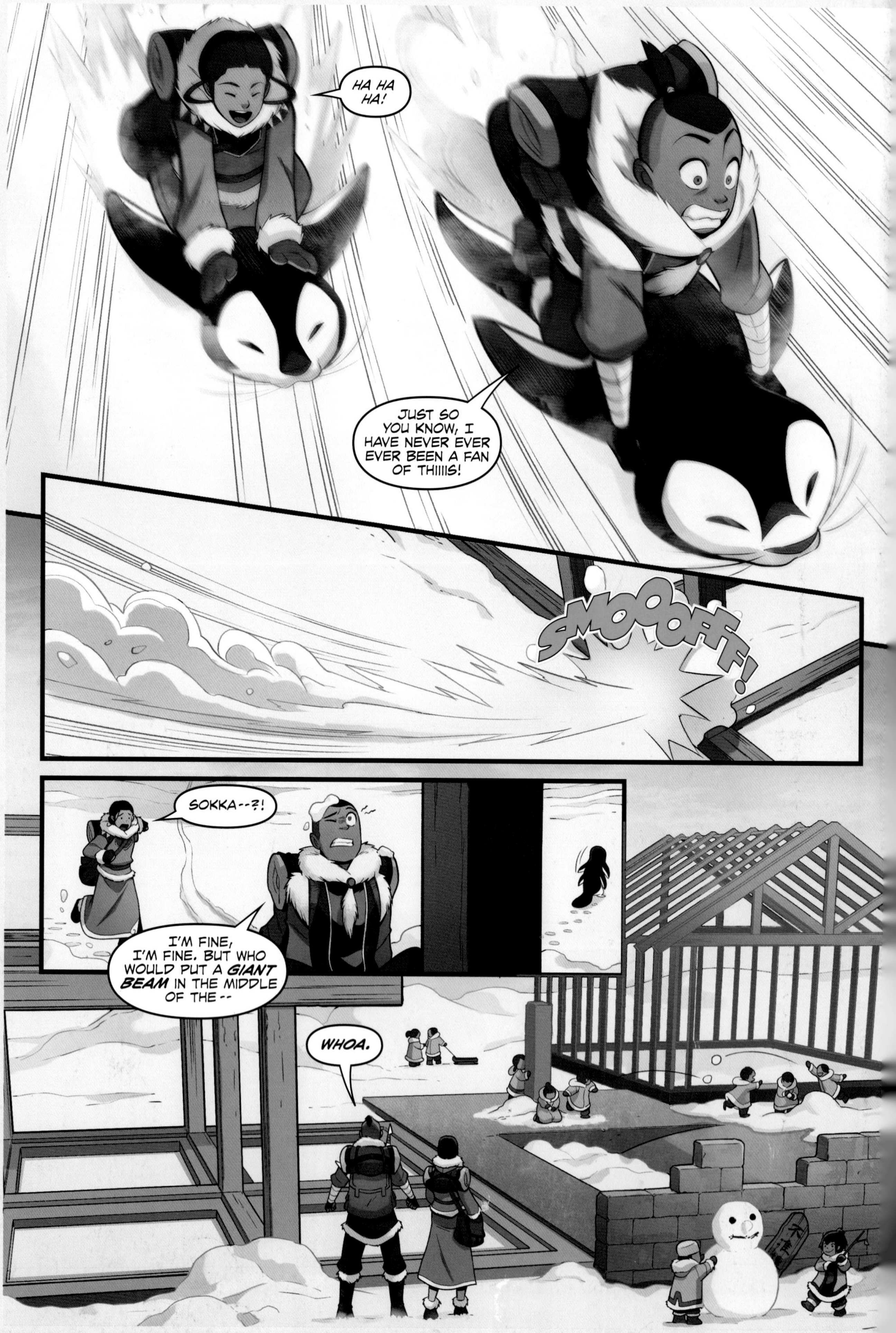
HA HA HA!
JUST SO YOU KNOW, I HAVE NEVER EVER EVER BEEN A FAN OF THIIIIS!
SMOOOOFFF!
SOKKA--?!
I'M FINE, I'M FINE. BUT WHO WOULD PUT A GIANT BEAM IN THE MIDDLE OF THE --
WHOA.

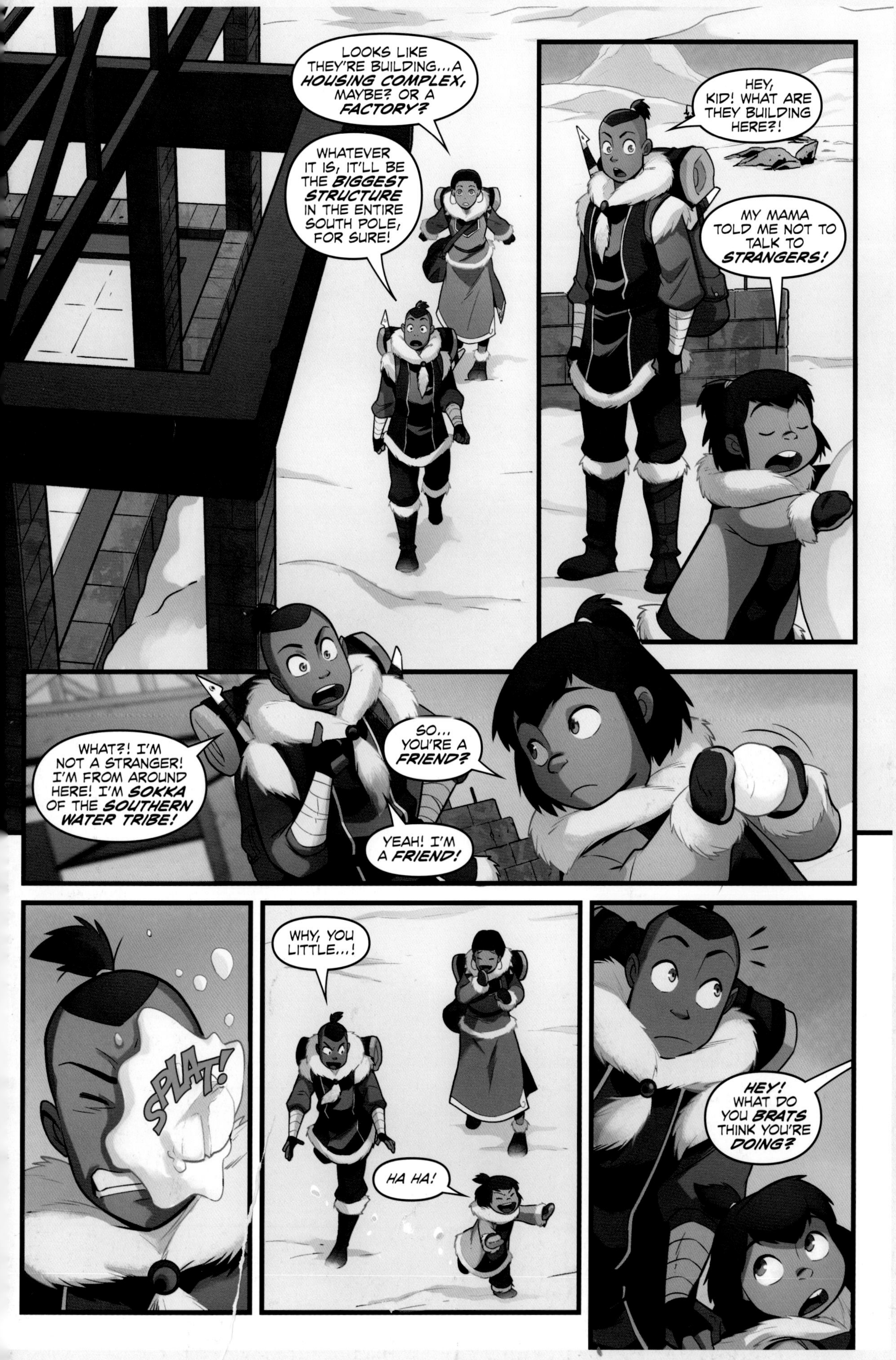
LOOKS LIKE THEY'RE BUILDING...A HOUSING COMPLEX, MAYBE? OR A FACTORY?
WHATEVER IT IS, IT'LL BE THE BIGGEST STRUCTURE IN THE ENTIRE SOUTH POLE, FOR SURE!
HEY, KID! WHAT ARE THEY BUILDING HERE?!
MY MAMA TOLD ME NOT TO TALK TO STRANGERS!
WHAT?! I'M NOT A STRANGER! I'M FROM AROUND HERE! I'M SOKKA OF THE SOUTHERN WATER TRIBE!
SO... YOU'RE A FRIEND?
YEAH! I'M A FRIEND!
SPLAT!
WHY, YOU LITTLE...!
HA HA!
HEY! WHAT DO YOU BRATS THINK YOU'RE DOING?

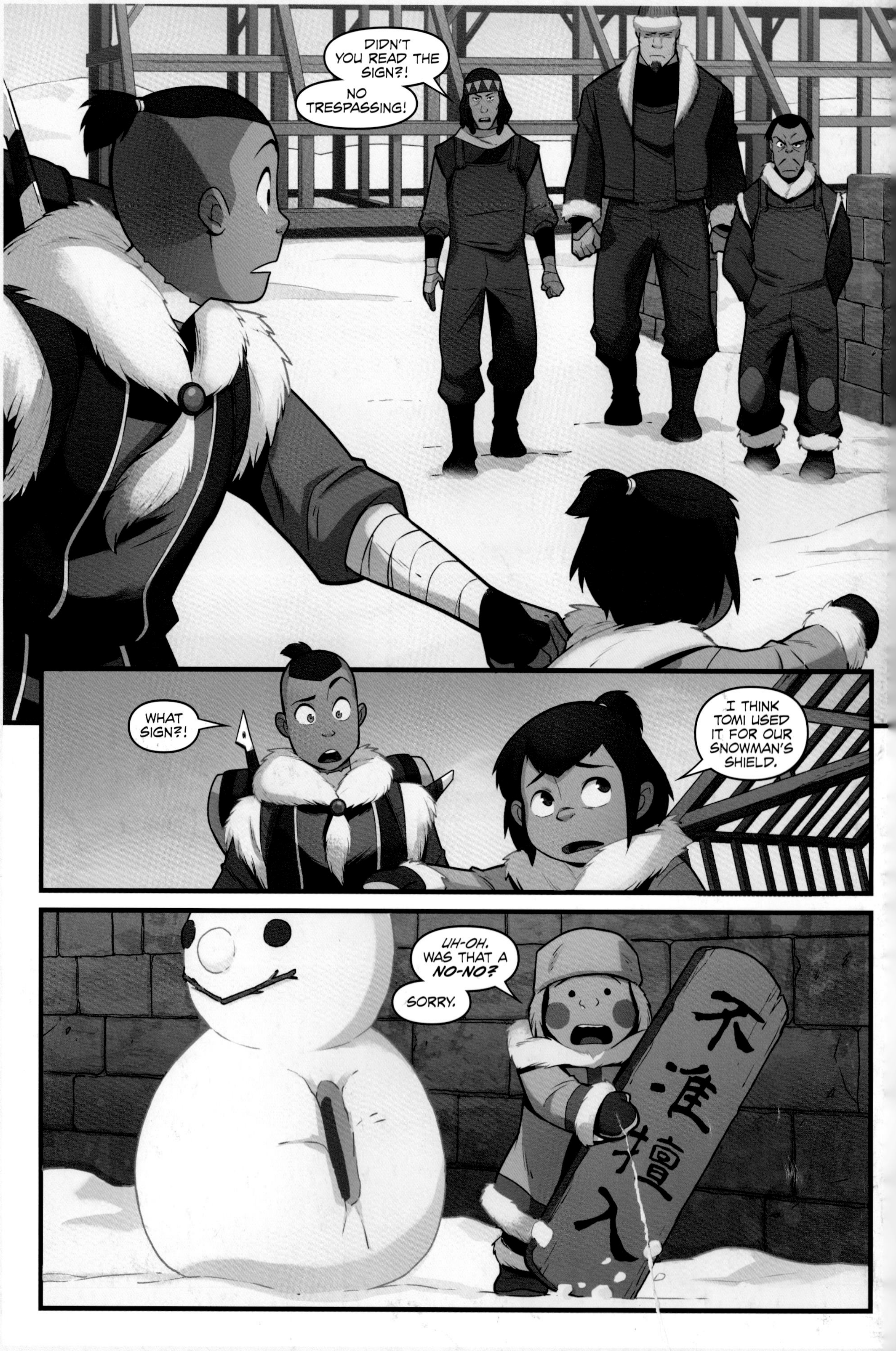
DIDN'T YOU READ THE SIGN?!
NO TRESPASSING!
WHAT SIGN?!
I THINK TOMI USED IT FOR OUR SNOWMAN'S SHIELD.
UH-OH. WAS THAT A *NO-NO?*
SORRY.
不准擅入

GLY: *In The Legend of Korra, the nations have gotten used to partnering together. We wanted to show the beginnings of that here by including an Earthbender in the construction crew.*

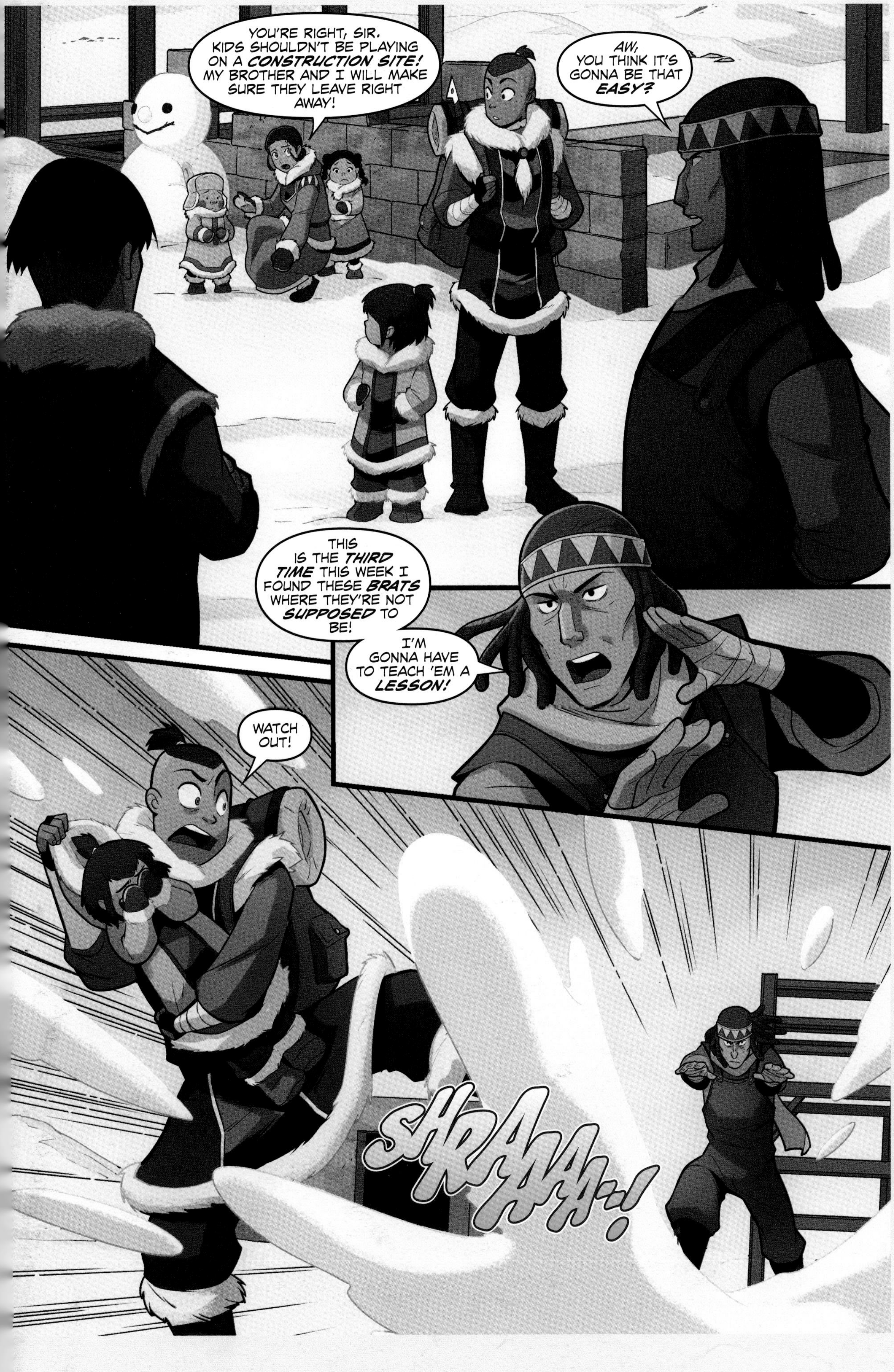
YOU'RE RIGHT, SIR. KIDS SHOULDN'T BE PLAYING ON A CONSTRUCTION SITE! MY BROTHER AND I WILL MAKE SURE THEY LEAVE RIGHT AWAY!
AW, YOU THINK IT'S GONNA BE THAT EASY?
THIS IS THE THIRD TIME THIS WEEK I FOUND THESE BRATS WHERE THEY'RE NOT SUPPOSED TO BE!
I'M GONNA HAVE TO TEACH 'EM A LESSON!
WATCH OUT!
SHRAAAA--!

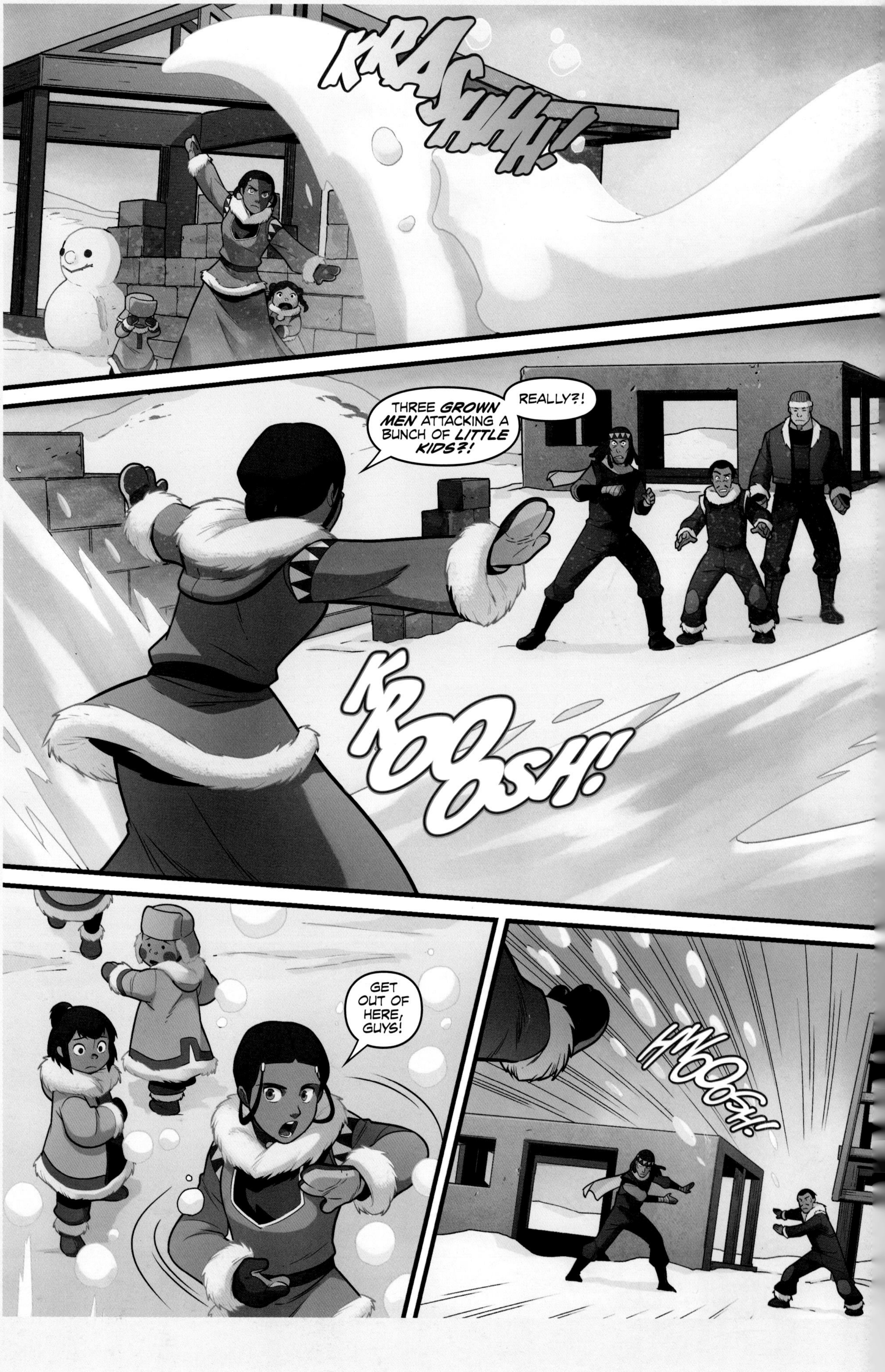
KRASHHH!
THREE GROWN MEN ATTACKING A BUNCH OF LITTLE KIDS?!
REALLY?!
KROOOSH!
GET OUT OF HERE, GUYS!
HWOOSH!

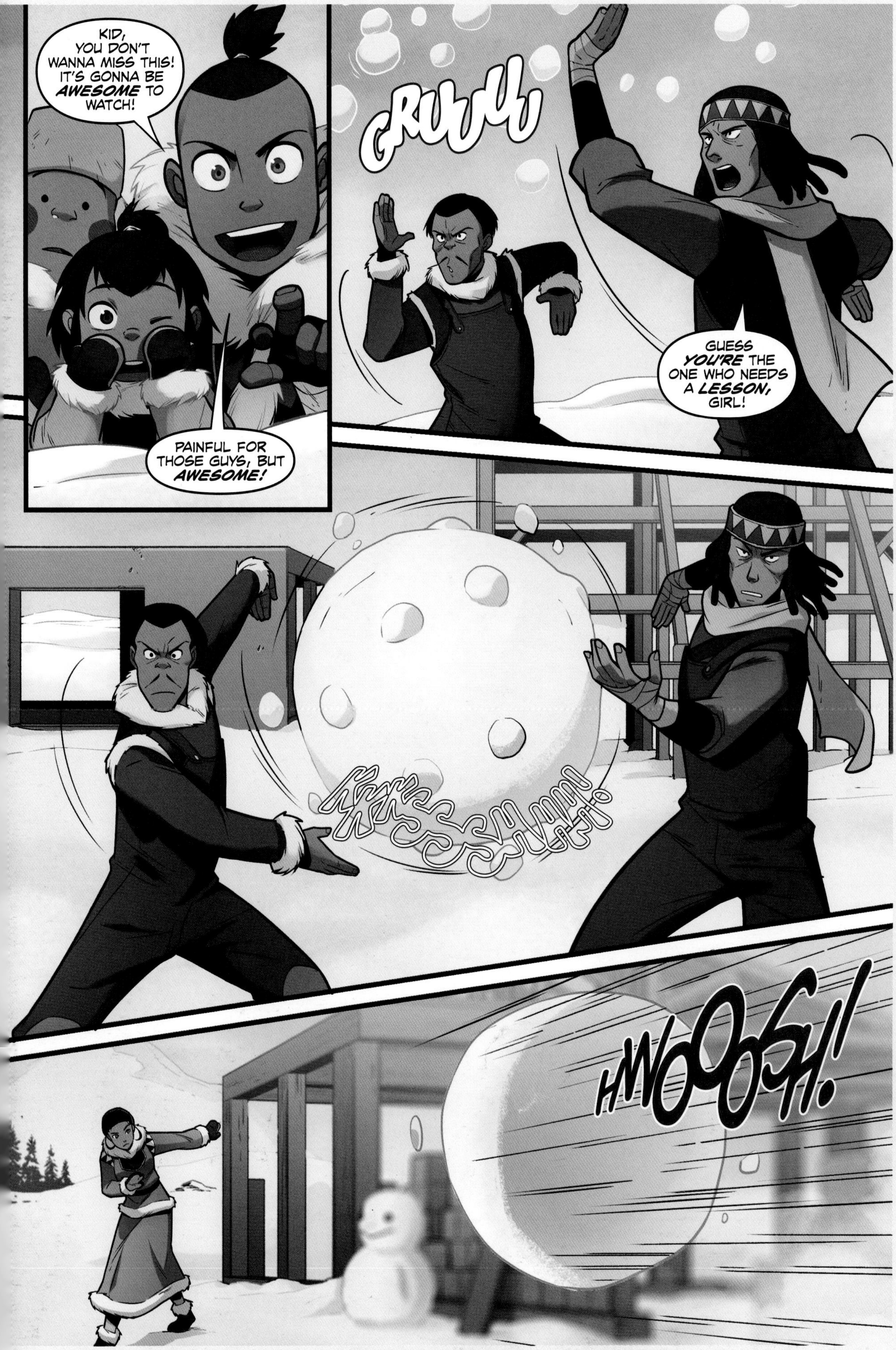
KID, YOU DON'T WANNA MISS THIS! IT'S GONNA BE AWESOME TO WATCH!
PAINFUL FOR THOSE GUYS, BUT AWESOME!
GRUUU
GUESS YOU'RE THE ONE WHO NEEDS A LESSON, GIRL!
HWOOOSH!

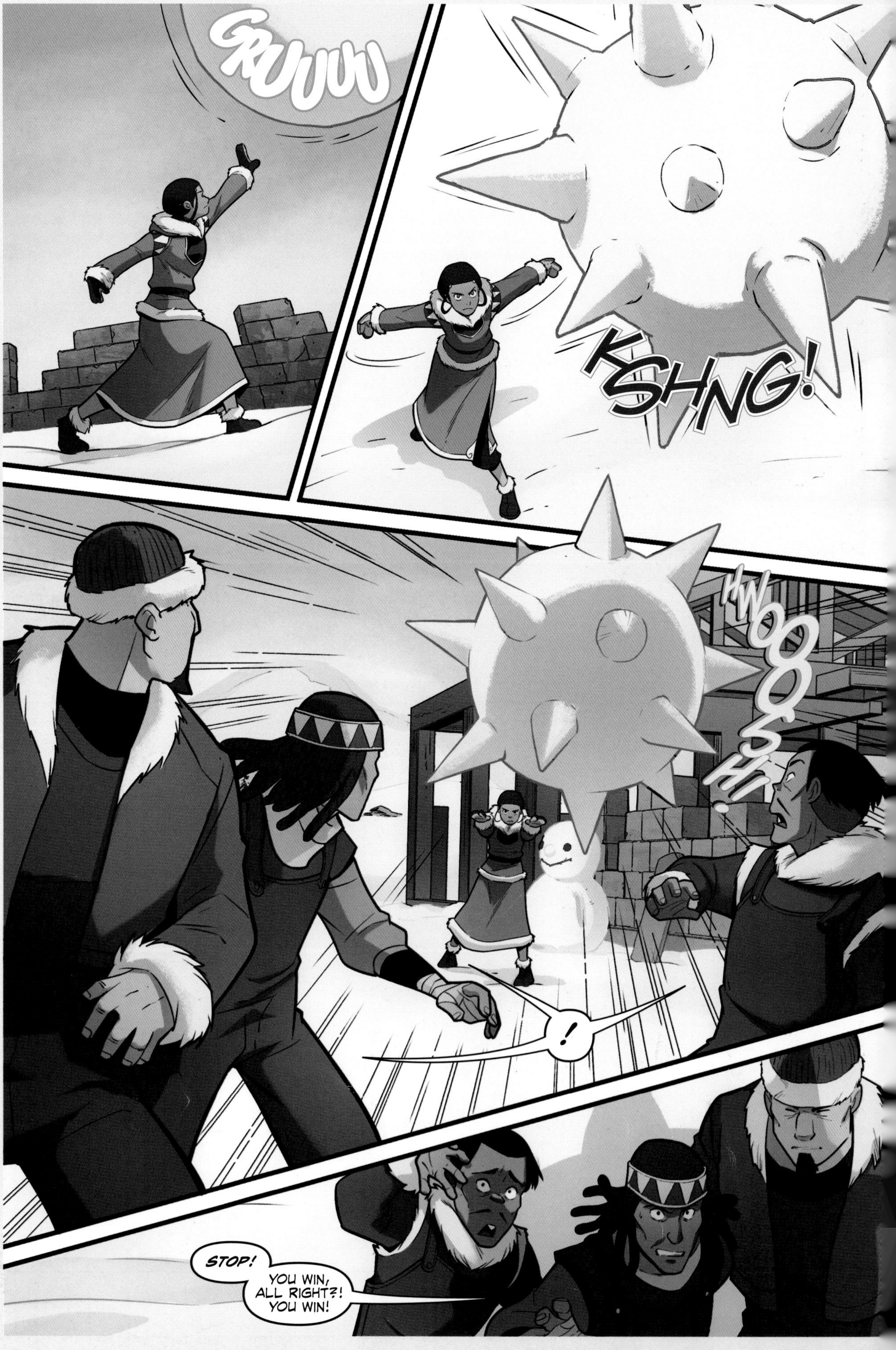
GRUUUU
KSHNG!
HWOOOSH!
!
STOP!
YOU WIN, ALL RIGHT?! YOU WIN!

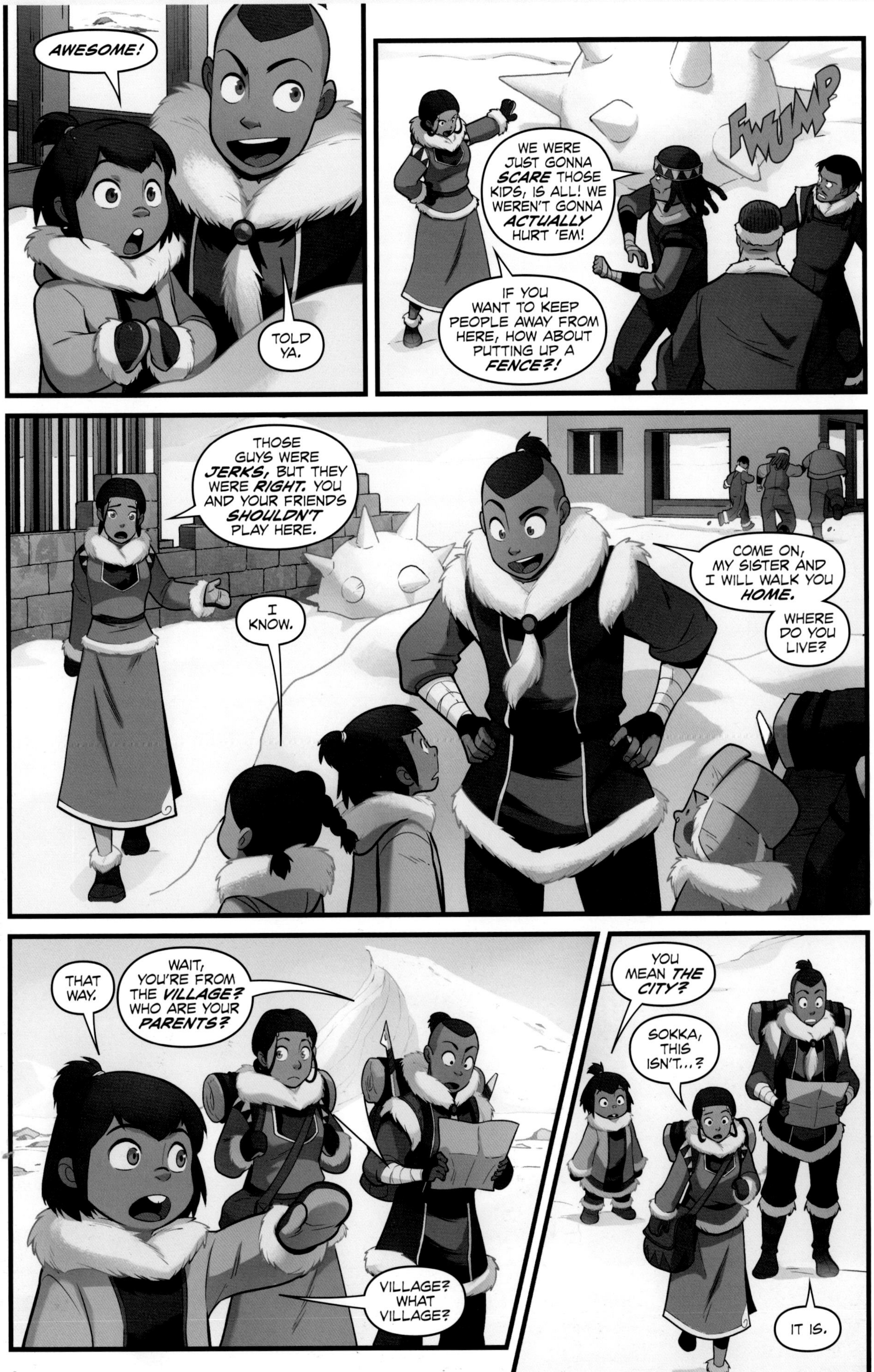
AWESOME!
TOLD YA.
FWUMP
WE WERE JUST GONNA SCARE THOSE KIDS, IS ALL! WE WEREN'T GONNA ACTUALLY HURT 'EM!
IF YOU WANT TO KEEP PEOPLE AWAY FROM HERE, HOW ABOUT PUTTING UP A FENCE?!
THOSE GUYS WERE JERKS, BUT THEY WERE RIGHT. YOU AND YOUR FRIENDS SHOULDN'T PLAY HERE.
I KNOW.
COME ON, MY SISTER AND I WILL WALK YOU HOME.
WHERE DO YOU LIVE?
THAT WAY.
WAIT, YOU'RE FROM THE VILLAGE? WHO ARE YOUR PARENTS?
VILLAGE? WHAT VILLAGE?
YOU MEAN THE CITY?
SOKKA, THIS ISN'T...?
IT IS.

GLY: *A recurring theme of the graphic novel series is modernization. What are the consequences of societal and technological development, both the good and the bad? In the real world, modernization often means "Westernization," a proliferation of Western culture. Even though there's no real "West" in the Avatar universe, we wanted to hint at some of the same dynamics.*

G: *It was hard to decide how much the Water Tribe has changed from being a small village. We imagined that the technology from the Northern Water Tribe and the Earth Kingdom both have affected the village, so while it may not be as big as the Northern Water Tribe, we made the city a bit bigger.*

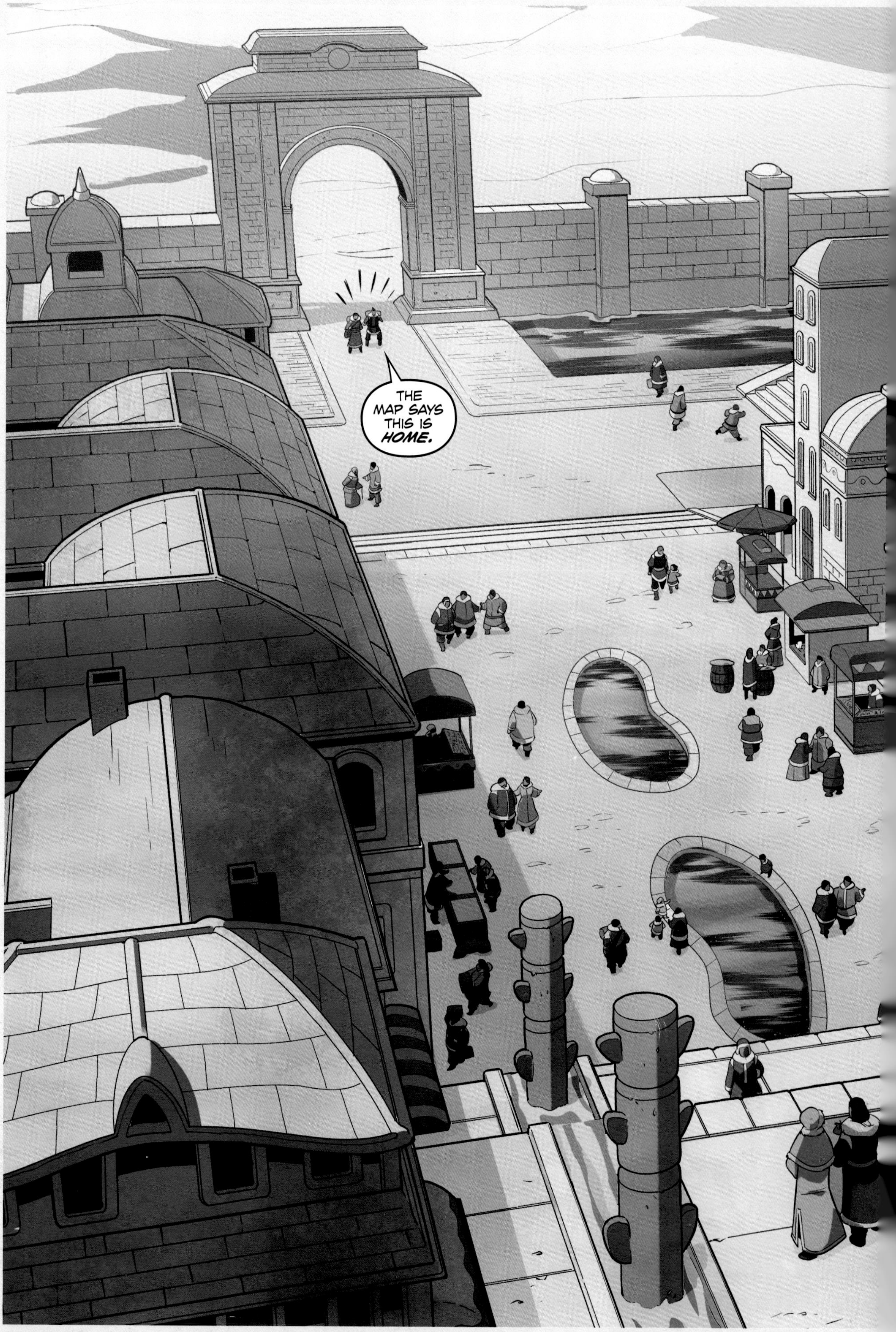
THE MAP SAYS THIS IS HOME.

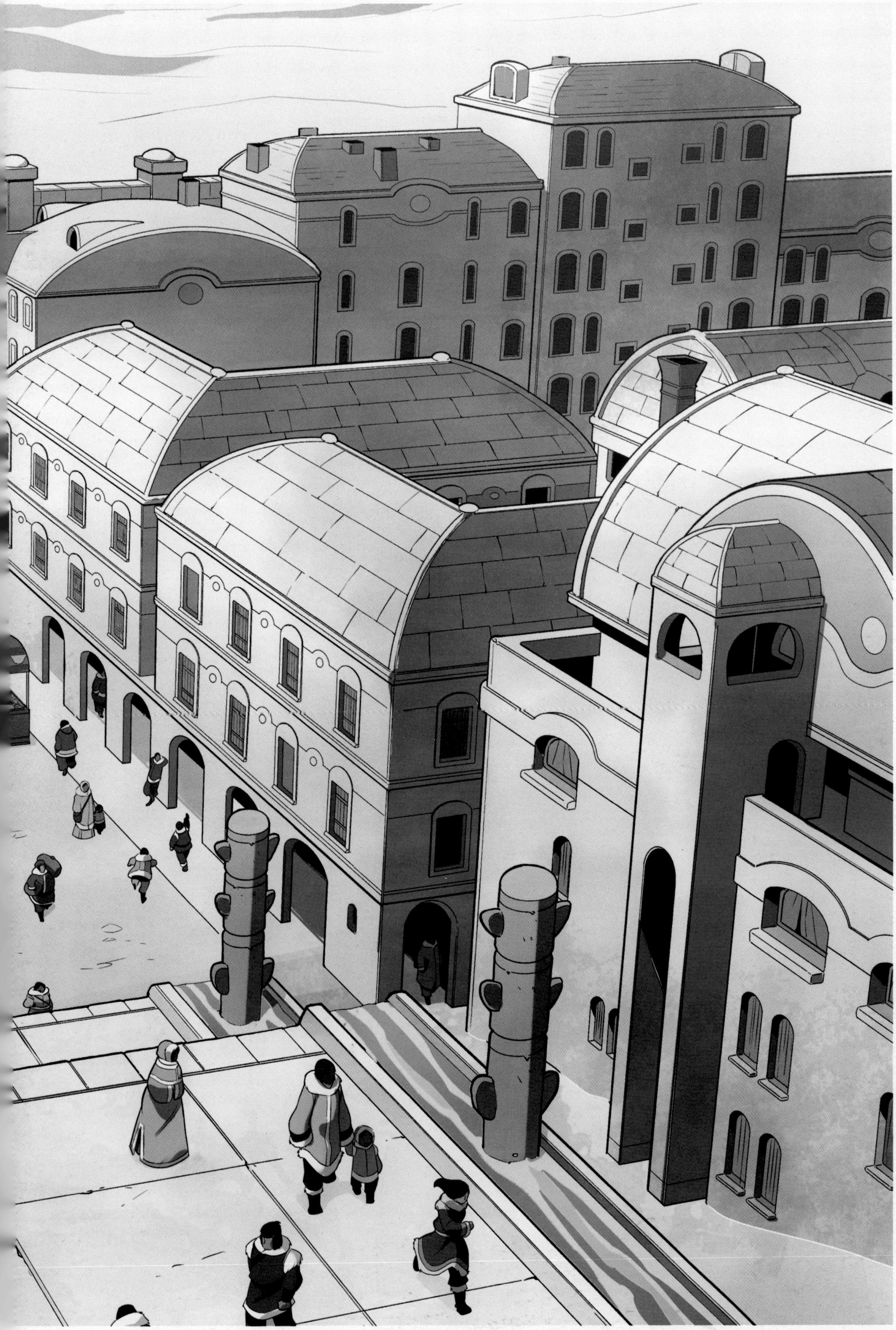

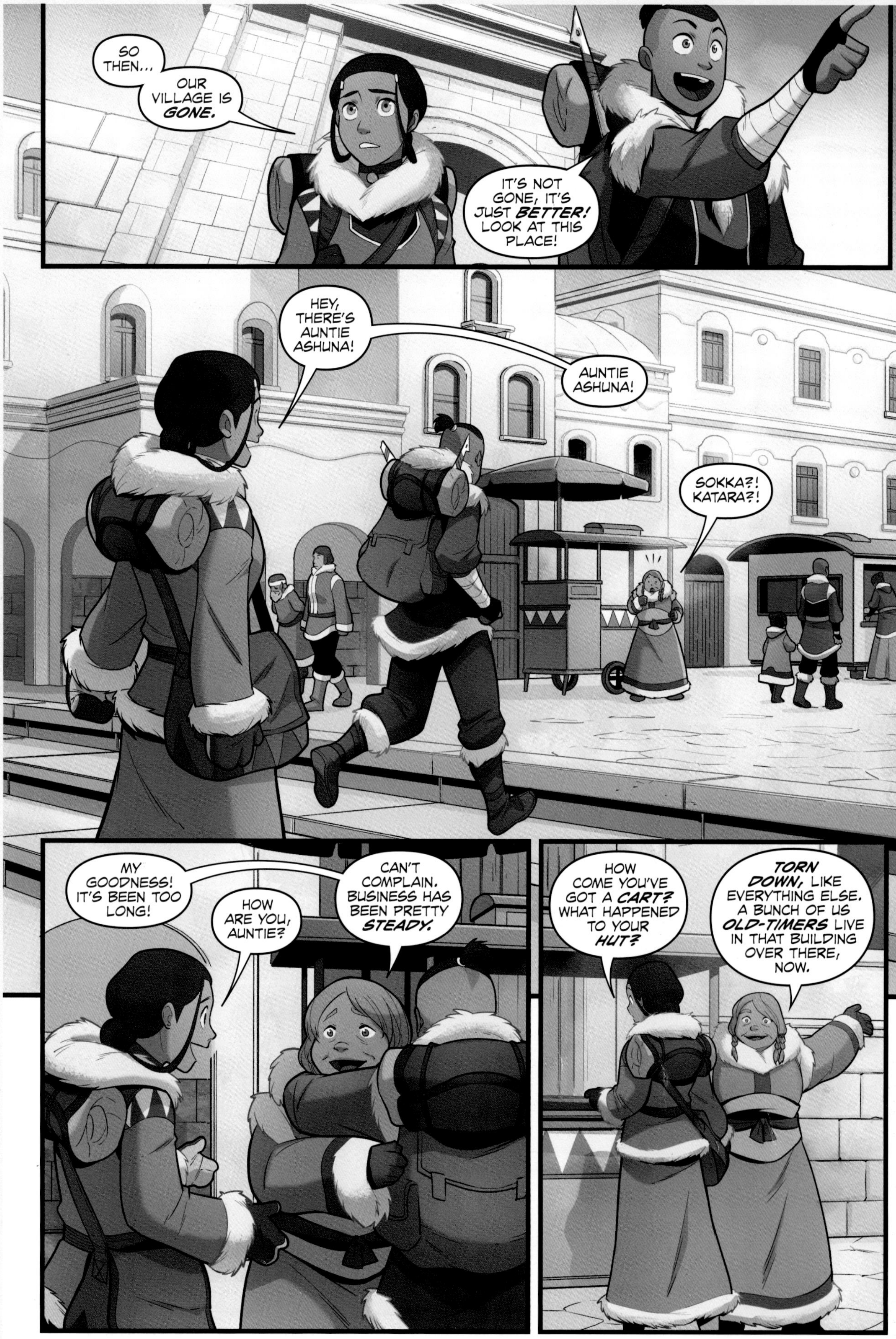
SO THEN...
OUR VILLAGE IS GONE.
IT'S NOT GONE, IT'S JUST BETTER! LOOK AT THIS PLACE!
HEY, THERE'S AUNTIE ASHUNA!
AUNTIE ASHUNA!
SOKKA?! KATARA?!
MY GOODNESS! IT'S BEEN TOO LONG!
HOW ARE YOU, AUNTIE?
CAN'T COMPLAIN. BUSINESS HAS BEEN PRETTY STEADY.
HOW COME YOU'VE GOT A CART? WHAT HAPPENED TO YOUR HUT?
TORN DOWN, LIKE EVERYTHING ELSE. A BUNCH OF US OLD-TIMERS LIVE IN THAT BUILDING OVER THERE, NOW.

GLY: *Auntie Ashuna was first mentioned in The Rift Part 3. This is our first look at her.*

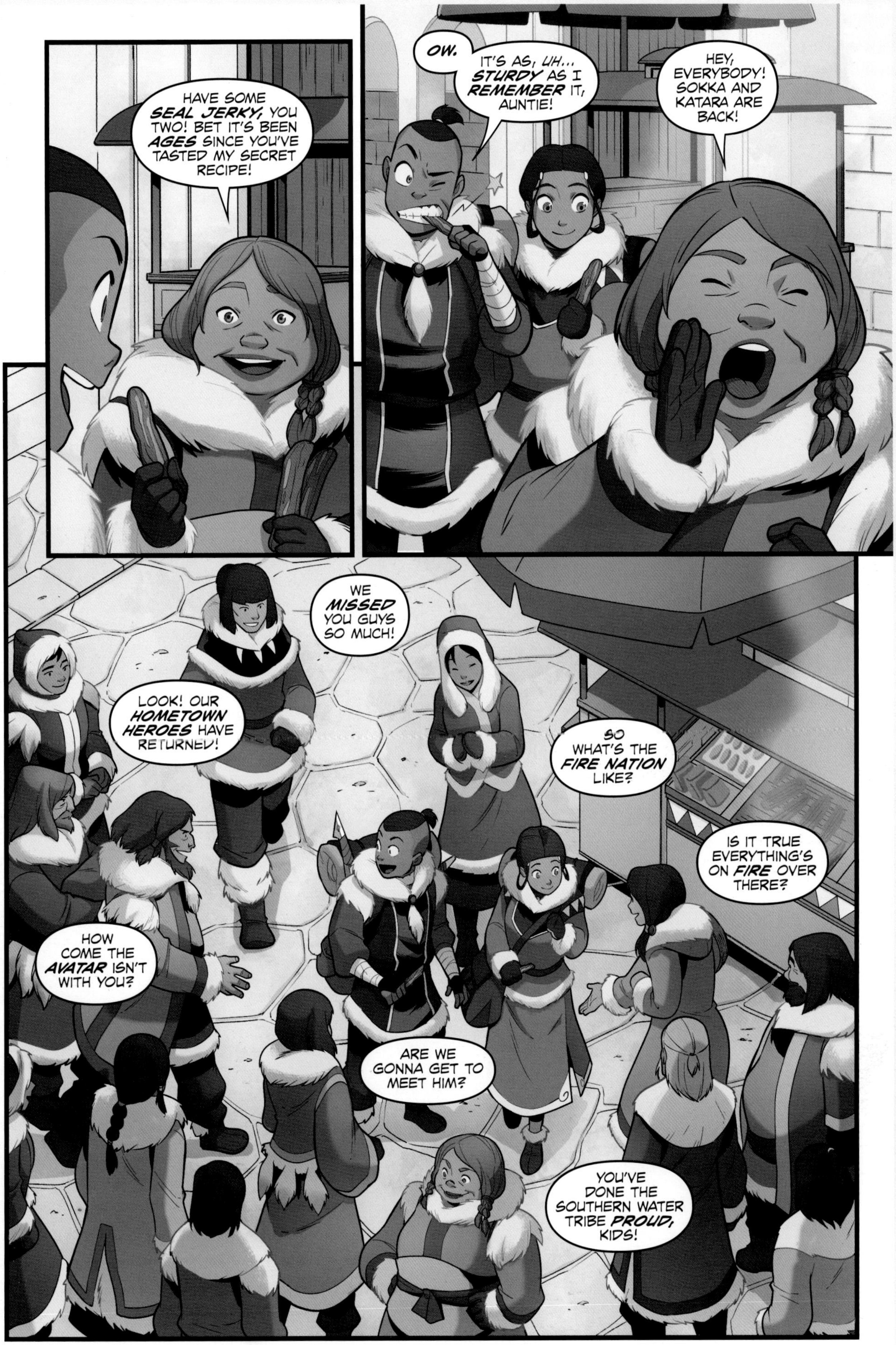
HAVE SOME SEAL JERKY, YOU TWO! BET IT'S BEEN AGES SINCE YOU'VE TASTED MY SECRET RECIPE!
OW.
IT'S AS, UH... STURDY AS I REMEMBER IT, AUNTIE!
HEY, EVERYBODY! SOKKA AND KATARA ARE BACK!
WE MISSED YOU GUYS SO MUCH!
LOOK! OUR HOMETOWN HEROES HAVE RETURNED!
SO WHAT'S THE FIRE NATION LIKE?
IS IT TRUE EVERYTHING'S ON FIRE OVER THERE?
HOW COME THE AVATAR ISN'T WITH YOU?
ARE WE GONNA GET TO MEET HIM?
YOU'VE DONE THE SOUTHERN WATER TRIBE PROUD, KIDS!

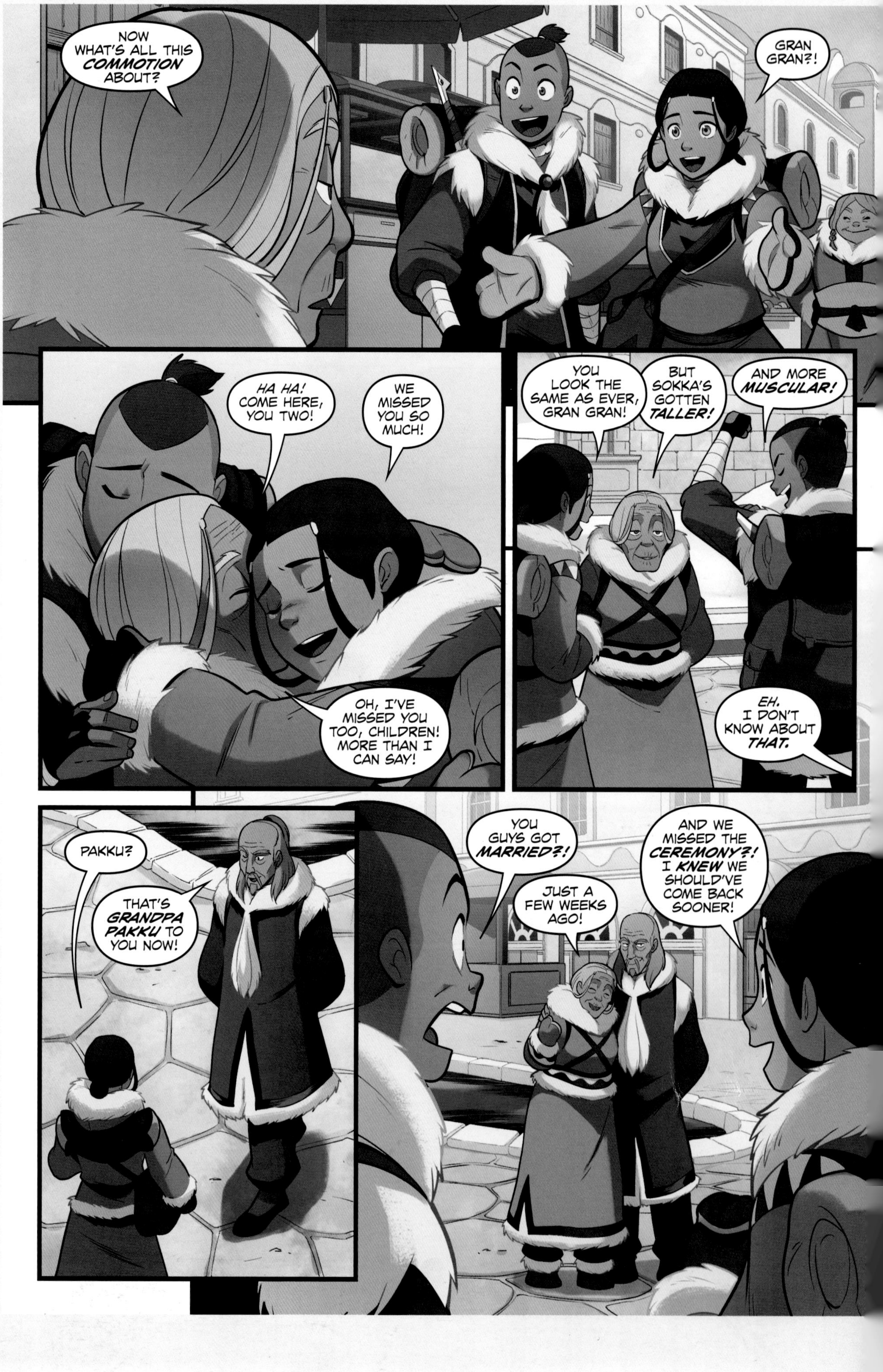
NOW WHAT'S ALL THIS COMMOTION ABOUT?
GRAN GRAN?!
HA HA! COME HERE, YOU TWO!
WE MISSED YOU SO MUCH!
OH, I'VE MISSED YOU TOO, CHILDREN! MORE THAN I CAN SAY!
YOU LOOK THE SAME AS EVER, GRAN GRAN!
BUT SOKKA'S GOTTEN TALLER!
AND MORE MUSCULAR!
EH. I DON'T KNOW ABOUT THAT.
PAKKU?
THAT'S GRANDPA PAKKU TO YOU NOW!
YOU GUYS GOT MARRIED?!
JUST A FEW WEEKS AGO!
AND WE MISSED THE CEREMONY?! I KNEW WE SHOULD'VE COME BACK SOONER!

GLY: *Pakku is Gran Gran's first love from back in the day. We saw the seeds of their renewed romance in the episode "The Waterbending Master." Here, we show that things worked out for them. You can never be too old to find love.*

NO, DEAR, THERE WASN'T A CEREMONY TO MISS! WE *ELOPED* TO THE MISTY PALMS OASIS!

WHICH, TO BE PERFECTLY BLUNT, DOESN'T LIVE UP TO ITS NAME.

BUT IT DIDN'T MATTER BECAUSE WE STILL HAD THE MOST *WONDERFUL* TIME! PAKKU'S SUCH A *ROMANTIC!*

HEE HEE!

KATARA, YOU OUGHT TO COME VISIT MY *SCHOOL!* I'M TRYING TO TRAIN UP NEW *WATERBENDERS* HERE IN THE SOUTH.

I COULD USE YOUR *HELP.*

YOU STARTED A SCHOOL?! BUT WHERE DID YOU FIND STUDENTS?

WELL... THAT'S THE *INTERESTING* PART. COME VISIT WHEN YOU GET THE CHANCE.

YOU KNOW, MASTER PAKKU, YOU COULD PROBABLY USE *MY* HELP, TOO.

BUT YOU'RE NOT A BENDER, SOKKA.

SEE, THAT'S WHERE YOU'RE WRONG! I *AM* A BENDER...A BENDER OF *MOTIVATION!*

HM.

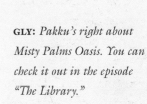

GLY: *Pakku's right about Misty Palms Oasis. You can check it out in the episode "The Library."*

YOUR FATHER WILL BE SO *THRILLED* TO SEE YOU TWO! HE'S SO *PROUD* OF YOU! WE *ALL* ARE!

HE TOLD US ABOUT HOW *BRAVE* SOKKA WAS ON THE *DAY OF BLACK SUN,* ABOUT WHAT AN *ACCOMPLISHED WATERBENDER* KATARA'S BECOME...

HE TALKS ABOUT YOU ALL THE TIME!

SERIOUSLY. *ALL THE TIME.*

DON'T GET ME WRONG, I LIKE YOU KIDS JUST FINE, BUT THERE ARE STILL *LIMITS,* YOU UNDERSTAND?

SO WHERE IS DAD?

IN HIS OFFICE.

DAD'S GOT AN *OFFICE?!*

YES, OVER IN THE *TOWN HALL.*

THERE'S A *TOWN HALL?!*

27

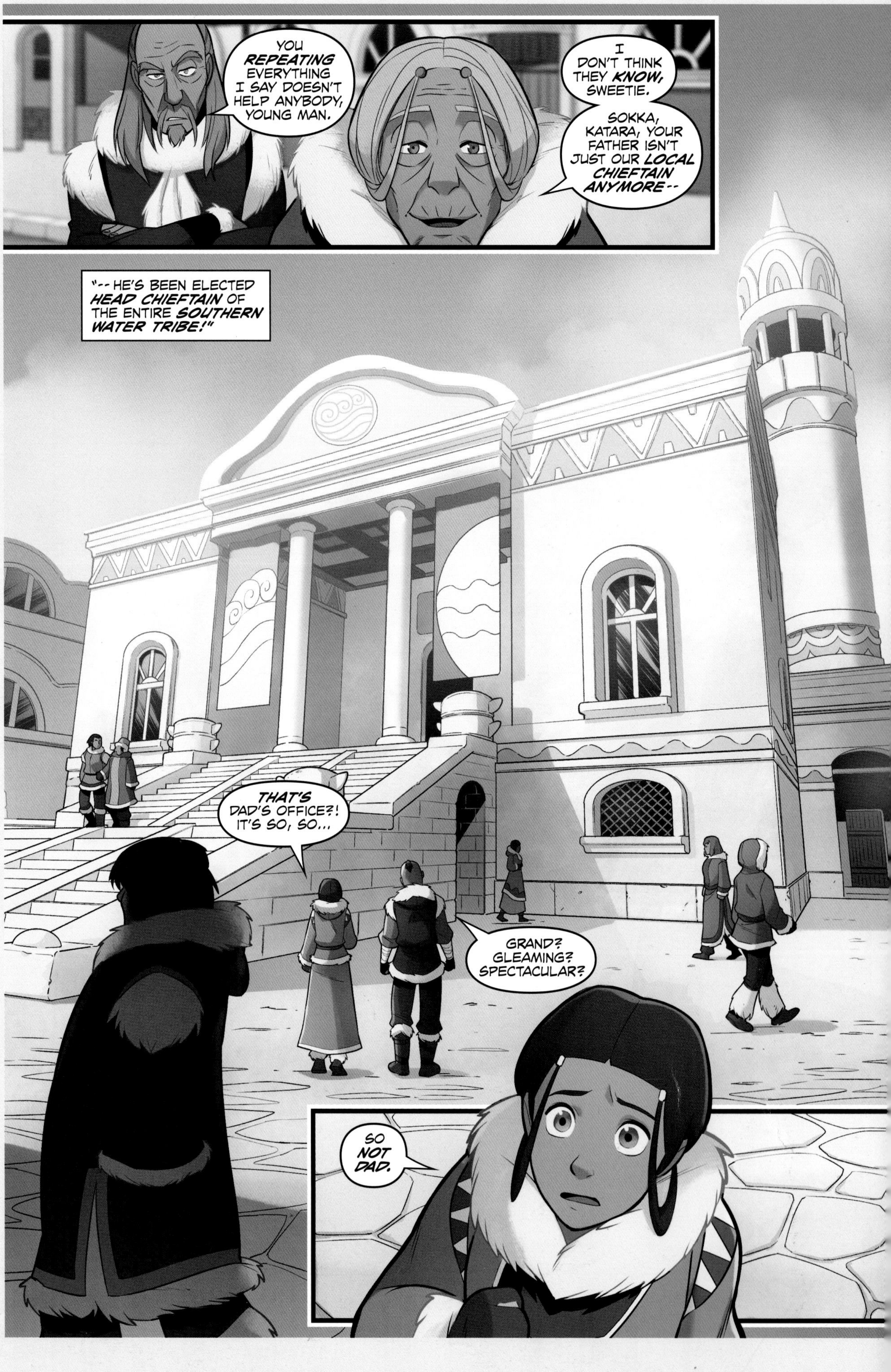
YOU REPEATING EVERYTHING I SAY DOESN'T HELP ANYBODY, YOUNG MAN.
I DON'T THINK THEY KNOW, SWEETIE.
SOKKA, KATARA, YOUR FATHER ISN'T JUST OUR LOCAL CHIEFTAIN ANYMORE--
"--HE'S BEEN ELECTED HEAD CHIEFTAIN OF THE ENTIRE SOUTHERN WATER TRIBE!"
THAT'S DAD'S OFFICE?! IT'S SO, SO...
GRAND? GLEAMING? SPECTACULAR?
SO NOT DAD.

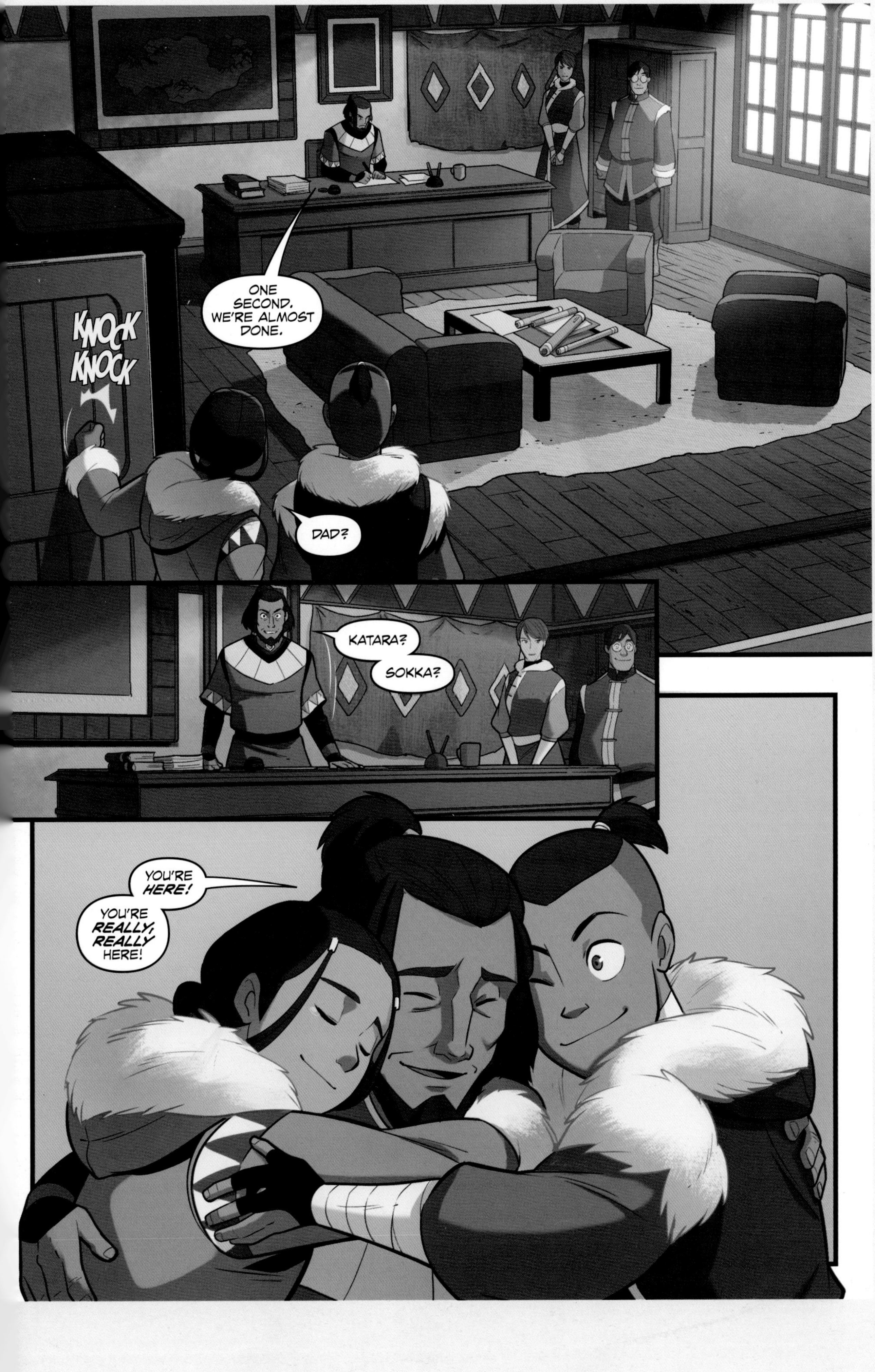
ONE SECOND. WE'RE ALMOST DONE.
KNOCK KNOCK
DAD?
KATARA?
SOKKA?
YOU'RE HERE!
YOU'RE REALLY, REALLY HERE!

GLY: *This volume is all about reunions for Katara and Sokka, one after another. We tried hard to differentiate the hugs. Not sure how successful we were. After all, hugs are hugs, you know?*

G: *We designed the Northern Water Tribe's costume to be simpler and more urban, while the Southern Water Tribe's costume is traditional and has more furs.*

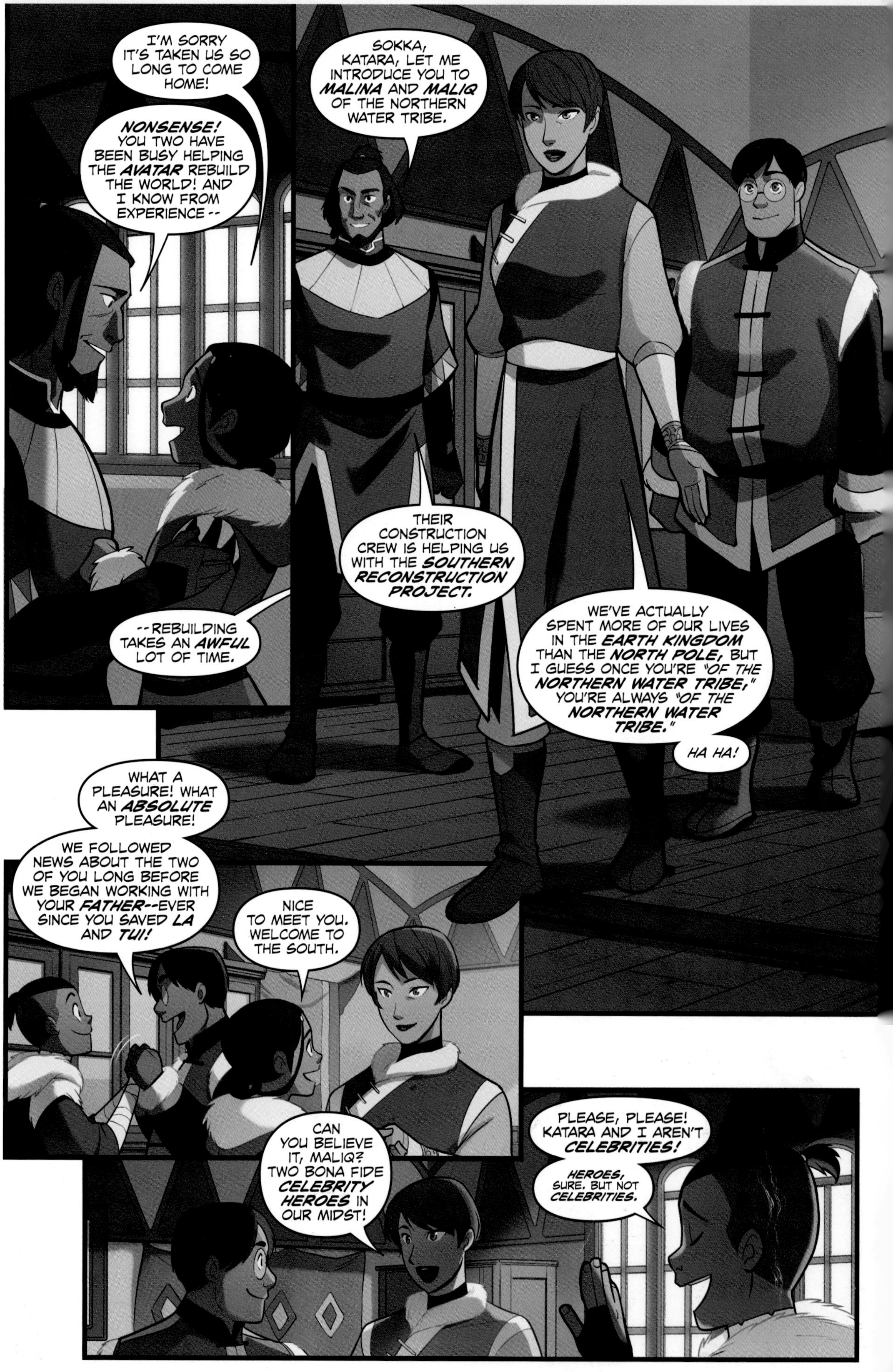
I'M SORRY IT'S TAKEN US SO LONG TO COME HOME!
NONSENSE! YOU TWO HAVE BEEN BUSY HELPING THE AVATAR REBUILD THE WORLD! AND I KNOW FROM EXPERIENCE--
--REBUILDING TAKES AN AWFUL LOT OF TIME.
SOKKA, KATARA, LET ME INTRODUCE YOU TO MALINA AND MALIQ OF THE NORTHERN WATER TRIBE.
THEIR CONSTRUCTION CREW IS HELPING US WITH THE SOUTHERN RECONSTRUCTION PROJECT.
WE'VE ACTUALLY SPENT MORE OF OUR LIVES IN THE EARTH KINGDOM THAN THE NORTH POLE, BUT I GUESS ONCE YOU'RE "OF THE NORTHERN WATER TRIBE," YOU'RE ALWAYS "OF THE NORTHERN WATER TRIBE."
HA HA!
WHAT A PLEASURE! WHAT AN ABSOLUTE PLEASURE!
WE FOLLOWED NEWS ABOUT THE TWO OF YOU LONG BEFORE WE BEGAN WORKING WITH YOUR FATHER--EVER SINCE YOU SAVED LA AND TUI!
NICE TO MEET YOU. WELCOME TO THE SOUTH.
CAN YOU BELIEVE IT, MALIQ? TWO BONA FIDE CELEBRITY HEROES IN OUR MIDST!
PLEASE, PLEASE! KATARA AND I AREN'T CELEBRITIES!
HEROES, SURE. BUT NOT CELEBRITIES.

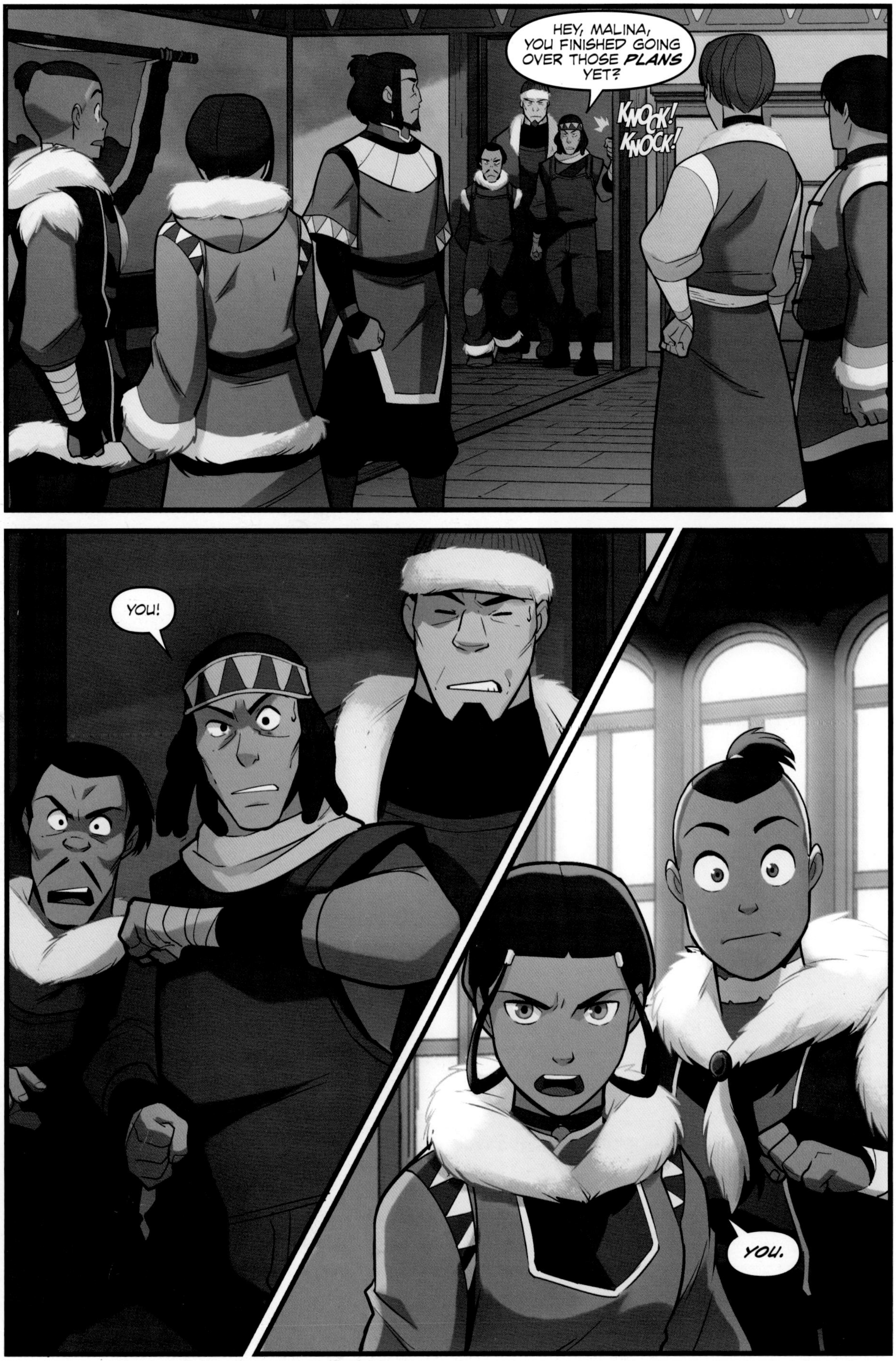
HEY, MALINA, YOU FINISHED GOING OVER THOSE PLANS YET?
KNOCK! KNOCK!
YOU!
YOU.

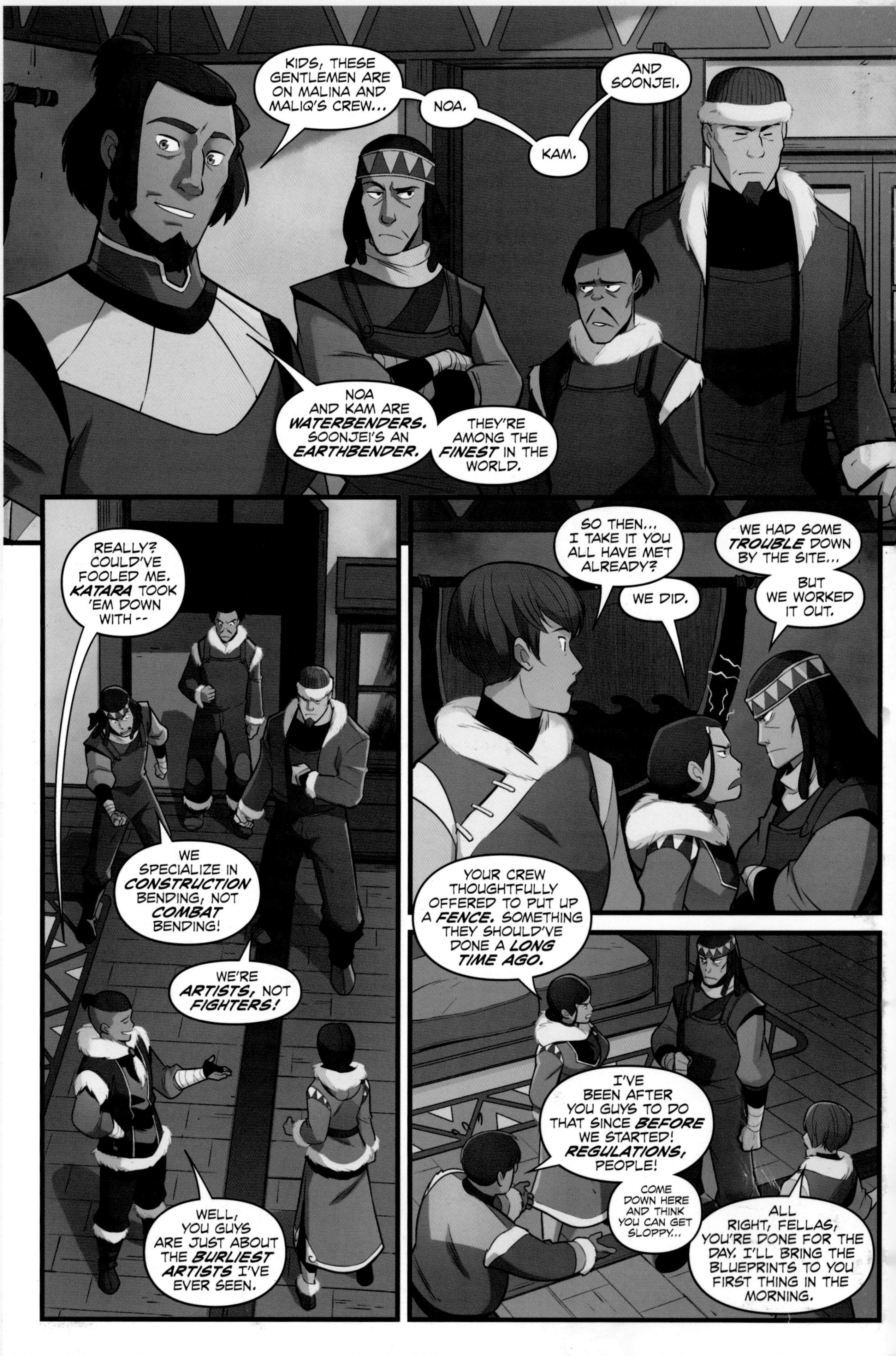
KIDS, THESE GENTLEMEN ARE ON MALINA AND MALIQ'S CREW...
NOA.
KAM.
AND SOONJEI.
NOA AND KAM ARE WATERBENDERS. SOONJEI'S AN EARTHBENDER.
THEY'RE AMONG THE FINEST IN THE WORLD.
REALLY? COULD'VE FOOLED ME. KATARA TOOK 'EM DOWN WITH --
WE SPECIALIZE IN CONSTRUCTION BENDING, NOT COMBAT BENDING!
WE'RE ARTISTS, NOT FIGHTERS!
WELL, YOU GUYS ARE JUST ABOUT THE BURLIEST ARTISTS I'VE EVER SEEN.
SO THEN... I TAKE IT YOU ALL HAVE MET ALREADY?
WE DID.
WE HAD SOME TROUBLE DOWN BY THE SITE...
BUT WE WORKED IT OUT.
YOUR CREW THOUGHTFULLY OFFERED TO PUT UP A FENCE. SOMETHING THEY SHOULD'VE DONE A LONG TIME AGO.
I'VE BEEN AFTER YOU GUYS TO DO THAT SINCE BEFORE WE STARTED! REGULATIONS, PEOPLE!
COME DOWN HERE AND THINK YOU CAN GET SLOPPY...
ALL RIGHT, FELLAS, YOU'RE DONE FOR THE DAY. I'LL BRING THE BLUEPRINTS TO YOU FIRST THING IN THE MORNING.

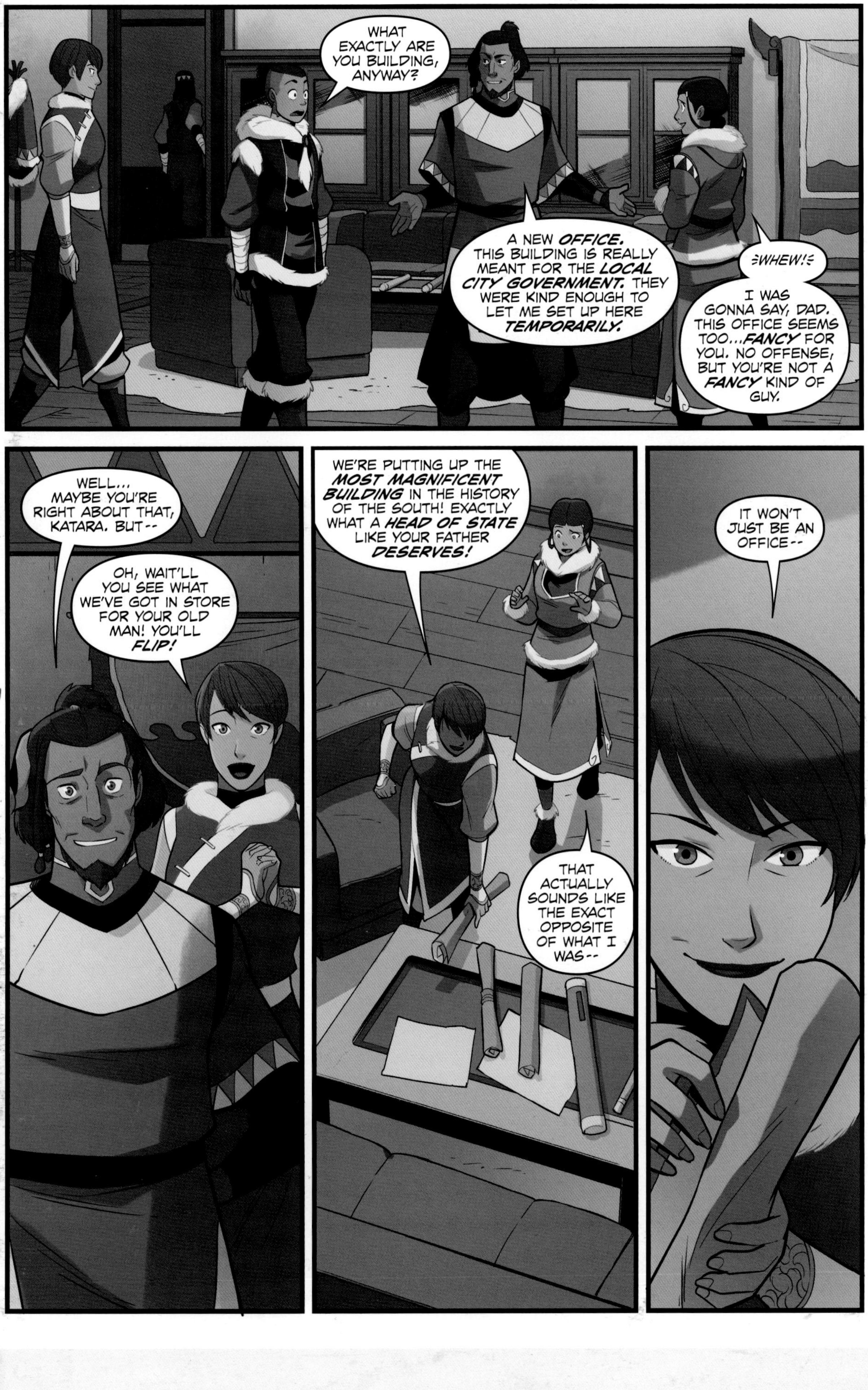
WHAT EXACTLY ARE YOU BUILDING, ANYWAY?
A NEW OFFICE. THIS BUILDING IS REALLY MEANT FOR THE LOCAL CITY GOVERNMENT. THEY WERE KIND ENOUGH TO LET ME SET UP HERE TEMPORARILY.
WHEW!
I WAS GONNA SAY, DAD. THIS OFFICE SEEMS TOO...FANCY FOR YOU. NO OFFENSE, BUT YOU'RE NOT A FANCY KIND OF GUY.
WELL... MAYBE YOU'RE RIGHT ABOUT THAT, KATARA. BUT--
OH, WAIT'LL YOU SEE WHAT WE'VE GOT IN STORE FOR YOUR OLD MAN! YOU'LL FLIP!
WE'RE PUTTING UP THE MOST MAGNIFICENT BUILDING IN THE HISTORY OF THE SOUTH! EXACTLY WHAT A HEAD OF STATE LIKE YOUR FATHER DESERVES!
THAT ACTUALLY SOUNDS LIKE THE EXACT OPPOSITE OF WHAT I WAS--
IT WON'T JUST BE AN OFFICE--

GLY: *In the first draft of the script, Malina was much more gruff. I'm thankful for Mike's note to tone it down. We really needed her to be right on the edge between likable and unlikable.*

G: *We gave Malina a short hairstyle based on Gene's request. She looks stylish and stands out among the Southern Water Tribe.*

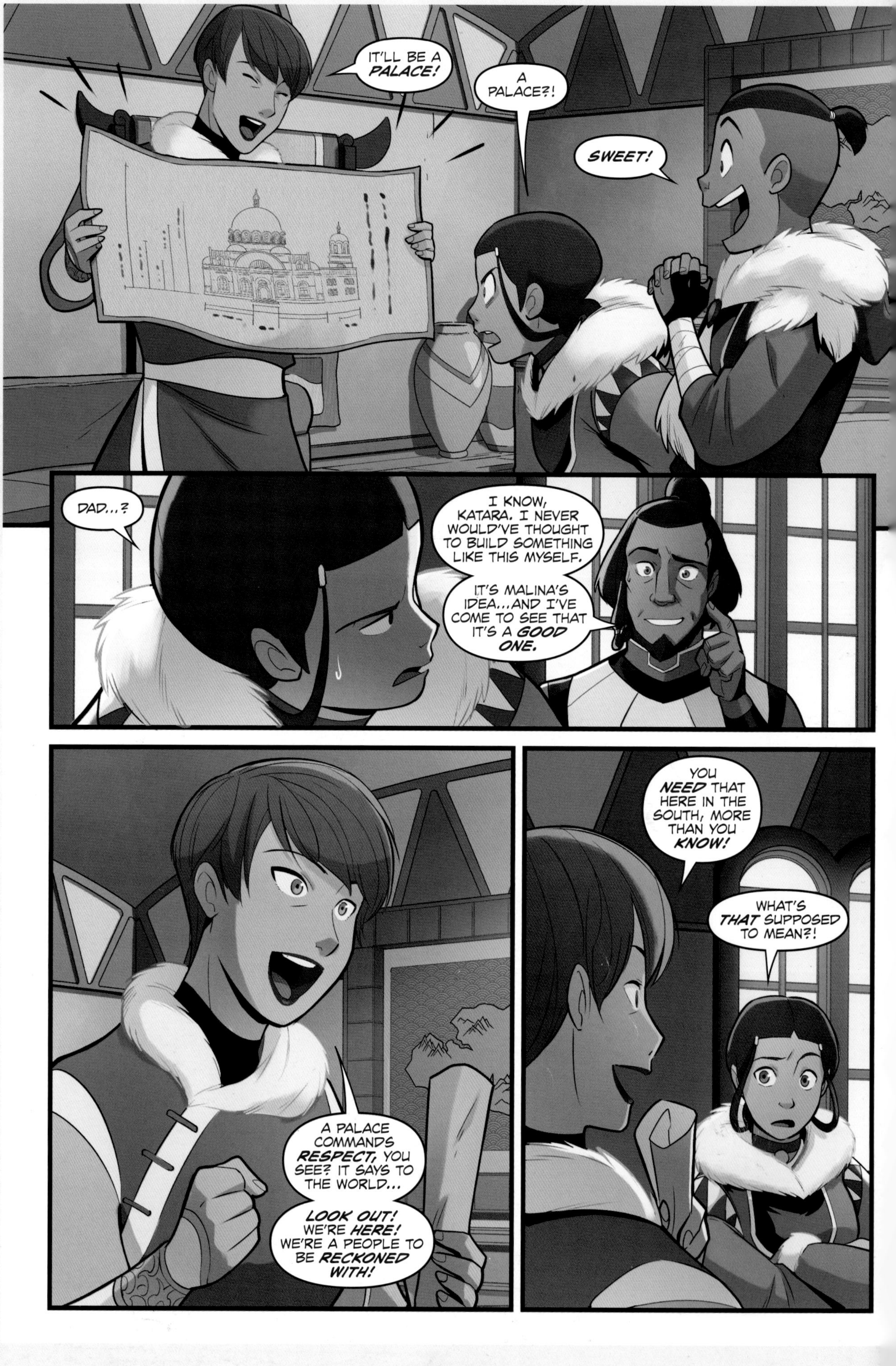

IT'LL BE A PALACE!
A PALACE?!
SWEET!
DAD...?
I KNOW, KATARA. I NEVER WOULD'VE THOUGHT TO BUILD SOMETHING LIKE THIS MYSELF.
IT'S MALINA'S IDEA...AND I'VE COME TO SEE THAT IT'S A GOOD ONE.
A PALACE COMMANDS RESPECT, YOU SEE? IT SAYS TO THE WORLD...
LOOK OUT! WE'RE HERE! WE'RE A PEOPLE TO BE RECKONED WITH!
YOU NEED THAT HERE IN THE SOUTH, MORE THAN YOU KNOW!
WHAT'S THAT SUPPOSED TO MEAN?!

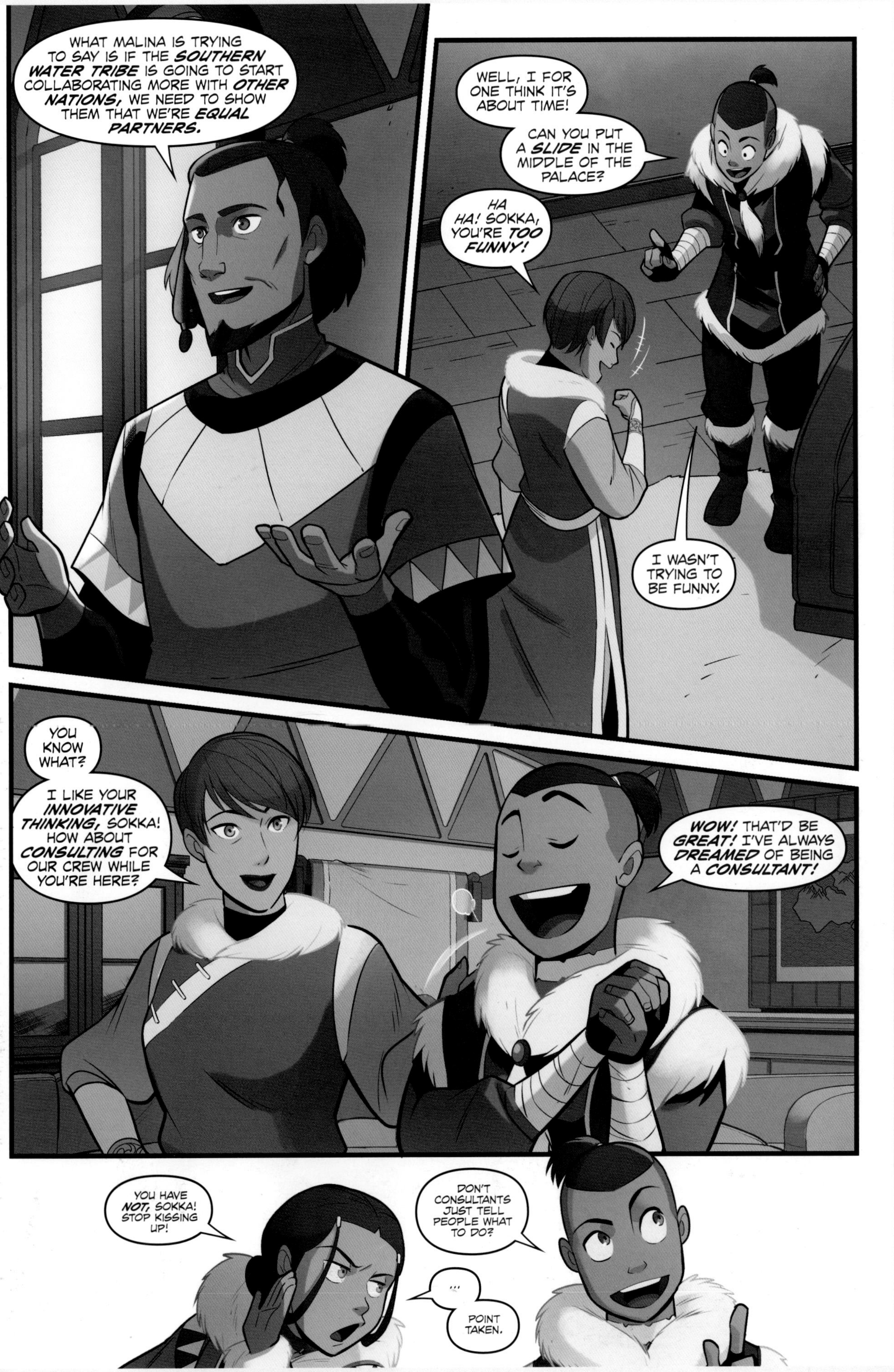
WHAT MALINA IS TRYING TO SAY IS IF THE SOUTHERN WATER TRIBE IS GOING TO START COLLABORATING MORE WITH OTHER NATIONS, WE NEED TO SHOW THEM THAT WE'RE EQUAL PARTNERS.
WELL, I FOR ONE THINK IT'S ABOUT TIME!
CAN YOU PUT A SLIDE IN THE MIDDLE OF THE PALACE?
HA HA! SOKKA, YOU'RE TOO FUNNY!
I WASN'T TRYING TO BE FUNNY.
YOU KNOW WHAT?
I LIKE YOUR INNOVATIVE THINKING, SOKKA! HOW ABOUT CONSULTING FOR OUR CREW WHILE YOU'RE HERE?
WOW! THAT'D BE GREAT! I'VE ALWAYS DREAMED OF BEING A CONSULTANT!
YOU HAVE NOT, SOKKA! STOP KISSING UP!
DON'T CONSULTANTS JUST TELL PEOPLE WHAT TO DO?
...
POINT TAKEN.

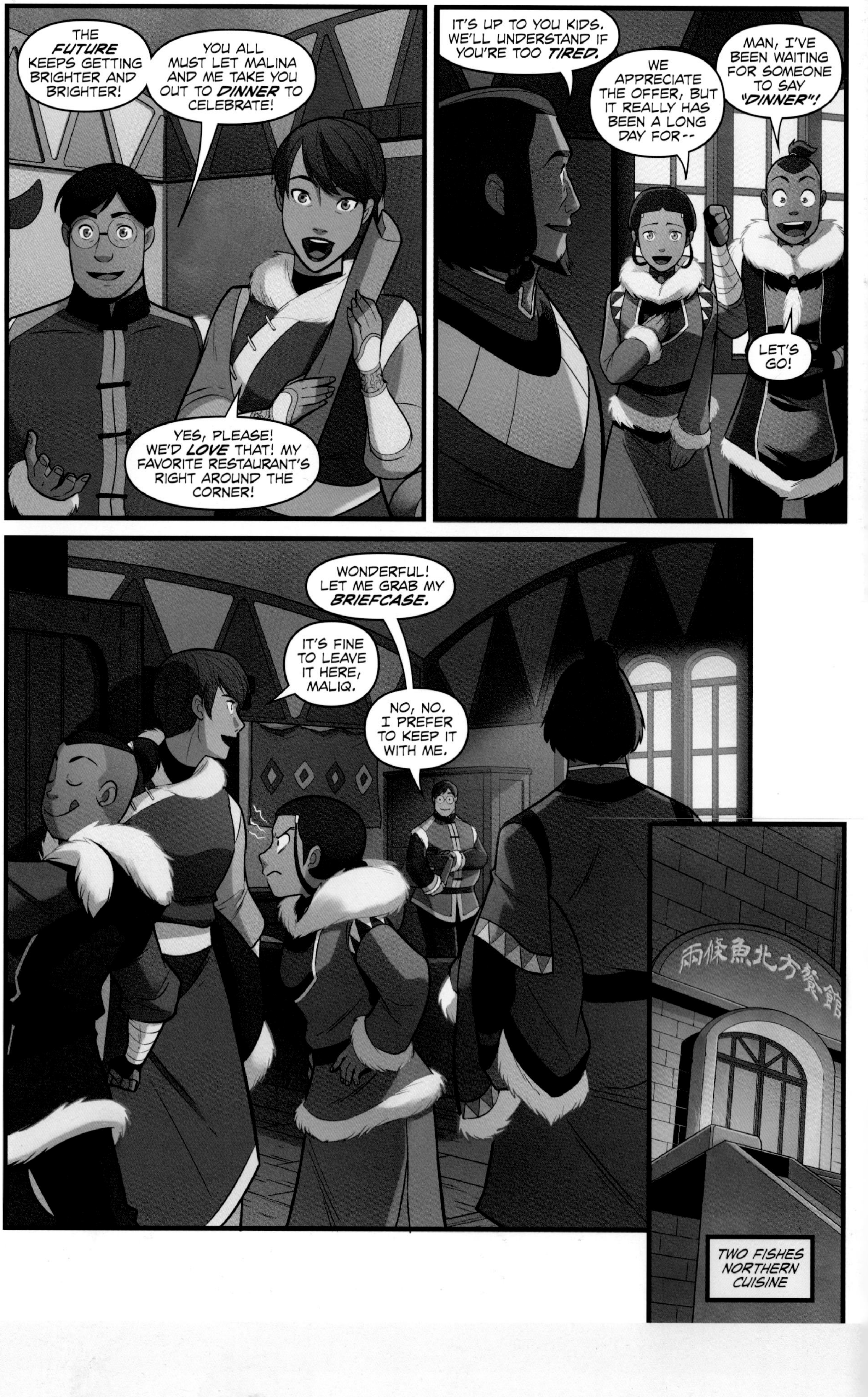
THE FUTURE KEEPS GETTING BRIGHTER AND BRIGHTER!
YOU ALL MUST LET MALINA AND ME TAKE YOU OUT TO DINNER TO CELEBRATE!
YES, PLEASE! WE'D LOVE THAT! MY FAVORITE RESTAURANT'S RIGHT AROUND THE CORNER!
IT'S UP TO YOU KIDS. WE'LL UNDERSTAND IF YOU'RE TOO TIRED.
WE APPRECIATE THE OFFER, BUT IT REALLY HAS BEEN A LONG DAY FOR--
MAN, I'VE BEEN WAITING FOR SOMEONE TO SAY "DINNER"!
LET'S GO!
WONDERFUL! LET ME GRAB MY BRIEFCASE.
IT'S FINE TO LEAVE IT HERE, MALIQ.
NO, NO. I PREFER TO KEEP IT WITH ME.
兩條魚北方餐館
TWO FISHES NORTHERN CUISINE

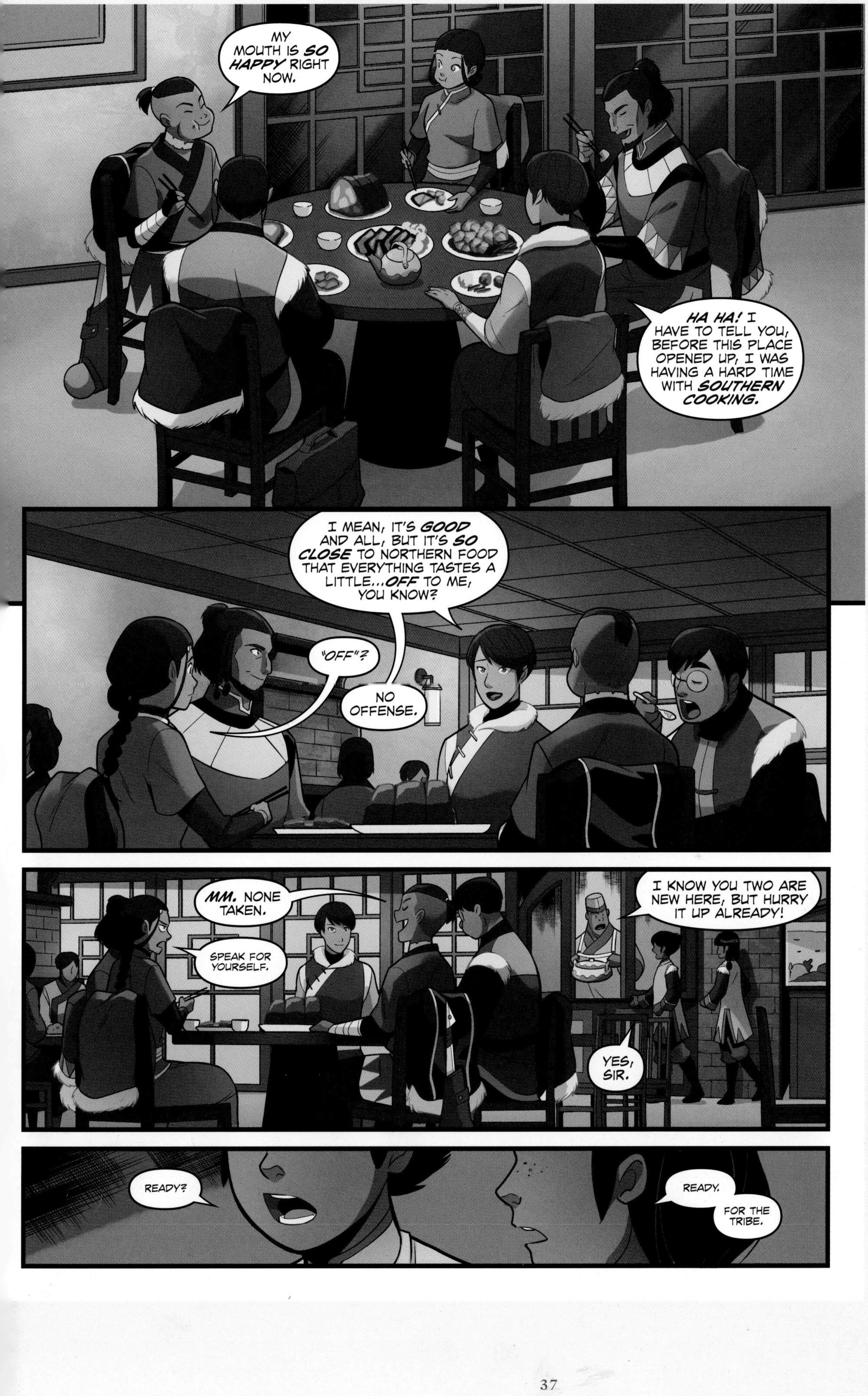
MY MOUTH IS SO HAPPY RIGHT NOW.
HA HA! I HAVE TO TELL YOU, BEFORE THIS PLACE OPENED UP, I WAS HAVING A HARD TIME WITH SOUTHERN COOKING.
I MEAN, IT'S GOOD AND ALL, BUT IT'S SO CLOSE TO NORTHERN FOOD THAT EVERYTHING TASTES A LITTLE...OFF TO ME, YOU KNOW?
"OFF"?
NO OFFENSE.
MM. NONE TAKEN.
SPEAK FOR YOURSELF.
I KNOW YOU TWO ARE NEW HERE, BUT HURRY IT UP ALREADY!
YES, SIR.
READY?
READY.
FOR THE TRIBE.

G: *We love drawing panels that include people having their meals. We came up with a menu centered on meat, based on Inuit dishes and other plates from cold regions.*

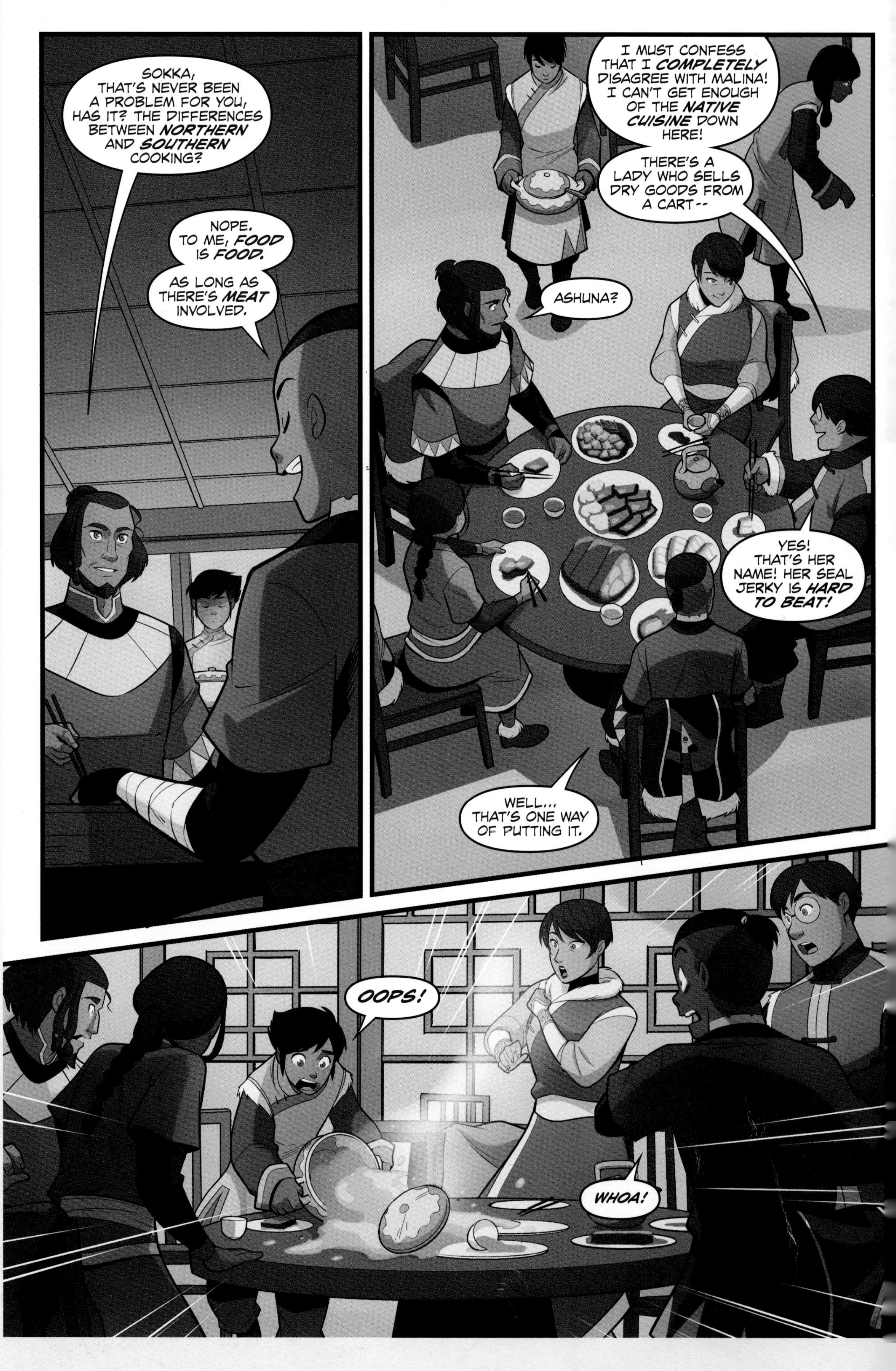
SOKKA, THAT'S NEVER BEEN A PROBLEM FOR YOU, HAS IT? THE DIFFERENCES BETWEEN NORTHERN AND SOUTHERN COOKING?
NOPE. TO ME, FOOD IS FOOD.
AS LONG AS THERE'S MEAT INVOLVED.
I MUST CONFESS THAT I COMPLETELY DISAGREE WITH MALINA! I CAN'T GET ENOUGH OF THE NATIVE CUISINE DOWN HERE!
THERE'S A LADY WHO SELLS DRY GOODS FROM A CART--
ASHUNA?
YES! THAT'S HER NAME! HER SEAL JERKY IS HARD TO BEAT!
WELL... THAT'S ONE WAY OF PUTTING IT.
OOPS!
WHOA!

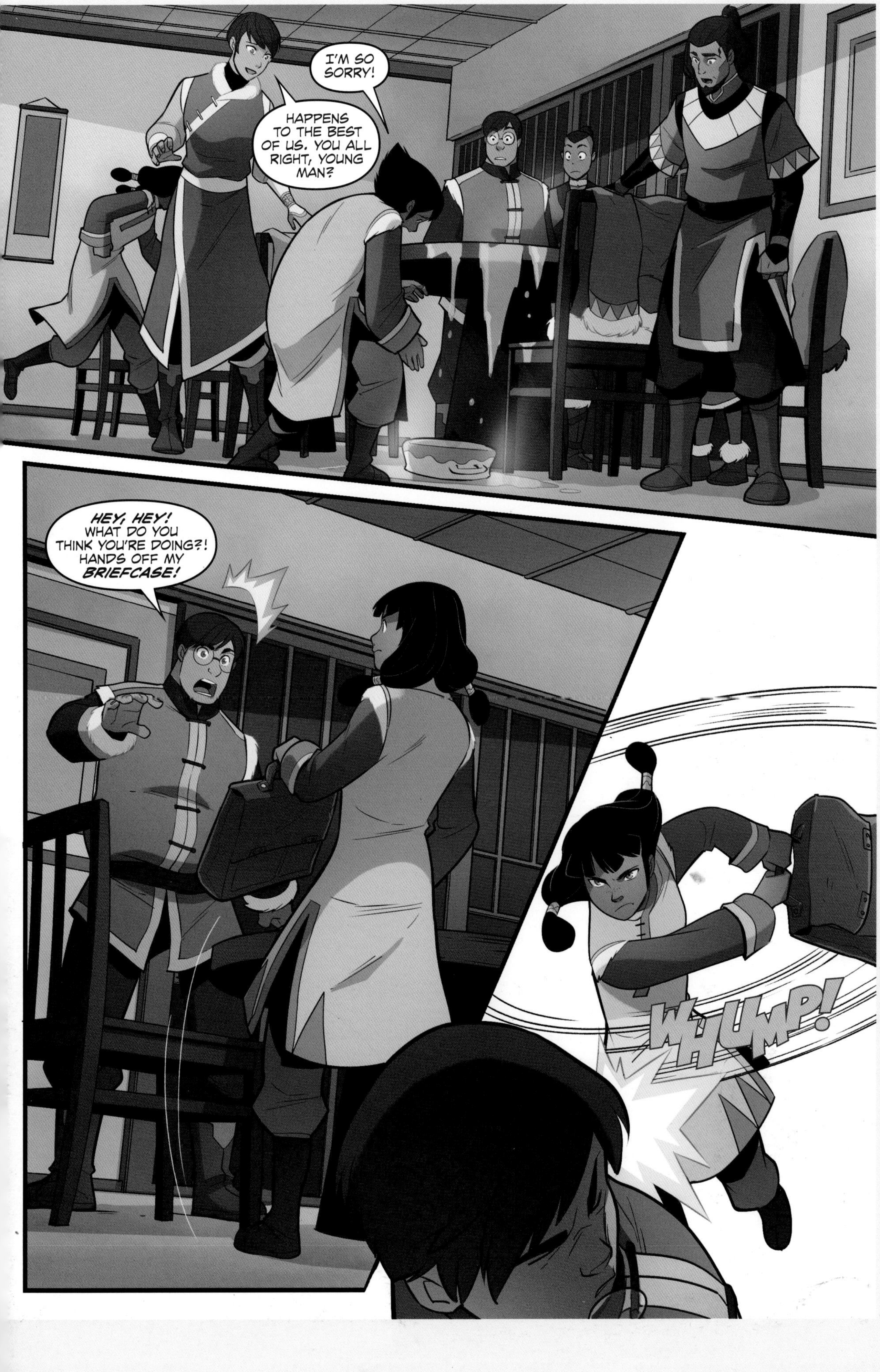
I'M SO SORRY!
HAPPENS TO THE BEST OF US. YOU ALL RIGHT, YOUNG MAN?
HEY, HEY! WHAT DO YOU THINK YOU'RE DOING?! HANDS OFF MY BRIEFCASE!
WHUMP!

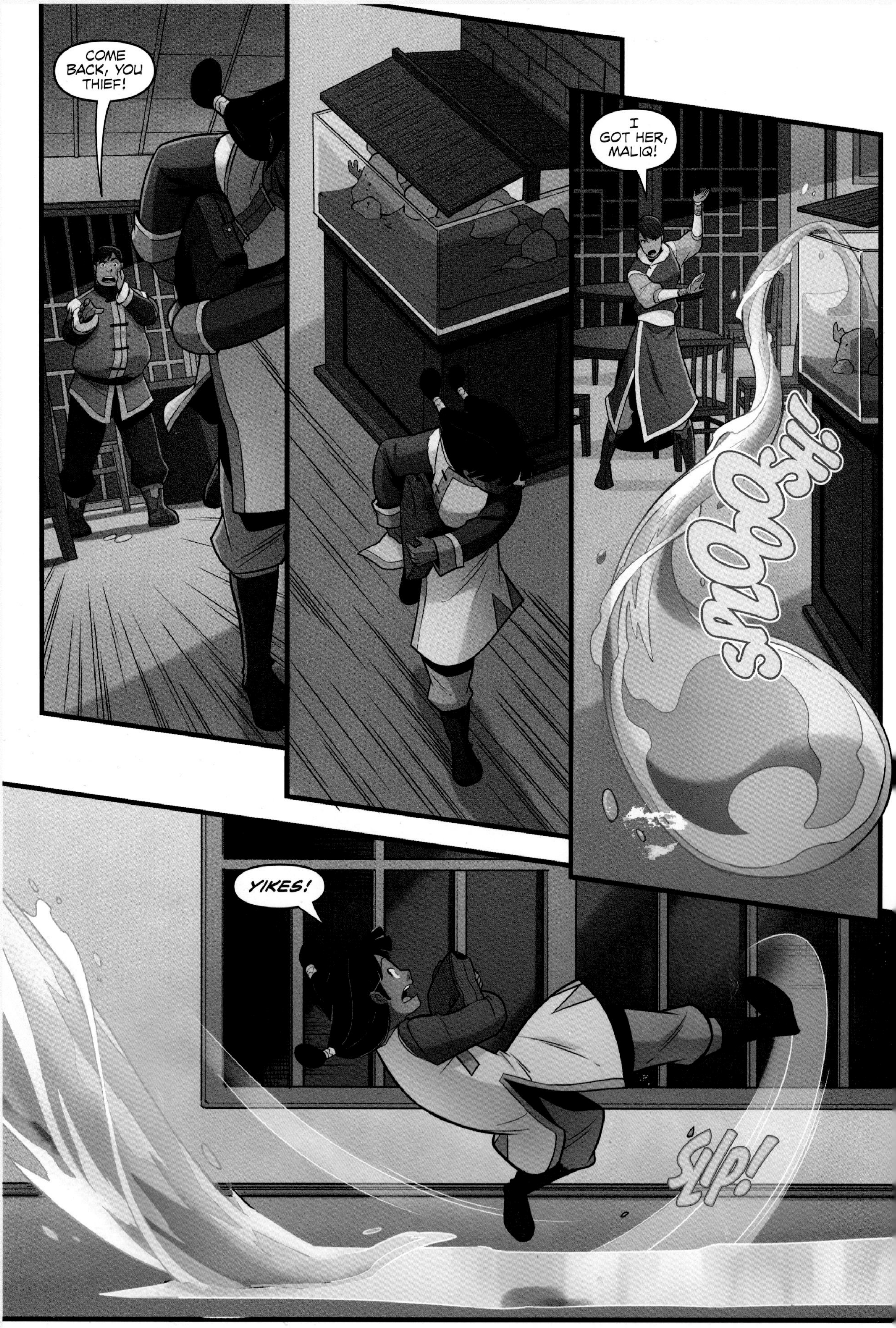
COME BACK, YOU THIEF!
I GOT HER, MALIQ!
SPLOOSH!
YIKES!
SLIP!

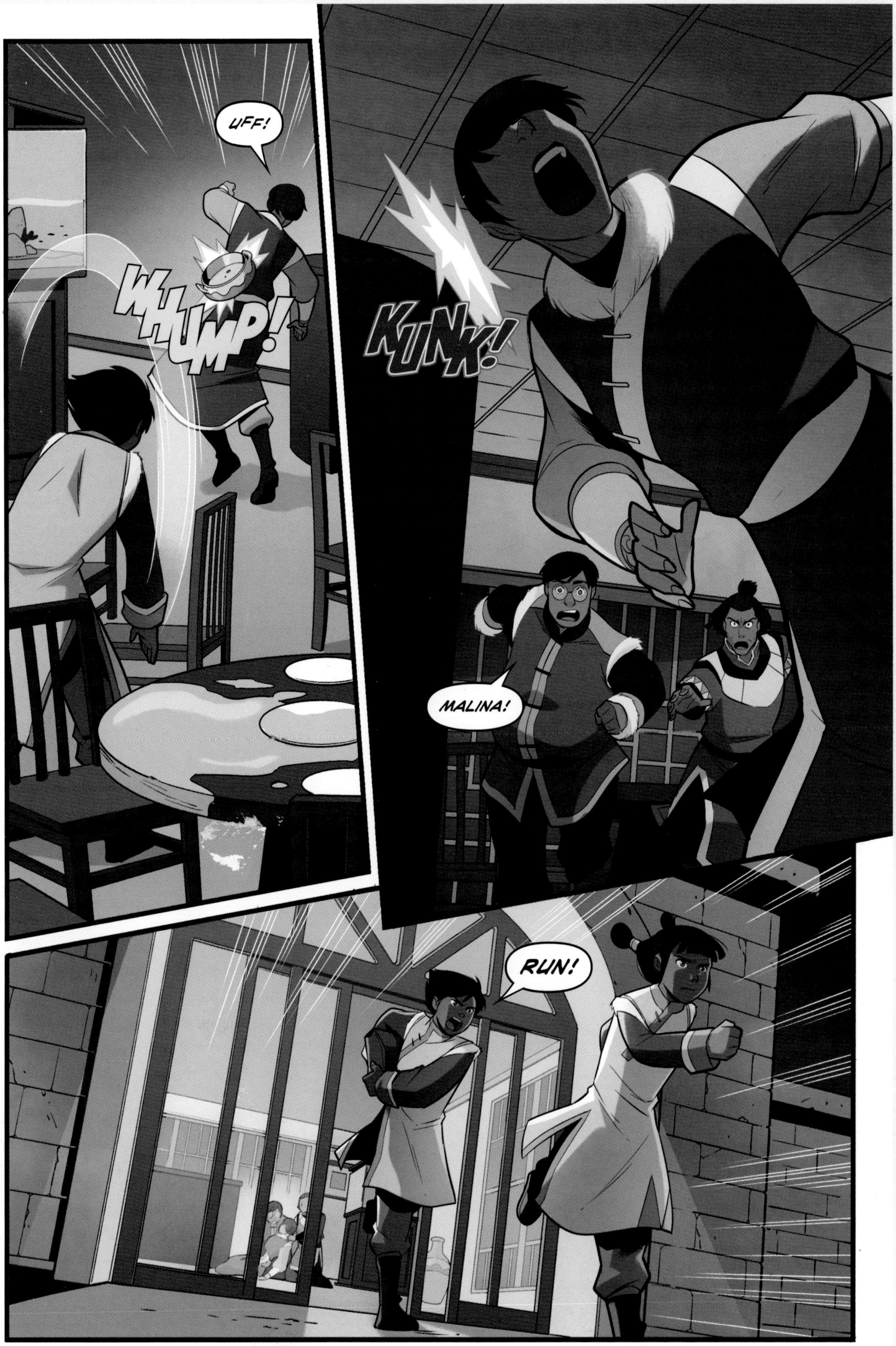
UFF!
WHUMP!
KUNK!
MALINA!
RUN!

GLY: *A snowmobile! Another instance of the growing influence of technology in the Avatar world.*

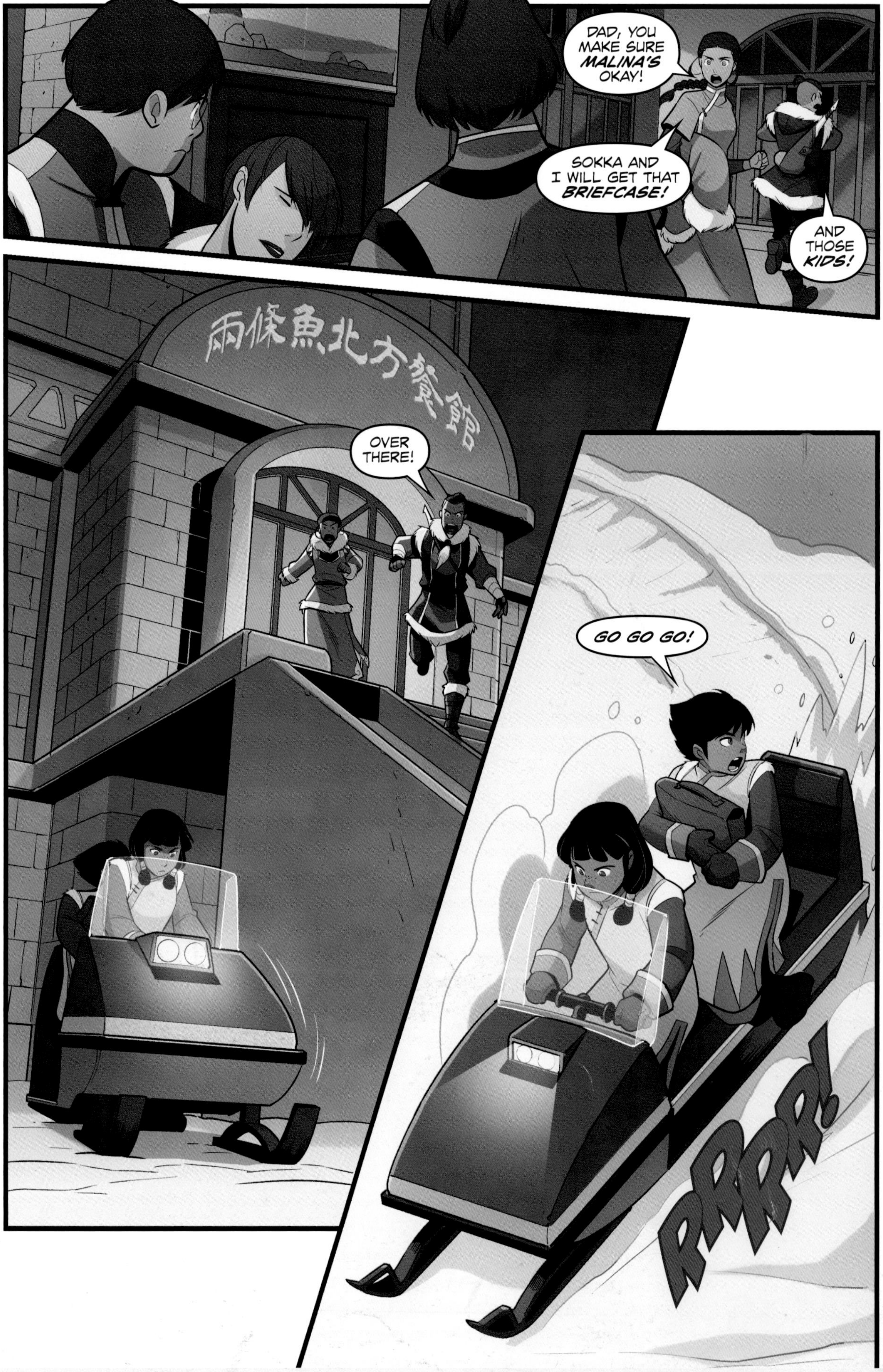
DAD, YOU MAKE SURE *MALINA'S* OKAY!
SOKKA AND I WILL GET THAT *BRIEFCASE!*
AND THOSE *KIDS!*
雨條魚北方餐館
OVER THERE!
GO GO GO!
RRRR!

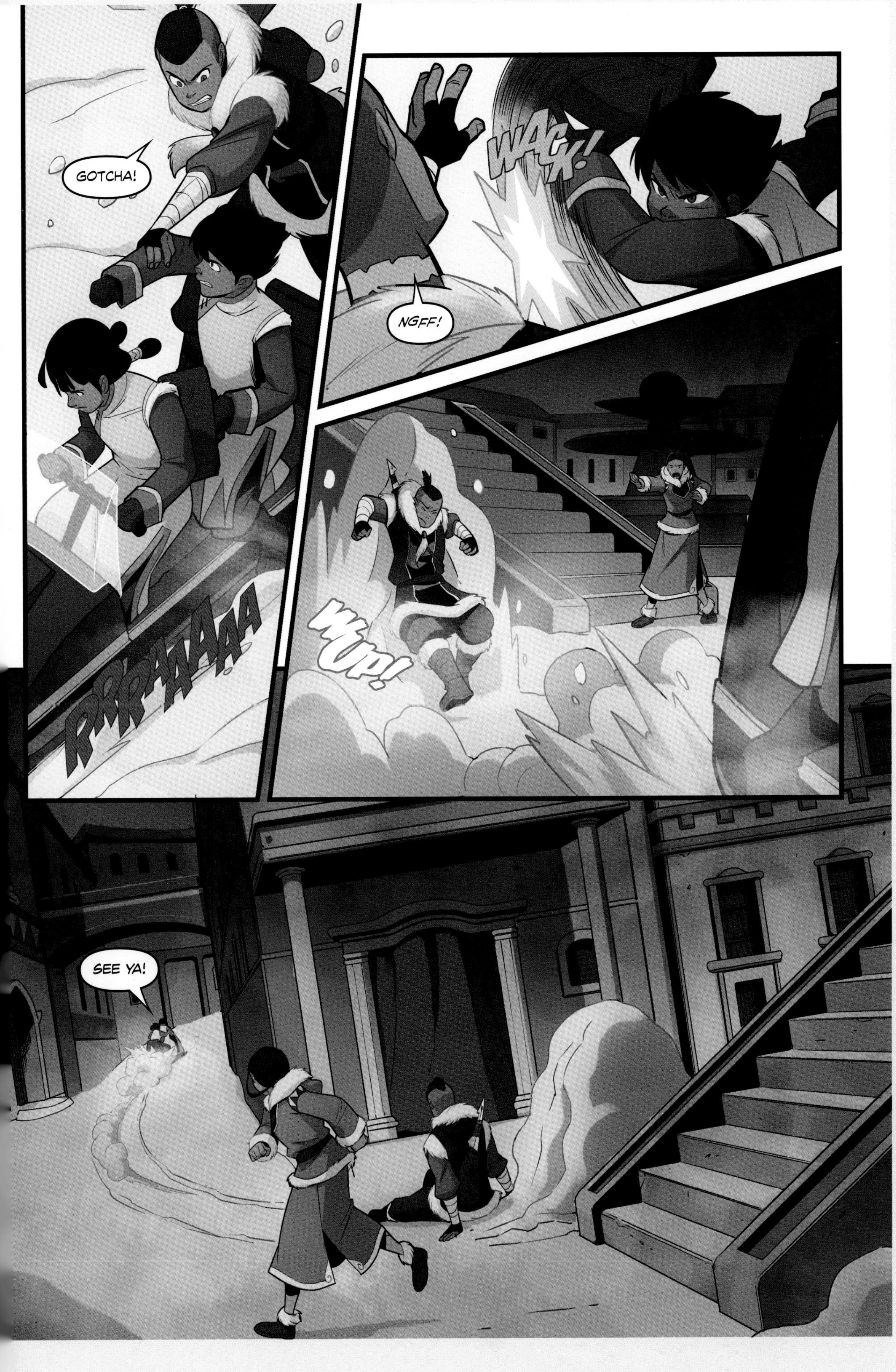
GOTCHA!
RRRAAAAA
WACK!
NGFF!
WUP!
SEE YA!

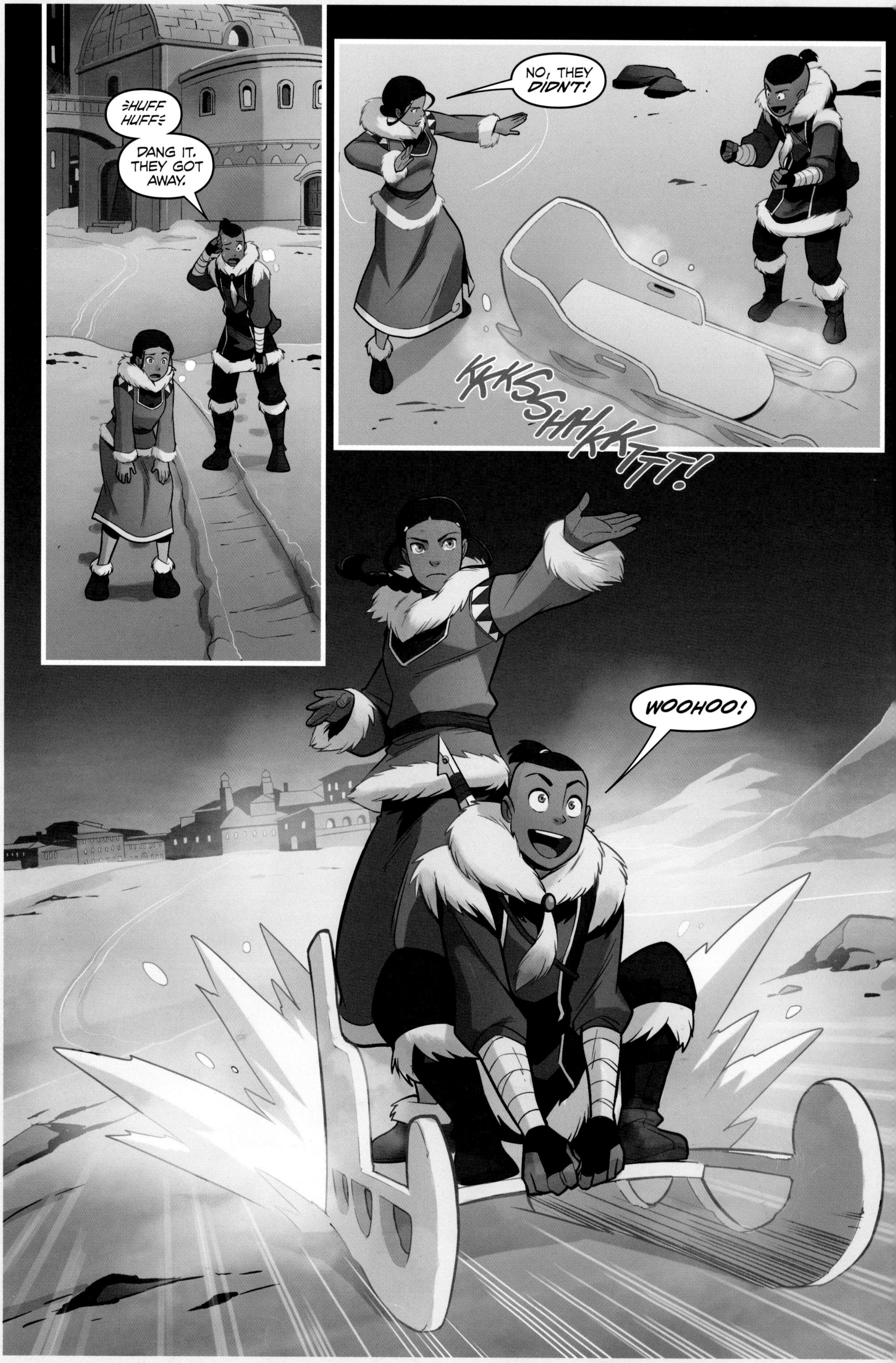
≷HUFF HUFF≶
DANG IT. THEY GOT AWAY.
NO, THEY DIDN'T!
KKKSSHHKKTTT!
WOOHOO!

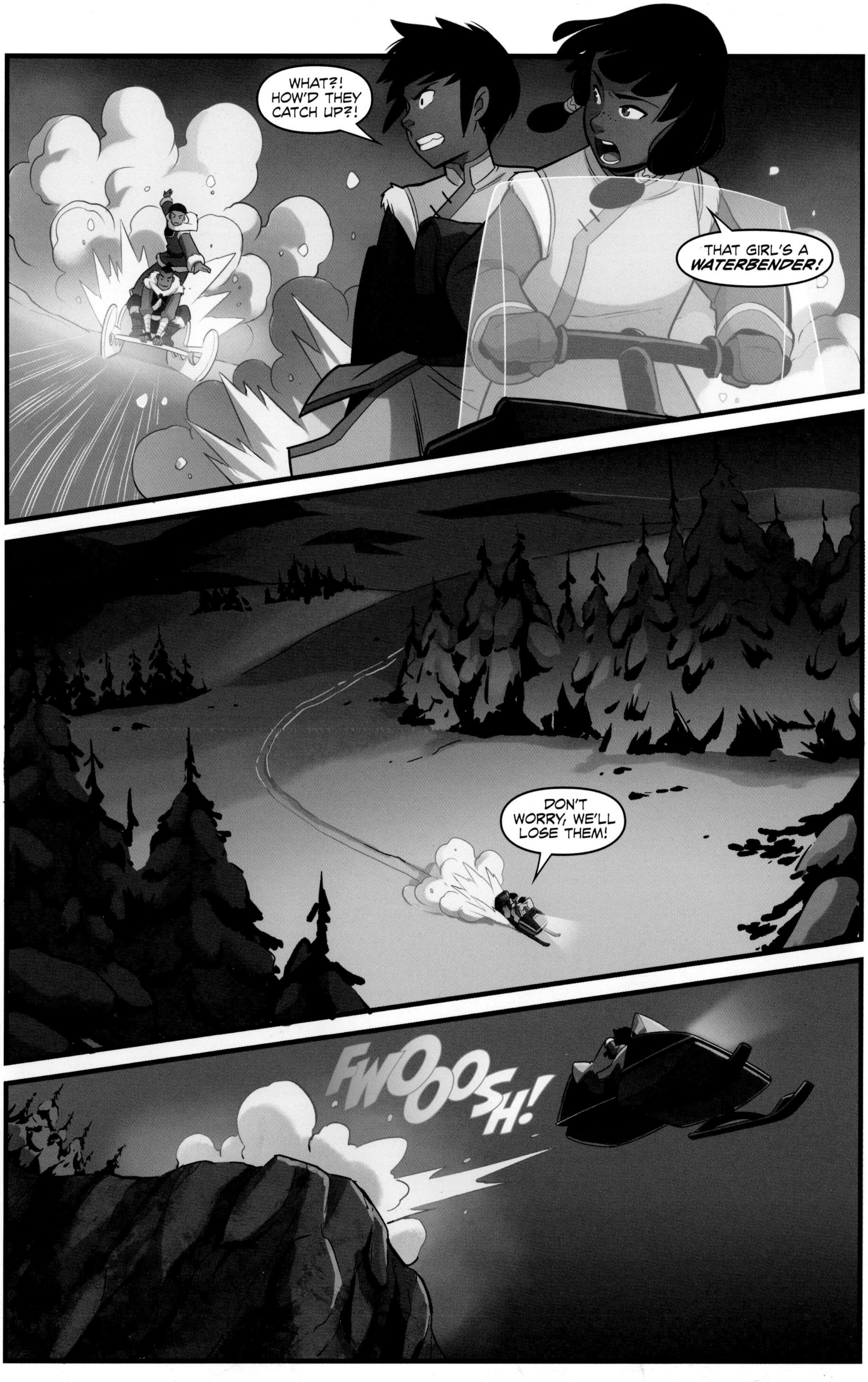
WHAT?! HOW'D THEY CATCH UP?!
THAT GIRL'S A *WATERBENDER!*
DON'T WORRY; WE'LL LOSE THEM!
FWOOOSH!

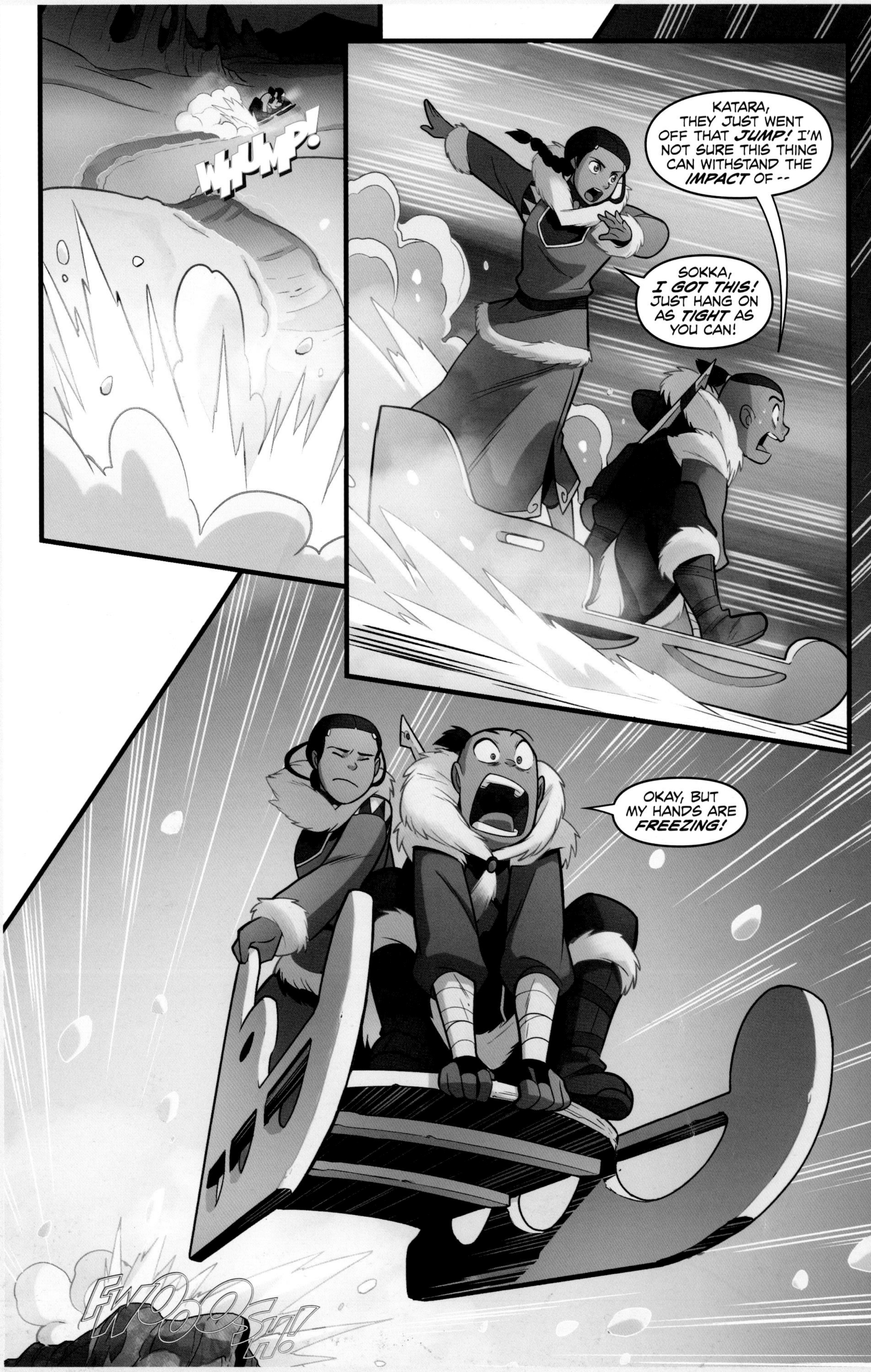
WHUMP!
KATARA, THEY JUST WENT OFF THAT JUMP! I'M NOT SURE THIS THING CAN WITHSTAND THE IMPACT OF --
SOKKA, I GOT THIS! JUST HANG ON AS TIGHT AS YOU CAN!
OKAY, BUT MY HANDS ARE FREEZING!
FWOOOSH!

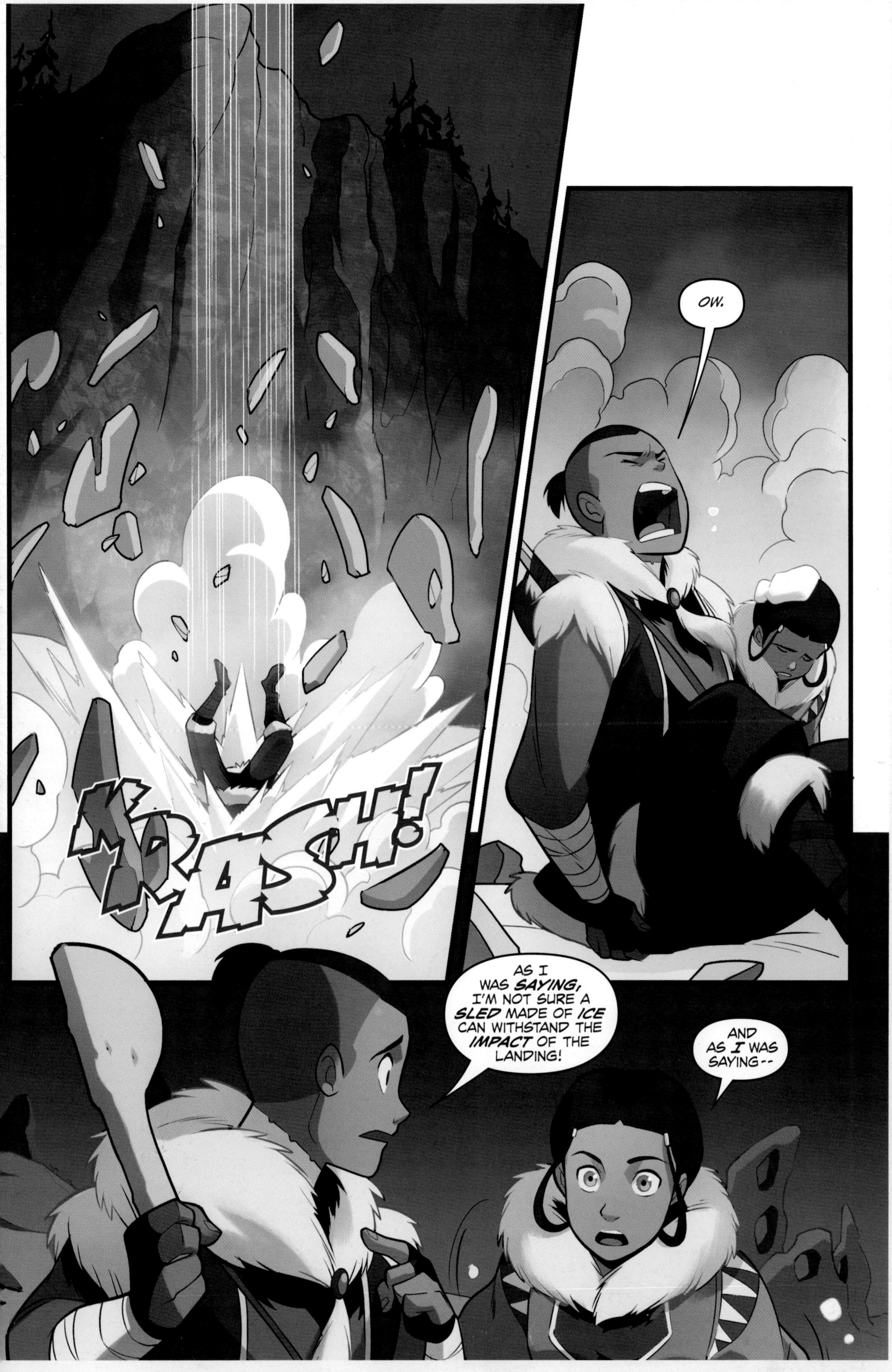
KRASH!
OW.
AS I WAS SAYING, I'M NOT SURE A SLED MADE OF ICE CAN WITHSTAND THE IMPACT OF THE LANDING!
AND AS I WAS SAYING--

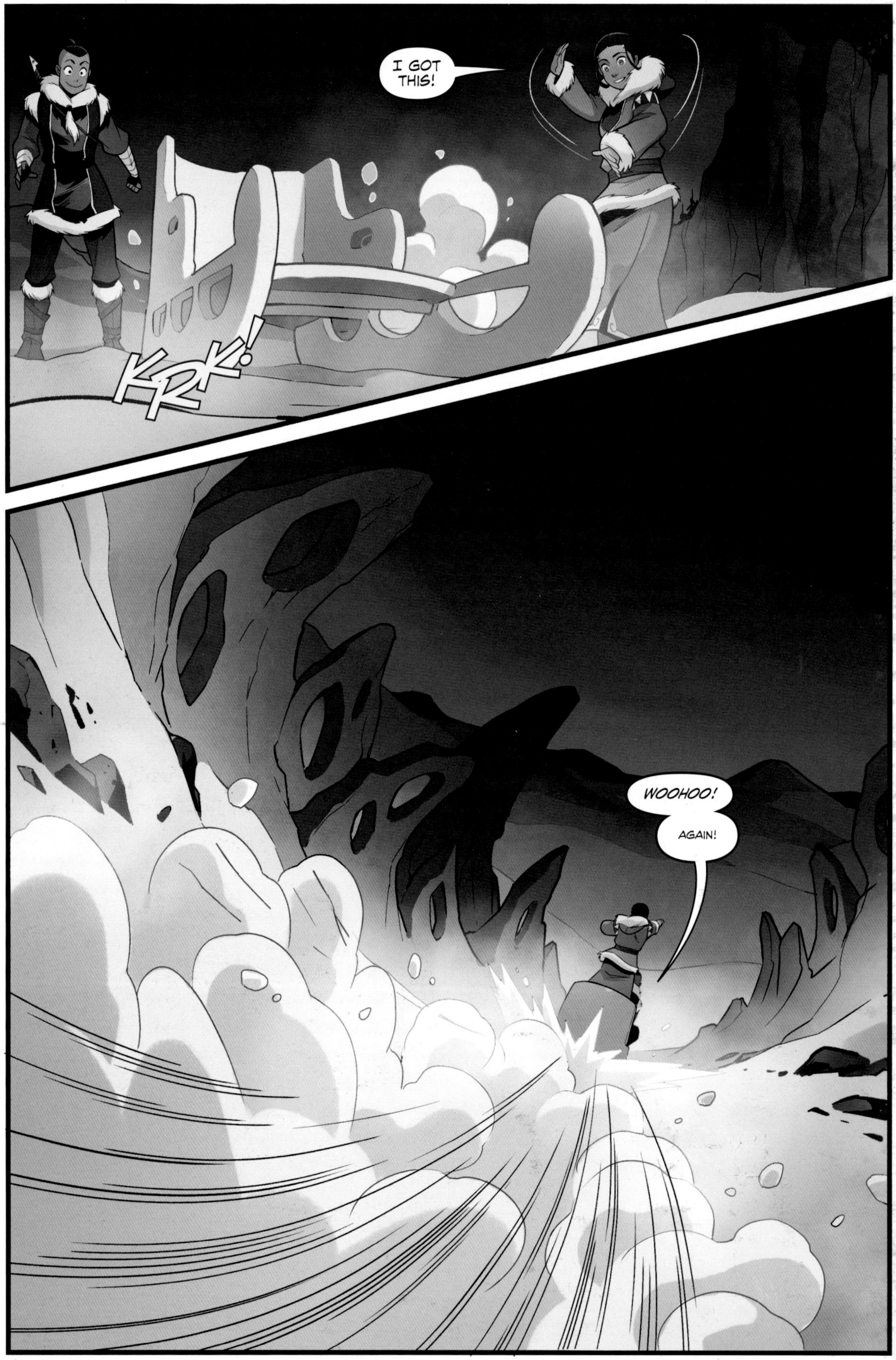
I GOT THIS!
KRK!
WOOHOO!
AGAIN!

GLY: *This scene totally depended on Gurihiru's ability to convey action. Obviously, they killed it.*

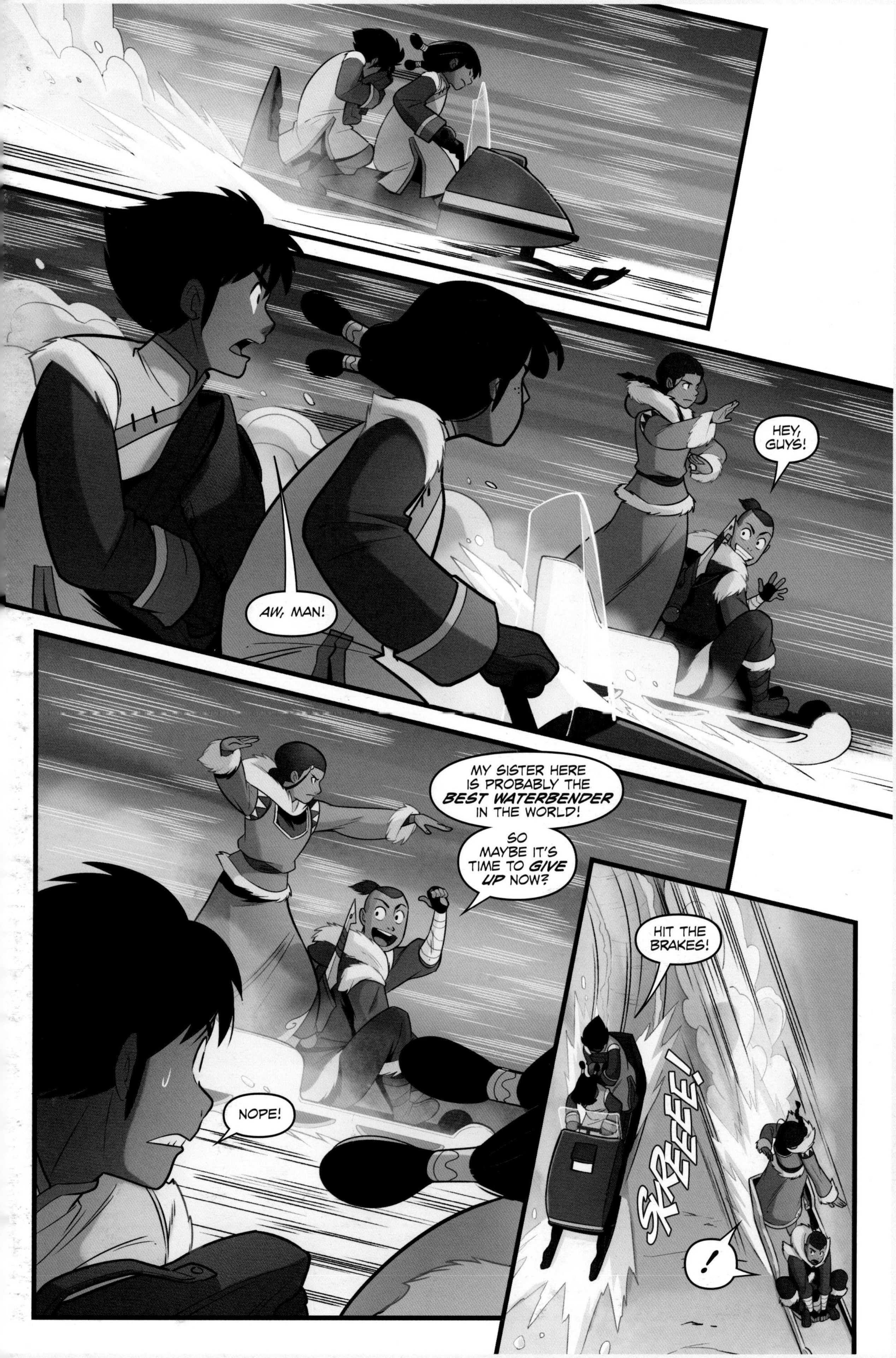
HEY, GUYS!
AW, MAN!
MY SISTER HERE IS PROBABLY THE BEST WATERBENDER IN THE WORLD!
SO MAYBE IT'S TIME TO GIVE UP NOW?
NOPE!
HIT THE BRAKES!
SKREEEEE!
!

G: *Since these pages continue with a simple chase through the snow, we laid out the panels creatively so readers would not get bored.*

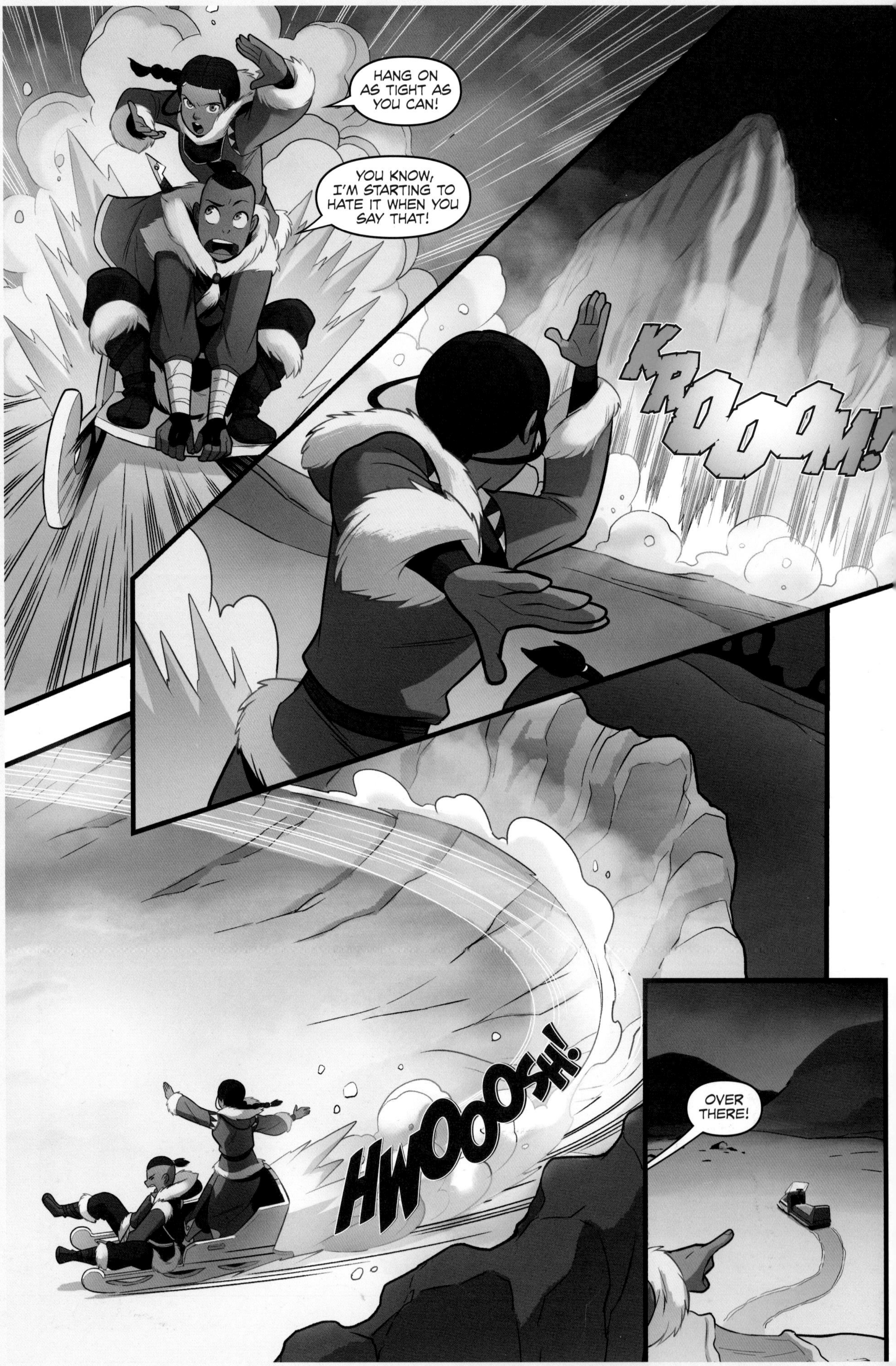
HANG ON AS TIGHT AS YOU CAN!
YOU KNOW, I'M STARTING TO HATE IT WHEN YOU SAY THAT!
KROOOM!
HWOOOSH!
OVER THERE!

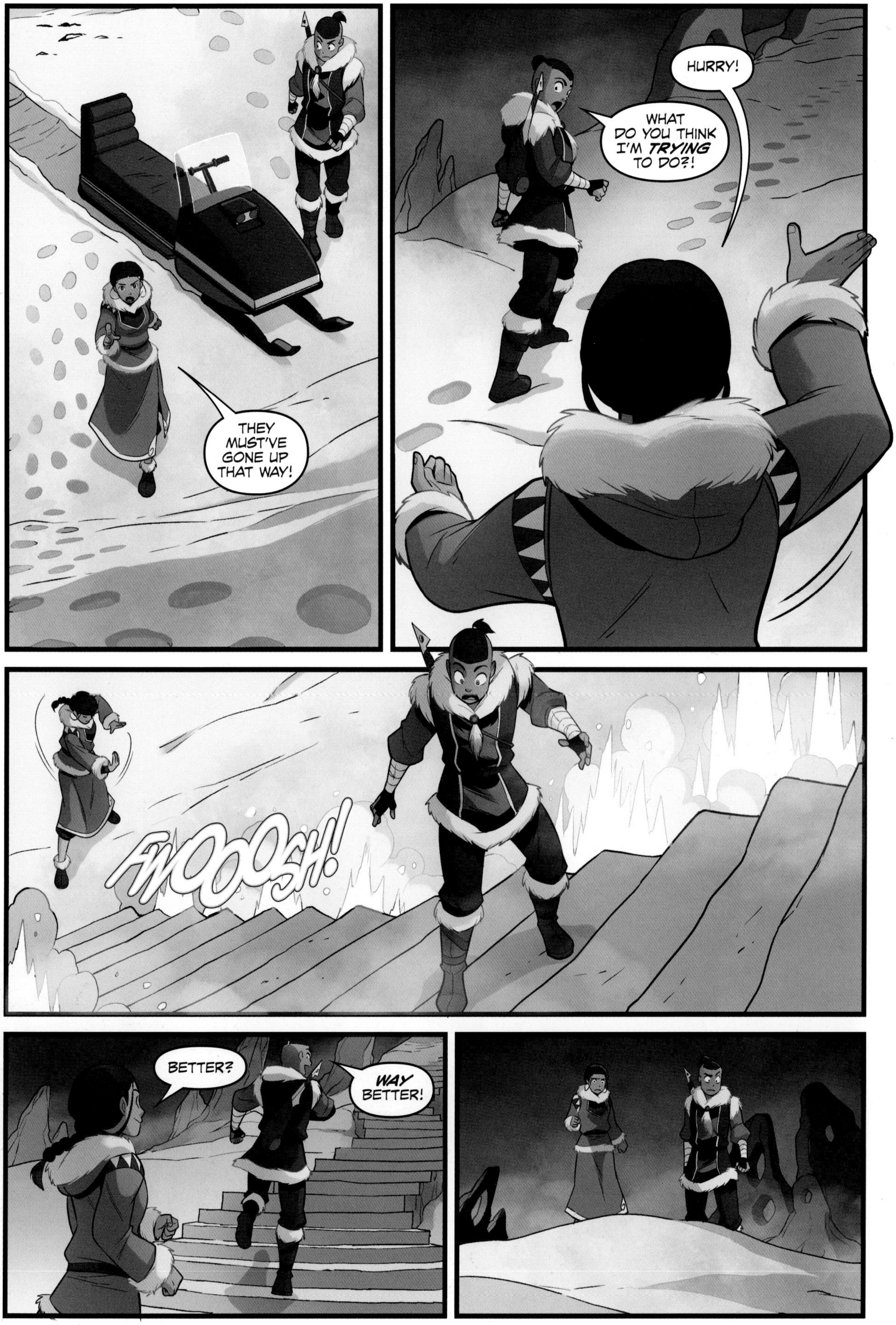
THEY MUST'VE GONE UP THAT WAY!
HURRY!
WHAT DO YOU THINK I'M *TRYING* TO DO?!
FWOOOSH!
BETTER?
WAY BETTER!

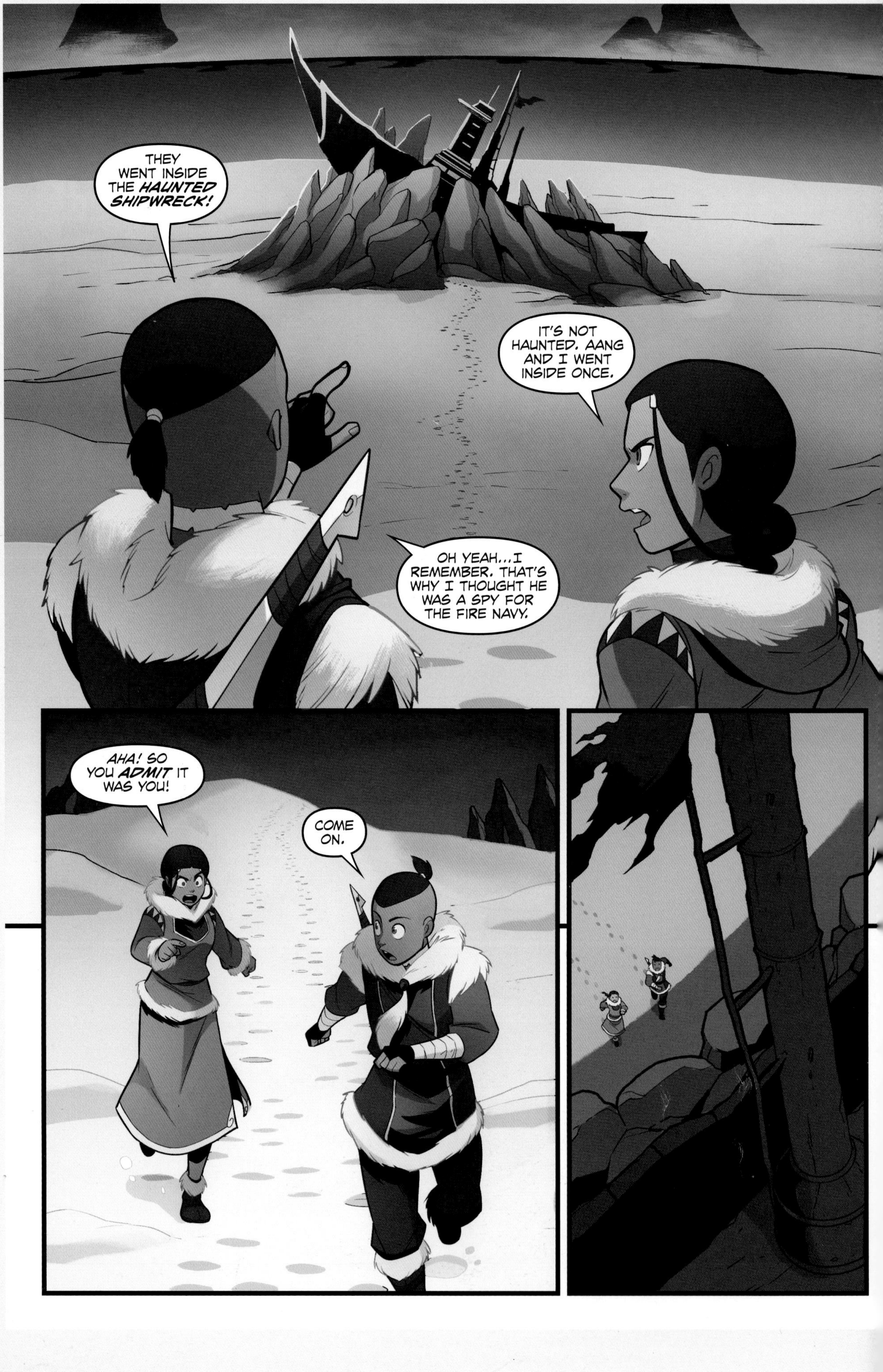
THEY WENT INSIDE THE HAUNTED SHIPWRECK!
IT'S NOT HAUNTED. AANG AND I WENT INSIDE ONCE.
OH YEAH...I REMEMBER. THAT'S WHY I THOUGHT HE WAS A SPY FOR THE FIRE NAVY.
AHA! SO YOU ADMIT IT WAS YOU!
COME ON.

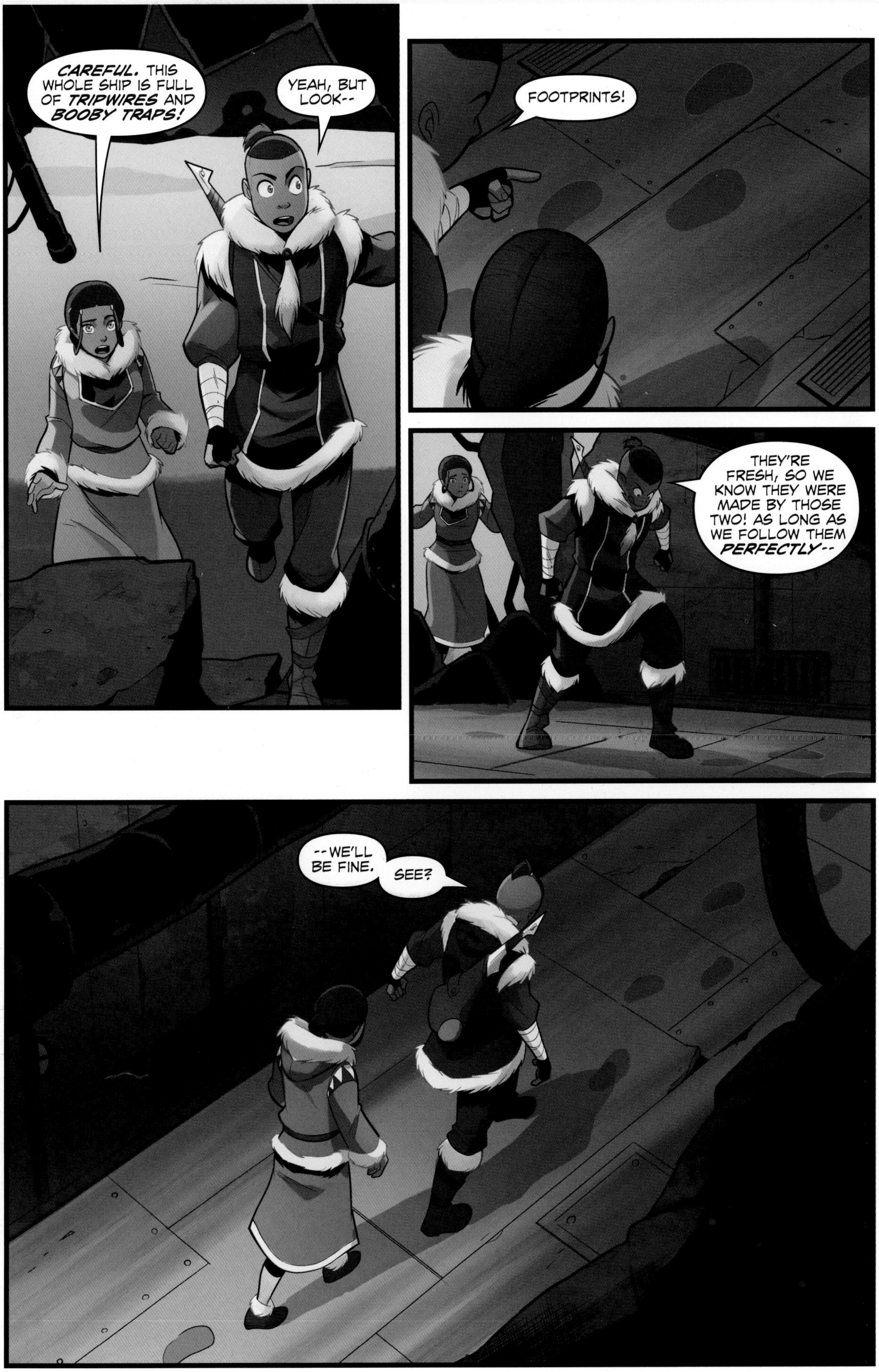
CAREFUL. THIS WHOLE SHIP IS FULL OF TRIPWIRES AND BOOBY TRAPS!
YEAH, BUT LOOK--
FOOTPRINTS!
THEY'RE FRESH, SO WE KNOW THEY WERE MADE BY THOSE TWO! AS LONG AS WE FOLLOW THEM PERFECTLY--
--WE'LL BE FINE.
SEE?

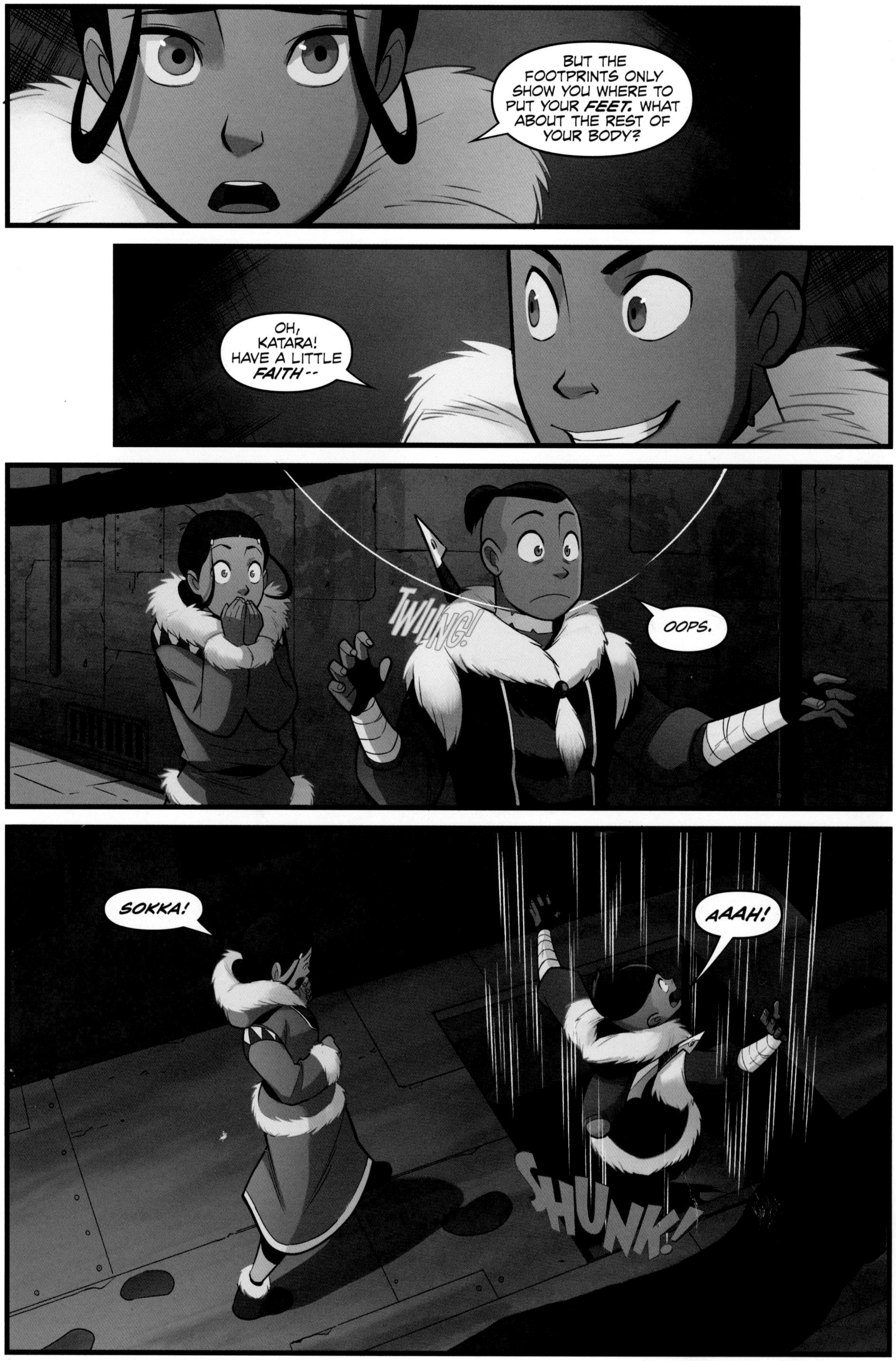
BUT THE FOOTPRINTS ONLY SHOW YOU WHERE TO PUT YOUR FEET. WHAT ABOUT THE REST OF YOUR BODY?
OH, KATARA! HAVE A LITTLE FAITH--
TWILING!
OOPS.
SOKKA!
AAAH!
SHUNK!

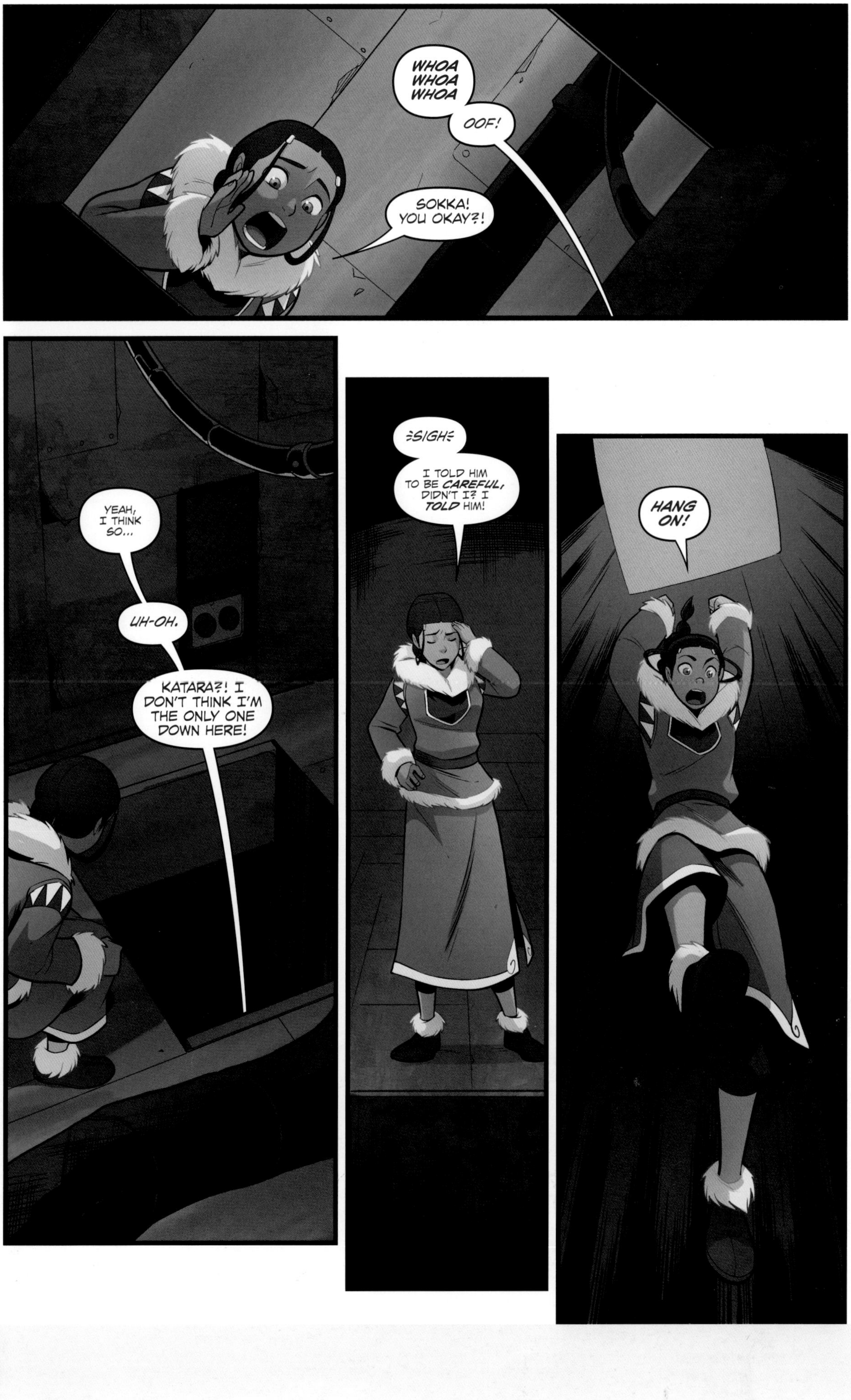
WHOA WHOA WHOA
OOF!
SOKKA! YOU OKAY?!
YEAH, I THINK SO...
UH-OH.
KATARA?! I DON'T THINK I'M THE ONLY ONE DOWN HERE!
=SIGH=
I TOLD HIM TO BE CAREFUL, DIDN'T I? I TOLD HIM!
HANG ON!

GLY: *The haunted shipwreck first appeared in "The Boy in the Iceberg." We thought it would be the perfect entry point to Gilak's secret hideout. The shipwreck is a symbol of colonialism, which is exactly what Gilak believes he's fighting against.*

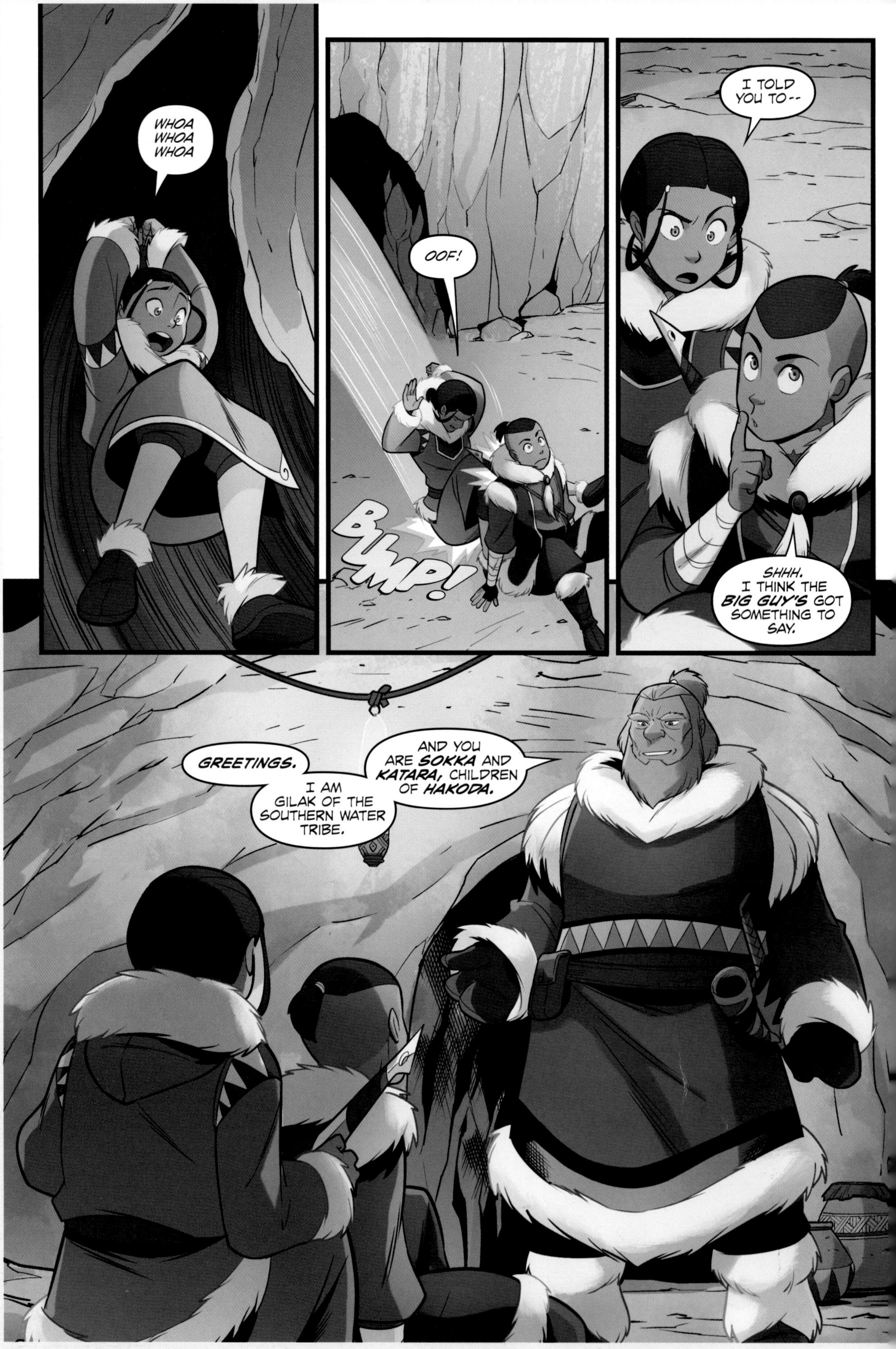
WHOA WHOA WHOA
OOF!
BUMP!
I TOLD YOU TO--
SHHH. I THINK THE BIG GUY'S GOT SOMETHING TO SAY.
GREETINGS.
I AM GILAK OF THE SOUTHERN WATER TRIBE.
AND YOU ARE SOKKA AND KATARA, CHILDREN OF HAKODA.

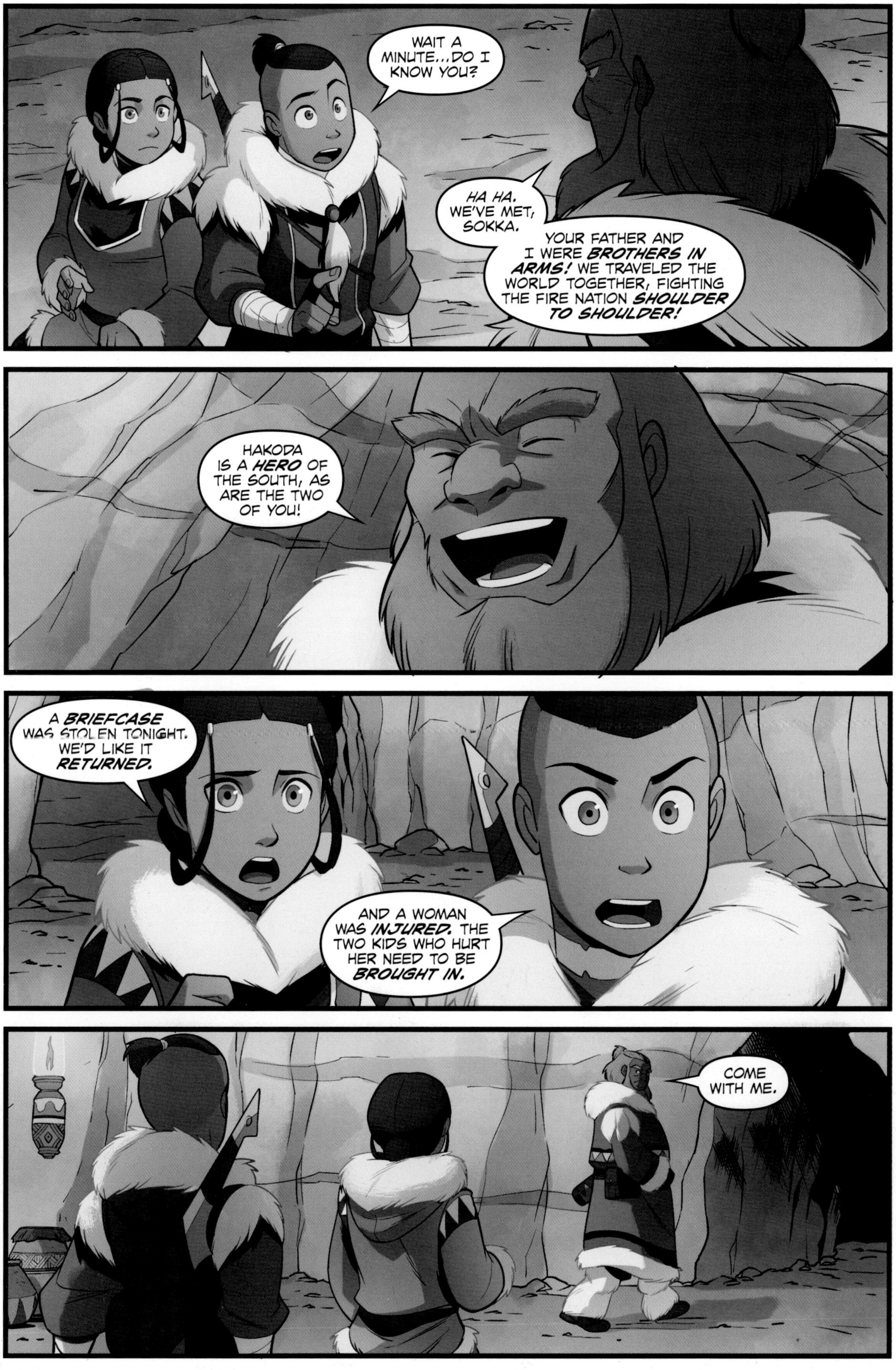
WAIT A MINUTE...DO I KNOW YOU?
HA HA. WE'VE MET, SOKKA.
YOUR FATHER AND I WERE BROTHERS IN ARMS! WE TRAVELED THE WORLD TOGETHER, FIGHTING THE FIRE NATION SHOULDER TO SHOULDER!
HAKODA IS A HERO OF THE SOUTH, AS ARE THE TWO OF YOU!
A BRIEFCASE WAS STOLEN TONIGHT. WE'D LIKE IT RETURNED.
AND A WOMAN WAS INJURED. THE TWO KIDS WHO HURT HER NEED TO BE BROUGHT IN.
COME WITH ME.

G: *The fact that Gilak and Hakoda used to fight together against the Fire Nation during the Hundred Year War is a reference to the TV show.*

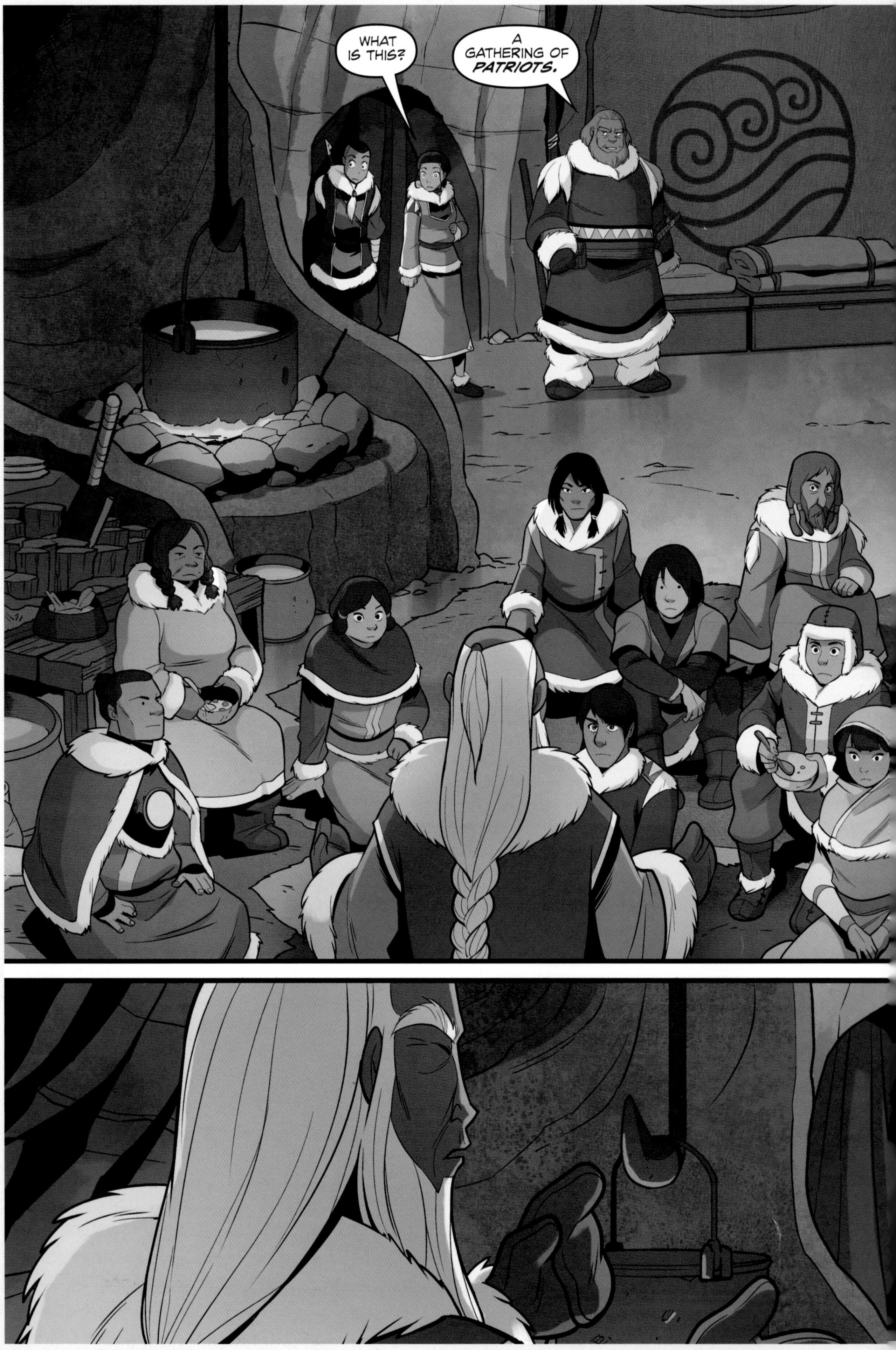
WHAT IS THIS?
A GATHERING OF *PATRIOTS.*

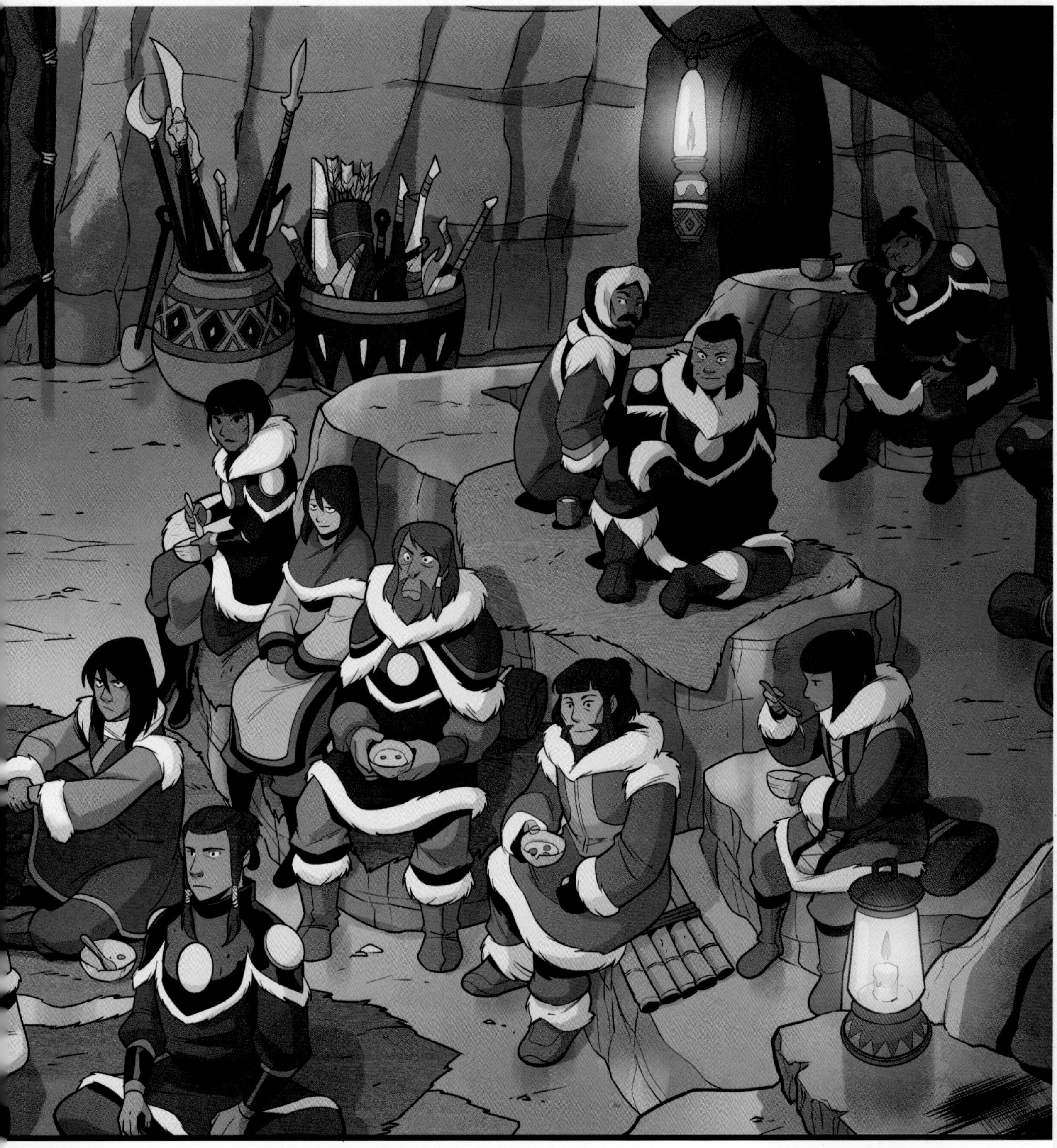

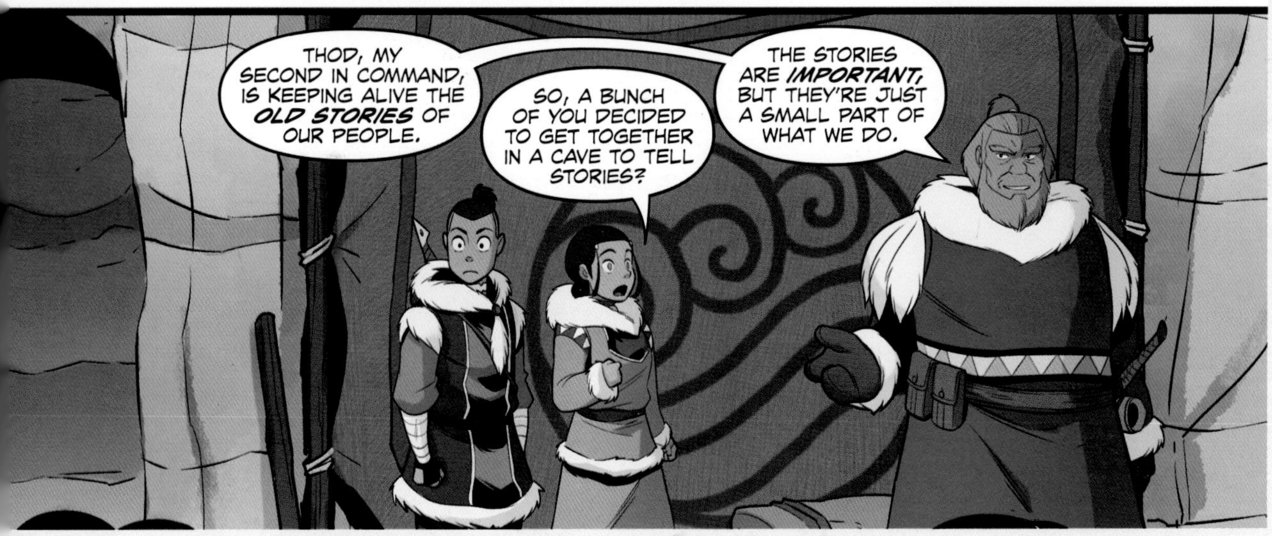
THOD, MY SECOND IN COMMAND, IS KEEPING ALIVE THE OLD STORIES OF OUR PEOPLE.
SO, A BUNCH OF YOU DECIDED TO GET TOGETHER IN A CAVE TO TELL STORIES?
THE STORIES ARE IMPORTANT, BUT THEY'RE JUST A SMALL PART OF WHAT WE DO.

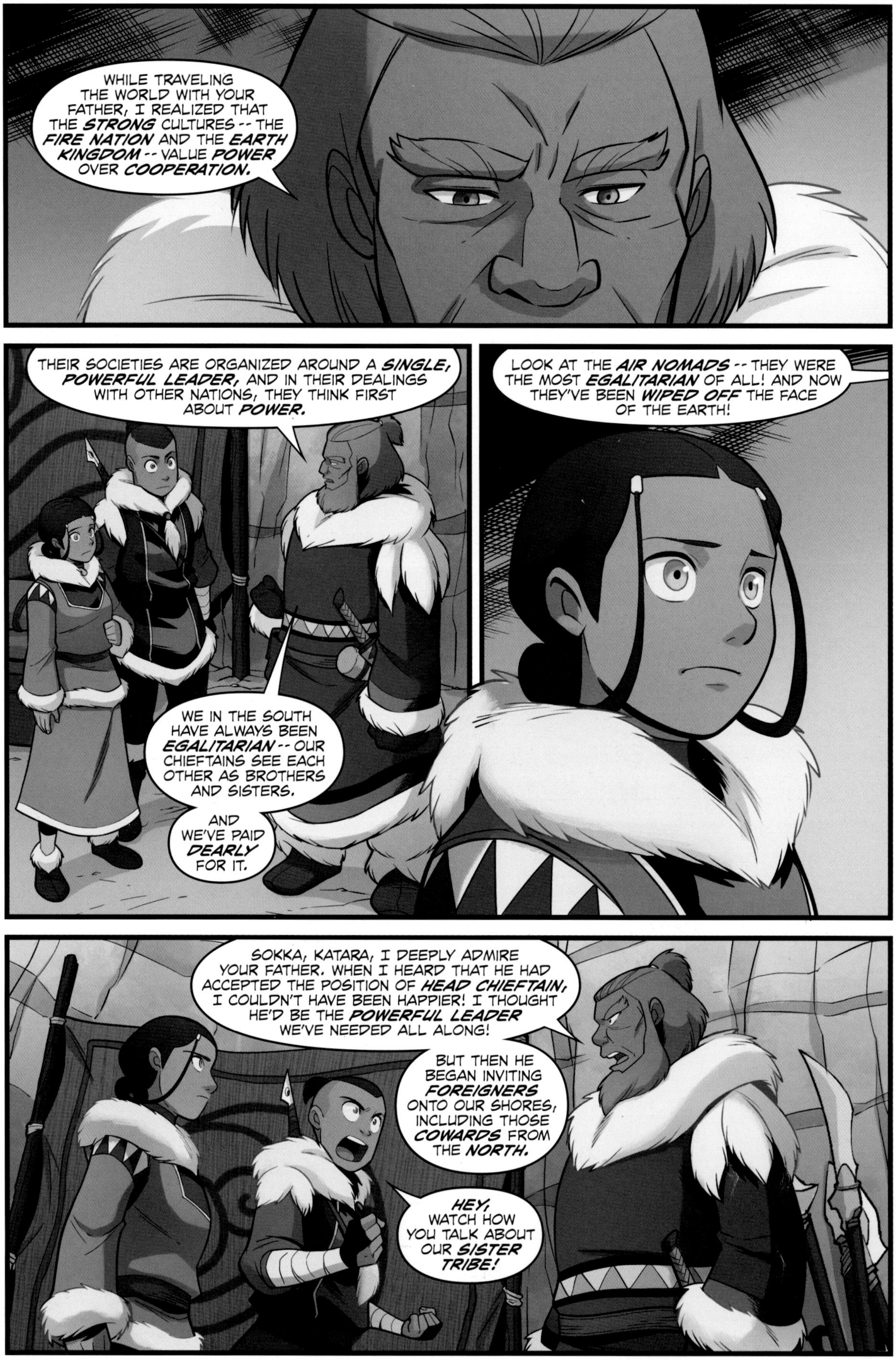
WHILE TRAVELING THE WORLD WITH YOUR FATHER, I REALIZED THAT THE *STRONG* CULTURES -- THE *FIRE NATION* AND THE *EARTH KINGDOM* -- VALUE *POWER* OVER *COOPERATION.*
THEIR SOCIETIES ARE ORGANIZED AROUND A *SINGLE, POWERFUL LEADER,* AND IN THEIR DEALINGS WITH OTHER NATIONS, THEY THINK FIRST ABOUT *POWER.*
WE IN THE SOUTH HAVE ALWAYS BEEN *EGALITARIAN* -- OUR CHIEFTAINS SEE EACH OTHER AS BROTHERS AND SISTERS.
AND WE'VE PAID *DEARLY* FOR IT.
LOOK AT THE *AIR NOMADS* -- THEY WERE THE MOST *EGALITARIAN* OF ALL! AND NOW THEY'VE BEEN *WIPED OFF* THE FACE OF THE EARTH!
SOKKA, KATARA, I DEEPLY ADMIRE YOUR FATHER. WHEN I HEARD THAT HE HAD ACCEPTED THE POSITION OF *HEAD CHIEFTAIN,* I COULDN'T HAVE BEEN HAPPIER! I THOUGHT HE'D BE THE *POWERFUL LEADER* WE'VE NEEDED ALL ALONG!
BUT THEN HE BEGAN INVITING *FOREIGNERS* ONTO OUR SHORES, INCLUDING THOSE *COWARDS* FROM THE *NORTH.*
HEY, WATCH HOW YOU TALK ABOUT OUR *SISTER TRIBE!*

GLY: *In the first draft of the script, Gilak's army wasn't an army. It was a religious cult. They wanted to bring about a Water Tribe Avatar as soon as possible because they believed that it would be the key to the South's cultural survival. As we went through the revision process, the religious element was dropped so that we could focus on the political element. Because Hakoda is a political figure, it seemed more appropriate.*

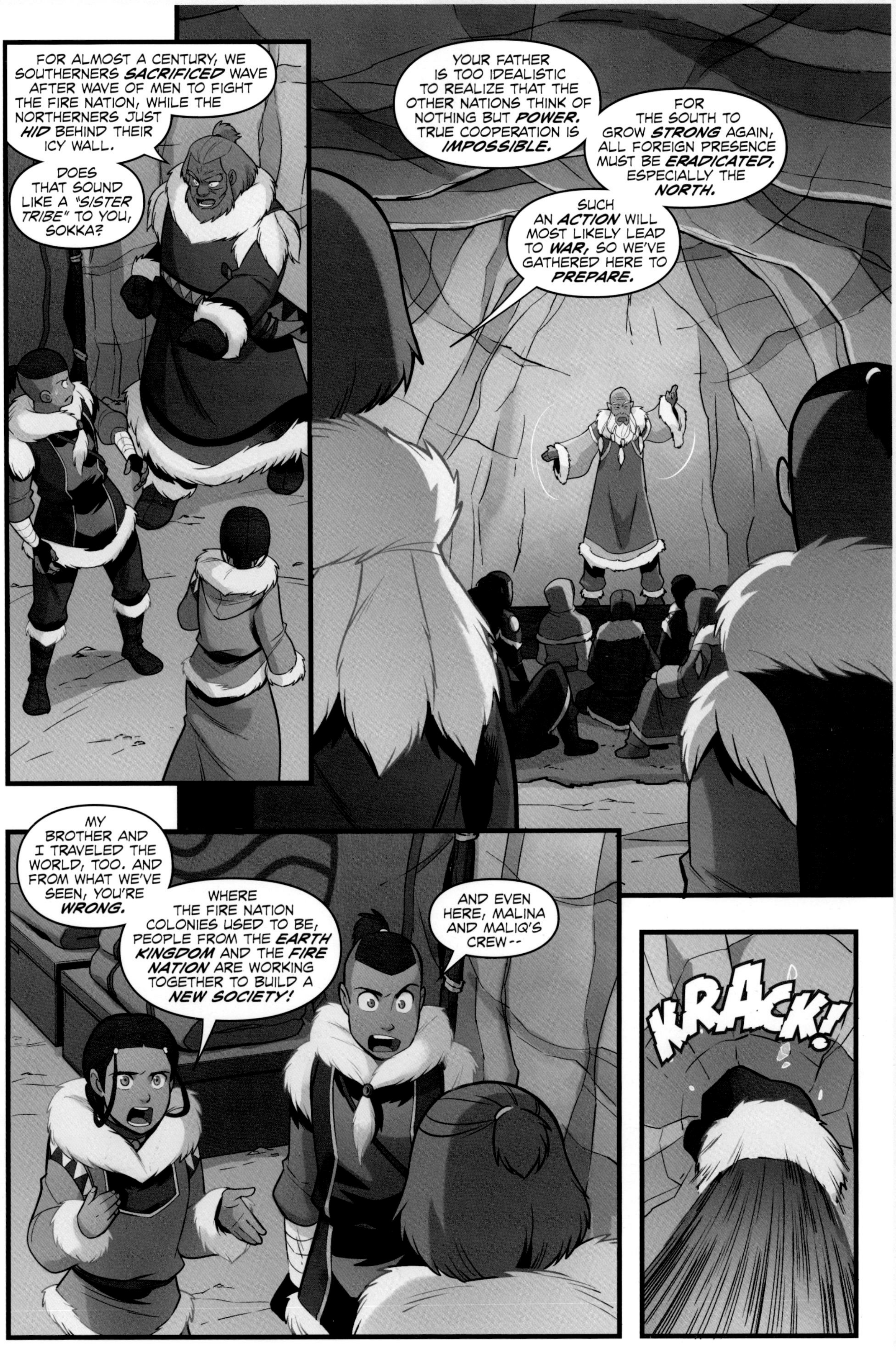
FOR ALMOST A CENTURY, WE SOUTHERNERS SACRIFICED WAVE AFTER WAVE OF MEN TO FIGHT THE FIRE NATION, WHILE THE NORTHERNERS JUST HID BEHIND THEIR ICY WALL.
DOES THAT SOUND LIKE A "SISTER TRIBE" TO YOU, SOKKA?
YOUR FATHER IS TOO IDEALISTIC TO REALIZE THAT THE OTHER NATIONS THINK OF NOTHING BUT POWER. TRUE COOPERATION IS IMPOSSIBLE.
FOR THE SOUTH TO GROW STRONG AGAIN, ALL FOREIGN PRESENCE MUST BE ERADICATED, ESPECIALLY THE NORTH.
SUCH AN ACTION WILL MOST LIKELY LEAD TO WAR, SO WE'VE GATHERED HERE TO PREPARE.
MY BROTHER AND I TRAVELED THE WORLD, TOO. AND FROM WHAT WE'VE SEEN, YOU'RE WRONG.
WHERE THE FIRE NATION COLONIES USED TO BE, PEOPLE FROM THE EARTH KINGDOM AND THE FIRE NATION ARE WORKING TOGETHER TO BUILD A NEW SOCIETY!
AND EVEN HERE, MALINA AND MALIQ'S CREW--
KRACK!

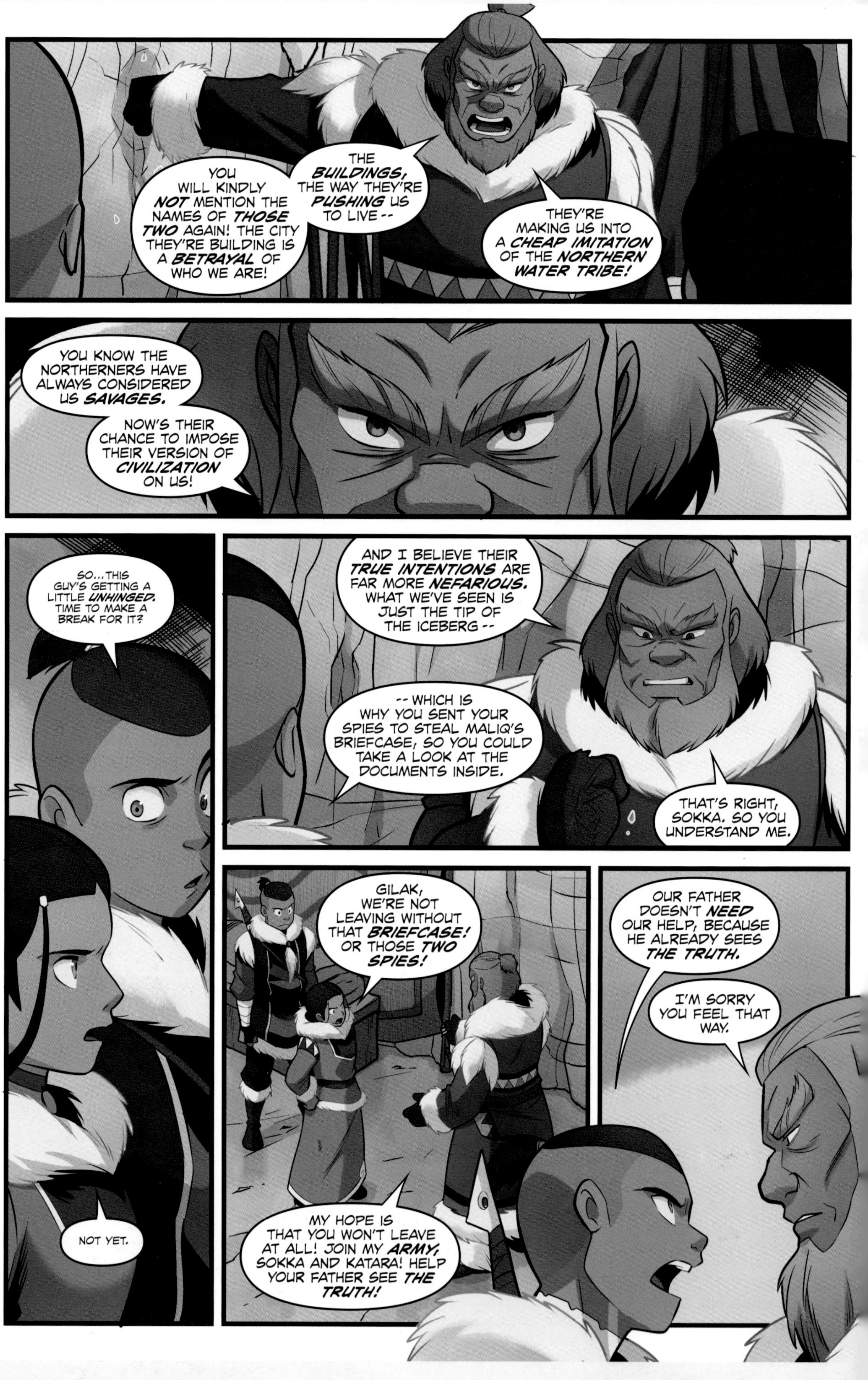
YOU WILL KINDLY NOT MENTION THE NAMES OF THOSE TWO AGAIN! THE CITY THEY'RE BUILDING IS A BETRAYAL OF WHO WE ARE!
THE BUILDINGS, THE WAY THEY'RE PUSHING US TO LIVE--
THEY'RE MAKING US INTO A CHEAP IMITATION OF THE NORTHERN WATER TRIBE!
YOU KNOW THE NORTHERNERS HAVE ALWAYS CONSIDERED US SAVAGES.
NOW'S THEIR CHANCE TO IMPOSE THEIR VERSION OF CIVILIZATION ON US!
SO...THIS GUY'S GETTING A LITTLE UNHINGED. TIME TO MAKE A BREAK FOR IT?
NOT YET.
AND I BELIEVE THEIR TRUE INTENTIONS ARE FAR MORE NEFARIOUS. WHAT WE'VE SEEN IS JUST THE TIP OF THE ICEBERG--
--WHICH IS WHY YOU SENT YOUR SPIES TO STEAL MALIQ'S BRIEFCASE, SO YOU COULD TAKE A LOOK AT THE DOCUMENTS INSIDE.
THAT'S RIGHT, SOKKA. SO YOU UNDERSTAND ME.
GILAK, WE'RE NOT LEAVING WITHOUT THAT BRIEFCASE! OR THOSE TWO SPIES!
MY HOPE IS THAT YOU WON'T LEAVE AT ALL! JOIN MY ARMY, SOKKA AND KATARA! HELP YOUR FATHER SEE THE TRUTH!
OUR FATHER DOESN'T NEED OUR HELP, BECAUSE HE ALREADY SEES THE TRUTH.
I'M SORRY YOU FEEL THAT WAY.

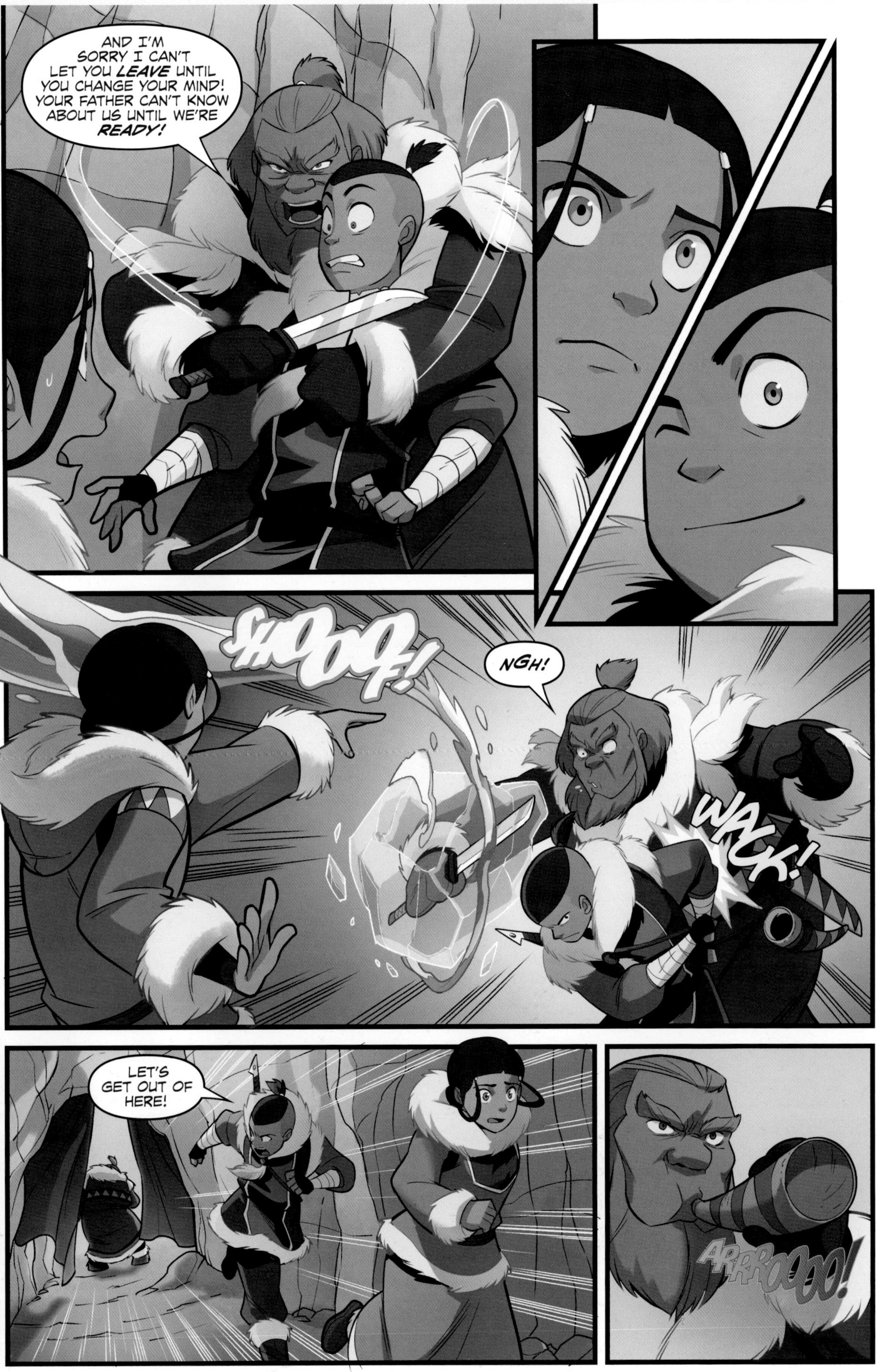
AND I'M SORRY I CAN'T LET YOU LEAVE UNTIL YOU CHANGE YOUR MIND! YOUR FATHER CAN'T KNOW ABOUT US UNTIL WE'RE READY!
SHOOOOF!
NGH!
WACK!
LET'S GET OUT OF HERE!
ARRROOOO!

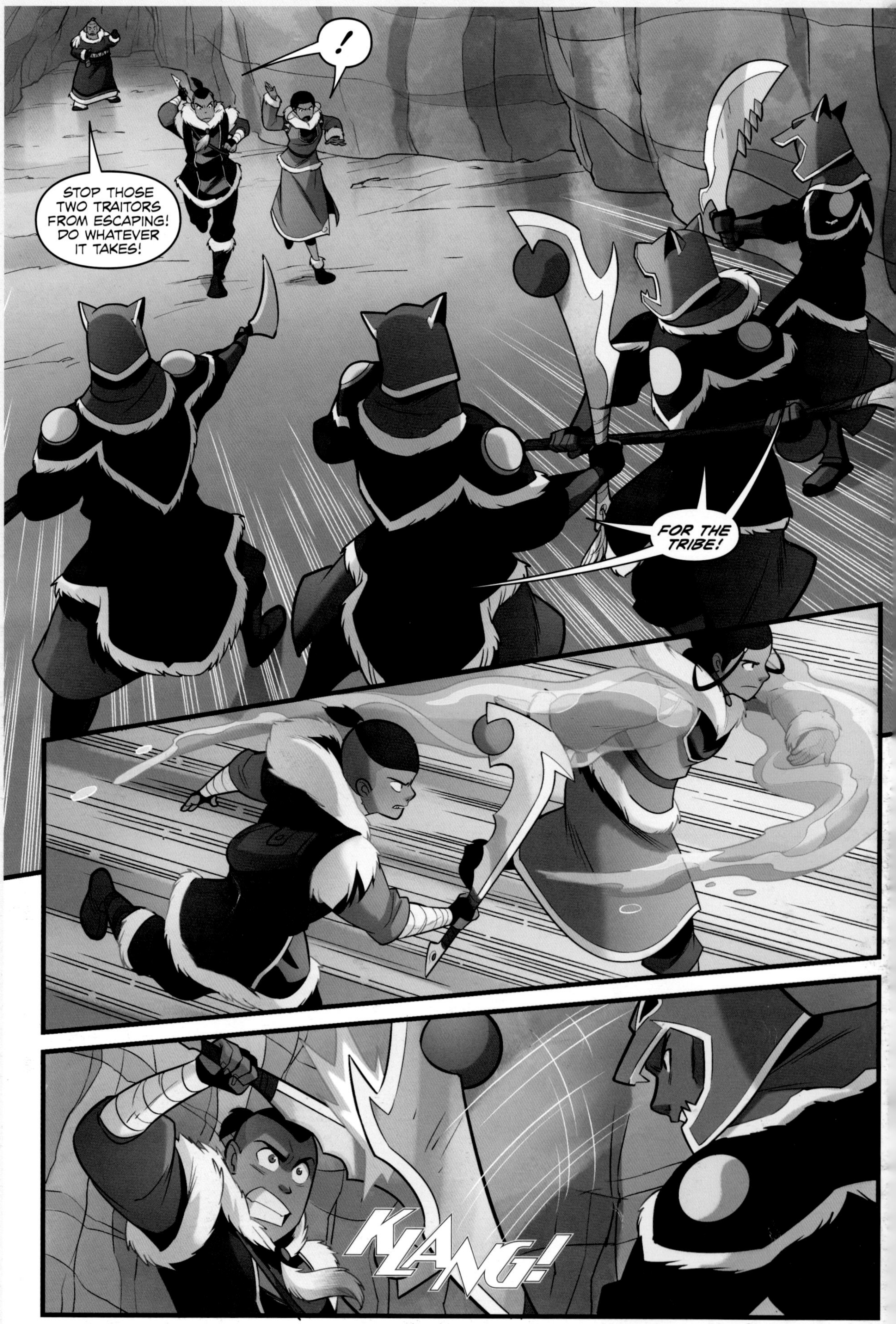
!
STOP THOSE TWO TRAITORS FROM ESCAPING! DO WHATEVER IT TAKES!
FOR THE TRIBE!
KLANG!

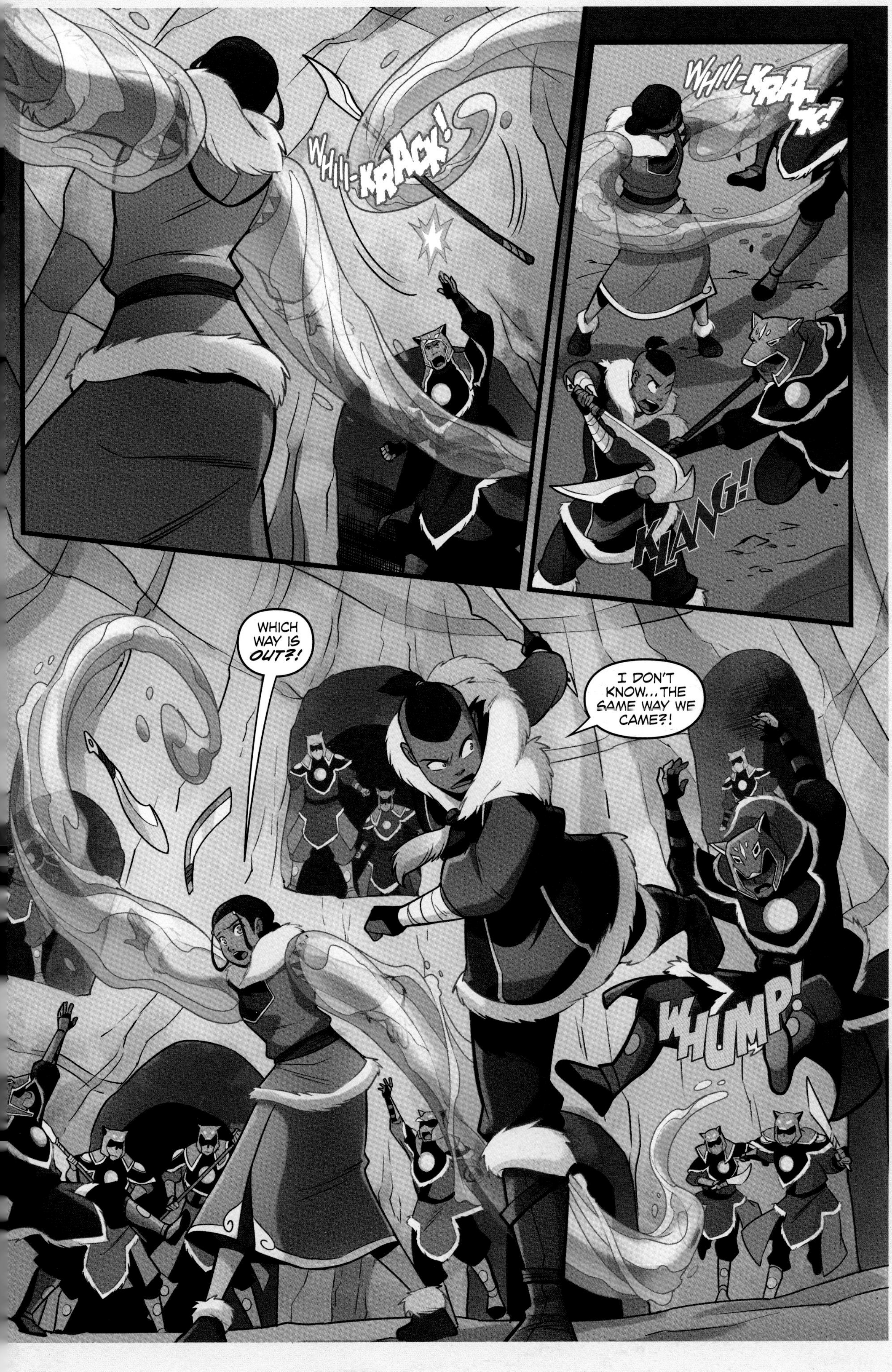
WHIII-KRACK!
WHIII-KRACK!
KLANG!
WHICH WAY IS OUT?!
I DON'T KNOW... THE SAME WAY WE CAME?!
WHUMP!

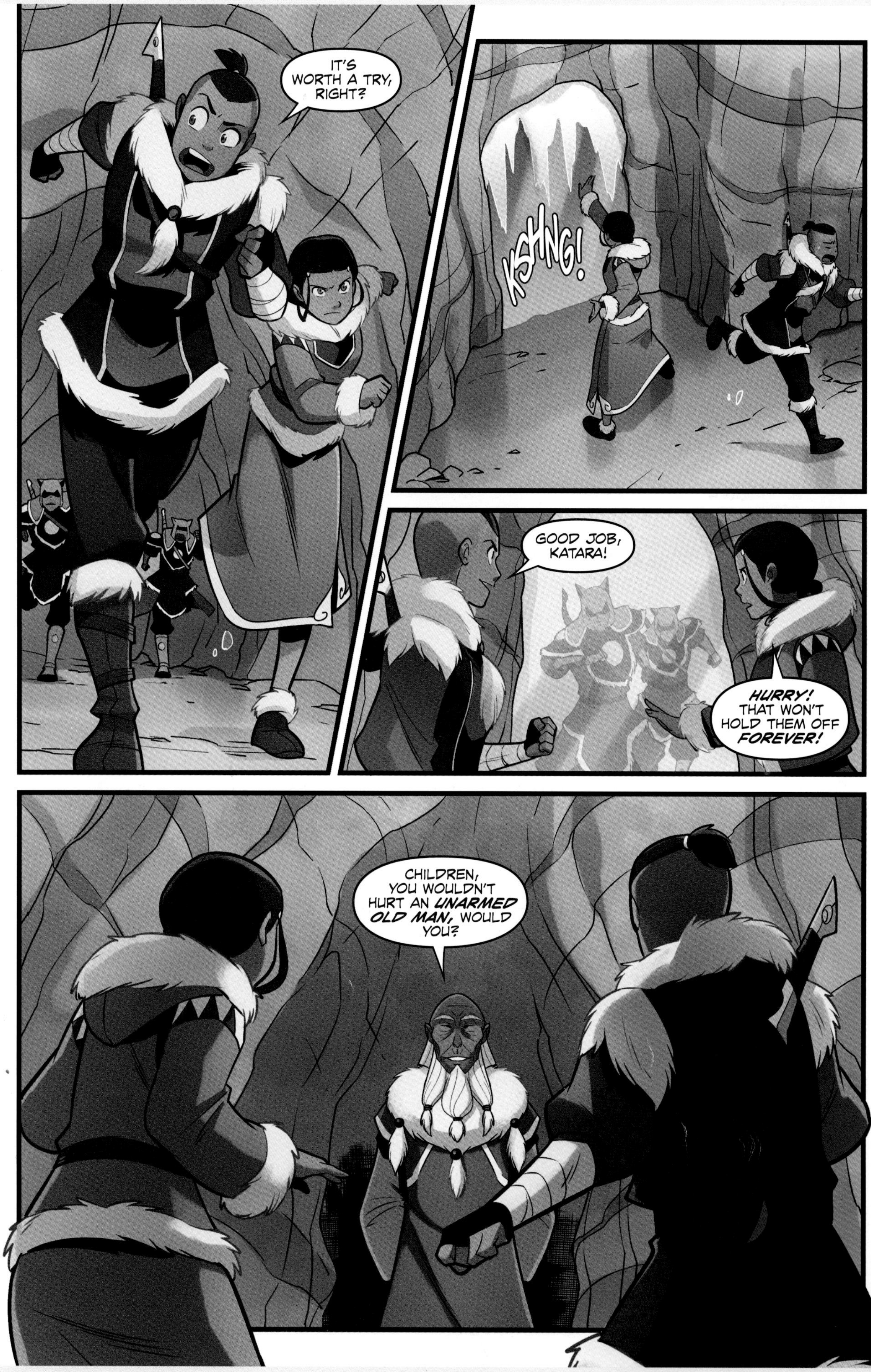
IT'S WORTH A TRY, RIGHT?
KSHNG!
GOOD JOB, KATARA!
HURRY! THAT WON'T HOLD THEM OFF FOREVER!
CHILDREN, YOU WOULDN'T HURT AN UNARMED OLD MAN, WOULD YOU?

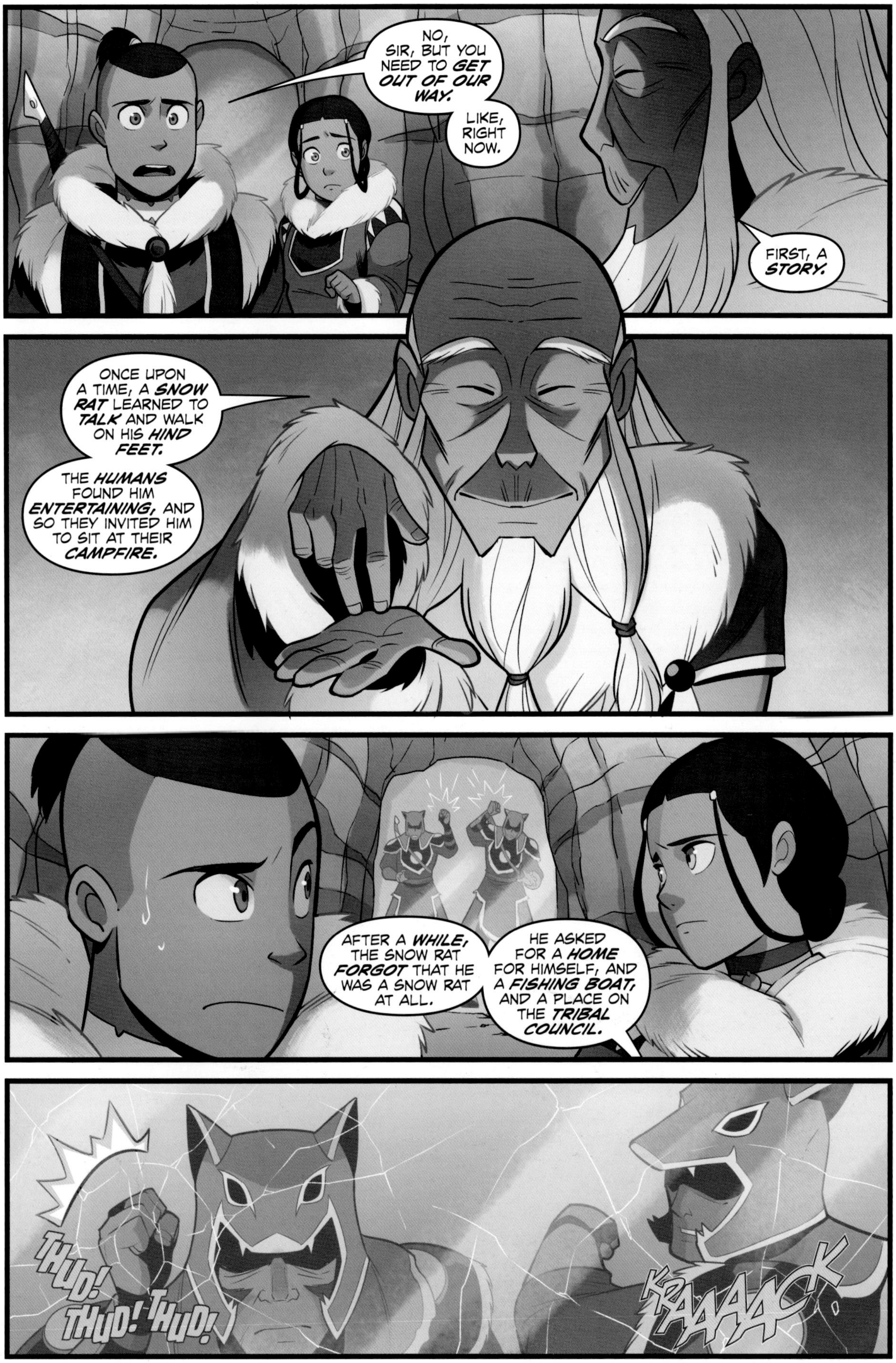
NO, SIR, BUT YOU NEED TO GET OUT OF OUR WAY.
LIKE, RIGHT NOW.
FIRST, A STORY.
ONCE UPON A TIME, A SNOW RAT LEARNED TO TALK AND WALK ON HIS HIND FEET.
THE HUMANS FOUND HIM ENTERTAINING, AND SO THEY INVITED HIM TO SIT AT THEIR CAMPFIRE.
AFTER A WHILE, THE SNOW RAT FORGOT THAT HE WAS A SNOW RAT AT ALL.
HE ASKED FOR A HOME FOR HIMSELF, AND A FISHING BOAT, AND A PLACE ON THE TRIBAL COUNCIL.
THUD! THUD! THUD!
KRAAAACK

GLY: *Originally, the protagonist of Thod's story was a wolf. We decided to change it to a rat because wolves are considered noble in Water Tribe culture.*

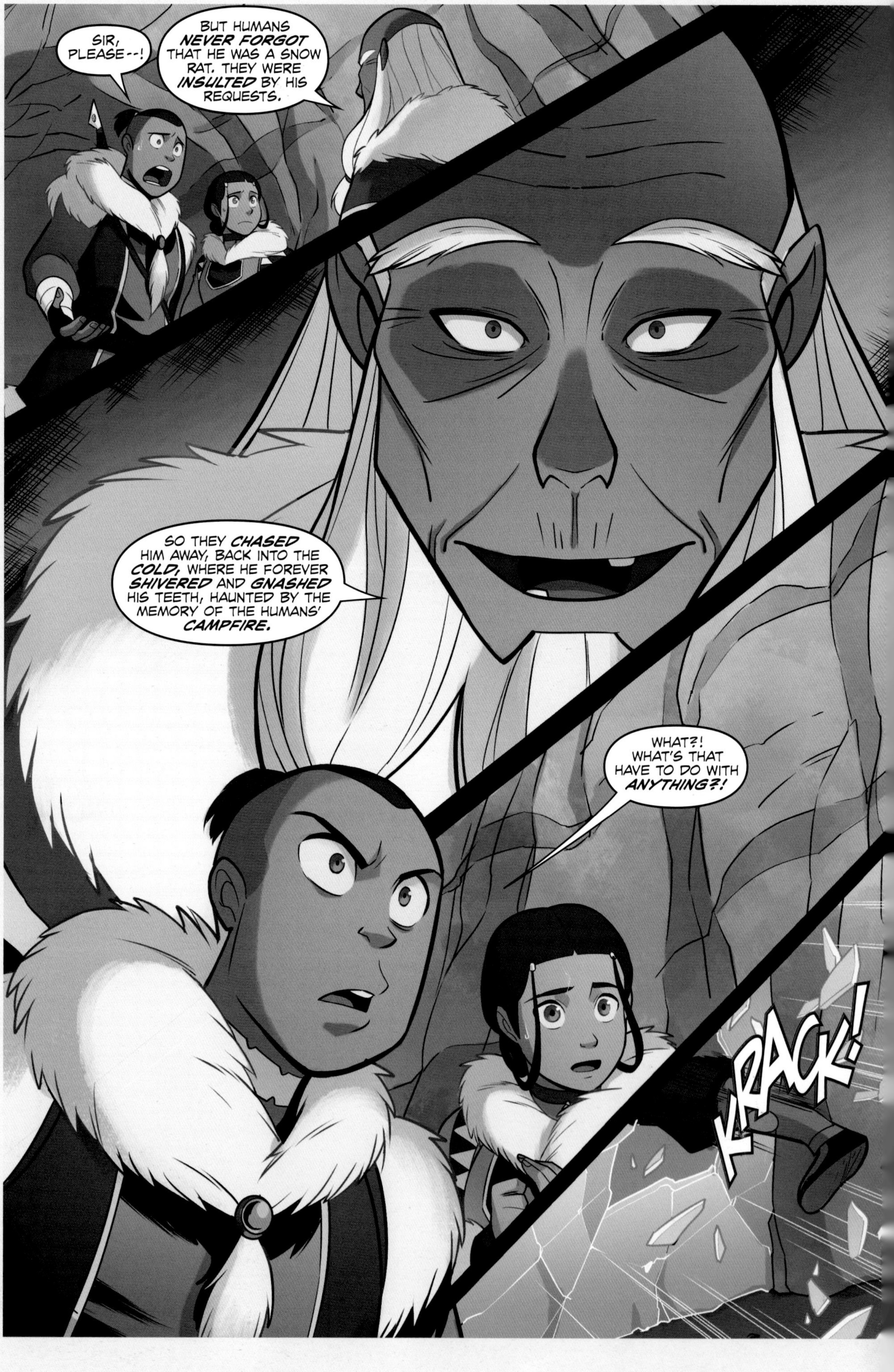
SIR, PLEASE--!
BUT HUMANS NEVER FORGOT THAT HE WAS A SNOW RAT. THEY WERE INSULTED BY HIS REQUESTS.
SO THEY CHASED HIM AWAY, BACK INTO THE COLD, WHERE HE FOREVER SHIVERED AND GNASHED HIS TEETH, HAUNTED BY THE MEMORY OF THE HUMANS' CAMPFIRE.
WHAT?! WHAT'S THAT HAVE TO DO WITH ANYTHING?!
KRACK!

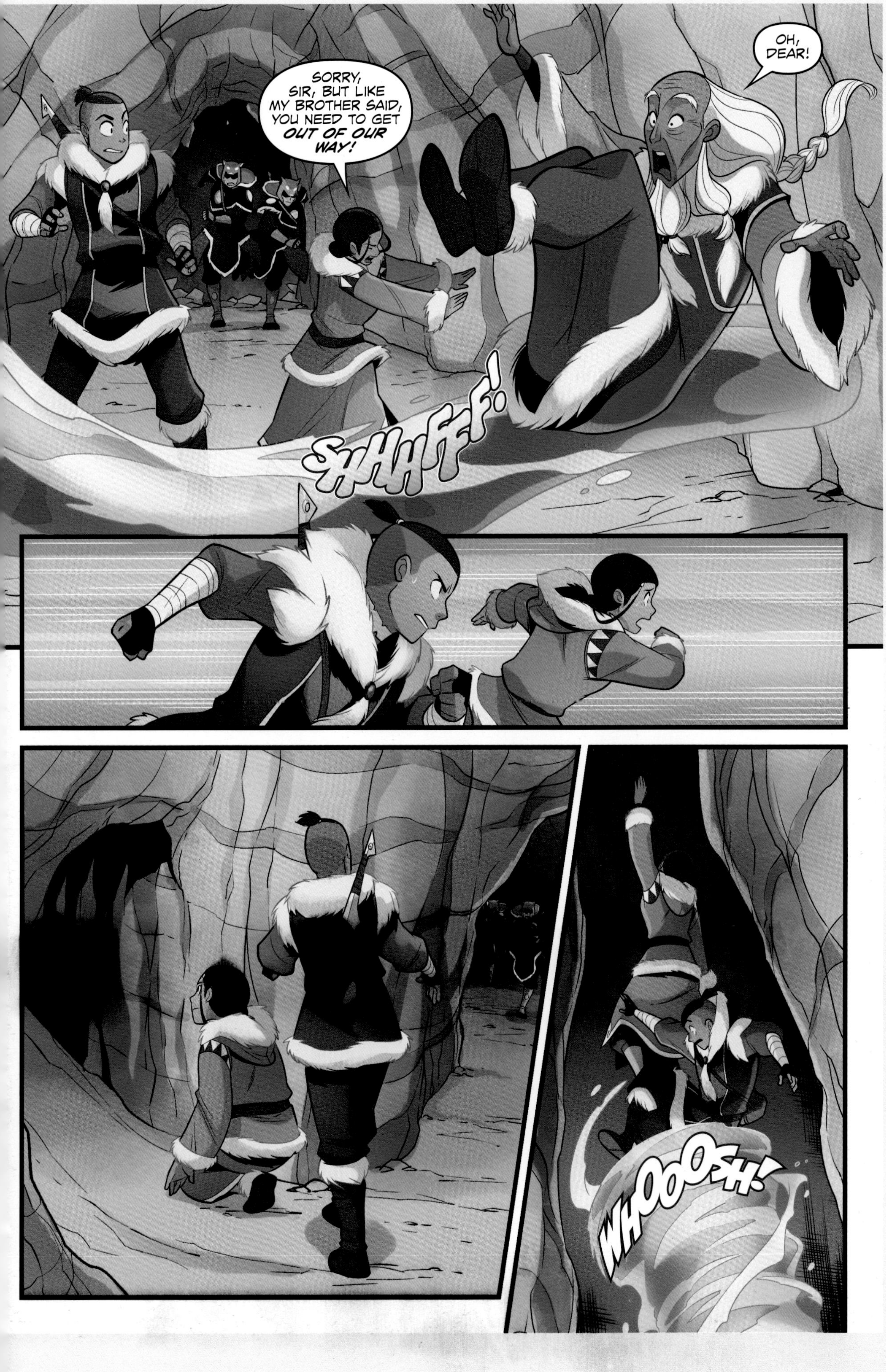
SORRY, SIR, BUT LIKE MY BROTHER SAID, YOU NEED TO GET OUT OF OUR WAY!
OH, DEAR!
SHHHFFF!
WHOOOSH!

GLY: *I love working with Gurihiru, in part because I get to throw out random combinations of animals, then sit back and see what they come up with. They never, ever disappoint. Snow leopard-caribou!*

G: *The two animals were originally supposed to be polar bear dogs, like Naga from The Legend of Korra, but we changed them to snow leopard-caribou instead.*

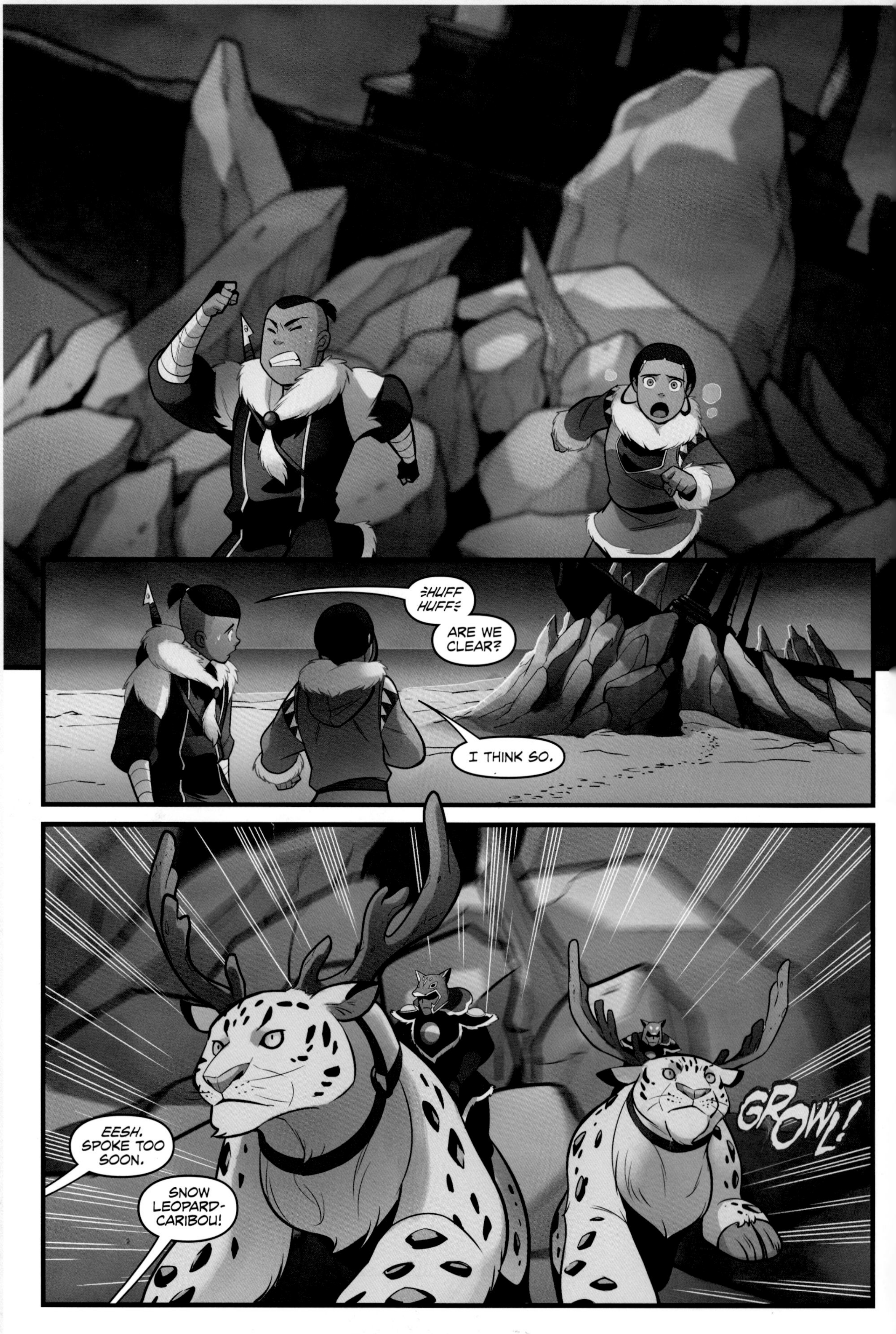
SHUFF HUFF
ARE WE CLEAR?
I THINK SO.
EESH. SPOKE TOO SOON.
SNOW LEOPARD-CARIBOU!
GROWL!

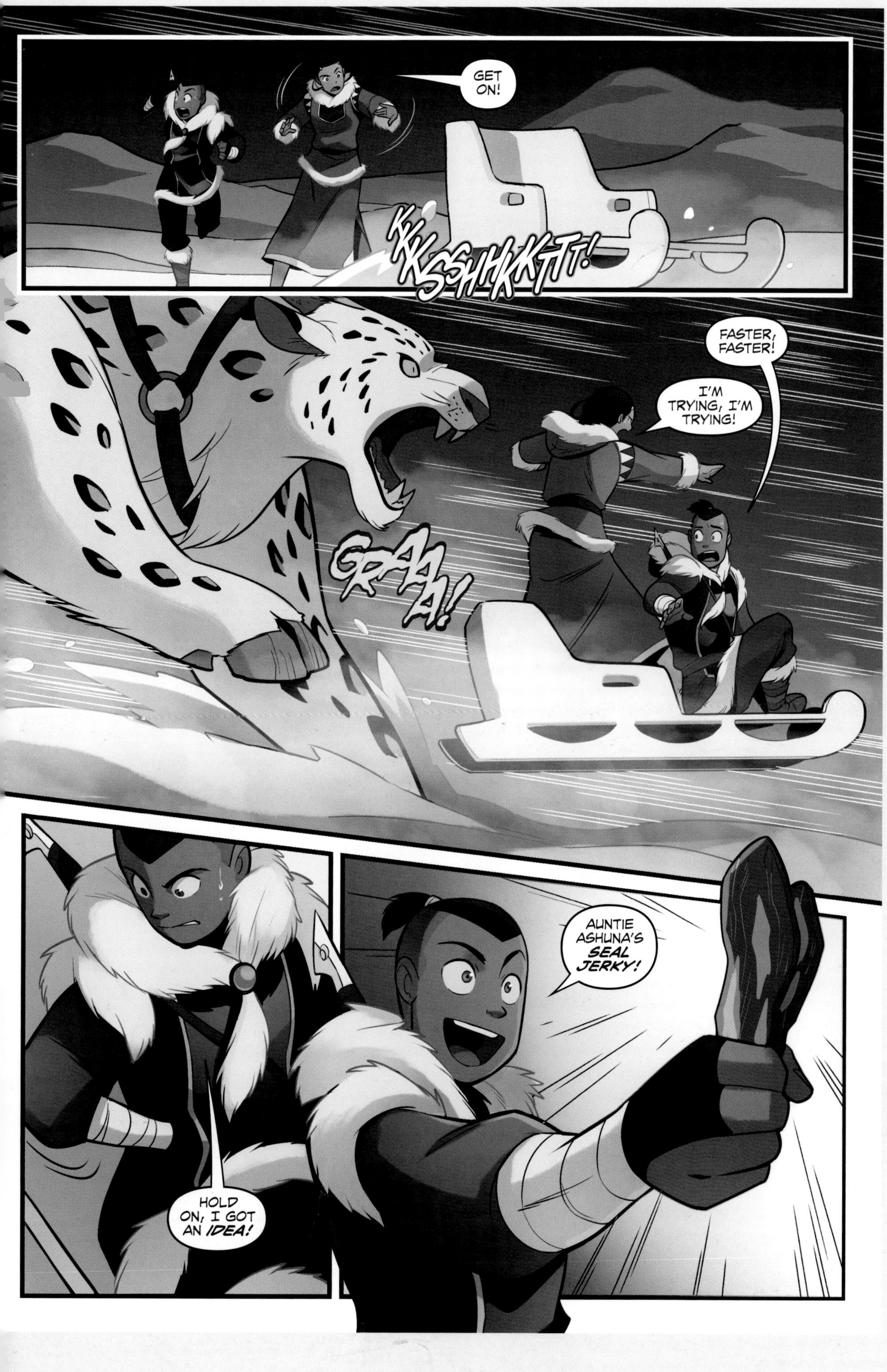
GET ON!
KKKSSHHKKKTTT!
FASTER, FASTER!
I'M TRYING, I'M TRYING!
GRAAAA!
HOLD ON, I GOT AN *IDEA!*
AUNTIE ASHUNA'S *SEAL JERKY!*

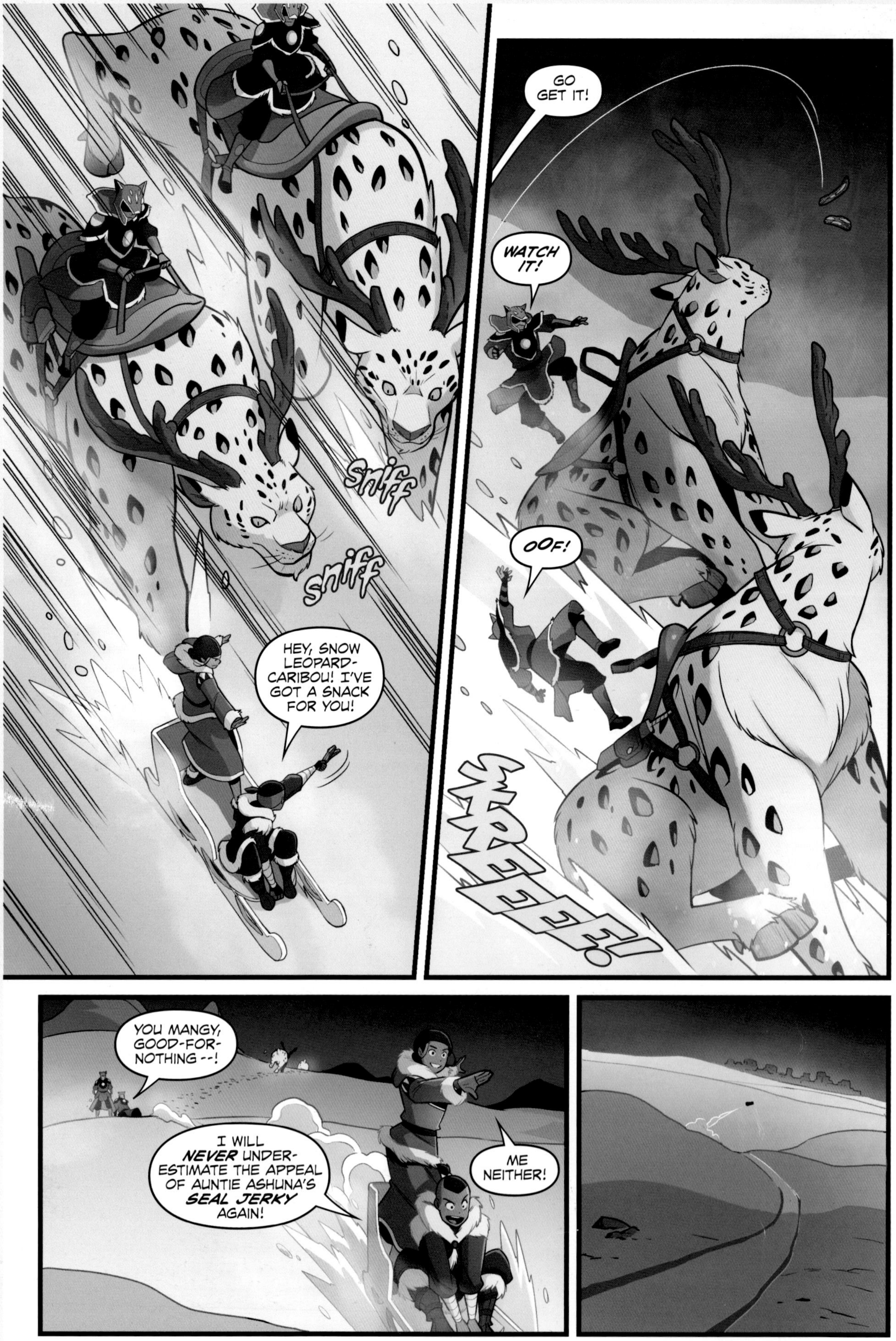
sniff
sniff
HEY, SNOW LEOPARD-CARIBOU! I'VE GOT A SNACK FOR YOU!
GO GET IT!
WATCH IT!
OOF!
SKREEEEE!
YOU MANGY, GOOD-FOR-NOTHING --!
I WILL NEVER UNDER-ESTIMATE THE APPEAL OF AUNTIE ASHUNA'S SEAL JERKY AGAIN!
ME NEITHER!

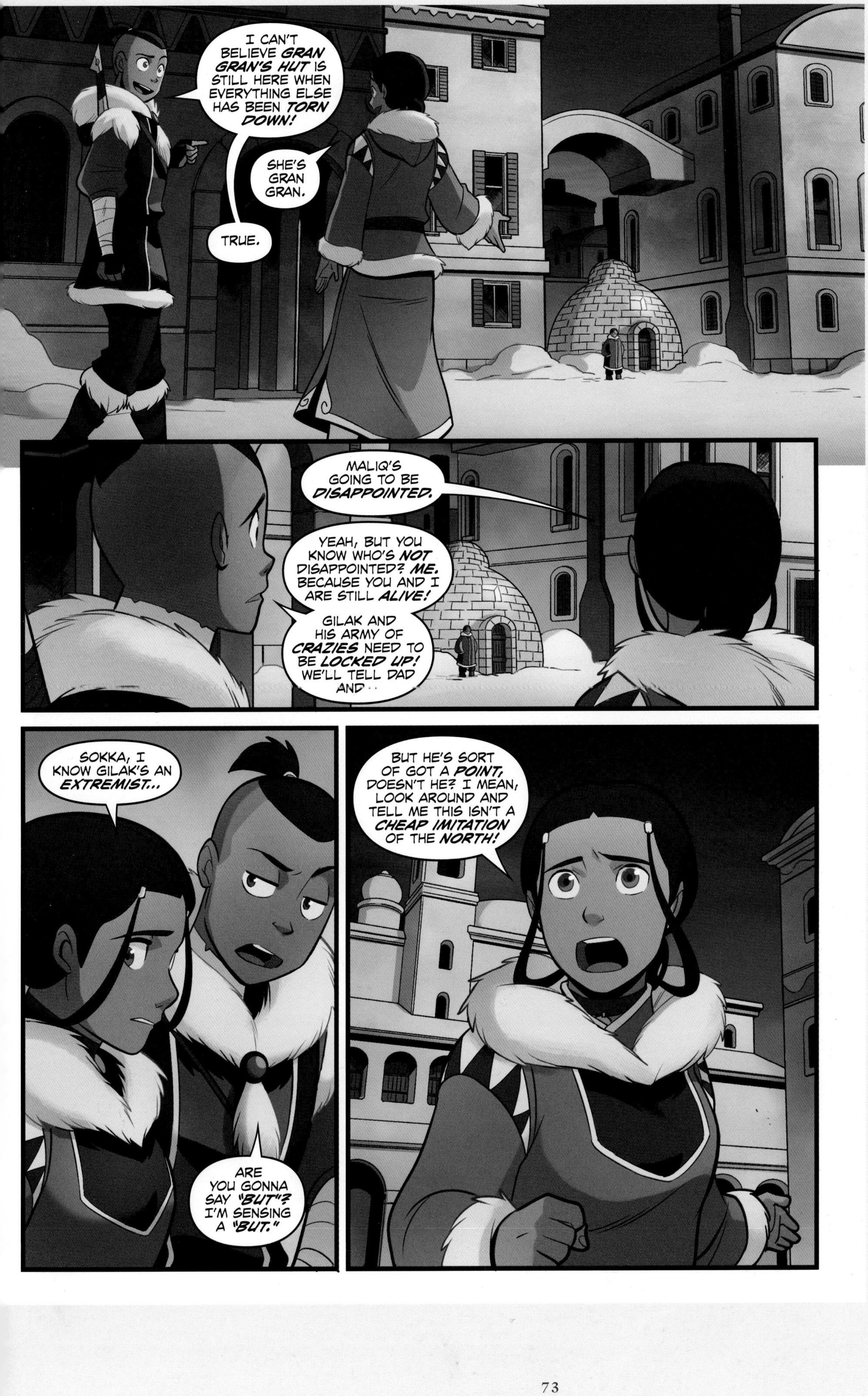
I CAN'T BELIEVE GRAN GRAN'S HUT IS STILL HERE WHEN EVERYTHING ELSE HAS BEEN TORN DOWN!
SHE'S GRAN GRAN.
TRUE.
MALIQ'S GOING TO BE DISAPPOINTED.
YEAH, BUT YOU KNOW WHO'S NOT DISAPPOINTED? ME. BECAUSE YOU AND I ARE STILL ALIVE!
GILAK AND HIS ARMY OF CRAZIES NEED TO BE LOCKED UP! WE'LL TELL DAD AND...
SOKKA, I KNOW GILAK'S AN EXTREMIST...
ARE YOU GONNA SAY "BUT"? I'M SENSING A "BUT."
BUT HE'S SORT OF GOT A POINT, DOESN'T HE? I MEAN, LOOK AROUND AND TELL ME THIS ISN'T A CHEAP IMITATION OF THE NORTH!

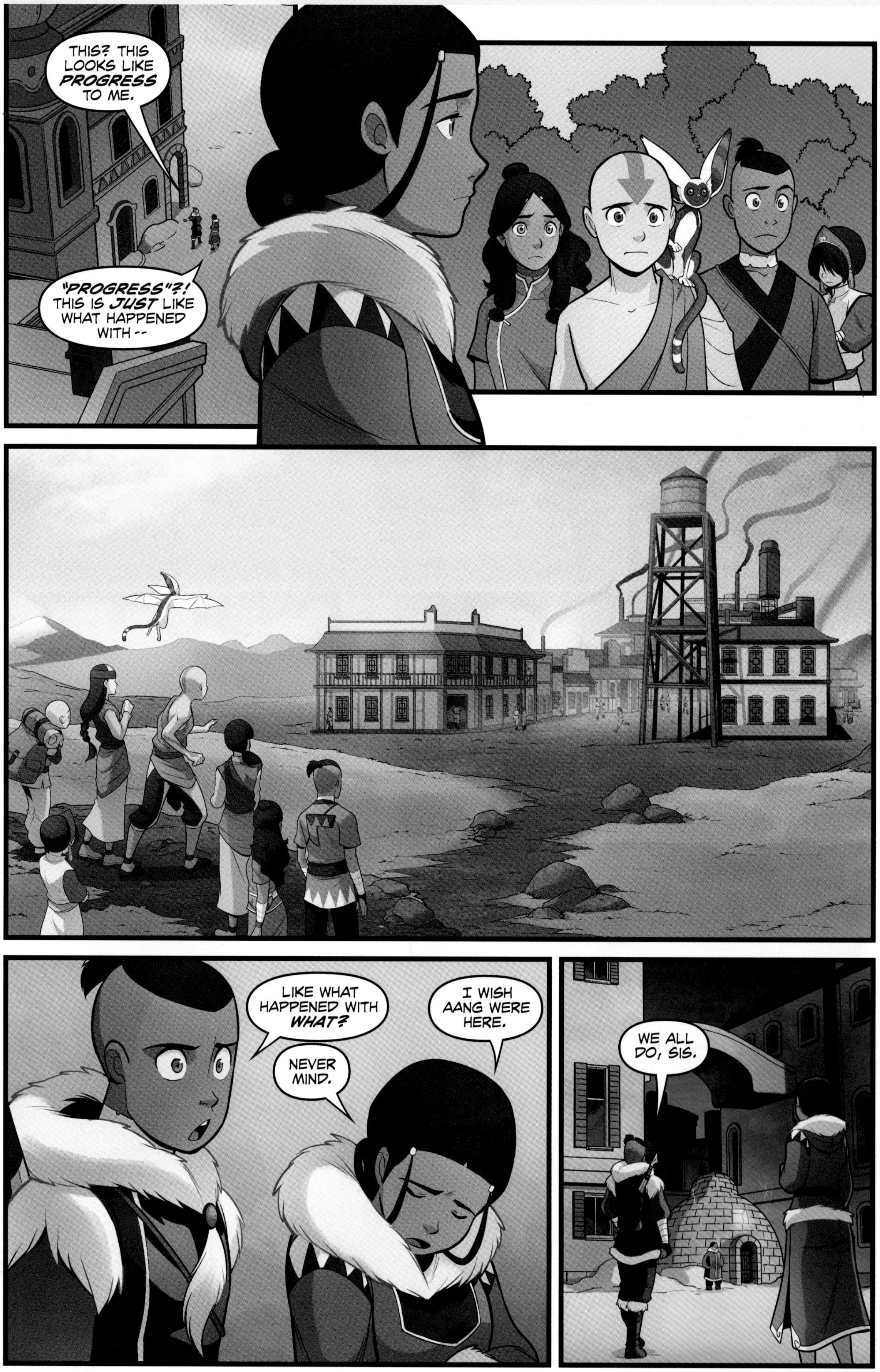
THIS? THIS LOOKS LIKE *PROGRESS* TO ME.
"*PROGRESS*"?! THIS IS *JUST* LIKE WHAT HAPPENED WITH --
LIKE WHAT HAPPENED WITH *WHAT?*
NEVER MIND.
I WISH AANG WERE HERE.
WE ALL DO, SIS.

GLY: *Katara is remembering a scene from The Rift.*

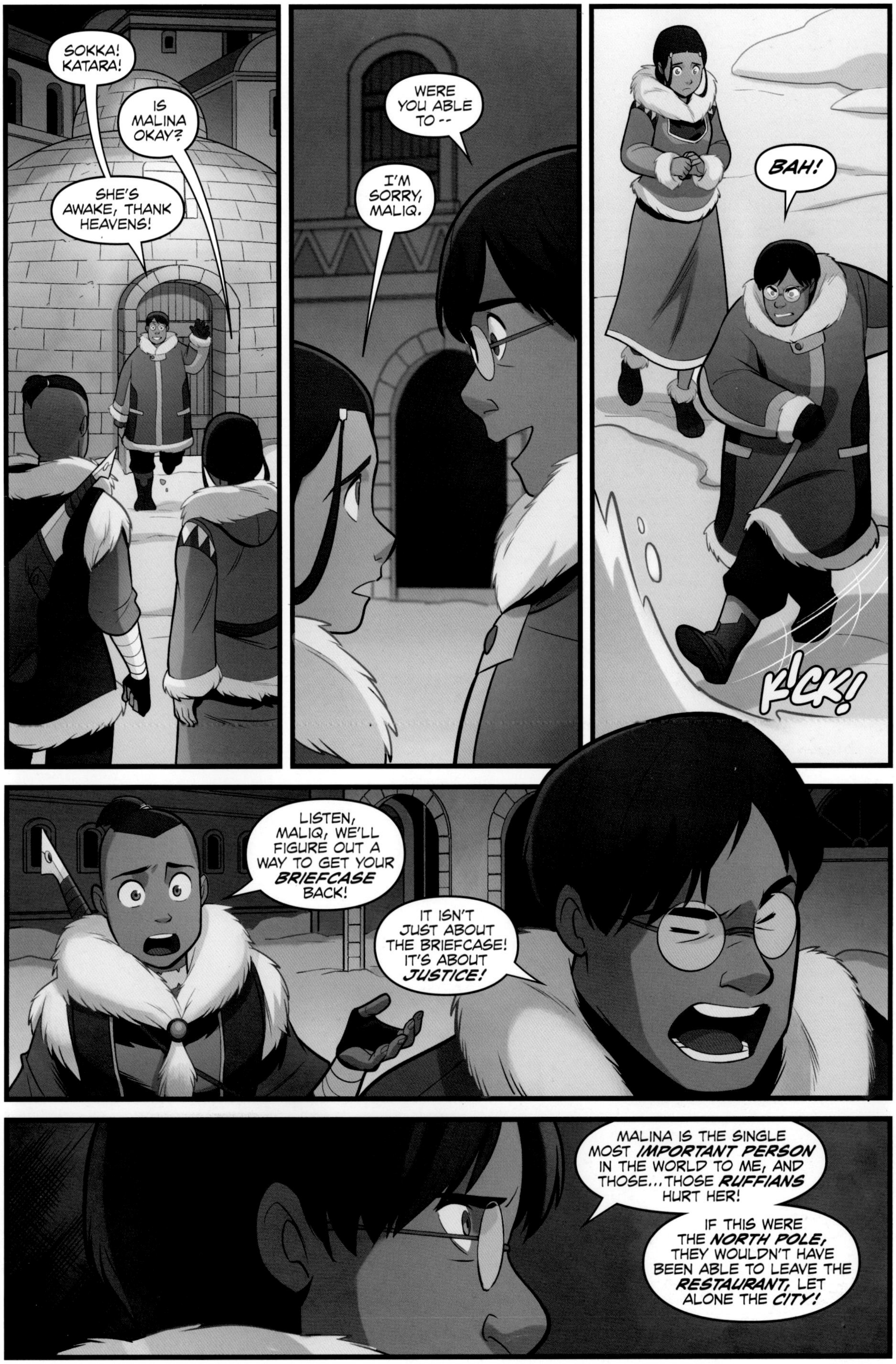
SOKKA! KATARA!
IS MALINA OKAY?
SHE'S AWAKE, THANK HEAVENS!
WERE YOU ABLE TO --
I'M SORRY, MALIQ.
BAH!
K'CK!
LISTEN, MALIQ, WE'LL FIGURE OUT A WAY TO GET YOUR BRIEFCASE BACK!
IT ISN'T JUST ABOUT THE BRIEFCASE! IT'S ABOUT JUSTICE!
MALINA IS THE SINGLE MOST IMPORTANT PERSON IN THE WORLD TO ME, AND THOSE... THOSE RUFFIANS HURT HER!
IF THIS WERE THE NORTH POLE, THEY WOULDN'T HAVE BEEN ABLE TO LEAVE THE RESTAURANT, LET ALONE THE CITY!

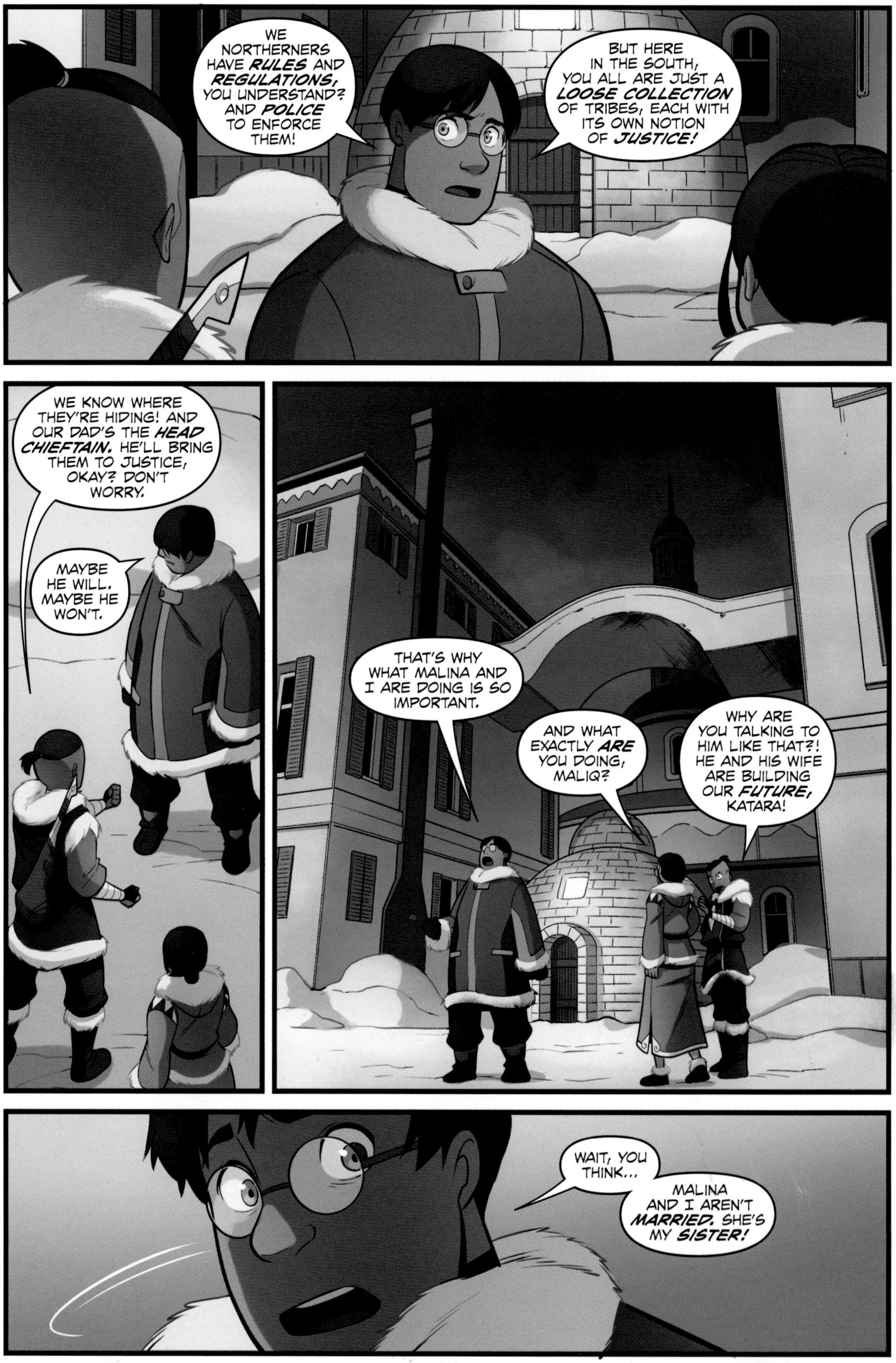
WE NORTHERNERS HAVE RULES AND REGULATIONS, YOU UNDERSTAND? AND POLICE TO ENFORCE THEM!
BUT HERE IN THE SOUTH, YOU ALL ARE JUST A LOOSE COLLECTION OF TRIBES, EACH WITH ITS OWN NOTION OF JUSTICE!
WE KNOW WHERE THEY'RE HIDING! AND OUR DAD'S THE HEAD CHIEFTAIN. HE'LL BRING THEM TO JUSTICE, OKAY? DON'T WORRY.
MAYBE HE WILL. MAYBE HE WON'T.
THAT'S WHY WHAT MALINA AND I ARE DOING IS SO IMPORTANT.
AND WHAT EXACTLY ARE YOU DOING, MALIQ?
WHY ARE YOU TALKING TO HIM LIKE THAT?! HE AND HIS WIFE ARE BUILDING OUR FUTURE, KATARA!
WAIT, YOU THINK...
MALINA AND I AREN'T MARRIED. SHE'S MY SISTER!

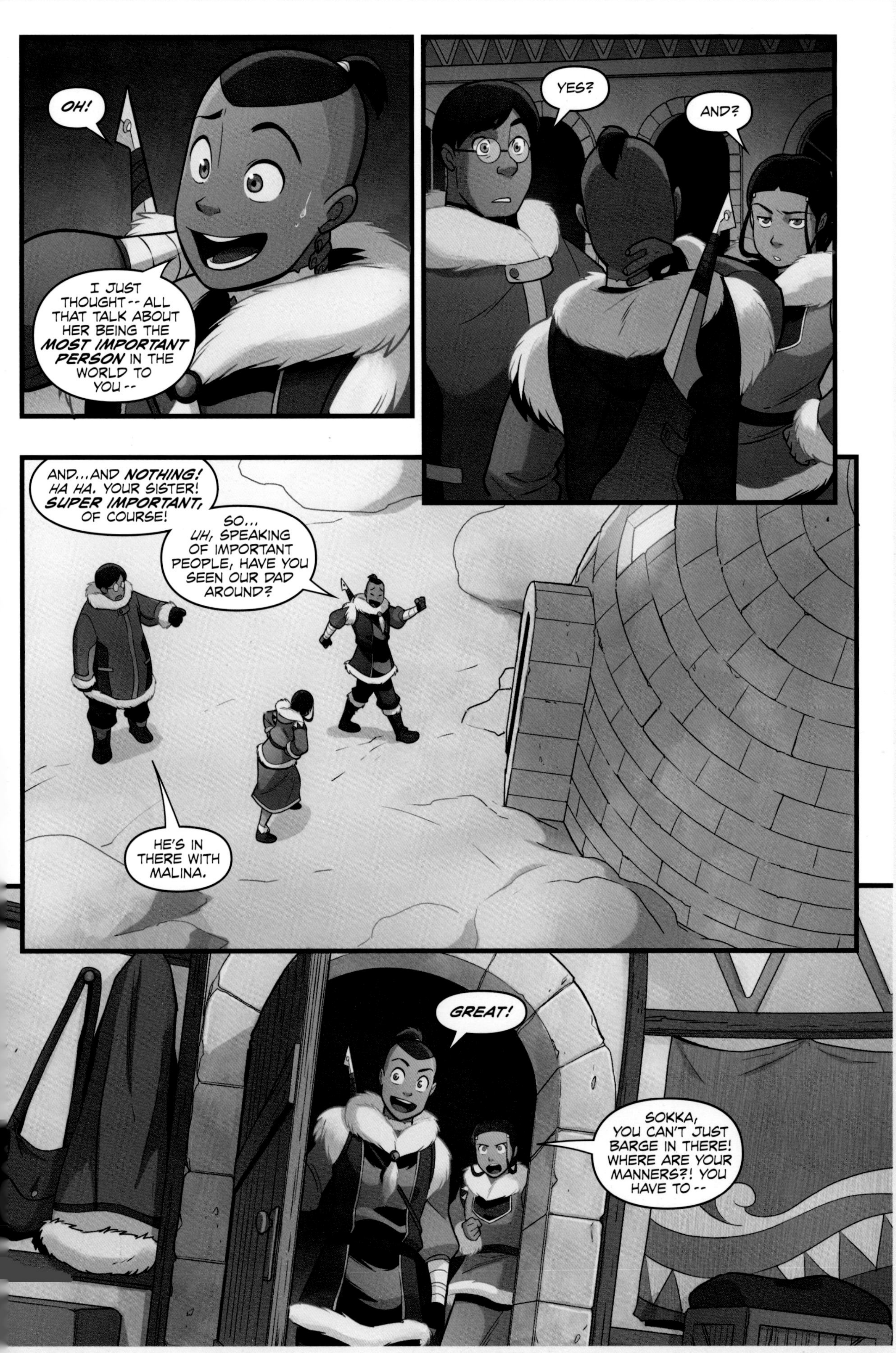
OH!
I JUST THOUGHT-- ALL THAT TALK ABOUT HER BEING THE MOST IMPORTANT PERSON IN THE WORLD TO YOU--
YES?
AND?
AND...AND NOTHING! HA HA. YOUR SISTER! SUPER IMPORTANT, OF COURSE!
SO... UH, SPEAKING OF IMPORTANT PEOPLE, HAVE YOU SEEN OUR DAD AROUND?
HE'S IN THERE WITH MALINA.
GREAT!
SOKKA, YOU CAN'T JUST BARGE IN THERE! WHERE ARE YOUR MANNERS?! YOU HAVE TO--

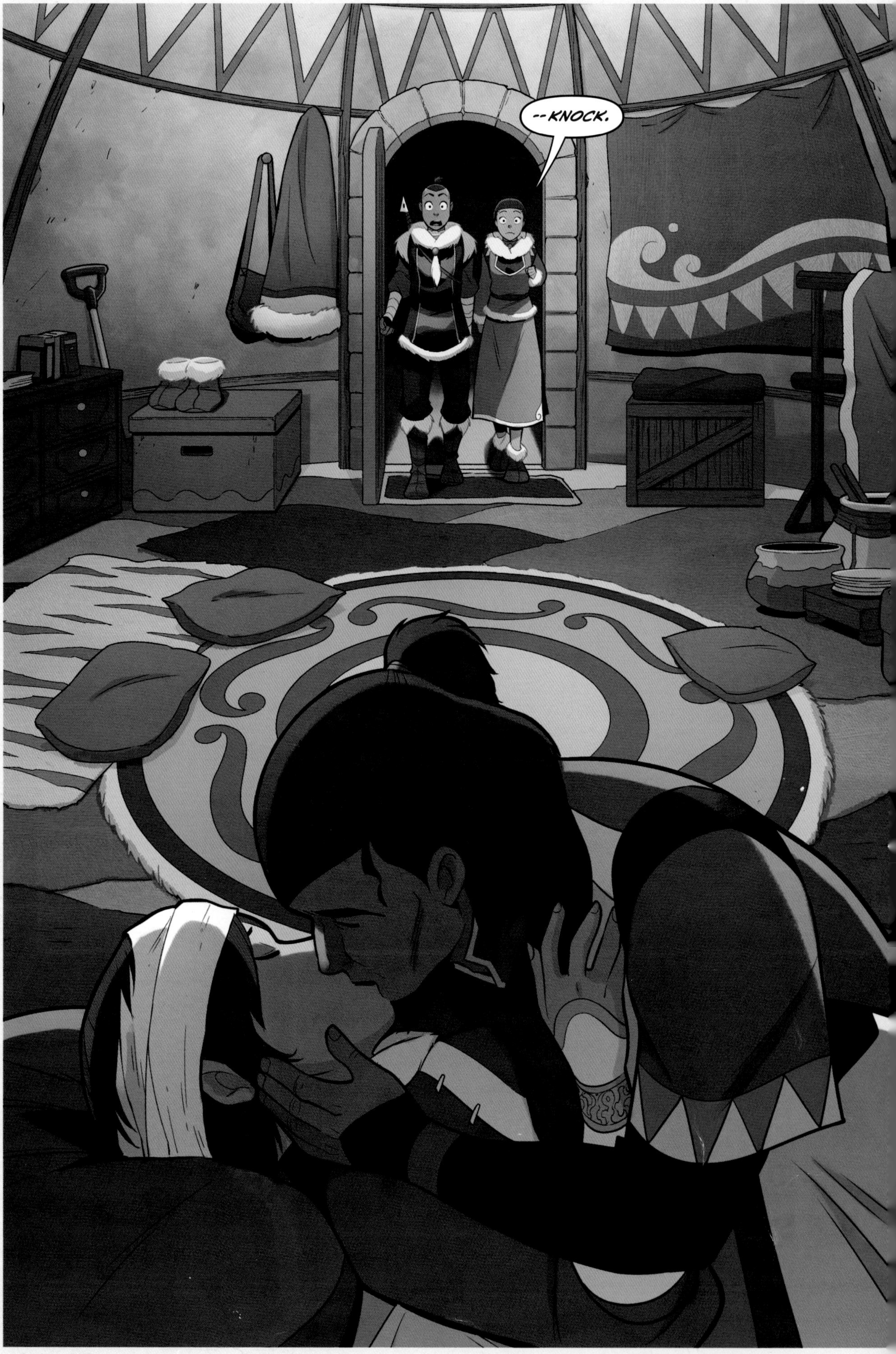
--KNOCK.

GLY: *It's gross to see your parents kissing, isn't it?* SO GROSS.

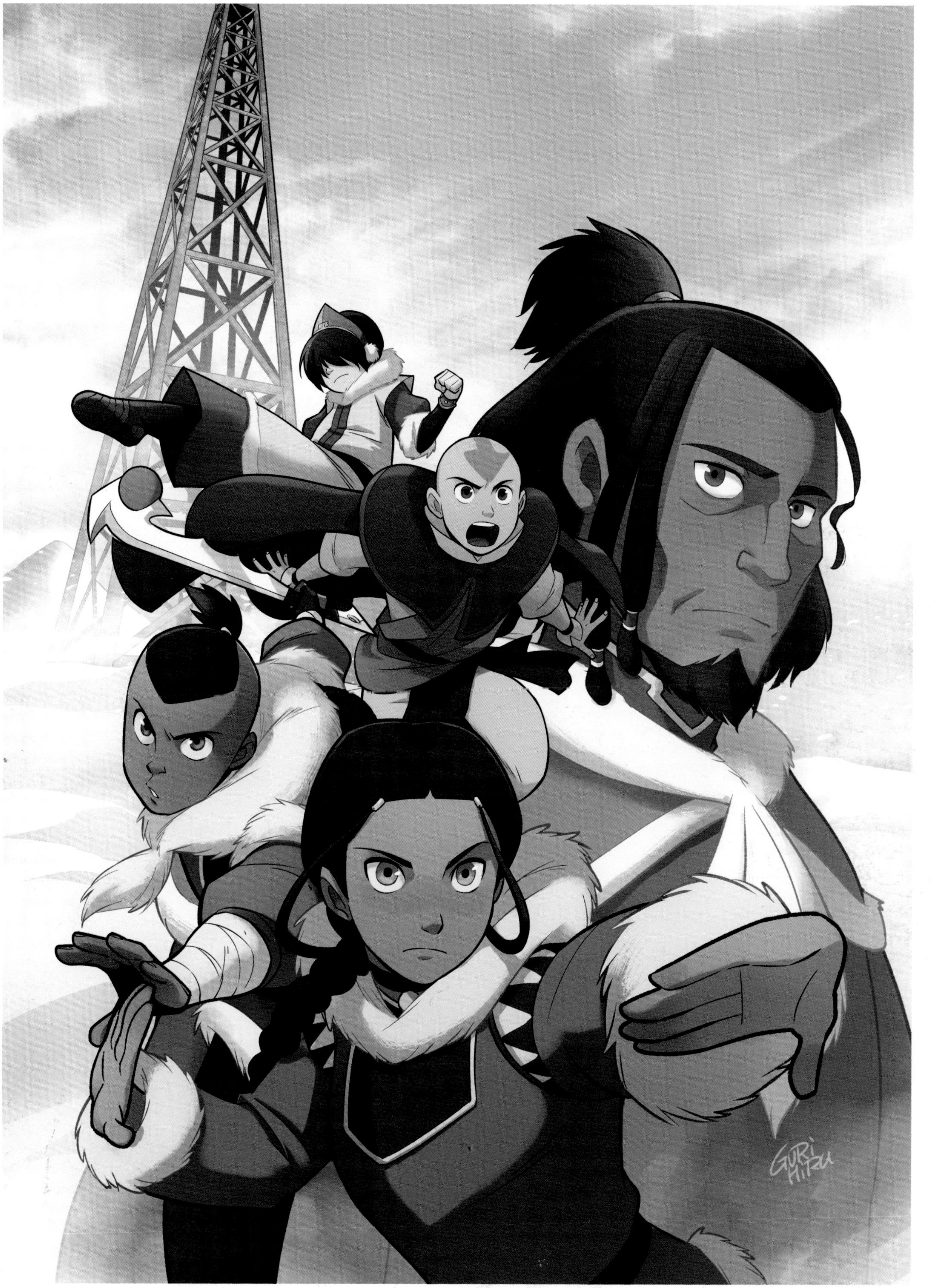
GURI HIRU

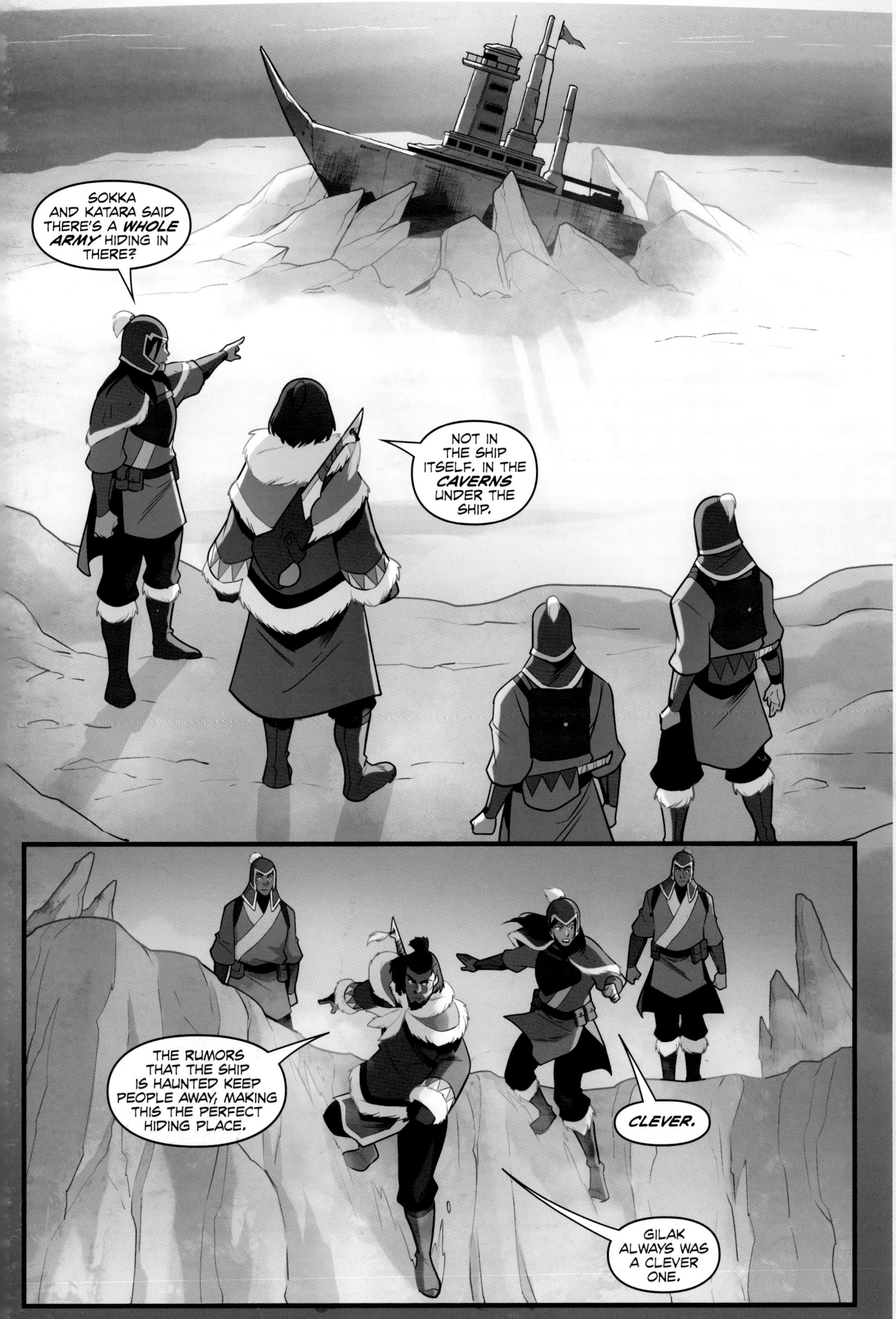
SOKKA AND KATARA SAID THERE'S A *WHOLE ARMY* HIDING IN THERE?
NOT IN THE SHIP ITSELF. IN THE *CAVERNS* UNDER THE SHIP.
THE RUMORS THAT THE SHIP IS HAUNTED KEEP PEOPLE AWAY, MAKING THIS THE PERFECT HIDING PLACE.
CLEVER.
GILAK ALWAYS WAS A CLEVER ONE.

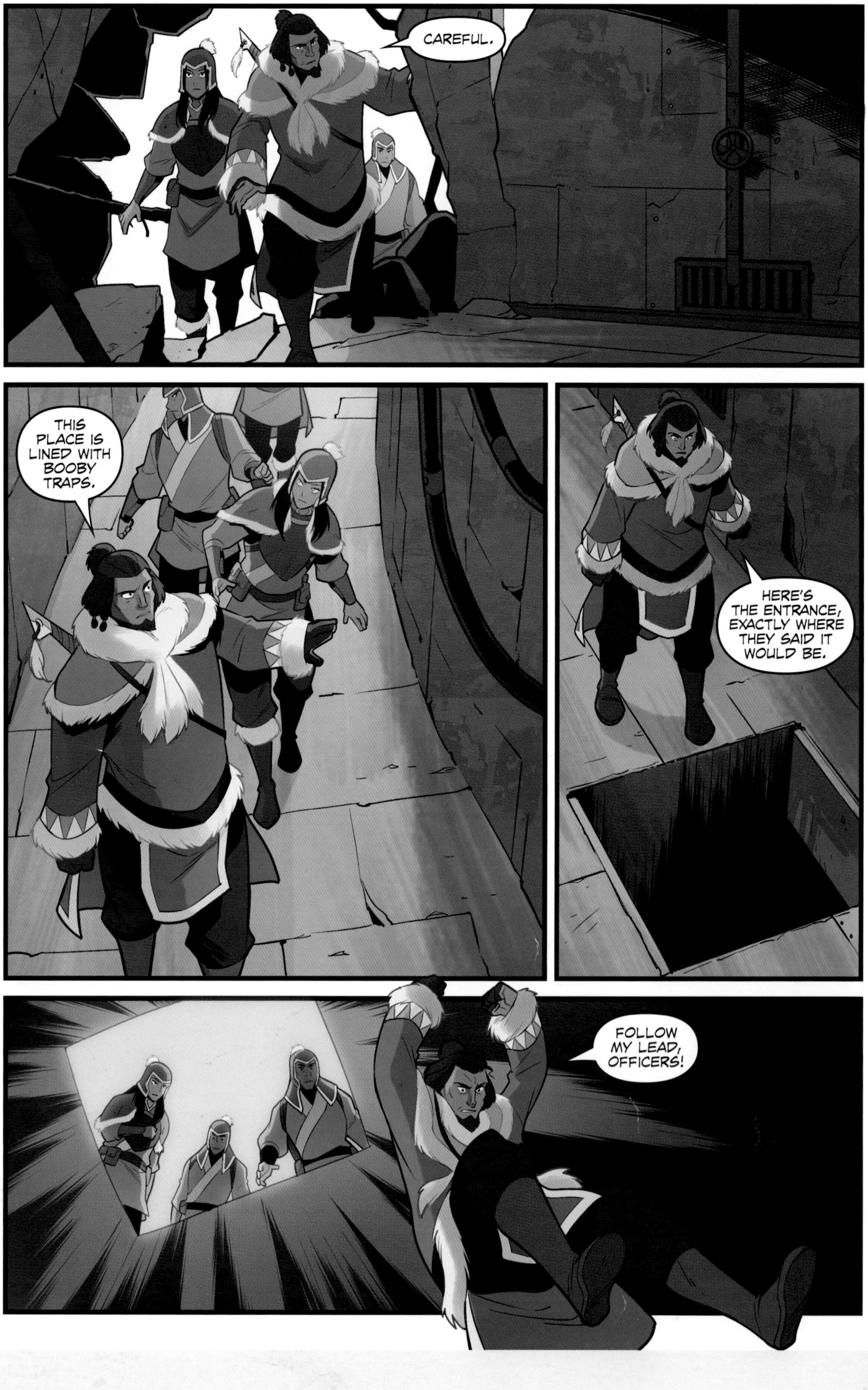
CAREFUL.
THIS PLACE IS LINED WITH BOOBY TRAPS.
HERE'S THE ENTRANCE, EXACTLY WHERE THEY SAID IT WOULD BE.
FOLLOW MY LEAD, OFFICERS!

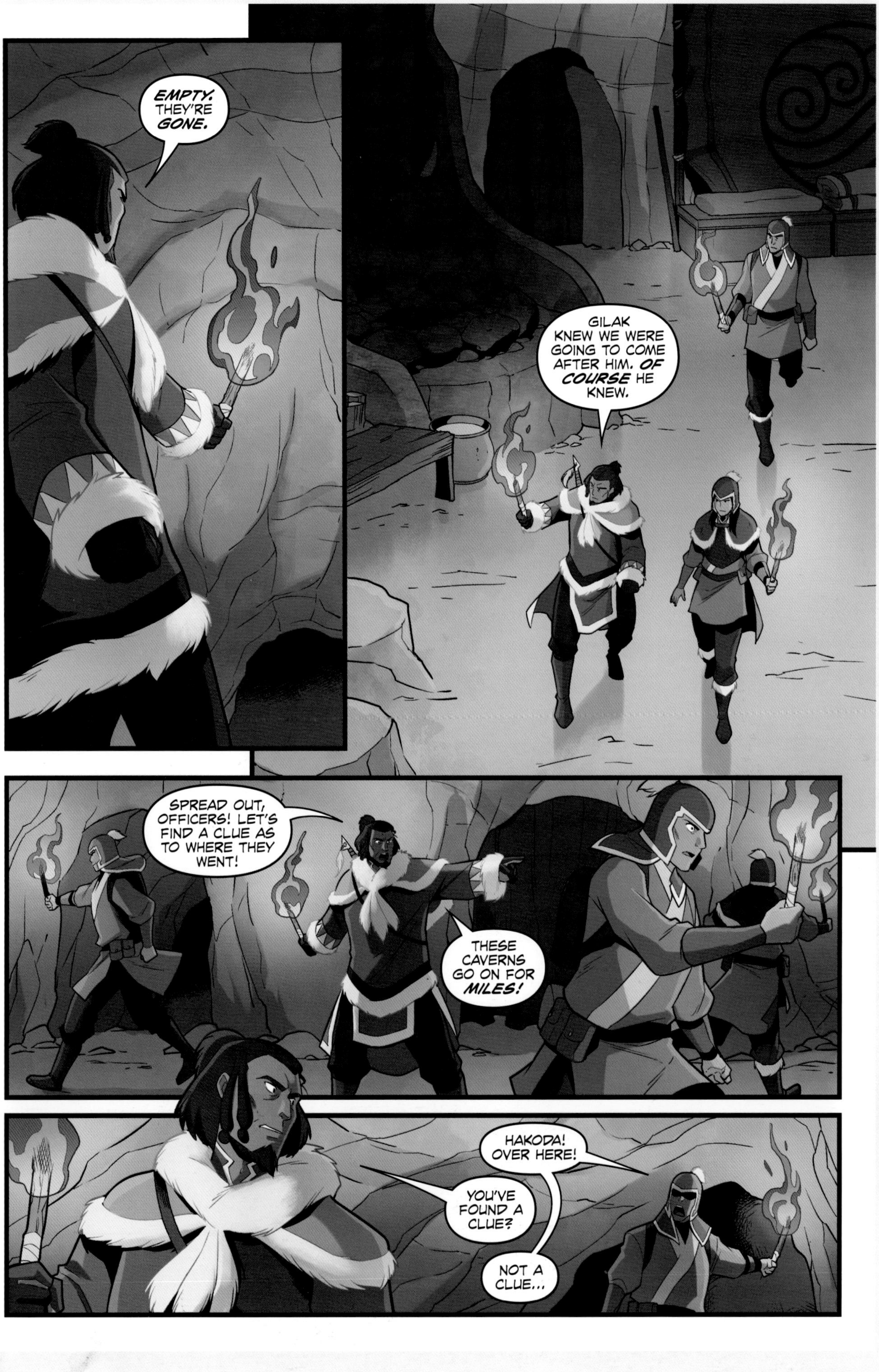
EMPTY. THEY'RE GONE.
GILAK KNEW WE WERE GOING TO COME AFTER HIM. OF COURSE HE KNEW.
SPREAD OUT, OFFICERS! LET'S FIND A CLUE AS TO WHERE THEY WENT!
THESE CAVERNS GO ON FOR MILES!
HAKODA! OVER HERE!
YOU'VE FOUND A CLUE?
NOT A CLUE...

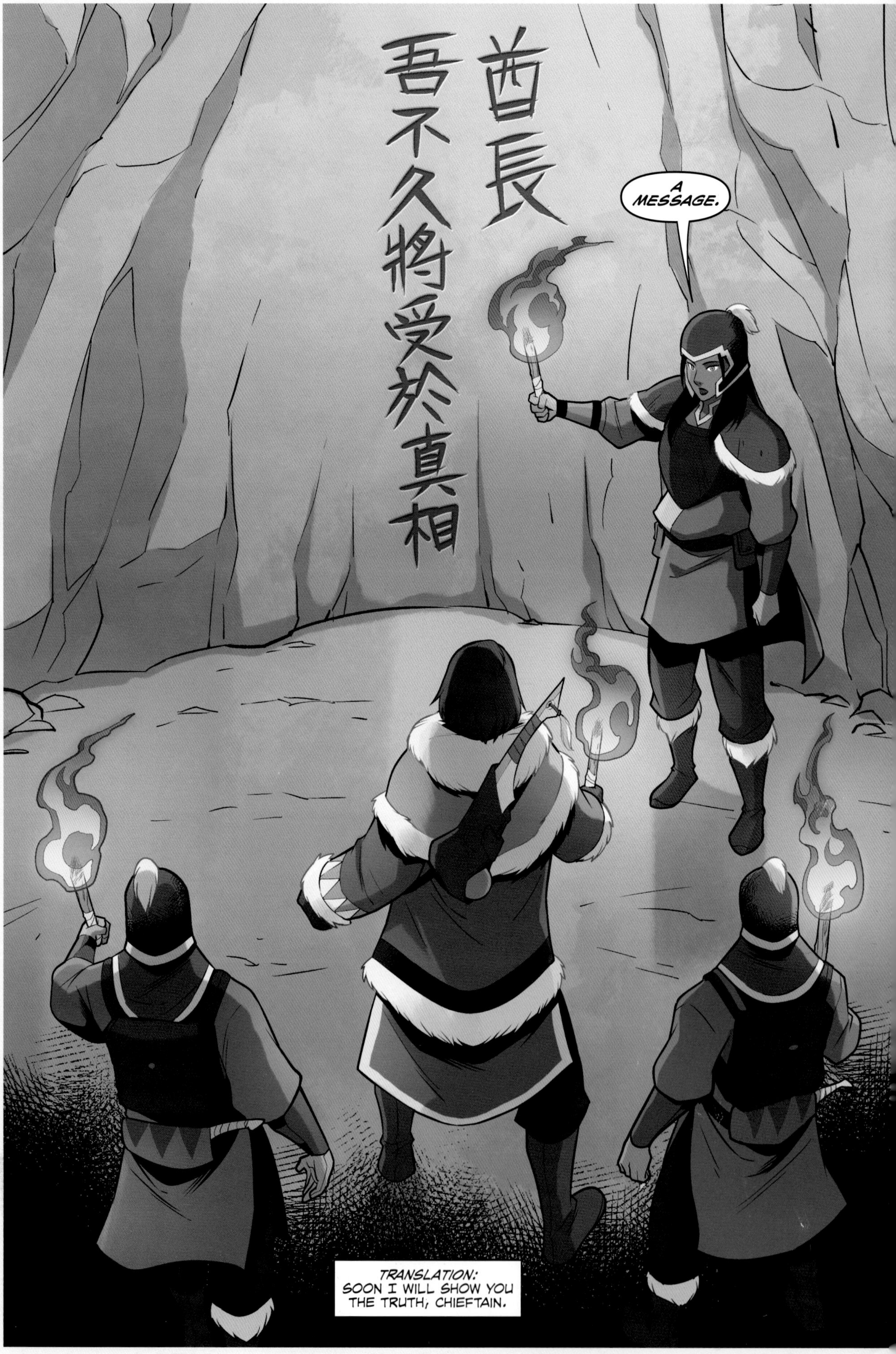
酋長
吾不久將受於真相
A MESSAGE.
TRANSLATION:
SOON I WILL SHOW YOU THE TRUTH, CHIEFTAIN.

GLY: *I had to ask my parents for help with all the Chinese translations. Thanks, Mom and Dad!*

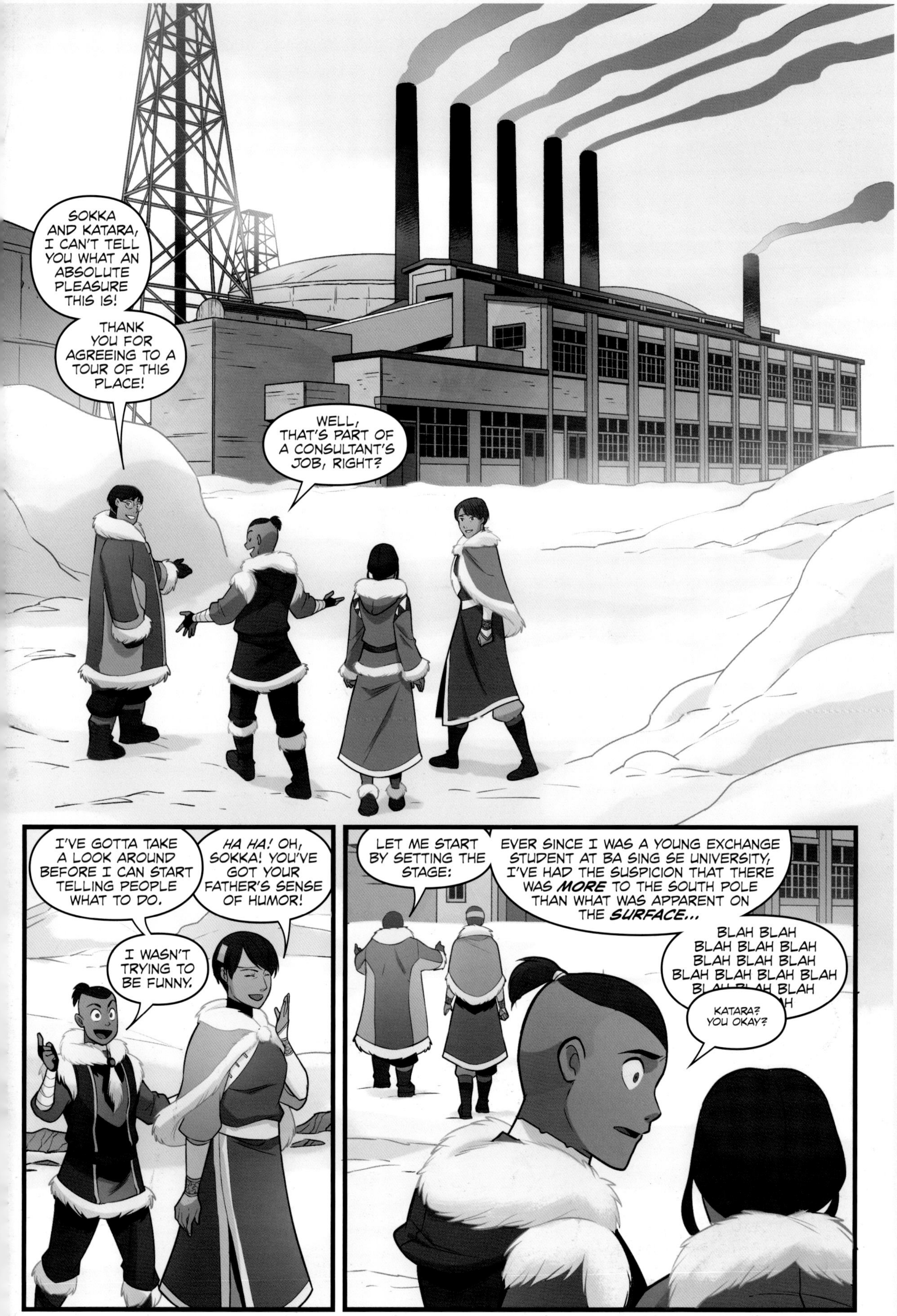
SOKKA AND KATARA, I CAN'T TELL YOU WHAT AN ABSOLUTE PLEASURE THIS IS!
THANK YOU FOR AGREEING TO A TOUR OF THIS PLACE!
WELL, THAT'S PART OF A CONSULTANT'S JOB, RIGHT?
I'VE GOTTA TAKE A LOOK AROUND BEFORE I CAN START TELLING PEOPLE WHAT TO DO.
HA HA! OH, SOKKA! YOU'VE GOT YOUR FATHER'S SENSE OF HUMOR!
I WASN'T TRYING TO BE FUNNY.
LET ME START BY SETTING THE STAGE:
EVER SINCE I WAS A YOUNG EXCHANGE STUDENT AT BA SING SE UNIVERSITY, I'VE HAD THE SUSPICION THAT THERE WAS MORE TO THE SOUTH POLE THAN WHAT WAS APPARENT ON THE SURFACE...
BLAH BLAH BLAH BLAH BLAH BLAH BLAH BLAH BLAH BLAH BLAH BLAH BLAH BLAH
KATARA? YOU OKAY?

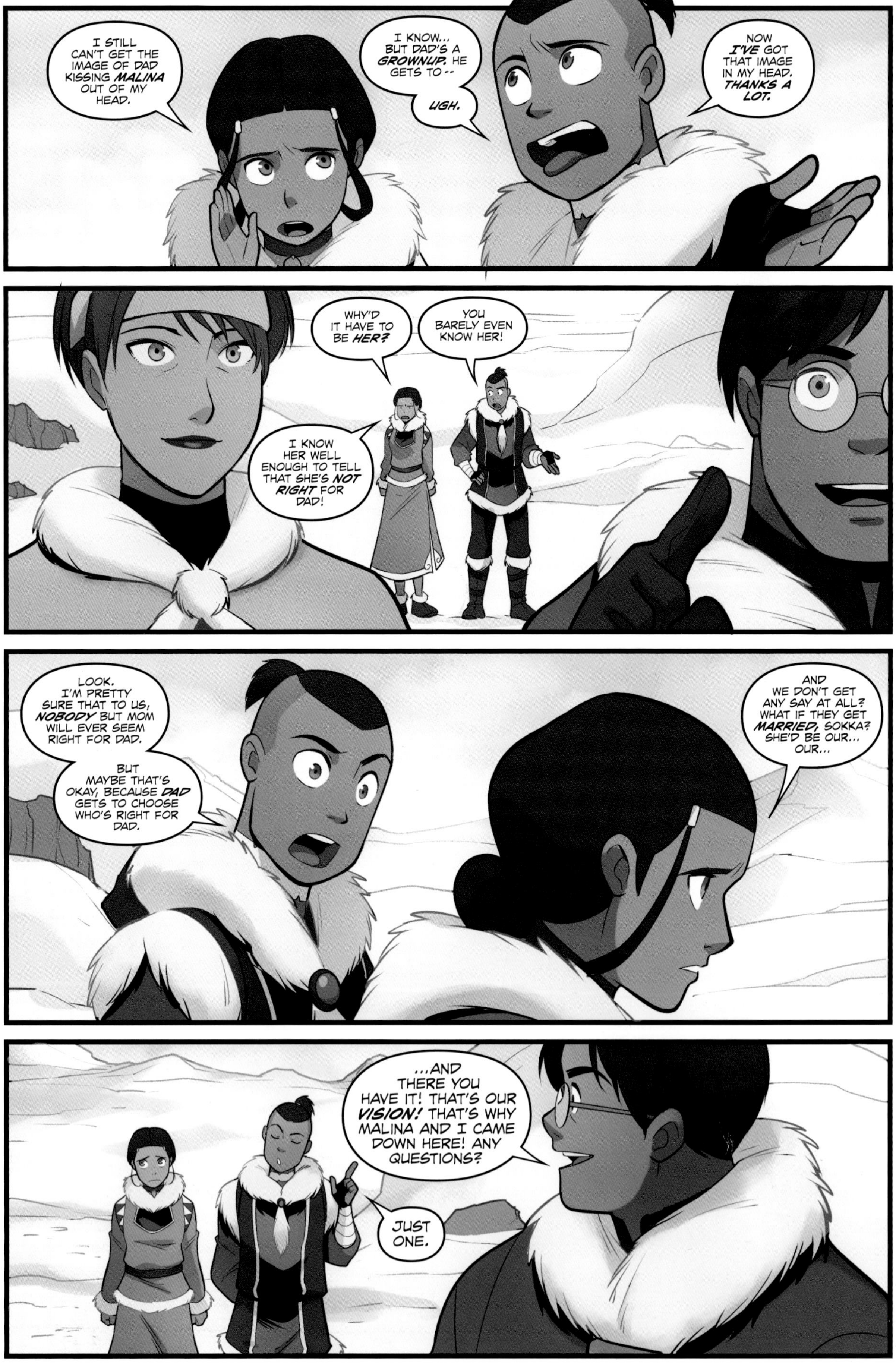
I STILL CAN'T GET THE IMAGE OF DAD KISSING *MALINA* OUT OF MY HEAD.
I KNOW... BUT DAD'S A *GROWNUP.* HE GETS TO --
UGH.
NOW *I'VE* GOT THAT IMAGE IN MY HEAD. *THANKS A LOT.*
WHY'D IT HAVE TO BE *HER?*
YOU BARELY EVEN KNOW HER!
I KNOW HER WELL ENOUGH TO TELL THAT SHE'S *NOT RIGHT* FOR DAD!
LOOK. I'M PRETTY SURE THAT TO US, *NOBODY* BUT MOM WILL EVER SEEM RIGHT FOR DAD.
BUT MAYBE THAT'S OKAY, BECAUSE *DAD* GETS TO CHOOSE WHO'S RIGHT FOR DAD.
AND WE DON'T GET ANY SAY AT ALL? WHAT IF THEY GET *MARRIED,* SOKKA? SHE'D BE OUR... OUR...
...AND THERE YOU HAVE IT! THAT'S OUR *VISION!* THAT'S WHY MALINA AND I CAME DOWN HERE! ANY QUESTIONS?
JUST ONE.

GLY: *Like I said before. Parents kissing? GROSS.*

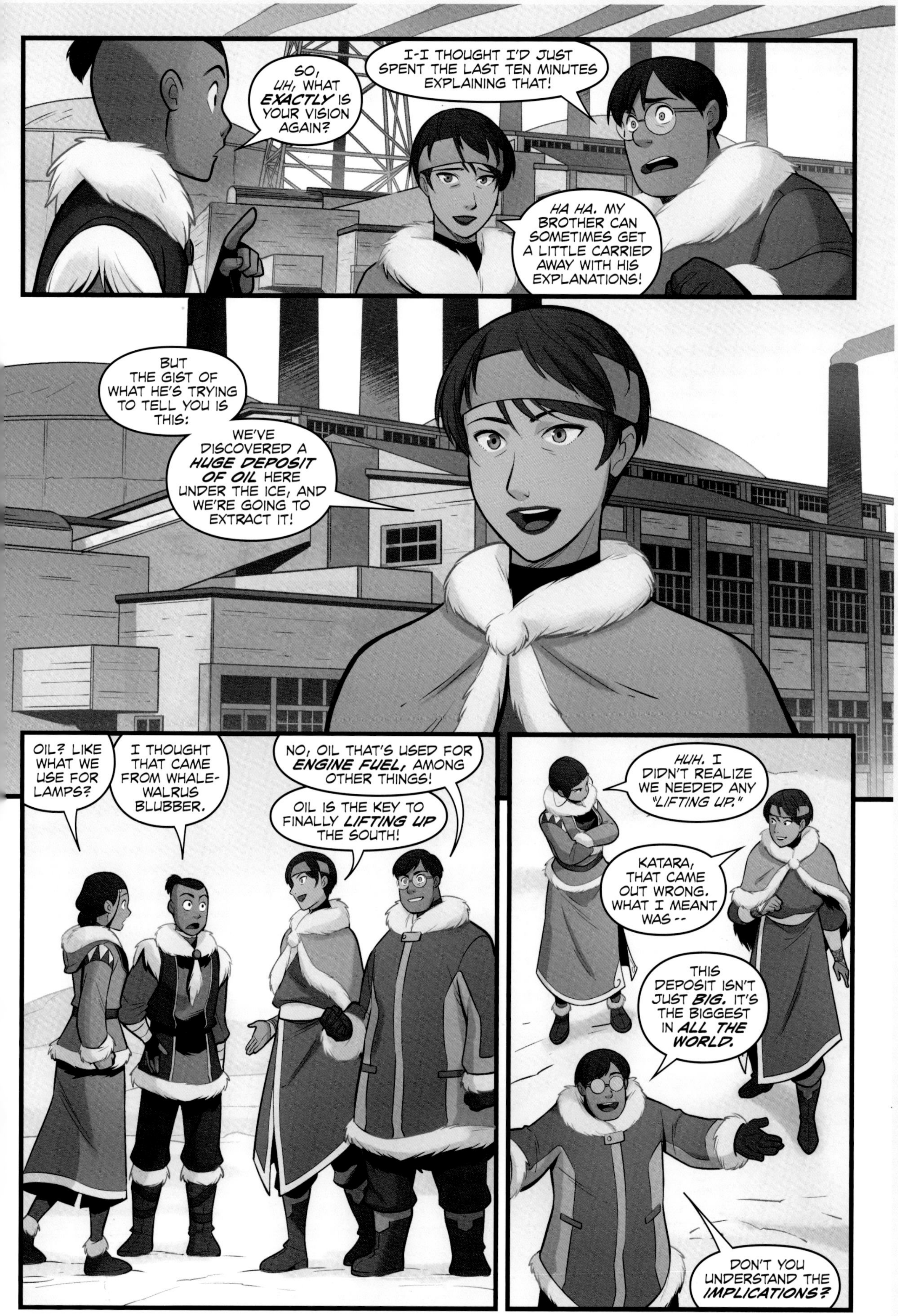
SO, UH, WHAT EXACTLY IS YOUR VISION AGAIN?
I-I THOUGHT I'D JUST SPENT THE LAST TEN MINUTES EXPLAINING THAT!
HA HA. MY BROTHER CAN SOMETIMES GET A LITTLE CARRIED AWAY WITH HIS EXPLANATIONS!
BUT THE GIST OF WHAT HE'S TRYING TO TELL YOU IS THIS:
WE'VE DISCOVERED A HUGE DEPOSIT OF OIL HERE UNDER THE ICE, AND WE'RE GOING TO EXTRACT IT!
OIL? LIKE WHAT WE USE FOR LAMPS?
I THOUGHT THAT CAME FROM WHALE-WALRUS BLUBBER.
NO, OIL THAT'S USED FOR ENGINE FUEL, AMONG OTHER THINGS!
OIL IS THE KEY TO FINALLY LIFTING UP THE SOUTH!
HUH. I DIDN'T REALIZE WE NEEDED ANY "LIFTING UP."
KATARA, THAT CAME OUT WRONG. WHAT I MEANT WAS --
THIS DEPOSIT ISN'T JUST BIG. IT'S THE BIGGEST IN ALL THE WORLD.
DON'T YOU UNDERSTAND THE IMPLICATIONS?

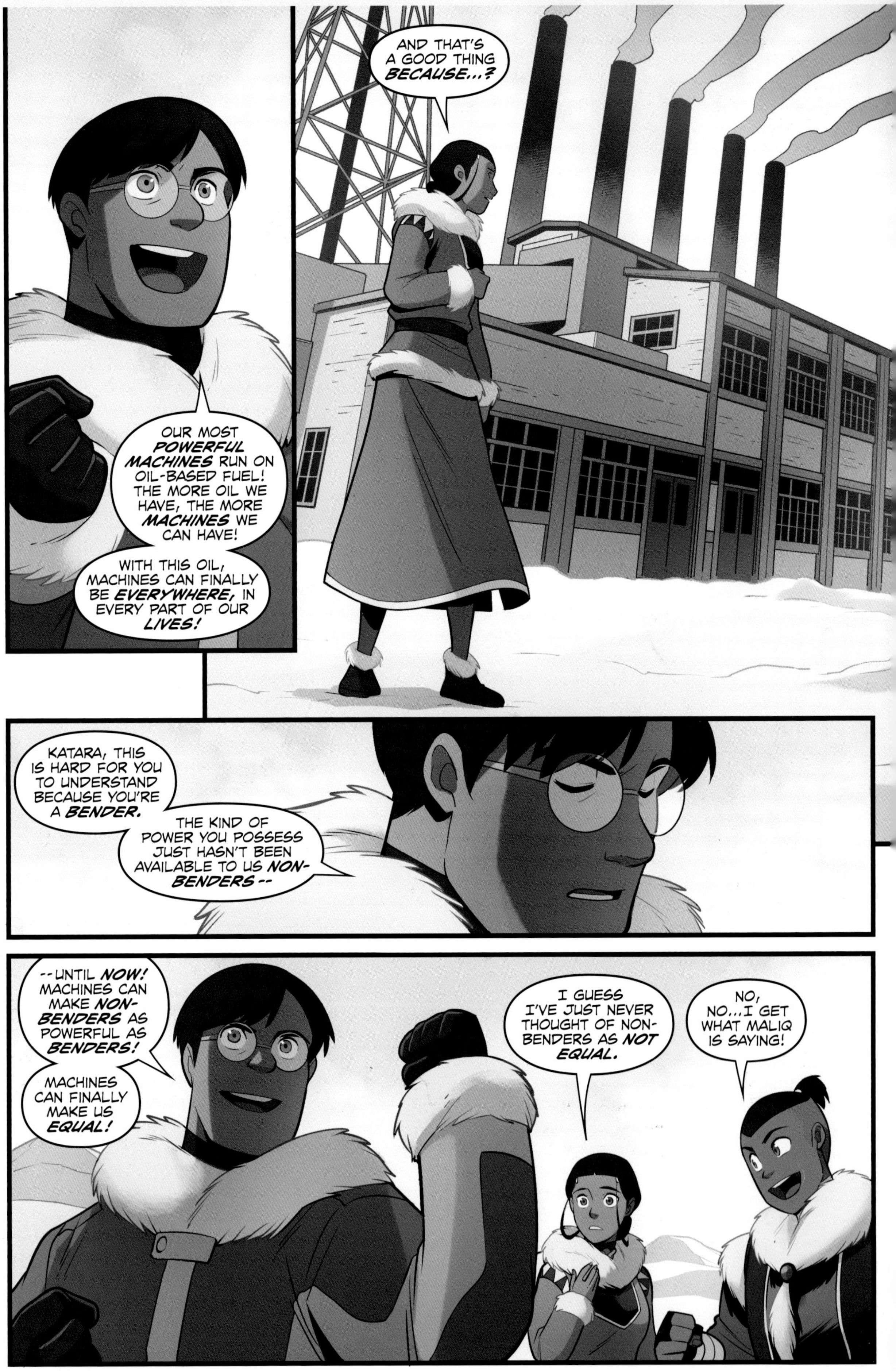
AND THAT'S A GOOD THING BECAUSE...?
OUR MOST POWERFUL MACHINES RUN ON OIL-BASED FUEL! THE MORE OIL WE HAVE, THE MORE MACHINES WE CAN HAVE!
WITH THIS OIL, MACHINES CAN FINALLY BE EVERYWHERE, IN EVERY PART OF OUR LIVES!
KATARA, THIS IS HARD FOR YOU TO UNDERSTAND BECAUSE YOU'RE A BENDER.
THE KIND OF POWER YOU POSSESS JUST HASN'T BEEN AVAILABLE TO US NON-BENDERS --
--UNTIL NOW! MACHINES CAN MAKE NON-BENDERS AS POWERFUL AS BENDERS!
MACHINES CAN FINALLY MAKE US EQUAL!
I GUESS I'VE JUST NEVER THOUGHT OF NON-BENDERS AS NOT EQUAL.
NO, NO...I GET WHAT MALIQ IS SAYING!

GLY: *I loved the Equalists in season one of The Legend of Korra. Even though they were bad guys, I found their point of view incredibly compelling. We're showing the beginnings of their philosophy here.*

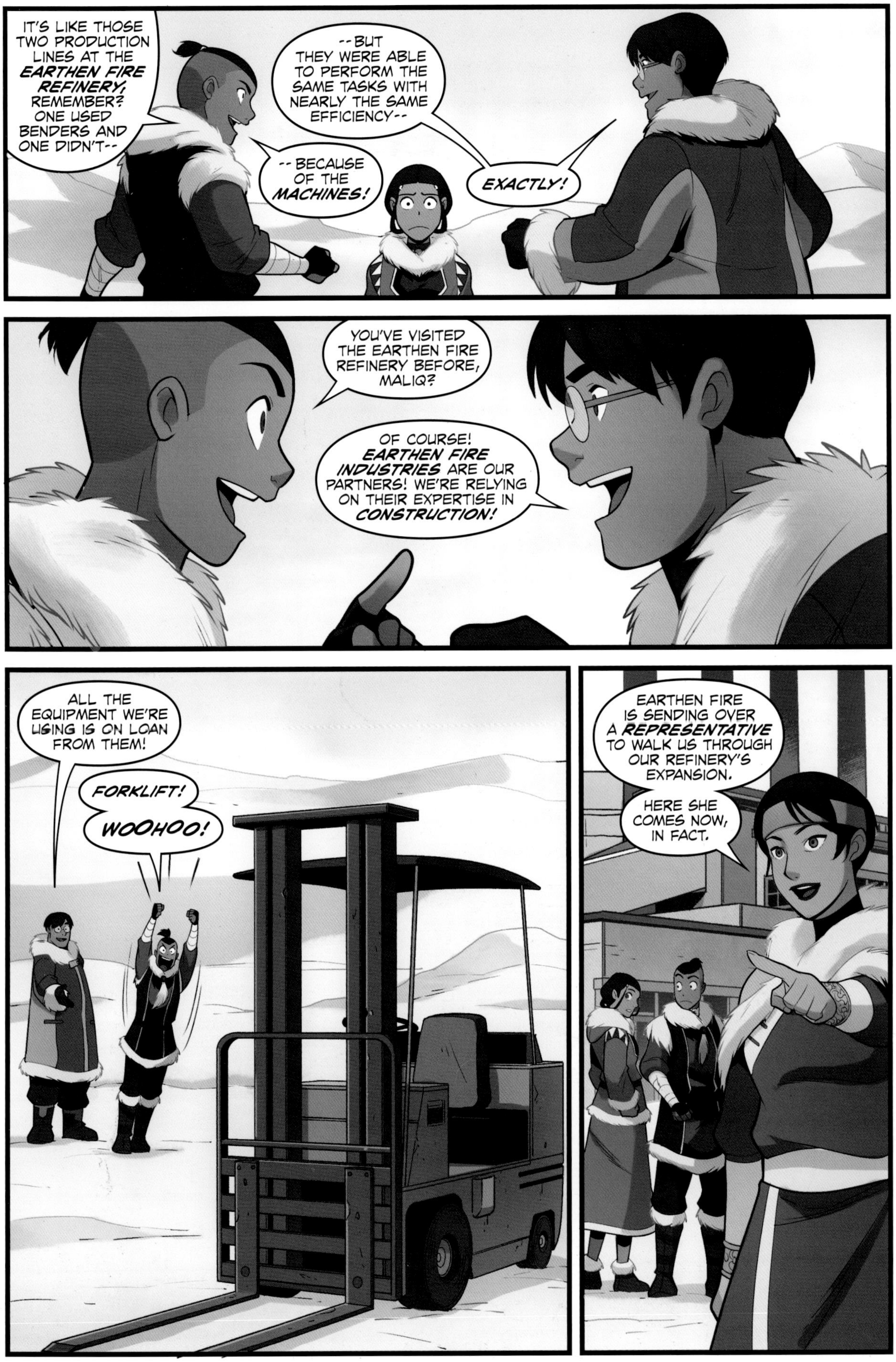
IT'S LIKE THOSE TWO PRODUCTION LINES AT THE EARTHEN FIRE REFINERY, REMEMBER? ONE USED BENDERS AND ONE DIDN'T--
--BUT THEY WERE ABLE TO PERFORM THE SAME TASKS WITH NEARLY THE SAME EFFICIENCY--
--BECAUSE OF THE MACHINES!
EXACTLY!
YOU'VE VISITED THE EARTHEN FIRE REFINERY BEFORE, MALIQ?
OF COURSE! EARTHEN FIRE INDUSTRIES ARE OUR PARTNERS! WE'RE RELYING ON THEIR EXPERTISE IN CONSTRUCTION!
ALL THE EQUIPMENT WE'RE USING IS ON LOAN FROM THEM!
FORKLIFT!
WOOHOO!
EARTHEN FIRE IS SENDING OVER A REPRESENTATIVE TO WALK US THROUGH OUR REFINERY'S EXPANSION.
HERE SHE COMES NOW, IN FACT.

G: *Here, we have another forklift.*

GLY: By the time we got to the scripting, Gurihiru and I knew that North and South would be our final Avatar: The Last Airbender story arc. We wanted to bring the whole team together so we could write and draw each of them one last time. Here's Toph!

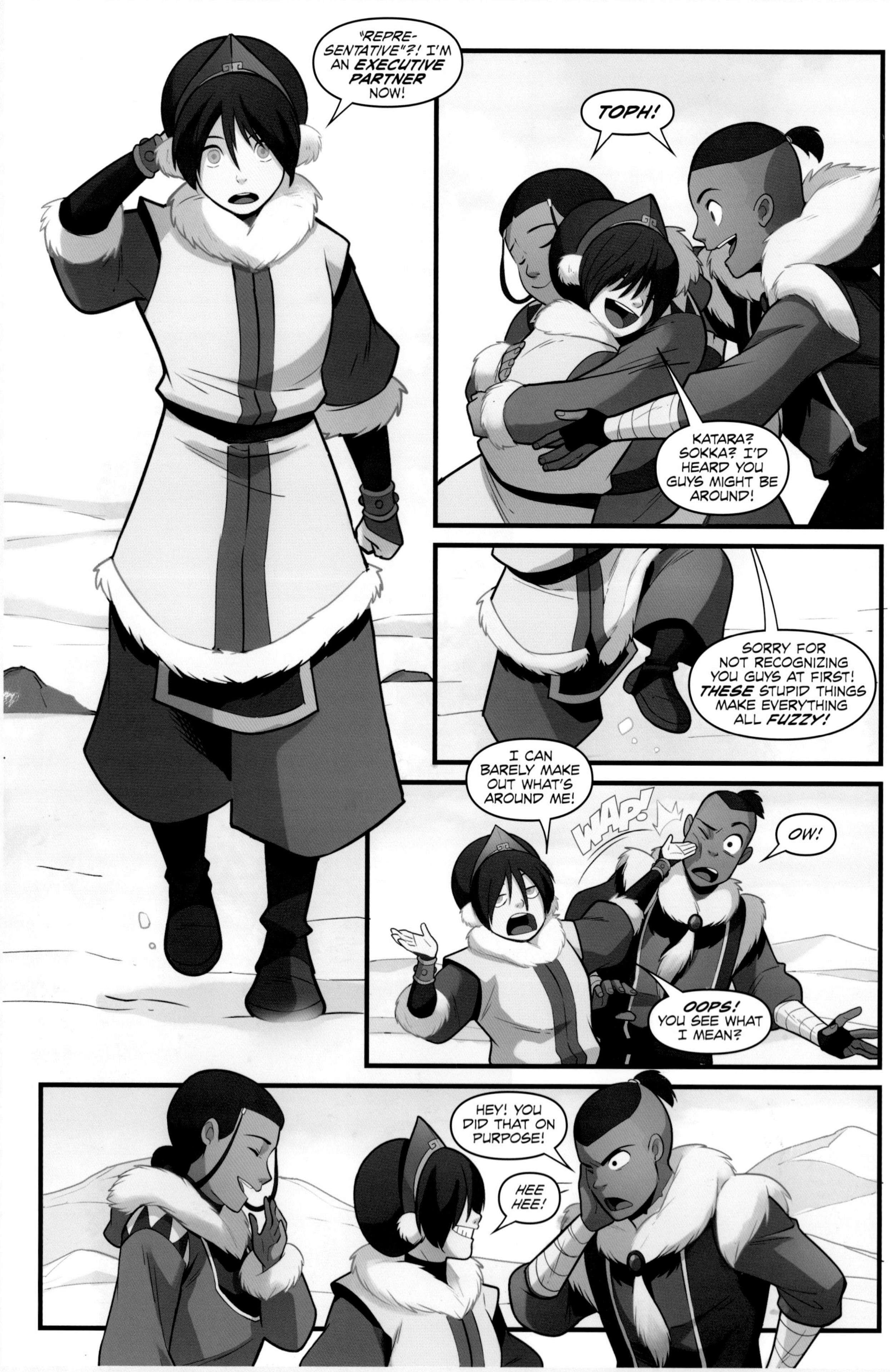
"REPRE-SENTATIVE"?! I'M AN EXECUTIVE PARTNER NOW!
TOPH!
KATARA? SOKKA? I'D HEARD YOU GUYS MIGHT BE AROUND!
SORRY FOR NOT RECOGNIZING YOU GUYS AT FIRST! THESE STUPID THINGS MAKE EVERYTHING ALL FUZZY!
I CAN BARELY MAKE OUT WHAT'S AROUND ME!
WAP!
OW!
OOPS! YOU SEE WHAT I MEAN?
HEY! YOU DID THAT ON PURPOSE!
HEE HEE!

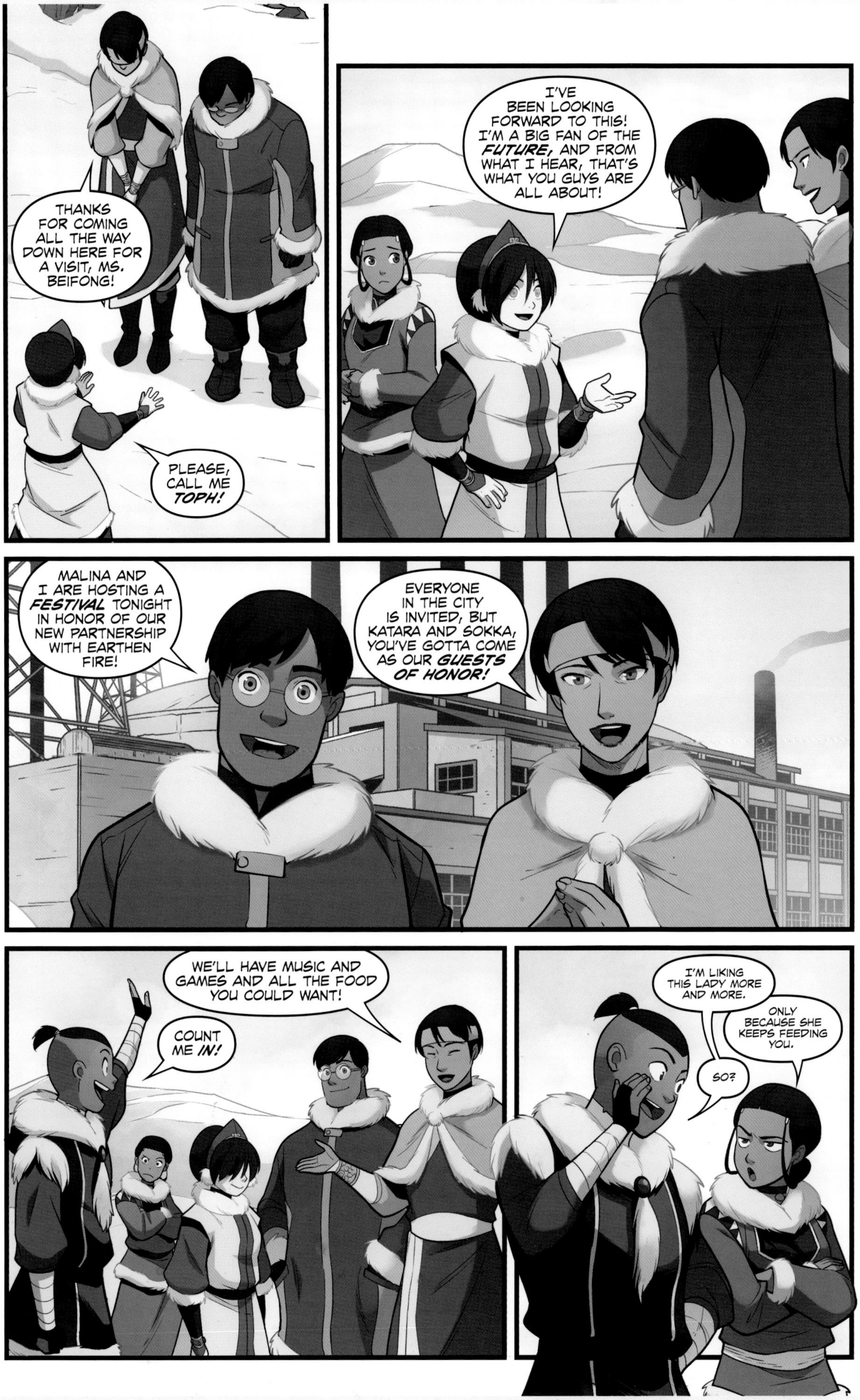
THANKS FOR COMING ALL THE WAY DOWN HERE FOR A VISIT, MS. BEIFONG!
PLEASE, CALL ME TOPH!
I'VE BEEN LOOKING FORWARD TO THIS! I'M A BIG FAN OF THE FUTURE, AND FROM WHAT I HEAR, THAT'S WHAT YOU GUYS ARE ALL ABOUT!
MALINA AND I ARE HOSTING A FESTIVAL TONIGHT IN HONOR OF OUR NEW PARTNERSHIP WITH EARTHEN FIRE!
EVERYONE IN THE CITY IS INVITED, BUT KATARA AND SOKKA, YOU'VE GOTTA COME AS OUR GUESTS OF HONOR!
WE'LL HAVE MUSIC AND GAMES AND ALL THE FOOD YOU COULD WANT!
COUNT ME IN!
I'M LIKING THIS LADY MORE AND MORE.
ONLY BECAUSE SHE KEEPS FEEDING YOU.
SO?

G: *The festival might have been a little too big.*

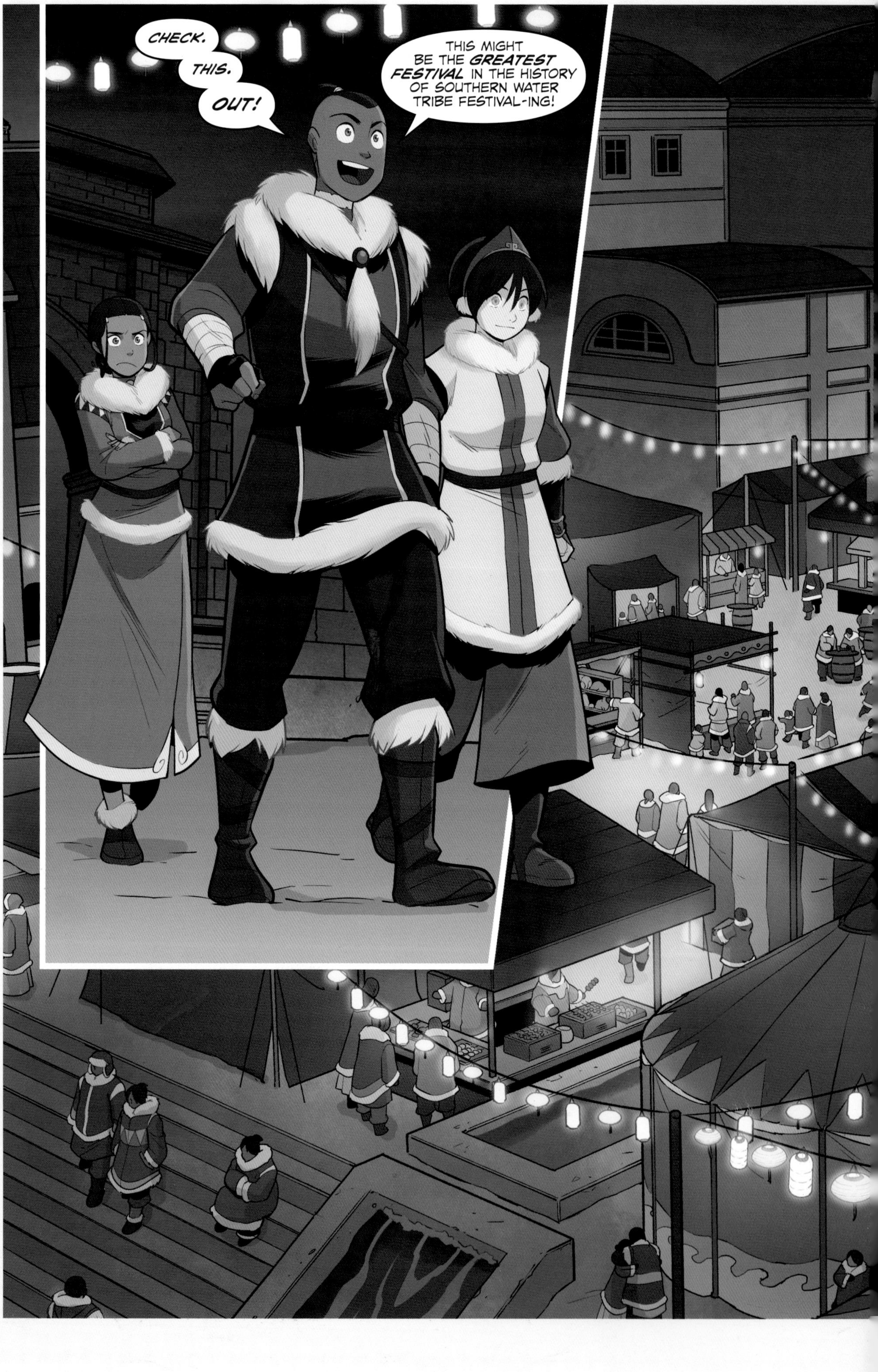
CHECK.
THIS.
OUT!
THIS MIGHT BE THE GREATEST FESTIVAL IN THE HISTORY OF SOUTHERN WATER TRIBE FESTIVAL-ING!

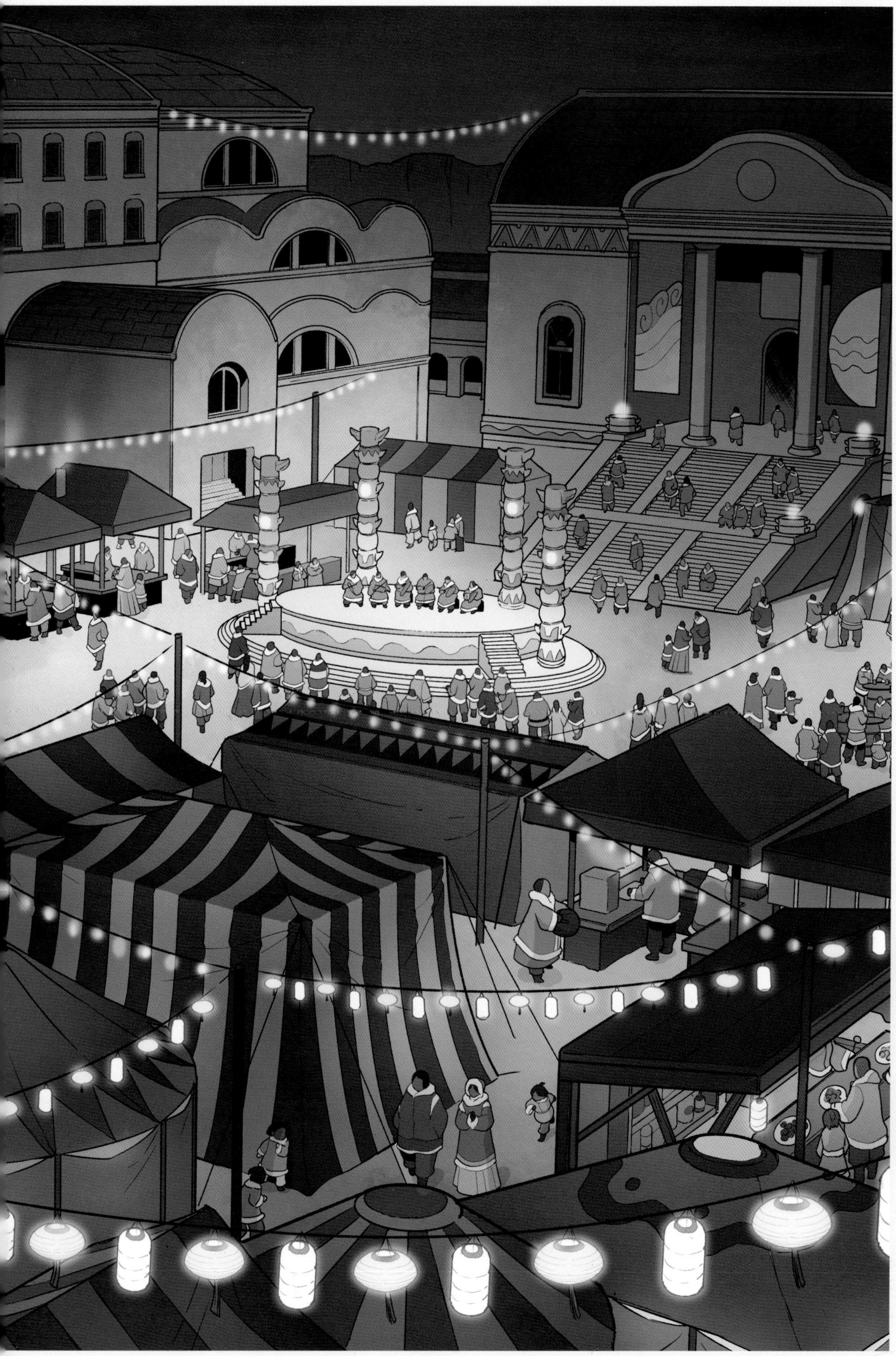

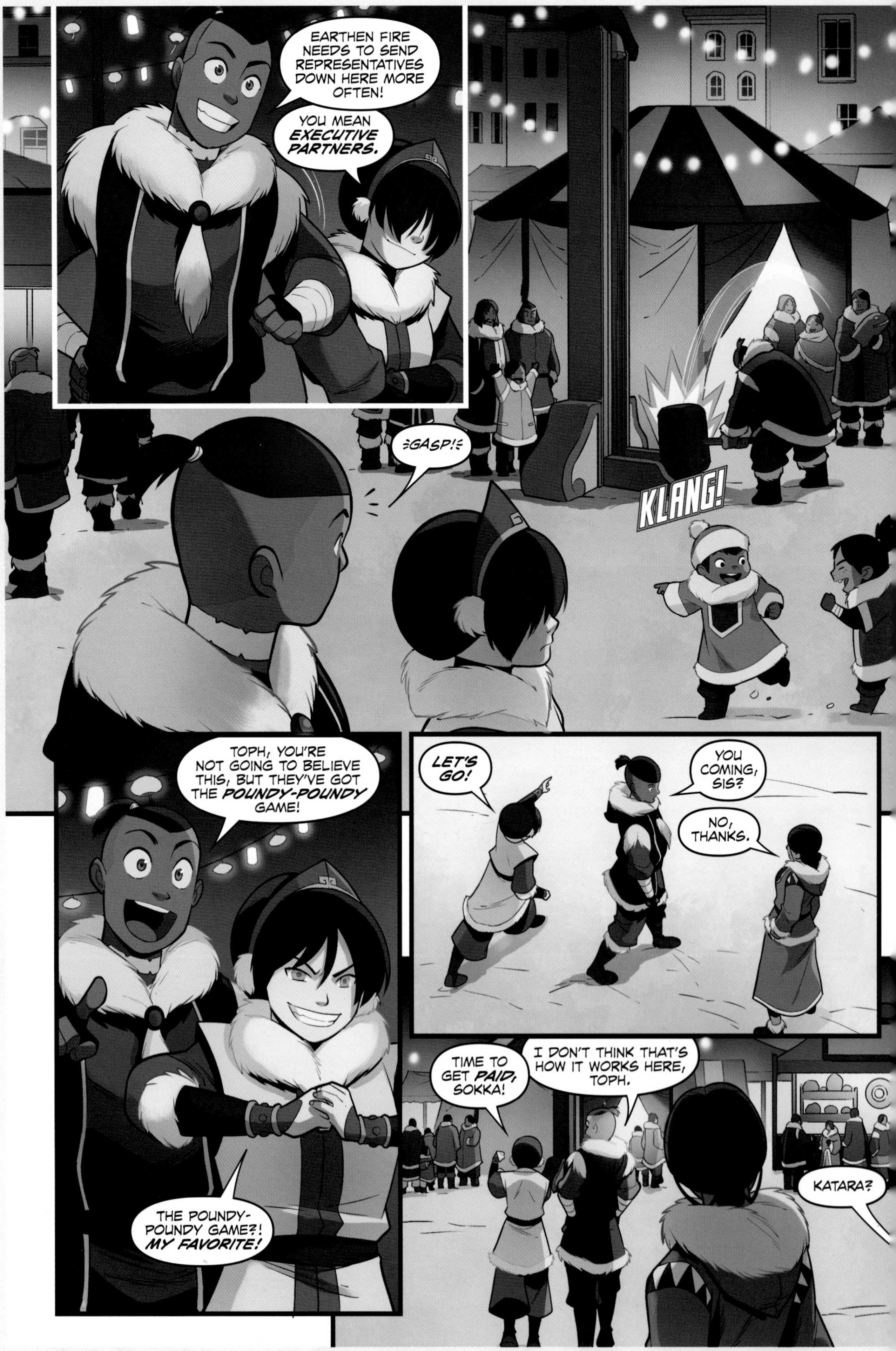
EARTHEN FIRE NEEDS TO SEND REPRESENTATIVES DOWN HERE MORE OFTEN!
YOU MEAN *EXECUTIVE PARTNERS.*
GASP!
KLANG!
TOPH, YOU'RE NOT GOING TO BELIEVE THIS, BUT THEY'VE GOT THE *POUNDY-POUNDY* GAME!
THE POUNDY-POUNDY GAME?! *MY FAVORITE!*
LET'S GO!
YOU COMING, SIS?
NO, THANKS.
TIME TO GET *PAID,* SOKKA!
I DON'T THINK THAT'S HOW IT WORKS HERE, TOPH.
KATARA?

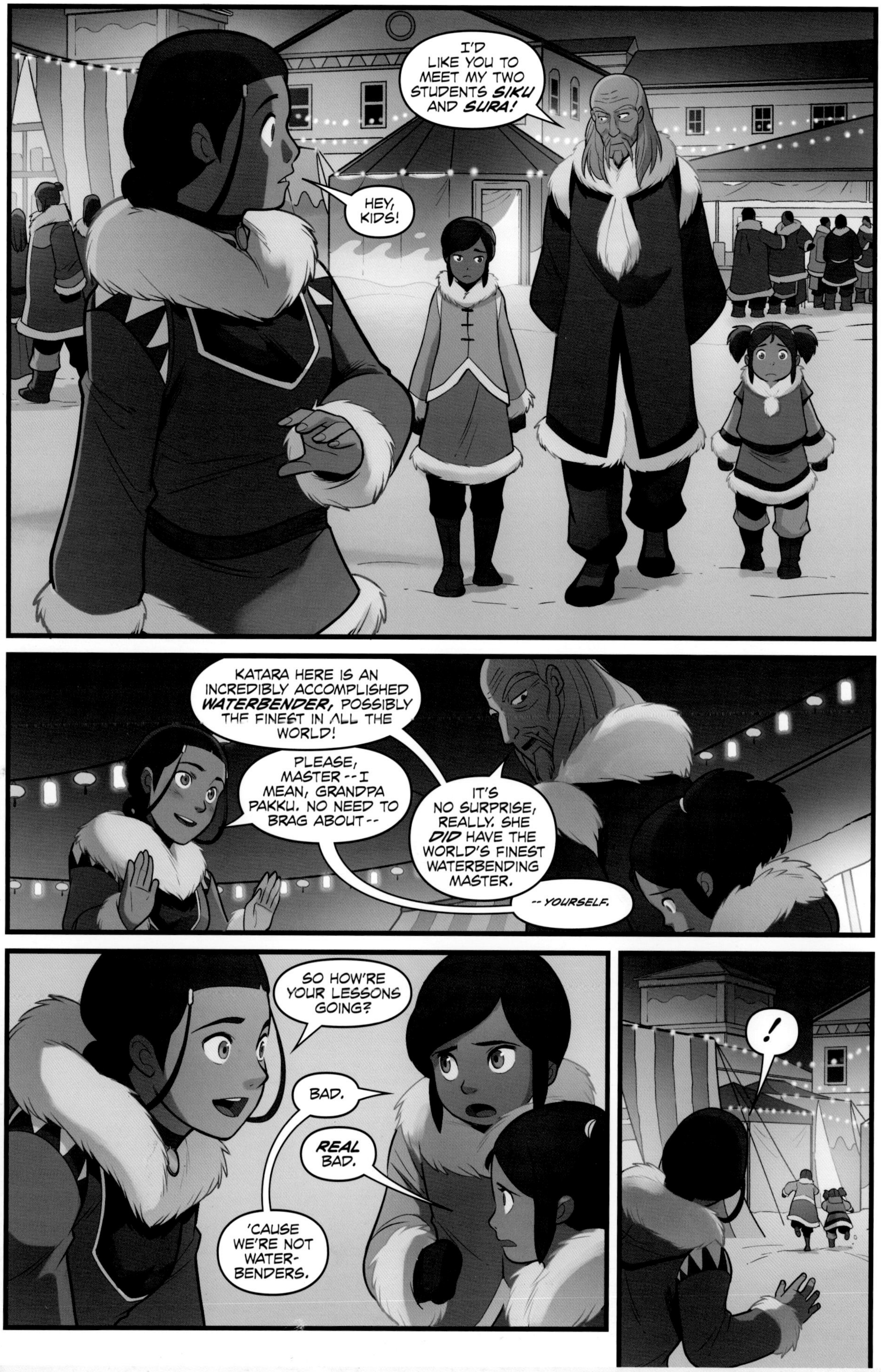
I'D LIKE YOU TO MEET MY TWO STUDENTS *SIKU* AND *SURA!*
HEY, KIDS!
KATARA HERE IS AN INCREDIBLY ACCOMPLISHED *WATERBENDER,* POSSIBLY THE FINEST IN ALL THE WORLD!
PLEASE, MASTER -- I MEAN, GRANDPA PAKKU. NO NEED TO BRAG ABOUT --
IT'S NO SURPRISE, REALLY. SHE *DID* HAVE THE WORLD'S FINEST WATERBENDING MASTER.
-- YOURSELF.
SO HOW'RE YOUR LESSONS GOING?
BAD.
REAL BAD.
'CAUSE WE'RE NOT WATER-BENDERS.
!

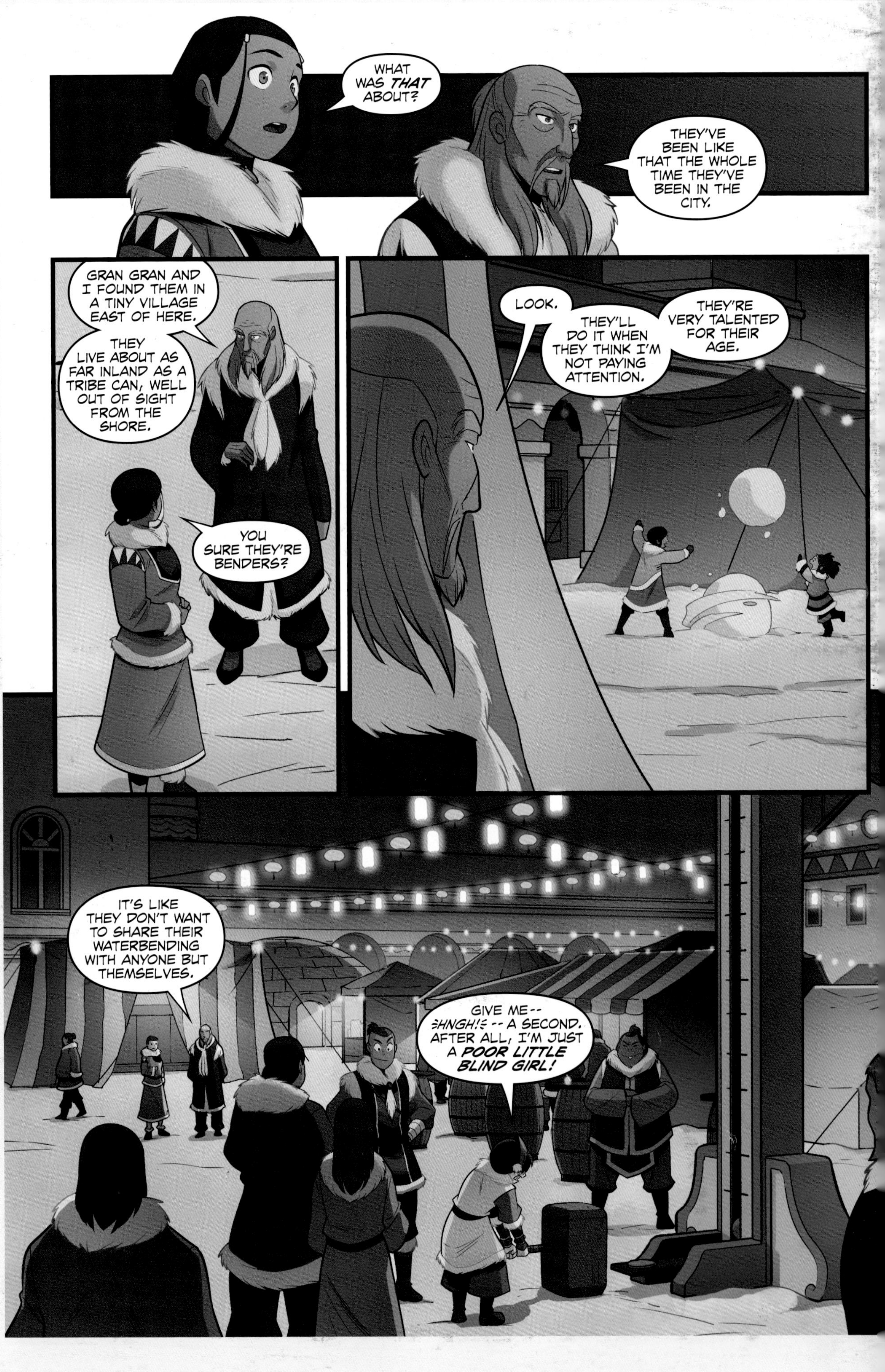
WHAT WAS *THAT* ABOUT?
THEY'VE BEEN LIKE THAT THE WHOLE TIME THEY'VE BEEN IN THE CITY.
GRAN GRAN AND I FOUND THEM IN A TINY VILLAGE EAST OF HERE.
THEY LIVE ABOUT AS FAR INLAND AS A TRIBE CAN, WELL OUT OF SIGHT FROM THE SHORE.
YOU SURE THEY'RE BENDERS?
LOOK.
THEY'LL DO IT WHEN THEY THINK I'M NOT PAYING ATTENTION.
THEY'RE VERY TALENTED FOR THEIR AGE.
IT'S LIKE THEY DON'T WANT TO SHARE THEIR WATERBENDING WITH ANYONE BUT THEMSELVES.
GIVE ME-- HNGH! --A SECOND. AFTER ALL, I'M JUST A *POOR LITTLE BLIND GIRL!*

GLY: *Toph and Sokka first played "the poundy-poundy game" in the episode "The Runaway," though it's not called that in the episode. I love that episode because it shows that although Aang is the Avatar, he's still just a kid. His love of fun can sometimes lead him to make bad decisions.*

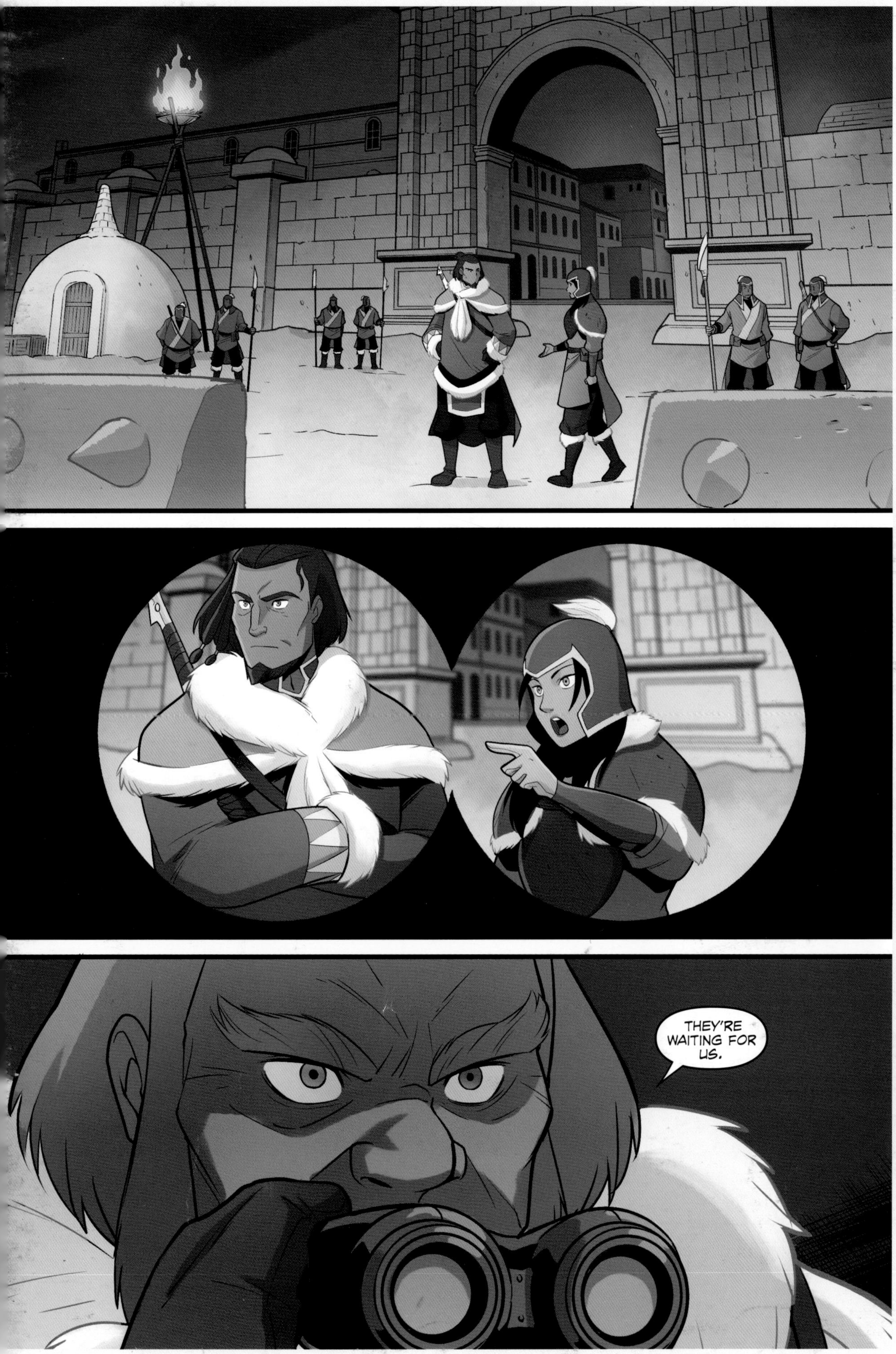
THEY'RE WAITING FOR US.

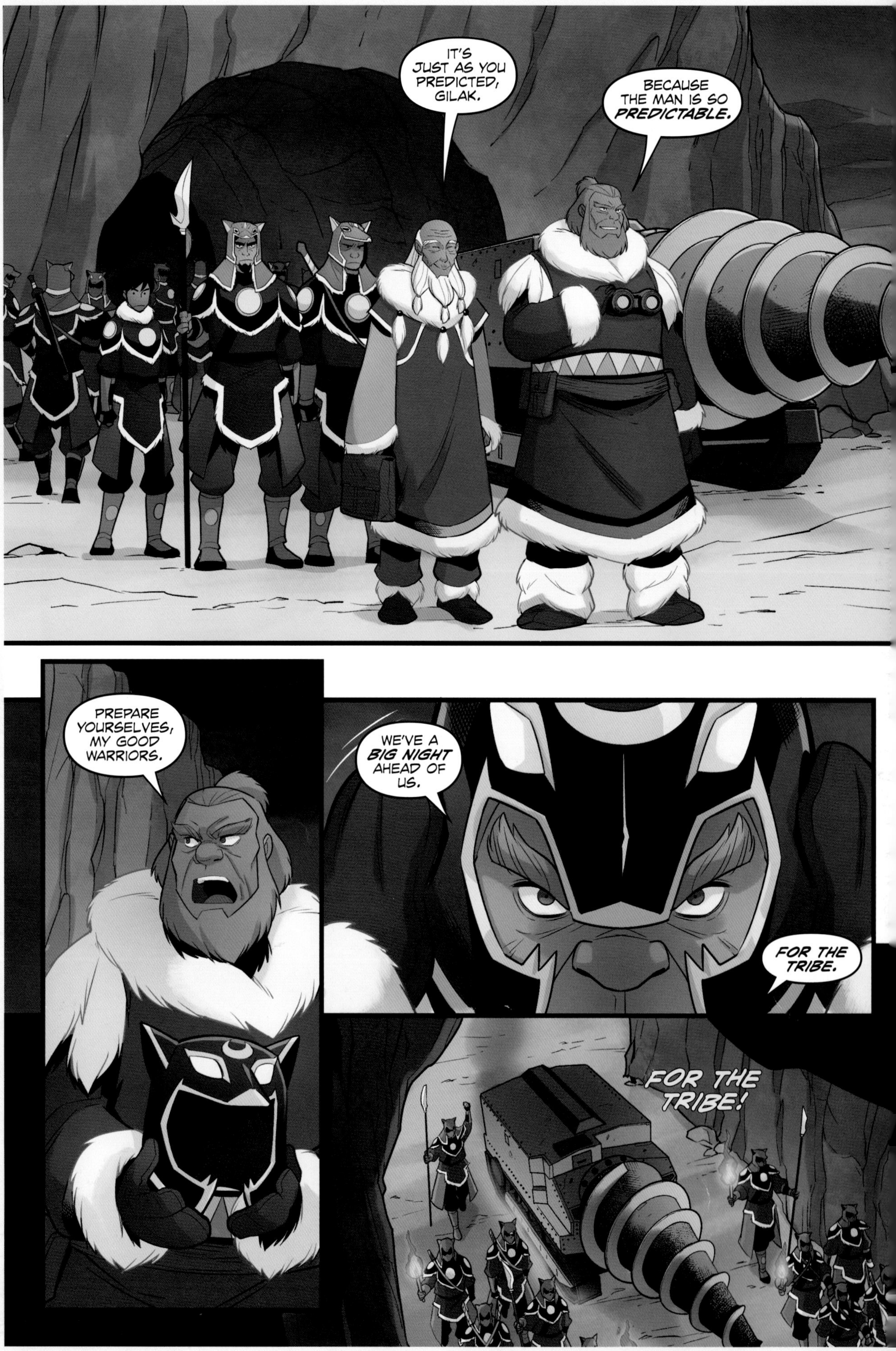
IT'S JUST AS YOU PREDICTED, GILAK.
BECAUSE THE MAN IS SO PREDICTABLE.
PREPARE YOURSELVES, MY GOOD WARRIORS.
WE'VE A BIG NIGHT AHEAD OF US.
FOR THE TRIBE.
FOR THE TRIBE!

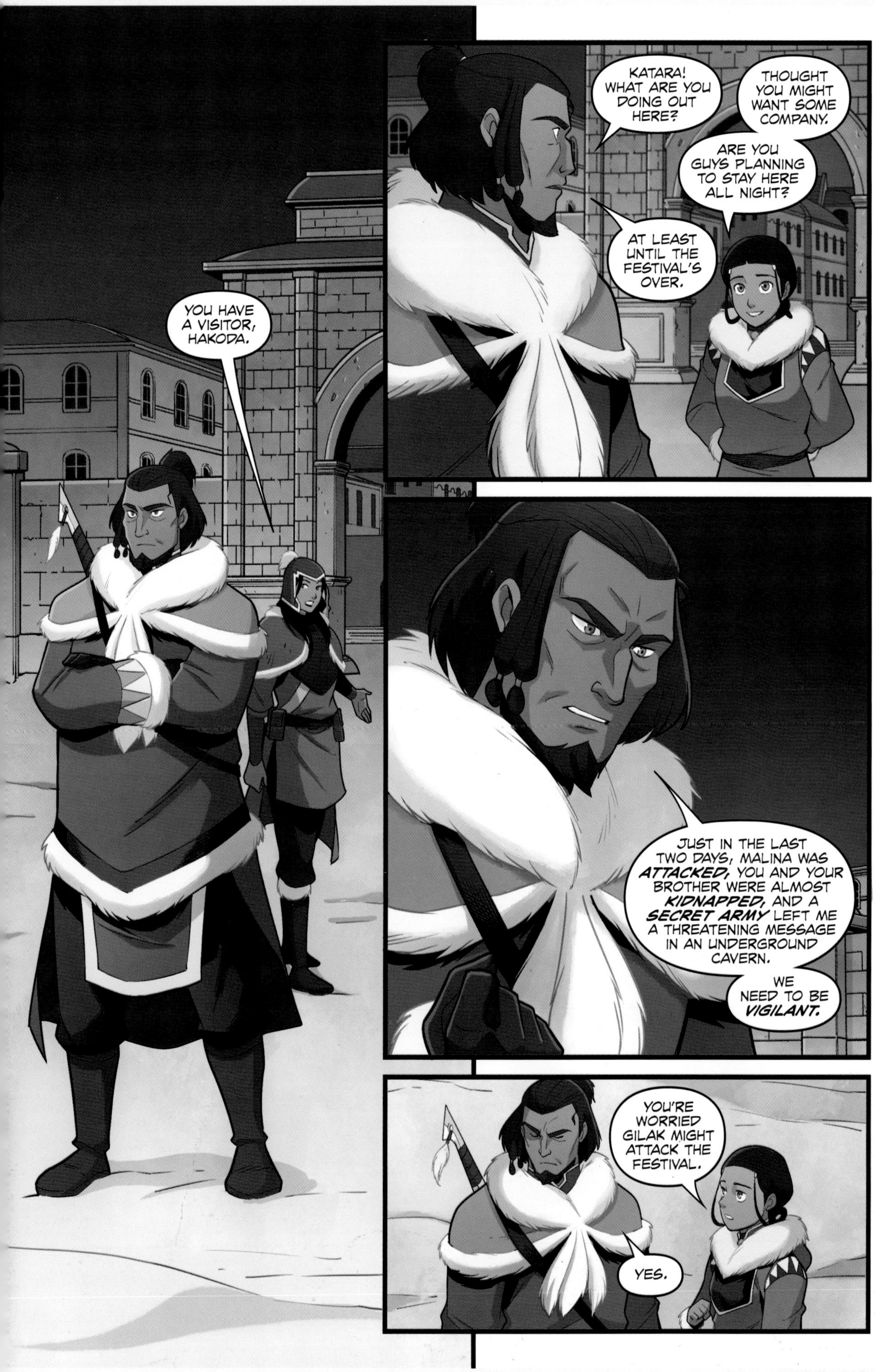
YOU HAVE A VISITOR, HAKODA.
KATARA! WHAT ARE YOU DOING OUT HERE?
THOUGHT YOU MIGHT WANT SOME COMPANY.
ARE YOU GUYS PLANNING TO STAY HERE ALL NIGHT?
AT LEAST UNTIL THE FESTIVAL'S OVER.
JUST IN THE LAST TWO DAYS, MALINA WAS ATTACKED, YOU AND YOUR BROTHER WERE ALMOST KIDNAPPED, AND A SECRET ARMY LEFT ME A THREATENING MESSAGE IN AN UNDERGROUND CAVERN.
WE NEED TO BE VIGILANT.
YOU'RE WORRIED GILAK MIGHT ATTACK THE FESTIVAL.
YES.

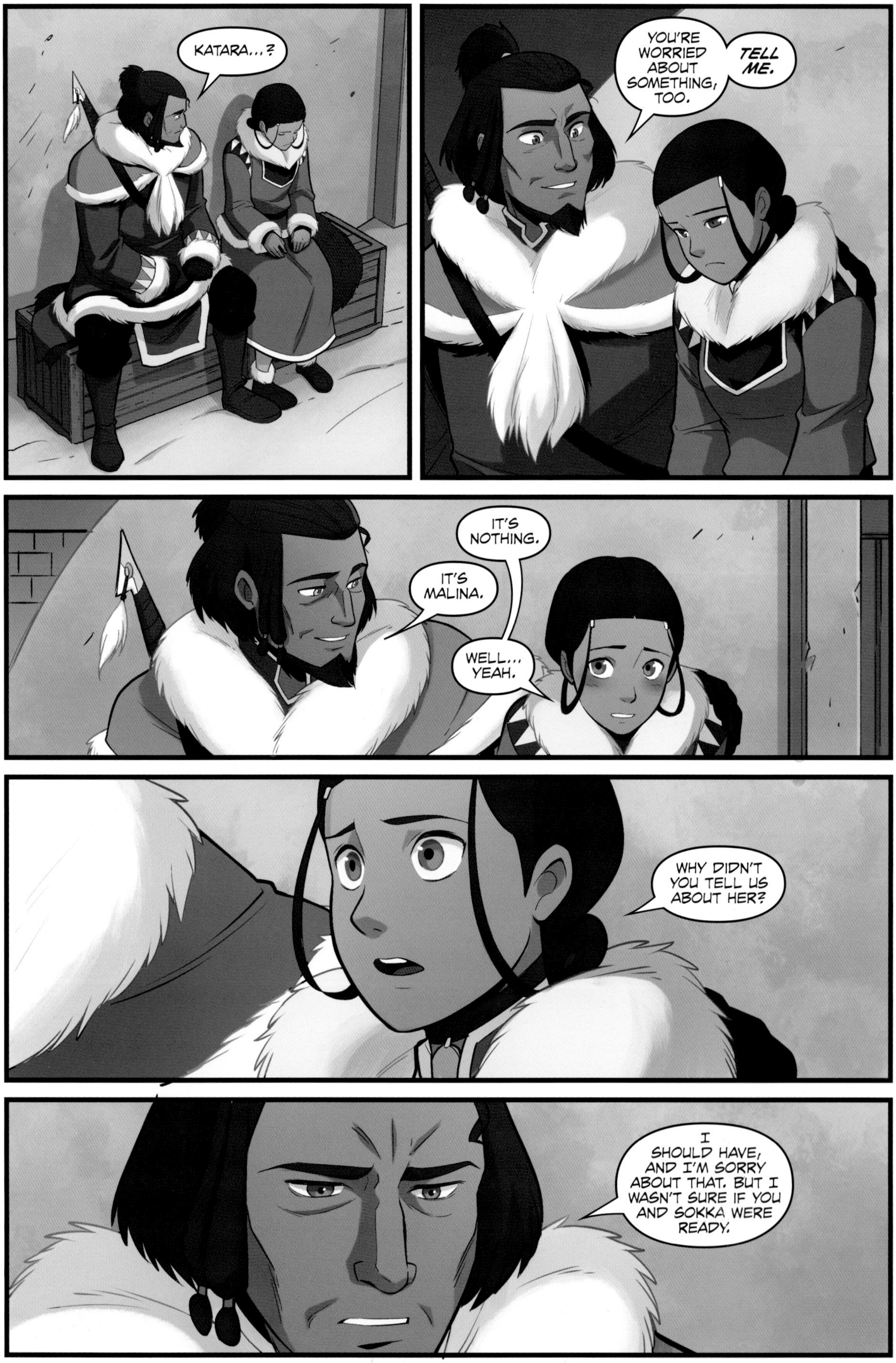
KATARA...?
YOU'RE WORRIED ABOUT SOMETHING, TOO.
TELL ME.
IT'S NOTHING.
IT'S MALINA.
WELL... YEAH.
WHY DIDN'T YOU TELL US ABOUT HER?
I SHOULD HAVE, AND I'M SORRY ABOUT THAT. BUT I WASN'T SURE IF YOU AND SOKKA WERE READY.

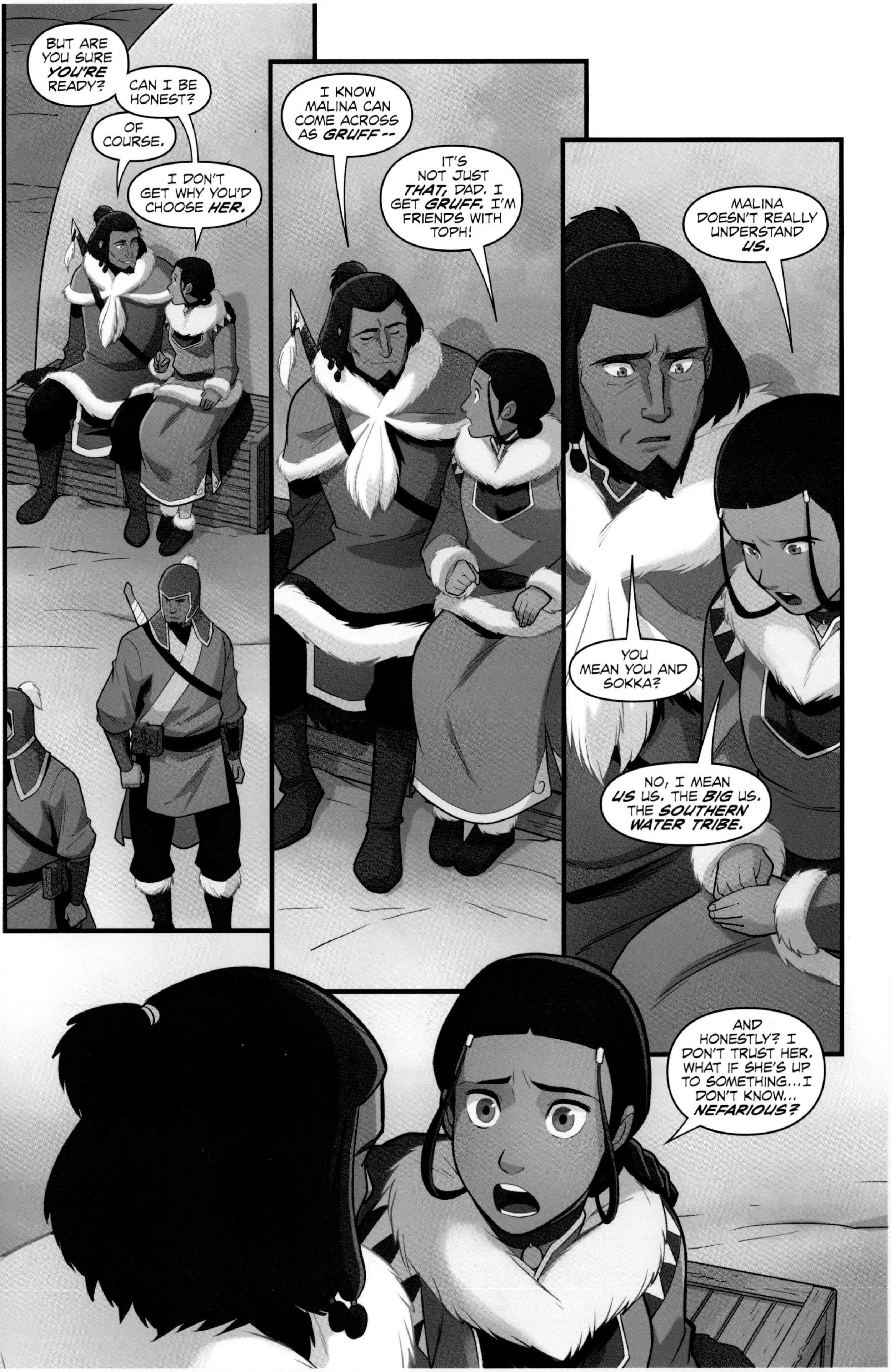
BUT ARE YOU SURE YOU'RE READY?
CAN I BE HONEST?
OF COURSE.
I DON'T GET WHY YOU'D CHOOSE HER.
I KNOW MALINA CAN COME ACROSS AS GRUFF --
IT'S NOT JUST THAT, DAD. I GET GRUFF. I'M FRIENDS WITH TOPH!
MALINA DOESN'T REALLY UNDERSTAND US.
YOU MEAN YOU AND SOKKA?
NO, I MEAN US US. THE BIG US. THE SOUTHERN WATER TRIBE.
AND HONESTLY? I DON'T TRUST HER. WHAT IF SHE'S UP TO SOMETHING... I DON'T KNOW... NEFARIOUS?

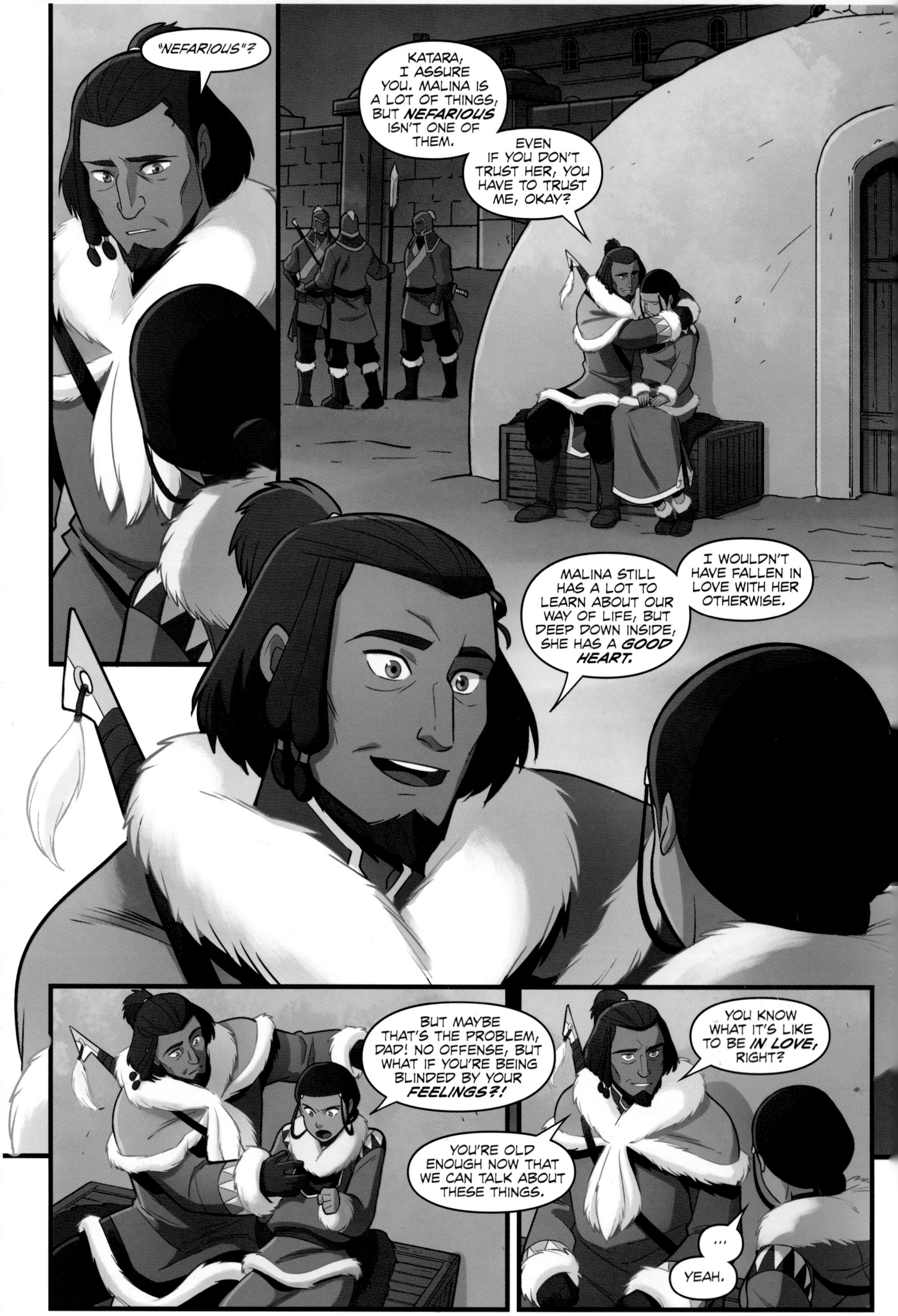
"NEFARIOUS"?
KATARA, I ASSURE YOU. MALINA IS A LOT OF THINGS, BUT NEFARIOUS ISN'T ONE OF THEM.
EVEN IF YOU DON'T TRUST HER, YOU HAVE TO TRUST ME, OKAY?
MALINA STILL HAS A LOT TO LEARN ABOUT OUR WAY OF LIFE, BUT DEEP DOWN INSIDE, SHE HAS A GOOD HEART.
I WOULDN'T HAVE FALLEN IN LOVE WITH HER OTHERWISE.
BUT MAYBE THAT'S THE PROBLEM, DAD! NO OFFENSE, BUT WHAT IF YOU'RE BEING BLINDED BY YOUR FEELINGS?!
YOU KNOW WHAT IT'S LIKE TO BE IN LOVE, RIGHT?
YOU'RE OLD ENOUGH NOW THAT WE CAN TALK ABOUT THESE THINGS.
...
YEAH.

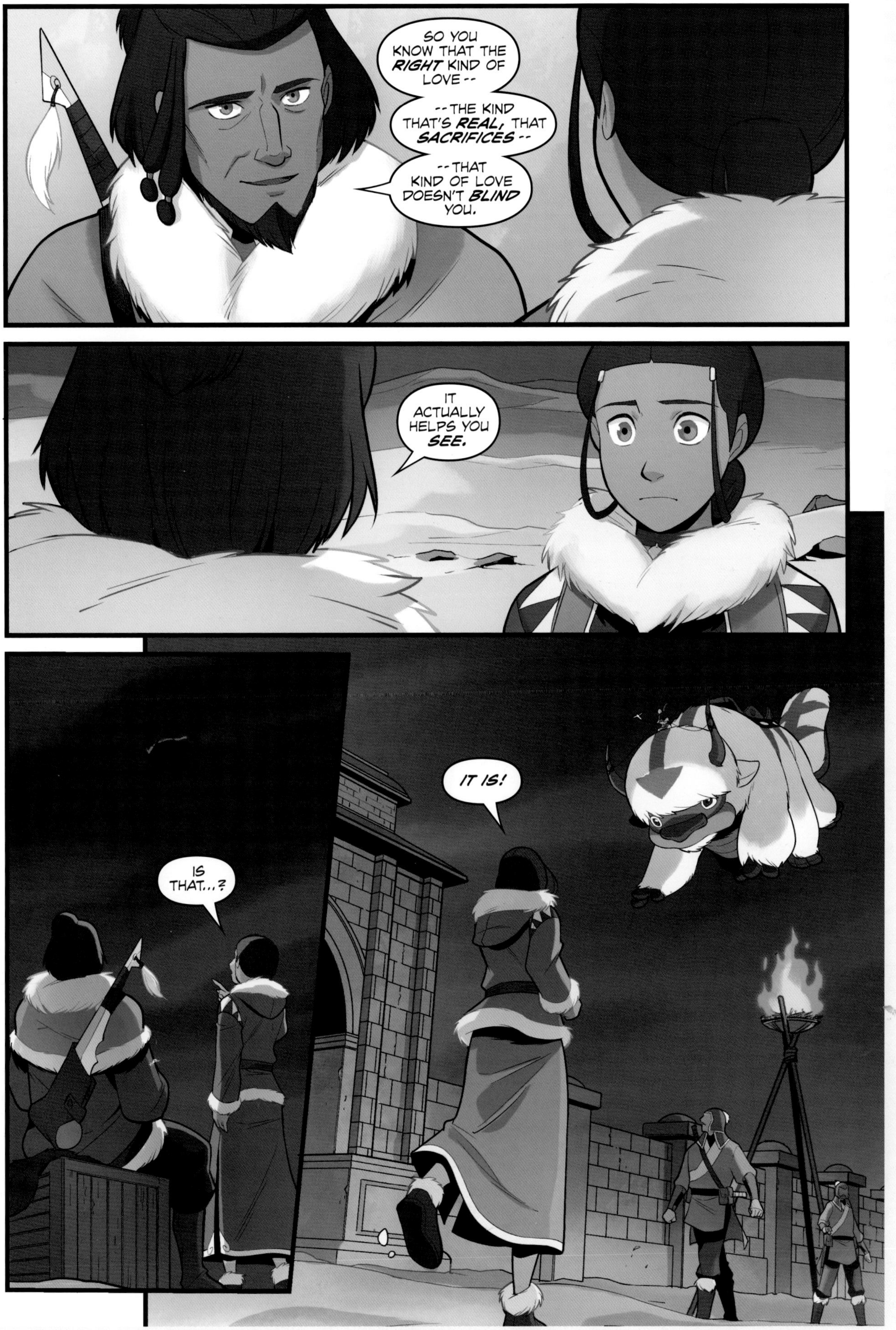
SO YOU KNOW THAT THE RIGHT KIND OF LOVE --
--THE KIND THAT'S REAL, THAT SACRIFICES --
--THAT KIND OF LOVE DOESN'T BLIND YOU.
IT ACTUALLY HELPS YOU SEE.
IS THAT...?
IT IS!

GLY: *We debated whether or not to bring Aang into the story earlier than this. We decided against it for a couple of reasons. First, we wanted the focus to firmly be on Katara and Sokka. Second, bringing Aang in earlier would have made the timeline tricky. The events of this story overlap with the events in Smoke and Shadow.*

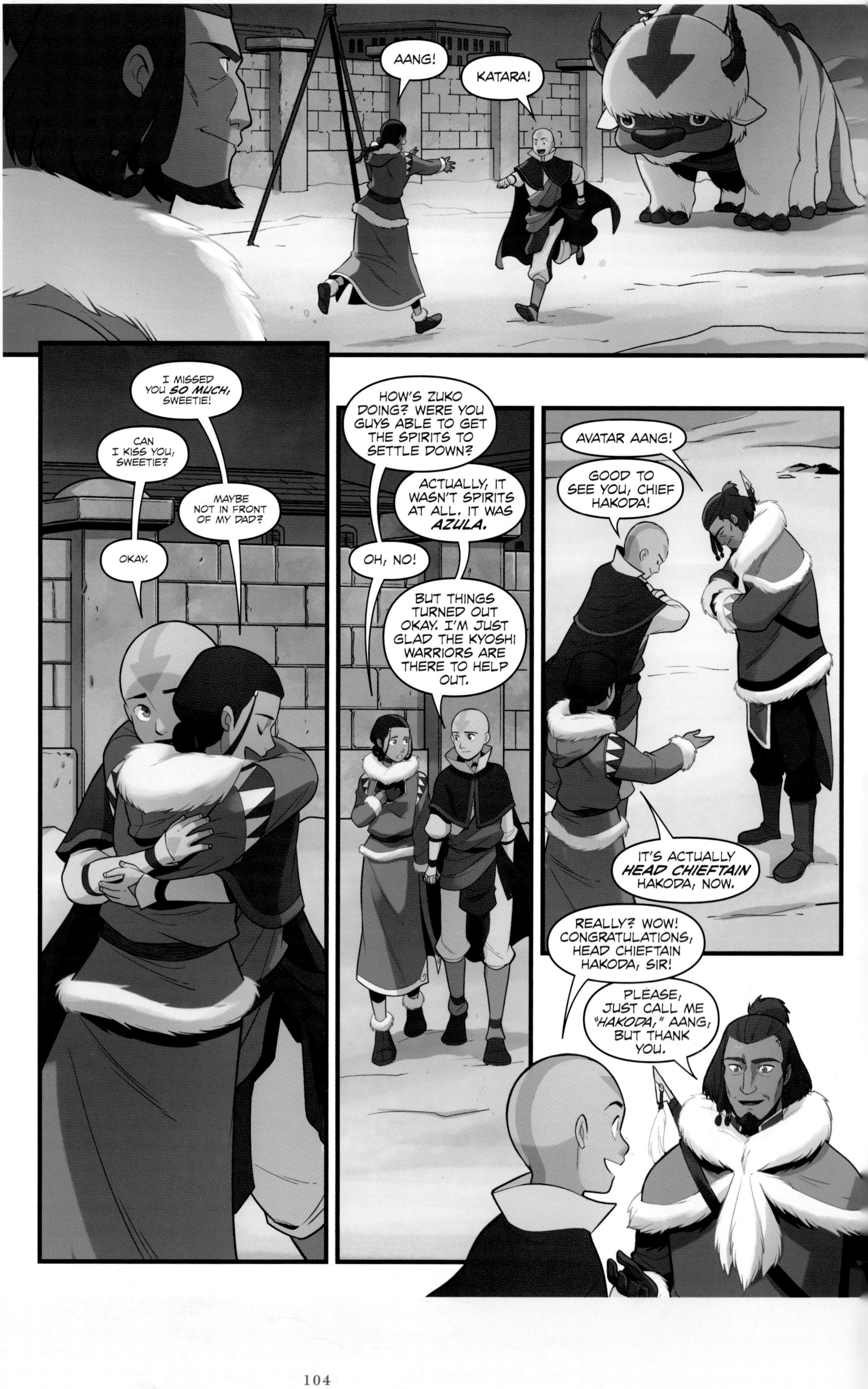
AANG!
KATARA!
I MISSED YOU *SO MUCH,* SWEETIE!
CAN I KISS YOU, SWEETIE?
MAYBE NOT IN FRONT OF MY DAD?
OKAY.
HOW'S ZUKO DOING? WERE YOU GUYS ABLE TO GET THE SPIRITS TO SETTLE DOWN?
ACTUALLY, IT WASN'T SPIRITS AT ALL. IT WAS *AZULA.*
OH, NO!
BUT THINGS TURNED OUT OKAY. I'M JUST GLAD THE KYOSHI WARRIORS ARE THERE TO HELP OUT.
AVATAR AANG!
GOOD TO SEE YOU, CHIEF HAKODA!
IT'S ACTUALLY *HEAD CHIEFTAIN* HAKODA, NOW.
REALLY? WOW! CONGRATULATIONS, HEAD CHIEFTAIN HAKODA, SIR!
PLEASE, JUST CALL ME *"HAKODA,"* AANG, BUT THANK YOU.

G: *Finally, our hero Aang is here! This might be his longest absence. Since Bryan and Mike told us an Airbender does not need to wear too much to keep warm, we made his clothing simple with just long sleeves and a cloak. The costume was drawn to look like the clothes worn by Tenzin, Aang's son from The Legend of Korra.*

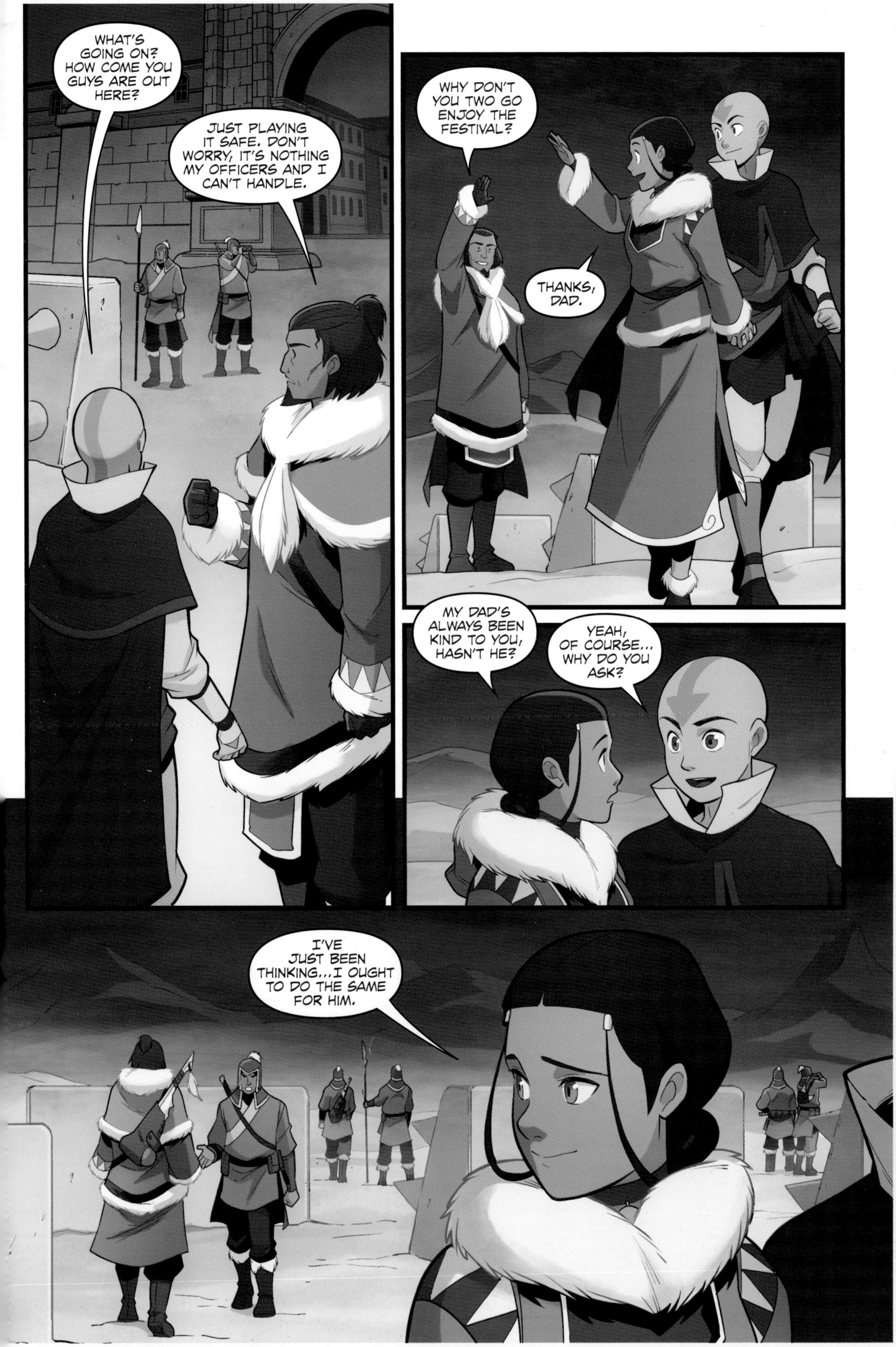
WHAT'S GOING ON? HOW COME YOU GUYS ARE OUT HERE?
JUST PLAYING IT SAFE. DON'T WORRY, IT'S NOTHING MY OFFICERS AND I CAN'T HANDLE.
WHY DON'T YOU TWO GO ENJOY THE FESTIVAL?
THANKS, DAD.
MY DAD'S ALWAYS BEEN KIND TO YOU, HASN'T HE?
YEAH, OF COURSE... WHY DO YOU ASK?
I'VE JUST BEEN THINKING... I OUGHT TO DO THE SAME FOR HIM.

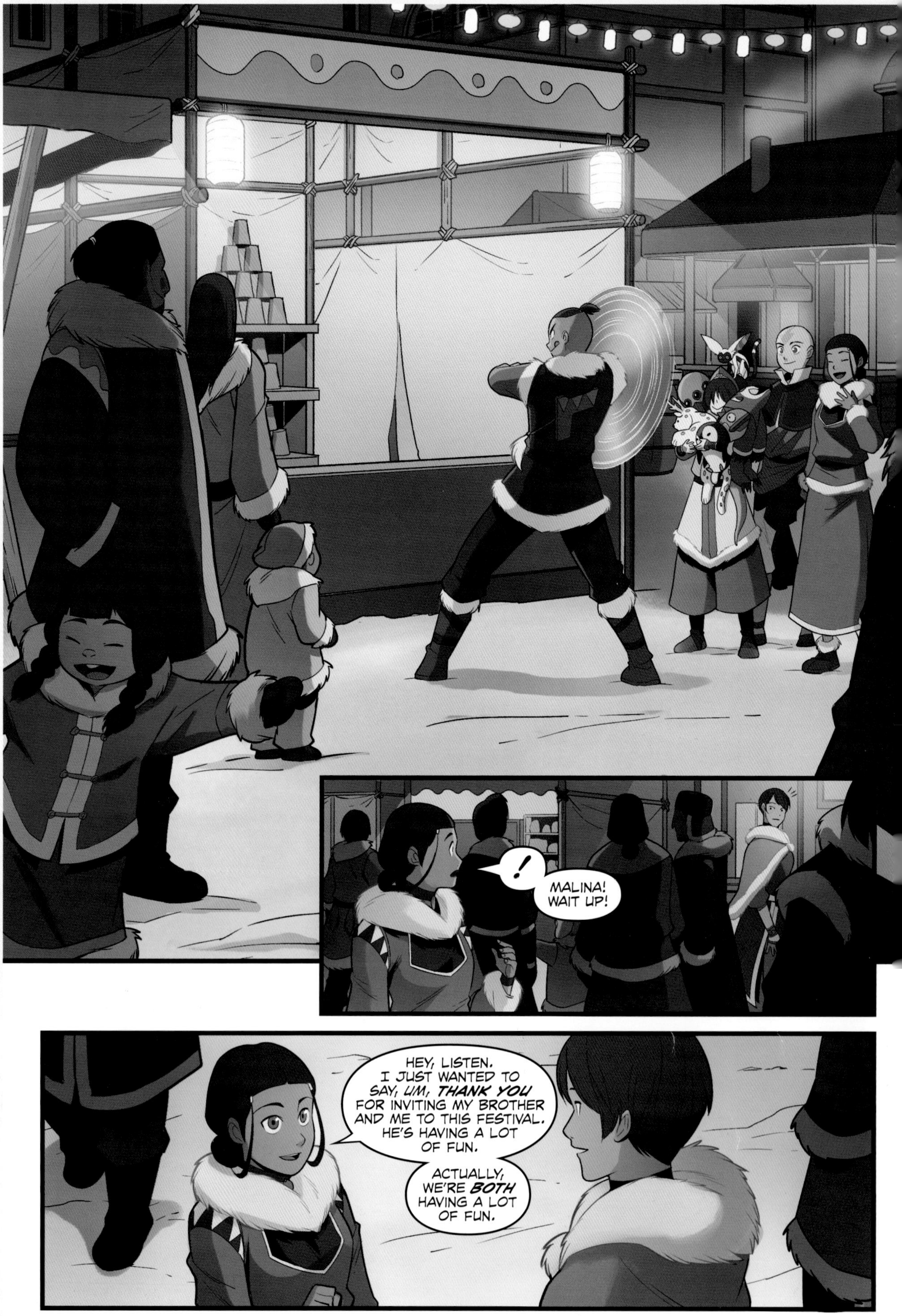
!
MALINA! WAIT UP!
HEY, LISTEN. I JUST WANTED TO SAY, UM, THANK YOU FOR INVITING MY BROTHER AND ME TO THIS FESTIVAL. HE'S HAVING A LOT OF FUN.
ACTUALLY, WE'RE BOTH HAVING A LOT OF FUN.

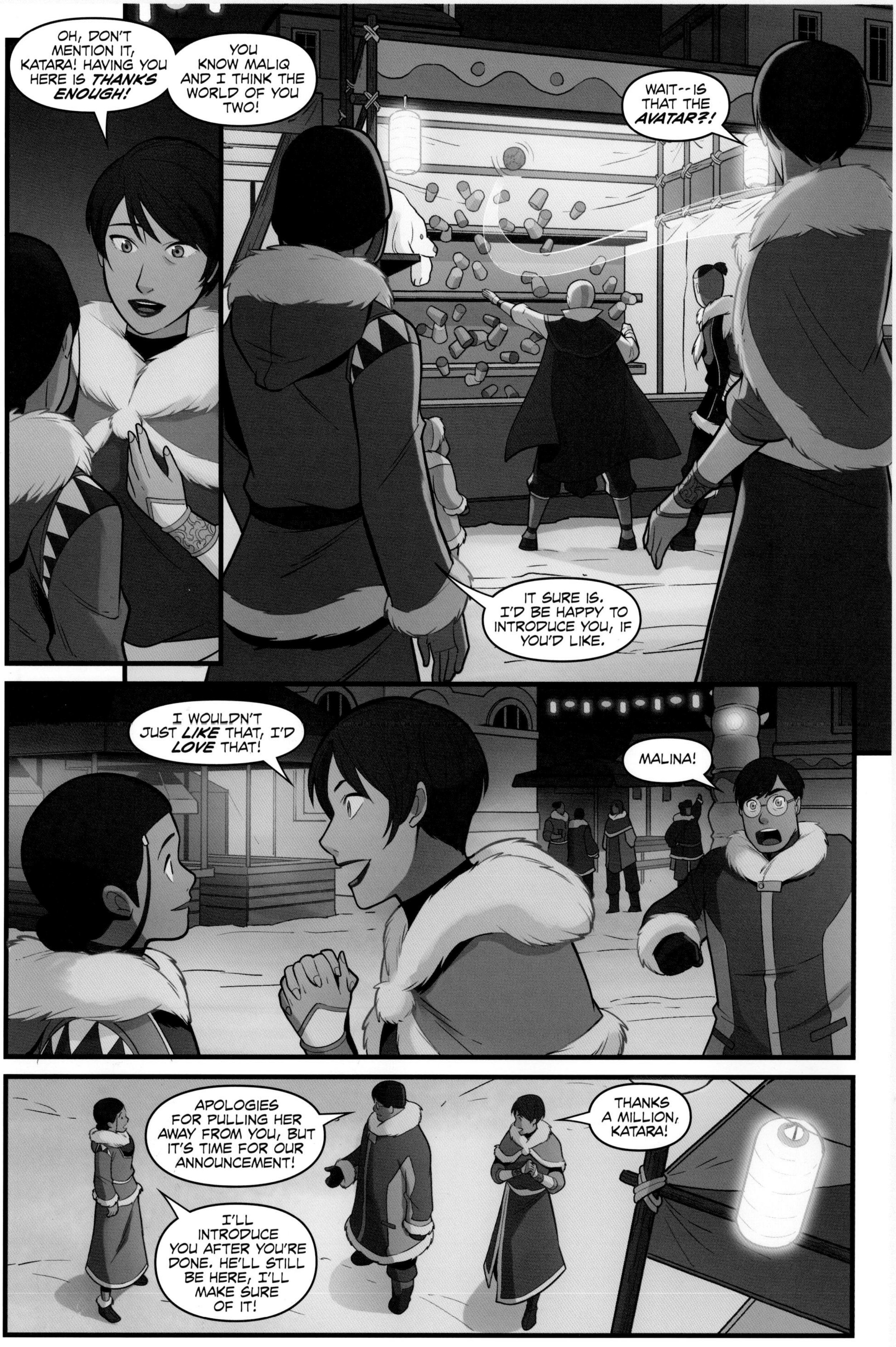
OH, DON'T MENTION IT, KATARA! HAVING YOU HERE IS THANKS ENOUGH!
YOU KNOW MALIQ AND I THINK THE WORLD OF YOU TWO!
WAIT--IS THAT THE AVATAR?!
IT SURE IS. I'D BE HAPPY TO INTRODUCE YOU, IF YOU'D LIKE.
I WOULDN'T JUST LIKE THAT, I'D LOVE THAT!
MALINA!
APOLOGIES FOR PULLING HER AWAY FROM YOU, BUT IT'S TIME FOR OUR ANNOUNCEMENT!
THANKS A MILLION, KATARA!
I'LL INTRODUCE YOU AFTER YOU'RE DONE. HE'LL STILL BE HERE, I'LL MAKE SURE OF IT!

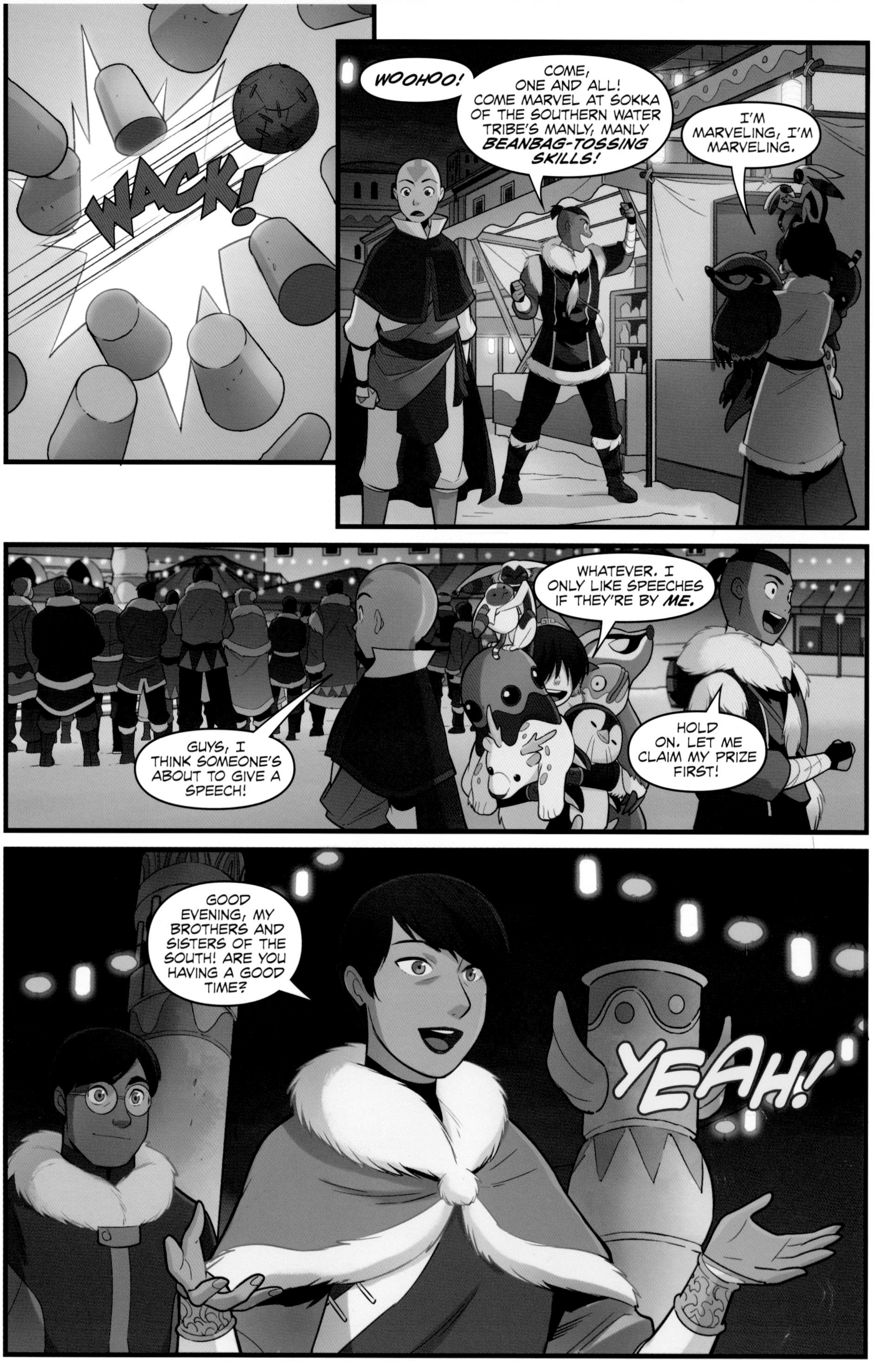
WACK!
WOOHOO!
COME, ONE AND ALL! COME MARVEL AT SOKKA OF THE SOUTHERN WATER TRIBE'S MANLY, MANLY **BEANBAG-TOSSING SKILLS!**
I'M MARVELING, I'M MARVELING.
GUYS, I THINK SOMEONE'S ABOUT TO GIVE A SPEECH!
WHATEVER. I ONLY LIKE SPEECHES IF THEY'RE BY **ME.**
HOLD ON. LET ME CLAIM MY PRIZE FIRST!
GOOD EVENING, MY BROTHERS AND SISTERS OF THE SOUTH! ARE YOU HAVING A GOOD TIME?
YEAH!

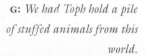

G: *We had Toph hold a pile of stuffed animals from this world.*

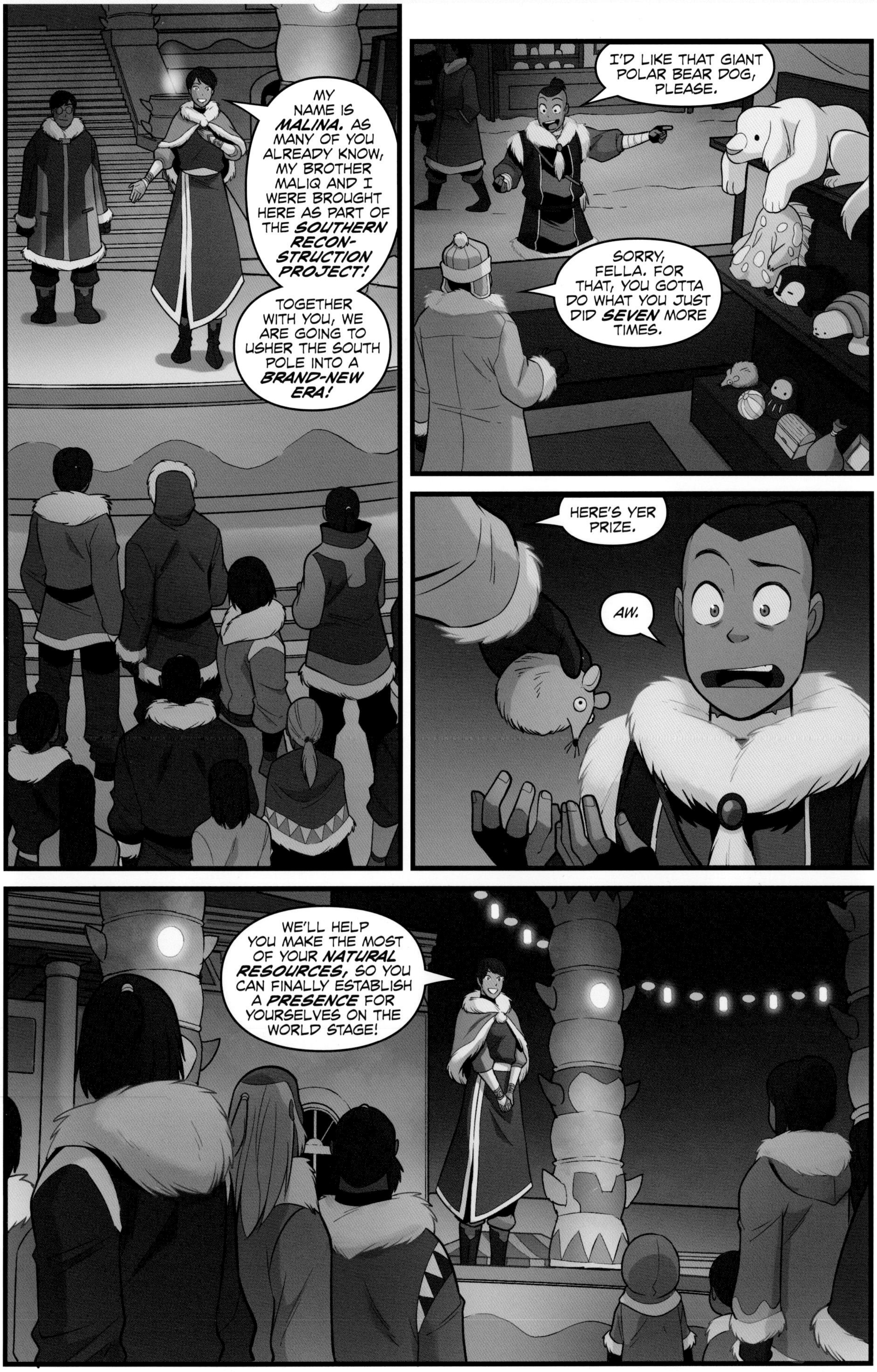
MY NAME IS MALINA. AS MANY OF YOU ALREADY KNOW, MY BROTHER MALIQ AND I WERE BROUGHT HERE AS PART OF THE SOUTHERN RECON-STRUCTION PROJECT!
TOGETHER WITH YOU, WE ARE GOING TO USHER THE SOUTH POLE INTO A BRAND-NEW ERA!
I'D LIKE THAT GIANT POLAR BEAR DOG, PLEASE.
SORRY, FELLA. FOR THAT, YOU GOTTA DO WHAT YOU JUST DID SEVEN MORE TIMES.
HERE'S YER PRIZE.
AW.
WE'LL HELP YOU MAKE THE MOST OF YOUR NATURAL RESOURCES, SO YOU CAN FINALLY ESTABLISH A PRESENCE FOR YOURSELVES ON THE WORLD STAGE!

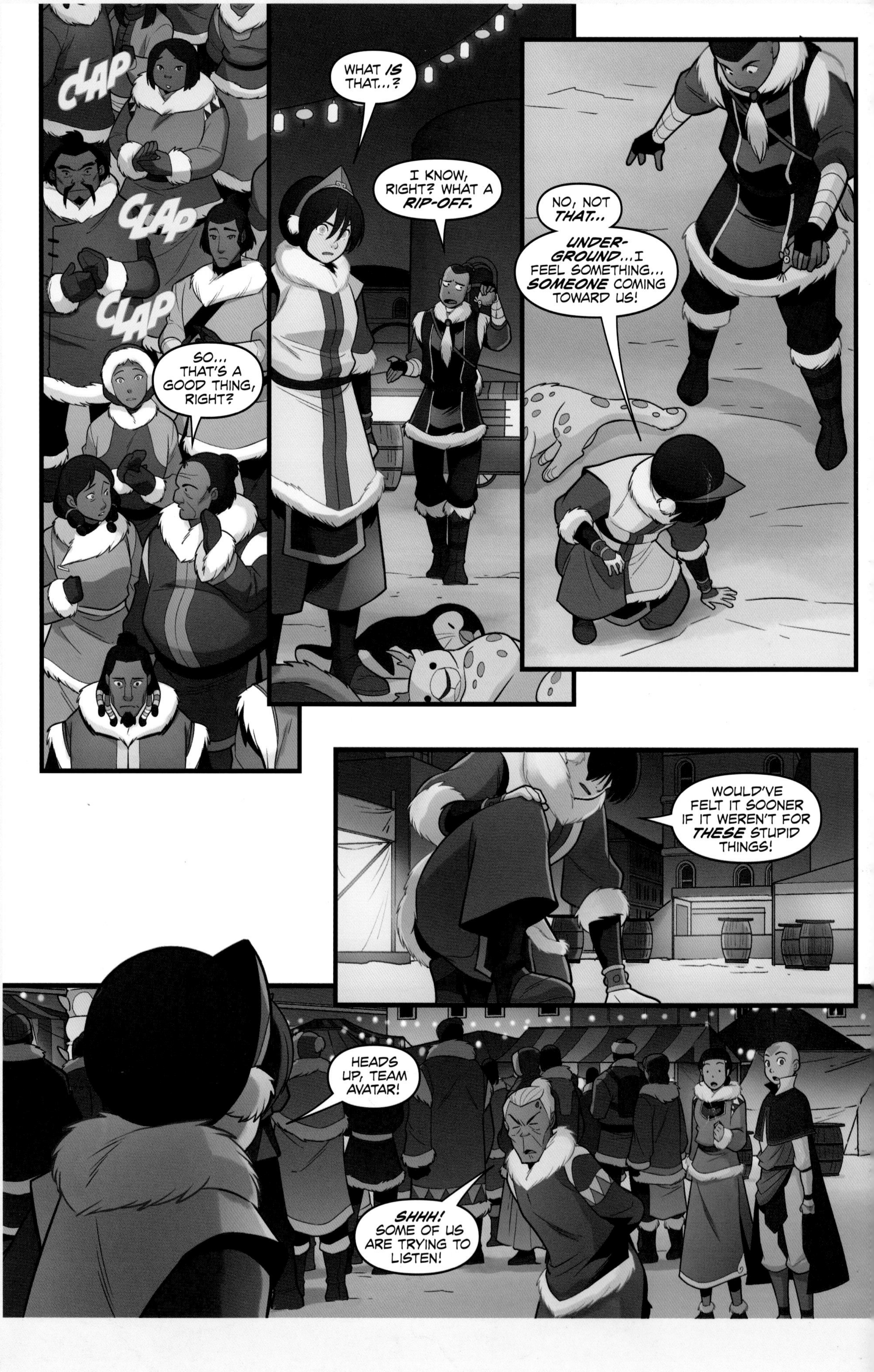
CLAP
CLAP
CLAP
SO... THAT'S A GOOD THING, RIGHT?
WHAT *IS* THAT...?
I KNOW, RIGHT? WHAT A *RIP-OFF.*
NO, NOT *THAT...*
UNDER-GROUND...I FEEL SOMETHING... *SOMEONE* COMING TOWARD US!
WOULD'VE FELT IT SOONER IF IT WEREN'T FOR *THESE* STUPID THINGS!
HEADS UP, TEAM AVATAR!
SHHH! SOME OF US ARE TRYING TO LISTEN!

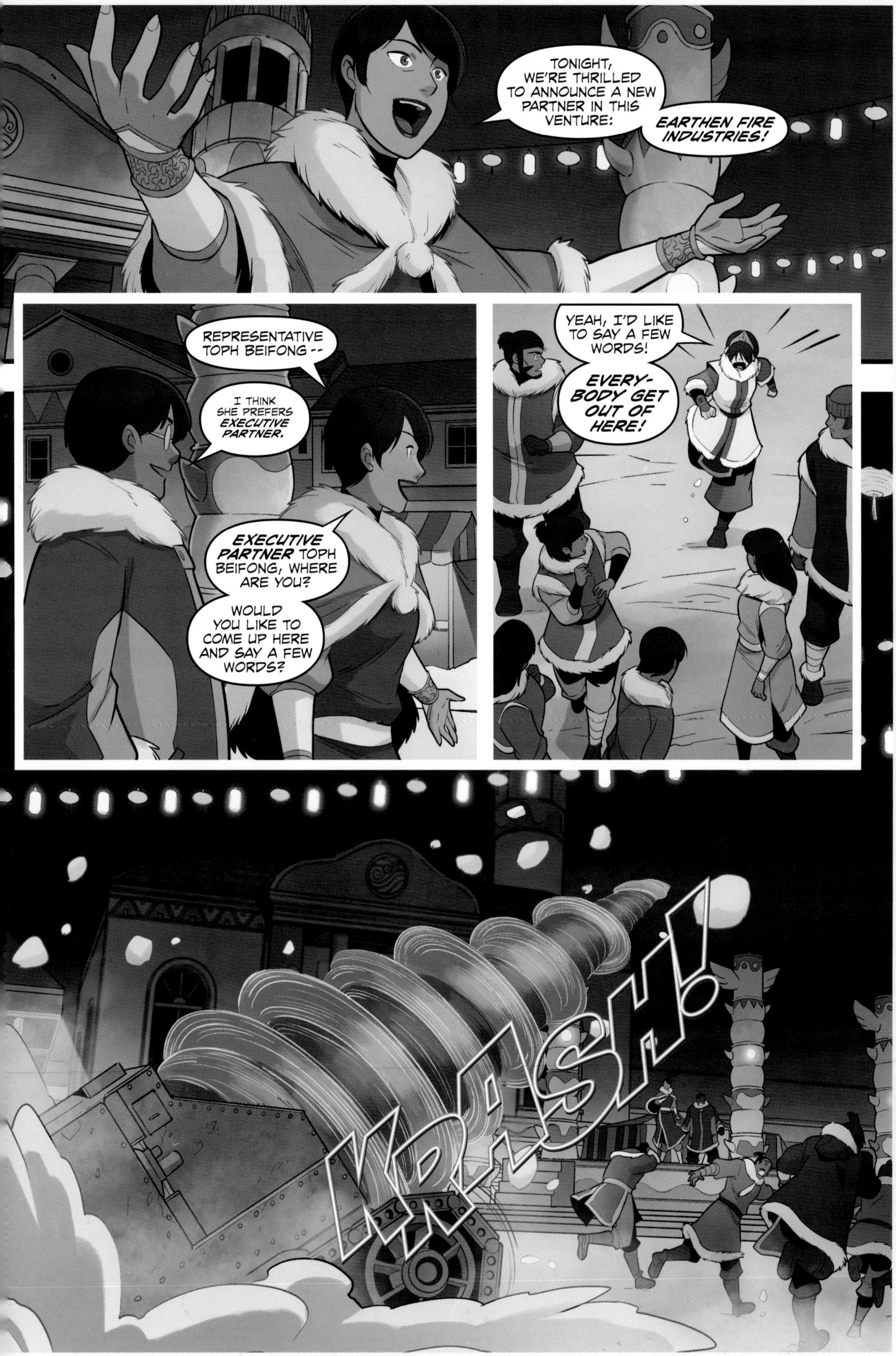
TONIGHT, WE'RE THRILLED TO ANNOUNCE A NEW PARTNER IN THIS VENTURE:
EARTHEN FIRE INDUSTRIES!
REPRESENTATIVE TOPH BEIFONG --
I THINK SHE PREFERS EXECUTIVE PARTNER.
EXECUTIVE PARTNER TOPH BEIFONG, WHERE ARE YOU?
WOULD YOU LIKE TO COME UP HERE AND SAY A FEW WORDS?
YEAH, I'D LIKE TO SAY A FEW WORDS!
EVERY-BODY GET OUT OF HERE!
KRASH!

GLY: *Maybe I have a thing for giant drills? One shows up in The Promise, too.*

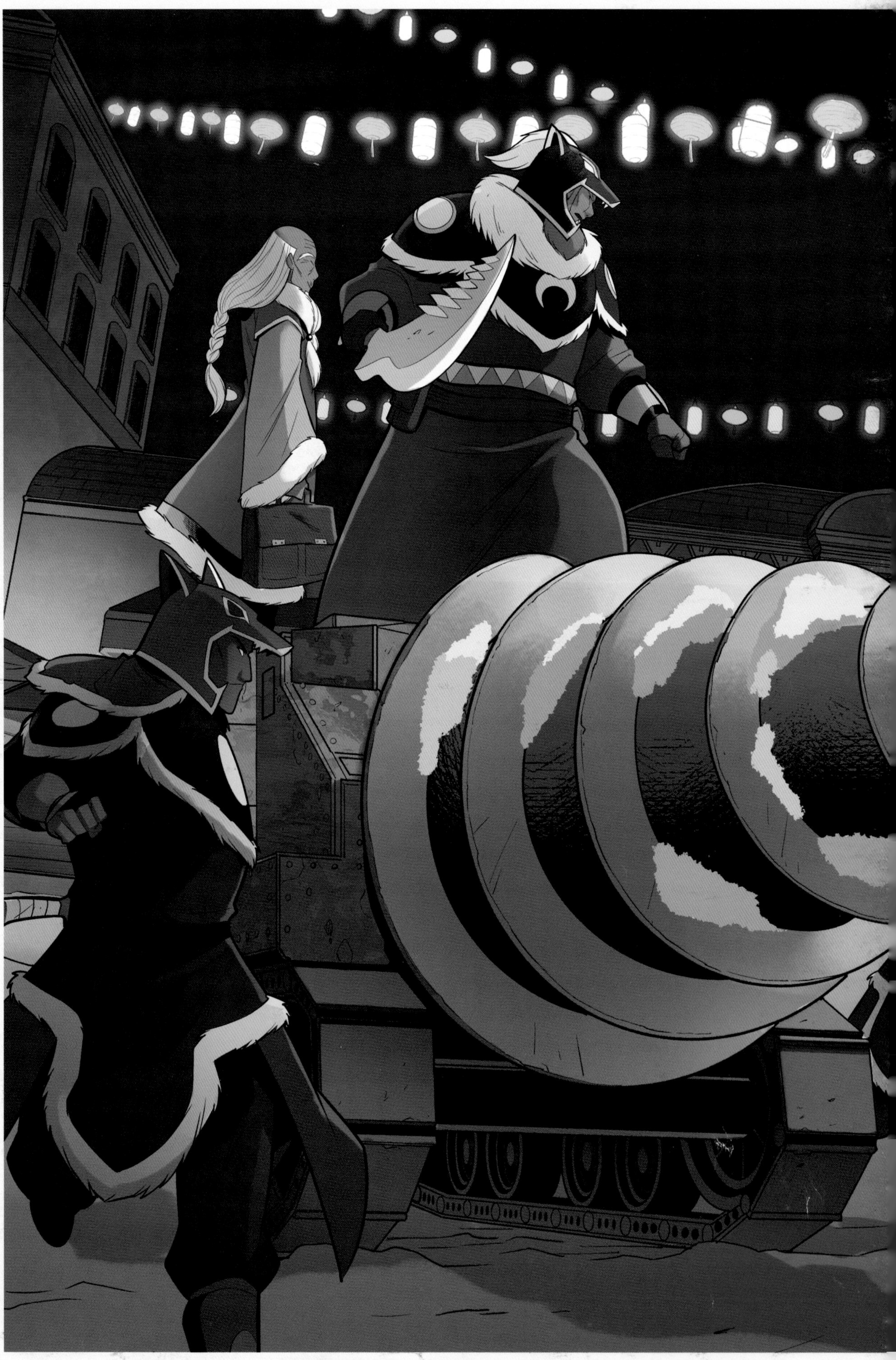

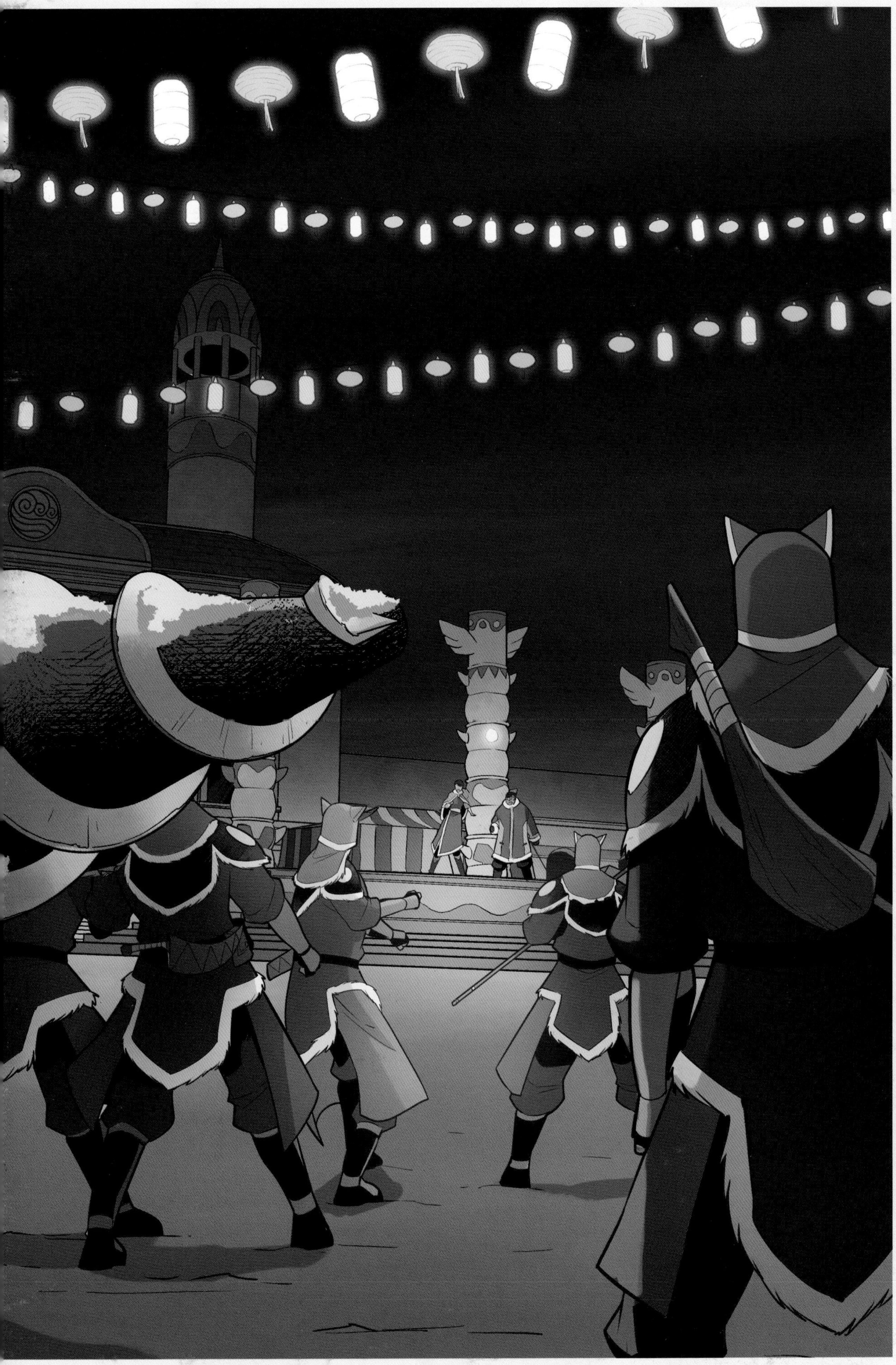

GLY: *The central tension of this story arc (and a few of the other story arcs by Gurihiru and me) is between cultural identity and diversity. Is it possible to keep one's own cultural identity in an increasingly diverse world? Can "small" cultures—small in terms of economic and military might, not in terms of dignity and importance—stay true to themselves while interacting with "larger" cultures? Gilak believes the answer is no. I sympathize with his position, but I hope he's wrong.*

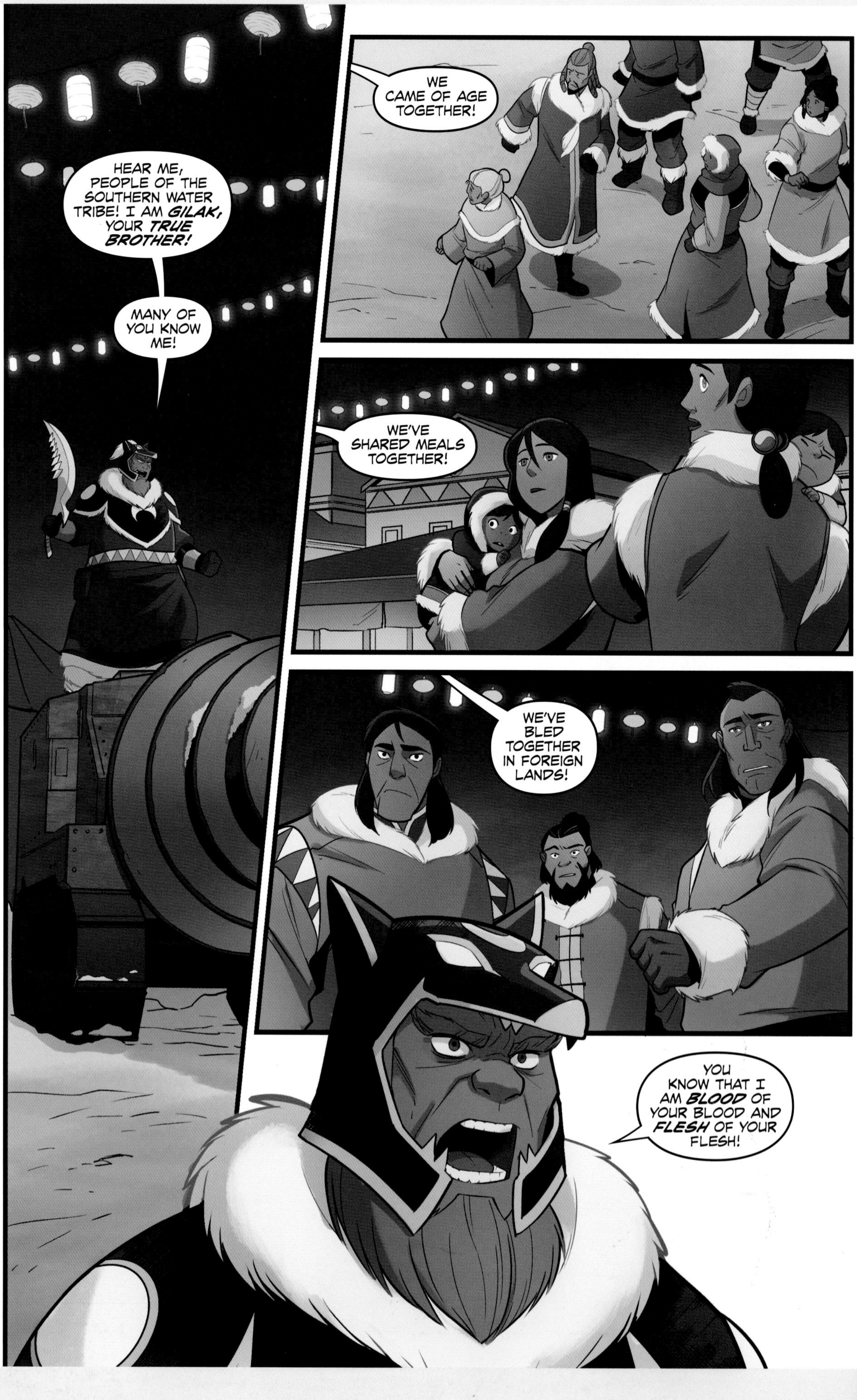
HEAR ME, PEOPLE OF THE SOUTHERN WATER TRIBE! I AM GILAK, YOUR TRUE BROTHER!
MANY OF YOU KNOW ME!
WE CAME OF AGE TOGETHER!
WE'VE SHARED MEALS TOGETHER!
WE'VE BLED TOGETHER IN FOREIGN LANDS!
YOU KNOW THAT I AM BLOOD OF YOUR BLOOD AND FLESH OF YOUR FLESH!

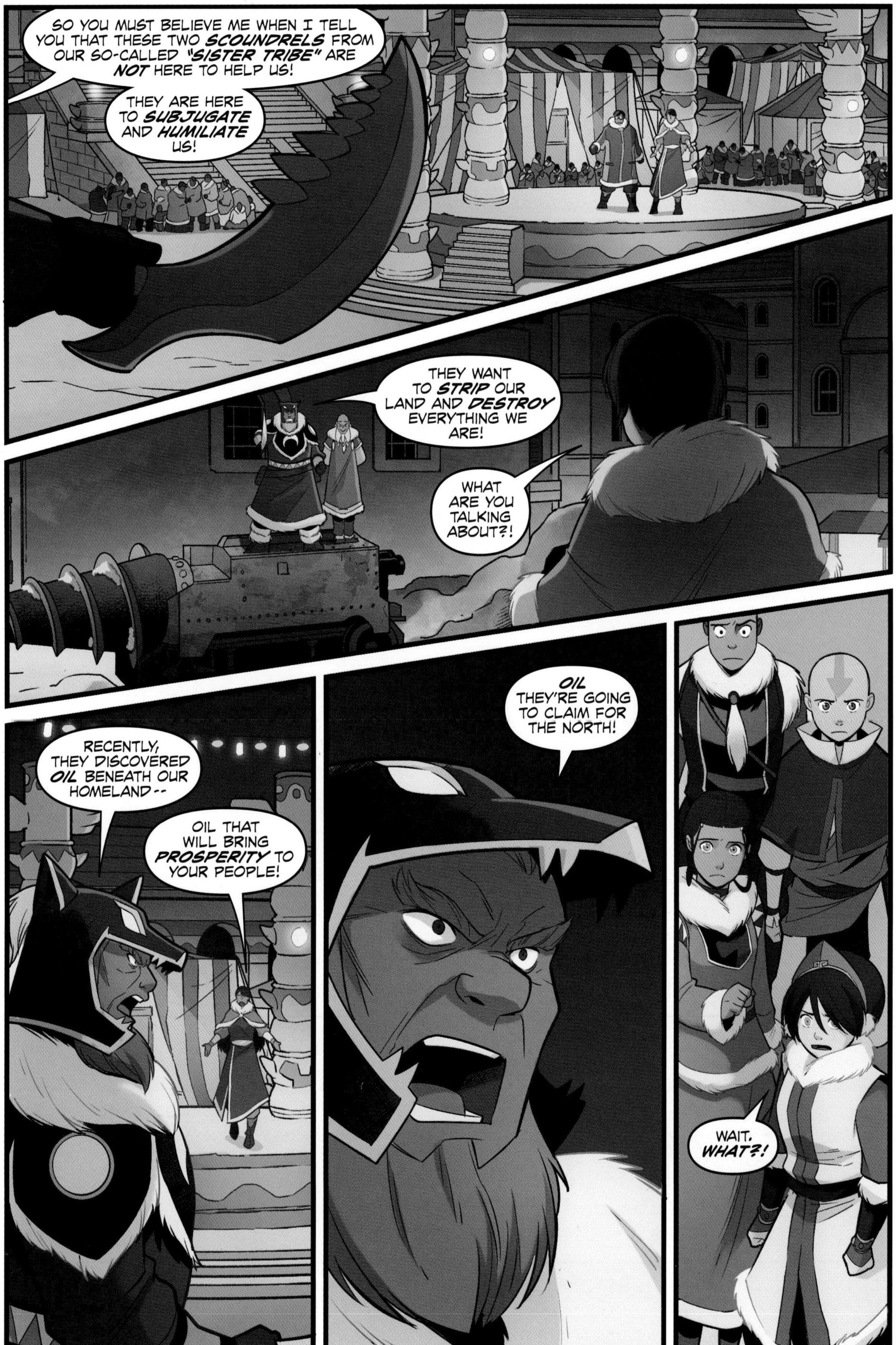
SO YOU MUST BELIEVE ME WHEN I TELL YOU THAT THESE TWO SCOUNDRELS FROM OUR SO-CALLED "SISTER TRIBE" ARE NOT HERE TO HELP US!
THEY ARE HERE TO SUBJUGATE AND HUMILIATE US!
THEY WANT TO STRIP OUR LAND AND DESTROY EVERYTHING WE ARE!
WHAT ARE YOU TALKING ABOUT?!
RECENTLY, THEY DISCOVERED OIL BENEATH OUR HOMELAND--
OIL THAT WILL BRING PROSPERITY TO YOUR PEOPLE!
OIL THEY'RE GOING TO CLAIM FOR THE NORTH!
WAIT. WHAT?!

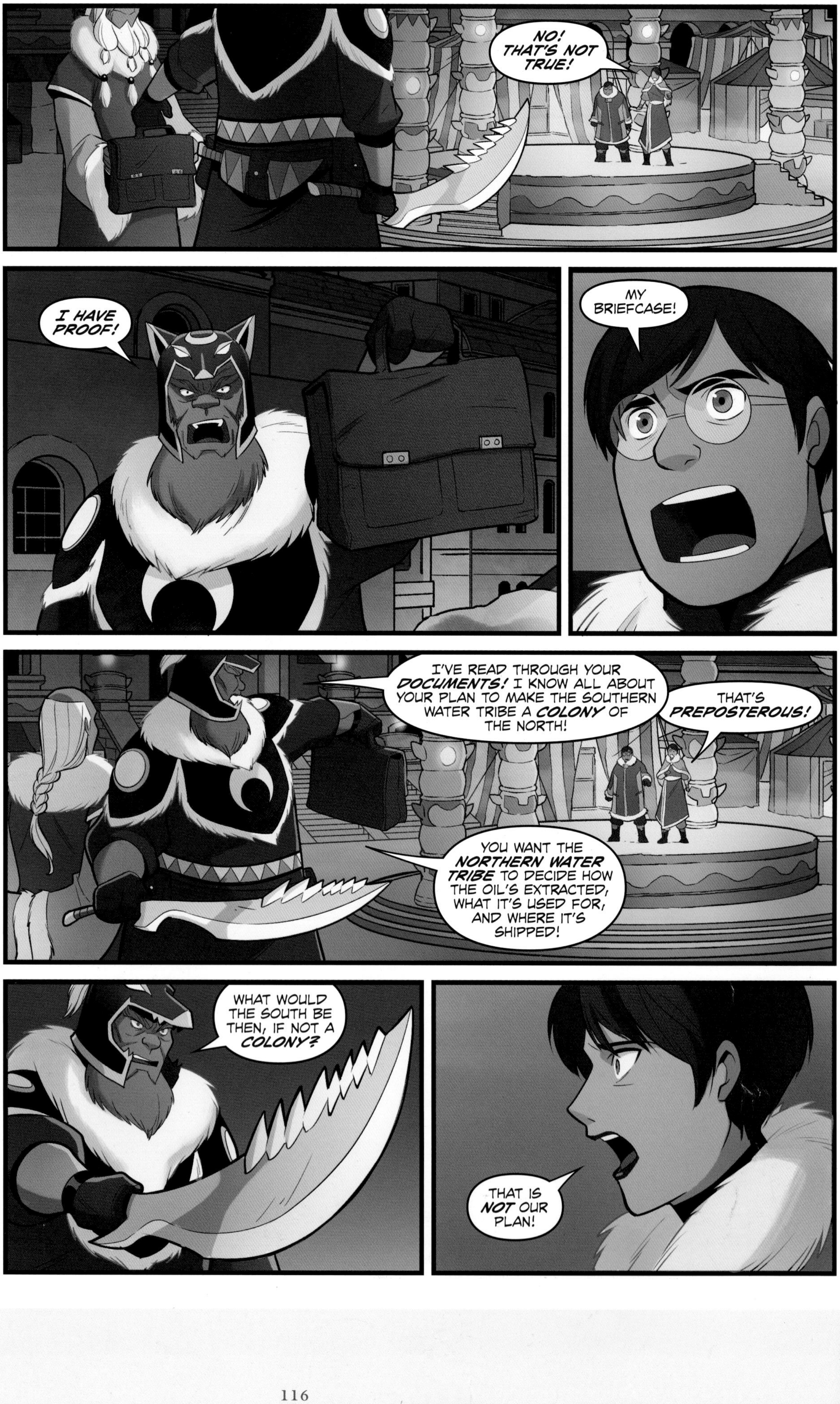
NO! THAT'S NOT TRUE!
I HAVE PROOF!
MY BRIEFCASE!
I'VE READ THROUGH YOUR DOCUMENTS! I KNOW ALL ABOUT YOUR PLAN TO MAKE THE SOUTHERN WATER TRIBE A COLONY OF THE NORTH!
THAT'S PREPOSTEROUS!
YOU WANT THE NORTHERN WATER TRIBE TO DECIDE HOW THE OIL'S EXTRACTED, WHAT IT'S USED FOR, AND WHERE IT'S SHIPPED!
WHAT WOULD THE SOUTH BE THEN, IF NOT A COLONY?
THAT IS NOT OUR PLAN!

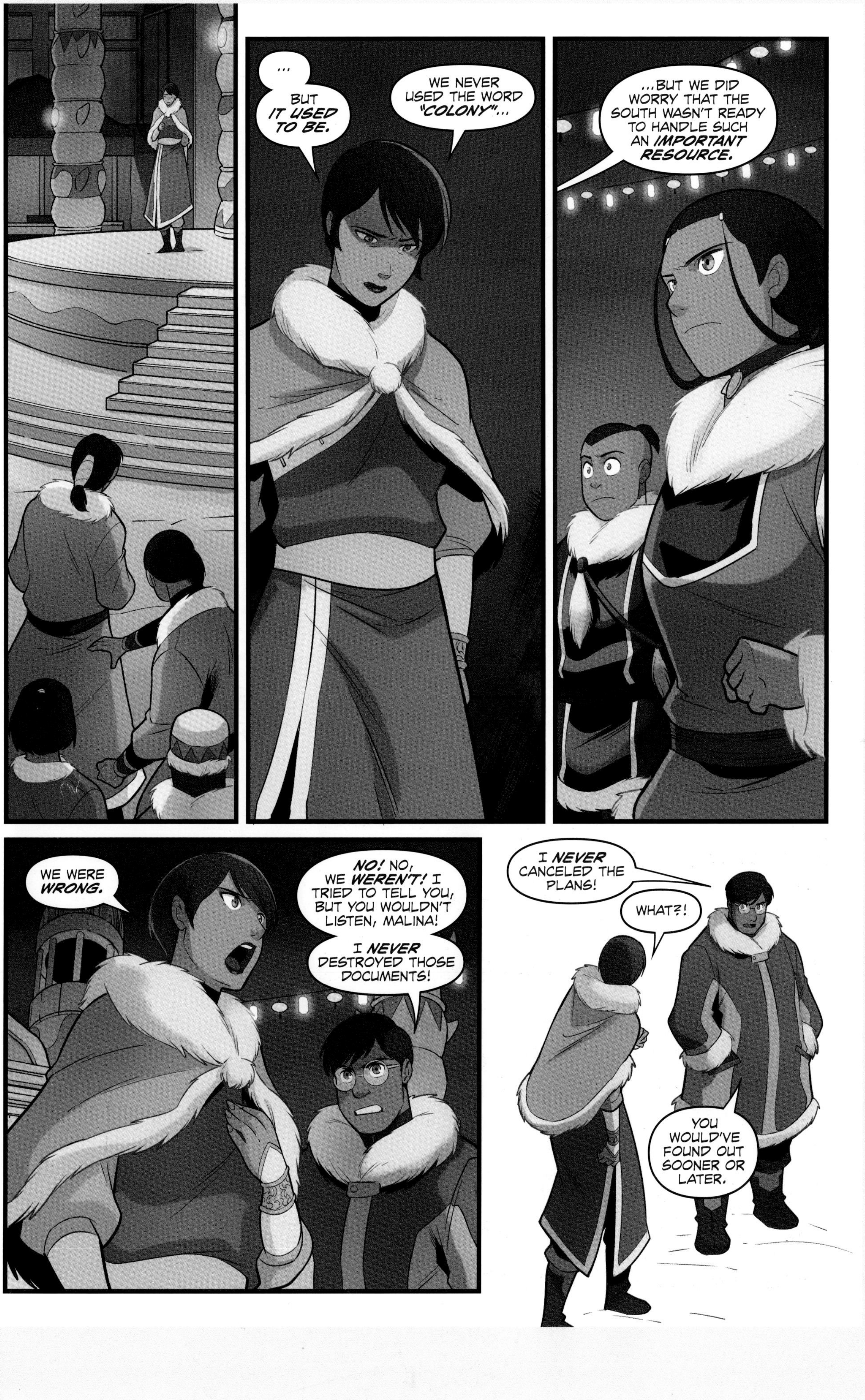
...
BUT IT USED TO BE.
WE NEVER USED THE WORD "COLONY"...
...BUT WE DID WORRY THAT THE SOUTH WASN'T READY TO HANDLE SUCH AN IMPORTANT RESOURCE.
WE WERE WRONG.
NO! NO, WE WEREN'T! I TRIED TO TELL YOU, BUT YOU WOULDN'T LISTEN, MALINA!
I NEVER DESTROYED THOSE DOCUMENTS!
I NEVER CANCELED THE PLANS!
WHAT?!
YOU WOULD'VE FOUND OUT SOONER OR LATER.

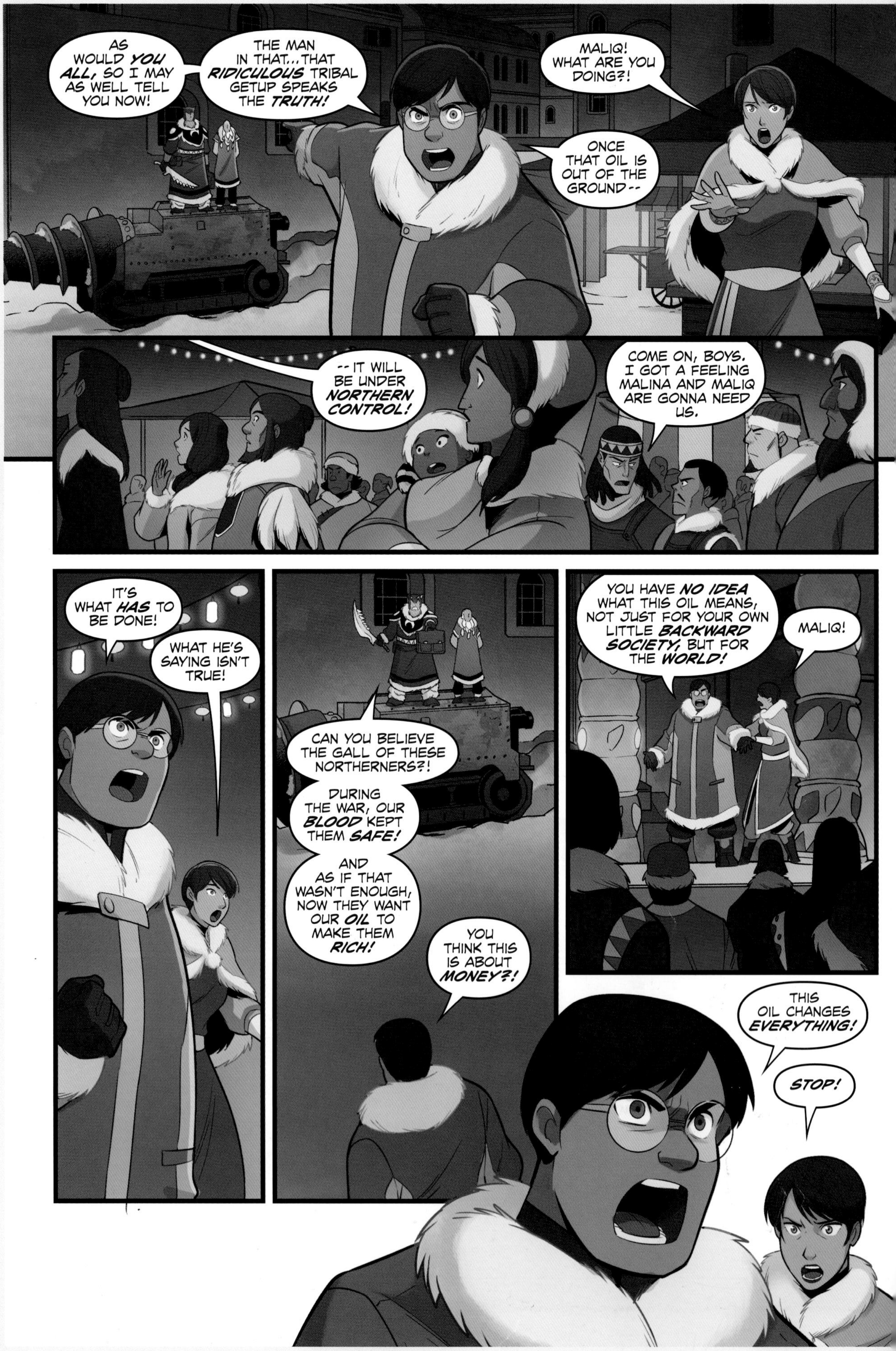
AS WOULD YOU ALL, SO I MAY AS WELL TELL YOU NOW!
THE MAN IN THAT...THAT RIDICULOUS TRIBAL GETUP SPEAKS THE TRUTH!
MALIQ! WHAT ARE YOU DOING?!
ONCE THAT OIL IS OUT OF THE GROUND--
--IT WILL BE UNDER NORTHERN CONTROL!
COME ON, BOYS. I GOT A FEELING MALINA AND MALIQ ARE GONNA NEED US.
IT'S WHAT HAS TO BE DONE!
WHAT HE'S SAYING ISN'T TRUE!
CAN YOU BELIEVE THE GALL OF THESE NORTHERNERS?!
DURING THE WAR, OUR BLOOD KEPT THEM SAFE!
AND AS IF THAT WASN'T ENOUGH, NOW THEY WANT OUR OIL TO MAKE THEM RICH!
YOU THINK THIS IS ABOUT MONEY?!
YOU HAVE NO IDEA WHAT THIS OIL MEANS, NOT JUST FOR YOUR OWN LITTLE BACKWARD SOCIETY, BUT FOR THE WORLD!
MALIQ!
THIS OIL CHANGES EVERYTHING!
STOP!

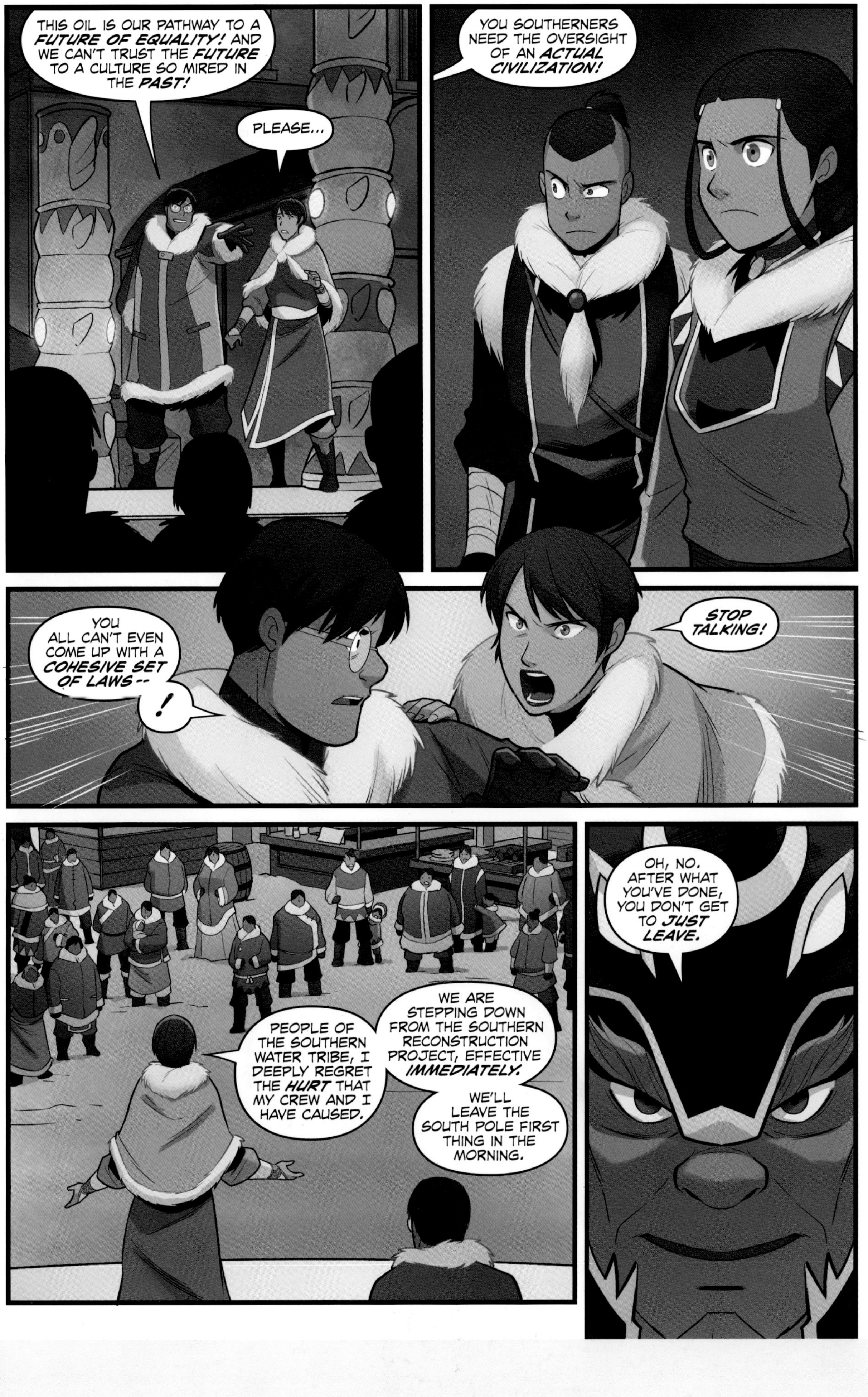
THIS OIL IS OUR PATHWAY TO A FUTURE OF EQUALITY! AND WE CAN'T TRUST THE FUTURE TO A CULTURE SO MIRED IN THE PAST!
PLEASE...
YOU SOUTHERNERS NEED THE OVERSIGHT OF AN ACTUAL CIVILIZATION!
YOU ALL CAN'T EVEN COME UP WITH A COHESIVE SET OF LAWS --
!
STOP TALKING!
PEOPLE OF THE SOUTHERN WATER TRIBE, I DEEPLY REGRET THE HURT THAT MY CREW AND I HAVE CAUSED.
WE ARE STEPPING DOWN FROM THE SOUTHERN RECONSTRUCTION PROJECT, EFFECTIVE IMMEDIATELY.
WE'LL LEAVE THE SOUTH POLE FIRST THING IN THE MORNING.
OH, NO. AFTER WHAT YOU'VE DONE, YOU DON'T GET TO JUST LEAVE.

GLY: *In The Legend of Korra, the Northern and Southern Water Tribes are at each other's throats. Here's where it all starts.*

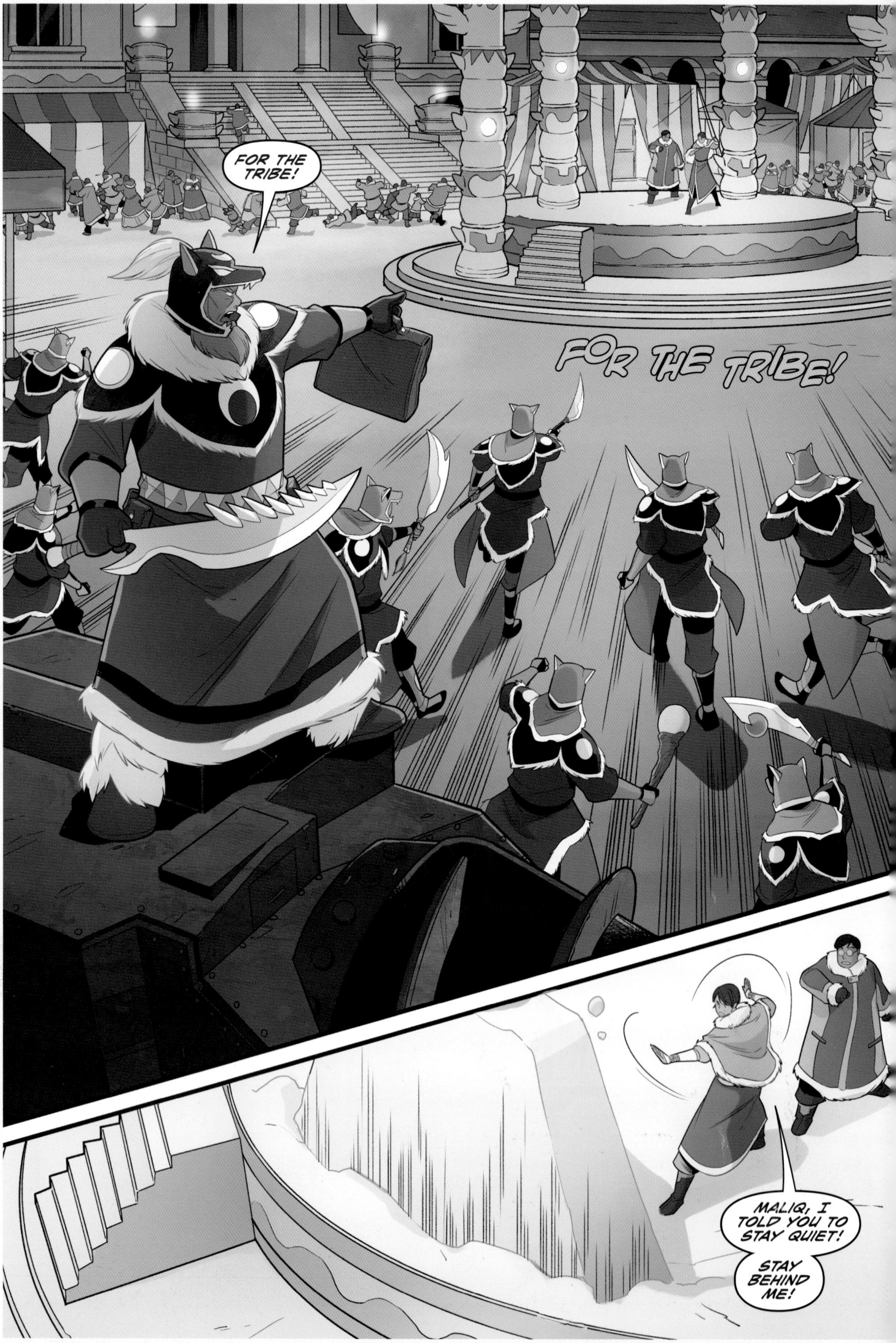
FOR THE TRIBE!
FOR THE TRIBE!
MALIQ, I TOLD YOU TO STAY QUIET!
STAY BEHIND ME!

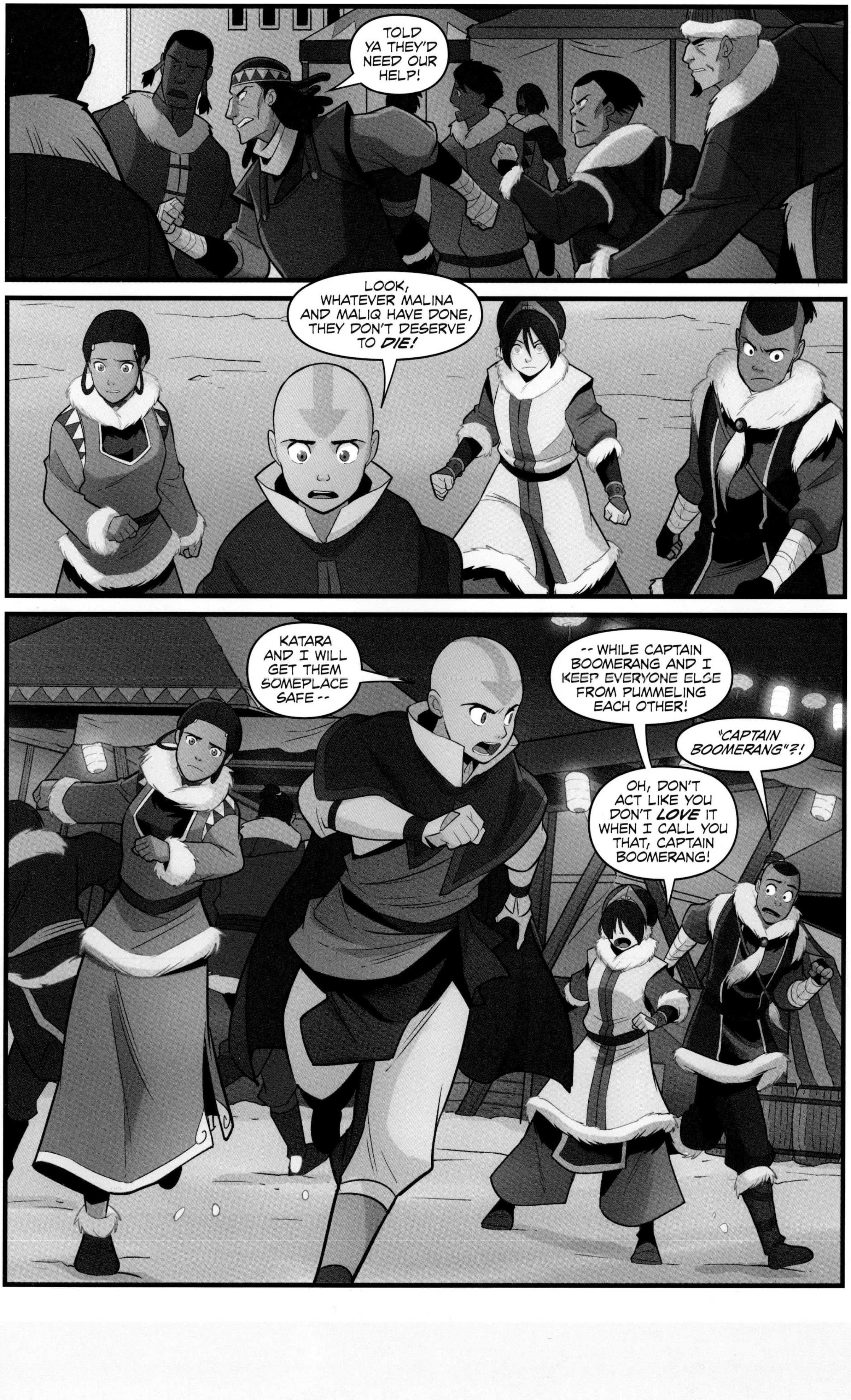
TOLD YA THEY'D NEED OUR HELP!
LOOK, WHATEVER MALINA AND MALIQ HAVE DONE, THEY DON'T DESERVE TO DIE!
KATARA AND I WILL GET THEM SOMEPLACE SAFE --
-- WHILE CAPTAIN BOOMERANG AND I KEEP EVERYONE ELSE FROM PUMMELING EACH OTHER!
"CAPTAIN BOOMERANG"?!
OH, DON'T ACT LIKE YOU DON'T LOVE IT WHEN I CALL YOU THAT, CAPTAIN BOOMERANG!

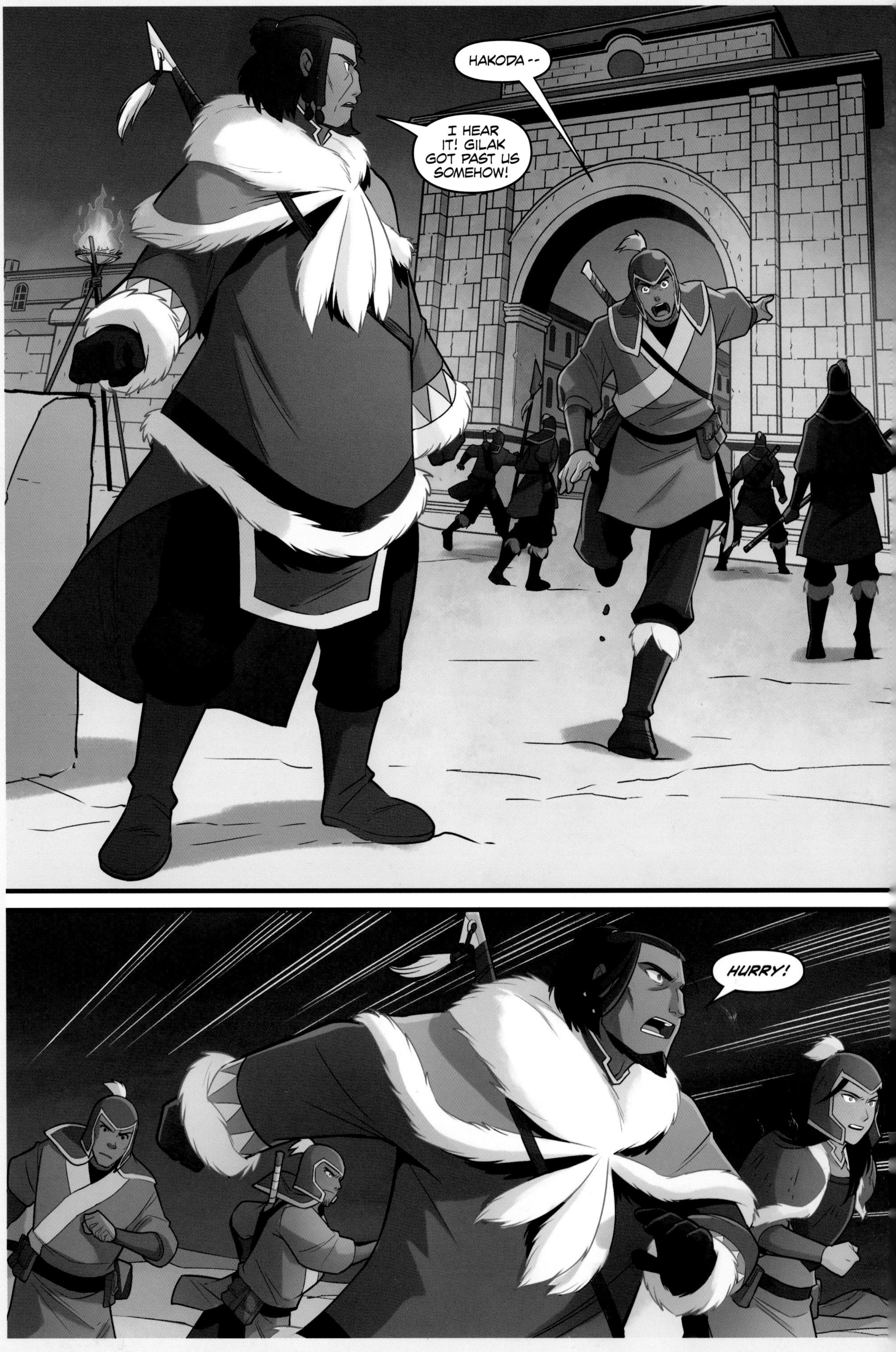
HAKODA --
I HEAR IT! GILAK GOT PAST US SOMEHOW!
HURRY!

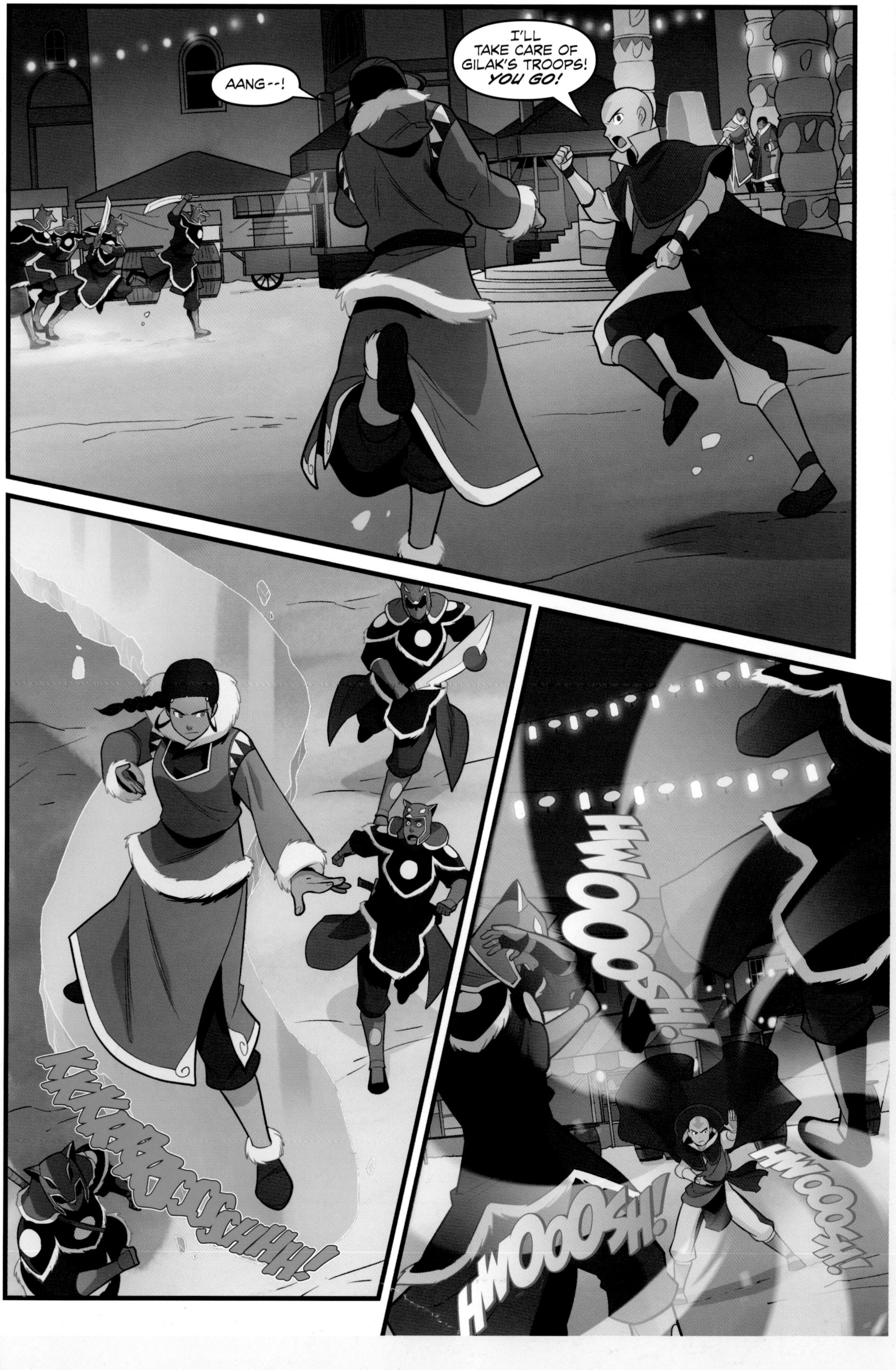
AANG--!
I'LL TAKE CARE OF GILAK'S TROOPS! YOU GO!
HWOOOSH!
HWOOOSH!
HWOOOSH!

GLY: *Yet another scene that relies heavily on the absolute awesomeness of Guribiru.*

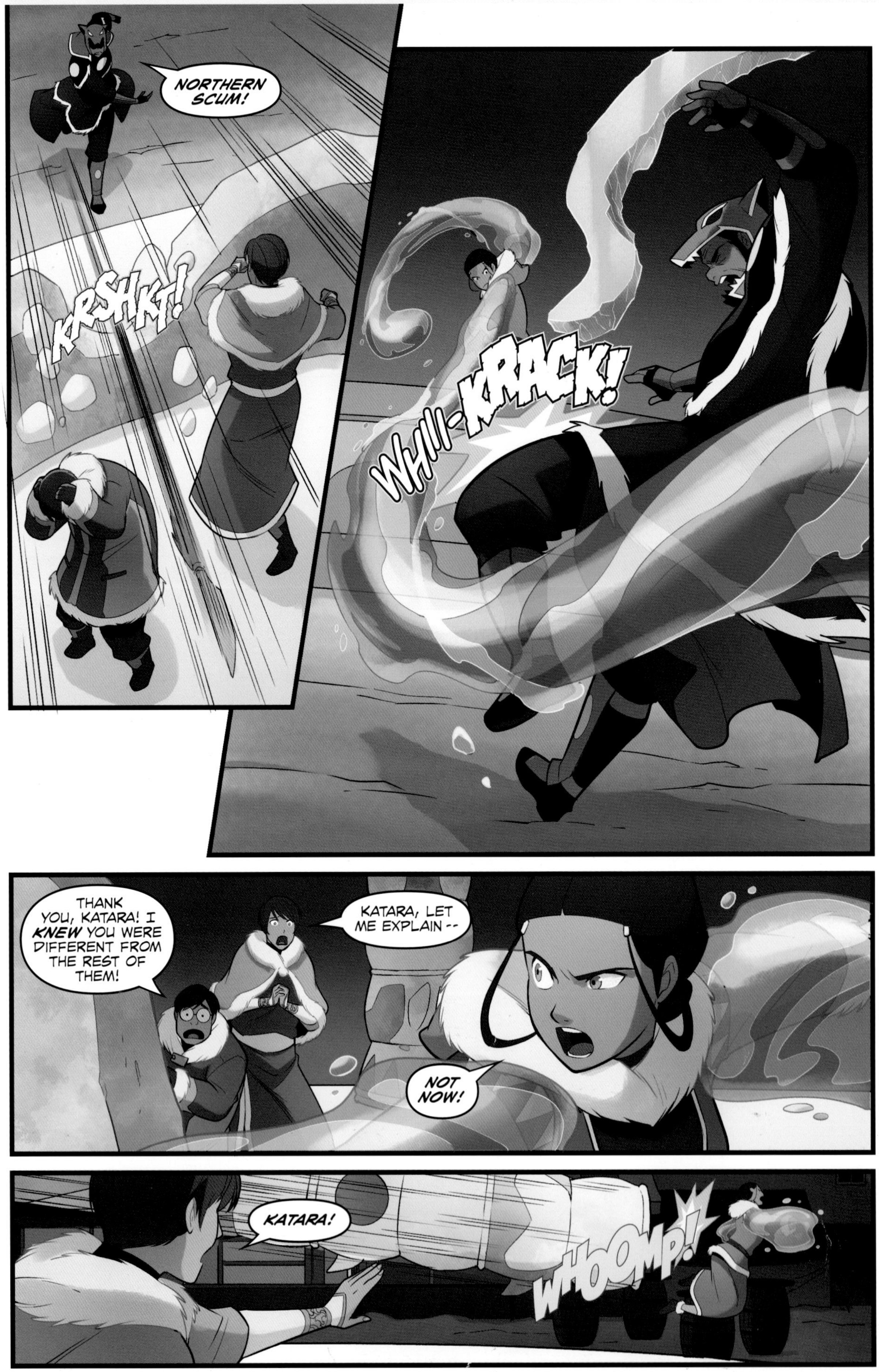
NORTHERN SCUM!
KRSHKT!
WHIII-KRACK!
THANK YOU, KATARA! I **KNEW** YOU WERE DIFFERENT FROM THE REST OF THEM!
KATARA, LET ME EXPLAIN --
NOT NOW!
KATARA!
WHOOMP!

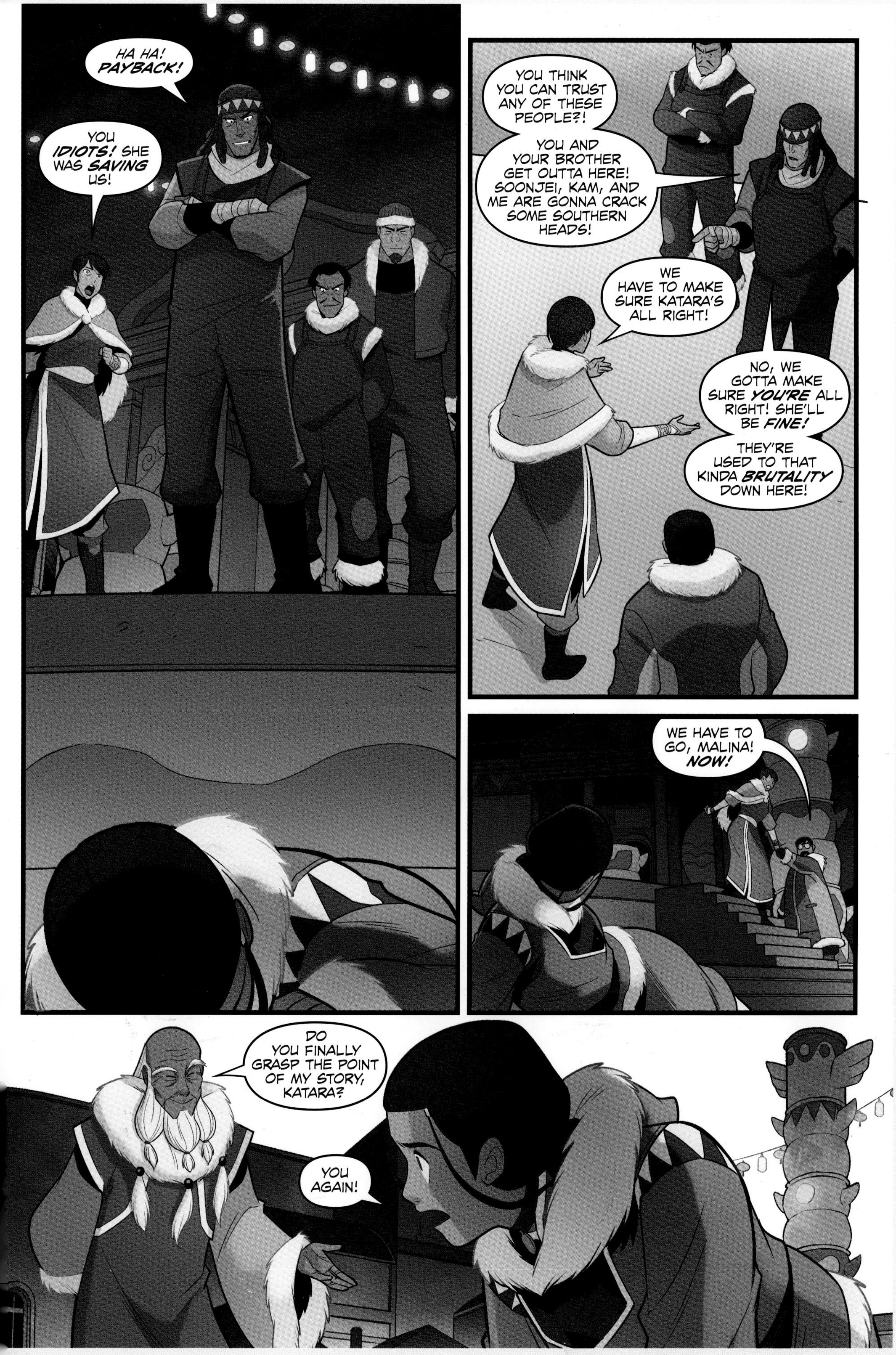
HA HA! PAYBACK!
YOU IDIOTS! SHE WAS SAVING US!
YOU THINK YOU CAN TRUST ANY OF THESE PEOPLE?!
YOU AND YOUR BROTHER GET OUTTA HERE! SOONJEI, KAM, AND ME ARE GONNA CRACK SOME SOUTHERN HEADS!
WE HAVE TO MAKE SURE KATARA'S ALL RIGHT!
NO, WE GOTTA MAKE SURE YOU'RE ALL RIGHT! SHE'LL BE FINE!
THEY'RE USED TO THAT KINDA BRUTALITY DOWN HERE!
WE HAVE TO GO, MALINA! NOW!
DO YOU FINALLY GRASP THE POINT OF MY STORY, KATARA?
YOU AGAIN!

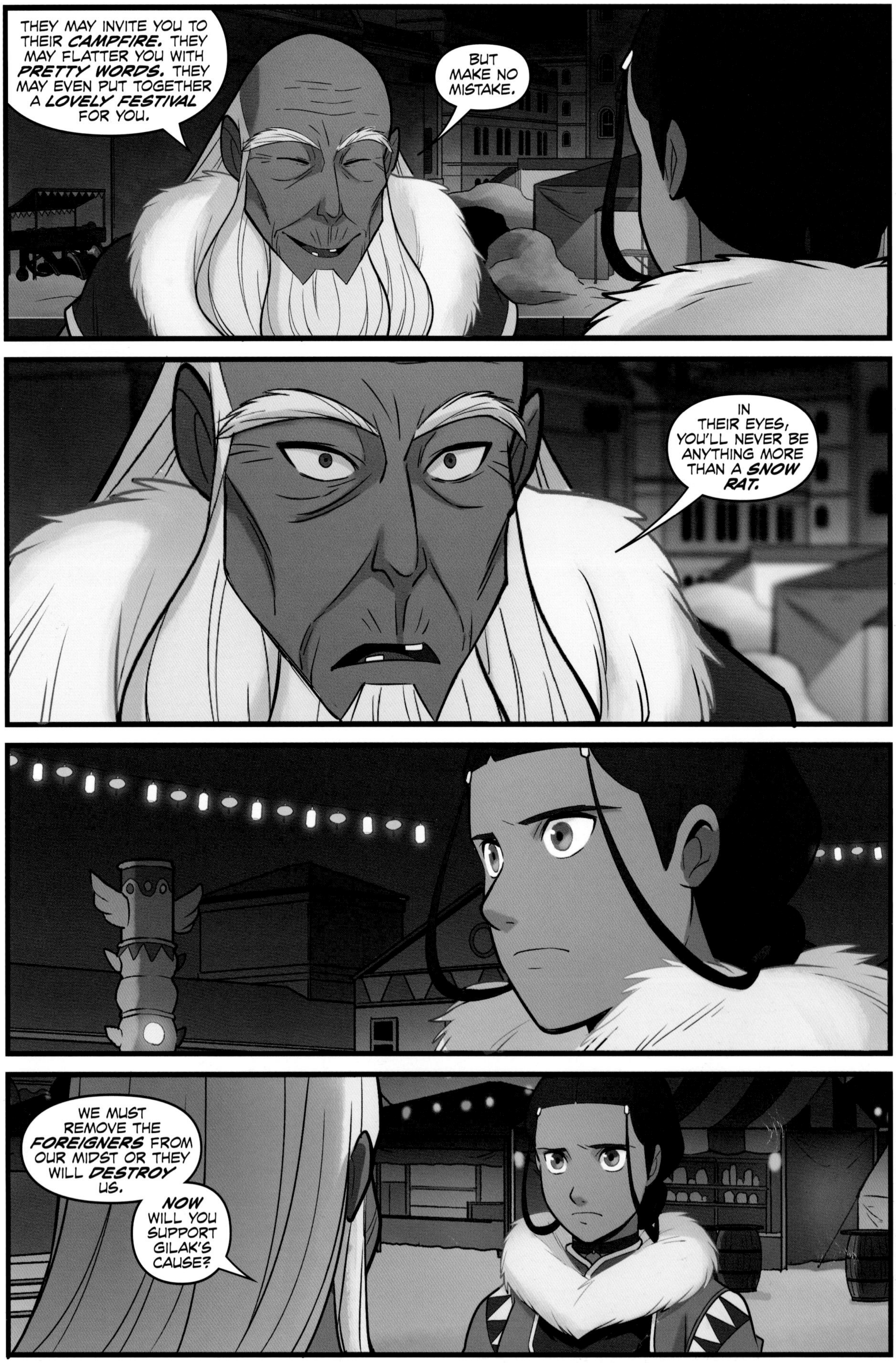
THEY MAY INVITE YOU TO THEIR CAMPFIRE. THEY MAY FLATTER YOU WITH PRETTY WORDS. THEY MAY EVEN PUT TOGETHER A LOVELY FESTIVAL FOR YOU.
BUT MAKE NO MISTAKE.
IN THEIR EYES, YOU'LL NEVER BE ANYTHING MORE THAN A SNOW RAT.
WE MUST REMOVE THE FOREIGNERS FROM OUR MIDST OR THEY WILL DESTROY US.
NOW WILL YOU SUPPORT GILAK'S CAUSE?

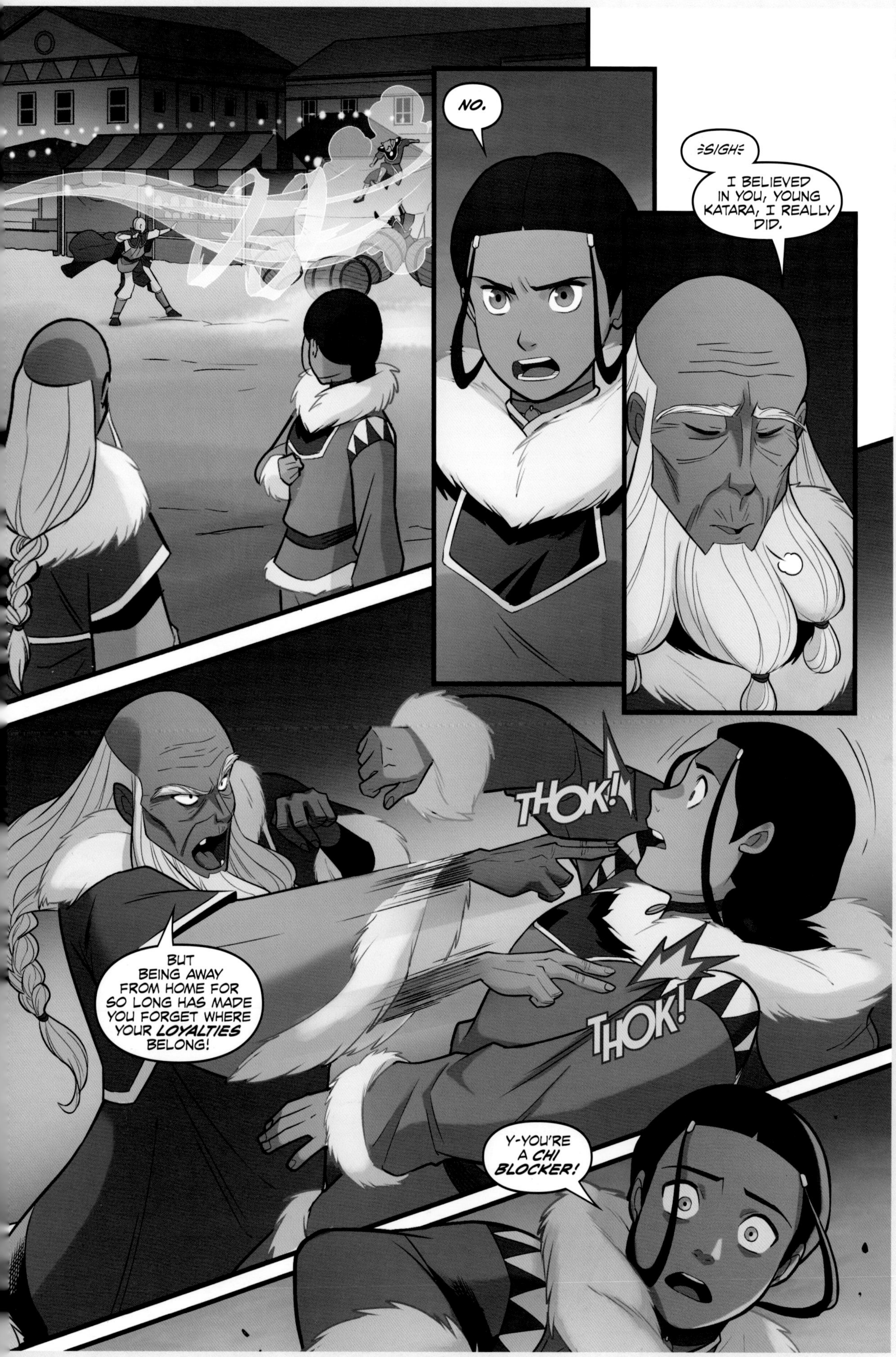
NO.
SIGH
I BELIEVED IN YOU, YOUNG KATARA, I REALLY DID.
THOK!
BUT BEING AWAY FROM HOME FOR SO LONG HAS MADE YOU FORGET WHERE YOUR *LOYALTIES* BELONG!
THOK!
Y-YOU'RE A *CHI BLOCKER!*

GLY: *Chi blocking is one of my favorite concepts in the Avatar universe, maybe because I like Ty Lee so much. The Korra creative team did a great job upping the stakes to make chi blocking downright scary.*

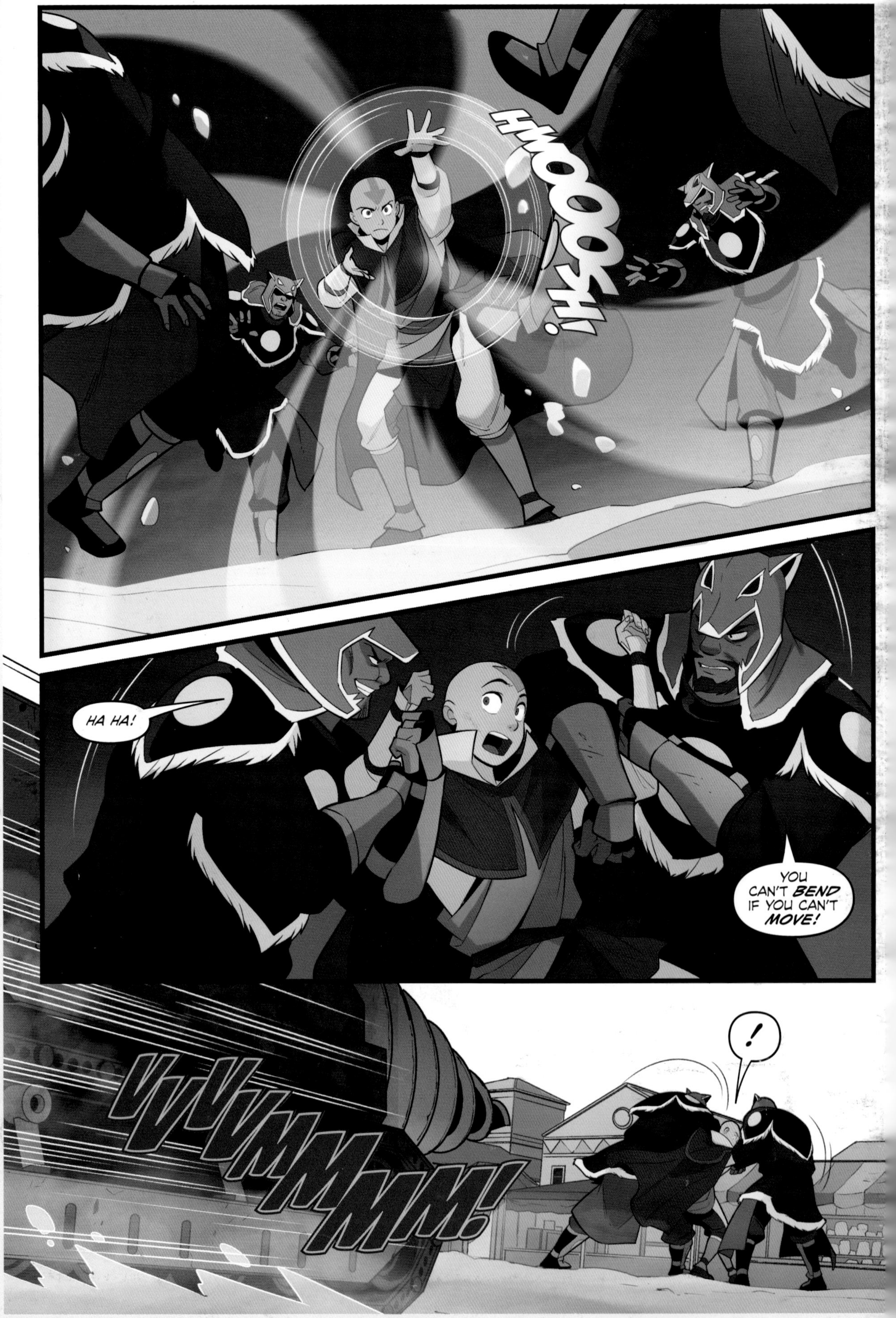
HWOOOSH!
HA HA!
YOU CAN'T BEND IF YOU CAN'T MOVE!
VVVVMMMMMM!
!

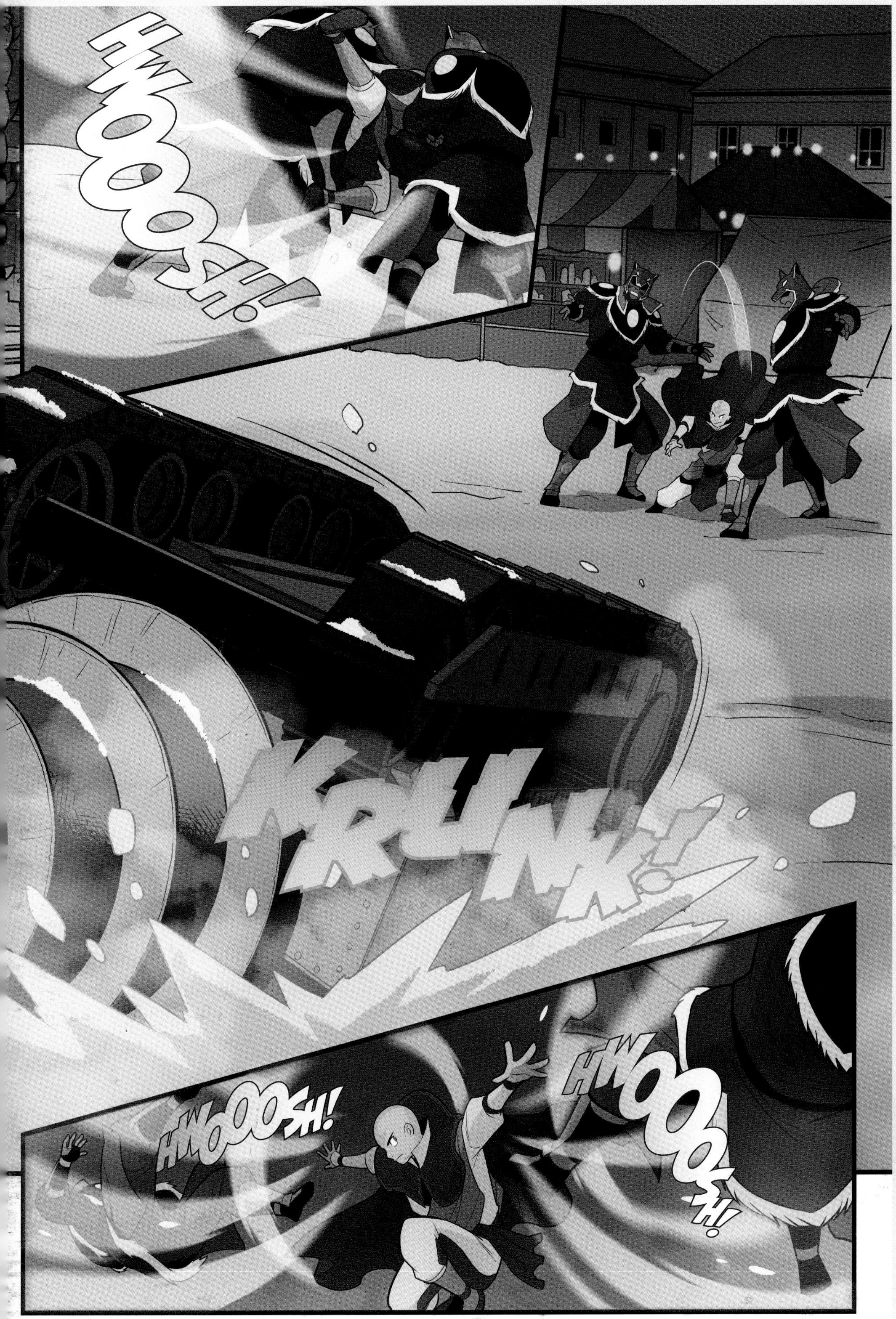
HWOOOSH!
KRUNK!
HWOOOSH!
HWOOOOSH!

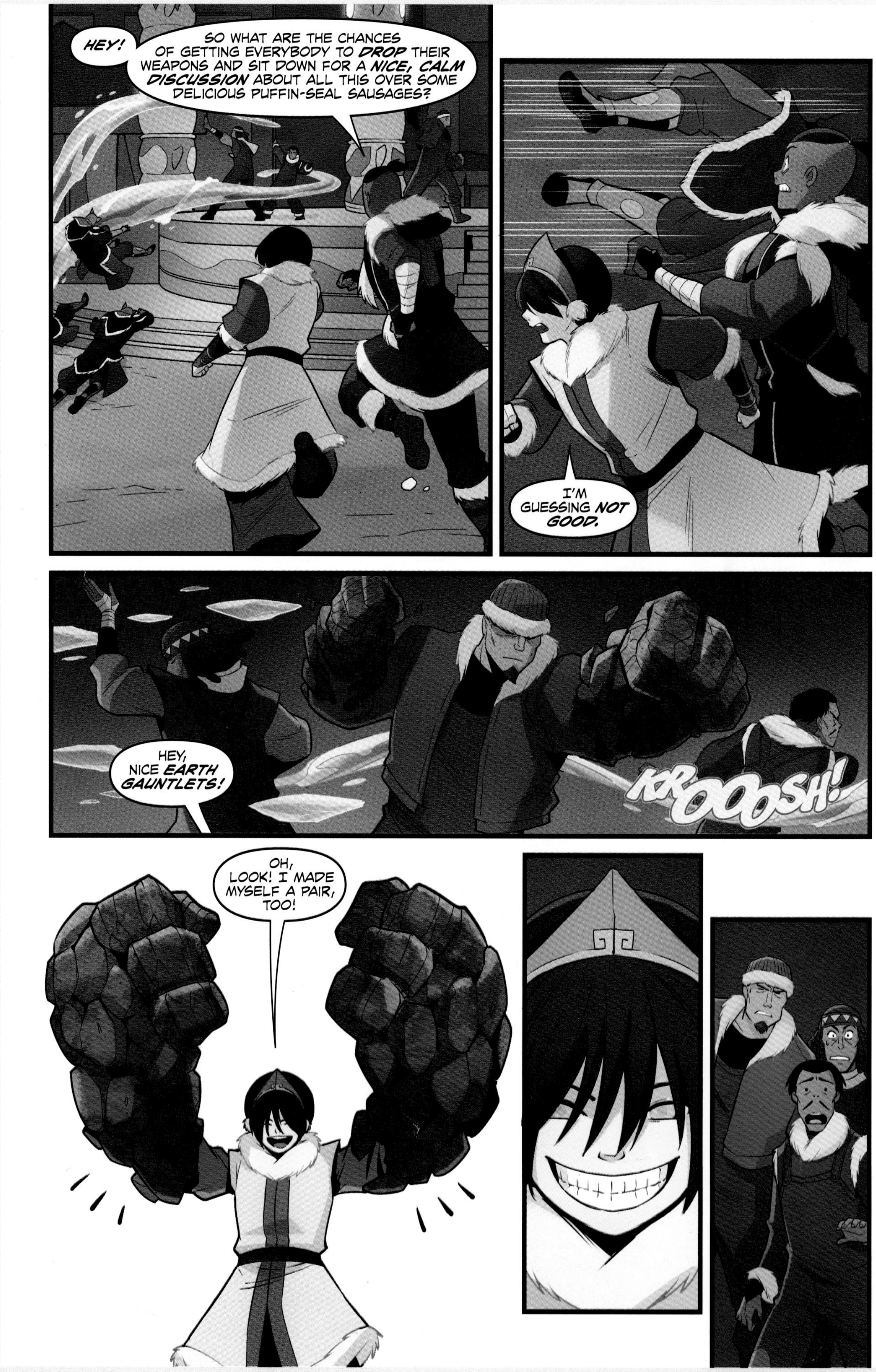
HEY!
SO WHAT ARE THE CHANCES OF GETTING EVERYBODY TO DROP THEIR WEAPONS AND SIT DOWN FOR A NICE, CALM DISCUSSION ABOUT ALL THIS OVER SOME DELICIOUS PUFFIN-SEAL SAUSAGES?
I'M GUESSING NOT GOOD.
HEY, NICE EARTH GAUNTLETS!
KRROOOSH!
OH, LOOK! I MADE MYSELF A PAIR, TOO!

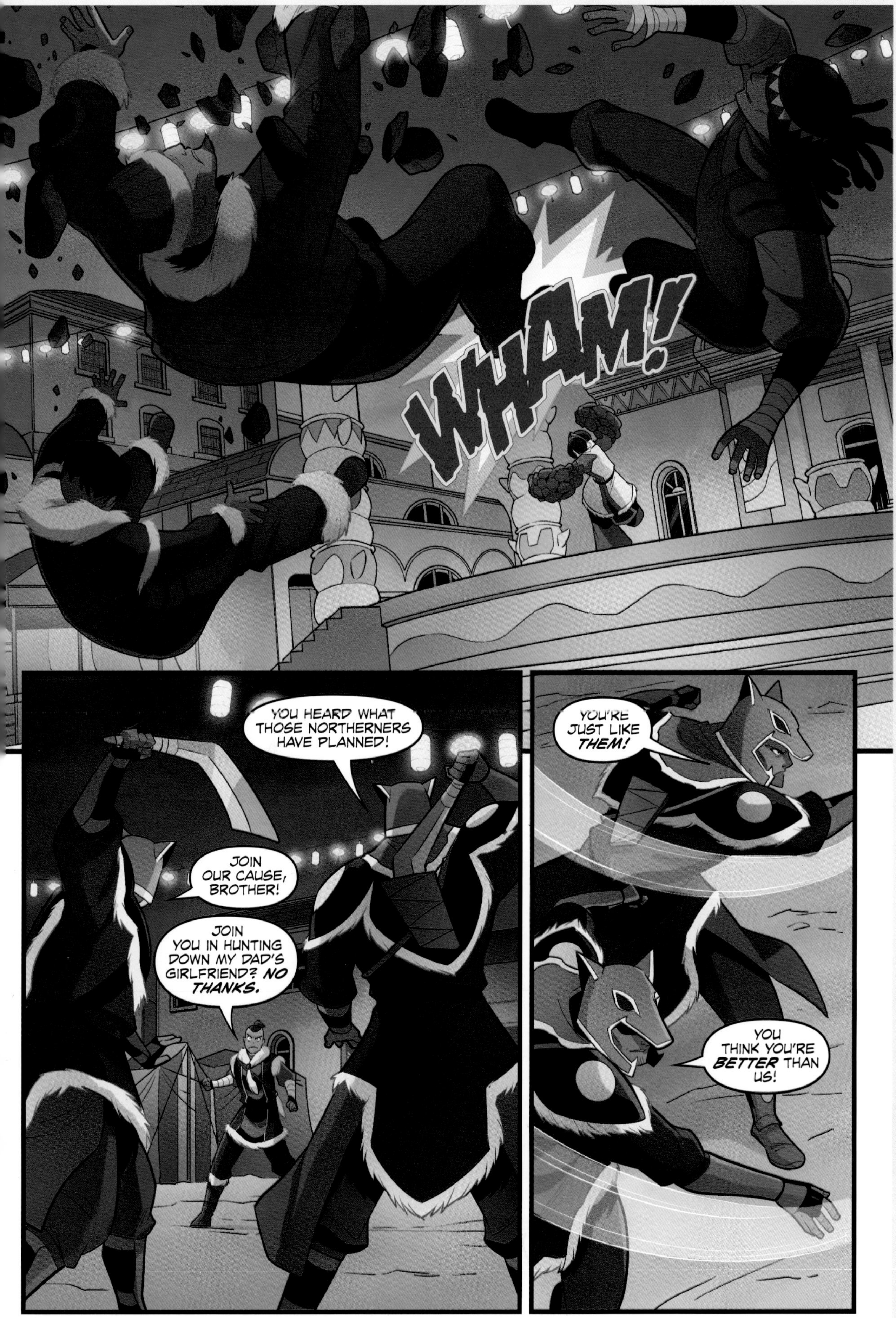
WHAM!
YOU HEARD WHAT THOSE NORTHERNERS HAVE PLANNED!
JOIN OUR CAUSE, BROTHER!
JOIN YOU IN HUNTING DOWN MY DAD'S GIRLFRIEND? NO THANKS.
YOU'RE JUST LIKE THEM!
YOU THINK YOU'RE BETTER THAN US!

GLY: *I was really, really tempted to have Toph yell, "It's clobberin' time!" But thankfully, I resisted.*

GLY: *Yes, Captain Boomerang is a character in the DC universe. He's a member of the Suicide Squad. But it's also an established phrase in the Avatar universe. Toph first calls Sokka "Captain Boomerang" in one of the final episodes of the series, "Sozin's Comet, Part 3: Into the Inferno."*

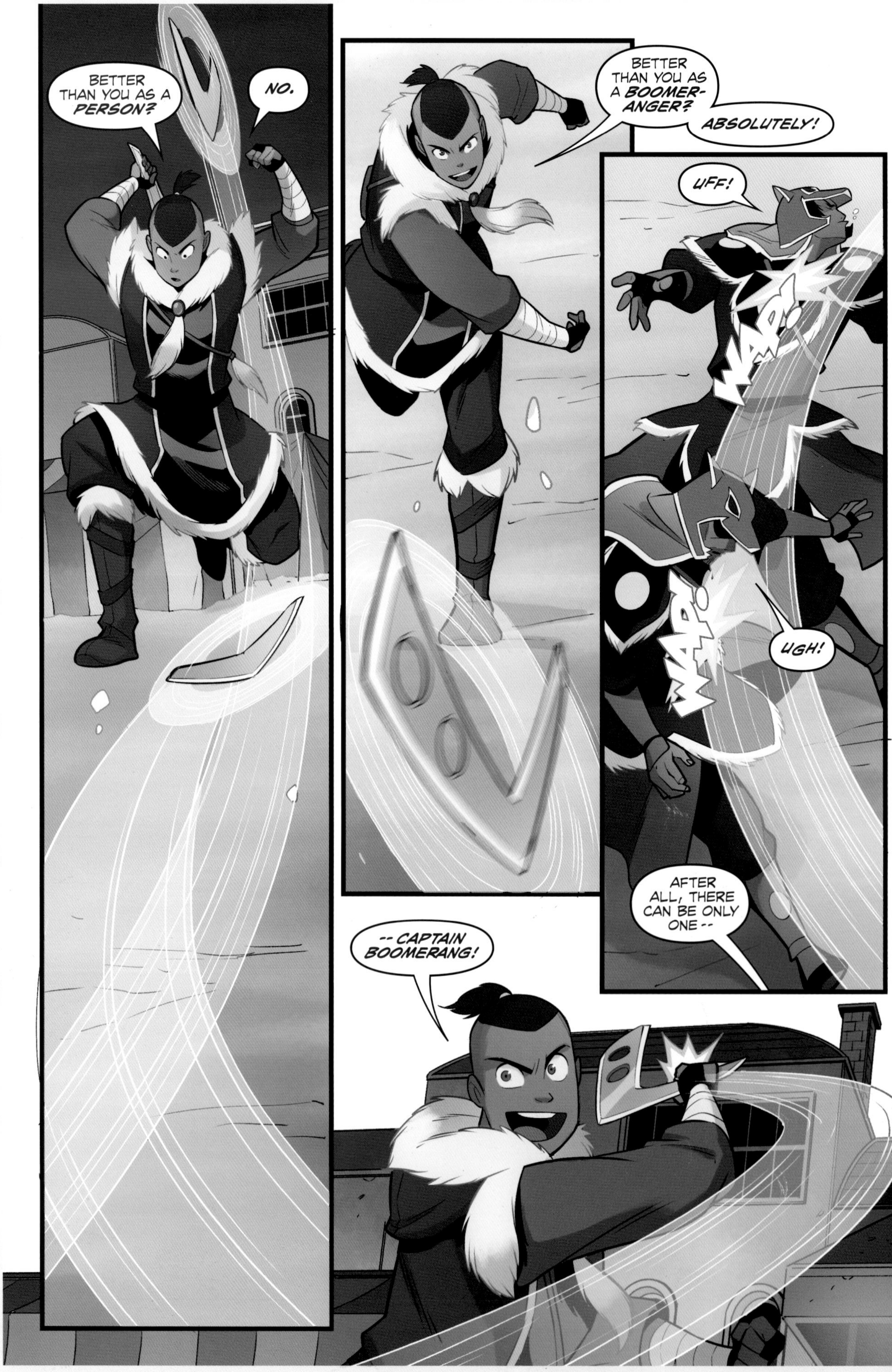
BETTER THAN YOU AS A PERSON?
NO.
BETTER THAN YOU AS A BOOMER-ANGER?
ABSOLUTELY!
UFF!
WAP!
WAP!
UGH!
AFTER ALL, THERE CAN BE ONLY ONE --
-- CAPTAIN BOOMERANG!

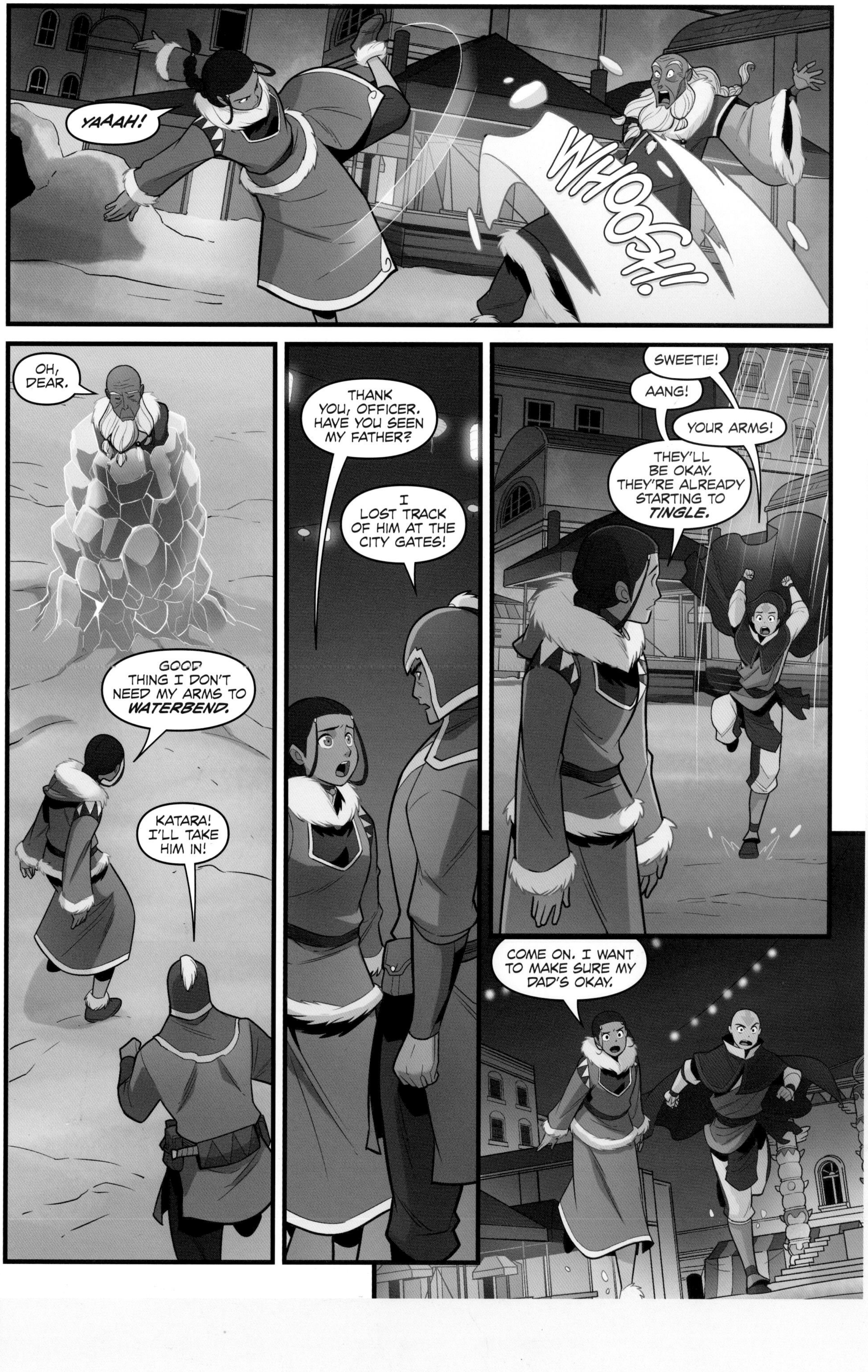
YAAAH!
WHOOSH!
OH, DEAR.
GOOD THING I DON'T NEED MY ARMS TO WATERBEND.
KATARA! I'LL TAKE HIM IN!
THANK YOU, OFFICER. HAVE YOU SEEN MY FATHER?
I LOST TRACK OF HIM AT THE CITY GATES!
SWEETIE!
AANG!
YOUR ARMS!
THEY'LL BE OKAY. THEY'RE ALREADY STARTING TO TINGLE.
COME ON. I WANT TO MAKE SURE MY DAD'S OKAY.

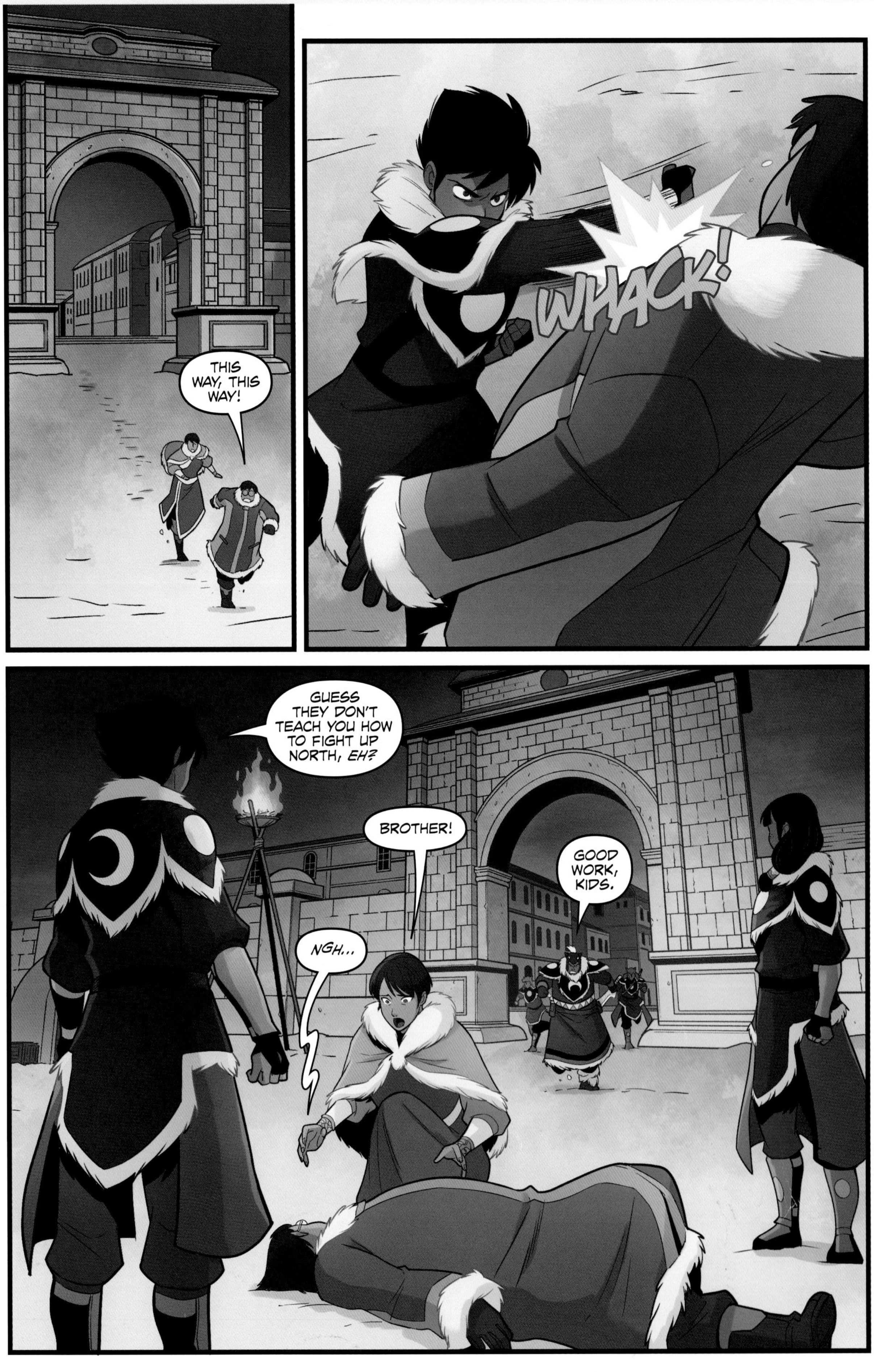
THIS WAY, THIS WAY!
WHACK!
GUESS THEY DON'T TEACH YOU HOW TO FIGHT UP NORTH, *EH?*
BROTHER!
GOOD WORK, KIDS.
NGH...

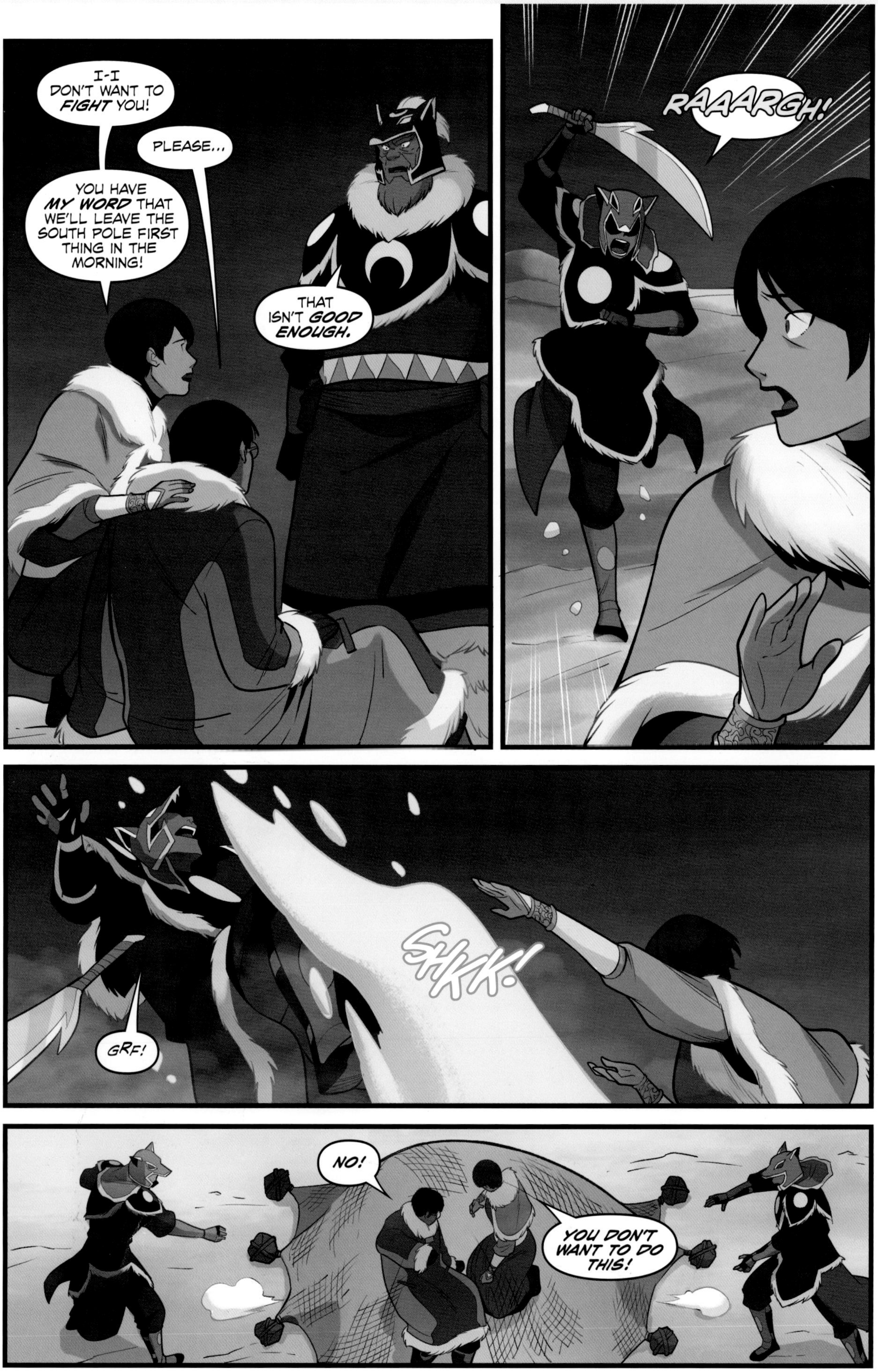
I-I DON'T WANT TO FIGHT YOU!
PLEASE...
YOU HAVE MY WORD THAT WE'LL LEAVE THE SOUTH POLE FIRST THING IN THE MORNING!
THAT ISN'T GOOD ENOUGH.
RAAARGH!
SHKK!
GRF!
NO!
YOU DON'T WANT TO DO THIS!

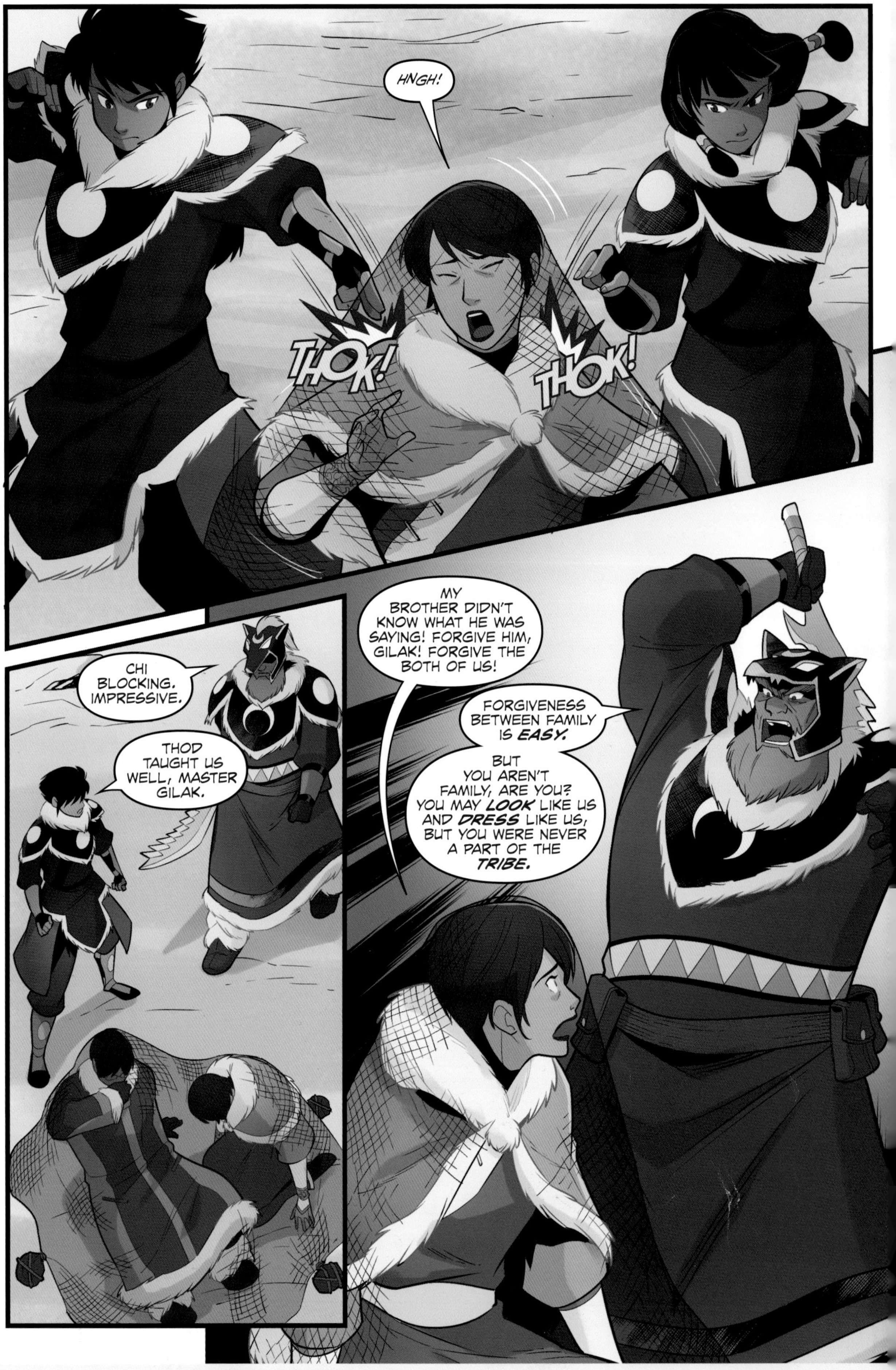
HNGH!
THOK!
THOK!
CHI BLOCKING. IMPRESSIVE.
THOD TAUGHT US WELL, MASTER GILAK.
MY BROTHER DIDN'T KNOW WHAT HE WAS SAYING! FORGIVE HIM, GILAK! FORGIVE THE BOTH OF US!
FORGIVENESS BETWEEN FAMILY IS EASY.
BUT YOU AREN'T FAMILY, ARE YOU? YOU MAY LOOK LIKE US AND DRESS LIKE US, BUT YOU WERE NEVER A PART OF THE TRIBE.

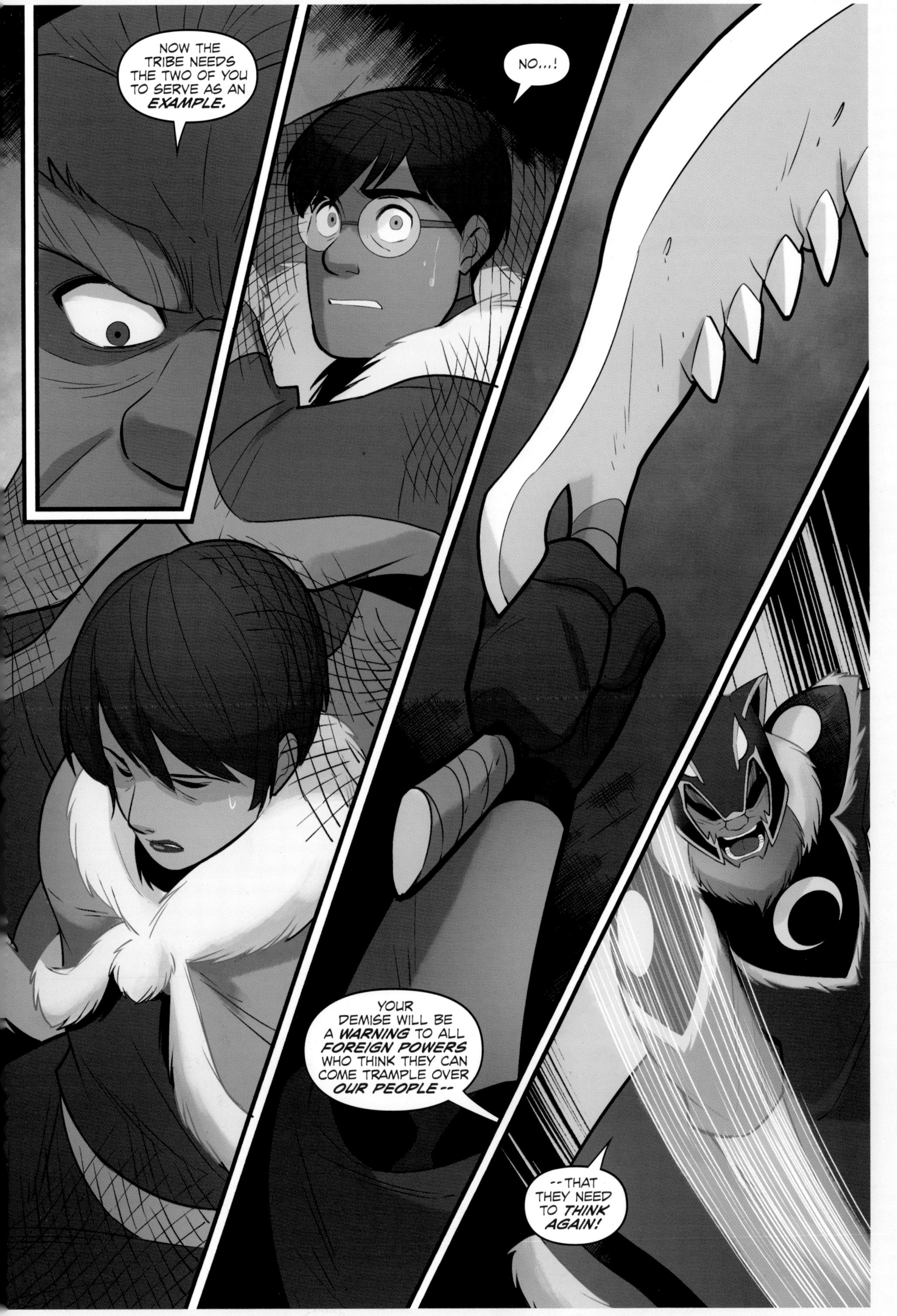
NOW THE TRIBE NEEDS THE TWO OF YOU TO SERVE AS AN EXAMPLE.
NO...!
YOUR DEMISE WILL BE A WARNING TO ALL FOREIGN POWERS WHO THINK THEY CAN COME TRAMPLE OVER OUR PEOPLE--
--THAT THEY NEED TO THINK AGAIN!

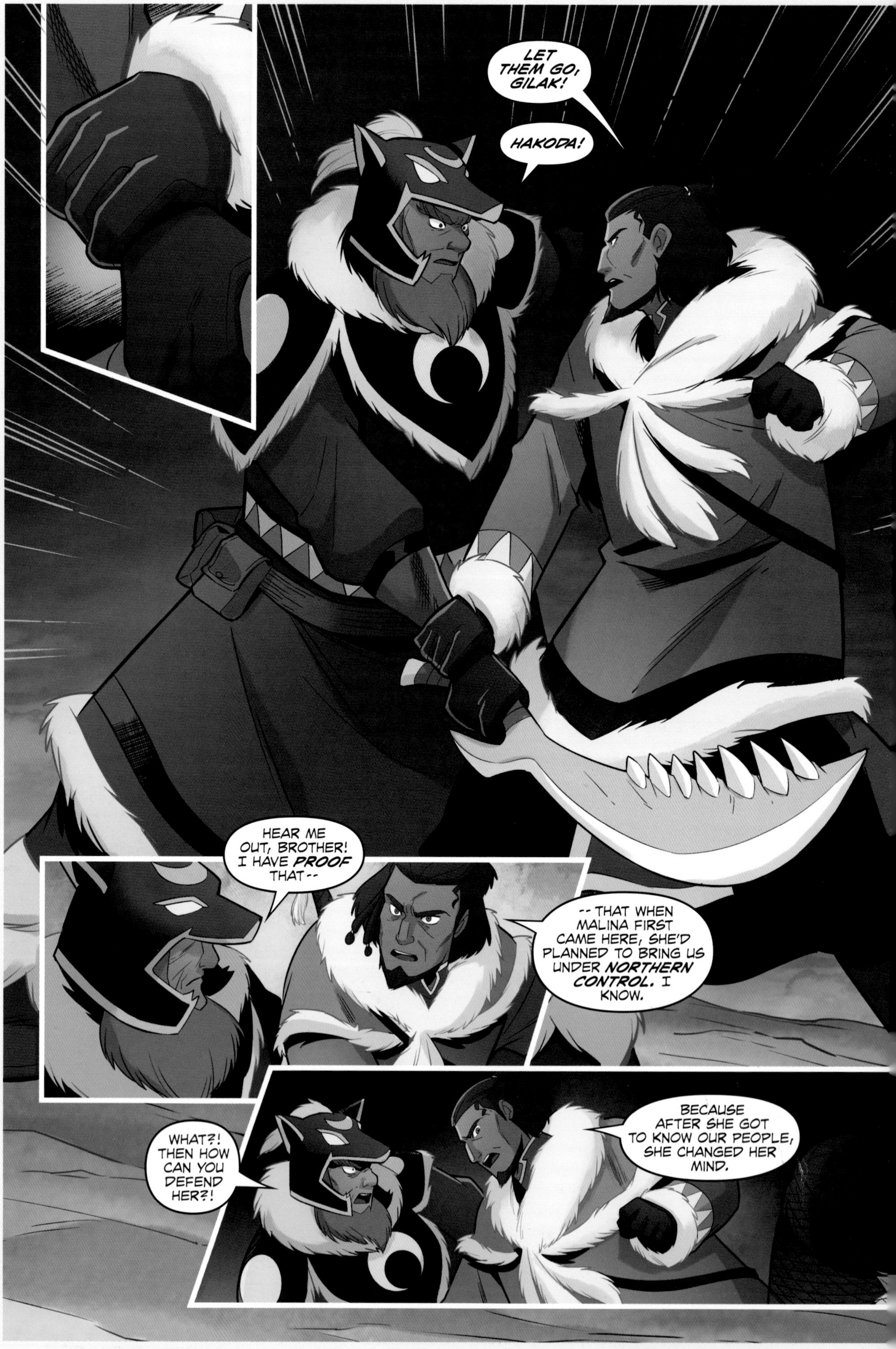
LET THEM GO, GILAK!
HAKODA!
HEAR ME OUT, BROTHER! I HAVE PROOF THAT--
-- THAT WHEN MALINA FIRST CAME HERE, SHE'D PLANNED TO BRING US UNDER NORTHERN CONTROL. I KNOW.
WHAT?! THEN HOW CAN YOU DEFEND HER?!
BECAUSE AFTER SHE GOT TO KNOW OUR PEOPLE, SHE CHANGED HER MIND.

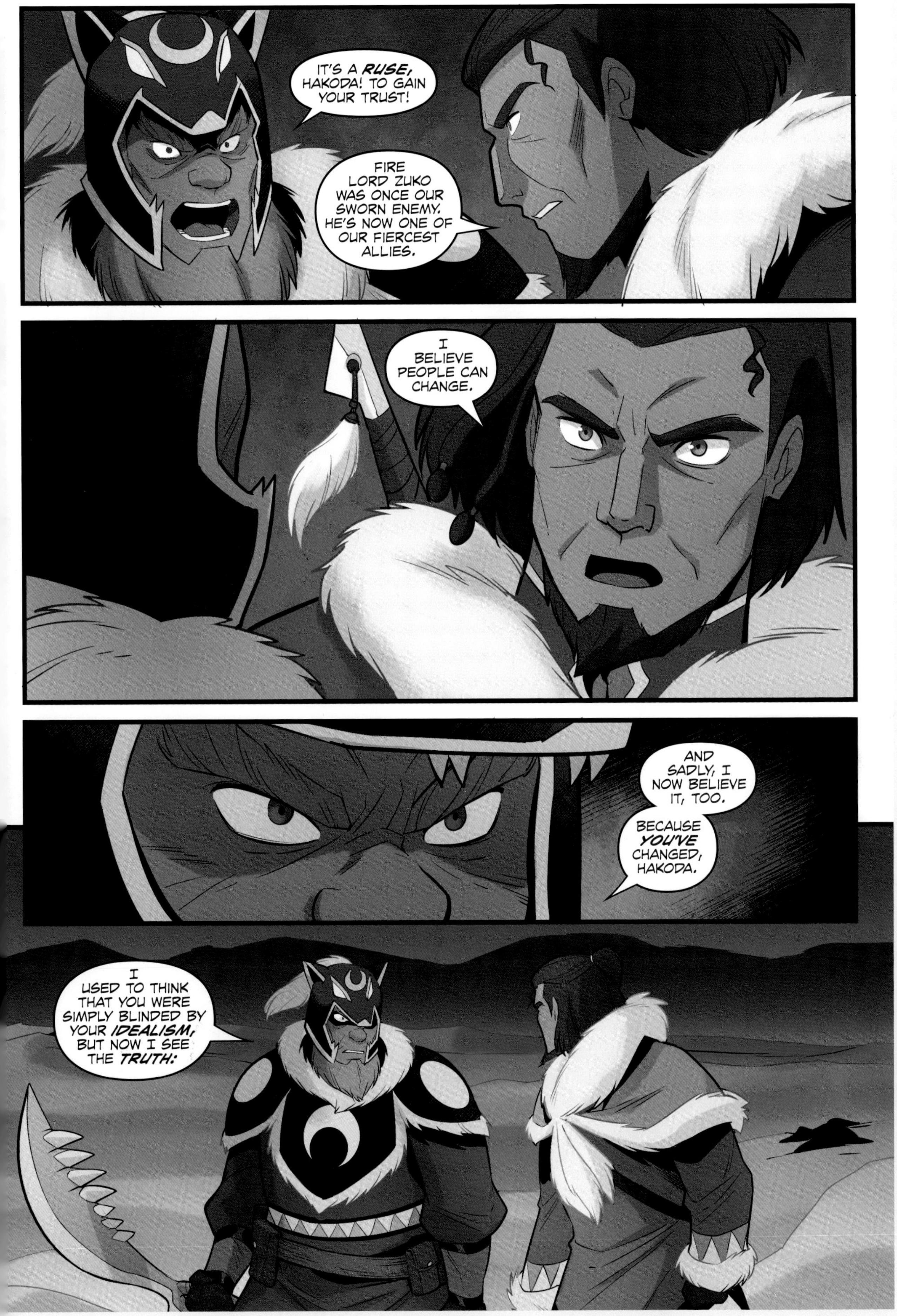
IT'S A RUSE, HAKODA! TO GAIN YOUR TRUST!
FIRE LORD ZUKO WAS ONCE OUR SWORN ENEMY. HE'S NOW ONE OF OUR FIERCEST ALLIES.
I BELIEVE PEOPLE CAN CHANGE.
AND SADLY, I NOW BELIEVE IT, TOO.
BECAUSE YOU'VE CHANGED, HAKODA.
I USED TO THINK THAT YOU WERE SIMPLY BLINDED BY YOUR IDEALISM, BUT NOW I SEE THE TRUTH:

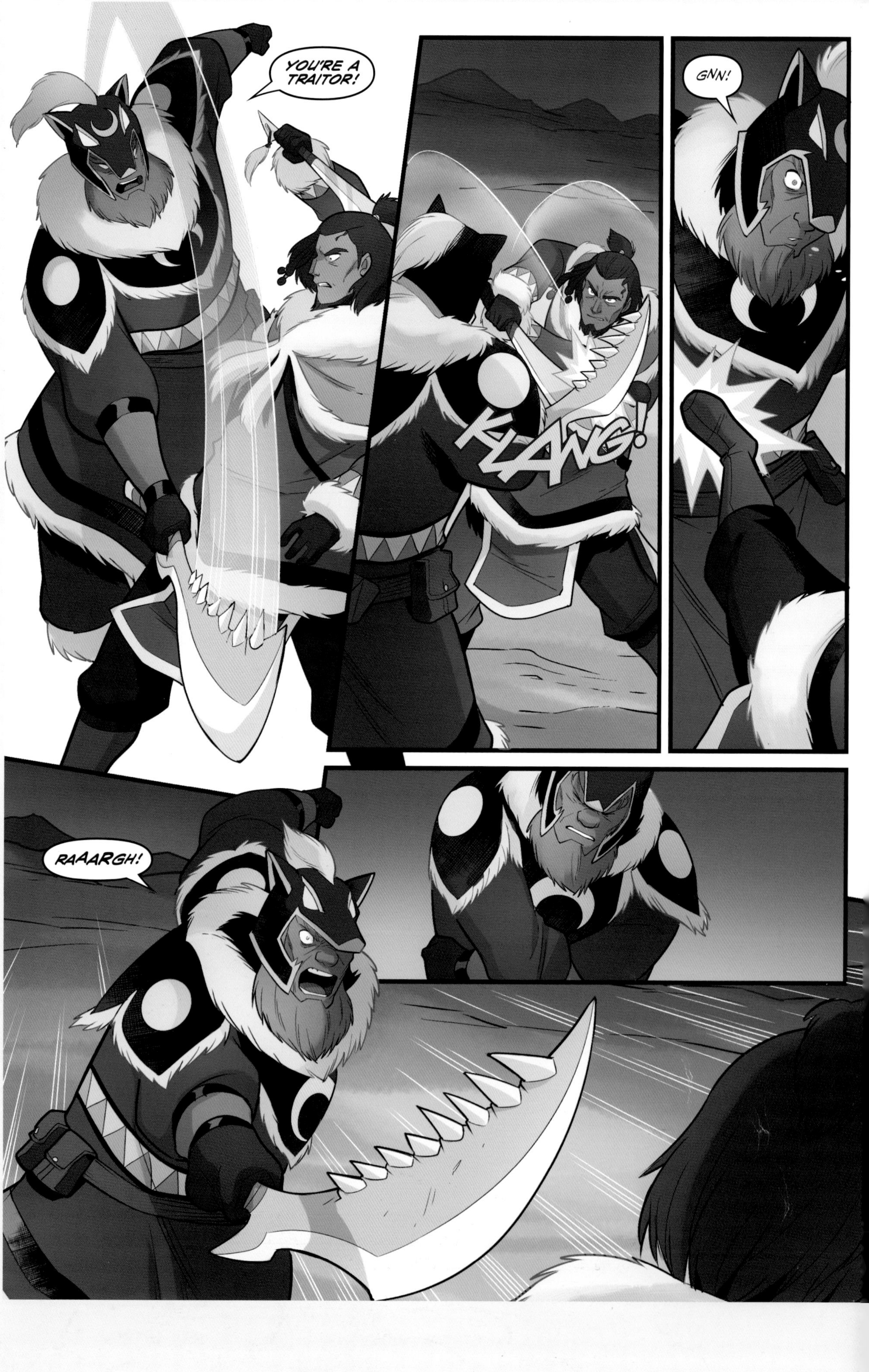
YOU'RE A TRAITOR!
GNN!
KLANG!
RAAARGH!

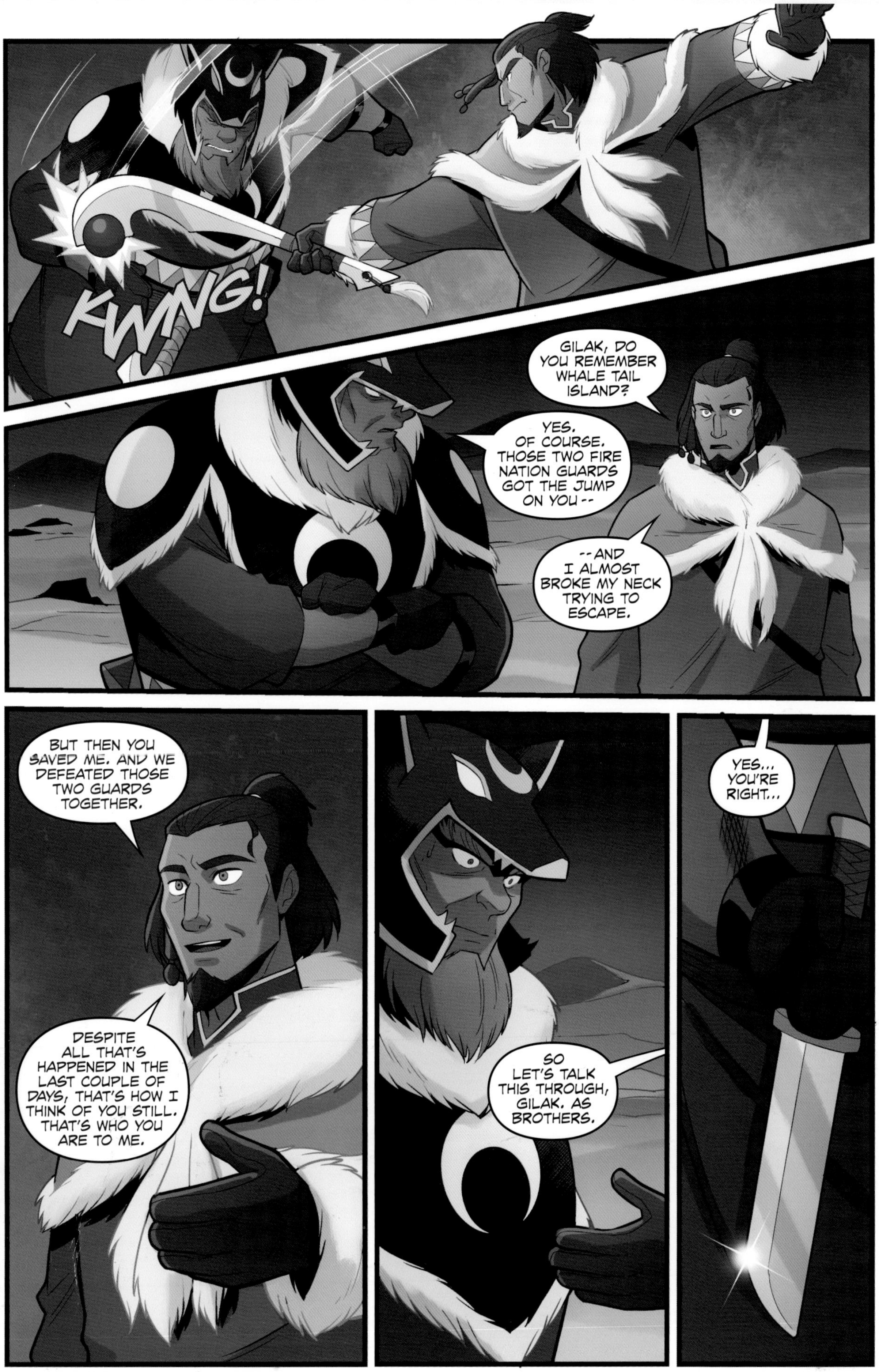
KWNG!
GILAK, DO YOU REMEMBER WHALE TAIL ISLAND?
YES. OF COURSE. THOSE TWO FIRE NATION GUARDS GOT THE JUMP ON YOU --
--AND I ALMOST BROKE MY NECK TRYING TO ESCAPE.
BUT THEN YOU SAVED ME. AND WE DEFEATED THOSE TWO GUARDS TOGETHER.
DESPITE ALL THAT'S HAPPENED IN THE LAST COUPLE OF DAYS, THAT'S HOW I THINK OF YOU STILL. THAT'S WHO YOU ARE TO ME.
SO LET'S TALK THIS THROUGH, GILAK. AS BROTHERS.
YES... YOU'RE RIGHT...

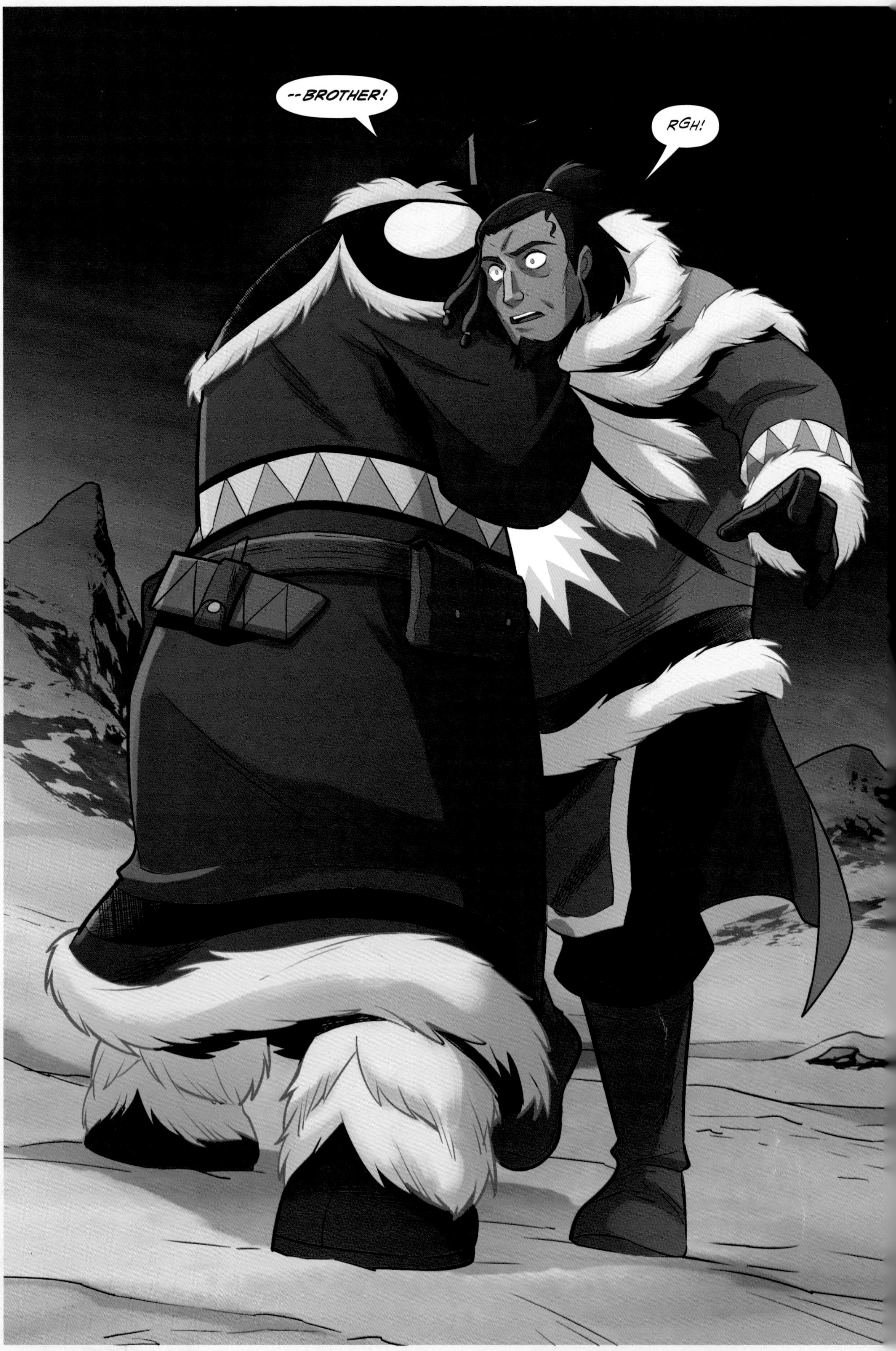
--BROTHER!
RGH!

G: *Since this is an important, dramatic scene where Gilak defeats Hakoda, we spent a lot of time redrawing the layout to get it right.*

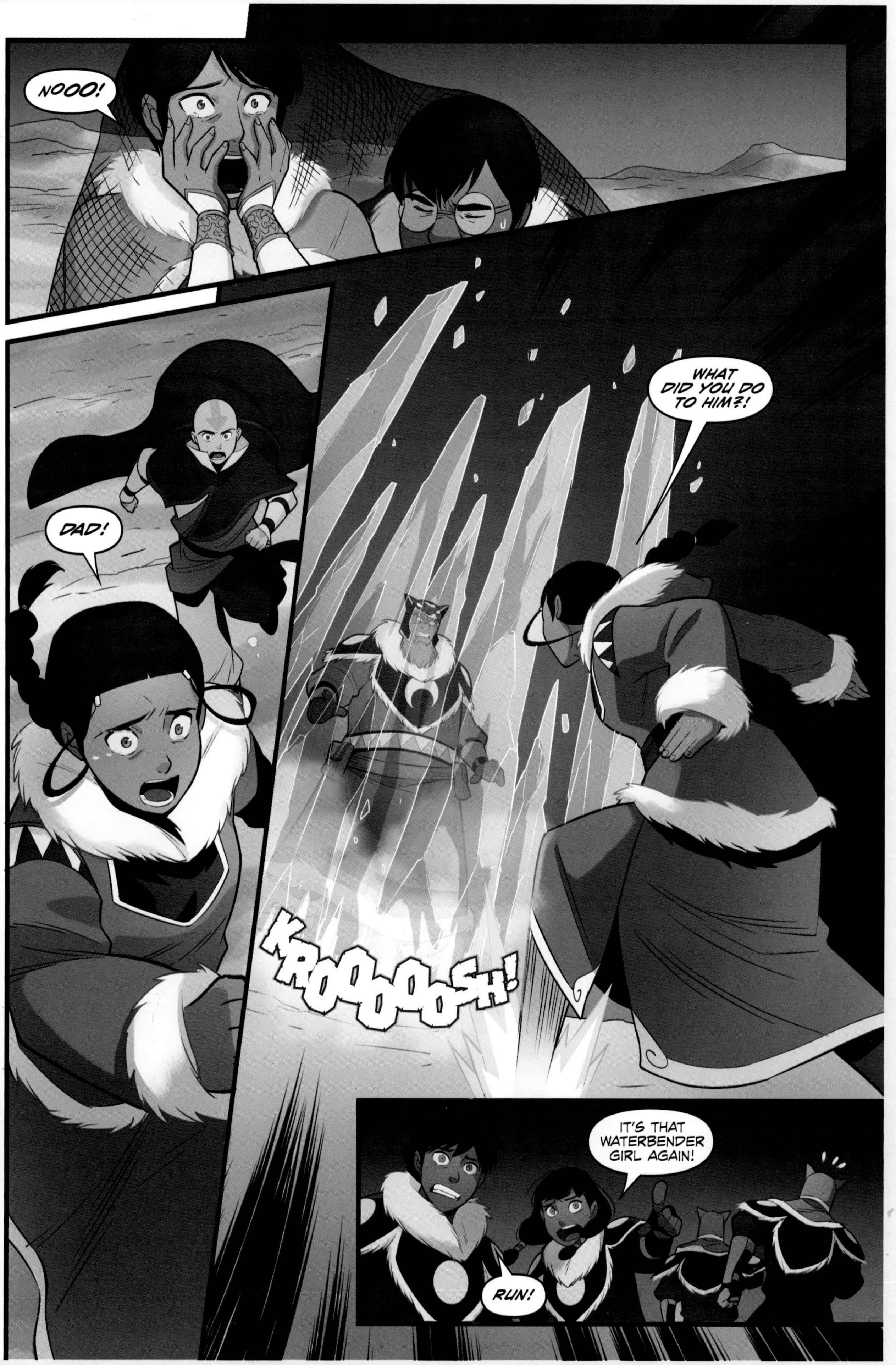
NOOO!
DAD!
WHAT DID YOU DO TO HIM?!
KROOOOOOSH!
IT'S THAT WATERBENDER GIRL AGAIN!
RUN!

G: *We expressed Katara's fury with her bending pose rather than her facial expression.*

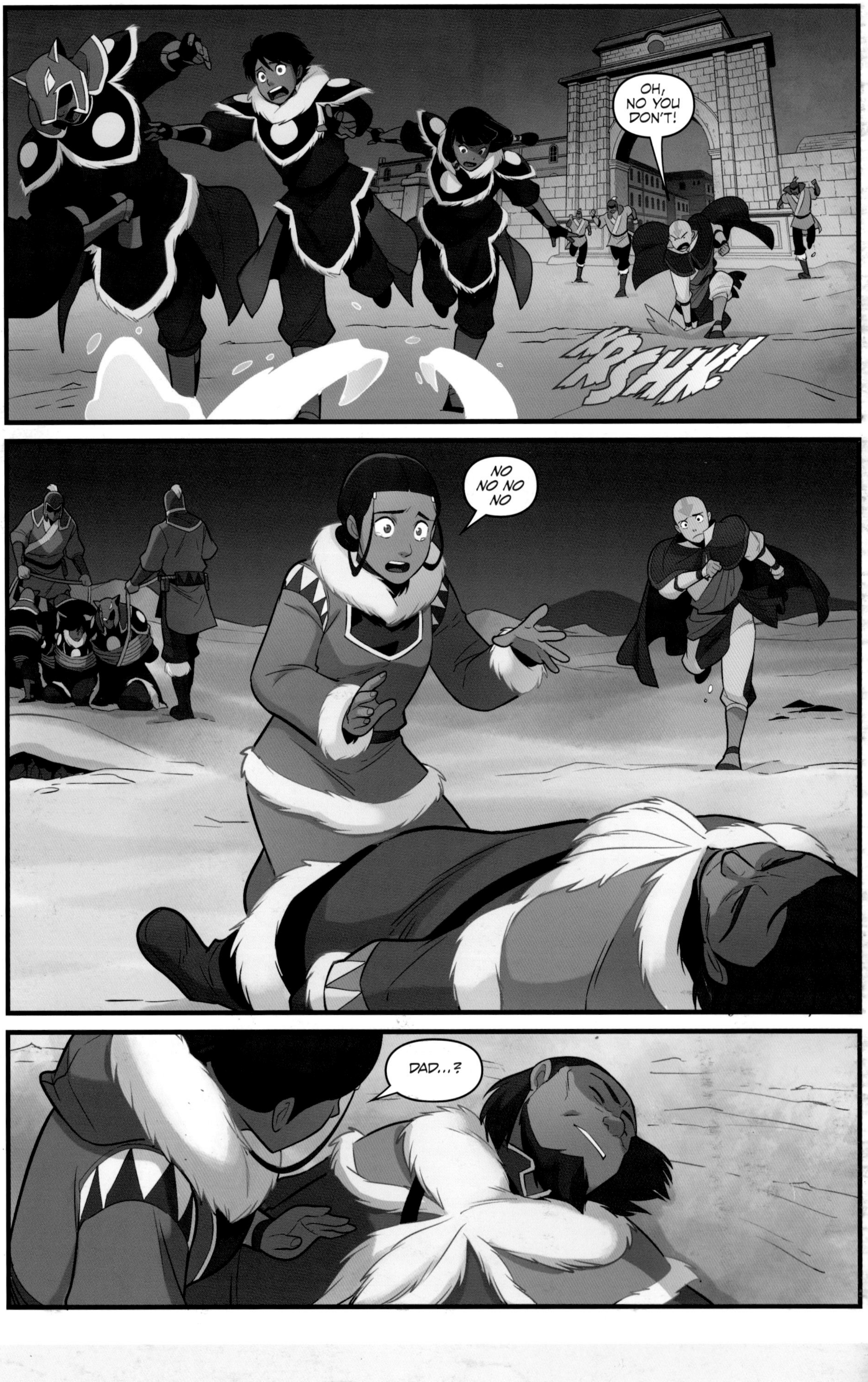
OH, NO YOU DON'T!
KRSHK!
NO NO NO NO NO
DAD...?

DADDY...?
I'M HERE, DADDY. STAY WITH ME.
STAY WITH ME.

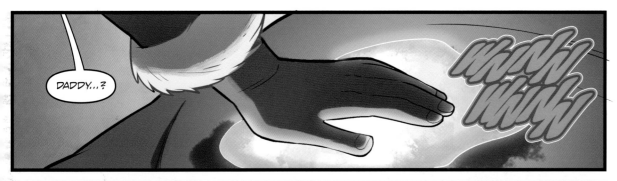

GLY: *Wasn't totally sure how to handle water-healing sounds. Wnnn seemed to work, even though it sounds kind of goofy when you say it out loud. Try it. Right now. Wnnn.*

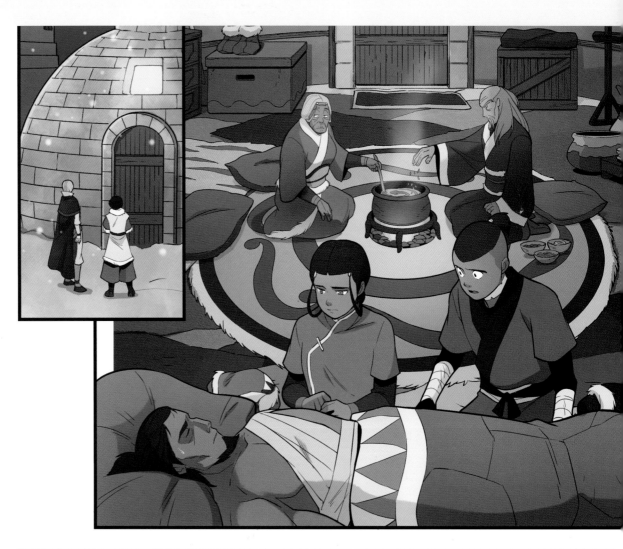

KATARA...

DAD!

YOU... SAVED MY LIFE.

THANK YOU...FOR BEING HERE... KIDS.

YOU HAD US SCARED FOR A BIT, DAD.

DON'T YOU WORRY. PAKKU AND I WILL TAKE GOOD CARE OF HIM.

LET HIM REST. YOU CAN COME SEE HIM IN THE MORNING.

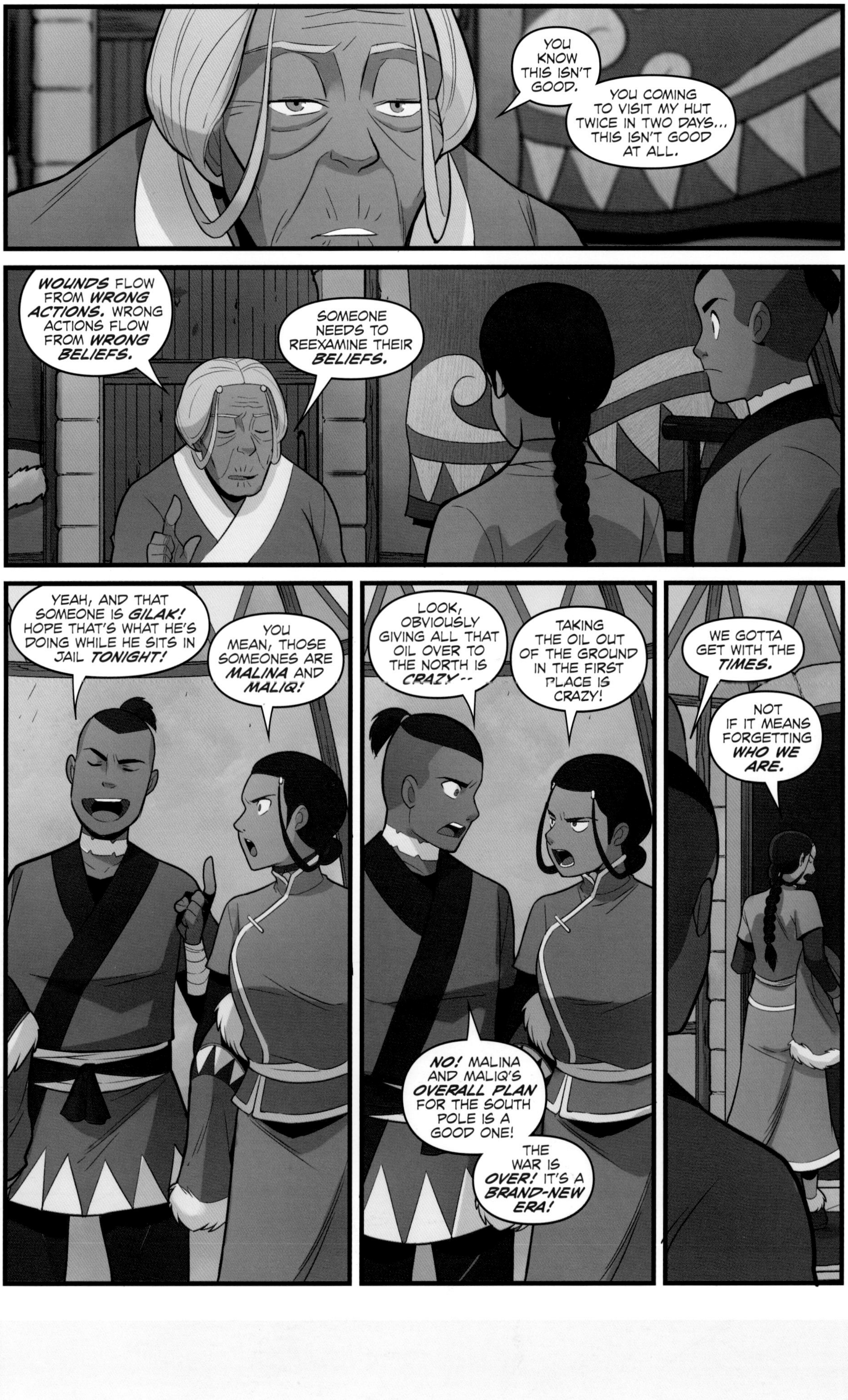
YOU KNOW THIS ISN'T GOOD.
YOU COMING TO VISIT MY HUT TWICE IN TWO DAYS... THIS ISN'T GOOD AT ALL.
WOUNDS FLOW FROM WRONG ACTIONS. WRONG ACTIONS FLOW FROM WRONG BELIEFS.
SOMEONE NEEDS TO REEXAMINE THEIR BELIEFS.
YEAH, AND THAT SOMEONE IS GILAK! HOPE THAT'S WHAT HE'S DOING WHILE HE SITS IN JAIL TONIGHT!
YOU MEAN, THOSE SOMEONES ARE MALINA AND MALIQ!
LOOK, OBVIOUSLY GIVING ALL THAT OIL OVER TO THE NORTH IS CRAZY--
TAKING THE OIL OUT OF THE GROUND IN THE FIRST PLACE IS CRAZY!
NO! MALINA AND MALIQ'S OVERALL PLAN FOR THE SOUTH POLE IS A GOOD ONE!
THE WAR IS OVER! IT'S A BRAND-NEW ERA!
WE GOTTA GET WITH THE TIMES.
NOT IF IT MEANS FORGETTING WHO WE ARE.

GLY: *The relationship between action and belief is a recurring topic in Eastern philosophies. Probably all philosophies. For an interesting take that's different from Gran Gran's, google search "unity of knowledge and action." It's the philosophy of a sixteenth-century Chinese general named Wang Yangming.*

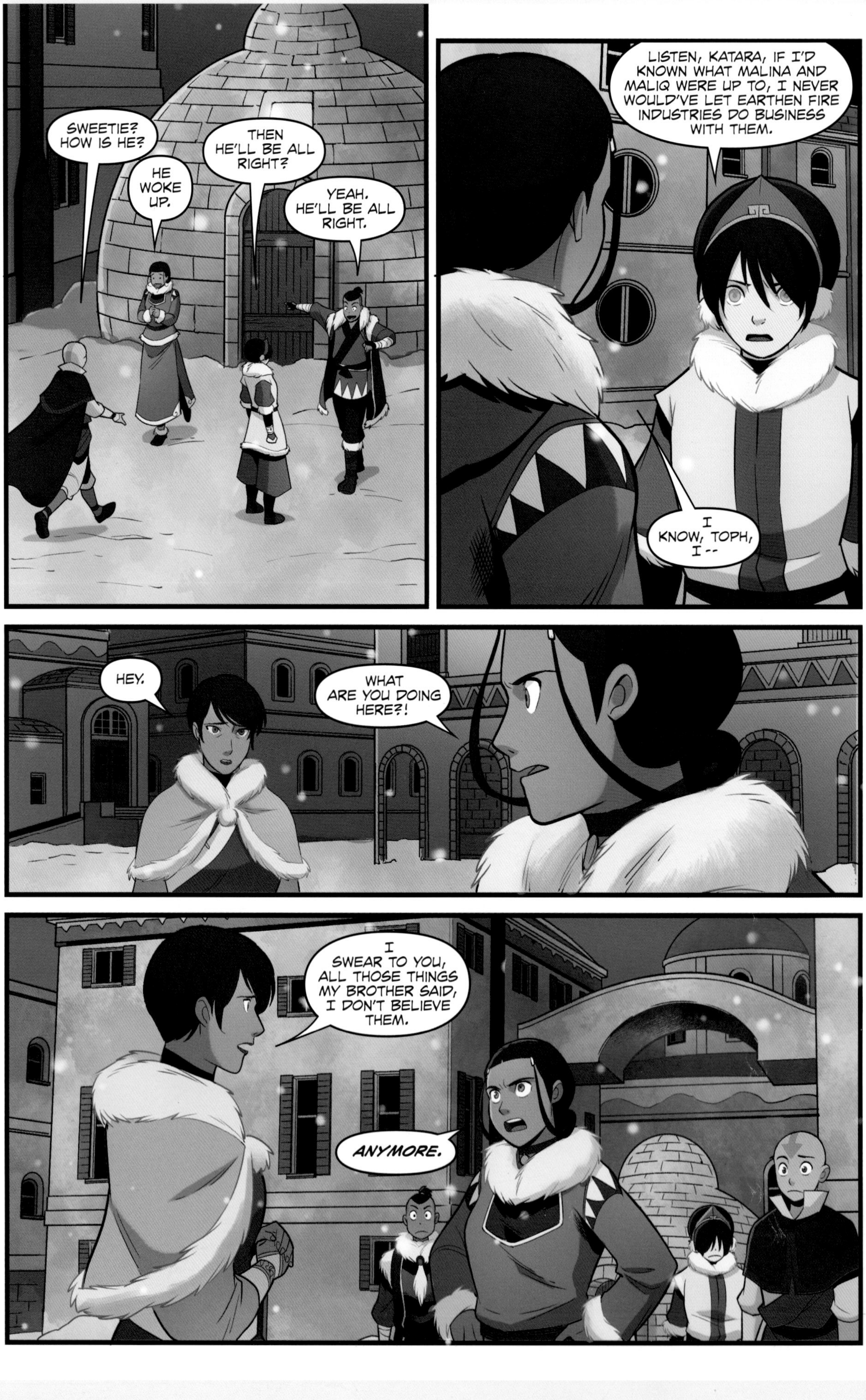
SWEETIE? HOW IS HE?
HE WOKE UP.
THEN HE'LL BE ALL RIGHT?
YEAH. HE'LL BE ALL RIGHT.
LISTEN, KATARA, IF I'D KNOWN WHAT MALINA AND MALIQ WERE UP TO, I NEVER WOULD'VE LET EARTHEN FIRE INDUSTRIES DO BUSINESS WITH THEM.
I KNOW, TOPH, I--
HEY.
WHAT ARE YOU DOING HERE?!
I SWEAR TO YOU, ALL THOSE THINGS MY BROTHER SAID, I DON'T BELIEVE THEM.
ANYMORE.

WHAT DO YOU MEAN?

YOU DON'T BELIEVE THEM *ANYMORE*, NOT AFTER YOU "FELL *IN LOVE*" WITH MY DAD.

BUT WHAT HAPPENS WHEN YOU FALL *OUT* OF LOVE, MALINA?

KATARA, IT GOES DEEPER THAN THAT.

I'M GOING TO ASK YOU AGAIN -- WHAT ARE YOU DOING HERE?!

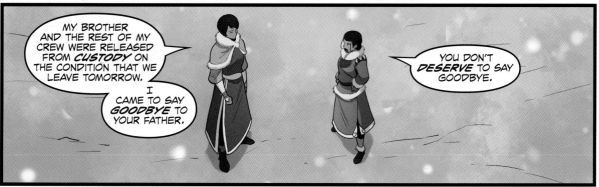

MY BROTHER AND THE REST OF MY CREW WERE RELEASED FROM *CUSTODY* ON THE CONDITION THAT WE LEAVE TOMORROW.

I CAME TO SAY *GOODBYE* TO YOUR FATHER.

YOU DON'T *DESERVE* TO SAY GOODBYE.

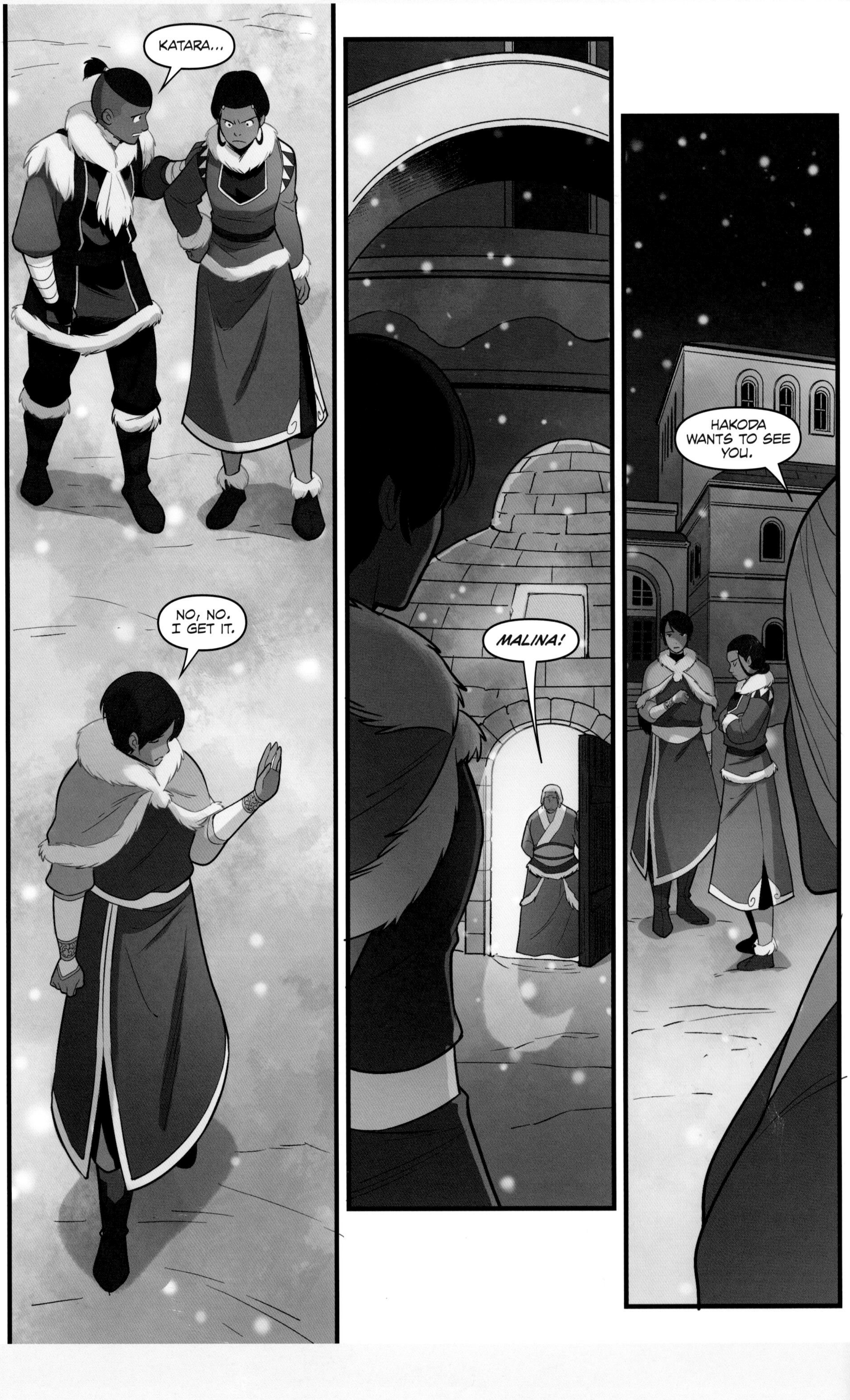
KATARA...
NO, NO. I GET IT.
MALINA!
HAKODA WANTS TO SEE YOU.

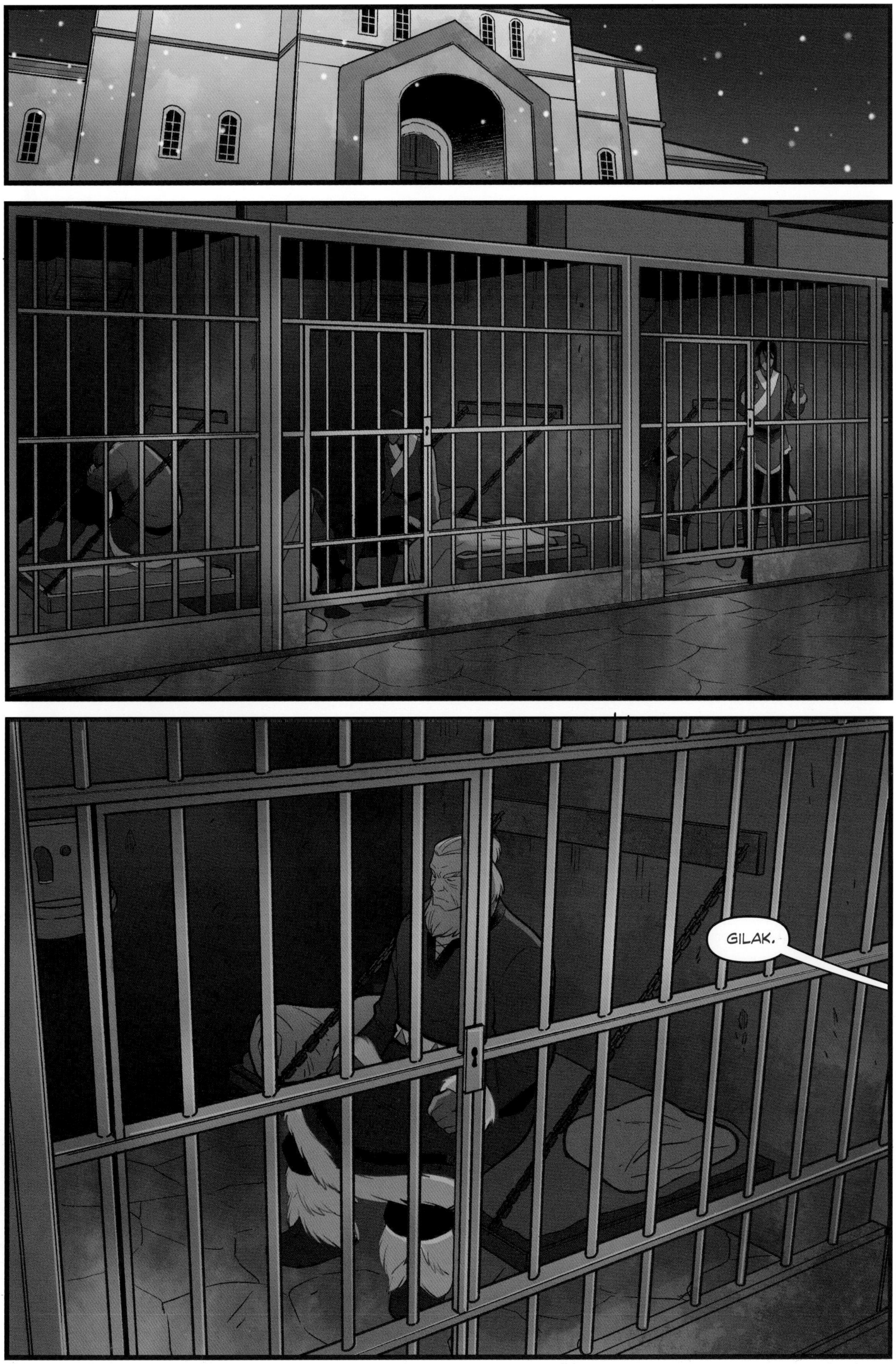
GILAK.

GLY: *In the first version of the script, the guard hid the key in a book. Mike suggested hiding it under a bowl of food, which works so much better.*

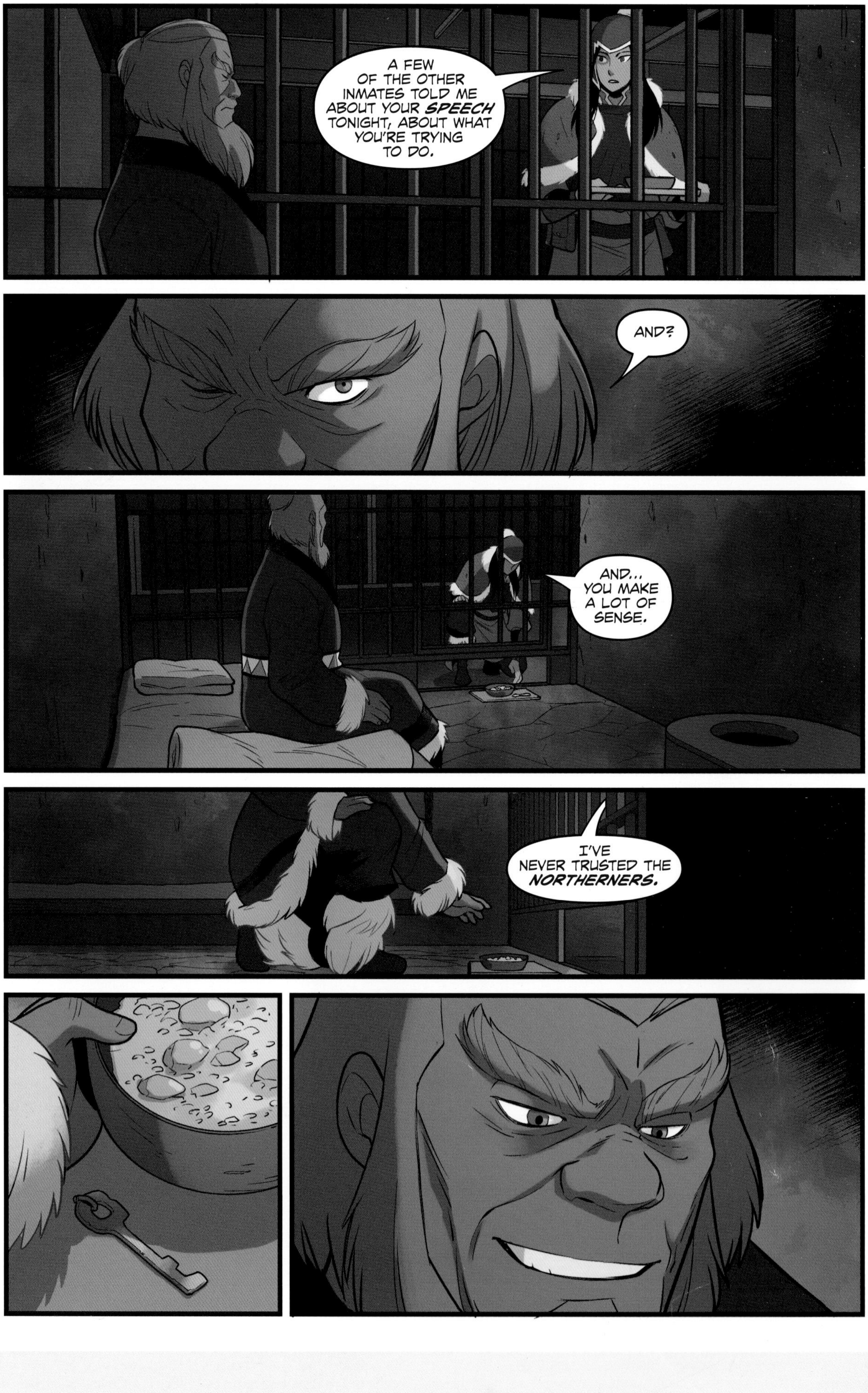
A FEW OF THE OTHER INMATES TOLD ME ABOUT YOUR ***SPEECH*** TONIGHT, ABOUT WHAT YOU'RE TRYING TO DO.
AND?
AND... YOU MAKE A LOT OF SENSE.
I'VE NEVER TRUSTED THE ***NORTHERNERS.***

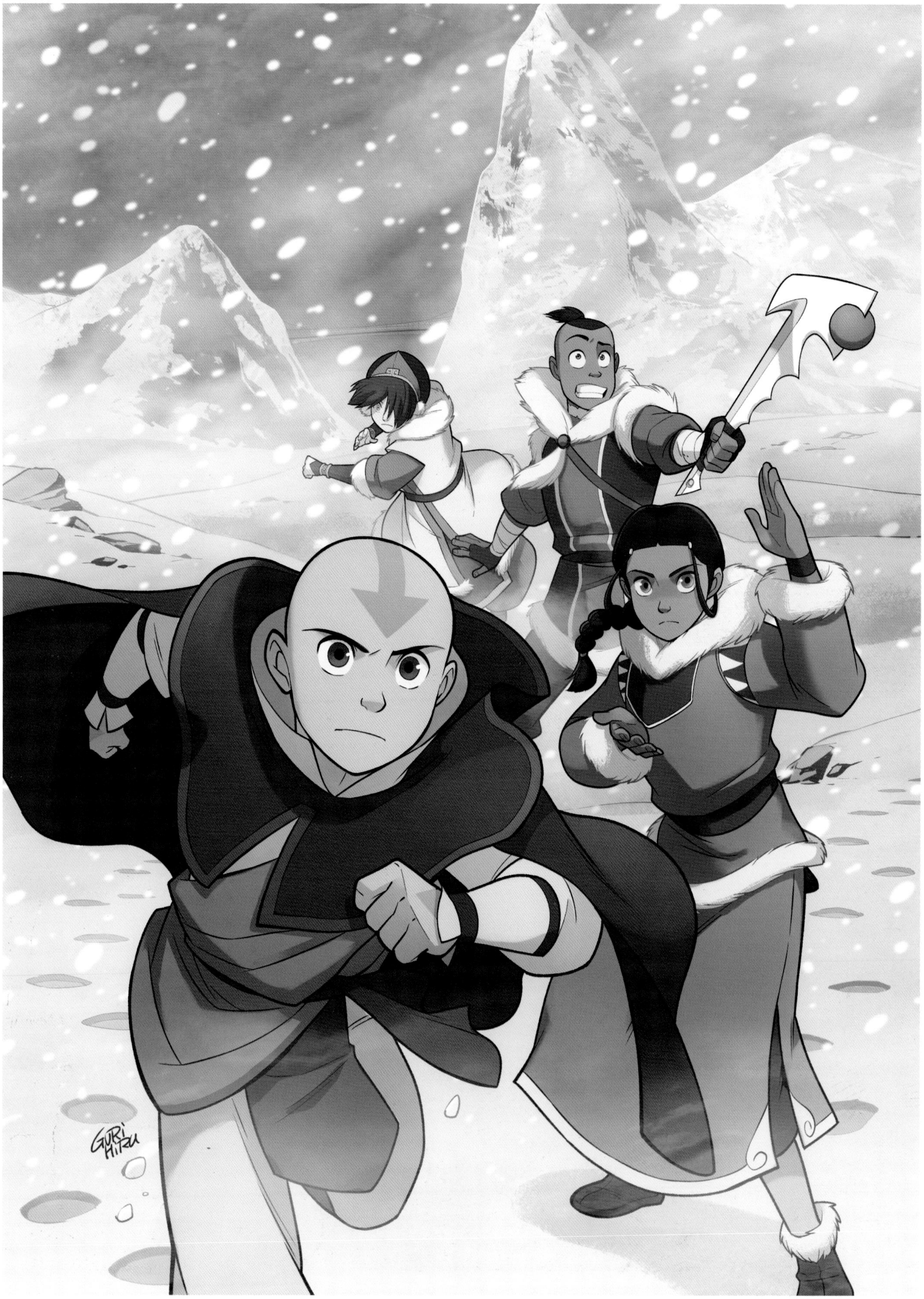
GURIHIRU

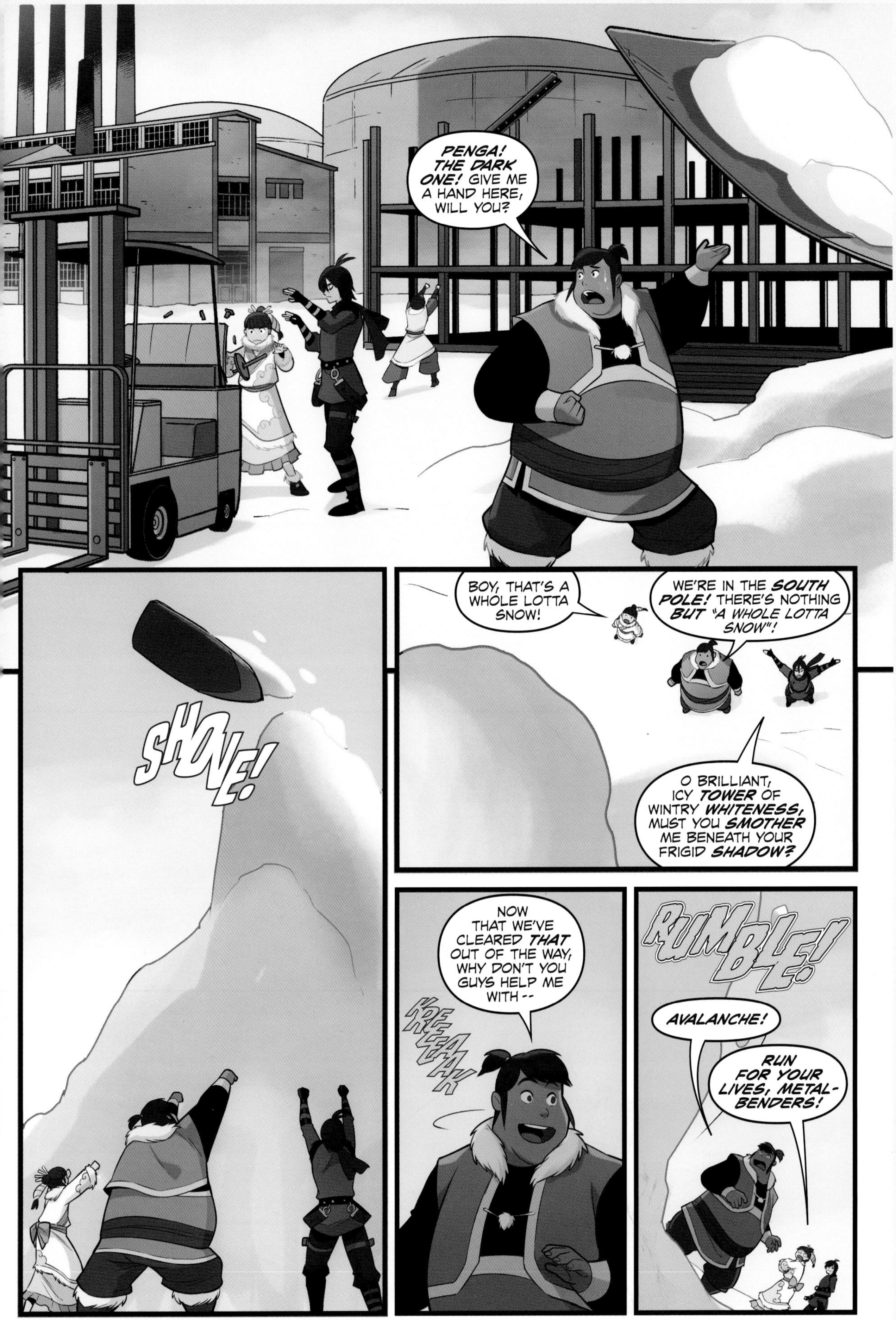
PENGA! THE DARK ONE! GIVE ME A HAND HERE, WILL YOU?
SHOVE!
BOY, THAT'S A WHOLE LOTTA SNOW!
WE'RE IN THE SOUTH POLE! THERE'S NOTHING BUT "A WHOLE LOTTA SNOW"!
O BRILLIANT, ICY TOWER OF WINTRY WHITENESS, MUST YOU SMOTHER ME BENEATH YOUR FRIGID SHADOW?
NOW THAT WE'VE CLEARED THAT OUT OF THE WAY, WHY DON'T YOU GUYS HELP ME WITH --
KREEAK
RUMBLE!
AVALANCHE!
RUN FOR YOUR LIVES, METAL-BENDERS!

G: *We were happy to see Toph's three students again. Since they are in a cold land, we drew them wearing warm clothes.*

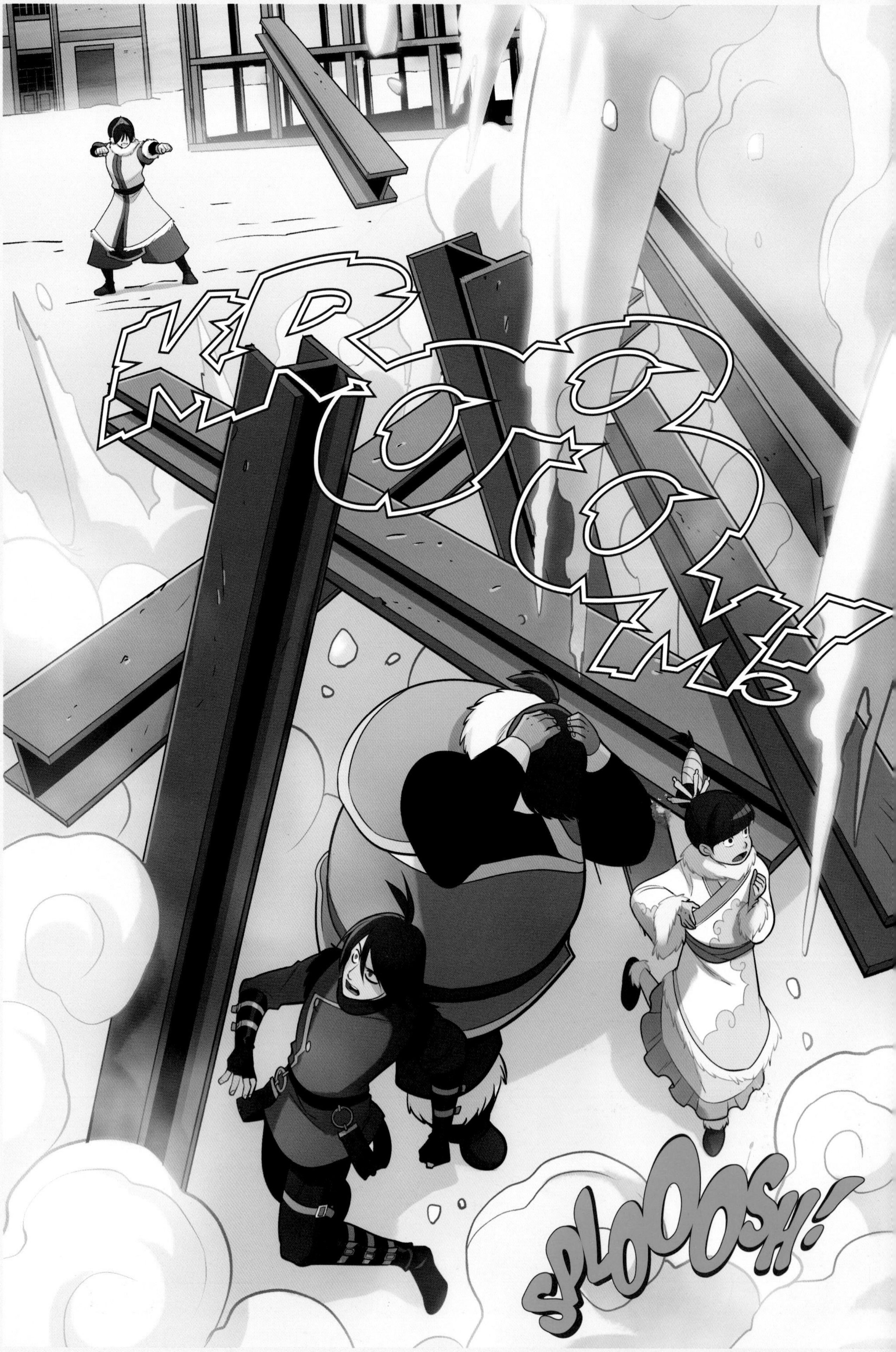
KROOOM!
SPLOOOSH!

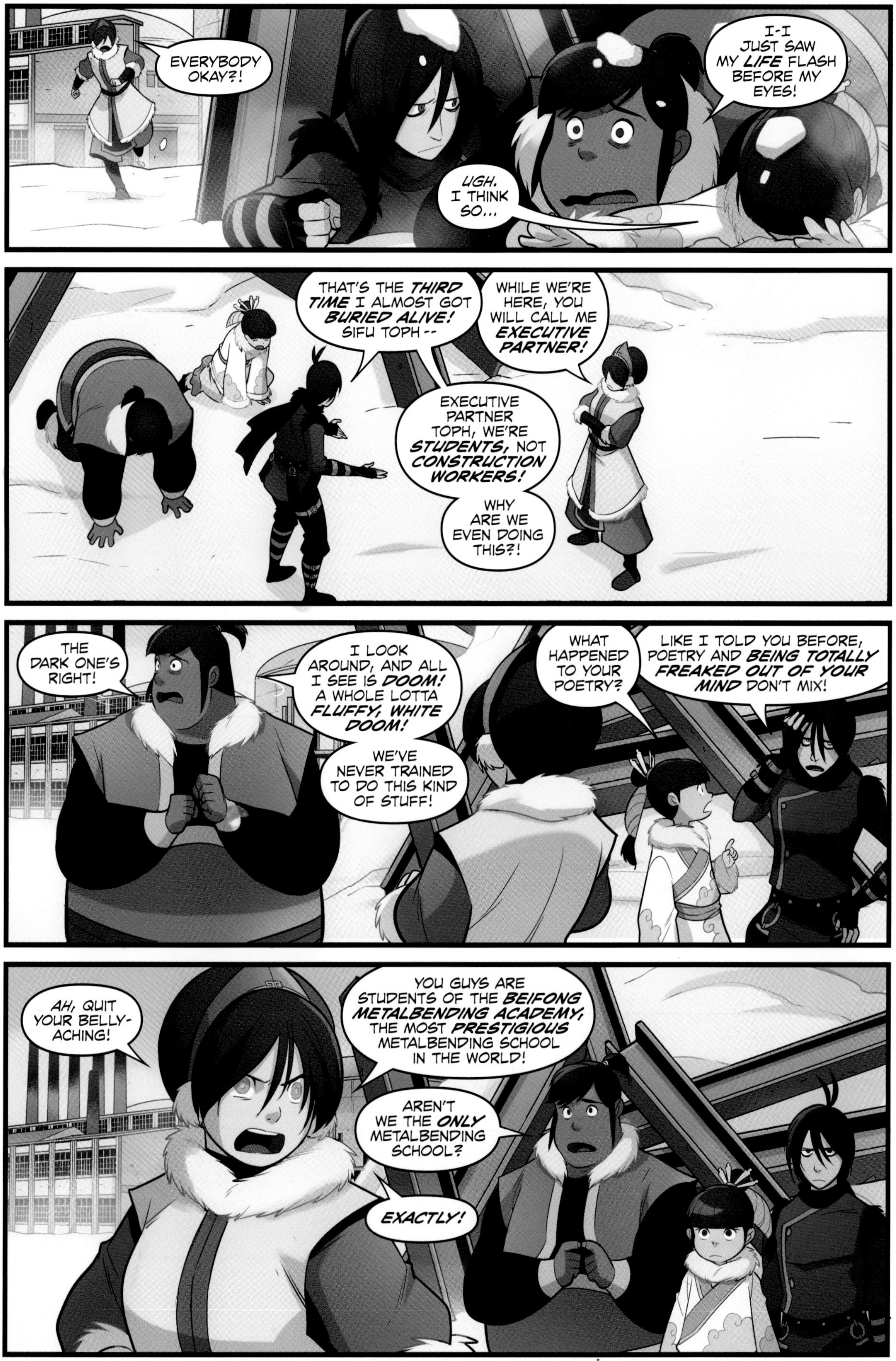
EVERYBODY OKAY?!
I-I JUST SAW MY *LIFE* FLASH BEFORE MY EYES!
UGH. I THINK SO...
THAT'S THE *THIRD TIME* I ALMOST GOT *BURIED ALIVE!* SIFU TOPH --
WHILE WE'RE HERE, YOU WILL CALL ME *EXECUTIVE PARTNER!*
EXECUTIVE PARTNER TOPH, WE'RE *STUDENTS,* NOT *CONSTRUCTION WORKERS!*
WHY ARE WE EVEN DOING THIS?!
THE DARK ONE'S RIGHT!
I LOOK AROUND, AND ALL I SEE IS *DOOM!* A WHOLE LOTTA *FLUFFY, WHITE DOOM!*
WE'VE NEVER TRAINED TO DO THIS KIND OF STUFF!
WHAT HAPPENED TO YOUR POETRY?
LIKE I TOLD YOU BEFORE, POETRY AND *BEING TOTALLY FREAKED OUT OF YOUR MIND* DON'T MIX!
AH, QUIT YOUR BELLY-ACHING!
YOU GUYS ARE STUDENTS OF THE *BEIFONG METALBENDING ACADEMY,* THE MOST *PRESTIGIOUS* METALBENDING SCHOOL IN THE WORLD!
AREN'T WE THE *ONLY* METALBENDING SCHOOL?
EXACTLY!

GLY: *What the Dark One says is true. Poetry and fear don't mix. Actually, creativity and fear don't mix. If you want to finish a creative project, you have to get over your fear. Maybe we all need a Sifu Toph in our lives yelling pep talks at us.*

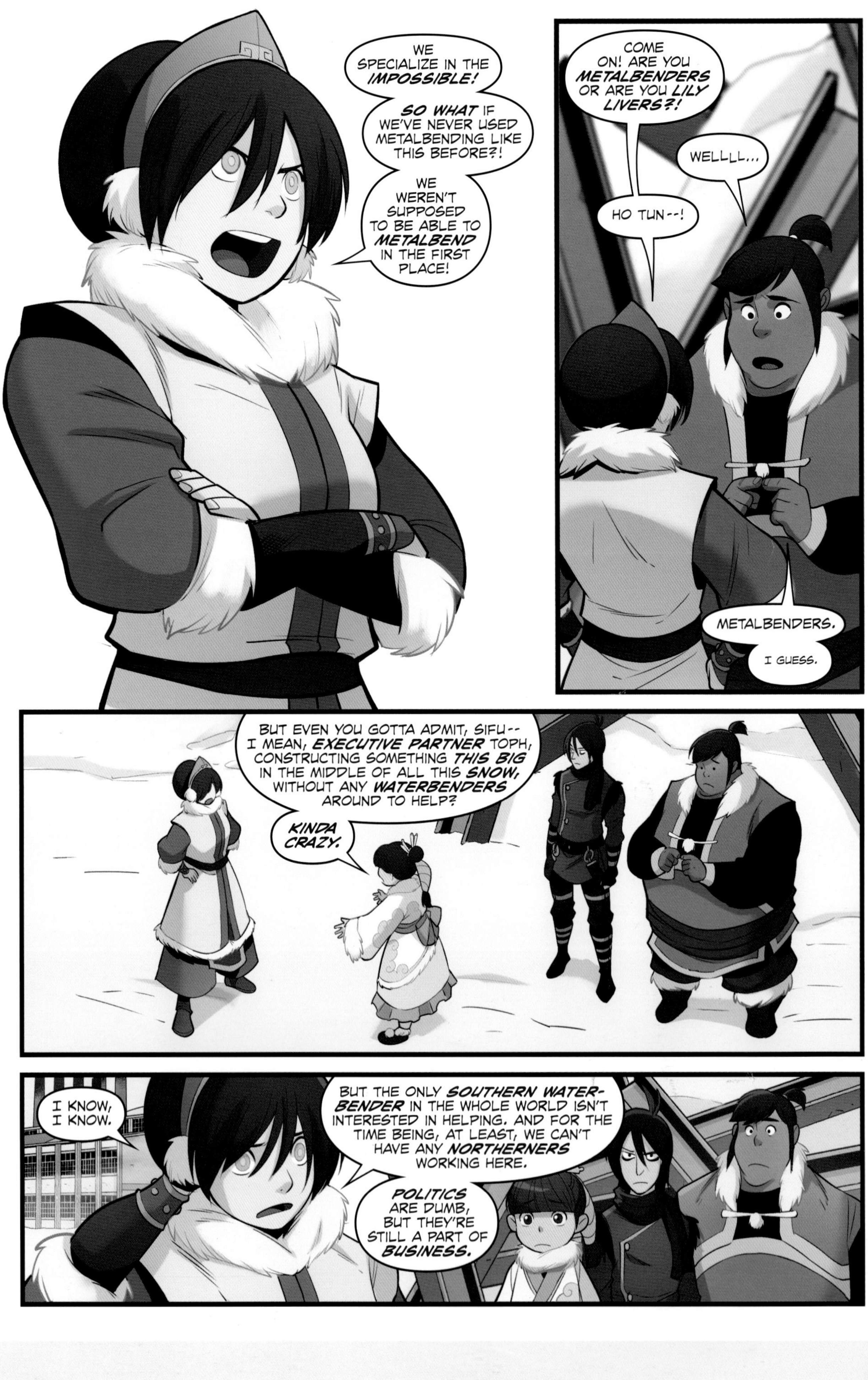
WE SPECIALIZE IN THE *IMPOSSIBLE!*
SO WHAT IF WE'VE NEVER USED METALBENDING LIKE THIS BEFORE?!
WE WEREN'T SUPPOSED TO BE ABLE TO *METALBEND* IN THE FIRST PLACE!
COME ON! ARE YOU *METALBENDERS* OR ARE YOU *LILY LIVERS?!*
HO TUN--!
WELLLL...
METALBENDERS.
I GUESS.
BUT EVEN YOU GOTTA ADMIT, SIFU-- I MEAN, *EXECUTIVE PARTNER* TOPH, CONSTRUCTING SOMETHING *THIS BIG* IN THE MIDDLE OF ALL THIS *SNOW*, WITHOUT ANY *WATERBENDERS* AROUND TO HELP?
KINDA CRAZY.
I KNOW, I KNOW.
BUT THE ONLY *SOUTHERN WATER-BENDER* IN THE WHOLE WORLD ISN'T INTERESTED IN HELPING. AND FOR THE TIME BEING, AT LEAST, WE CAN'T HAVE ANY *NORTHERNERS* WORKING HERE.
POLITICS ARE DUMB, BUT THEY'RE STILL A PART OF *BUSINESS.*

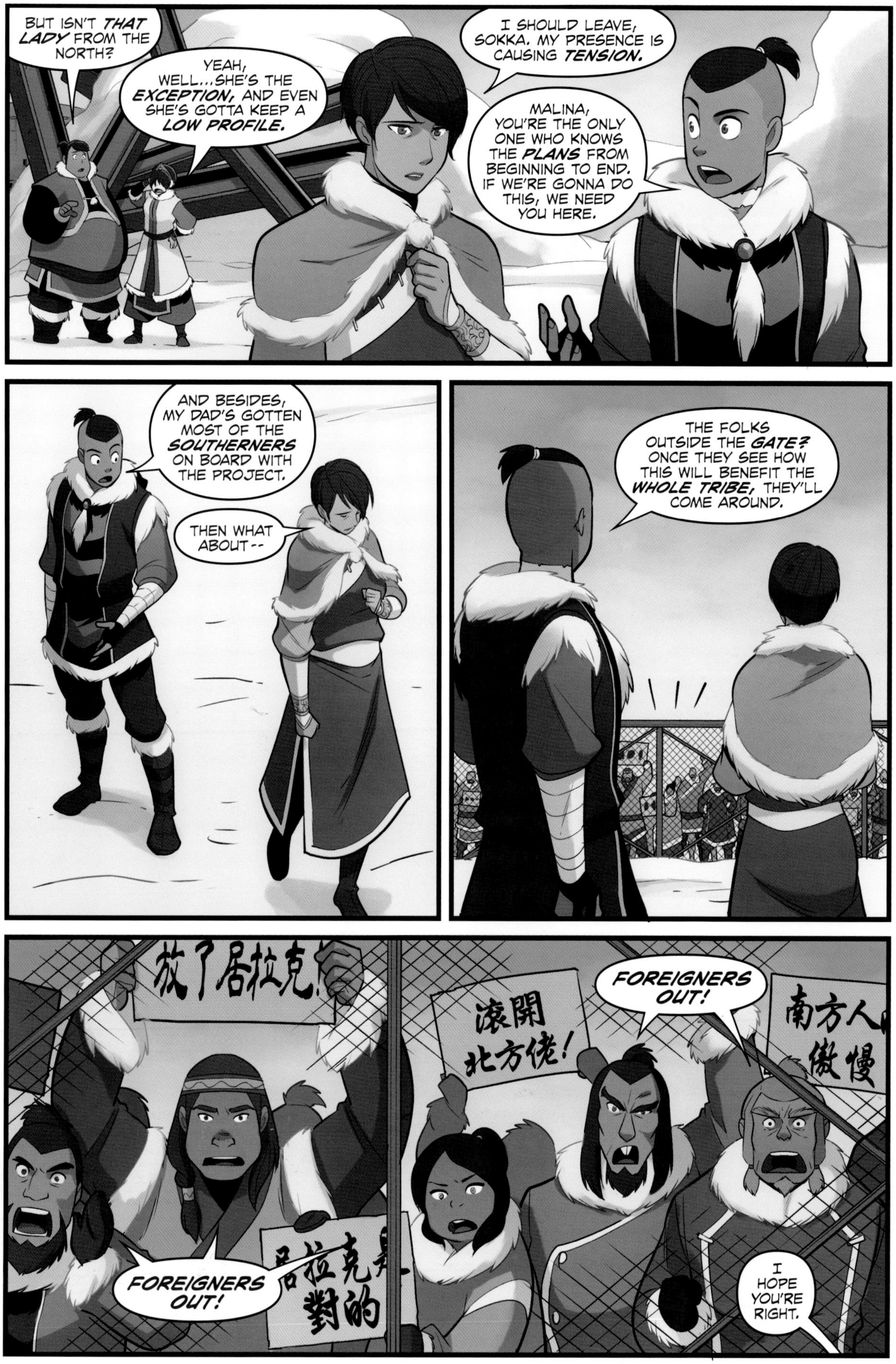

BUT ISN'T THAT LADY FROM THE NORTH?
YEAH, WELL...SHE'S THE EXCEPTION, AND EVEN SHE'S GOTTA KEEP A LOW PROFILE.
I SHOULD LEAVE, SOKKA. MY PRESENCE IS CAUSING TENSION.
MALINA, YOU'RE THE ONLY ONE WHO KNOWS THE PLANS FROM BEGINNING TO END. IF WE'RE GONNA DO THIS, WE NEED YOU HERE.
AND BESIDES, MY DAD'S GOTTEN MOST OF THE SOUTHERNERS ON BOARD WITH THE PROJECT.
THEN WHAT ABOUT--
THE FOLKS OUTSIDE THE GATE? ONCE THEY SEE HOW THIS WILL BENEFIT THE WHOLE TRIBE, THEY'LL COME AROUND.
放了居拉克
滾開北方佬!
FOREIGNERS OUT!
南方人
傲慢
FOREIGNERS OUT!
對的
I HOPE YOU'RE RIGHT.

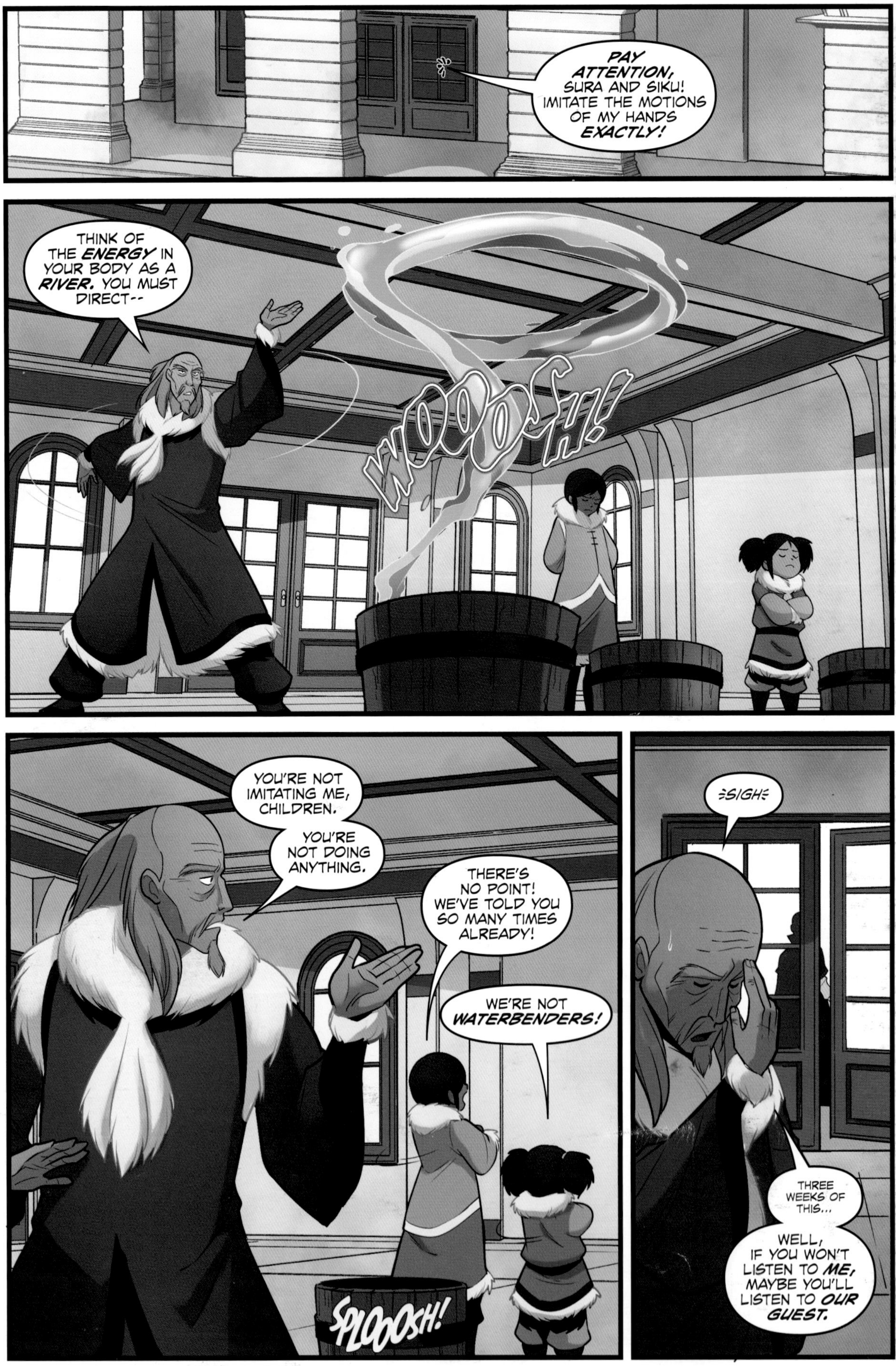
PAY ATTENTION, SURA AND SIKU! IMITATE THE MOTIONS OF MY HANDS EXACTLY!
THINK OF THE ENERGY IN YOUR BODY AS A RIVER. YOU MUST DIRECT--
WOOOOSH!
YOU'RE NOT IMITATING ME, CHILDREN.
YOU'RE NOT DOING ANYTHING.
THERE'S NO POINT! WE'VE TOLD YOU SO MANY TIMES ALREADY!
WE'RE NOT WATERBENDERS!
SPLOOOSH!
SIGH
THREE WEEKS OF THIS...
WELL, IF YOU WON'T LISTEN TO ME, MAYBE YOU'LL LISTEN TO OUR GUEST.

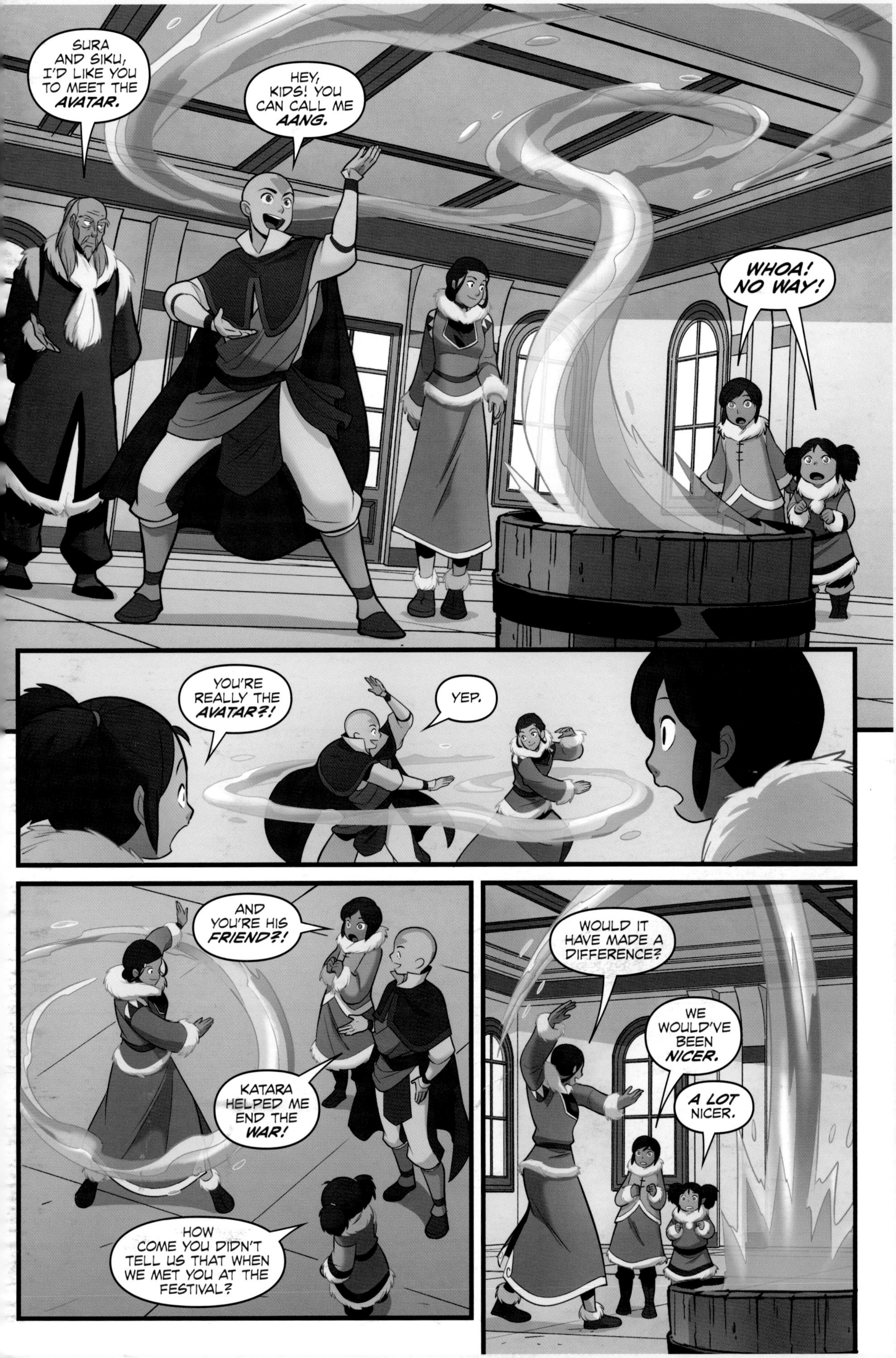
SURA AND SIKU, I'D LIKE YOU TO MEET THE AVATAR.
HEY, KIDS! YOU CAN CALL ME AANG.
WHOA! NO WAY!
YOU'RE REALLY THE AVATAR?!
YEP.
AND YOU'RE HIS FRIEND?!
KATARA HELPED ME END THE WAR!
HOW COME YOU DIDN'T TELL US THAT WHEN WE MET YOU AT THE FESTIVAL?
WOULD IT HAVE MADE A DIFFERENCE?
WE WOULD'VE BEEN NICER.
A LOT NICER.

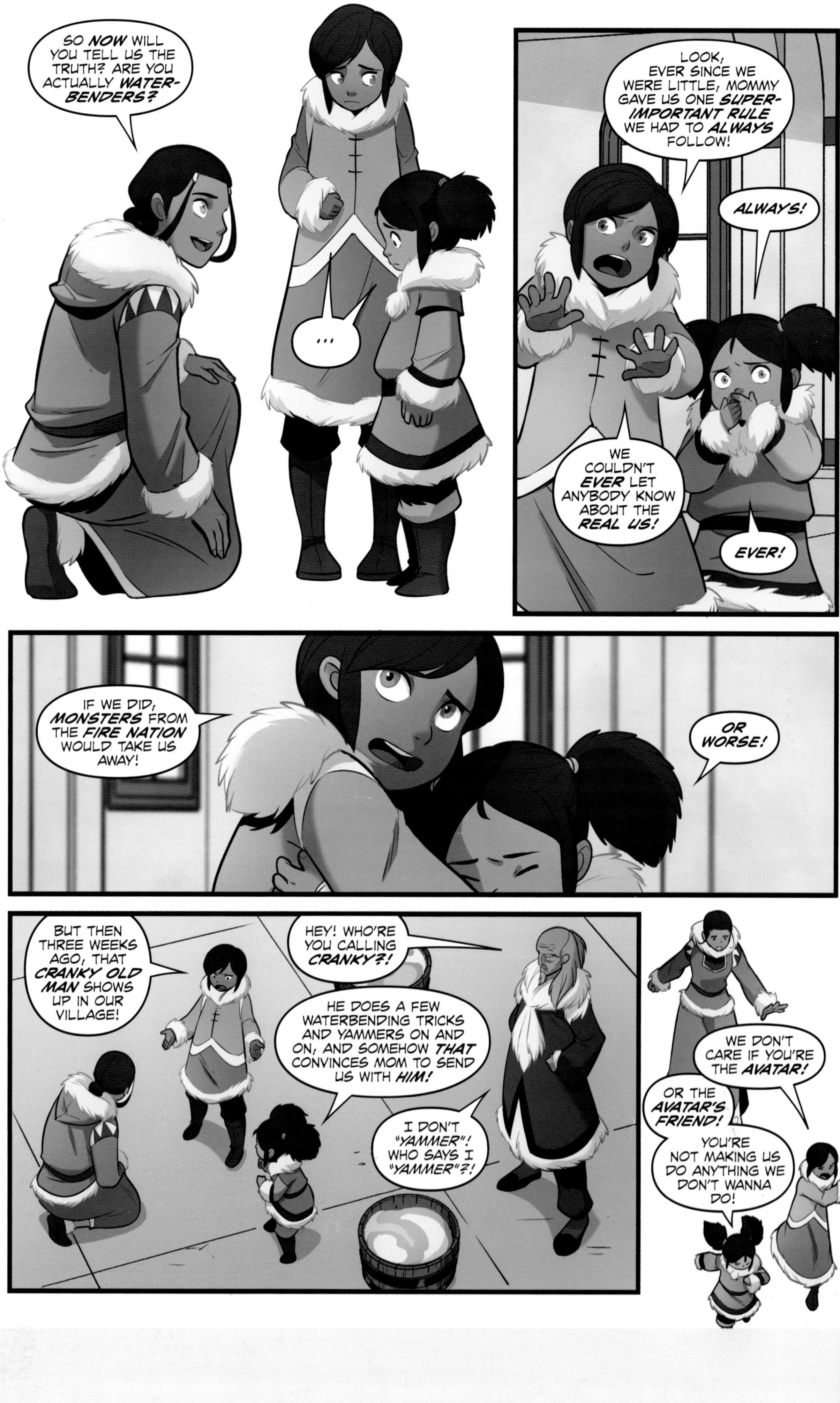
SO NOW WILL YOU TELL US THE TRUTH? ARE YOU ACTUALLY WATER-BENDERS?
...
LOOK, EVER SINCE WE WERE LITTLE, MOMMY GAVE US ONE SUPER-IMPORTANT RULE WE HAD TO ALWAYS FOLLOW!
ALWAYS!
WE COULDN'T EVER LET ANYBODY KNOW ABOUT THE REAL US!
EVER!
IF WE DID, MONSTERS FROM THE FIRE NATION WOULD TAKE US AWAY!
OR WORSE!
BUT THEN THREE WEEKS AGO, THAT CRANKY OLD MAN SHOWS UP IN OUR VILLAGE!
HEY! WHO'RE YOU CALLING CRANKY?!
HE DOES A FEW WATERBENDING TRICKS AND YAMMERS ON AND ON, AND SOMEHOW THAT CONVINCES MOM TO SEND US WITH HIM!
I DON'T "YAMMER"! WHO SAYS I "YAMMER"?!
WE DON'T CARE IF YOU'RE THE AVATAR!
OR THE AVATAR'S FRIEND!
YOU'RE NOT MAKING US DO ANYTHING WE DON'T WANNA DO!

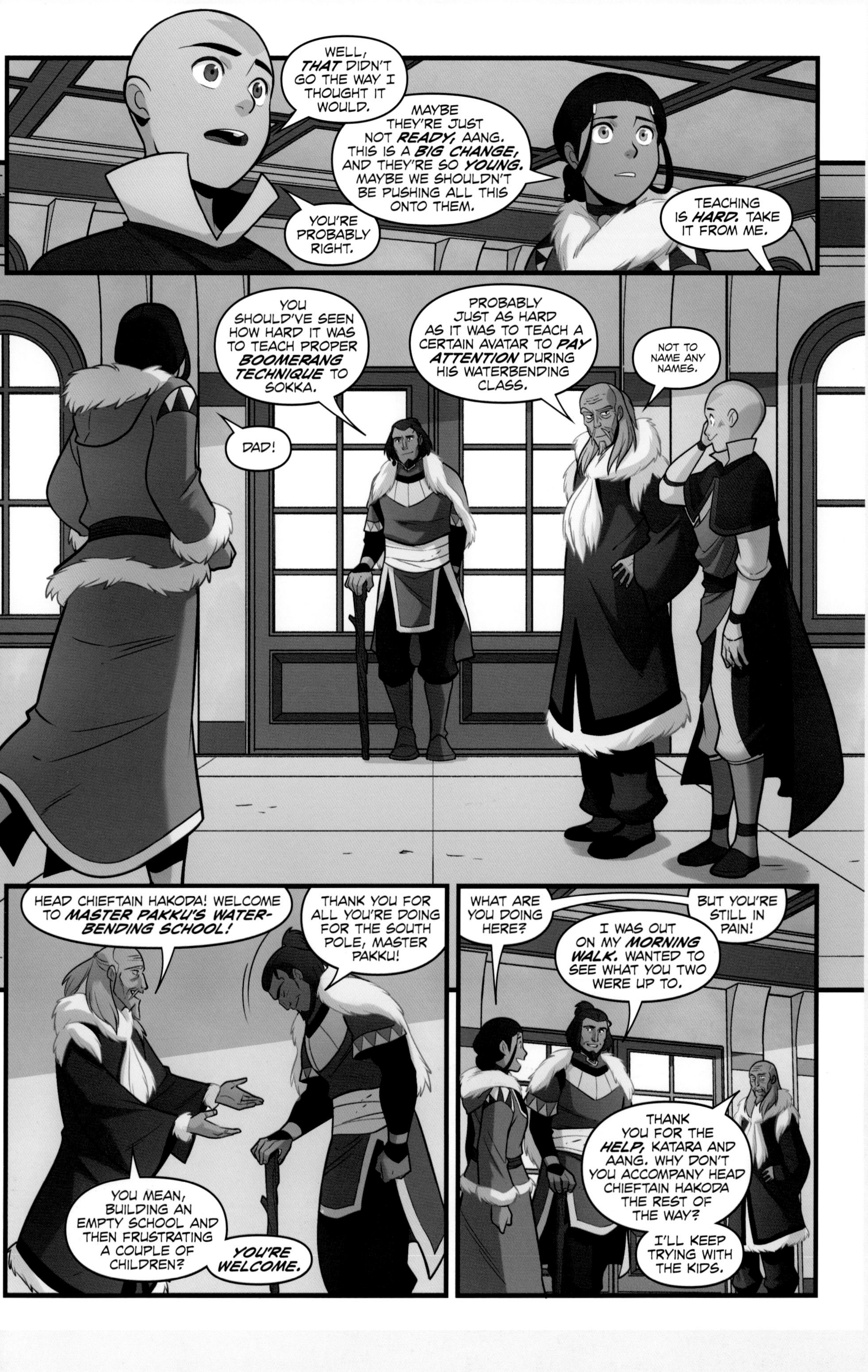
WELL, THAT DIDN'T GO THE WAY I THOUGHT IT WOULD.
MAYBE THEY'RE JUST NOT READY, AANG. THIS IS A BIG CHANGE, AND THEY'RE SO YOUNG. MAYBE WE SHOULDN'T BE PUSHING ALL THIS ONTO THEM.
YOU'RE PROBABLY RIGHT.
TEACHING IS HARD. TAKE IT FROM ME.
YOU SHOULD'VE SEEN HOW HARD IT WAS TO TEACH PROPER BOOMERANG TECHNIQUE TO SOKKA.
DAD!
PROBABLY JUST AS HARD AS IT WAS TO TEACH A CERTAIN AVATAR TO PAY ATTENTION DURING HIS WATERBENDING CLASS.
NOT TO NAME ANY NAMES.
HEAD CHIEFTAIN HAKODA! WELCOME TO MASTER PAKKU'S WATER-BENDING SCHOOL!
THANK YOU FOR ALL YOU'RE DOING FOR THE SOUTH POLE, MASTER PAKKU!
YOU MEAN, BUILDING AN EMPTY SCHOOL AND THEN FRUSTRATING A COUPLE OF CHILDREN?
YOU'RE WELCOME.
WHAT ARE YOU DOING HERE?
BUT YOU'RE STILL IN PAIN!
I WAS OUT ON MY MORNING WALK. WANTED TO SEE WHAT YOU TWO WERE UP TO.
THANK YOU FOR THE HELP, KATARA AND AANG. WHY DON'T YOU ACCOMPANY HEAD CHIEFTAIN HAKODA THE REST OF THE WAY?
I'LL KEEP TRYING WITH THE KIDS.

GLY: *Pakku is referring to events in the episode "The Siege of the North, Part 1." That was when Katara's hard work outpaced Aang's natural talent.*

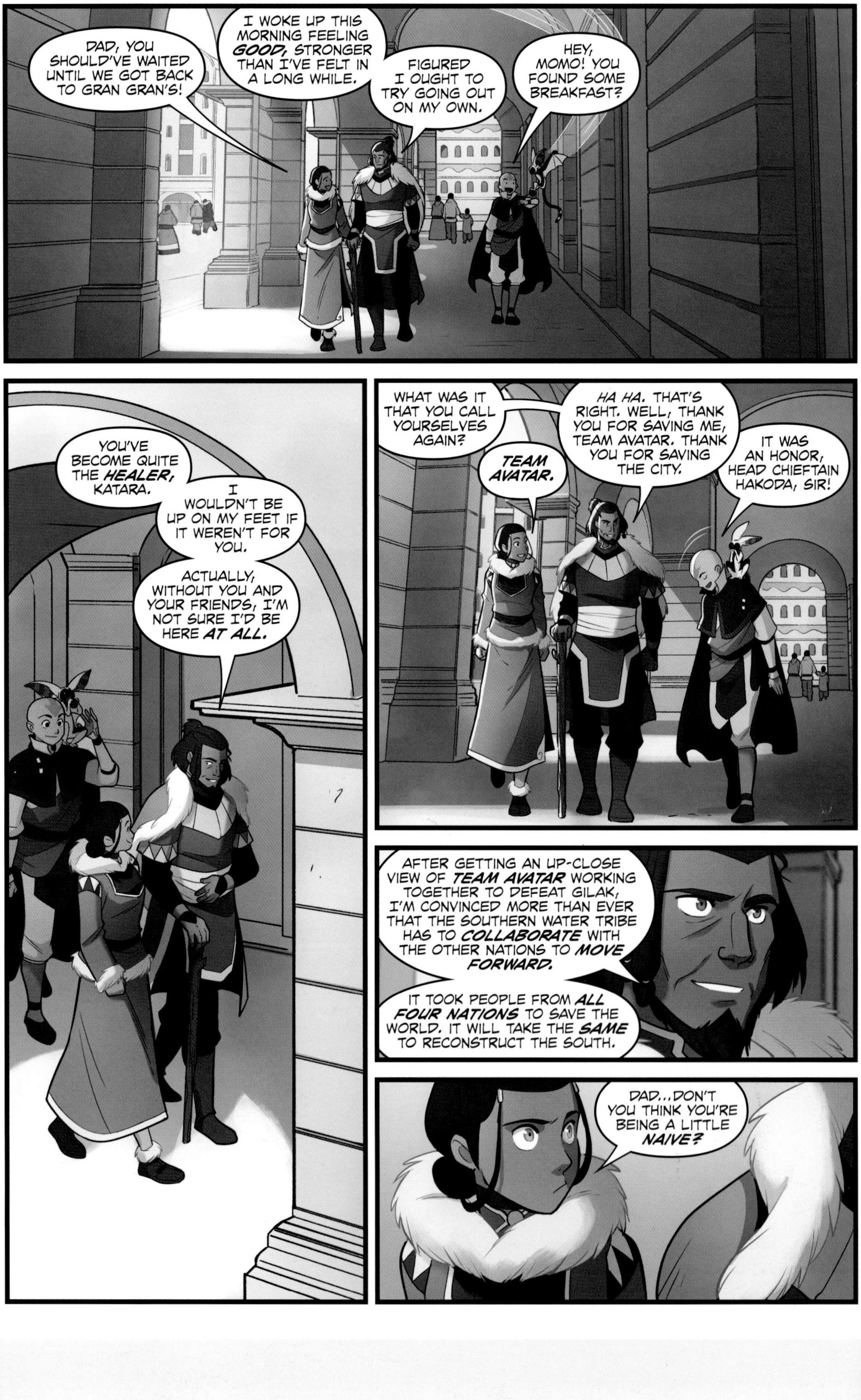
DAD, YOU SHOULD'VE WAITED UNTIL WE GOT BACK TO GRAN GRAN'S!
I WOKE UP THIS MORNING FEELING GOOD, STRONGER THAN I'VE FELT IN A LONG WHILE.
FIGURED I OUGHT TO TRY GOING OUT ON MY OWN.
HEY, MOMO! YOU FOUND SOME BREAKFAST?
YOU'VE BECOME QUITE THE HEALER, KATARA.
I WOULDN'T BE UP ON MY FEET IF IT WEREN'T FOR YOU.
ACTUALLY, WITHOUT YOU AND YOUR FRIENDS, I'M NOT SURE I'D BE HERE AT ALL.
WHAT WAS IT THAT YOU CALL YOURSELVES AGAIN?
TEAM AVATAR.
HA HA. THAT'S RIGHT. WELL, THANK YOU FOR SAVING ME, TEAM AVATAR. THANK YOU FOR SAVING THE CITY.
IT WAS AN HONOR, HEAD CHIEFTAIN HAKODA, SIR!
AFTER GETTING AN UP-CLOSE VIEW OF TEAM AVATAR WORKING TOGETHER TO DEFEAT GILAK, I'M CONVINCED MORE THAN EVER THAT THE SOUTHERN WATER TRIBE HAS TO COLLABORATE WITH THE OTHER NATIONS TO MOVE FORWARD.
IT TOOK PEOPLE FROM ALL FOUR NATIONS TO SAVE THE WORLD. IT WILL TAKE THE SAME TO RECONSTRUCT THE SOUTH.
DAD...DON'T YOU THINK YOU'RE BEING A LITTLE NAIVE?

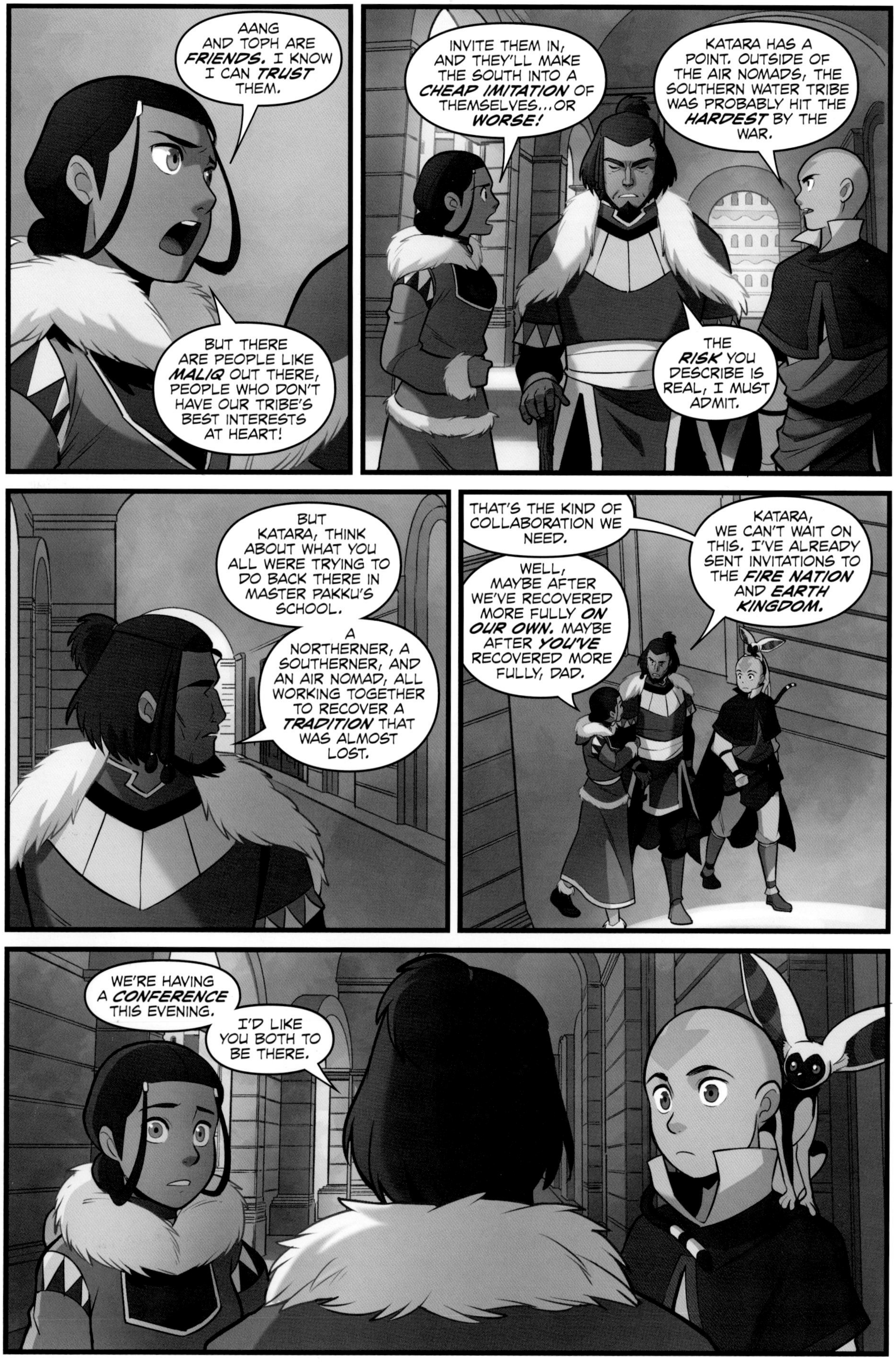
AANG AND TOPH ARE FRIENDS. I KNOW I CAN TRUST THEM.
BUT THERE ARE PEOPLE LIKE MALIQ OUT THERE, PEOPLE WHO DON'T HAVE OUR TRIBE'S BEST INTERESTS AT HEART!
INVITE THEM IN, AND THEY'LL MAKE THE SOUTH INTO A CHEAP IMITATION OF THEMSELVES...OR WORSE!
KATARA HAS A POINT. OUTSIDE OF THE AIR NOMADS, THE SOUTHERN WATER TRIBE WAS PROBABLY HIT THE HARDEST BY THE WAR.
THE RISK YOU DESCRIBE IS REAL, I MUST ADMIT.
BUT KATARA, THINK ABOUT WHAT YOU ALL WERE TRYING TO DO BACK THERE IN MASTER PAKKU'S SCHOOL.
A NORTHERNER, A SOUTHERNER, AND AN AIR NOMAD, ALL WORKING TOGETHER TO RECOVER A TRADITION THAT WAS ALMOST LOST.
THAT'S THE KIND OF COLLABORATION WE NEED.
WELL, MAYBE AFTER WE'VE RECOVERED MORE FULLY ON OUR OWN. MAYBE AFTER YOU'VE RECOVERED MORE FULLY, DAD.
KATARA, WE CAN'T WAIT ON THIS. I'VE ALREADY SENT INVITATIONS TO THE FIRE NATION AND EARTH KINGDOM.
WE'RE HAVING A CONFERENCE THIS EVENING.
I'D LIKE YOU BOTH TO BE THERE.

GLY: *Check out how Gurihiru draw airships! They're so good at drawing airships!*

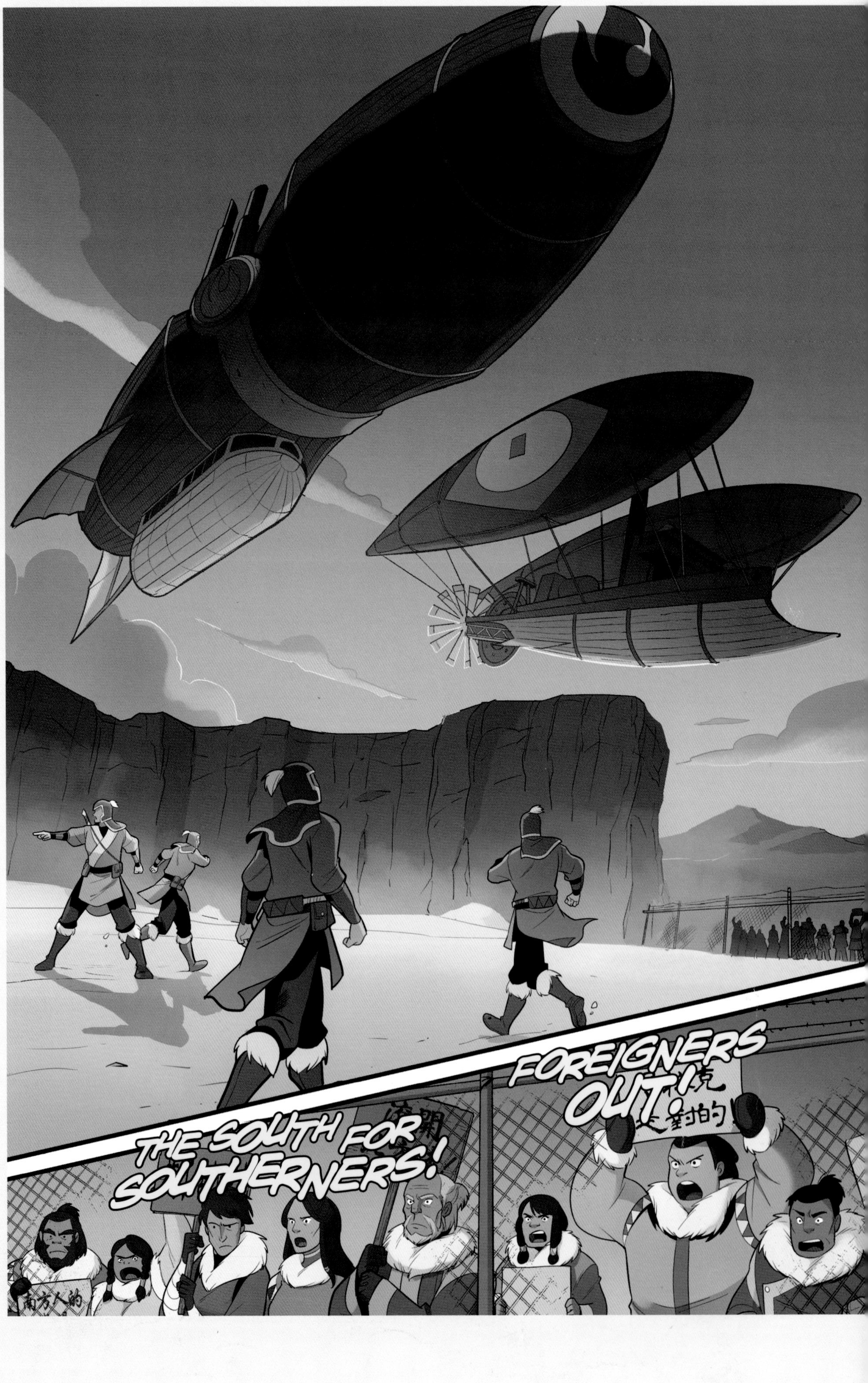
FOREIGNERS OUT!
THE SOUTH FOR SOUTHERNERS!

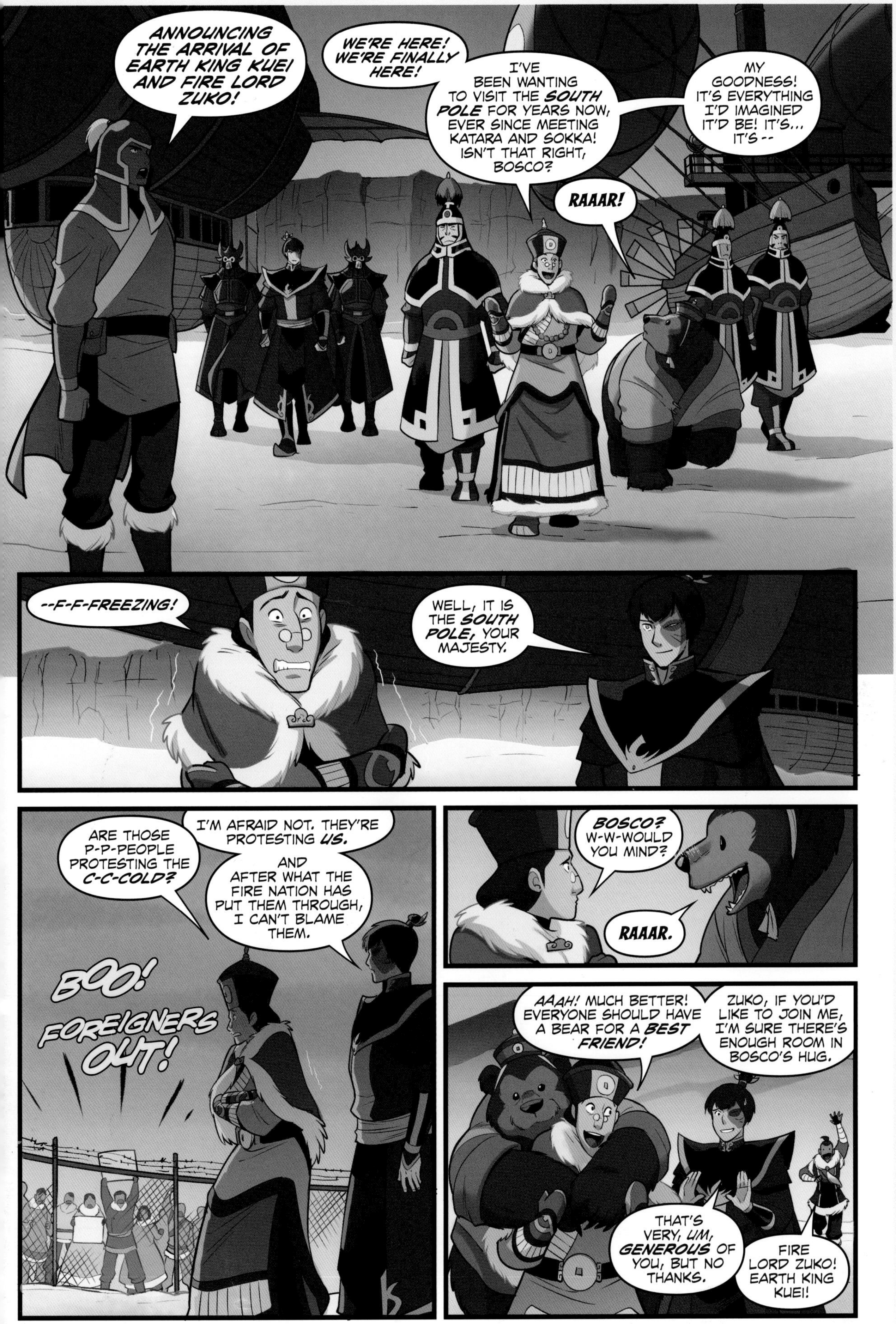
ANNOUNCING THE ARRIVAL OF EARTH KING KUEI AND FIRE LORD ZUKO!
WE'RE HERE! WE'RE FINALLY HERE!
I'VE BEEN WANTING TO VISIT THE SOUTH POLE FOR YEARS NOW, EVER SINCE MEETING KATARA AND SOKKA! ISN'T THAT RIGHT, BOSCO?
RAAAR!
MY GOODNESS! IT'S EVERYTHING I'D IMAGINED IT'D BE! IT'S... IT'S --
--F-F-FREEZING!
WELL, IT IS THE SOUTH POLE, YOUR MAJESTY.
ARE THOSE P-P-PEOPLE PROTESTING THE C-C-COLD?
I'M AFRAID NOT. THEY'RE PROTESTING US.
AND AFTER WHAT THE FIRE NATION HAS PUT THEM THROUGH, I CAN'T BLAME THEM.
BOO!
FOREIGNERS OUT!
BOSCO? W-W-WOULD YOU MIND?
RAAAR.
AAAH! MUCH BETTER! EVERYONE SHOULD HAVE A BEAR FOR A BEST FRIEND!
ZUKO, IF YOU'D LIKE TO JOIN ME, I'M SURE THERE'S ENOUGH ROOM IN BOSCO'S HUG.
THAT'S VERY, UM, GENEROUS OF YOU, BUT NO THANKS.
FIRE LORD ZUKO! EARTH KING KUEI!

GLY: *Like I mentioned before, Gurihiru and I knew that this was going to be our last venture into the Avatar universe. We needed to gather the whole team together. Here's Zuko!*

G: *It's been a while since we last drew Kuei! We enjoy drawing the little moments between Bosco and Kuei.*

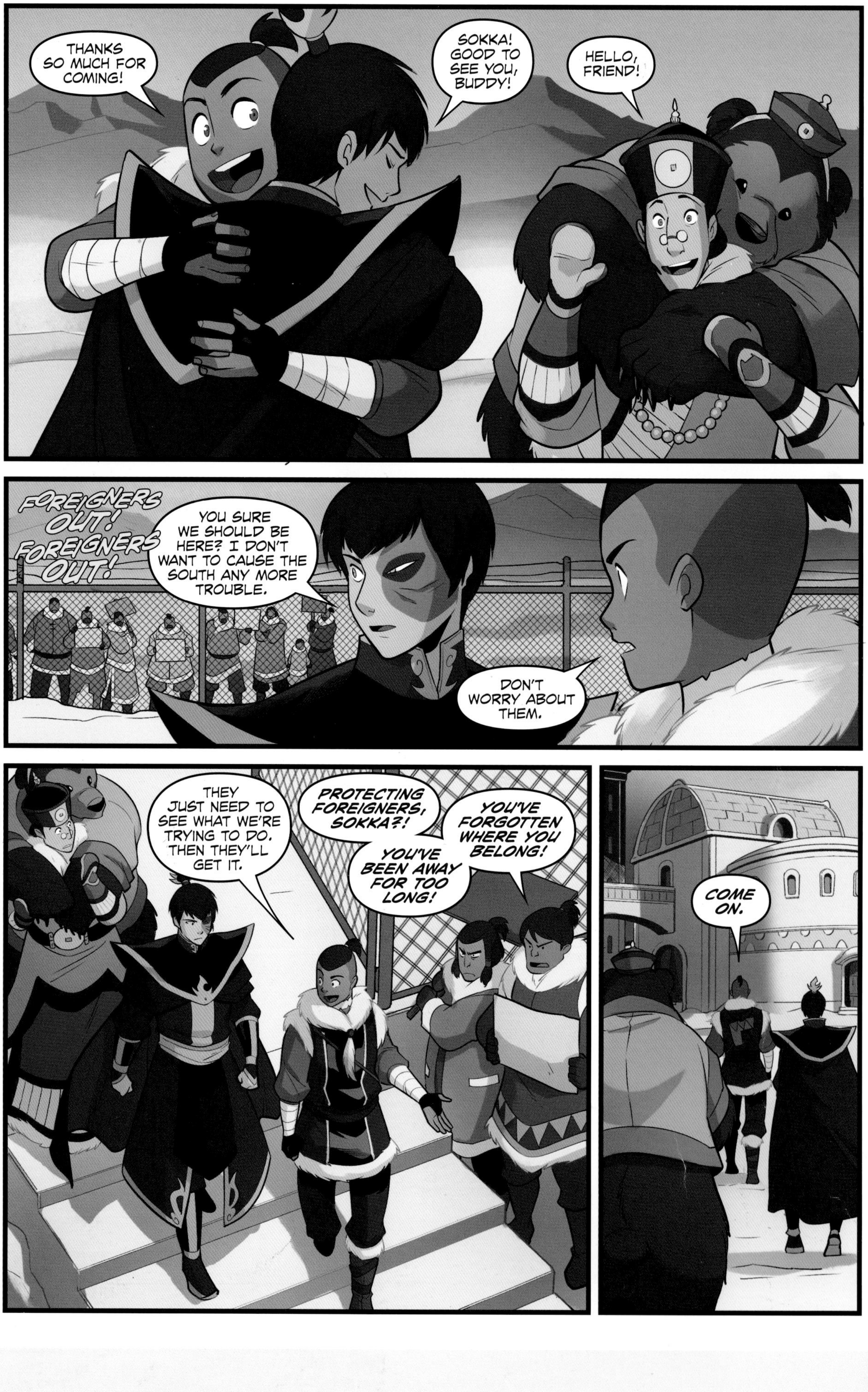
THANKS SO MUCH FOR COMING!
SOKKA! GOOD TO SEE YOU, BUDDY!
HELLO, FRIEND!
FOREIGNERS OUT! FOREIGNERS OUT!
YOU SURE WE SHOULD BE HERE? I DON'T WANT TO CAUSE THE SOUTH ANY MORE TROUBLE.
DON'T WORRY ABOUT THEM.
THEY JUST NEED TO SEE WHAT WE'RE TRYING TO DO. THEN THEY'LL GET IT.
PROTECTING FOREIGNERS, SOKKA?!
YOU'VE BEEN AWAY FOR TOO LONG!
YOU'VE FORGOTTEN WHERE YOU BELONG!
COME ON.

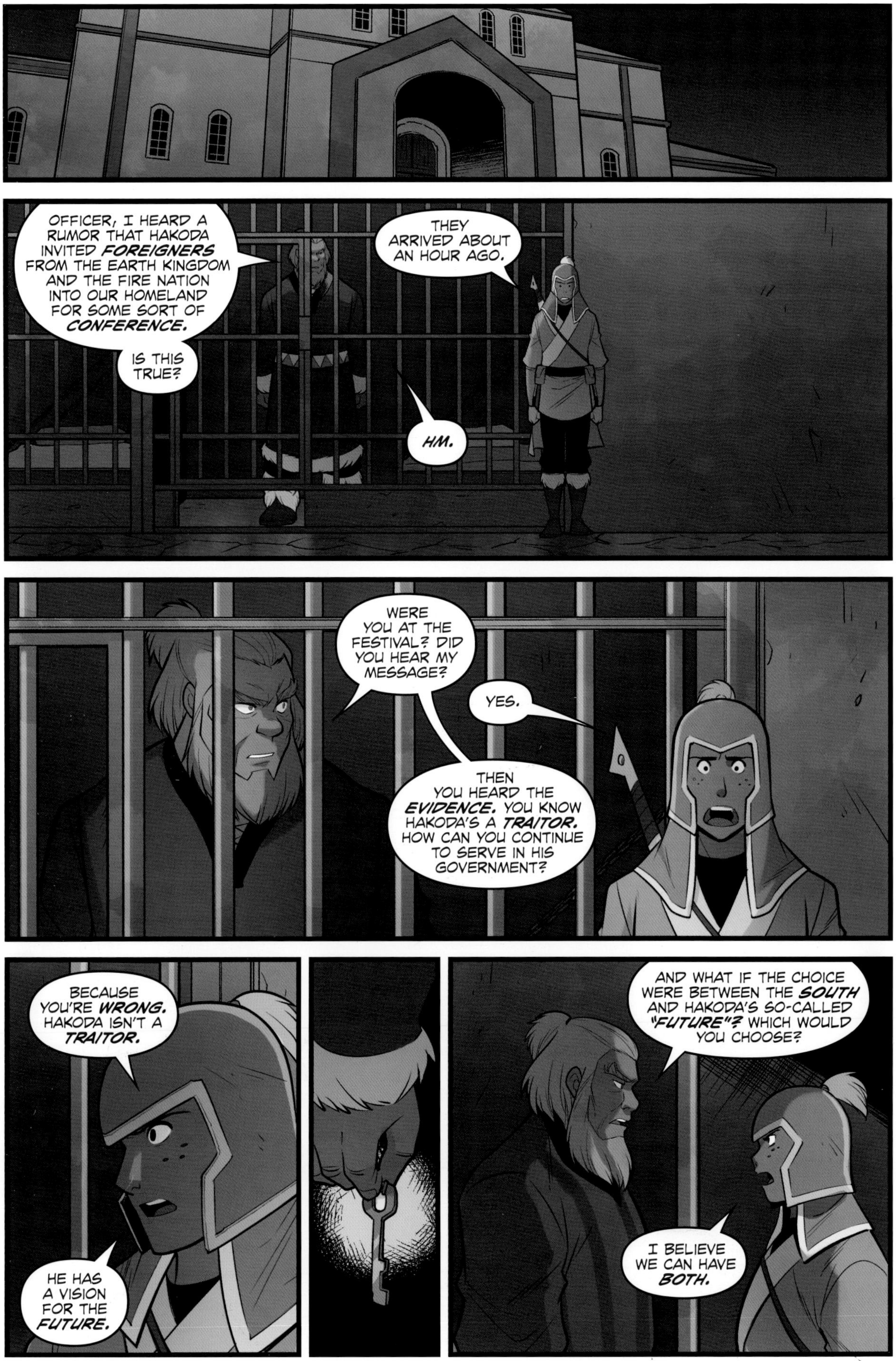
OFFICER, I HEARD A RUMOR THAT HAKODA INVITED FOREIGNERS FROM THE EARTH KINGDOM AND THE FIRE NATION INTO OUR HOMELAND FOR SOME SORT OF CONFERENCE.
IS THIS TRUE?
THEY ARRIVED ABOUT AN HOUR AGO.
HM.
WERE YOU AT THE FESTIVAL? DID YOU HEAR MY MESSAGE?
YES.
THEN YOU HEARD THE EVIDENCE. YOU KNOW HAKODA'S A TRAITOR. HOW CAN YOU CONTINUE TO SERVE IN HIS GOVERNMENT?
BECAUSE YOU'RE WRONG. HAKODA ISN'T A TRAITOR.
HE HAS A VISION FOR THE FUTURE.
AND WHAT IF THE CHOICE WERE BETWEEN THE SOUTH AND HAKODA'S SO-CALLED "FUTURE"? WHICH WOULD YOU CHOOSE?
I BELIEVE WE CAN HAVE BOTH.

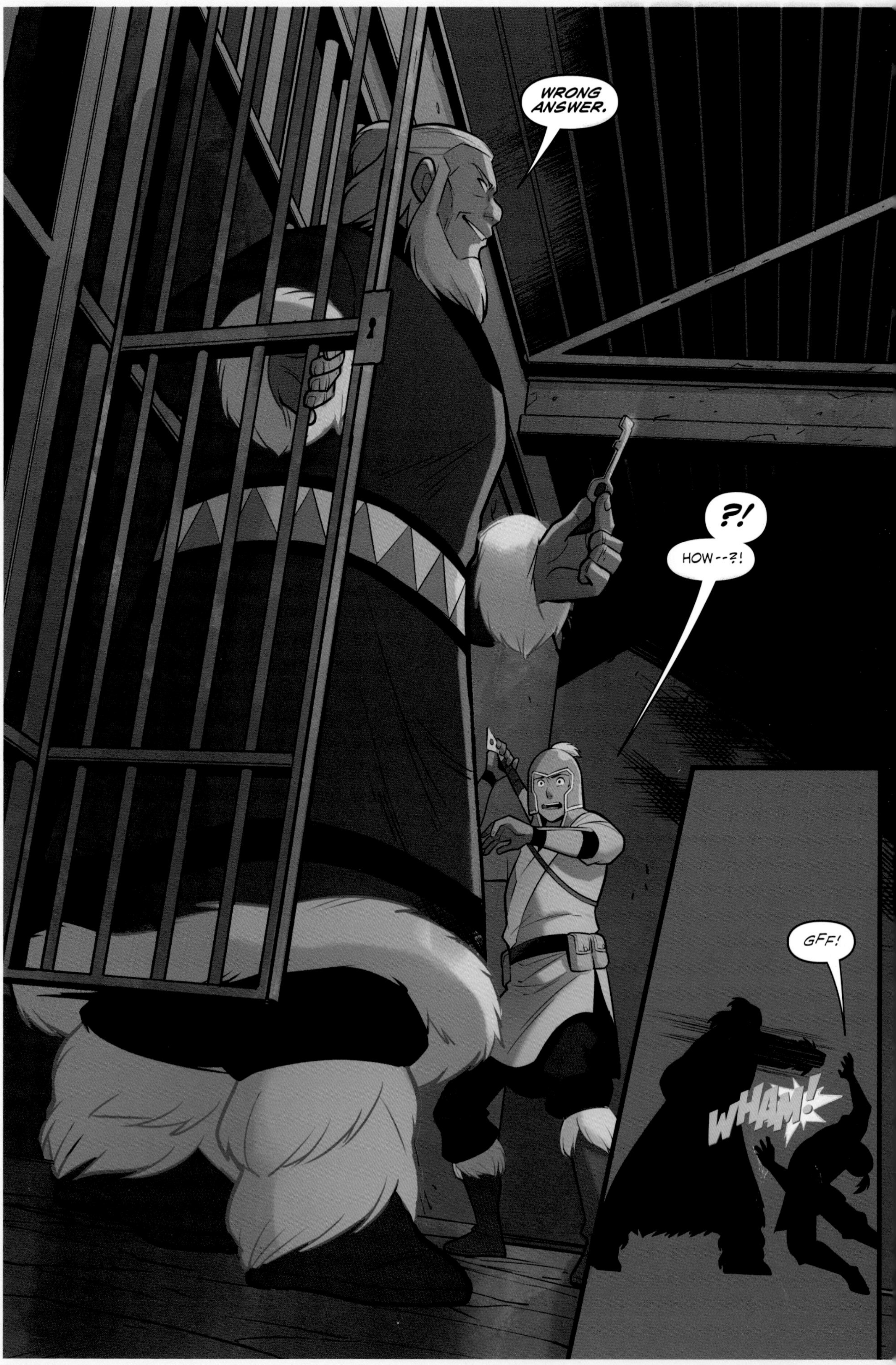
WRONG ANSWER.
?!
HOW--?!
GFF!
WHAM!

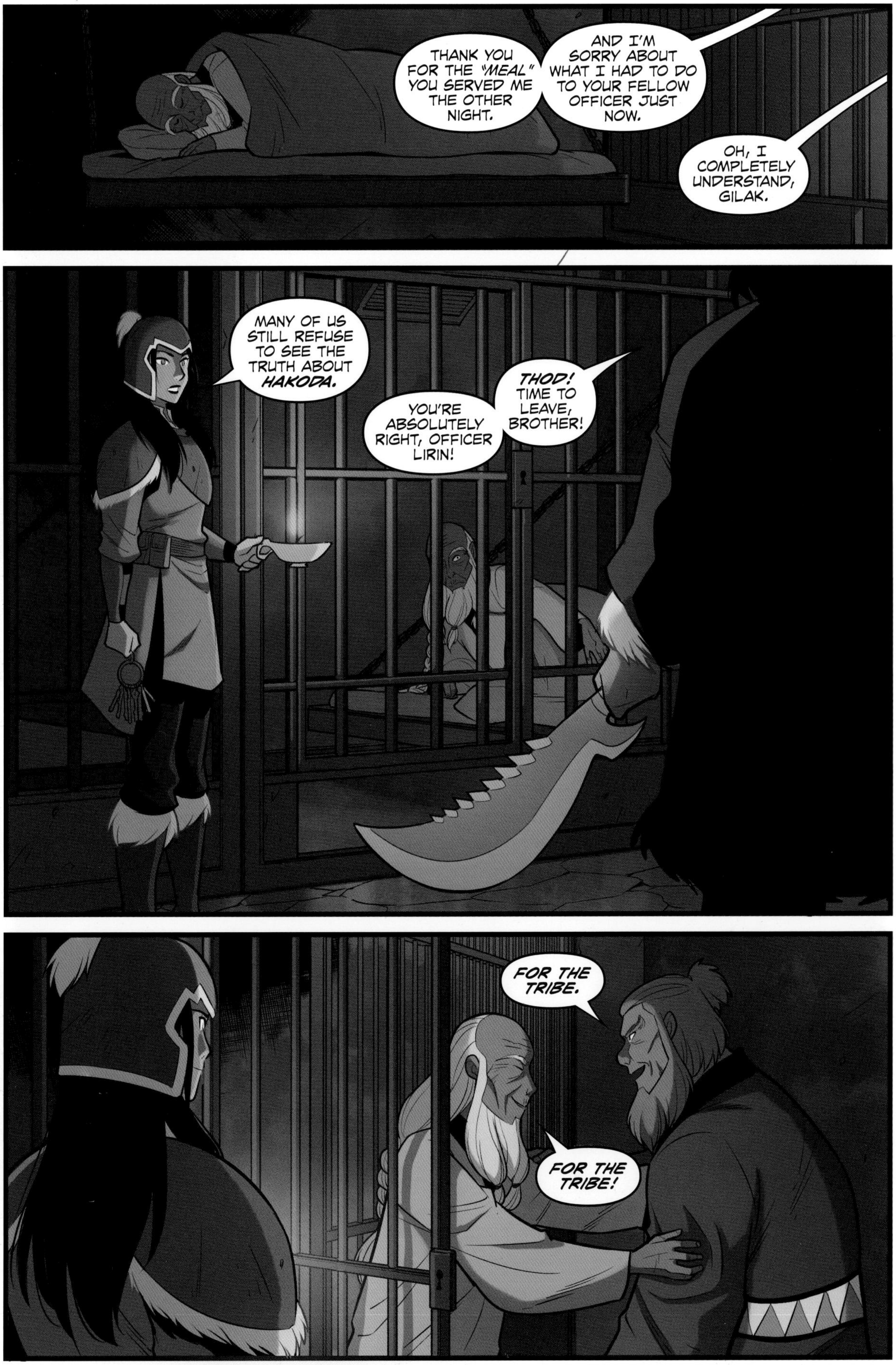
THANK YOU FOR THE "MEAL" YOU SERVED ME THE OTHER NIGHT.
AND I'M SORRY ABOUT WHAT I HAD TO DO TO YOUR FELLOW OFFICER JUST NOW.
OH, I COMPLETELY UNDERSTAND, GILAK.
MANY OF US STILL REFUSE TO SEE THE TRUTH ABOUT HAKODA.
YOU'RE ABSOLUTELY RIGHT, OFFICER LIRIN!
THOD! TIME TO LEAVE, BROTHER!
FOR THE TRIBE.
FOR THE TRIBE!

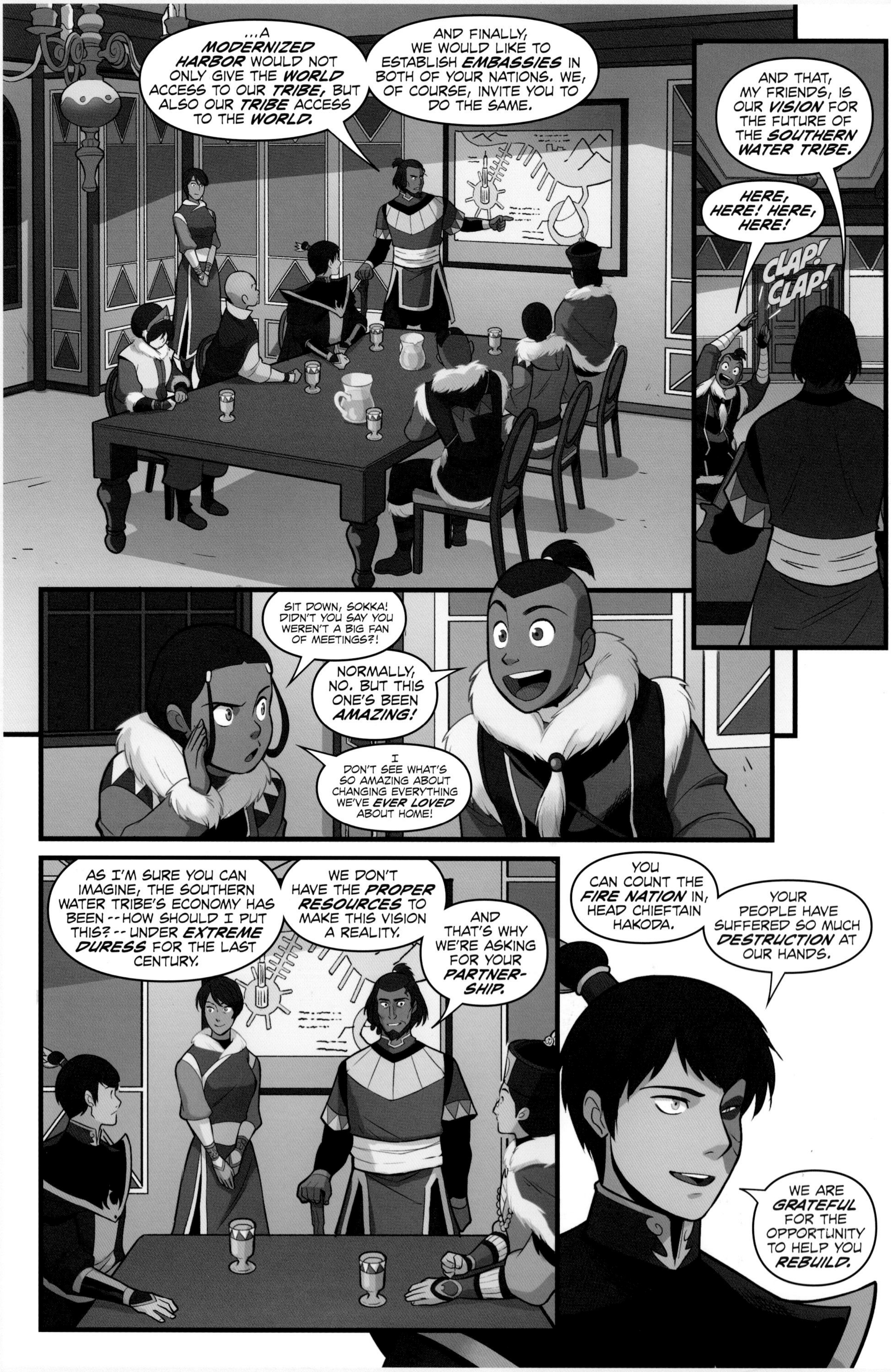
...A MODERNIZED HARBOR WOULD NOT ONLY GIVE THE WORLD ACCESS TO OUR TRIBE, BUT ALSO OUR TRIBE ACCESS TO THE WORLD.
AND FINALLY, WE WOULD LIKE TO ESTABLISH EMBASSIES IN BOTH OF YOUR NATIONS. WE, OF COURSE, INVITE YOU TO DO THE SAME.
AND THAT, MY FRIENDS, IS OUR VISION FOR THE FUTURE OF THE SOUTHERN WATER TRIBE.
HERE, HERE! HERE, HERE!
CLAP! CLAP!
SIT DOWN, SOKKA! DIDN'T YOU SAY YOU WEREN'T A BIG FAN OF MEETINGS?!
NORMALLY, NO. BUT THIS ONE'S BEEN AMAZING!
I DON'T SEE WHAT'S SO AMAZING ABOUT CHANGING EVERYTHING WE'VE EVER LOVED ABOUT HOME!
AS I'M SURE YOU CAN IMAGINE, THE SOUTHERN WATER TRIBE'S ECONOMY HAS BEEN -- HOW SHOULD I PUT THIS? -- UNDER EXTREME DURESS FOR THE LAST CENTURY.
WE DON'T HAVE THE PROPER RESOURCES TO MAKE THIS VISION A REALITY.
AND THAT'S WHY WE'RE ASKING FOR YOUR PARTNERSHIP.
YOU CAN COUNT THE FIRE NATION IN, HEAD CHIEFTAIN HAKODA.
YOUR PEOPLE HAVE SUFFERED SO MUCH DESTRUCTION AT OUR HANDS.
WE ARE GRATEFUL FOR THE OPPORTUNITY TO HELP YOU REBUILD.

G: *The map on the wall is a Southern Water Tribe port, but we drew it to look like the port from The Legend of Korra so it would have a visual connection.*

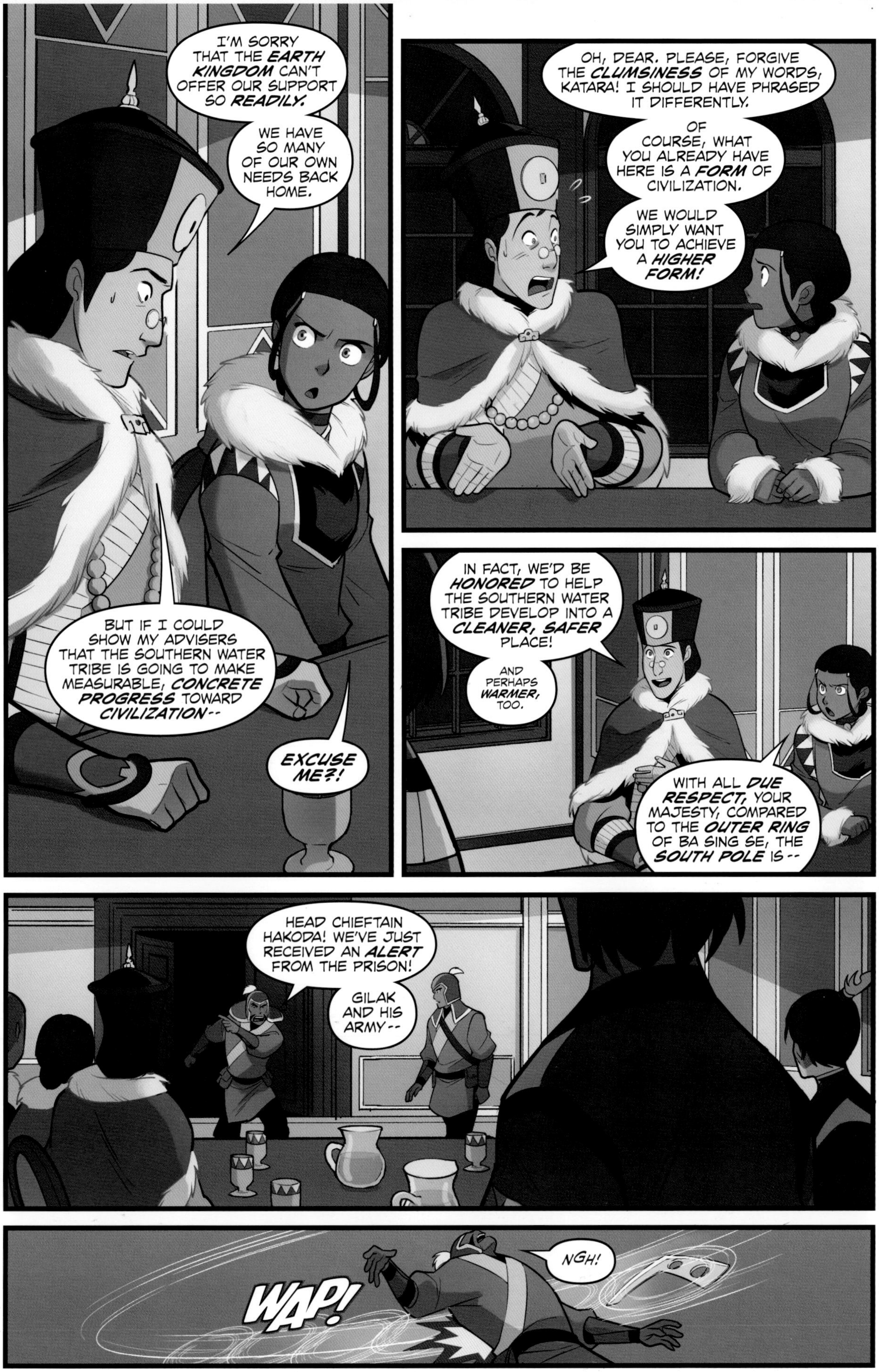
I'M SORRY THAT THE EARTH KINGDOM CAN'T OFFER OUR SUPPORT SO READILY.
WE HAVE SO MANY OF OUR OWN NEEDS BACK HOME.
BUT IF I COULD SHOW MY ADVISERS THAT THE SOUTHERN WATER TRIBE IS GOING TO MAKE MEASURABLE, CONCRETE PROGRESS TOWARD CIVILIZATION--
EXCUSE ME?!
OH, DEAR. PLEASE, FORGIVE THE CLUMSINESS OF MY WORDS, KATARA! I SHOULD HAVE PHRASED IT DIFFERENTLY.
OF COURSE, WHAT YOU ALREADY HAVE HERE IS A FORM OF CIVILIZATION.
WE WOULD SIMPLY WANT YOU TO ACHIEVE A HIGHER FORM!
IN FACT, WE'D BE HONORED TO HELP THE SOUTHERN WATER TRIBE DEVELOP INTO A CLEANER, SAFER PLACE!
AND PERHAPS WARMER, TOO.
WITH ALL DUE RESPECT, YOUR MAJESTY, COMPARED TO THE OUTER RING OF BA SING SE, THE SOUTH POLE IS--
HEAD CHIEFTAIN HAKODA! WE'VE JUST RECEIVED AN ALERT FROM THE PRISON!
GILAK AND HIS ARMY--
NGH!
WAP!

GLY: *In an earlier draft, Earth King Kuei was much more of a hard-liner. He looked down on the Southern Water Tribe and intentionally talked about them as a "lesser" form of civilization. Mike felt that it didn't line up with Kuei's portrayal in the show. I totally agree. I like this dynamic between Kuei and Katara so much better.*

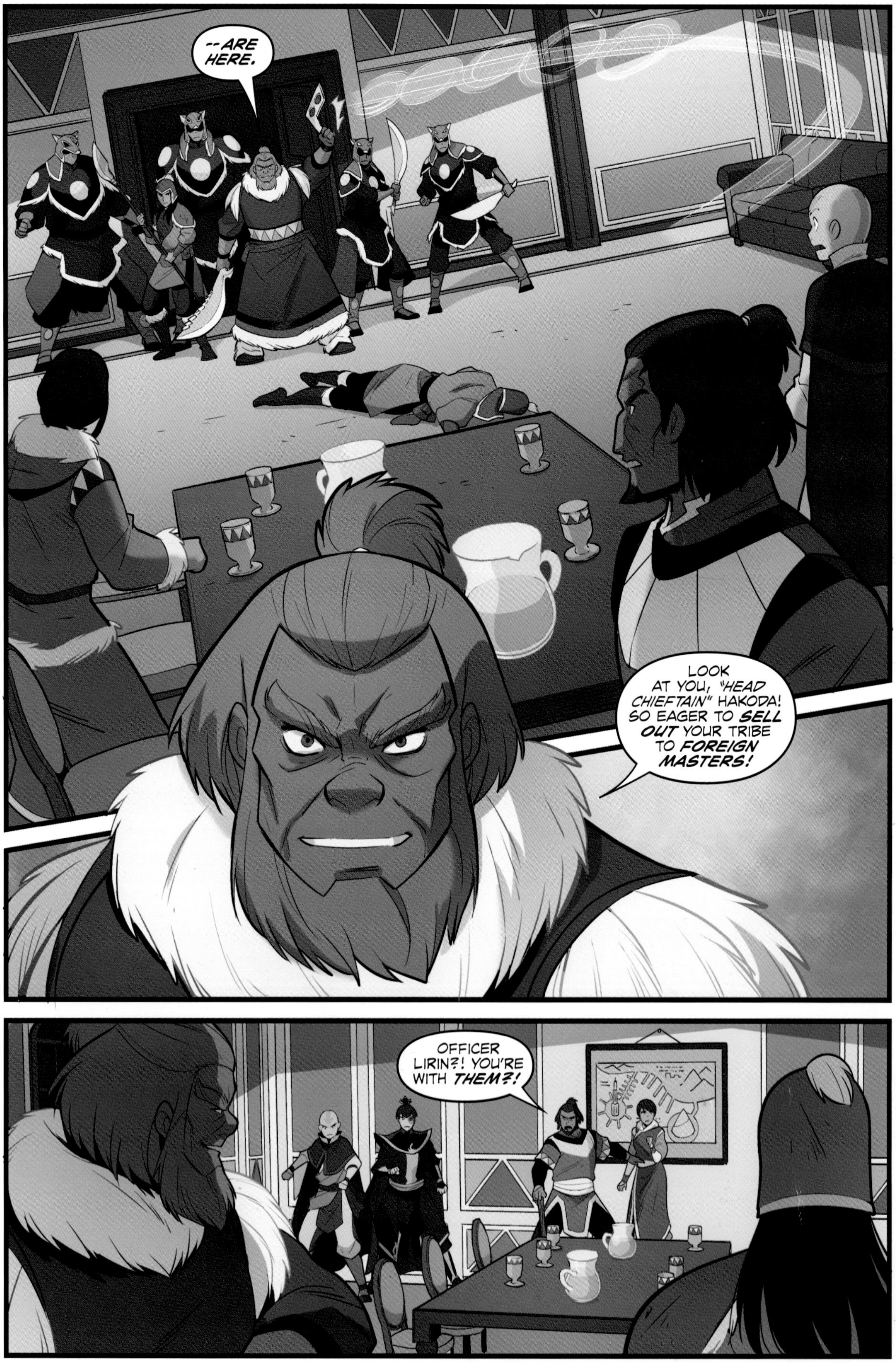
--ARE HERE.
LOOK AT YOU, "HEAD CHIEFTAIN" HAKODA! SO EAGER TO SELL OUT YOUR TRIBE TO FOREIGN MASTERS!
OFFICER LIRIN?! YOU'RE WITH THEM?!

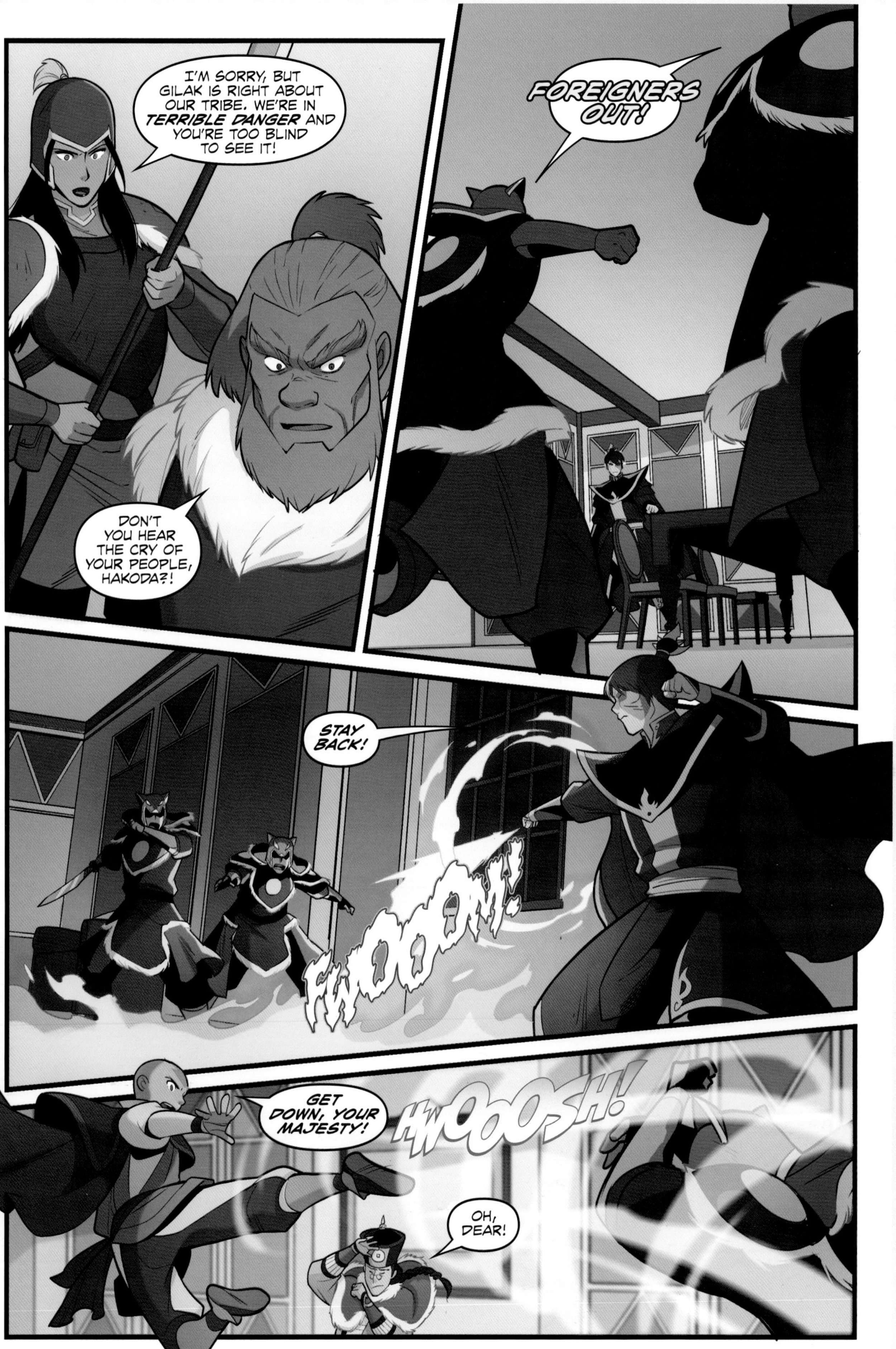
I'M SORRY, BUT GILAK IS RIGHT ABOUT OUR TRIBE. WE'RE IN TERRIBLE DANGER AND YOU'RE TOO BLIND TO SEE IT!
DON'T YOU HEAR THE CRY OF YOUR PEOPLE, HAKODA?!
FOREIGNERS OUT!
STAY BACK!
FWOOOM!
GET DOWN, YOUR MAJESTY!
HWOOOSH!
OH, DEAR!

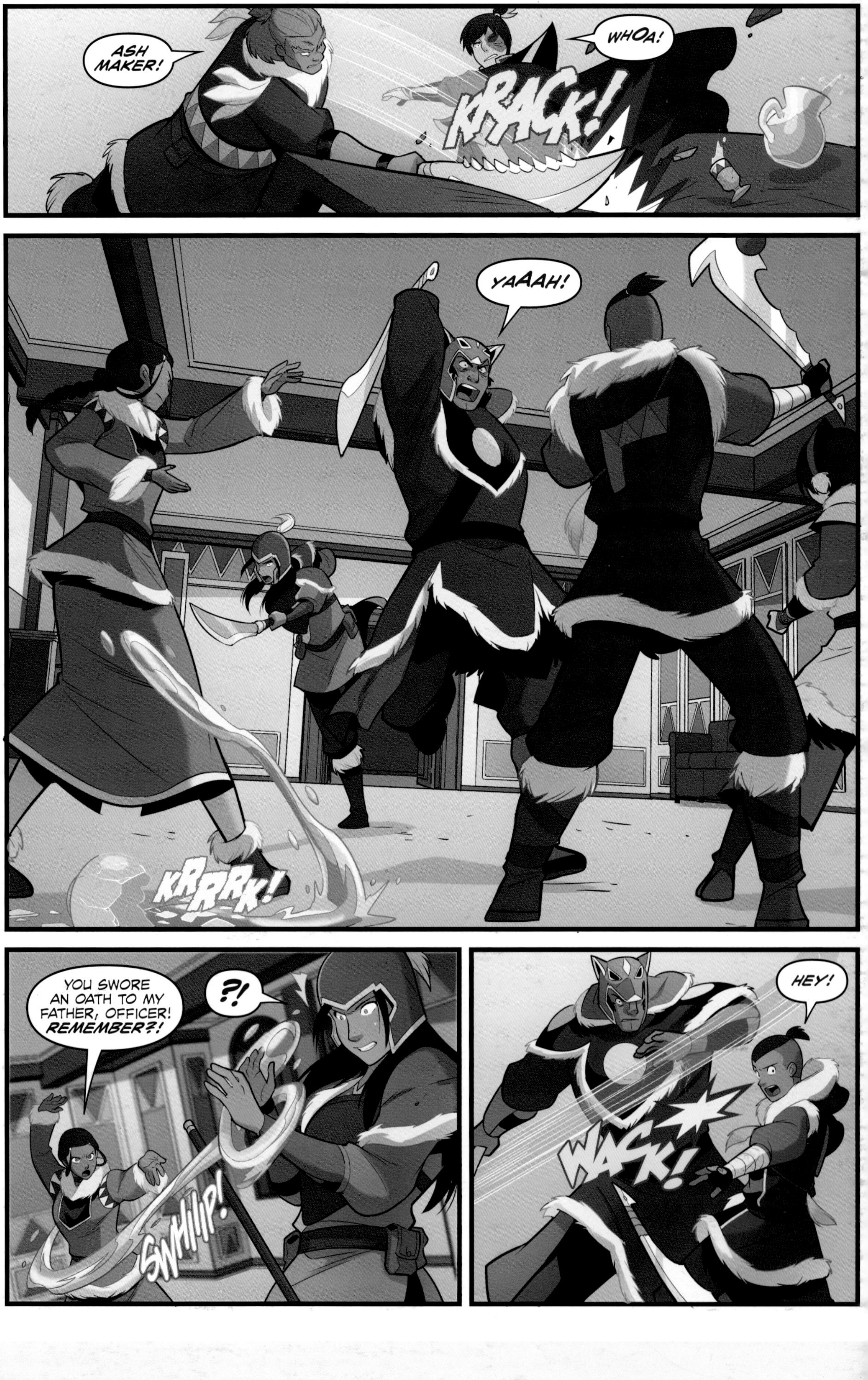
ASH MAKER!
WHOA!
KRACK!
YAAAH!
KRRRK!
YOU SWORE AN OATH TO MY FATHER, OFFICER! REMEMBER?!
?!
SWHIP!
HEY!
WACK!

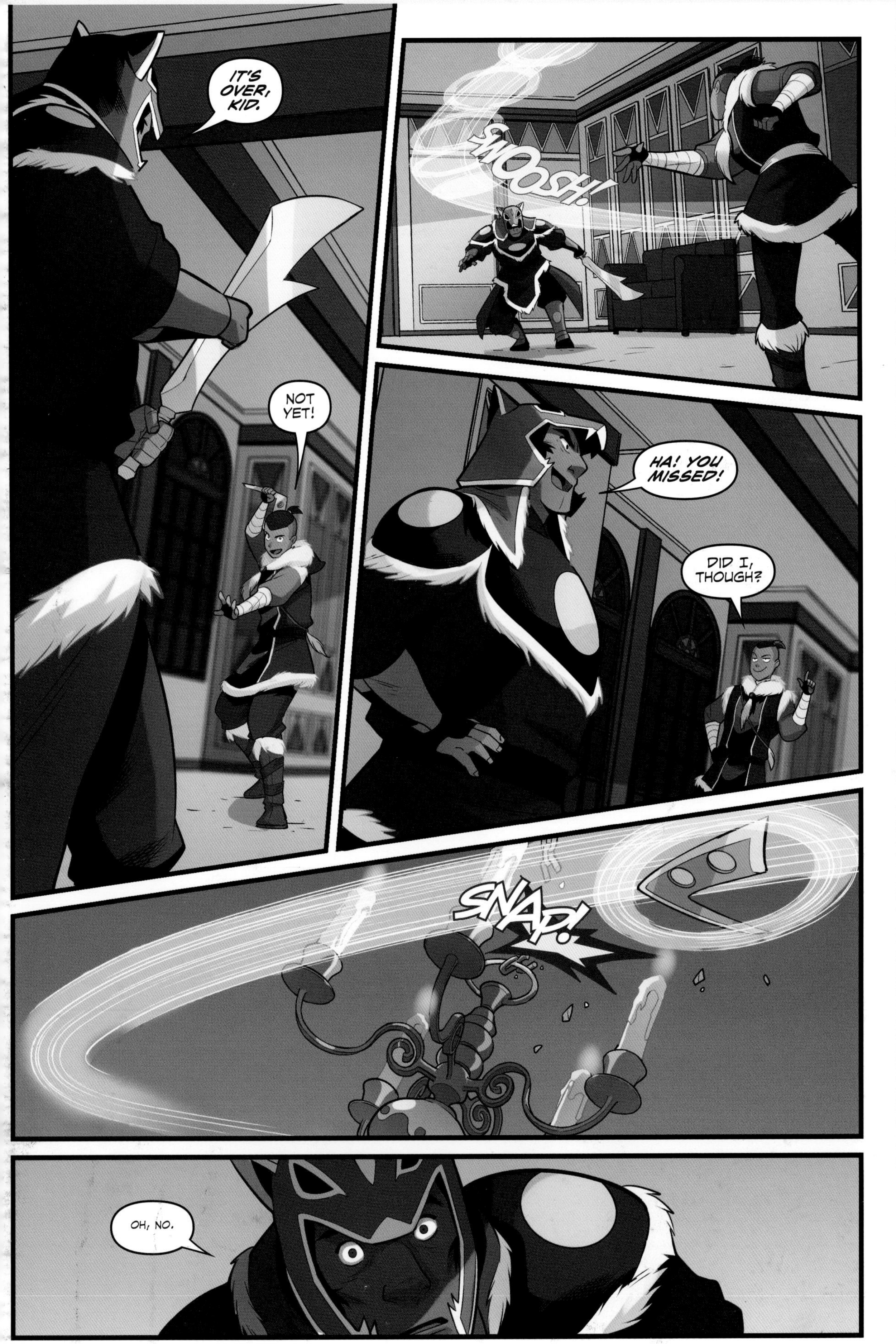
IT'S OVER, KID.
NOT YET!
SWOOSH!
HA! YOU MISSED!
DID I, THOUGH?
SNAP!
OH, NO.

GLY: *Toph's space rock shows up in The Promise. I wanted to use it one more time because I love it so much. I wish someone would sell physical replicas on Etsy.*

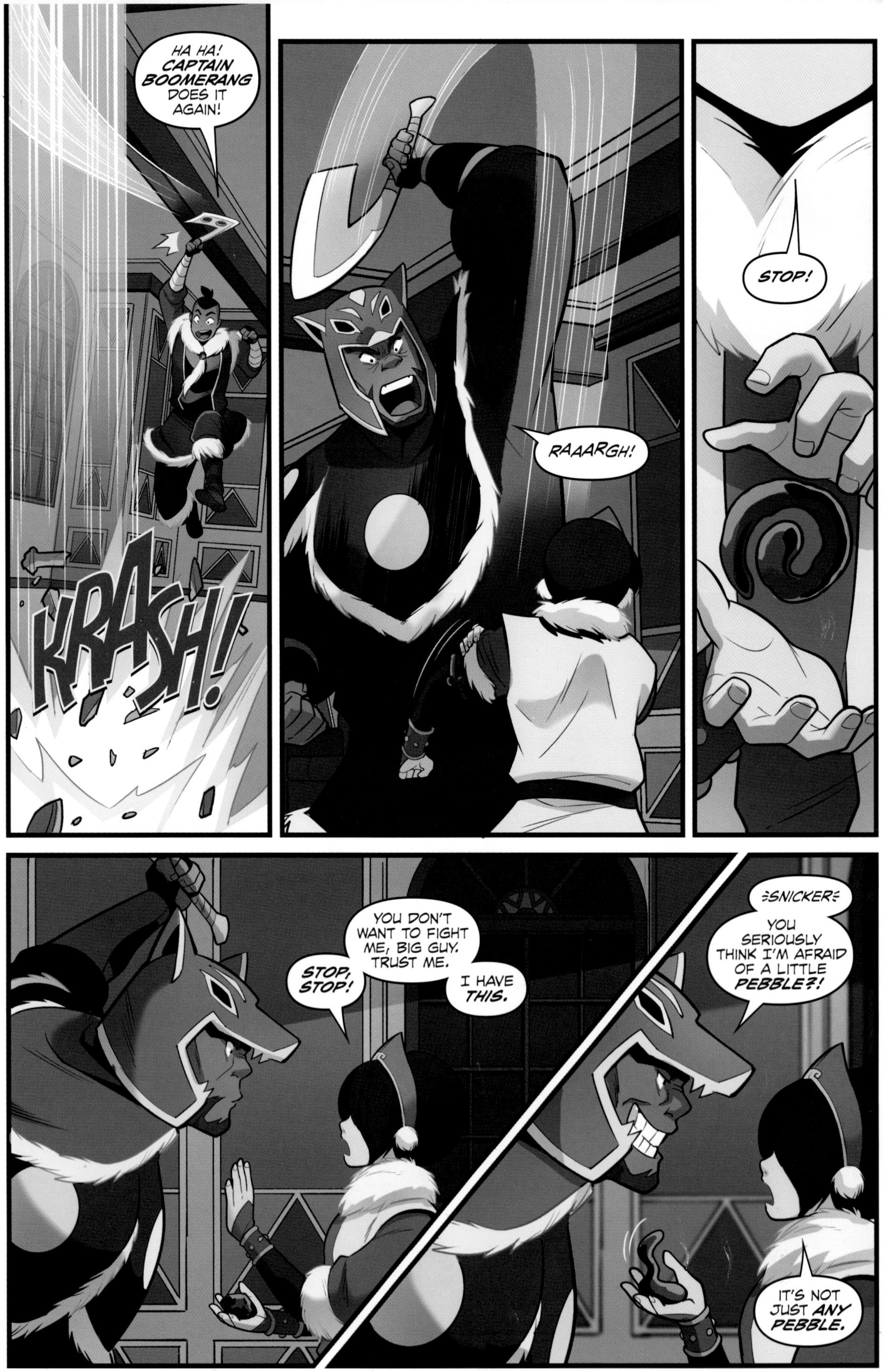
HA HA! CAPTAIN BOOMERANG DOES IT AGAIN!
KRASH!
RAAARGH!
STOP!
STOP, STOP!
YOU DON'T WANT TO FIGHT ME, BIG GUY. TRUST ME.
I HAVE THIS.
SNICKER
YOU SERIOUSLY THINK I'M AFRAID OF A LITTLE PEBBLE?!
IT'S NOT JUST ANY PEBBLE.

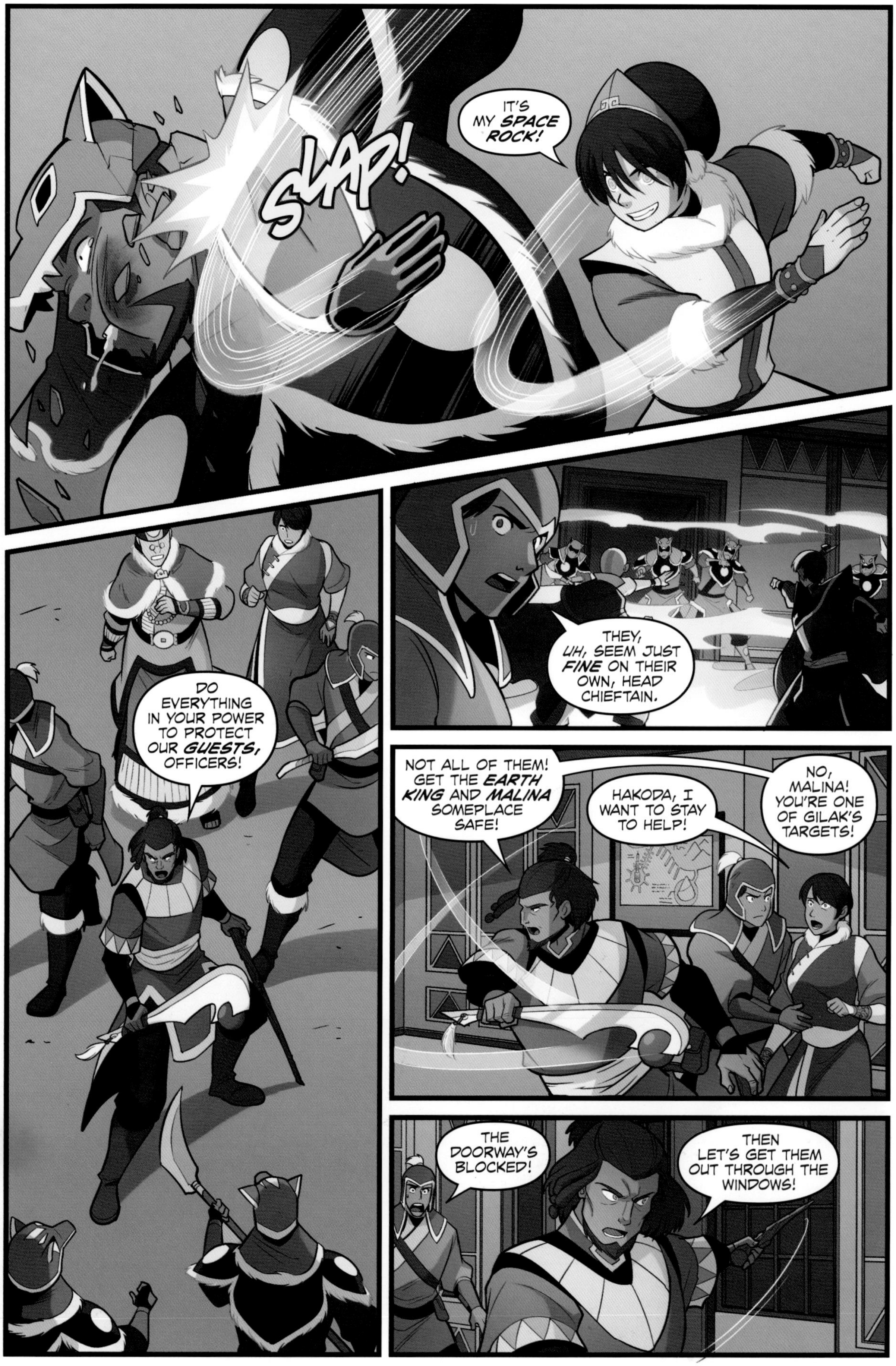
IT'S MY SPACE ROCK!
SLAP!
THEY, UH, SEEM JUST FINE ON THEIR OWN, HEAD CHIEFTAIN.
DO EVERYTHING IN YOUR POWER TO PROTECT OUR GUESTS, OFFICERS!
NOT ALL OF THEM! GET THE EARTH KING AND MALINA SOMEPLACE SAFE!
HAKODA, I WANT TO STAY TO HELP!
NO, MALINA! YOU'RE ONE OF GILAK'S TARGETS!
THE DOORWAY'S BLOCKED!
THEN LET'S GET THEM OUT THROUGH THE WINDOWS!

G: *This is the first time in the comics that Toph used her meteor bracelet to attack.*

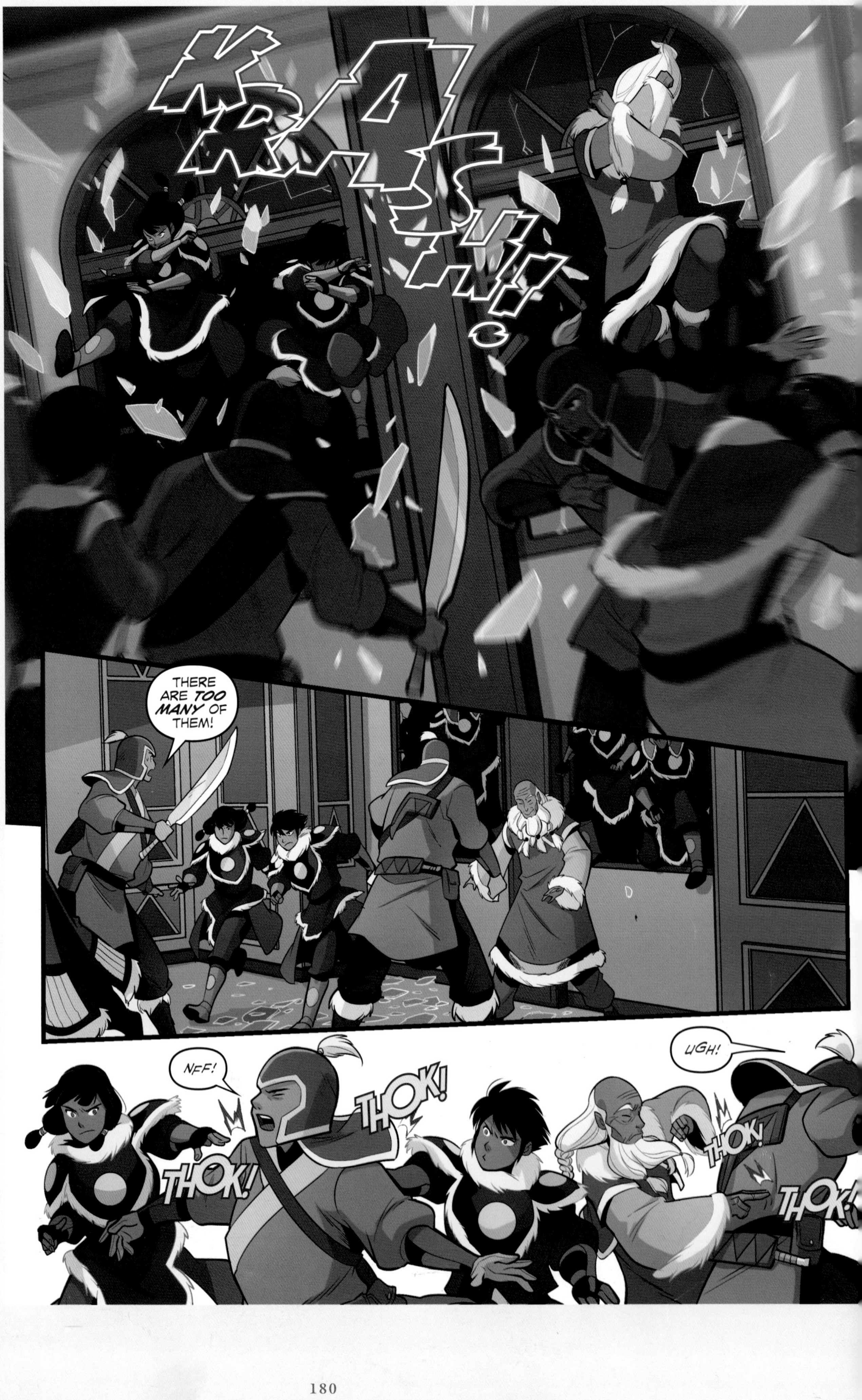
KRASSH!!
THERE ARE TOO MANY OF THEM!
NFF!
THOK!
UGH!
THOK!
THOK!
THOK!

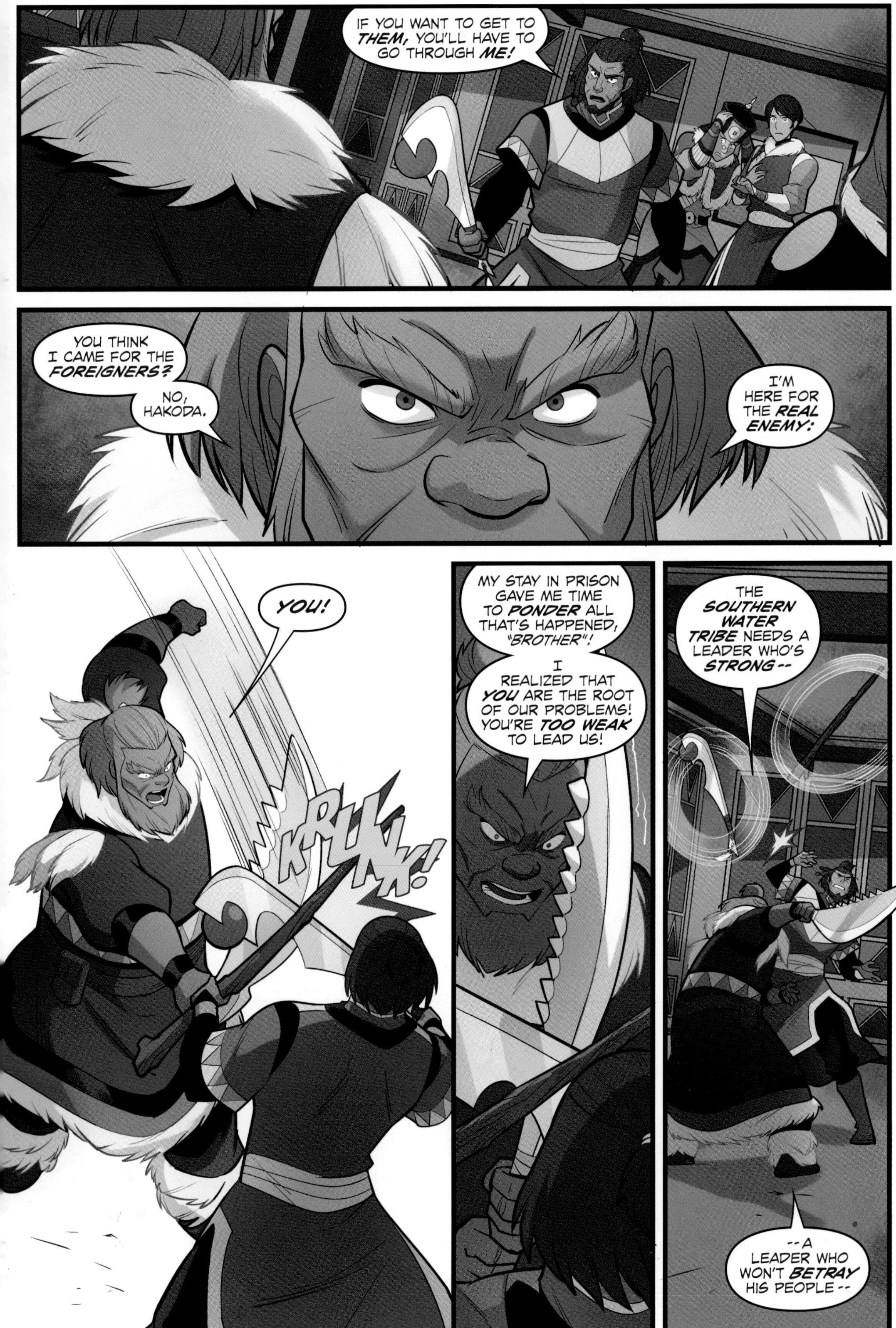
IF YOU WANT TO GET TO THEM, YOU'LL HAVE TO GO THROUGH ME!
YOU THINK I CAME FOR THE FOREIGNERS?
NO, HAKODA.
I'M HERE FOR THE REAL ENEMY:
YOU!
KRUNK!
MY STAY IN PRISON GAVE ME TIME TO PONDER ALL THAT'S HAPPENED, "BROTHER"!
I REALIZED THAT YOU ARE THE ROOT OF OUR PROBLEMS! YOU'RE TOO WEAK TO LEAD US!
THE SOUTHERN WATER TRIBE NEEDS A LEADER WHO'S STRONG--
--A LEADER WHO WON'T BETRAY HIS PEOPLE--

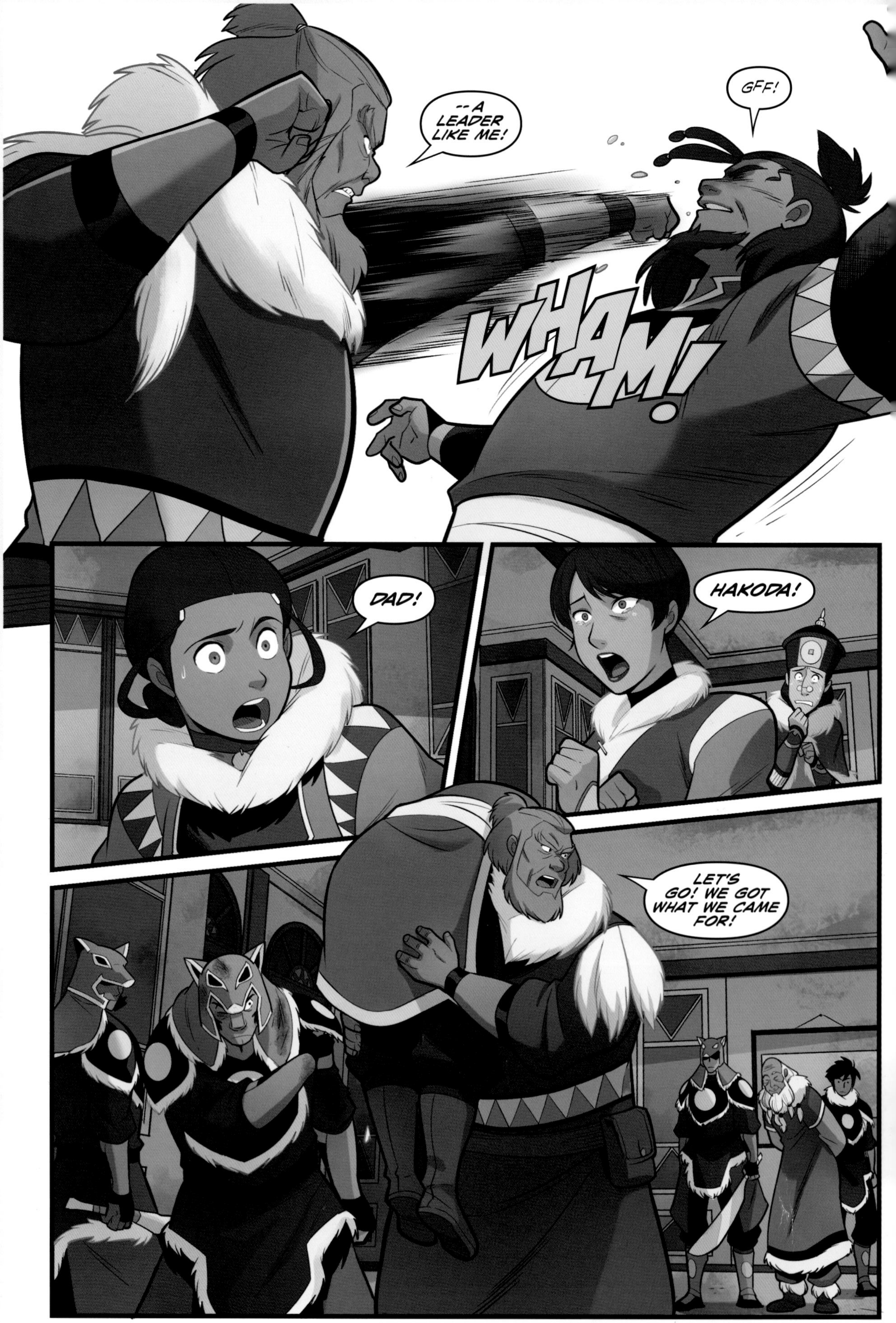
--A LEADER LIKE ME!
GFF!
WHAM!
DAD!
HAKODA!
LET'S GO! WE GOT WHAT WE CAME FOR!

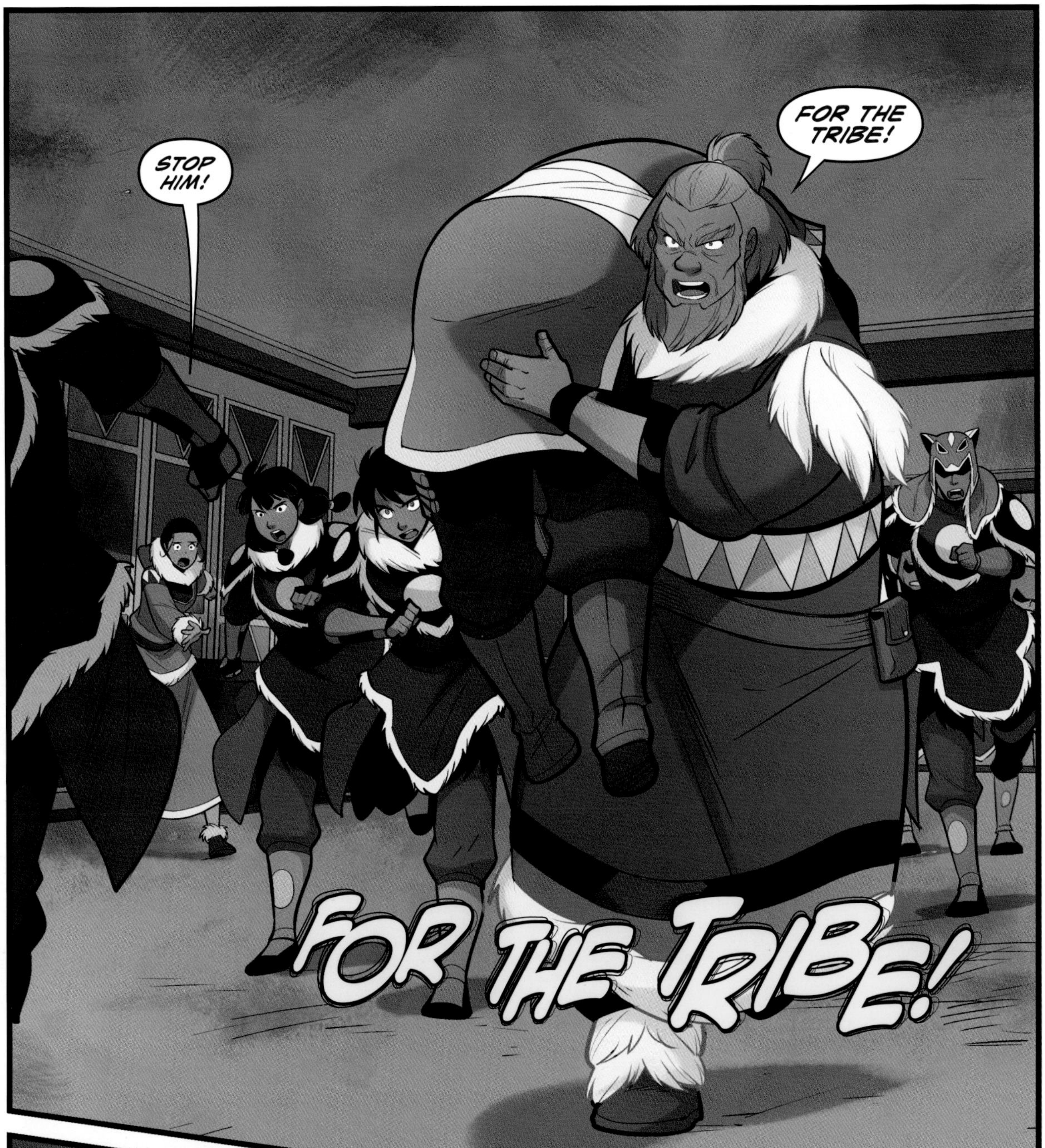
STOP HIM!
FOR THE TRIBE!
FOR THE TRIBE!

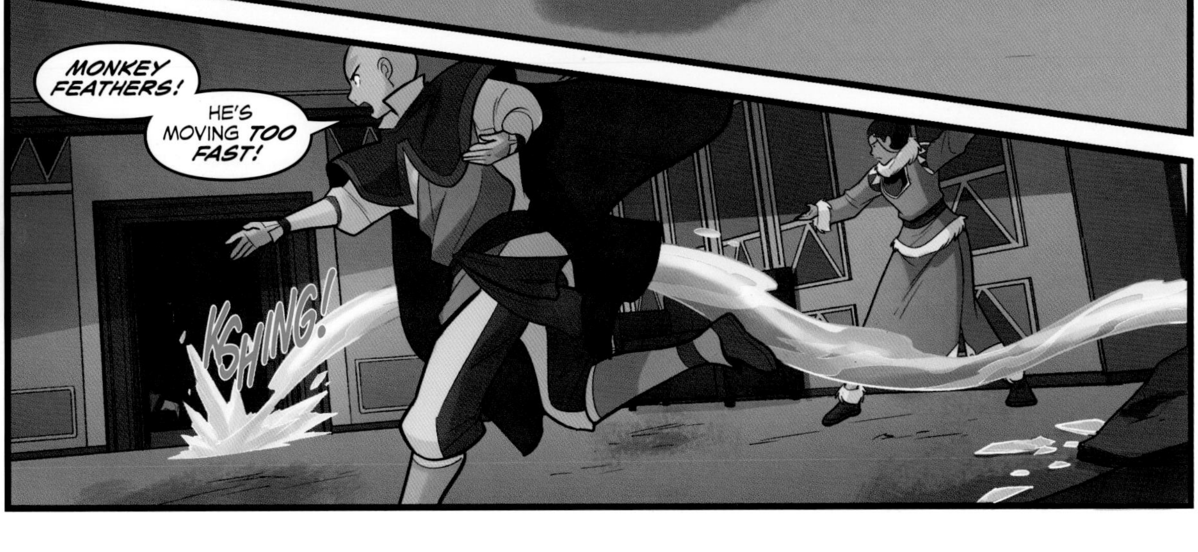
MONKEY FEATHERS!
HE'S MOVING TOO FAST!
KSHING!

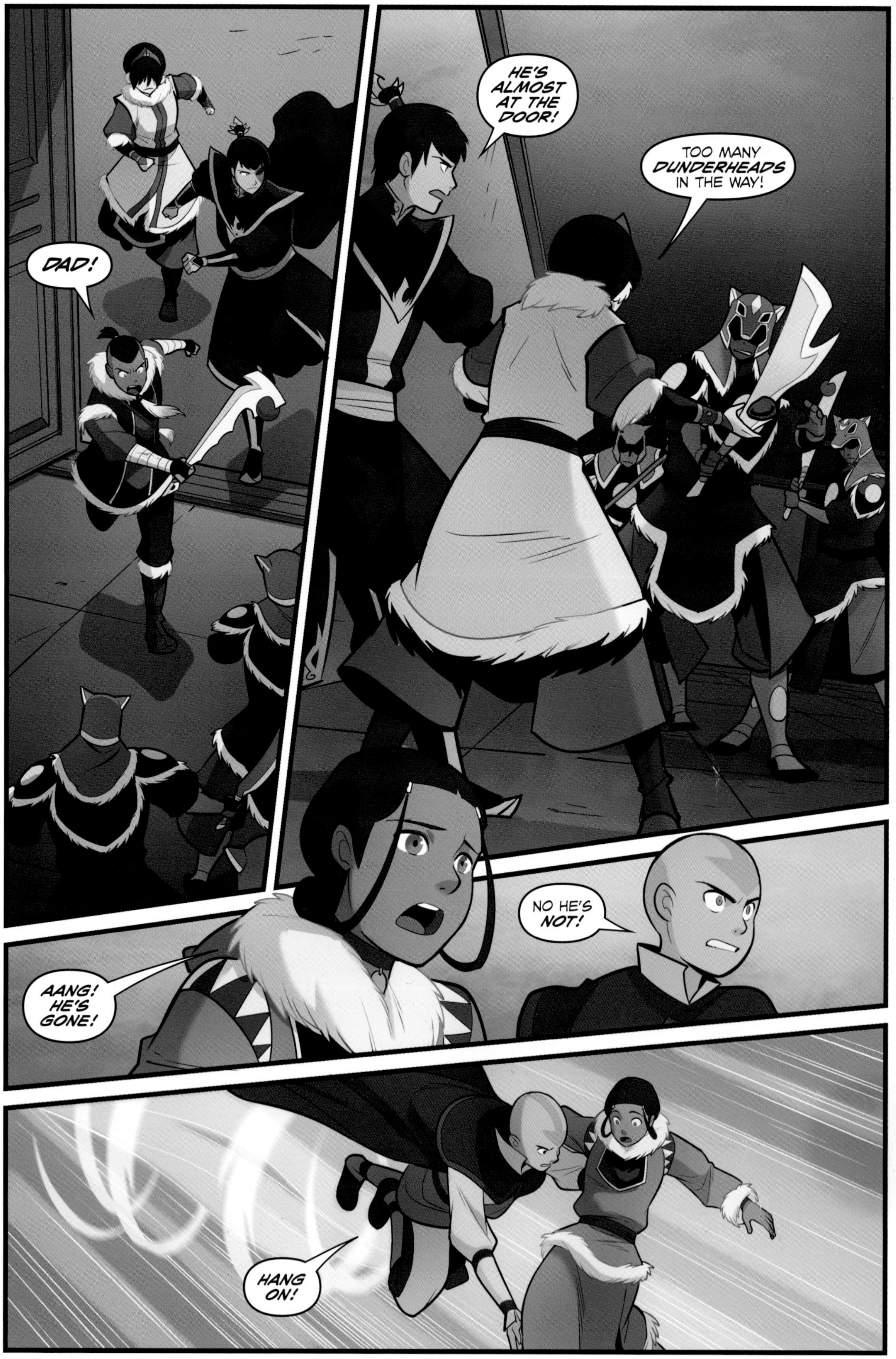
DAD!
HE'S ALMOST AT THE DOOR!
TOO MANY DUNDERHEADS IN THE WAY!
AANG! HE'S GONE!
NO HE'S NOT!
HANG ON!

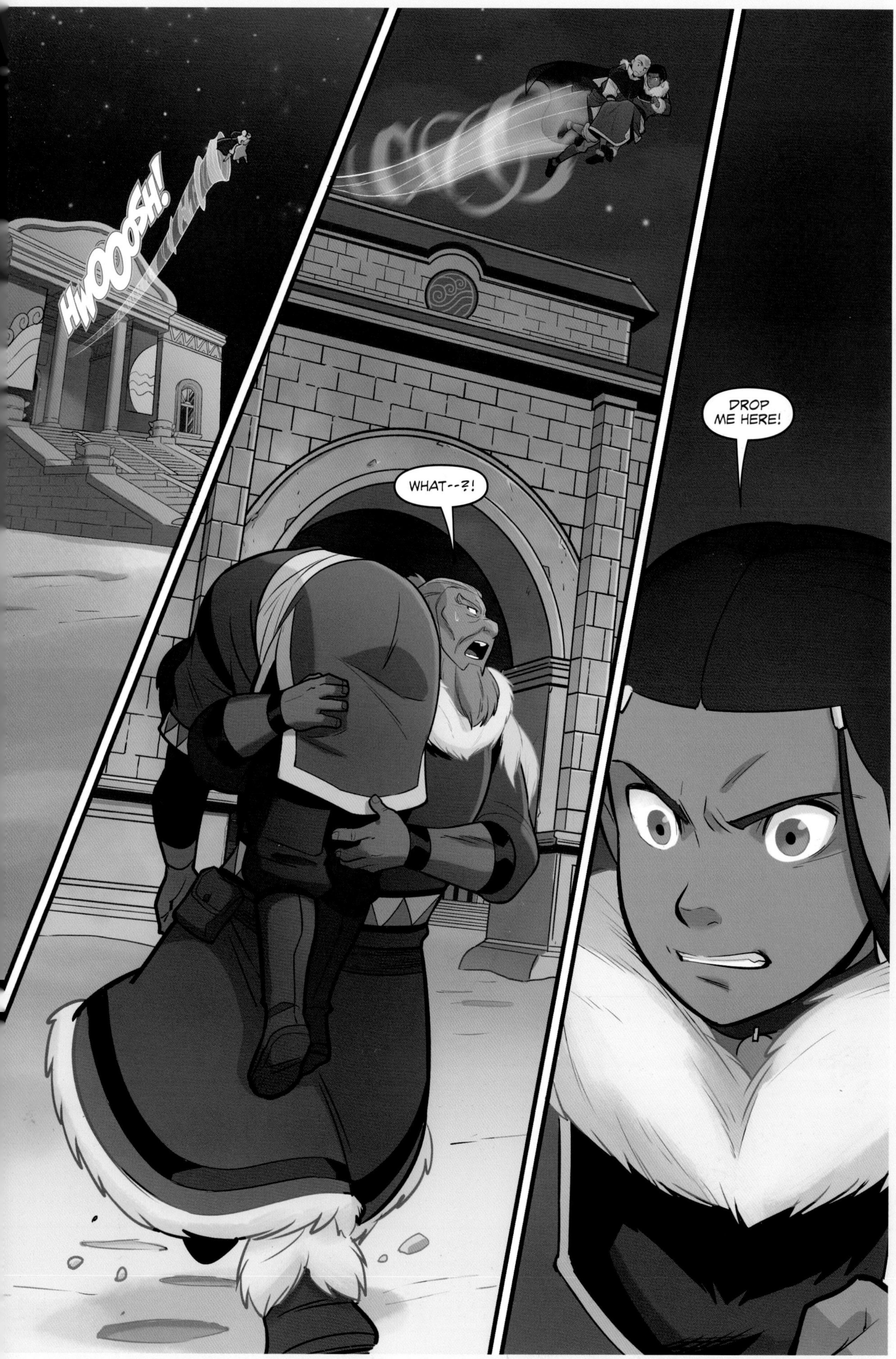
HWOOOSH!
WHAT--?!
DROP ME HERE!

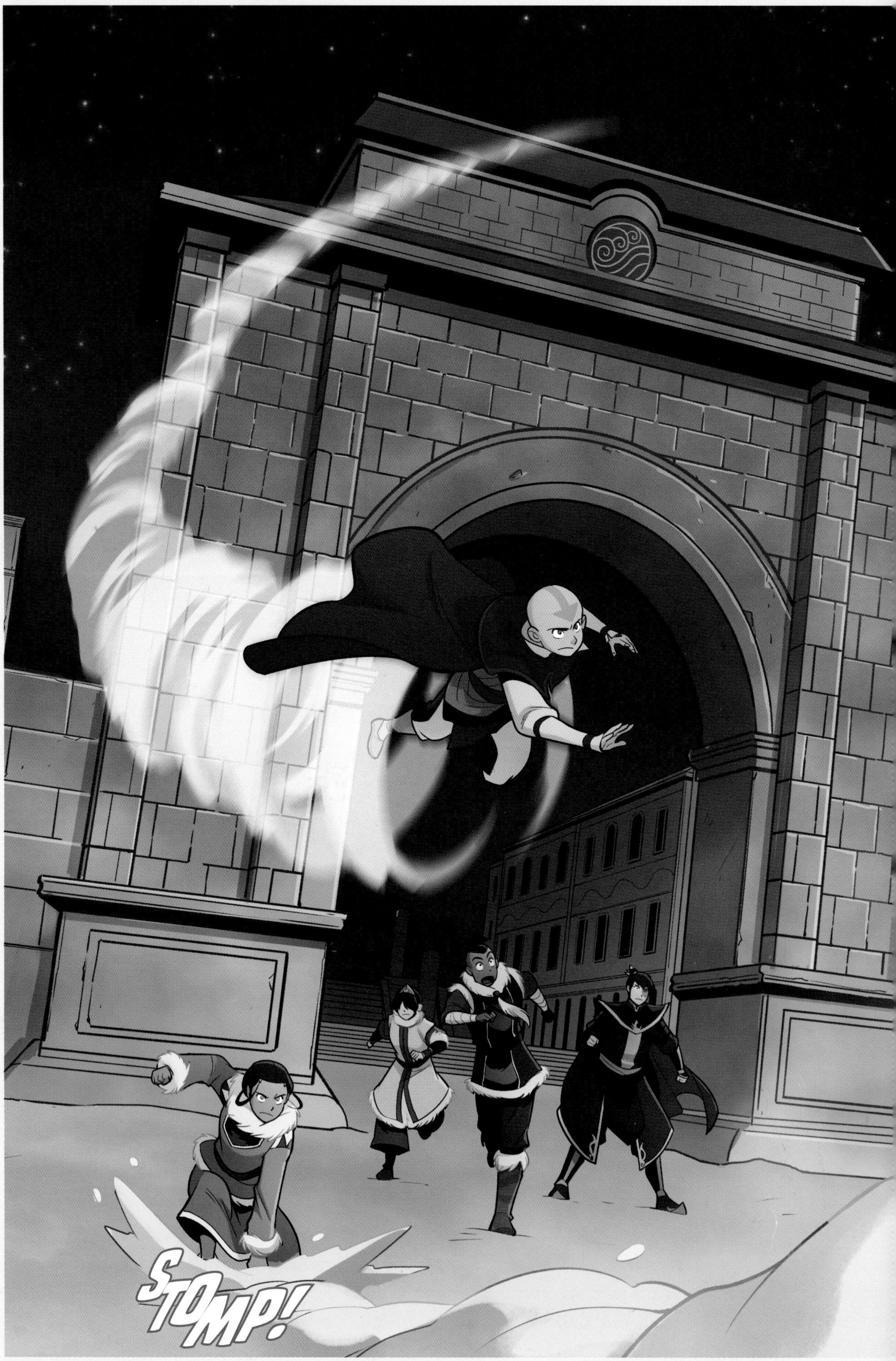
STOMP!

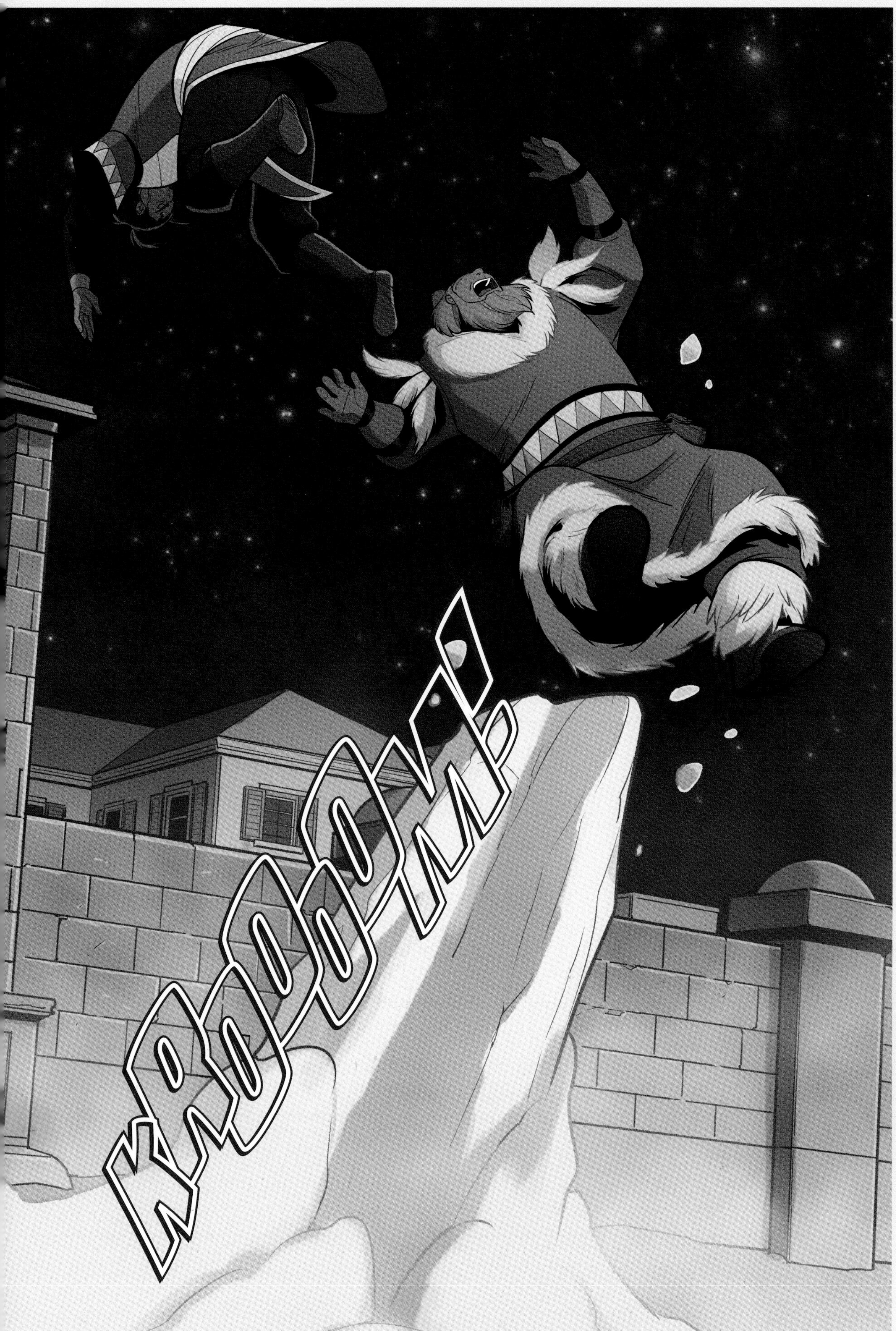
KROOOOM!

GLY: *Once we decided to focus this story arc on Katara and Sokka, I knew we had to give Katara a double-page spread to show off her skills. Here it is.*

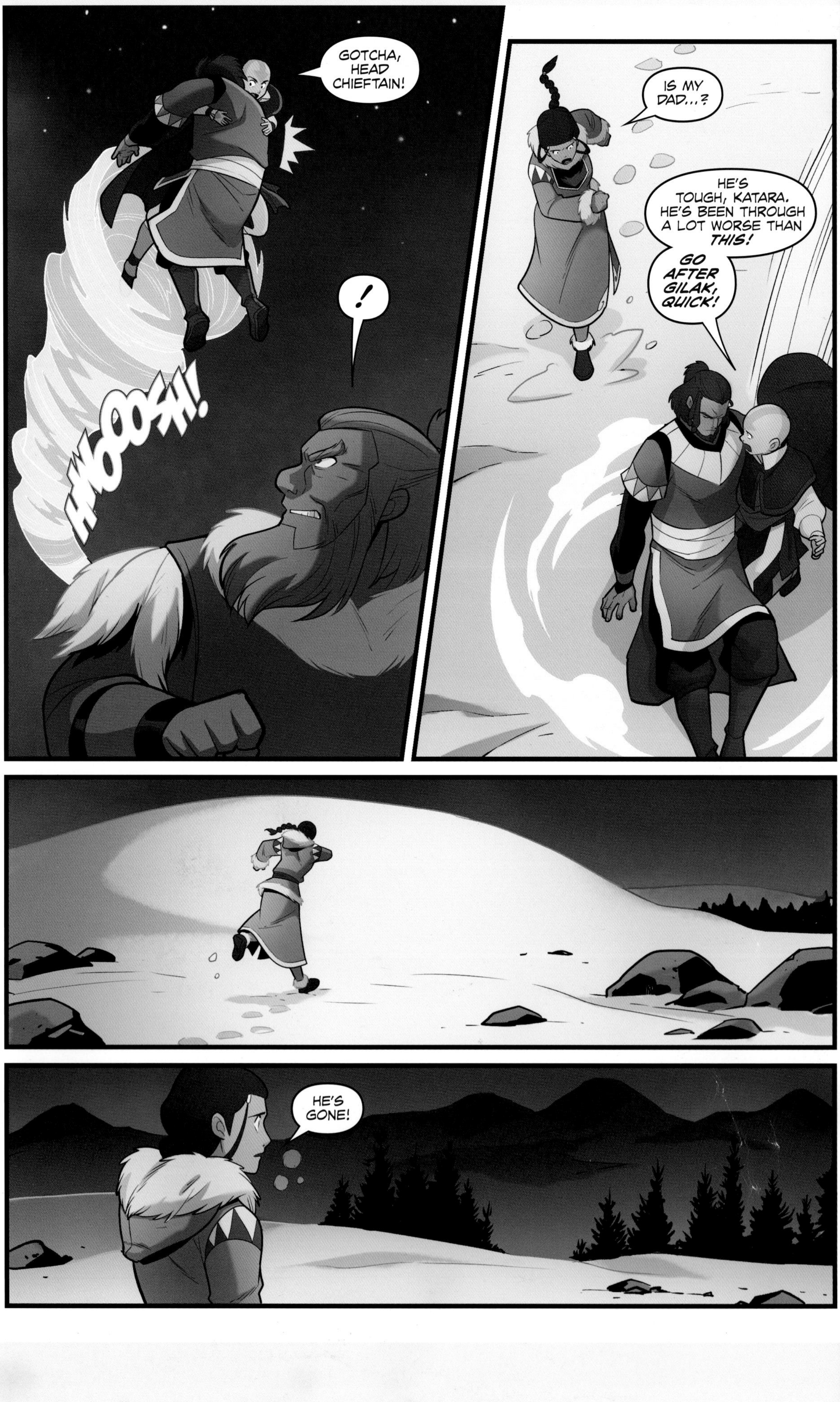
GOTCHA, HEAD CHIEFTAIN!
!
WHOOOSH!
IS MY DAD...?
HE'S TOUGH, KATARA. HE'S BEEN THROUGH A LOT WORSE THAN THIS!
GO AFTER GILAK, QUICK!
HE'S GONE!

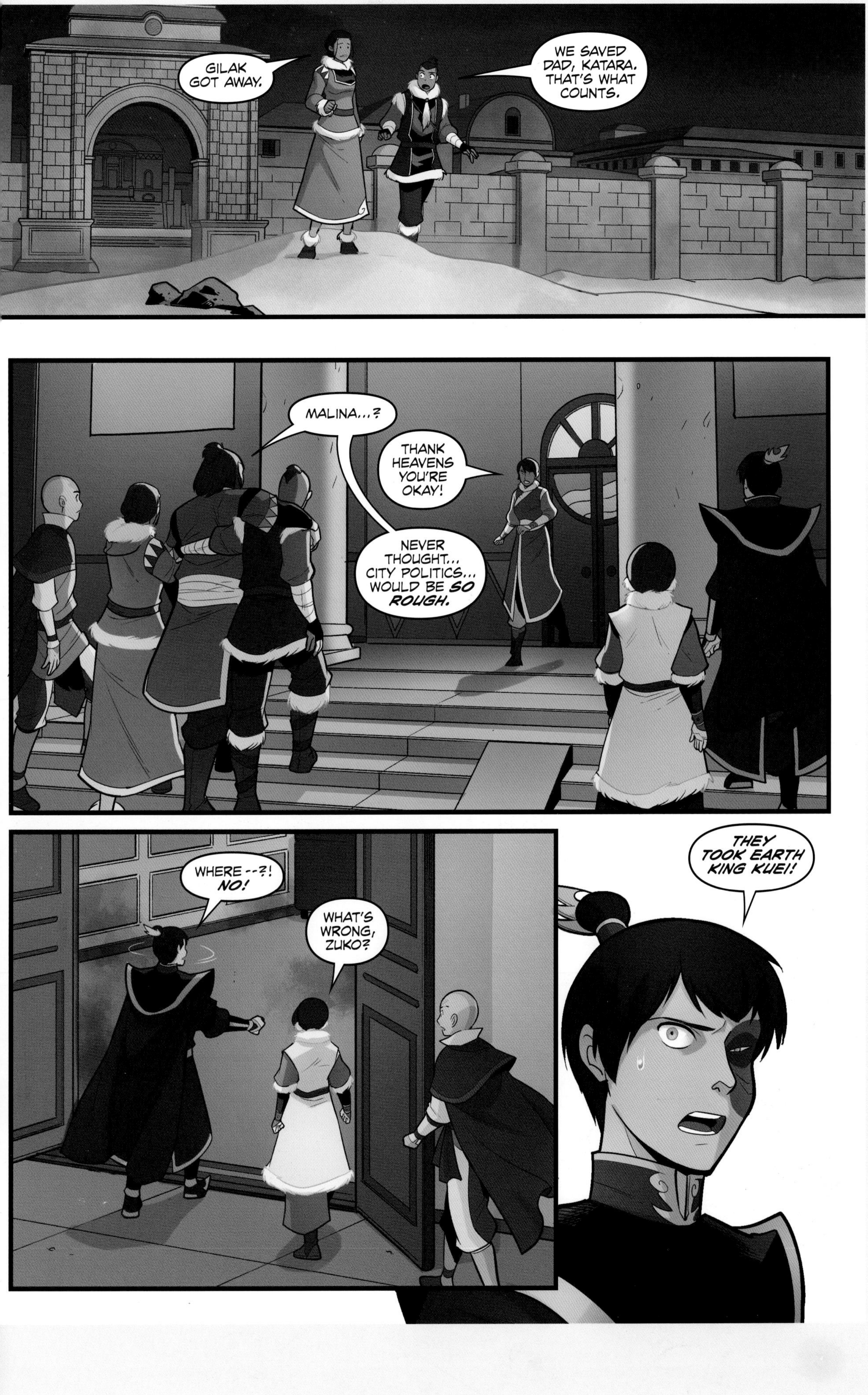
GILAK GOT AWAY.
WE SAVED DAD, KATARA. THAT'S WHAT COUNTS.
MALINA...?
THANK HEAVENS YOU'RE OKAY!
NEVER THOUGHT... CITY POLITICS... WOULD BE SO ROUGH.
WHERE--?! NO!
WHAT'S WRONG, ZUKO?
THEY TOOK EARTH KING KUEI!

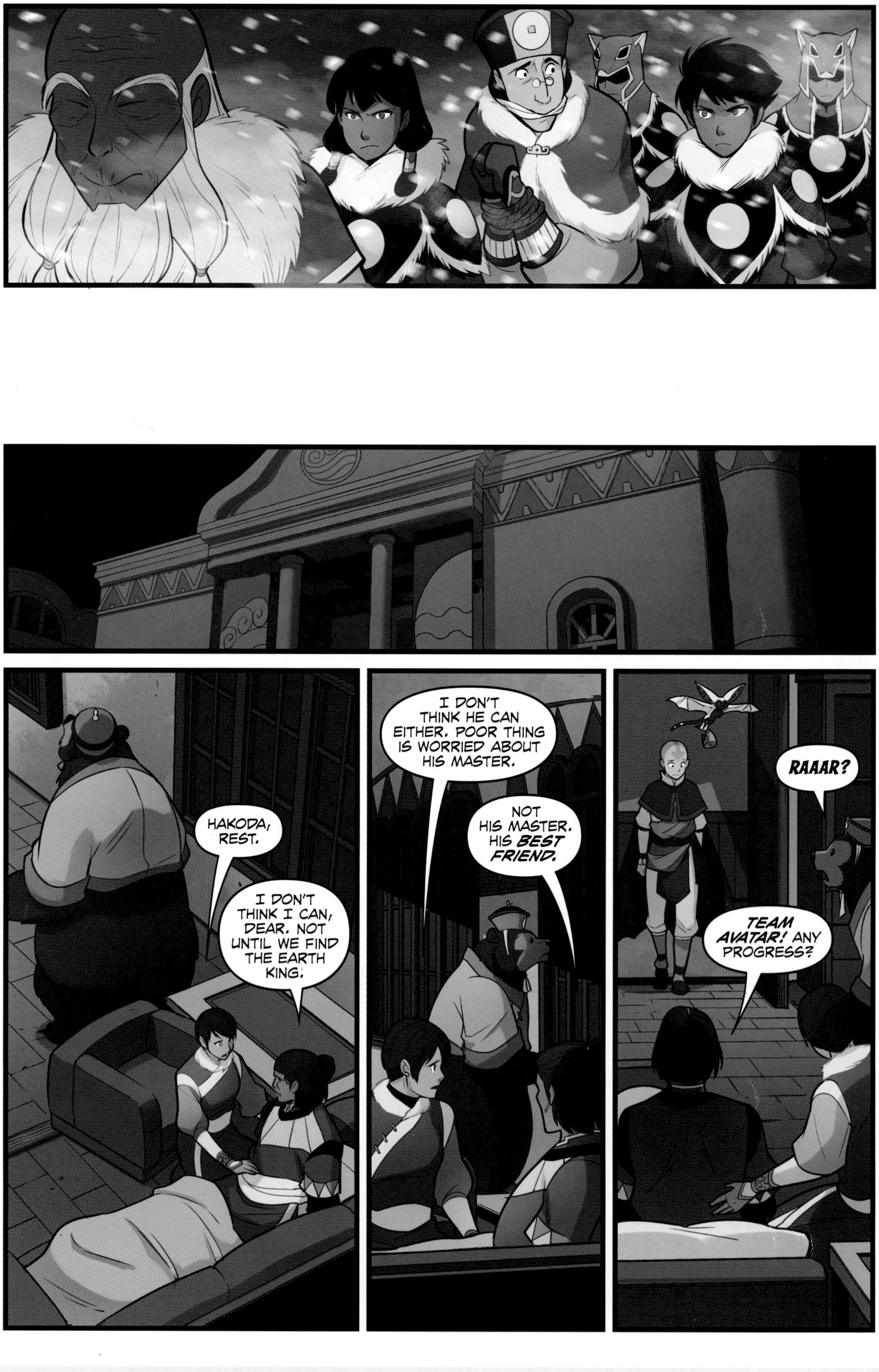
HAKODA, REST.
I DON'T THINK I CAN, DEAR. NOT UNTIL WE FIND THE EARTH KING.
I DON'T THINK HE CAN EITHER. POOR THING IS WORRIED ABOUT HIS MASTER.
NOT HIS MASTER. HIS BEST FRIEND.
RAAAR?
TEAM AVATAR! ANY PROGRESS?

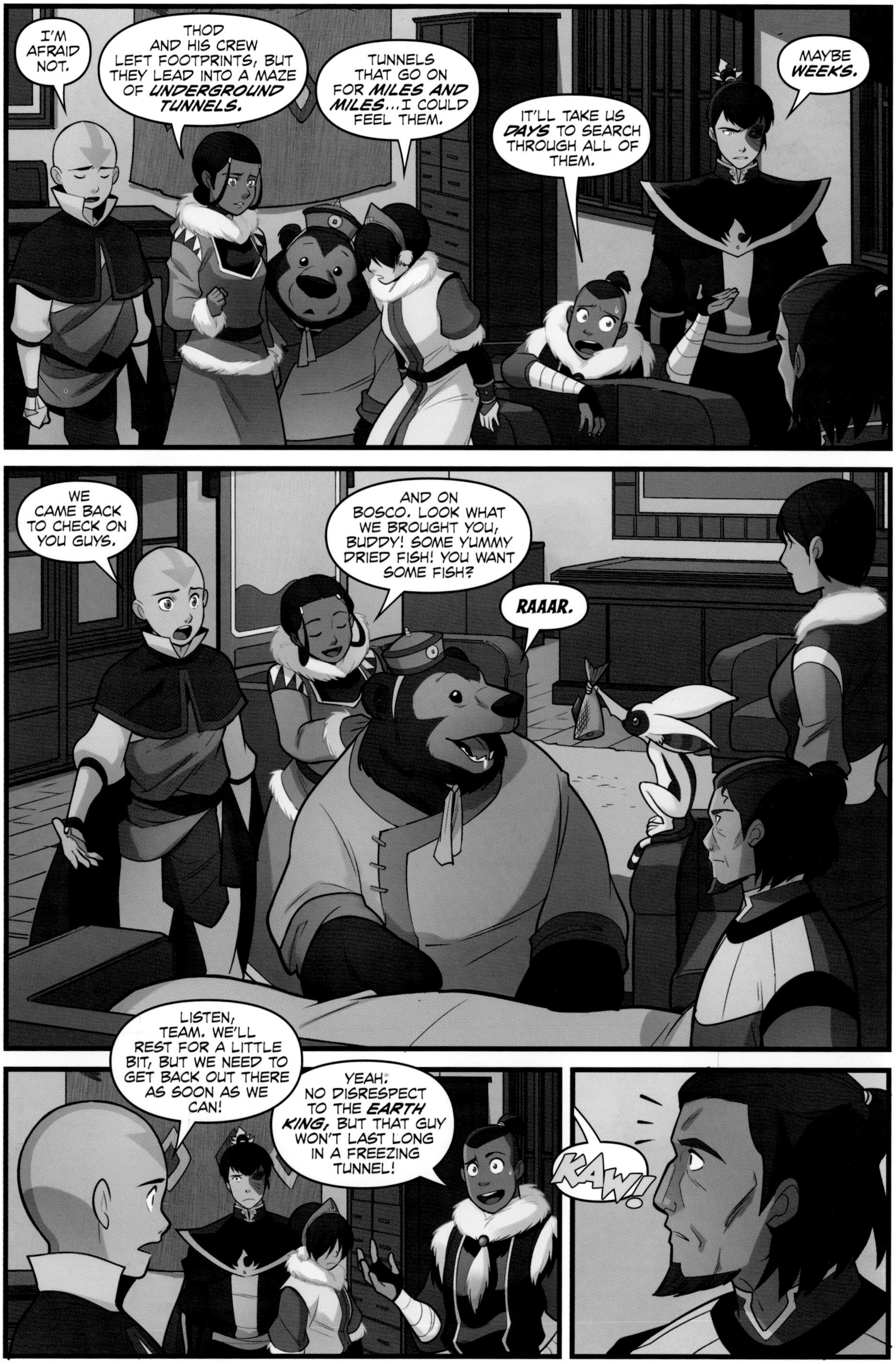
I'M AFRAID NOT.
THOD AND HIS CREW LEFT FOOTPRINTS, BUT THEY LEAD INTO A MAZE OF UNDERGROUND TUNNELS.
TUNNELS THAT GO ON FOR MILES AND MILES...I COULD FEEL THEM.
IT'LL TAKE US DAYS TO SEARCH THROUGH ALL OF THEM.
MAYBE WEEKS.
WE CAME BACK TO CHECK ON YOU GUYS.
AND ON BOSCO. LOOK WHAT WE BROUGHT YOU, BUDDY! SOME YUMMY DRIED FISH! YOU WANT SOME FISH?
RAAAR.
LISTEN, TEAM. WE'LL REST FOR A LITTLE BIT, BUT WE NEED TO GET BACK OUT THERE AS SOON AS WE CAN!
YEAH. NO DISRESPECT TO THE EARTH KING, BUT THAT GUY WON'T LAST LONG IN A FREEZING TUNNEL!
KAW!!

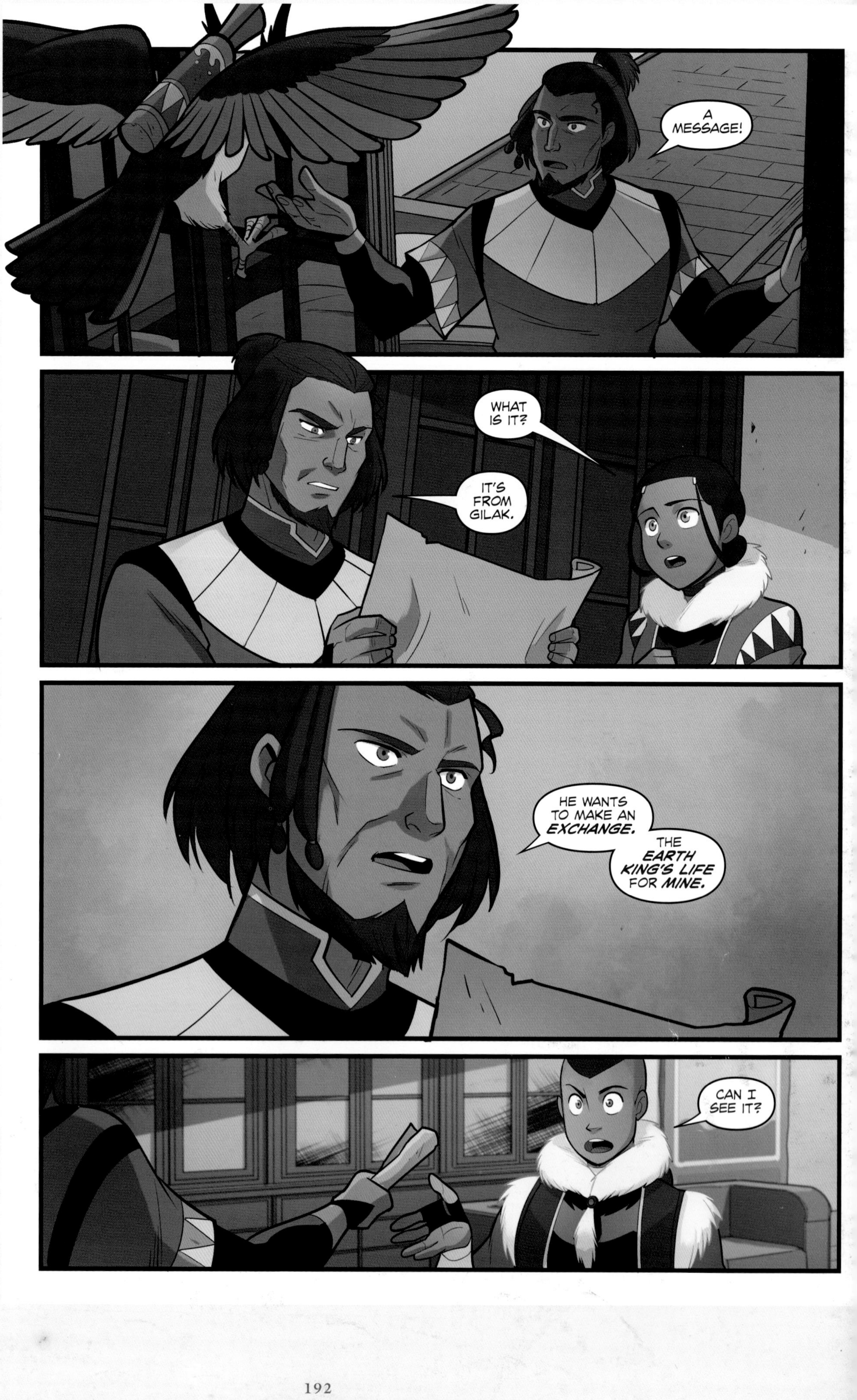
A MESSAGE!
WHAT IS IT?
IT'S FROM GILAK.
HE WANTS TO MAKE AN *EXCHANGE.*
THE *EARTH KING'S LIFE* FOR *MINE.*
CAN I SEE IT?

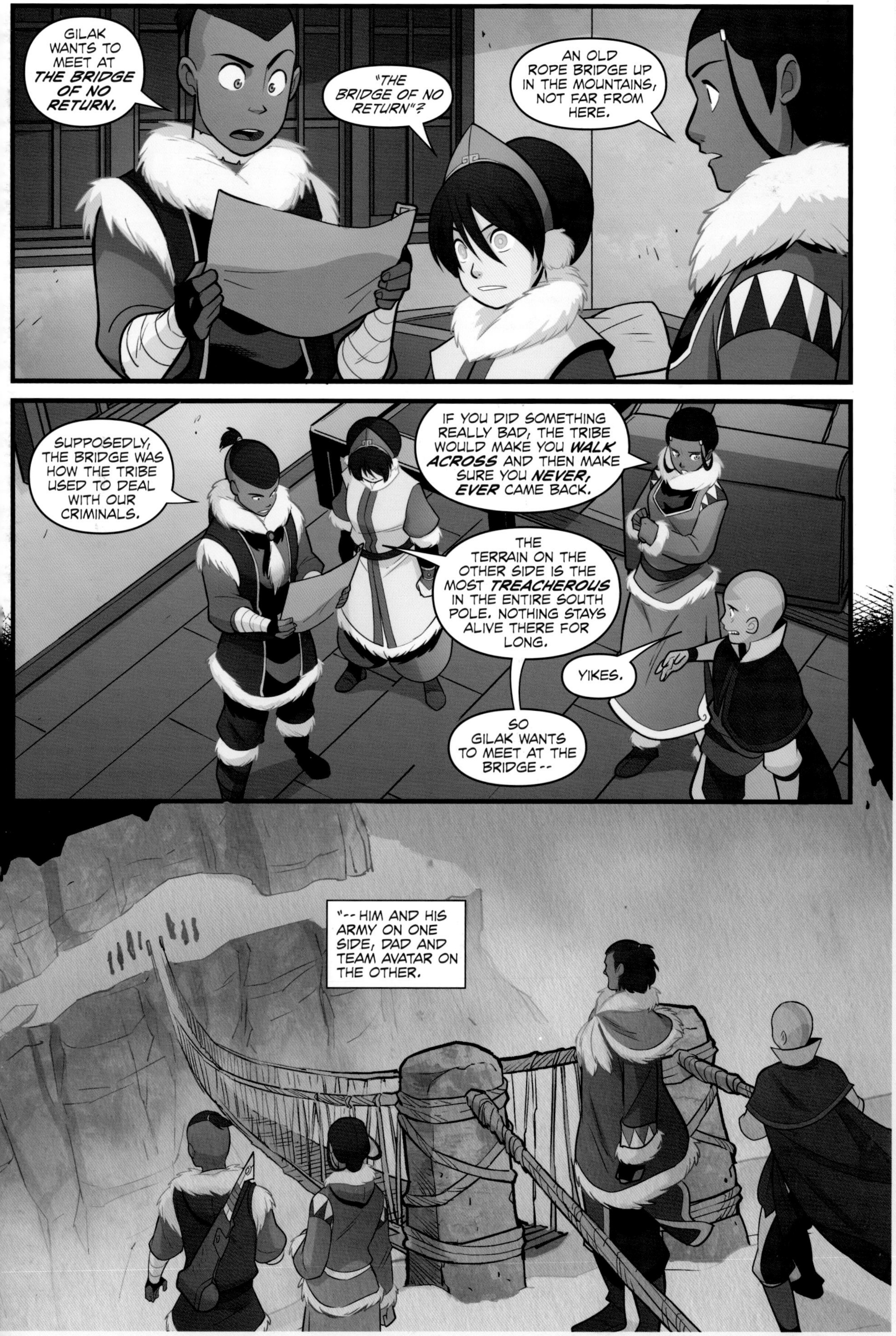
GILAK WANTS TO MEET AT THE BRIDGE OF NO RETURN.
"THE BRIDGE OF NO RETURN"?
AN OLD ROPE BRIDGE UP IN THE MOUNTAINS, NOT FAR FROM HERE.
SUPPOSEDLY, THE BRIDGE WAS HOW THE TRIBE USED TO DEAL WITH OUR CRIMINALS.
IF YOU DID SOMETHING REALLY BAD, THE TRIBE WOULD MAKE YOU WALK ACROSS AND THEN MAKE SURE YOU NEVER, EVER CAME BACK.
THE TERRAIN ON THE OTHER SIDE IS THE MOST TREACHEROUS IN THE ENTIRE SOUTH POLE. NOTHING STAYS ALIVE THERE FOR LONG.
YIKES.
SO GILAK WANTS TO MEET AT THE BRIDGE--
"--HIM AND HIS ARMY ON ONE SIDE, DAD AND TEAM AVATAR ON THE OTHER.

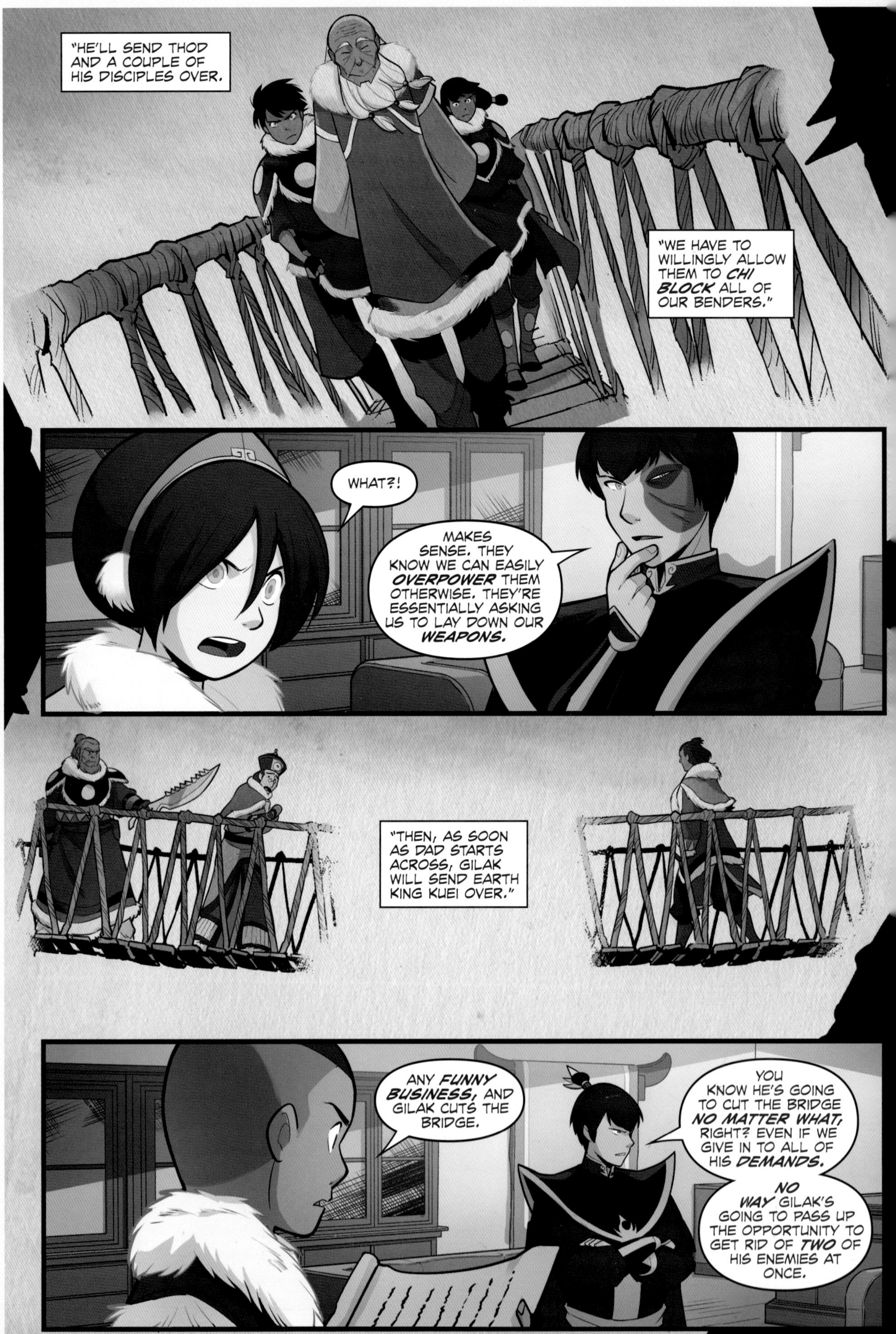
"HE'LL SEND THOD AND A COUPLE OF HIS DISCIPLES OVER.
"WE HAVE TO WILLINGLY ALLOW THEM TO CHI BLOCK ALL OF OUR BENDERS."
WHAT?!
MAKES SENSE. THEY KNOW WE CAN EASILY OVERPOWER THEM OTHERWISE. THEY'RE ESSENTIALLY ASKING US TO LAY DOWN OUR WEAPONS.
"THEN, AS SOON AS DAD STARTS ACROSS, GILAK WILL SEND EARTH KING KUEI OVER."
ANY FUNNY BUSINESS, AND GILAK CUTS THE BRIDGE.
YOU KNOW HE'S GOING TO CUT THE BRIDGE NO MATTER WHAT, RIGHT? EVEN IF WE GIVE IN TO ALL OF HIS DEMANDS.
NO WAY GILAK'S GOING TO PASS UP THE OPPORTUNITY TO GET RID OF TWO OF HIS ENEMIES AT ONCE.

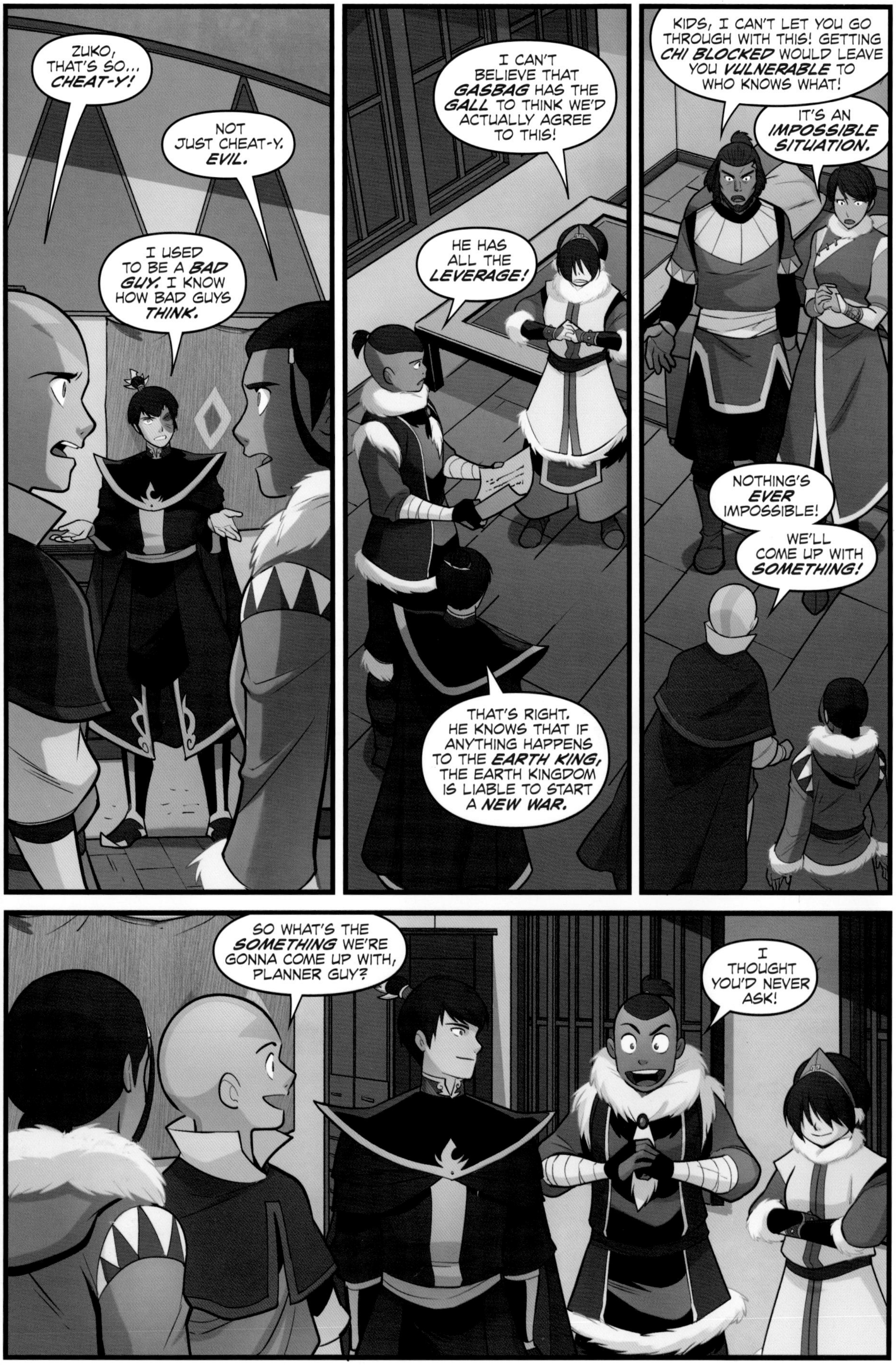
ZUKO, THAT'S SO... CHEAT-Y!
NOT JUST CHEAT-Y. EVIL.
I USED TO BE A BAD GUY. I KNOW HOW BAD GUYS THINK.
I CAN'T BELIEVE THAT GASBAG HAS THE GALL TO THINK WE'D ACTUALLY AGREE TO THIS!
HE HAS ALL THE LEVERAGE!
THAT'S RIGHT. HE KNOWS THAT IF ANYTHING HAPPENS TO THE EARTH KING, THE EARTH KINGDOM IS LIABLE TO START A NEW WAR.
KIDS, I CAN'T LET YOU GO THROUGH WITH THIS! GETTING CHI BLOCKED WOULD LEAVE YOU VULNERABLE TO WHO KNOWS WHAT!
IT'S AN IMPOSSIBLE SITUATION.
NOTHING'S EVER IMPOSSIBLE!
WE'LL COME UP WITH SOMETHING!
SO WHAT'S THE SOMETHING WE'RE GONNA COME UP WITH, PLANNER GUY?
I THOUGHT YOU'D NEVER ASK!

GLY: *Sokka is like the Avatar: The Last Airbender version of the A-Team. (Look it up on Wikipedia, kids.) The whole team, rolled into one teenage Water Tribe kid.*

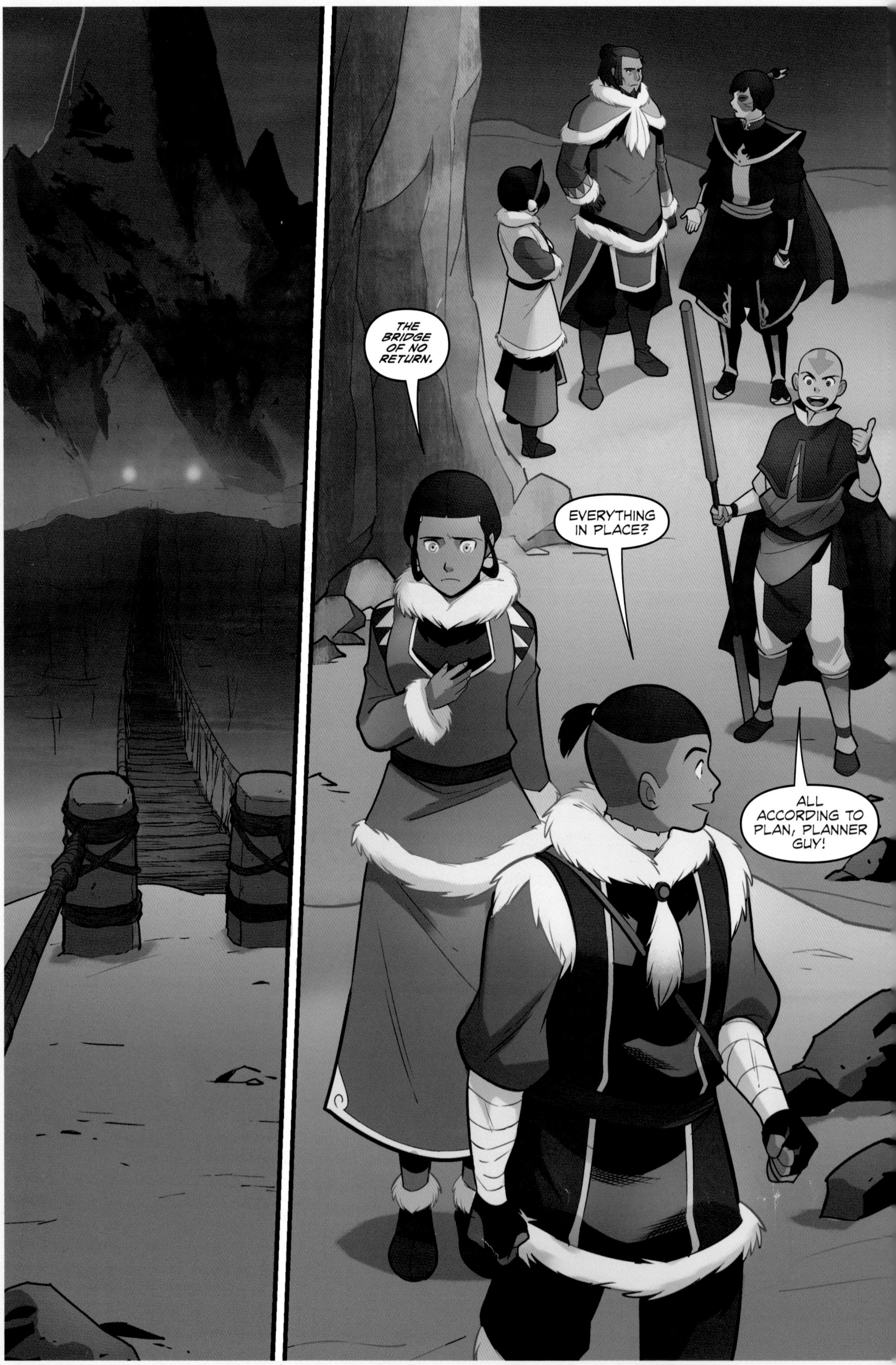
THE BRIDGE OF NO RETURN.
EVERYTHING IN PLACE?
ALL ACCORDING TO PLAN, PLANNER GUY!

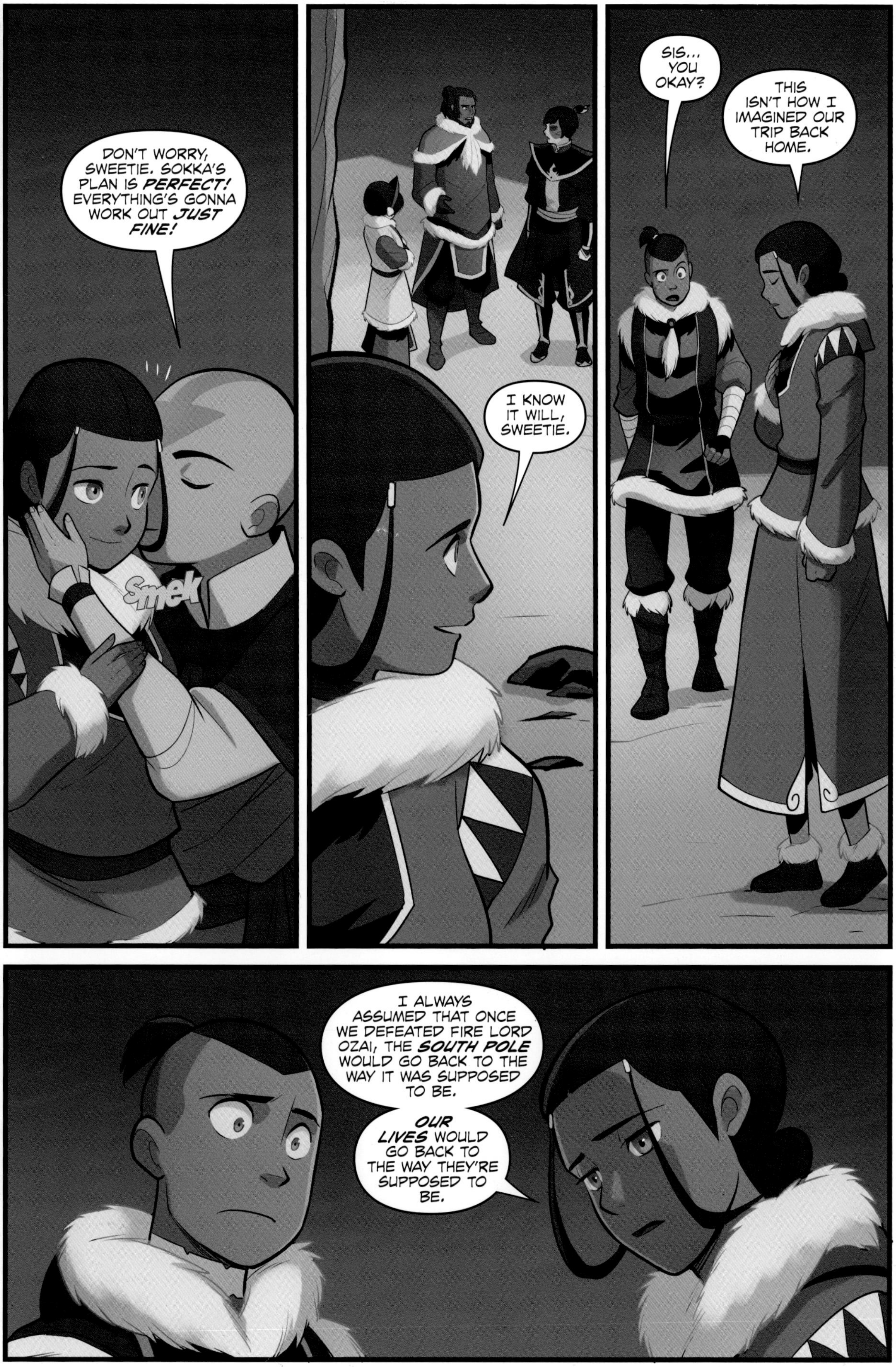
DON'T WORRY, SWEETIE. SOKKA'S PLAN IS PERFECT! EVERYTHING'S GONNA WORK OUT JUST FINE!
SMEK
I KNOW IT WILL, SWEETIE.
SIS... YOU OKAY?
THIS ISN'T HOW I IMAGINED OUR TRIP BACK HOME.
I ALWAYS ASSUMED THAT ONCE WE DEFEATED FIRE LORD OZAI, THE SOUTH POLE WOULD GO BACK TO THE WAY IT WAS SUPPOSED TO BE.
OUR LIVES WOULD GO BACK TO THE WAY THEY'RE SUPPOSED TO BE.

GLY: *What Katara is talking about here . . . I wonder about sometimes myself. I am definitely prone to nostalgia. I'm prone to believing in the myth of the "good ol' days." It drives a lot of my geek habits. I really enjoy reading comic books about characters I first fell in love with when I was twelve. I don't think there's anything wrong with that, as long as I also keep in mind that my memories of those stories are often idealized.*

That's one of the many reasons that I love Avatar: The Last Airbender so much. It wasn't around when I was twelve, but it proves that nostalgia isn't the only pathway to my heartstrings. New characters, especially characters who look different from the characters I grew up with, have a place. They can be just as compelling, just as influential, just as inspirational.

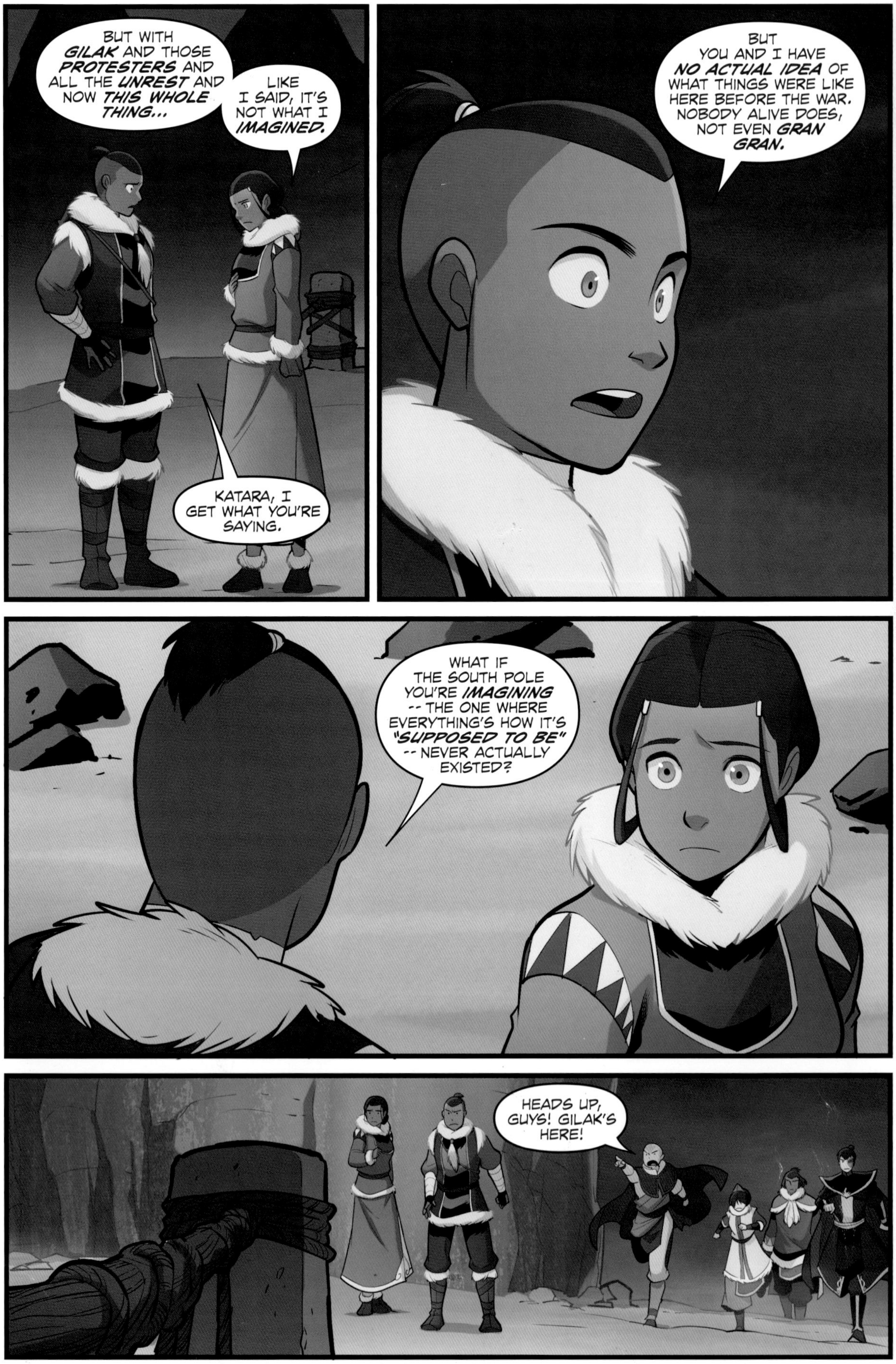
BUT WITH GILAK AND THOSE PROTESTERS AND ALL THE UNREST AND NOW THIS WHOLE THING...
LIKE I SAID, IT'S NOT WHAT I IMAGINED.
KATARA, I GET WHAT YOU'RE SAYING.
BUT YOU AND I HAVE NO ACTUAL IDEA OF WHAT THINGS WERE LIKE HERE BEFORE THE WAR. NOBODY ALIVE DOES, NOT EVEN GRAN GRAN.
WHAT IF THE SOUTH POLE YOU'RE IMAGINING -- THE ONE WHERE EVERYTHING'S HOW IT'S "SUPPOSED TO BE" -- NEVER ACTUALLY EXISTED?
HEADS UP, GUYS! GILAK'S HERE!

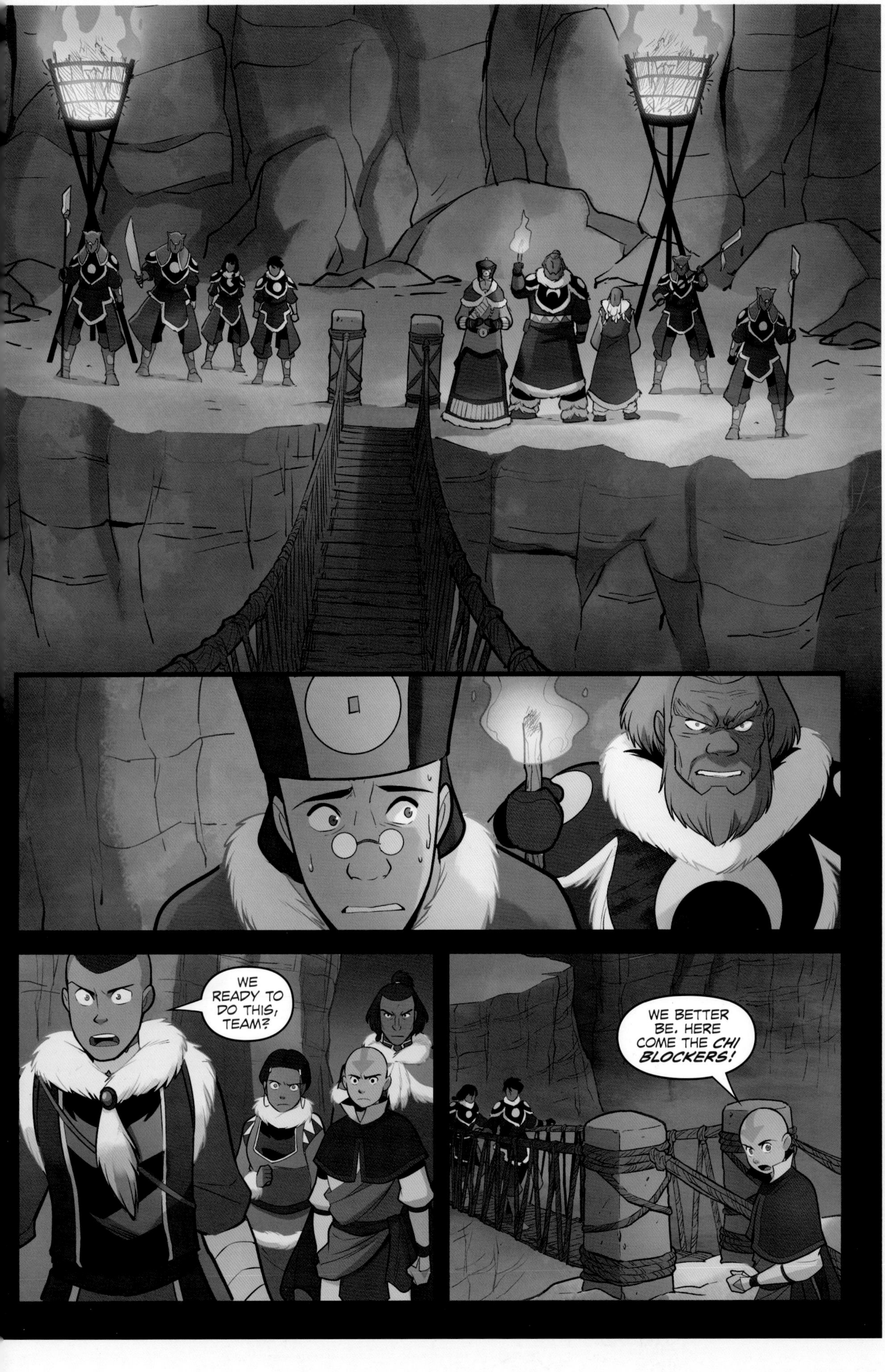
WE READY TO DO THIS, TEAM?
WE BETTER BE. HERE COME THE *CHI BLOCKERS!*

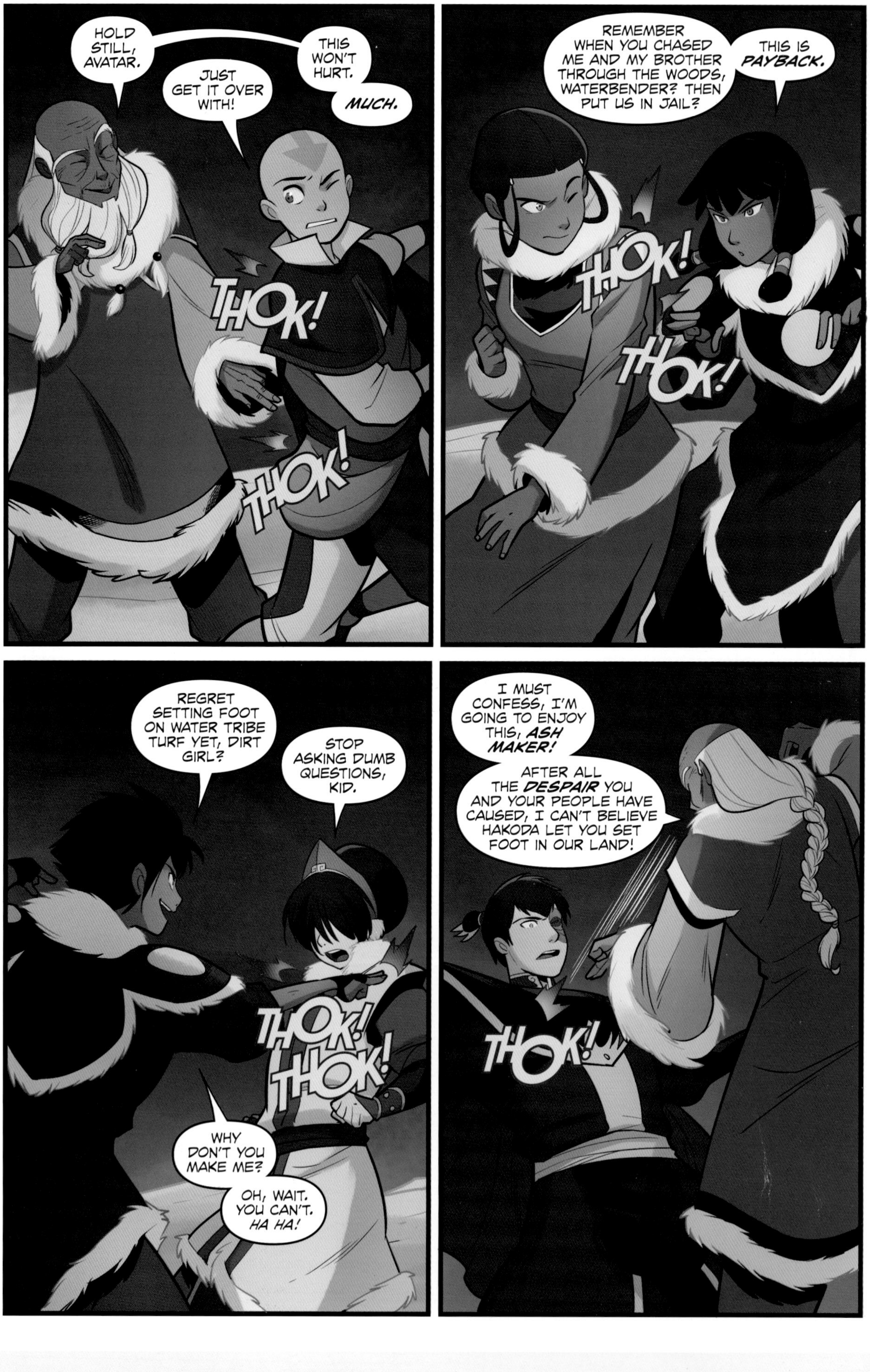
HOLD STILL, AVATAR.
THIS WON'T HURT.
MUCH.
JUST GET IT OVER WITH!
THOK!
THOK!
REMEMBER WHEN YOU CHASED ME AND MY BROTHER THROUGH THE WOODS, WATERBENDER? THEN PUT US IN JAIL?
THIS IS PAYBACK.
THOK!
THOK!
REGRET SETTING FOOT ON WATER TRIBE TURF YET, DIRT GIRL?
STOP ASKING DUMB QUESTIONS, KID.
THOK! THOK!
WHY DON'T YOU MAKE ME?
OH, WAIT. YOU CAN'T. HA HA!
I MUST CONFESS, I'M GOING TO ENJOY THIS, ASH MAKER!
AFTER ALL THE DESPAIR YOU AND YOUR PEOPLE HAVE CAUSED, I CAN'T BELIEVE HAKODA LET YOU SET FOOT IN OUR LAND!
THOK!

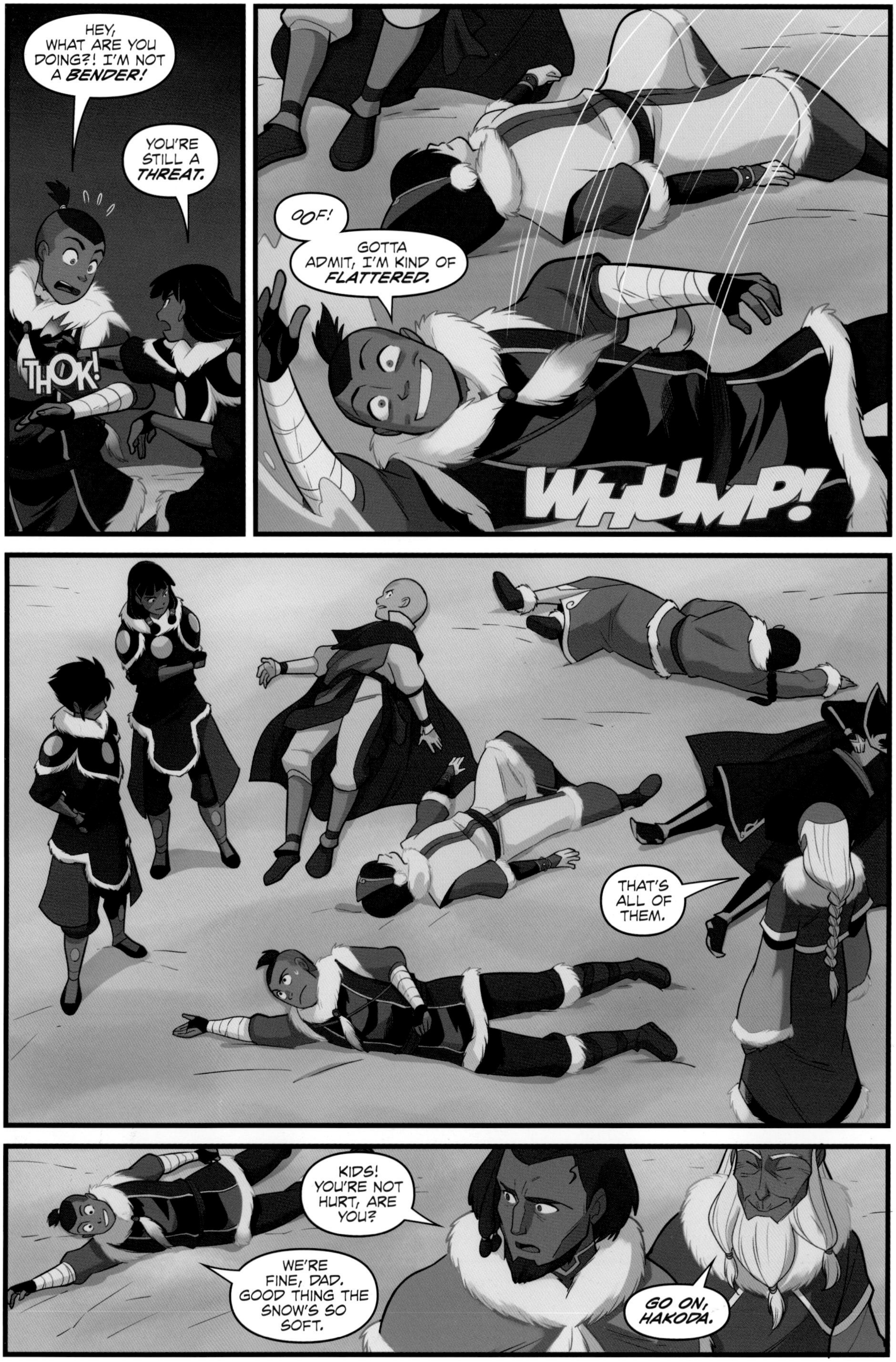
HEY, WHAT ARE YOU DOING?! I'M NOT A BENDER!
YOU'RE STILL A THREAT.
THOK!
OOF!
GOTTA ADMIT, I'M KIND OF FLATTERED.
WHUMP!
THAT'S ALL OF THEM.
KIDS! YOU'RE NOT HURT, ARE YOU?
WE'RE FINE, DAD. GOOD THING THE SNOW'S SO SOFT.
GO ON, HAKODA.

GLY: *Just remember, benders. Planner Guy is always a threat!*

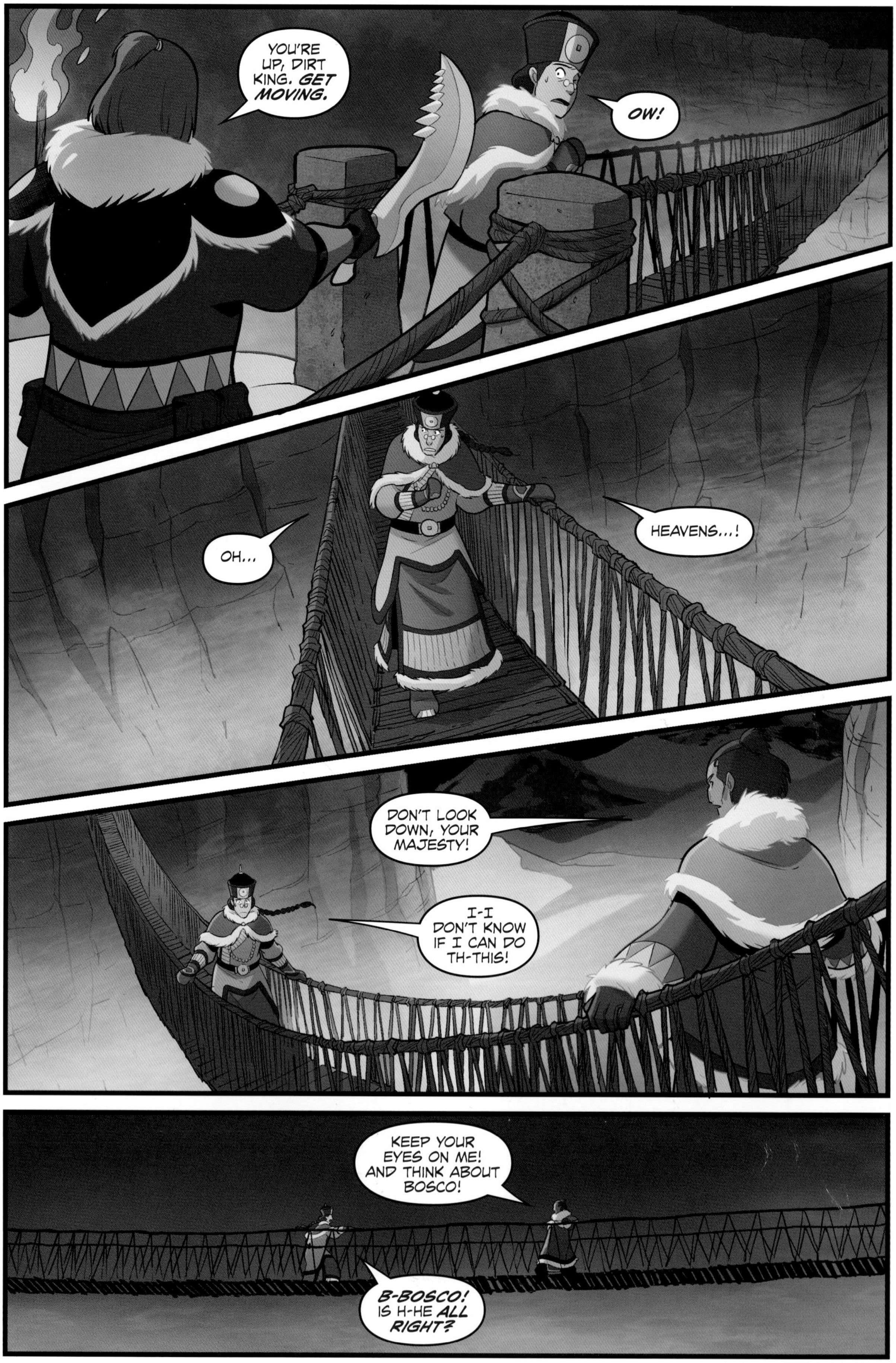
YOU'RE UP, DIRT KING. GET MOVING.
OW!
OH...
HEAVENS...!
DON'T LOOK DOWN, YOUR MAJESTY!
I-I DON'T KNOW IF I CAN DO TH-THIS!
KEEP YOUR EYES ON ME! AND THINK ABOUT BOSCO!
B-BOSCO! IS H-HE ALL RIGHT?

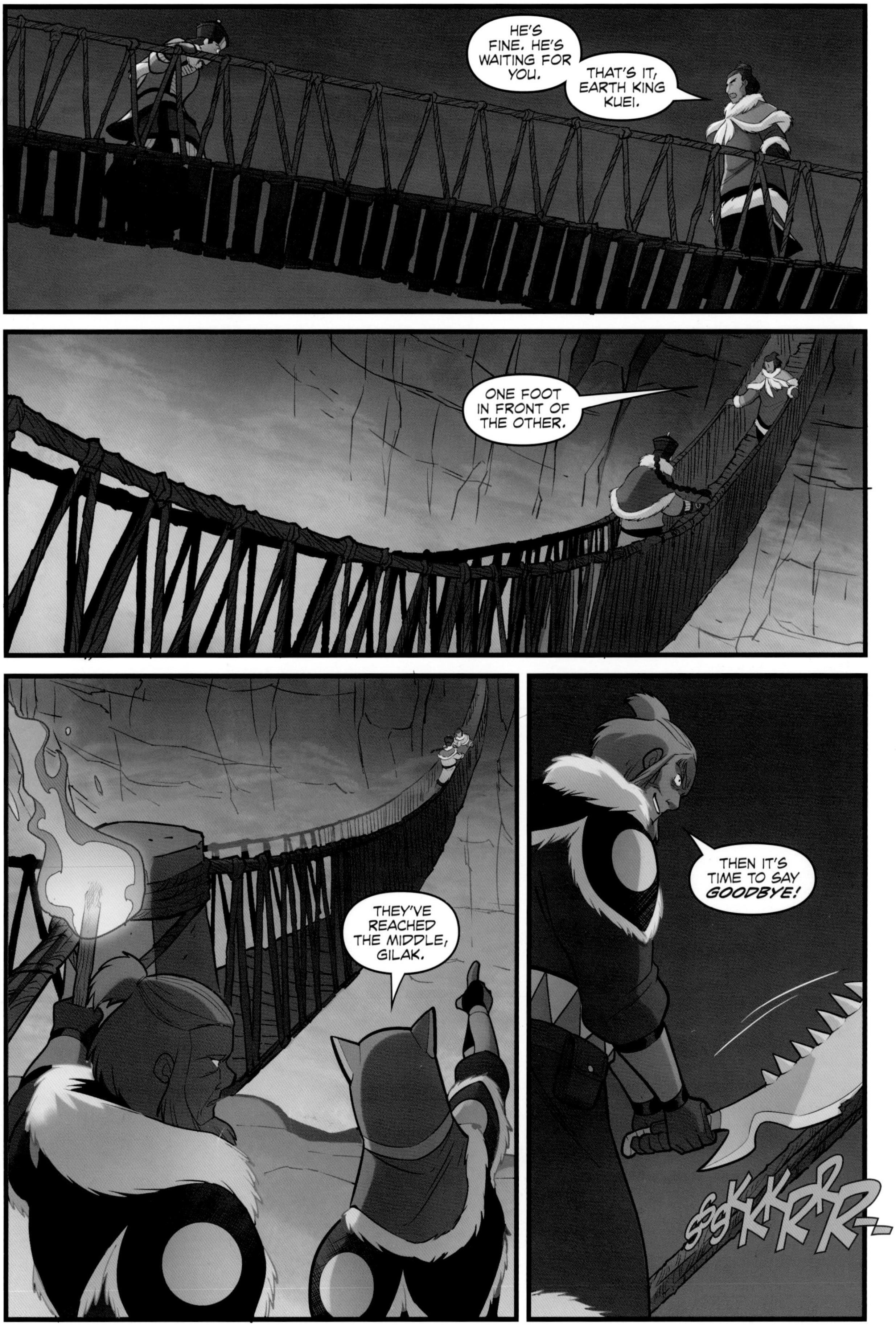
HE'S FINE. HE'S WAITING FOR YOU.
THAT'S IT, EARTH KING KUEI.
ONE FOOT IN FRONT OF THE OTHER.
THEY'VE REACHED THE MIDDLE, GILAK.
THEN IT'S TIME TO SAY GOODBYE!
SSGKKKRRR--

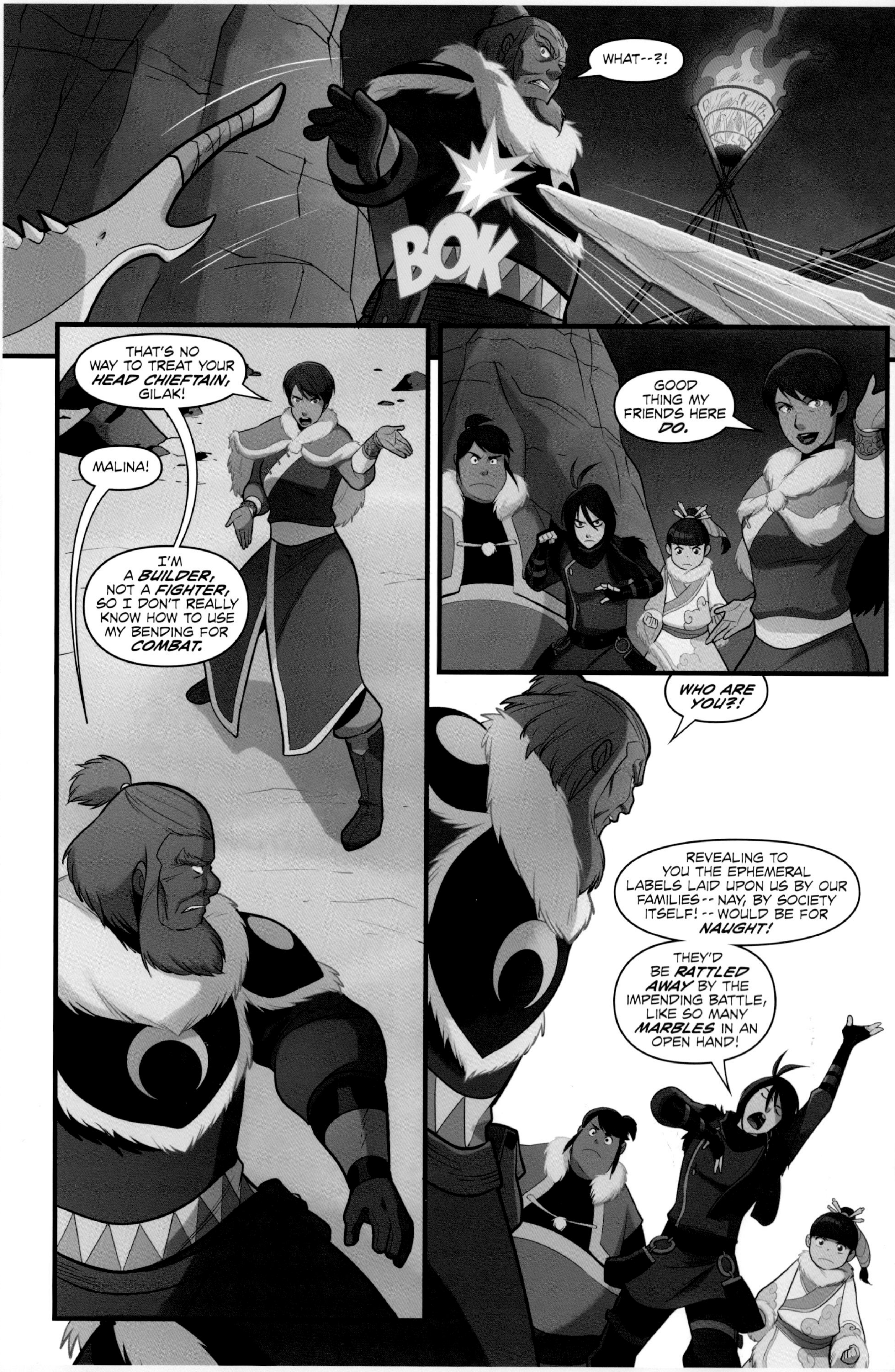
WHAT--?!
BOK
THAT'S NO WAY TO TREAT YOUR HEAD CHIEFTAIN, GILAK!
MALINA!
I'M A BUILDER, NOT A FIGHTER, SO I DON'T REALLY KNOW HOW TO USE MY BENDING FOR COMBAT.
GOOD THING MY FRIENDS HERE DO.
WHO ARE YOU?!
REVEALING TO YOU THE EPHEMERAL LABELS LAID UPON US BY OUR FAMILIES--NAY, BY SOCIETY ITSELF!--WOULD BE FOR NAUGHT!
THEY'D BE RATTLED AWAY BY THE IMPENDING BATTLE, LIKE SO MANY MARBLES IN AN OPEN HAND!

G: *We love the Dark One; he is always funny! Even when the story is tense, the scene lightens up and relaxes a bit when these three appear.*

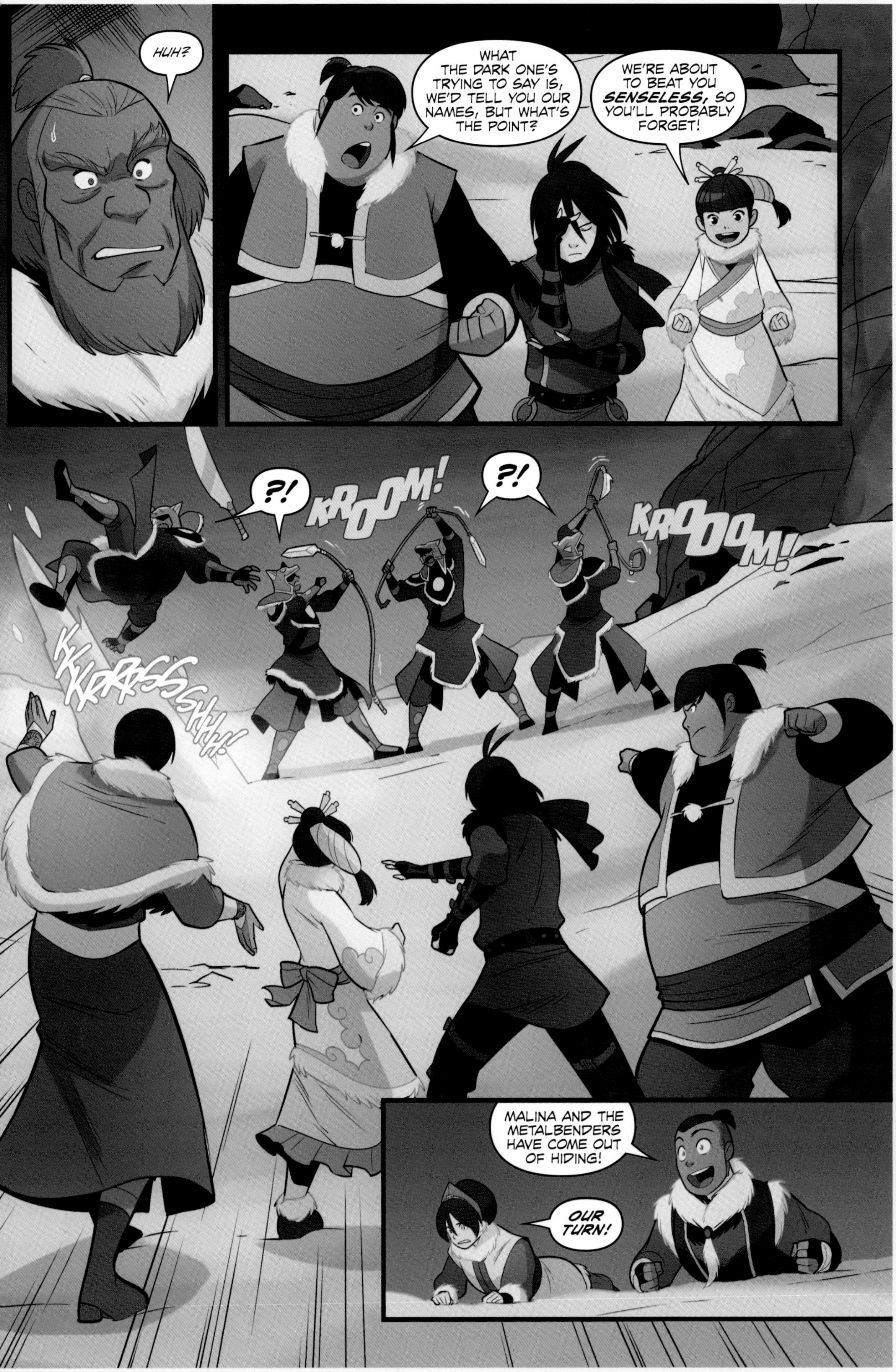
HUH?
WHAT THE DARK ONE'S TRYING TO SAY IS, WE'D TELL YOU OUR NAMES, BUT WHAT'S THE POINT?
WE'RE ABOUT TO BEAT YOU SENSELESS, SO YOU'LL PROBABLY FORGET!
?!
KROOOM!
?!
KROOOOM!
KKKRRRSSSHHH!
MALINA AND THE METALBENDERS HAVE COME OUT OF HIDING!
OUR TURN!

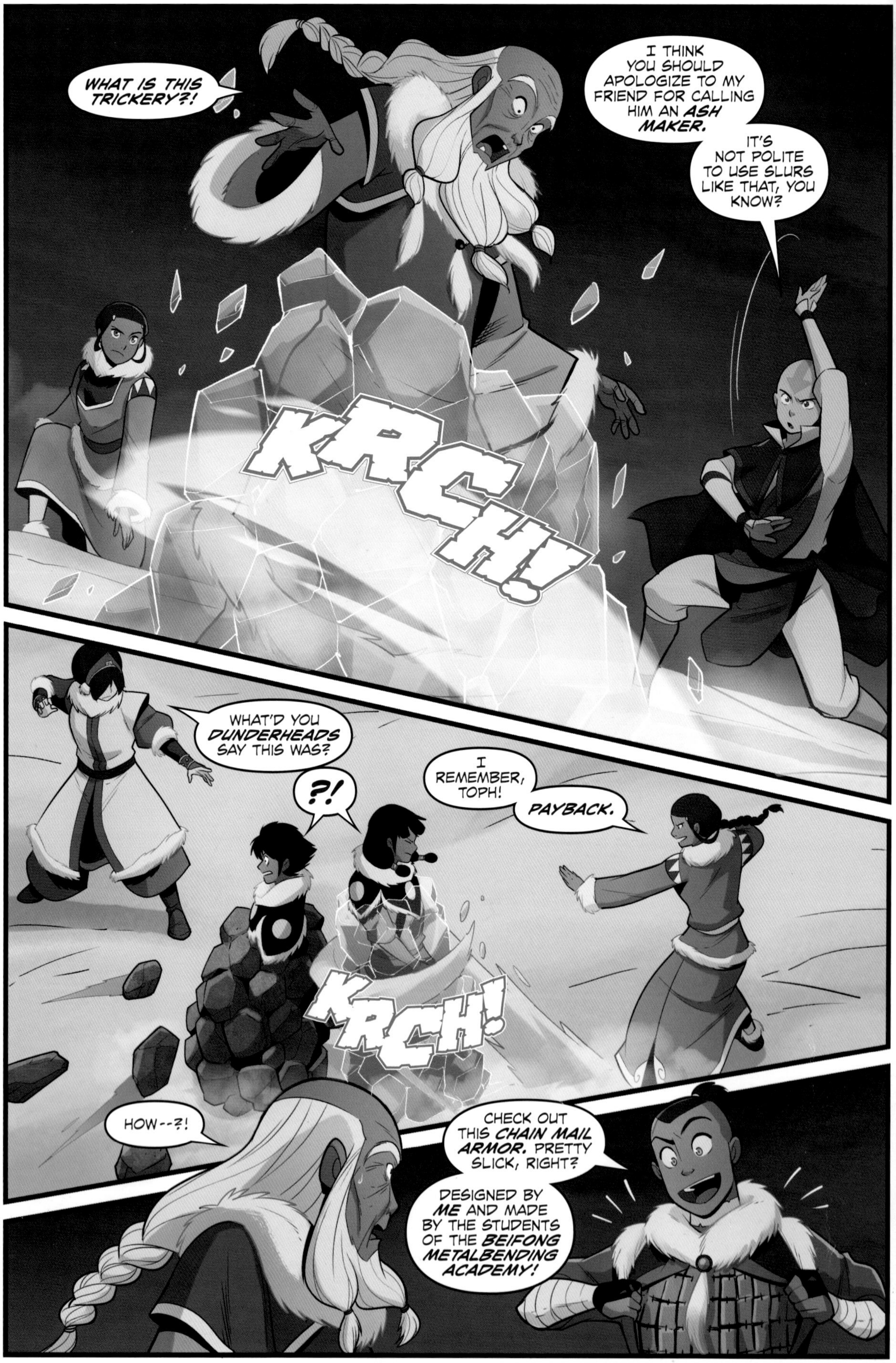
WHAT IS THIS TRICKERY?!
I THINK YOU SHOULD APOLOGIZE TO MY FRIEND FOR CALLING HIM AN ASH MAKER.
IT'S NOT POLITE TO USE SLURS LIKE THAT, YOU KNOW?
KRRCH!
WHAT'D YOU DUNDERHEADS SAY THIS WAS?
?!
I REMEMBER, TOPH!
PAYBACK.
KRCH!
HOW--?!
CHECK OUT THIS CHAIN MAIL ARMOR. PRETTY SLICK, RIGHT?
DESIGNED BY ME AND MADE BY THE STUDENTS OF THE BEIFONG METALBENDING ACADEMY!

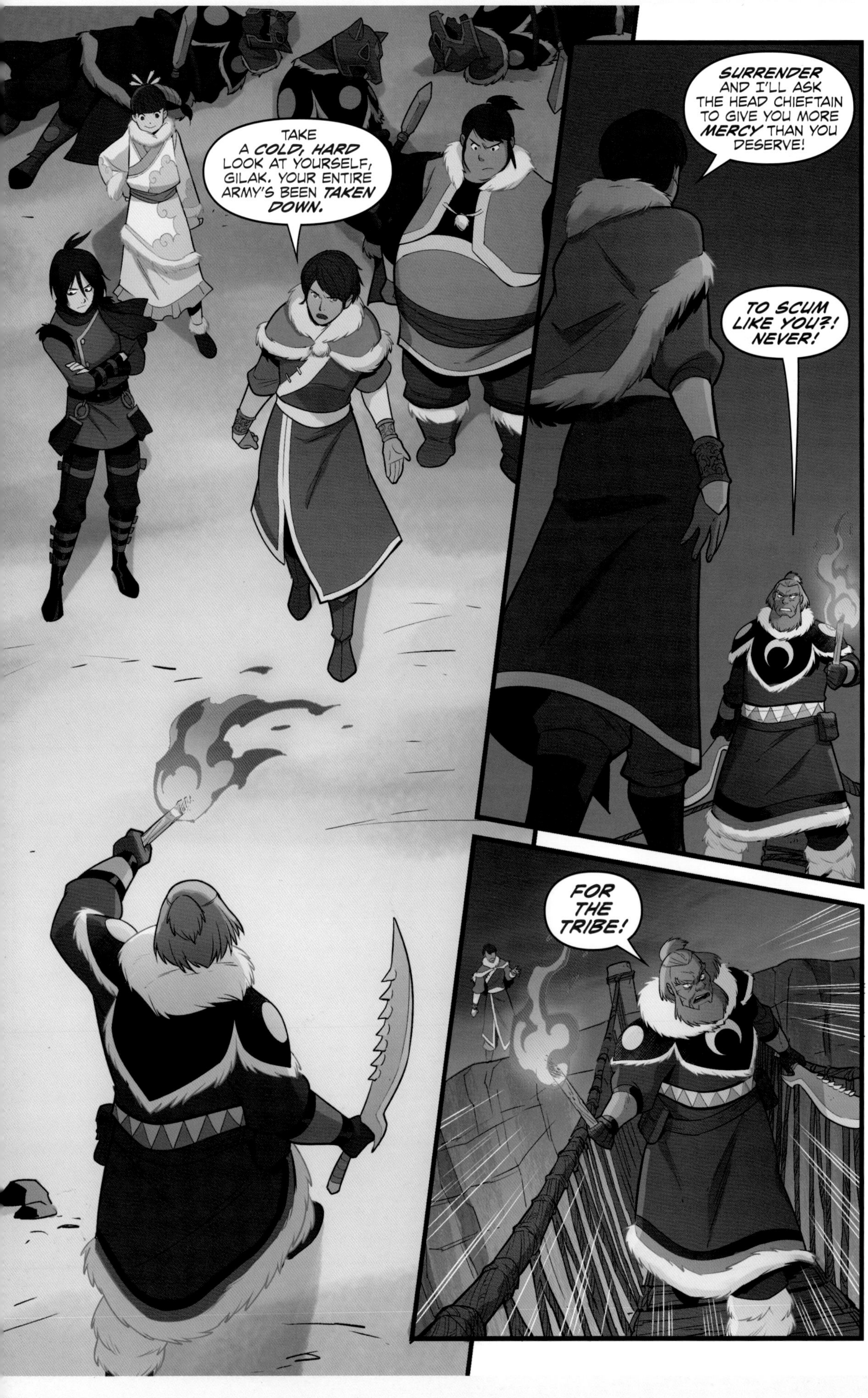
TAKE A COLD, HARD LOOK AT YOURSELF, GILAK. YOUR ENTIRE ARMY'S BEEN TAKEN DOWN.
SURRENDER AND I'LL ASK THE HEAD CHIEFTAIN TO GIVE YOU MORE MERCY THAN YOU DESERVE!
TO SCUM LIKE YOU?! NEVER!
FOR THE TRIBE!

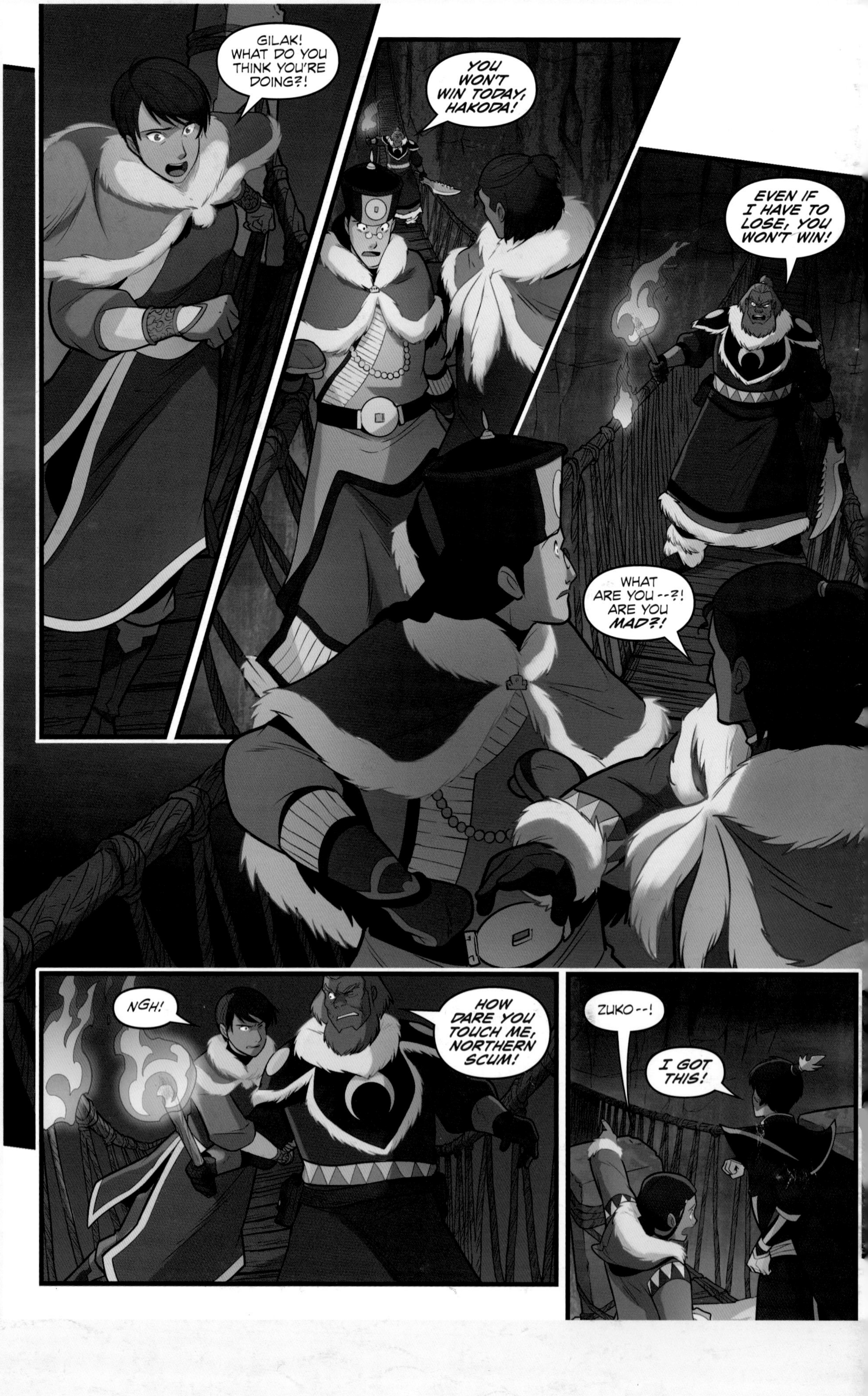
GILAK! WHAT DO YOU THINK YOU'RE DOING?!
YOU WON'T WIN TODAY, HAKODA!
EVEN IF I HAVE TO LOSE, YOU WON'T WIN!
WHAT ARE YOU --?! ARE YOU MAD?!
NGH!
HOW DARE YOU TOUCH ME, NORTHERN SCUM!
ZUKO--!
I GOT THIS!

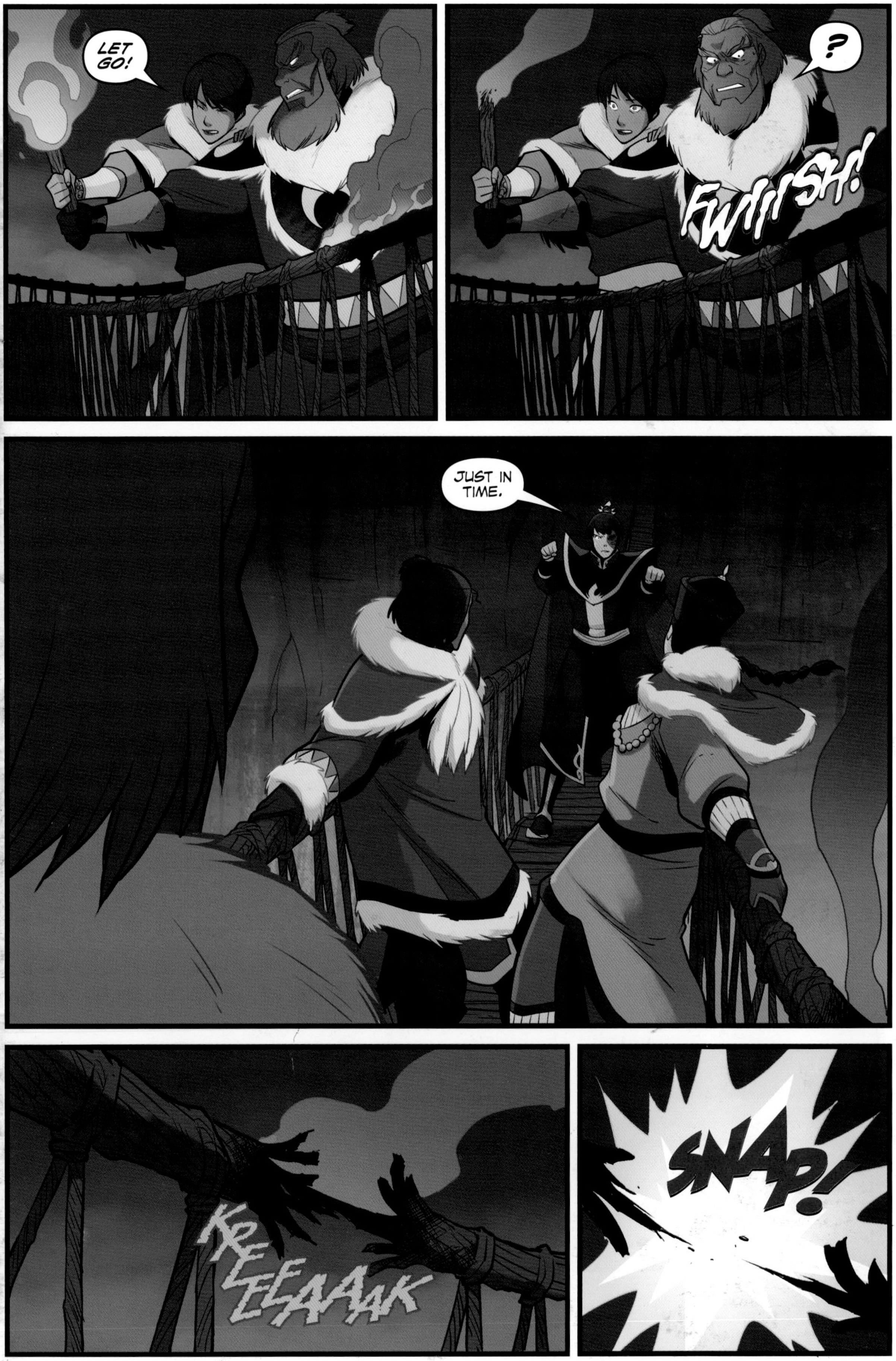
LET GO!
?
FWIIIISH!
JUST IN TIME.
KREEEEAAAAK
SNAP!

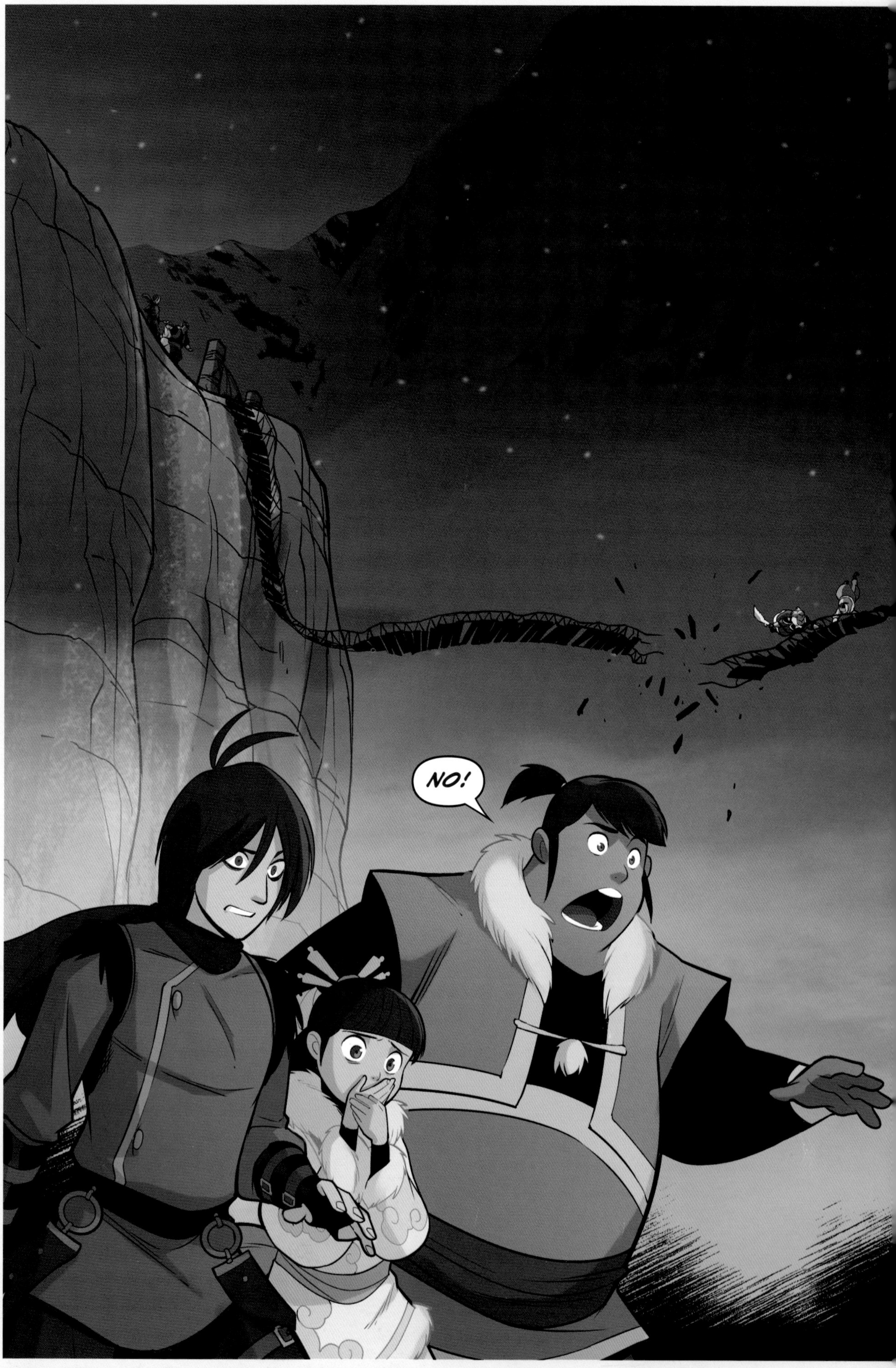
NO!

GLY: *I wasn't sure how to portray the emotion and the action in this scene. I love Gurihiru's solution. Juxtaposing the close-ups with the wide shot works great!*

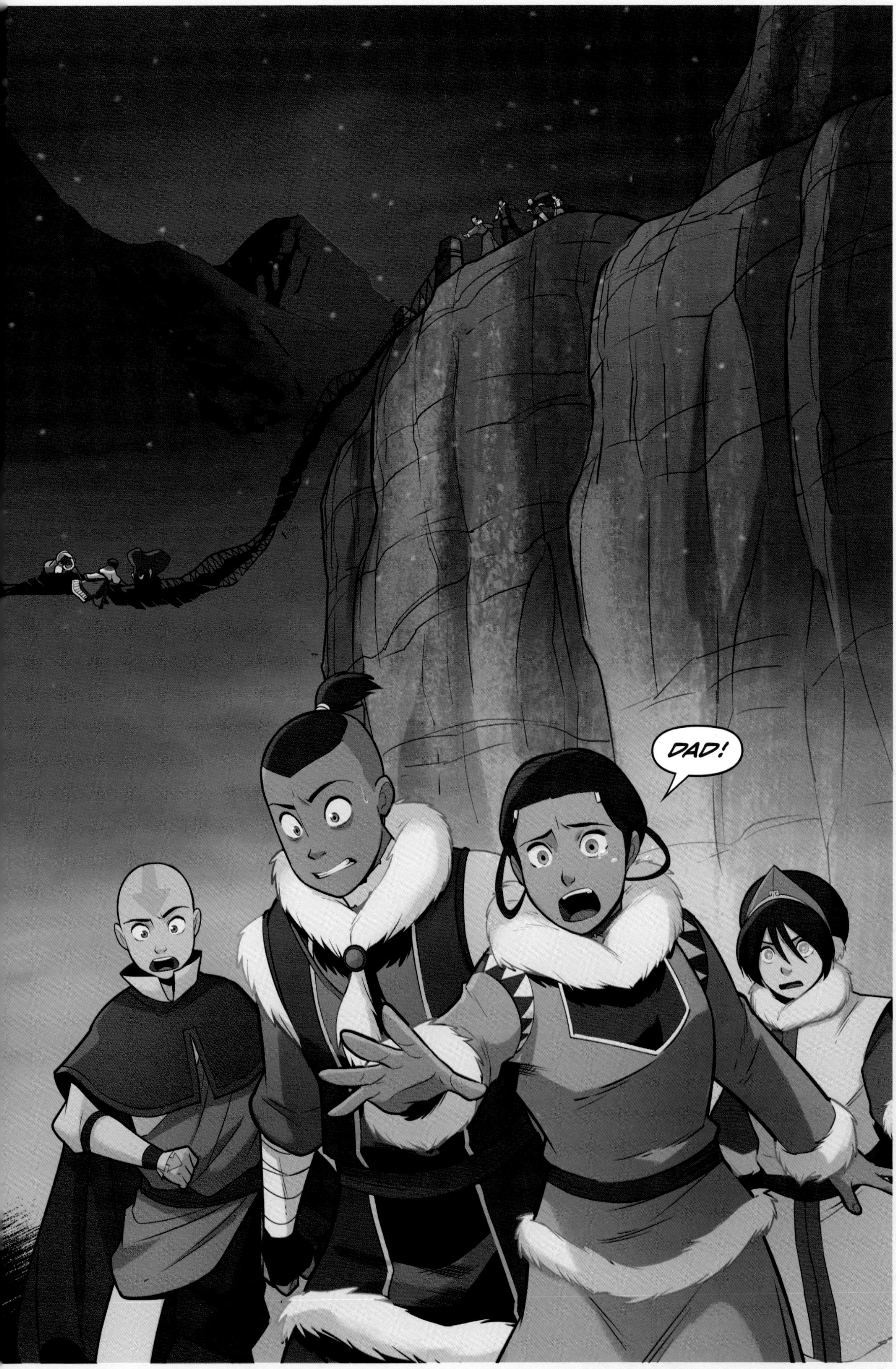
DAD!

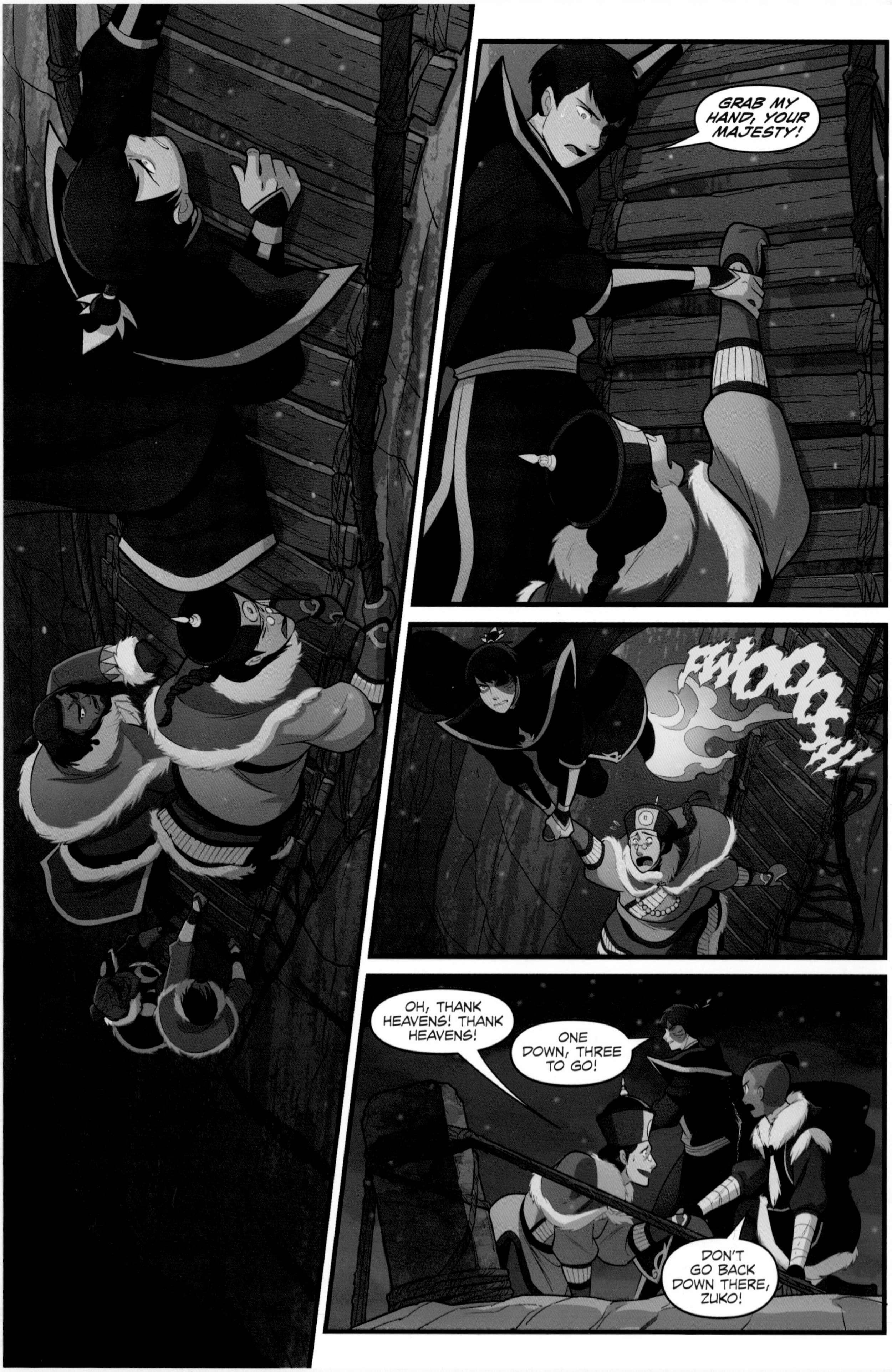
GRAB MY HAND, YOUR MAJESTY!
FWOOOSH!
OH, THANK HEAVENS! THANK HEAVENS!
ONE DOWN, THREE TO GO!
DON'T GO BACK DOWN THERE, ZUKO!

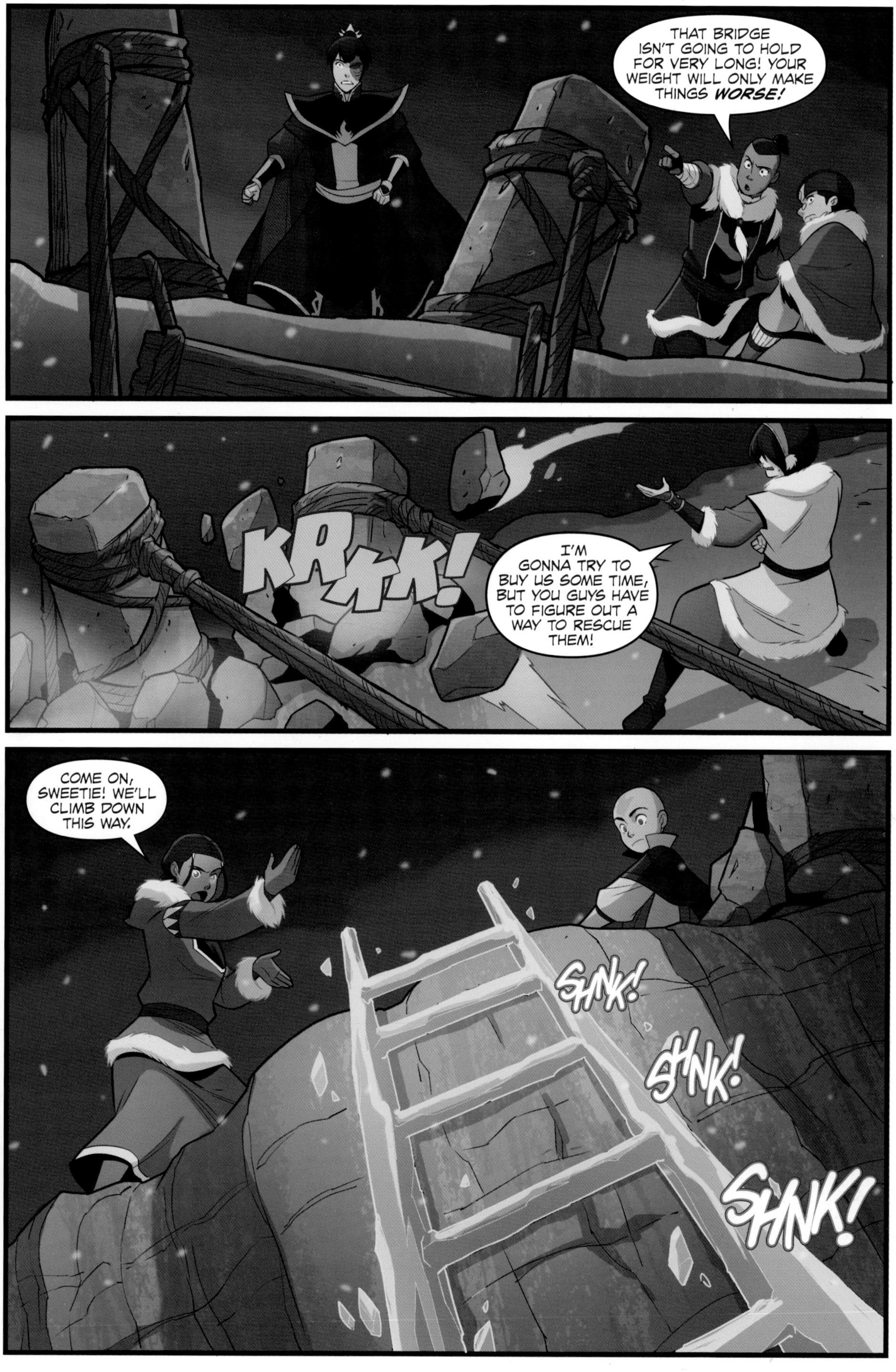
THAT BRIDGE ISN'T GOING TO HOLD FOR VERY LONG! YOUR WEIGHT WILL ONLY MAKE THINGS *WORSE!*
KRKK!
I'M GONNA TRY TO BUY US SOME TIME, BUT YOU GUYS HAVE TO FIGURE OUT A WAY TO RESCUE THEM!
COME ON, SWEETIE! WE'LL CLIMB DOWN THIS WAY.
SHNK!
SHNK!
SHNK!

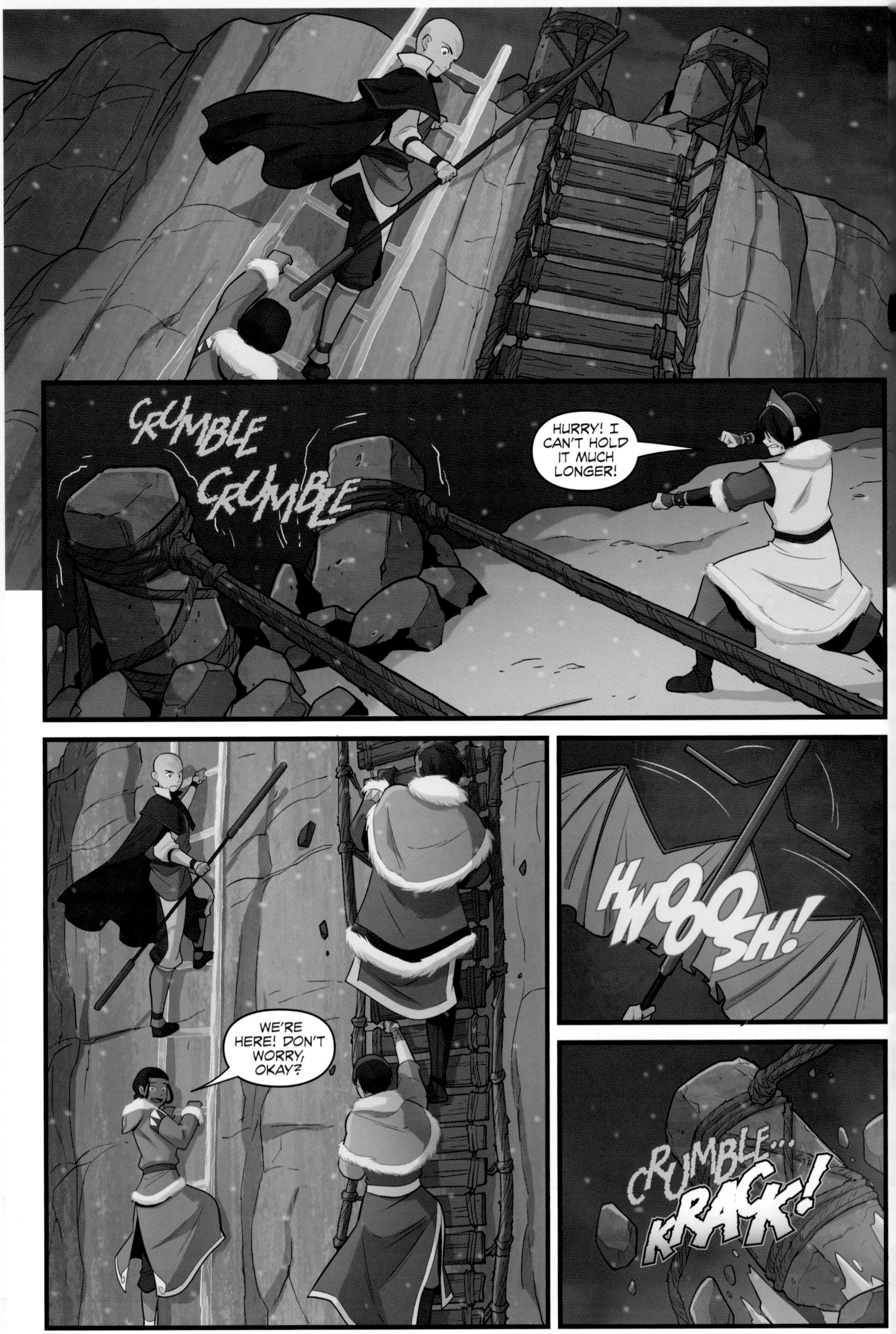
CRUMBLE
CRUMBLE
HURRY! I CAN'T HOLD IT MUCH LONGER!
WE'RE HERE! DON'T WORRY, OKAY?
HWOOOSH!
CRUMBLE...
KRACK!

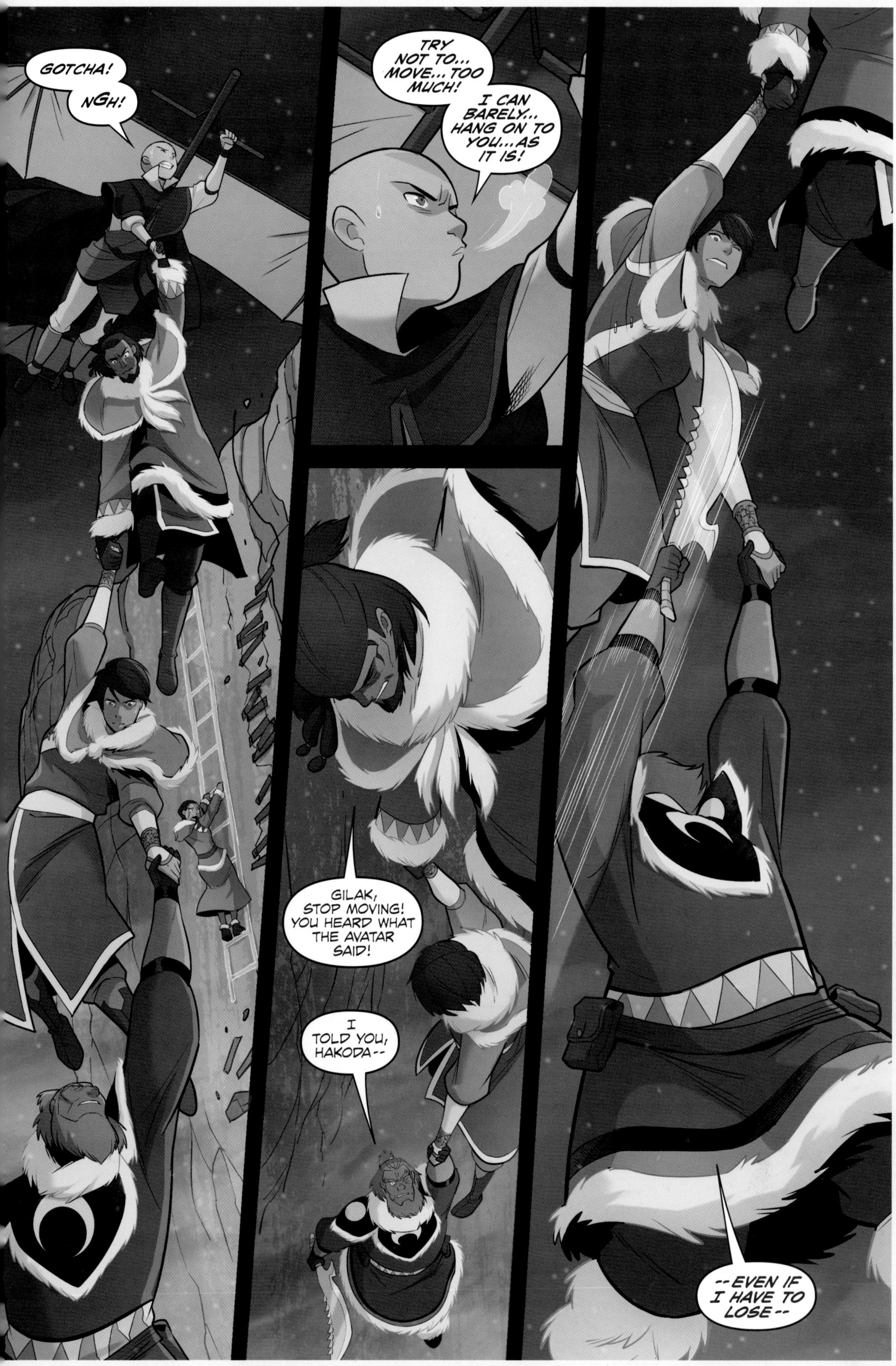
GOTCHA!
NGH!
TRY NOT TO... MOVE... TOO MUCH!
I CAN BARELY... HANG ON TO YOU... AS IT IS!
GILAK, STOP MOVING! YOU HEARD WHAT THE AVATAR SAID!
I TOLD YOU, HAKODA--
--EVEN IF I HAVE TO LOSE--

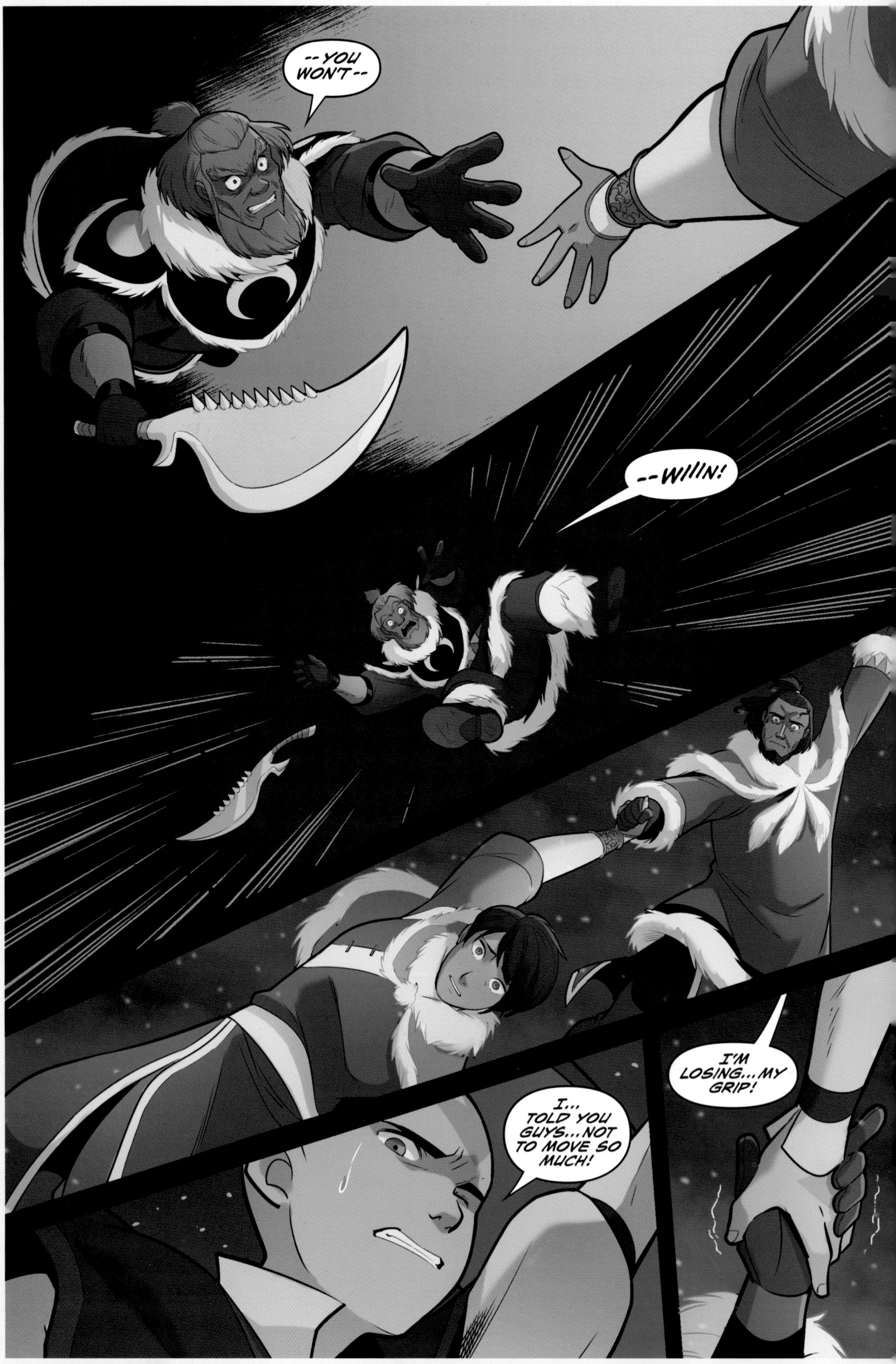
--YOU WON'T--
--WIIIN!
I'M LOSING... MY GRIP!
I... TOLD YOU GUYS... NOT TO MOVE SO MUCH!

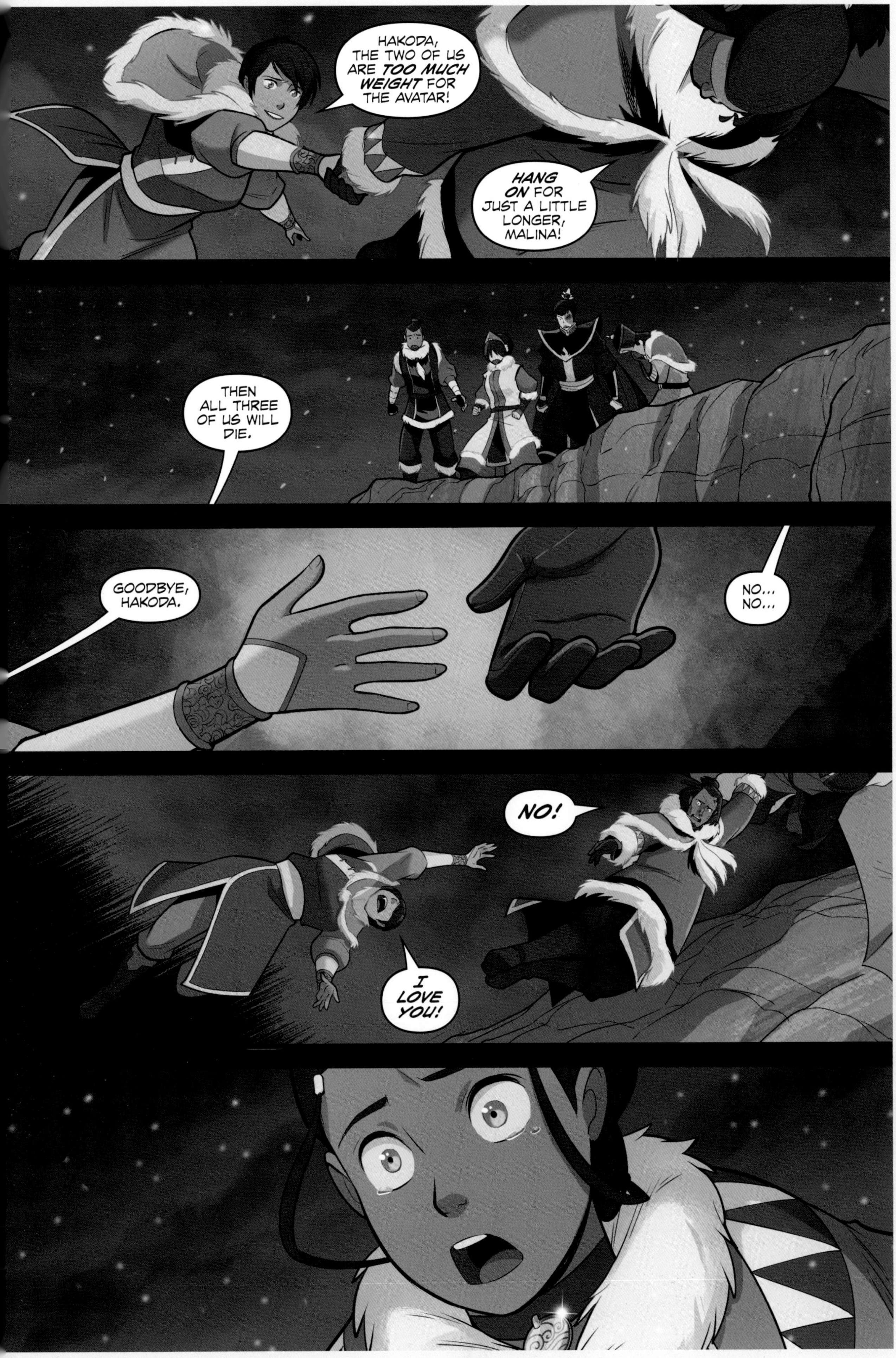
HAKODA, THE TWO OF US ARE TOO MUCH WEIGHT FOR THE AVATAR!
HANG ON FOR JUST A LITTLE LONGER, MALINA!
THEN ALL THREE OF US WILL DIE.
GOODBYE, HAKODA.
NO... NO...
NO!
I LOVE YOU!

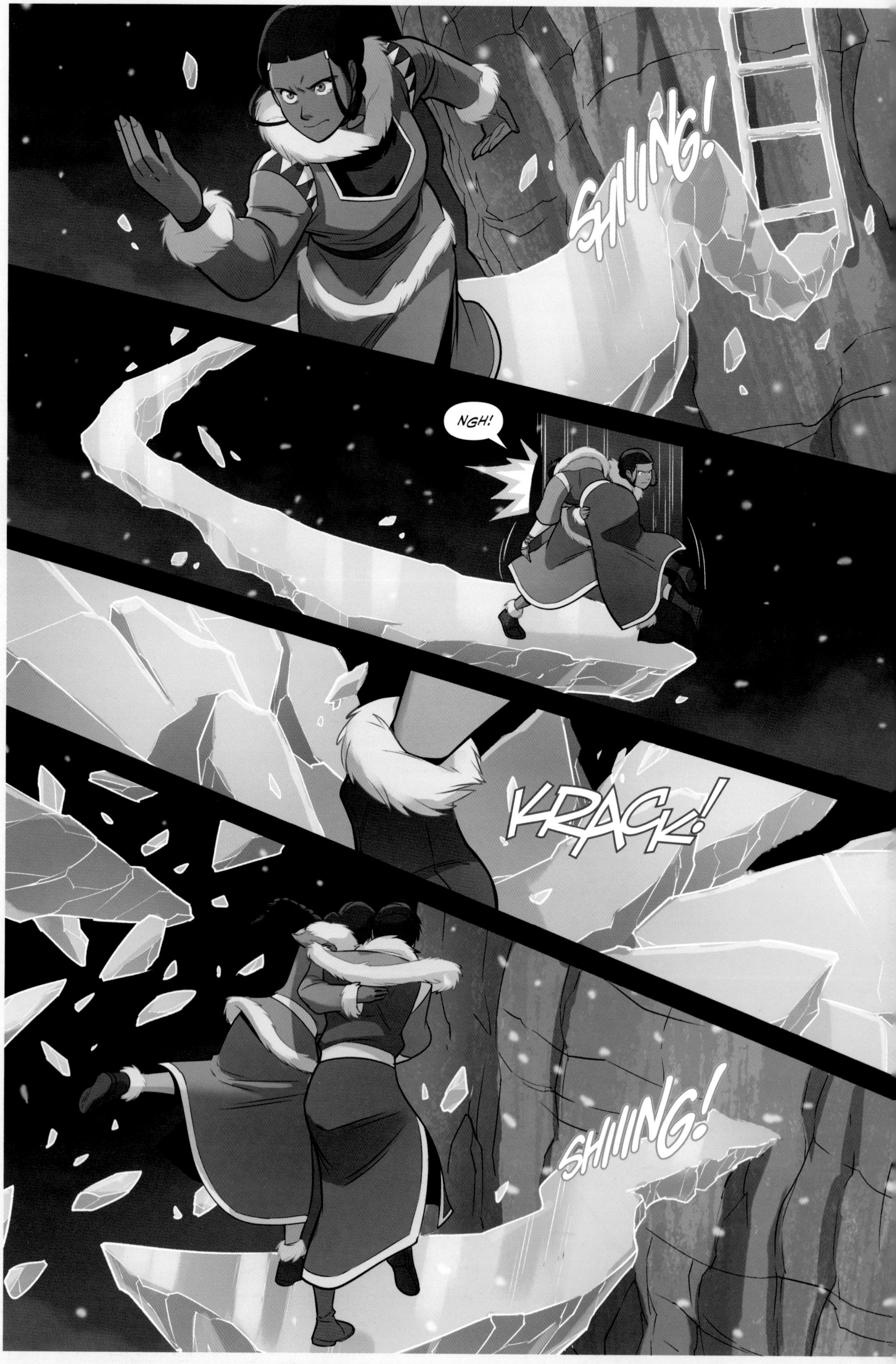
SHIIING!
NGH!
KRACK!
SHIIING!

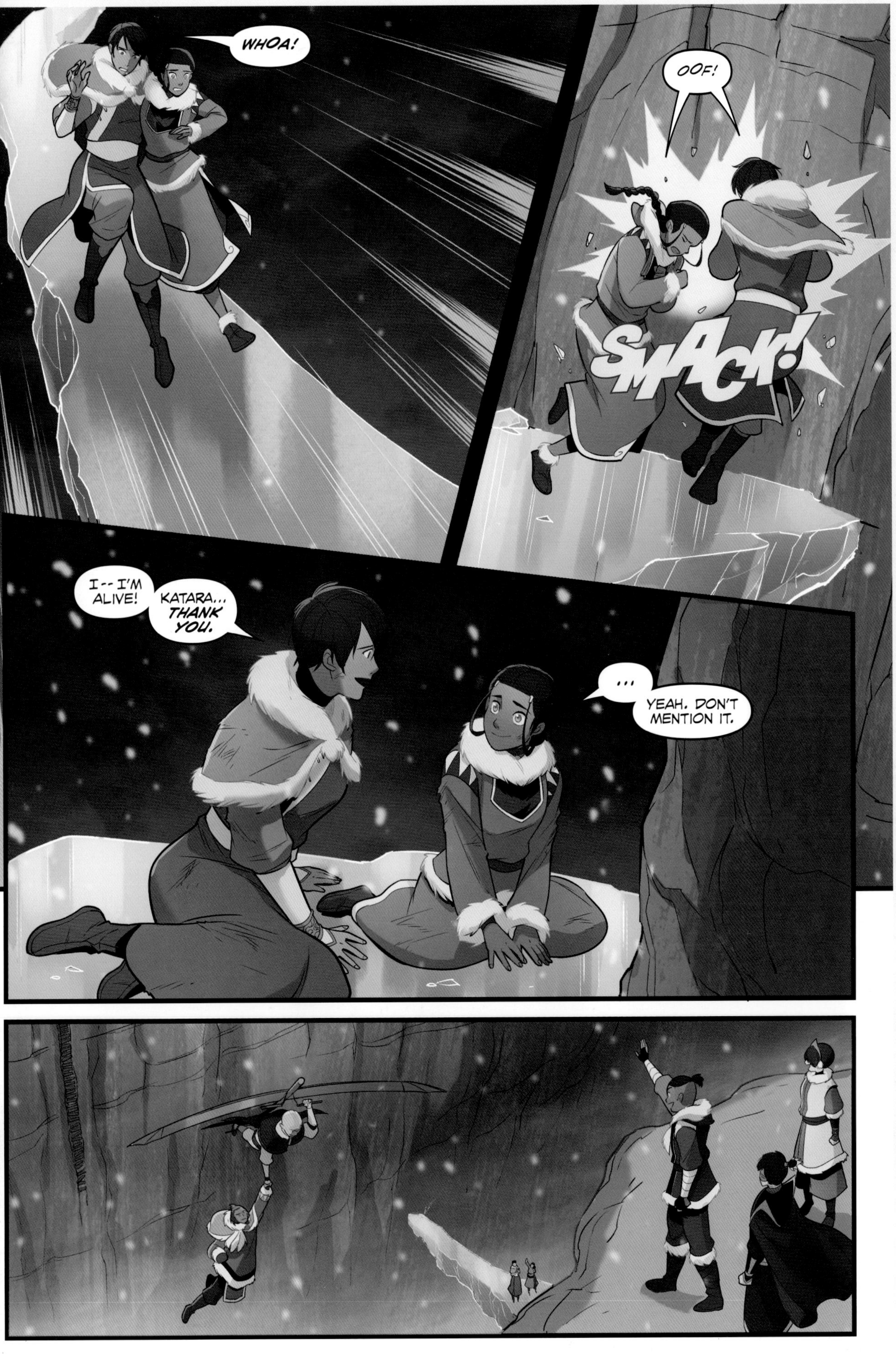
WHOA!
OOF!
SMACK!
I-- I'M ALIVE!
KATARA... THANK YOU.
...
YEAH. DON'T MENTION IT.

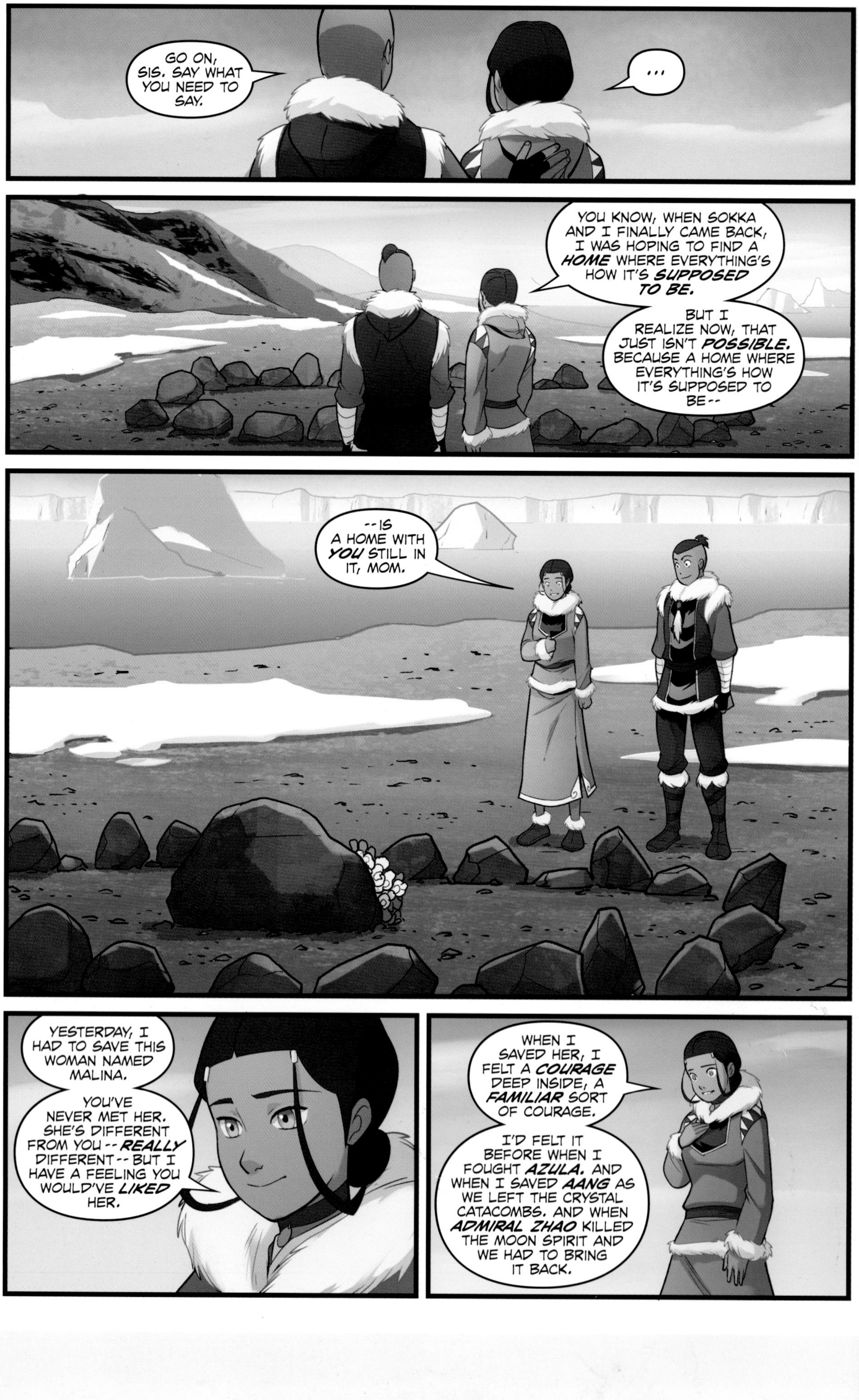
GO ON, SIS. SAY WHAT YOU NEED TO SAY.
...
YOU KNOW, WHEN SOKKA AND I FINALLY CAME BACK, I WAS HOPING TO FIND A HOME WHERE EVERYTHING'S HOW IT'S SUPPOSED TO BE.
BUT I REALIZE NOW, THAT JUST ISN'T POSSIBLE. BECAUSE A HOME WHERE EVERYTHING'S HOW IT'S SUPPOSED TO BE--
--IS A HOME WITH YOU STILL IN IT, MOM.
YESTERDAY, I HAD TO SAVE THIS WOMAN NAMED MALINA.
YOU'VE NEVER MET HER. SHE'S DIFFERENT FROM YOU--REALLY DIFFERENT--BUT I HAVE A FEELING YOU WOULD'VE LIKED HER.
WHEN I SAVED HER, I FELT A COURAGE DEEP INSIDE, A FAMILIAR SORT OF COURAGE.
I'D FELT IT BEFORE WHEN I FOUGHT AZULA. AND WHEN I SAVED AANG AS WE LEFT THE CRYSTAL CATACOMBS. AND WHEN ADMIRAL ZHAO KILLED THE MOON SPIRIT AND WE HAD TO BRING IT BACK.

GLY: *To write this scene, I researched what Inuit gravesites looked like.*

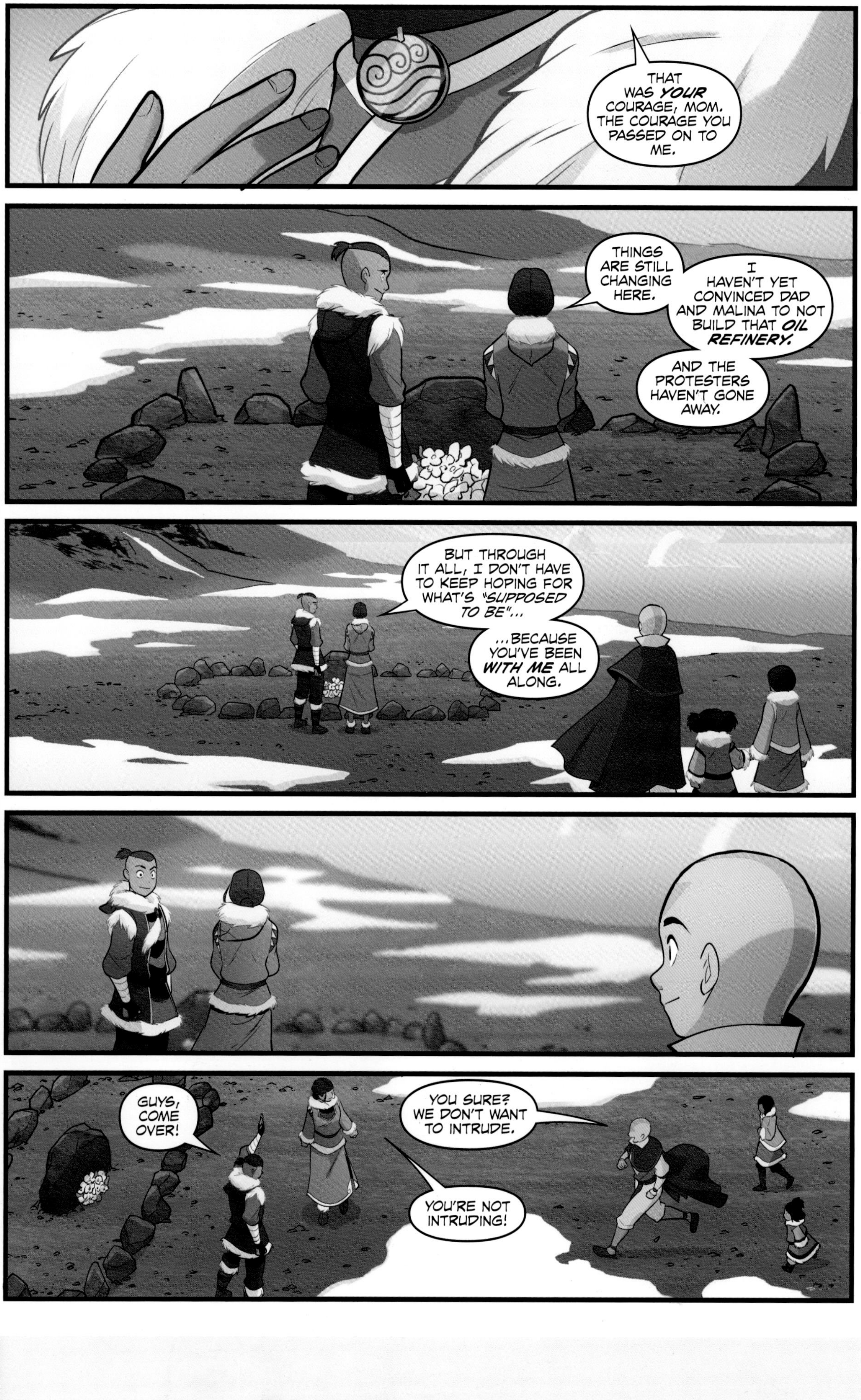
THAT WAS *YOUR* COURAGE, MOM. THE COURAGE YOU PASSED ON TO ME.
THINGS ARE STILL CHANGING HERE.
I HAVEN'T YET CONVINCED DAD AND MALINA TO NOT BUILD THAT *OIL REFINERY.*
AND THE PROTESTERS HAVEN'T GONE AWAY.
BUT THROUGH IT ALL, I DON'T HAVE TO KEEP HOPING FOR WHAT'S *"SUPPOSED TO BE"*...
...BECAUSE YOU'VE BEEN *WITH ME* ALL ALONG.
GUYS, COME OVER!
YOU SURE? WE DON'T WANT TO INTRUDE.
YOU'RE NOT INTRUDING!

G: *We used an Inuit grave as a model for Kya's grave.*

G: *Katara's expression had to show her sorrow about the past and hope for her future at the same time, which was very difficult to convey.*

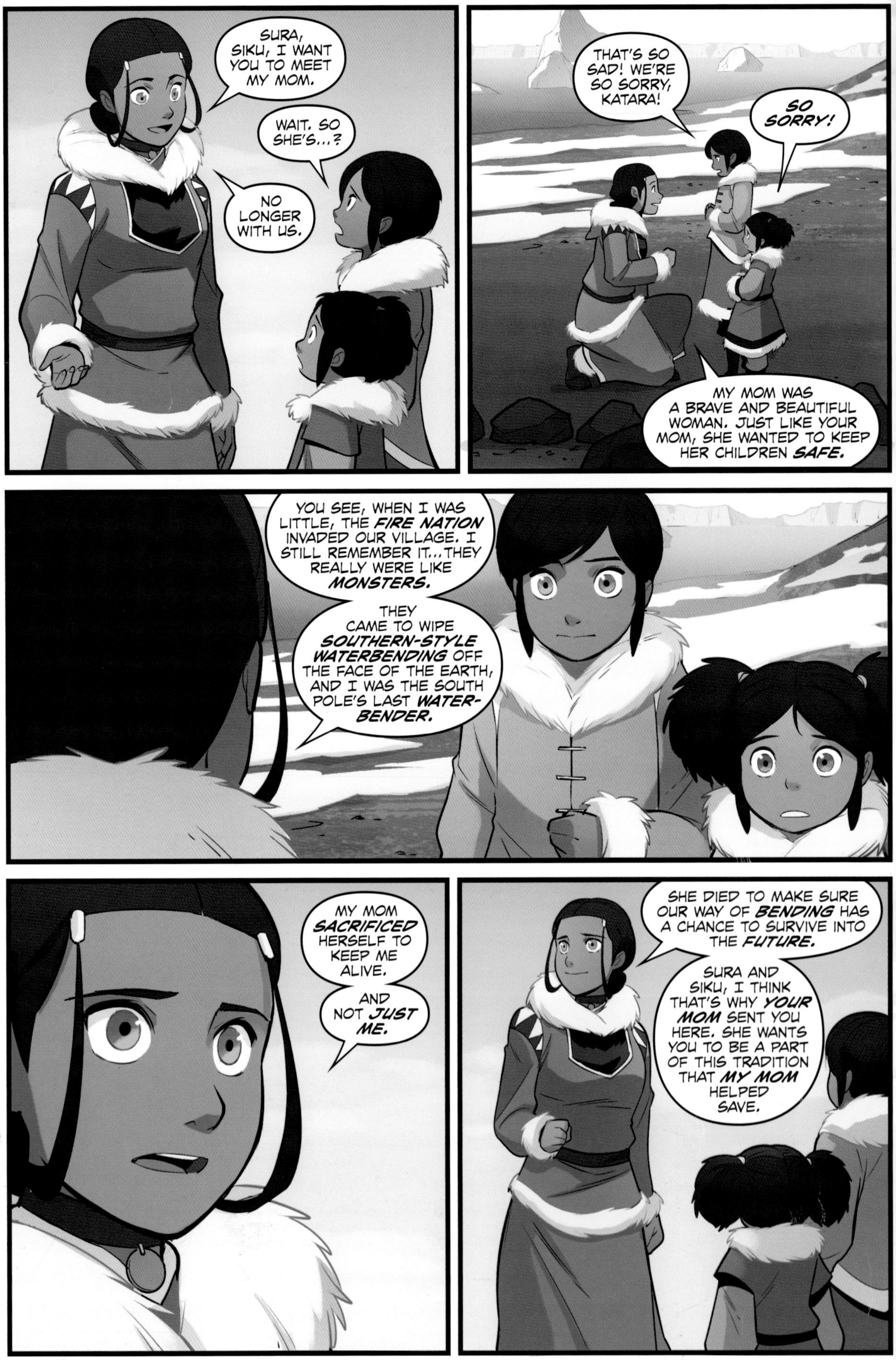
SURA, SIKU, I WANT YOU TO MEET MY MOM.
WAIT. SO SHE'S...?
NO LONGER WITH US.
THAT'S SO SAD! WE'RE SO SORRY, KATARA!
SO SORRY!
MY MOM WAS A BRAVE AND BEAUTIFUL WOMAN. JUST LIKE YOUR MOM, SHE WANTED TO KEEP HER CHILDREN SAFE.
YOU SEE, WHEN I WAS LITTLE, THE FIRE NATION INVADED OUR VILLAGE. I STILL REMEMBER IT...THEY REALLY WERE LIKE MONSTERS.
THEY CAME TO WIPE SOUTHERN-STYLE WATERBENDING OFF THE FACE OF THE EARTH, AND I WAS THE SOUTH POLE'S LAST WATER-BENDER.
MY MOM SACRIFICED HERSELF TO KEEP ME ALIVE.
AND NOT JUST ME.
SHE DIED TO MAKE SURE OUR WAY OF BENDING HAS A CHANCE TO SURVIVE INTO THE FUTURE.
SURA AND SIKU, I THINK THAT'S WHY YOUR MOM SENT YOU HERE. SHE WANTS YOU TO BE A PART OF THIS TRADITION THAT MY MOM HELPED SAVE.

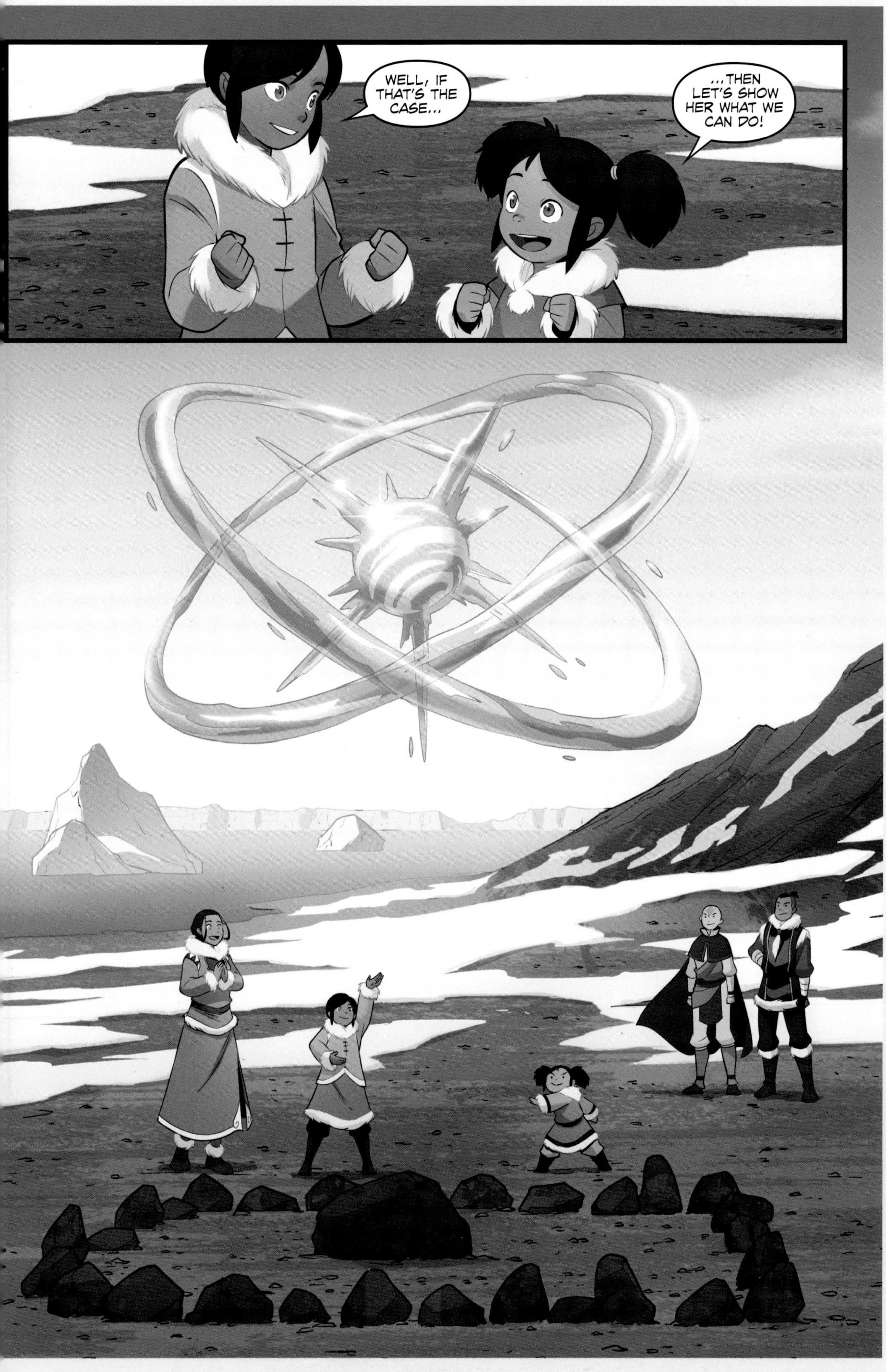
WELL, IF THAT'S THE CASE...
...THEN LET'S SHOW HER WHAT WE CAN DO!

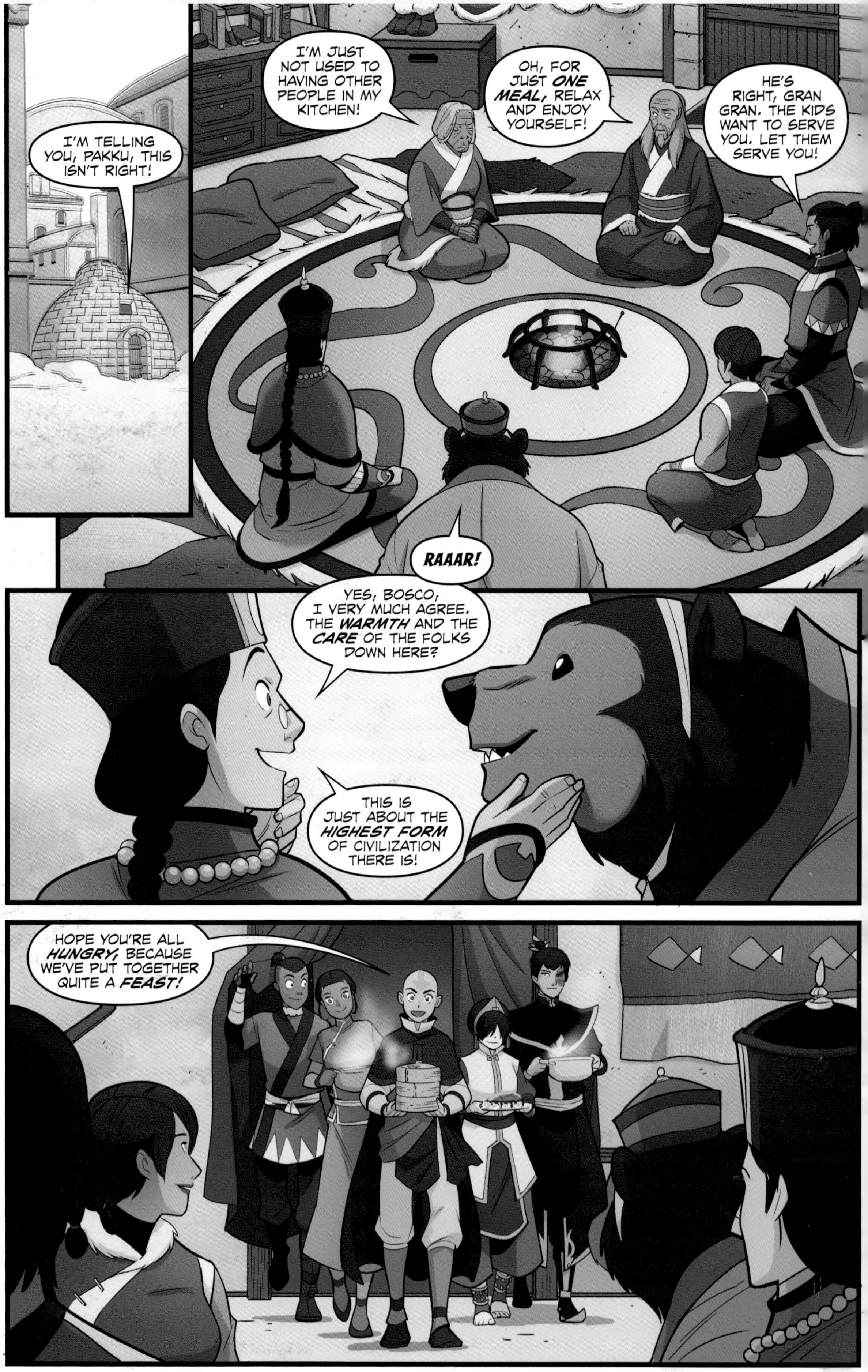
I'M TELLING YOU, PAKKU, THIS ISN'T RIGHT!
I'M JUST NOT USED TO HAVING OTHER PEOPLE IN MY KITCHEN!
OH, FOR JUST ONE MEAL, RELAX AND ENJOY YOURSELF!
HE'S RIGHT, GRAN GRAN. THE KIDS WANT TO SERVE YOU. LET THEM SERVE YOU!
RAAAR!
YES, BOSCO, I VERY MUCH AGREE. THE WARMTH AND THE CARE OF THE FOLKS DOWN HERE?
THIS IS JUST ABOUT THE HIGHEST FORM OF CIVILIZATION THERE IS!
HOPE YOU'RE ALL HUNGRY, BECAUSE WE'VE PUT TOGETHER QUITE A FEAST!

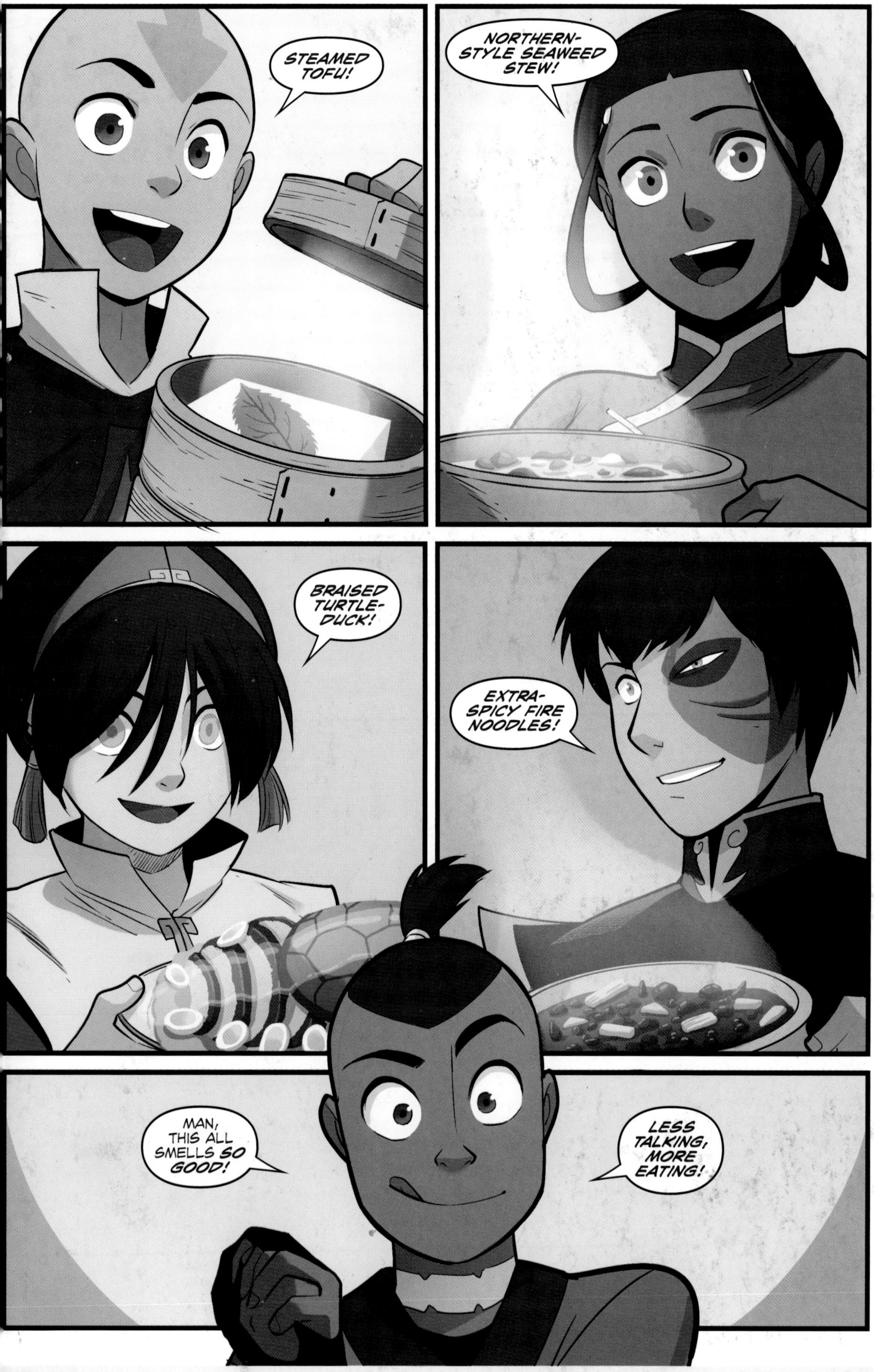
STEAMED TOFU!
NORTHERN-STYLE SEAWEED STEW!
BRAISED TURTLE-DUCK!
EXTRA-SPICY FIRE NOODLES!
MAN, THIS ALL SMELLS SO GOOD!
LESS TALKING, MORE EATING!

GLY: *Nothing like some amazing Avatar food to bring everybody together!*

G: Gene Yang's scripts have many scenes where the characters connect to their feelings and each other through eating, which gives depth to the story. We think these scenes are among the best ways to show the characters' feelings to the readers, and we tried to accomplish that here. We were happy to be able to draw this scene for our last page!

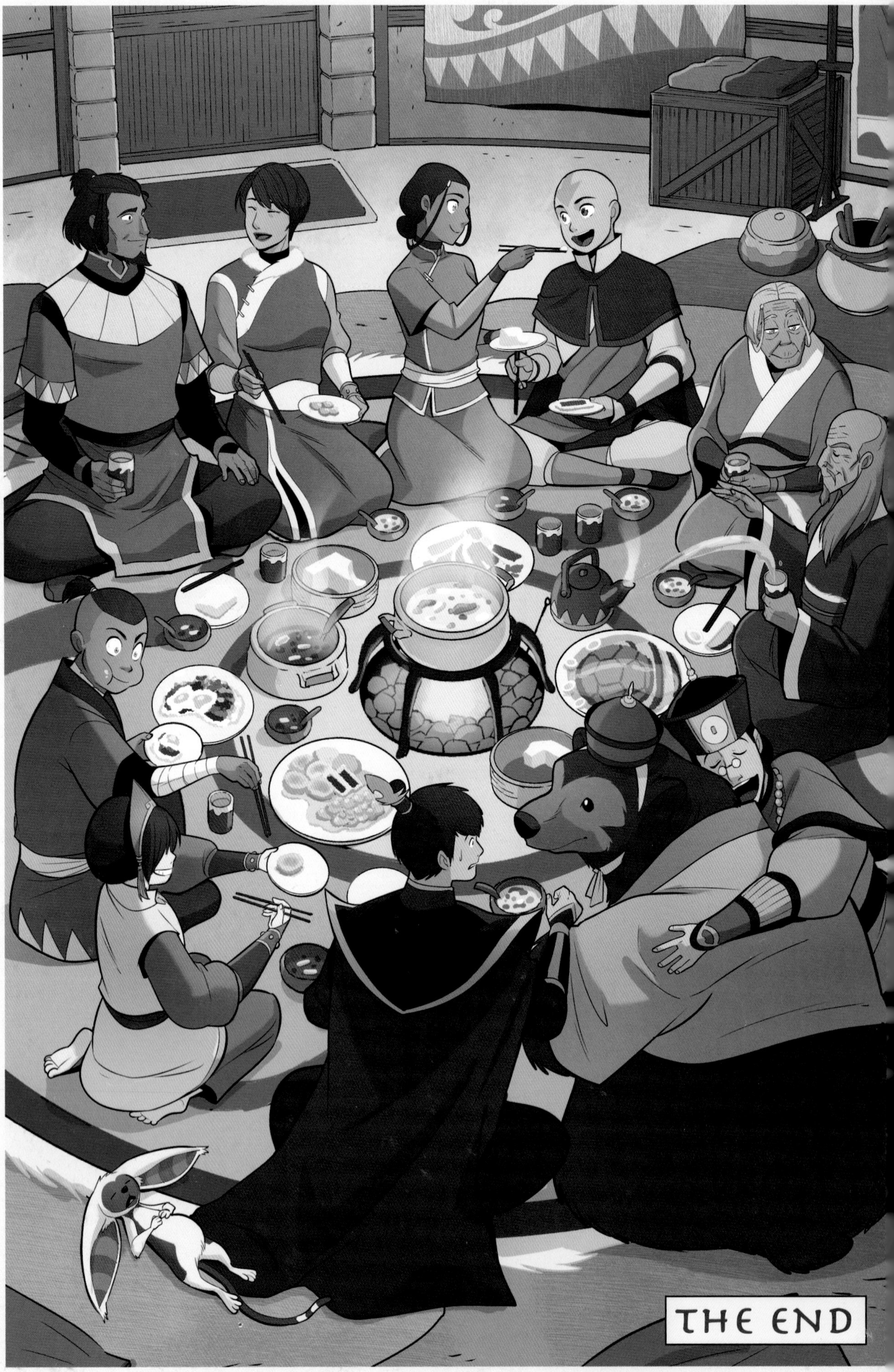
THE END

Five years ago, I got an email from an editor at Dark Horse. She told me that Nickelodeon was about to launch a sequel to *Avatar: The Last Airbender*. Dark Horse had just acquired the license to do a series of graphic novels that would fill in the gap between the two shows. Would I be interested in writing it?

It was a dream come true. I'd been an *Avatar* fan for a while by then. Getting to play in a corner of this universe I loved so much . . . what more could a guy ask for?

The actual job was better than I'd hoped. Gurihiru are, simply put, perfect for the series. Their art style is both true to the original show and entirely their own, a difficult blend they pulled off flawlessly.

Mike DiMartino and Bryan Konietzko were involved from day one. They gave feedback at every stage, and I got an up-close look at how these two world-class storytellers approached their craft. I learned so much from them.

Joan Hilty, Dave Marshall, the folks at Nickelodeon, and the folks at Dark Horse all loved this series into existence. You can tell by the care with which they handled every detail.

I'm deeply thankful for the readers who've come out to support the series. I've met so many passionate and creative fans at conventions and signings and shows. I've received *Avatar* plush dolls, Christmas tree ornaments, and bracelets as gifts. It just goes to show, *Avatar: The Last Airbender* is great art that inspires more great art.

I can't believe it's been five years. It's bittersweet to move on from a series and a team that I love so much. I will always cherish my time in the world of *Avatar: The Last Airbender*.

But I have to confess, I'm REALLY excited to see what's next for Aang, Katara, Sokka, Toph, and Zuko! Until then, flameo, hotpeople!

—Gene Luen Yang

Aang and Katara. Toph and Sokka. And of course Zuko...
The five years with these characters were very fun and precious for us.
We really felt that this story was loved by so many people.

We would like to thank Mike, Bryan, Gene, and all the staff at Dark Horse.
It was wonderful working with everyone.
And we would like to thank everyone who read this book from the bottom of our heart.

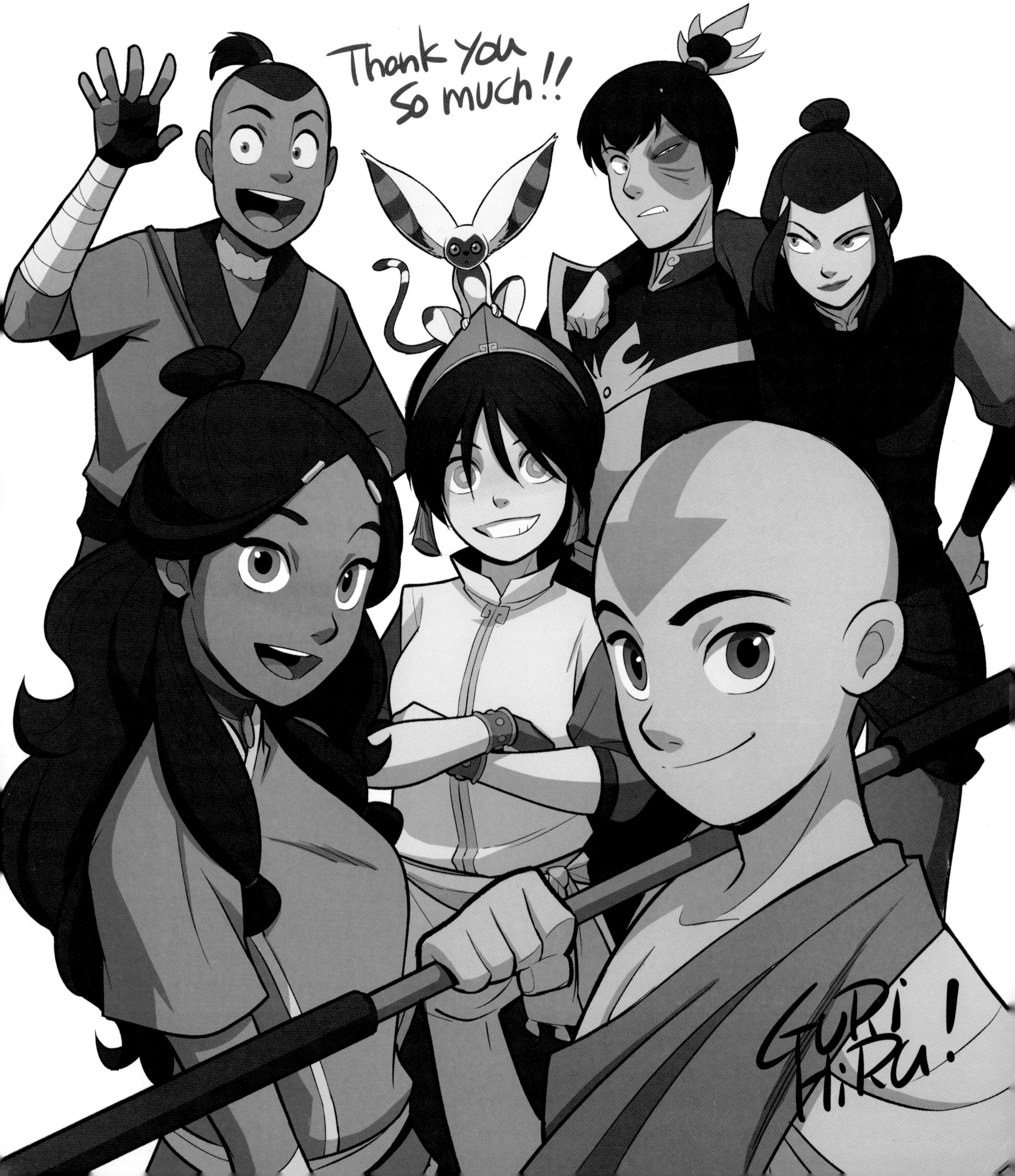
Thank You so much!!
GURI HIRU!

Artwork and captions by Gurihiru

HAKODA

Since Hakoda has become a more prominent leader in his tribe than he was before, we came up with costumes that fit his new role: one costume to wear indoors and one with a coat for outside.

TOPH

Even an Earthbender would be having a hard time in the cold. Toph cannot stand on the ice with bare feet, so we had her wear shoes. We think it was inconvenient for her.

KATARA

Katara plays a big role in this story. In order to connect her with her origins, we came up with the idea of drawing her with her original Water Tribe hairstyle. We suggested this to Mike and Bryan, and they gave us the go-ahead.

SOKKA

Rather than overthinking Sokka's outfit, we just gave him something warm to wear. In the end, we changed the number of furs around his chest from three to one.

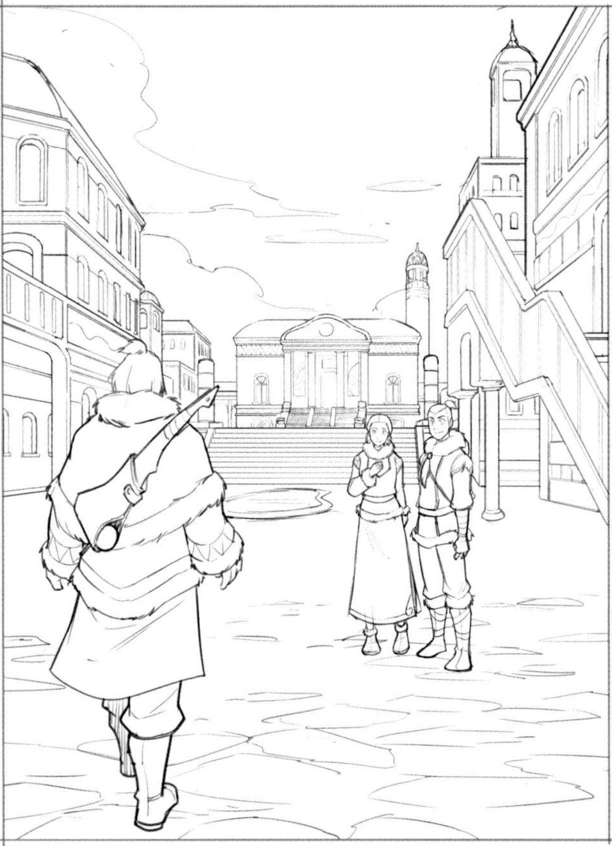

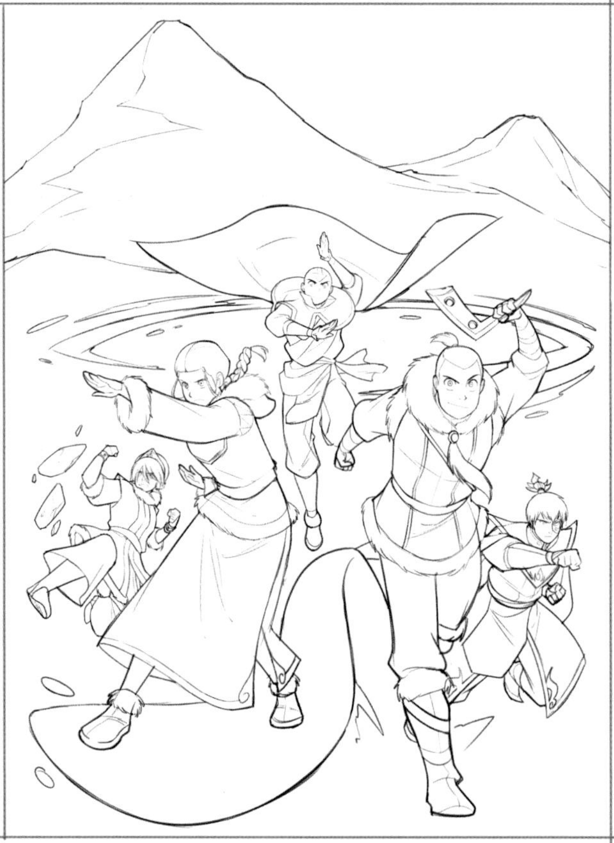

A

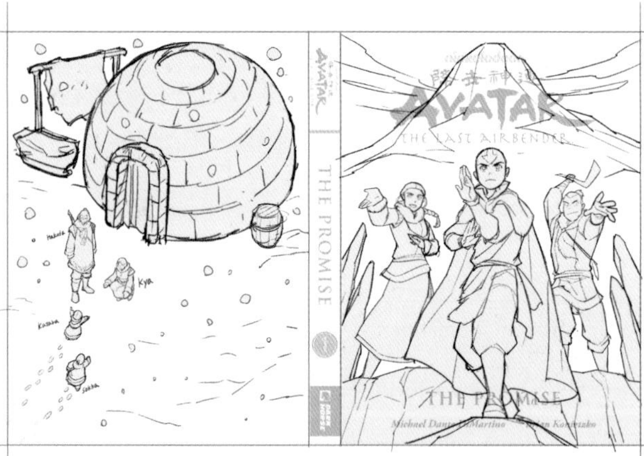
AVATAR
THE LAST AIRBENDER
THE PROMISE

B

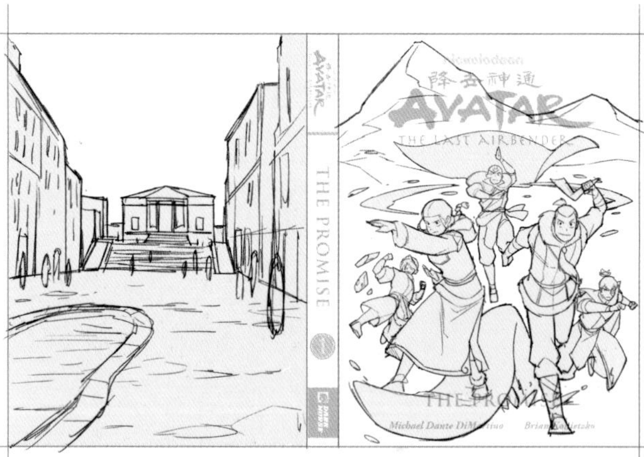
AVATAR
THE LAST AIRBENDER
THE PROMISE

C

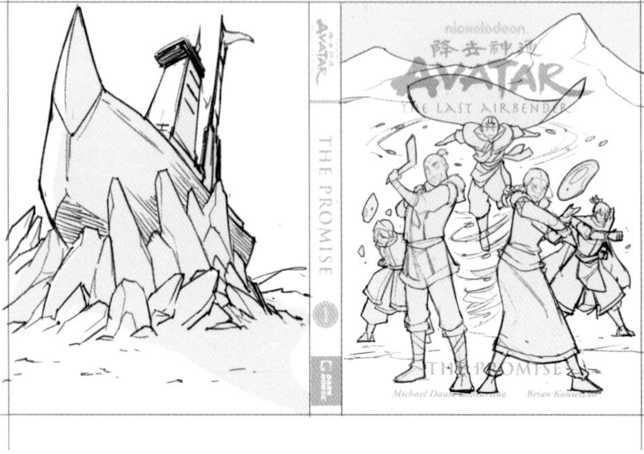
nickelodeon
AVATAR
THE LAST AIRBENDER
THE PROMISE

D

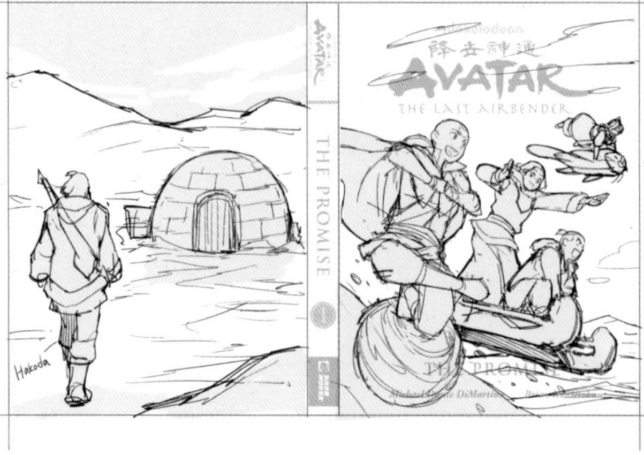
AVATAR
THE LAST AIRBENDER
THE PROMISE
Hakoda

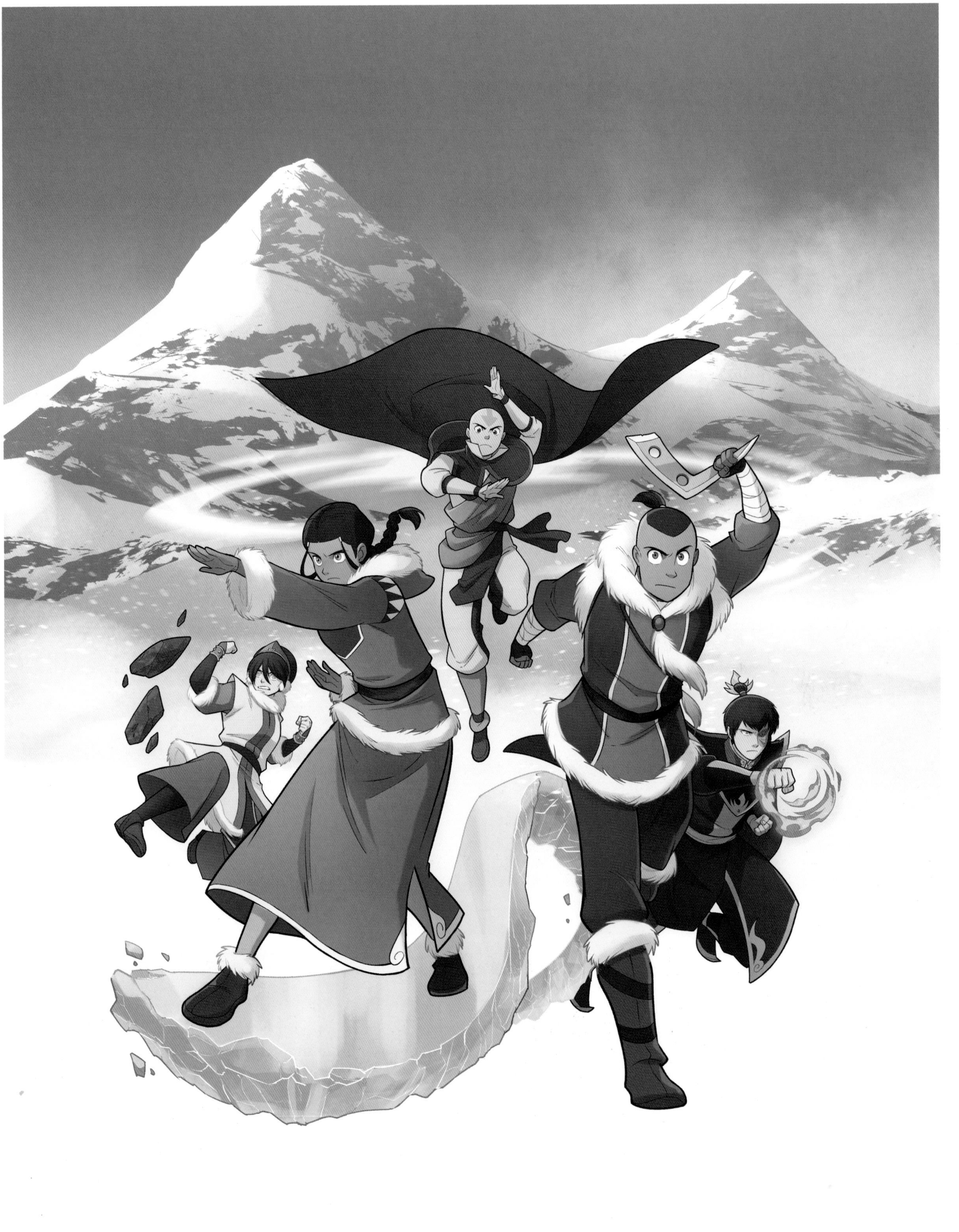

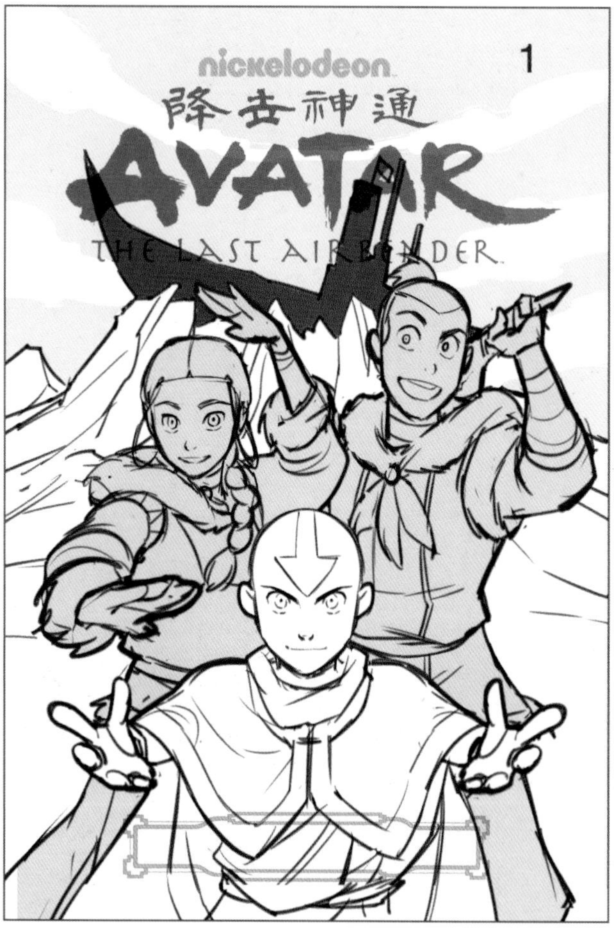
nickelodeon
1
降去神通
AVATAR
THE LAST AIRBENDER

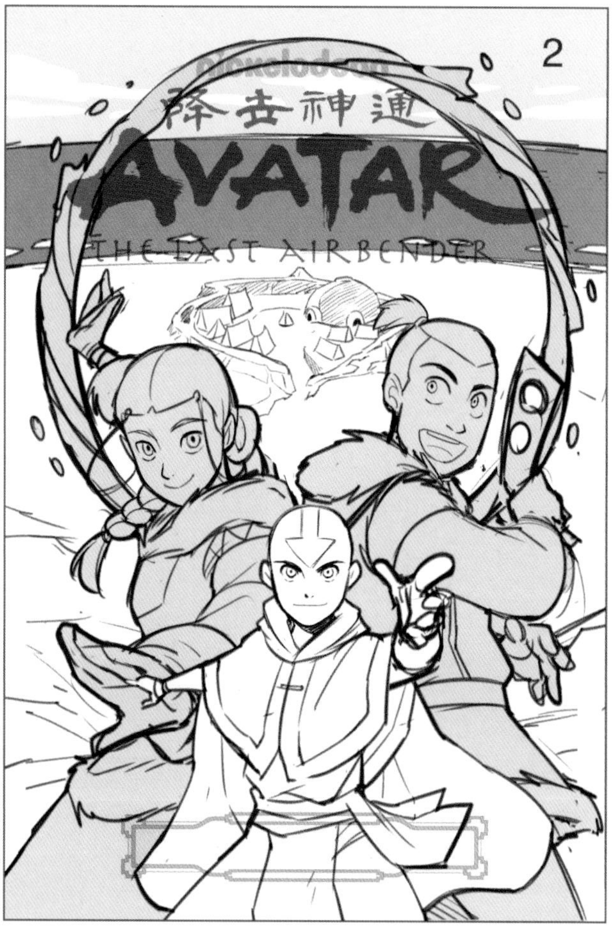
2
降去神通
AVATAR
THE LAST AIRBENDER

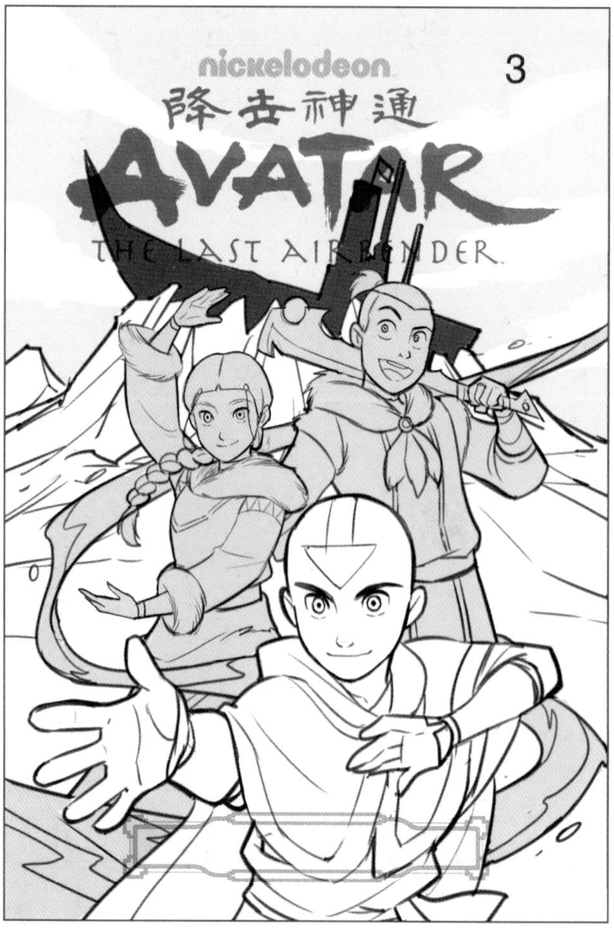
nickelodeon
3
降去神通
AVATAR
THE LAST AIRBENDER

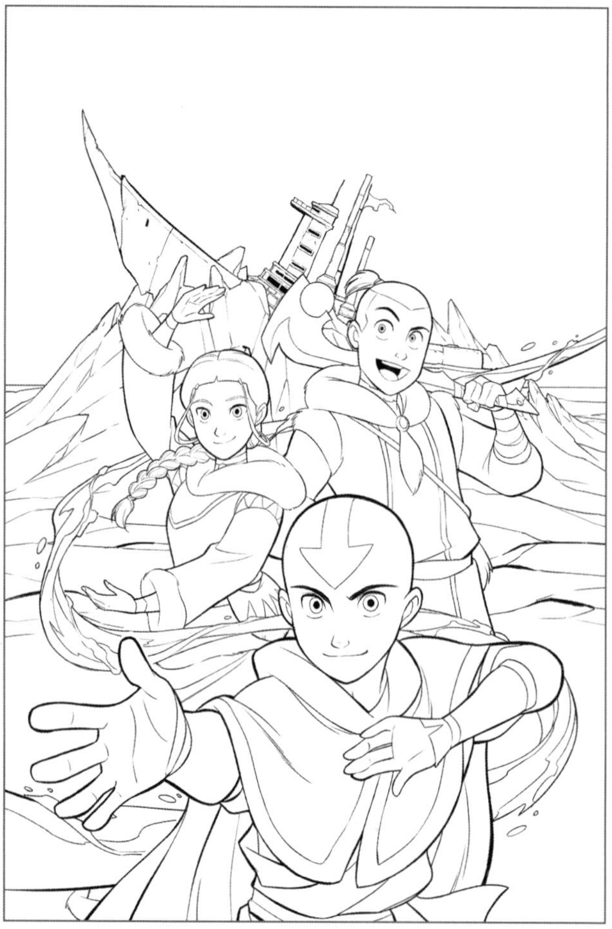

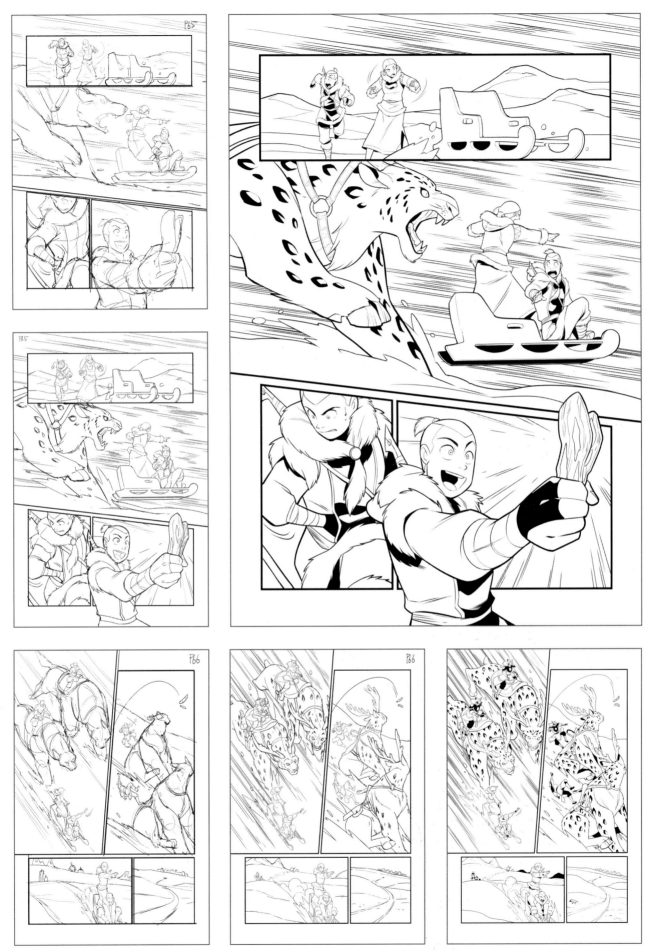

This Part One chase scene featured Polar Bear Dogs in the script and and page layouts. They were then changed to Snow-Leopard Caribou.

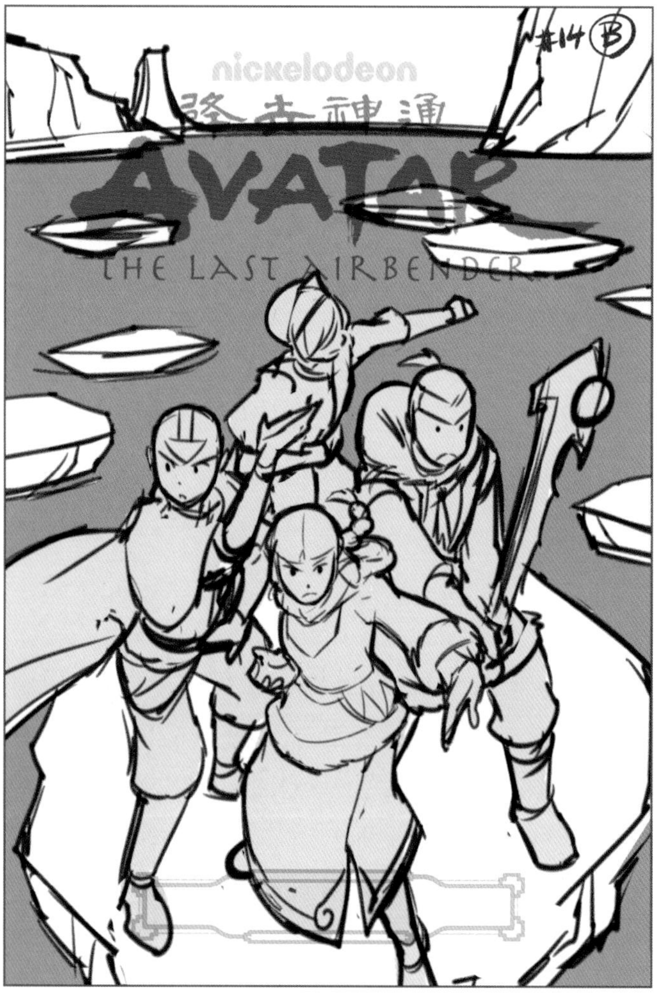
#14 B
nickelodeon
降世神通
AVATAR
THE LAST AIRBENDER

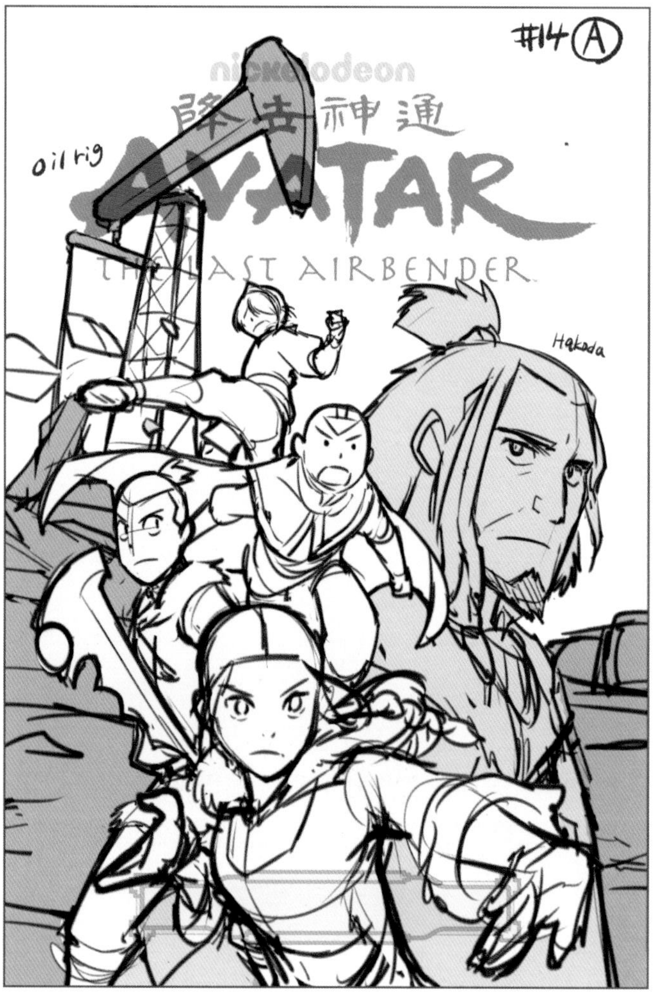
#14 A
nickelodeon
降世神通
Oil rig
AVATAR
THE LAST AIRBENDER
Hakoda

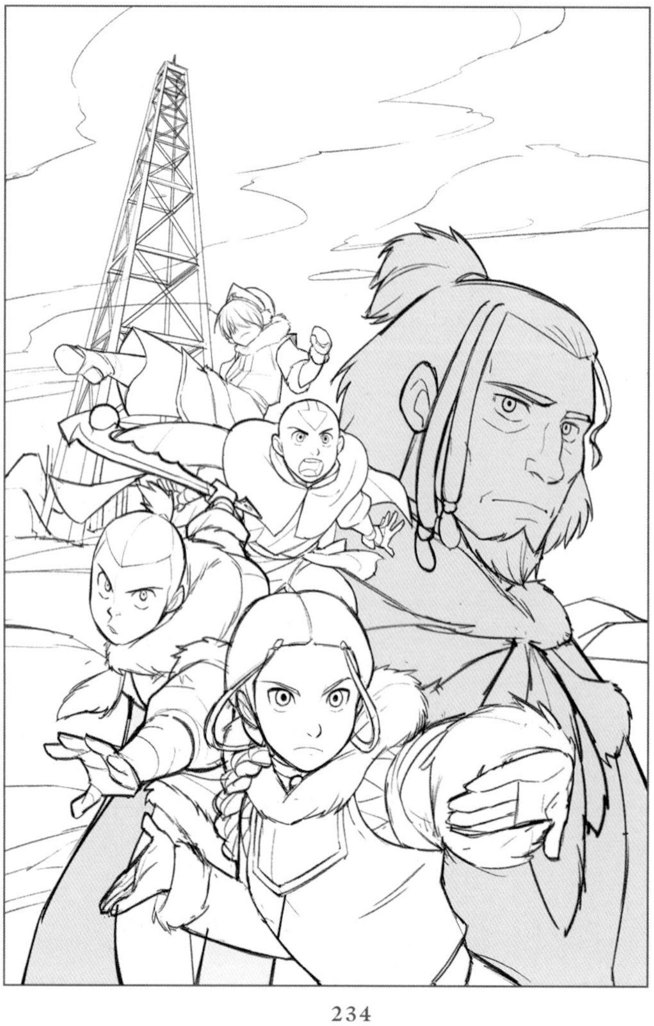

These scenes from Part Two changed between each drawing stage to get the angles and emotional impact just right.

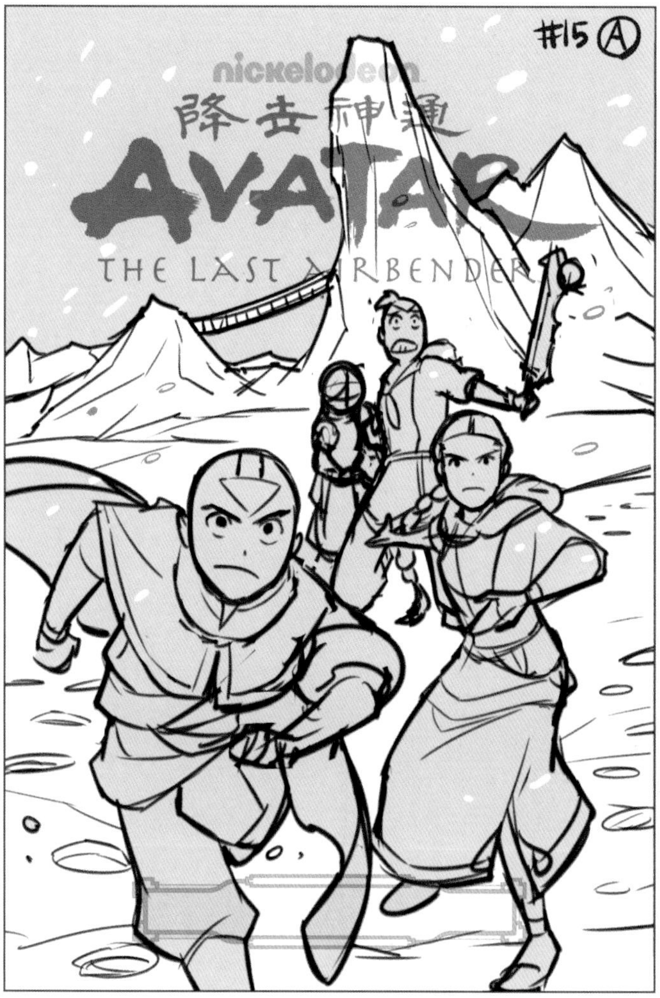
#15 A
nickelodeon
AVATAR
THE LAST AIRBENDER

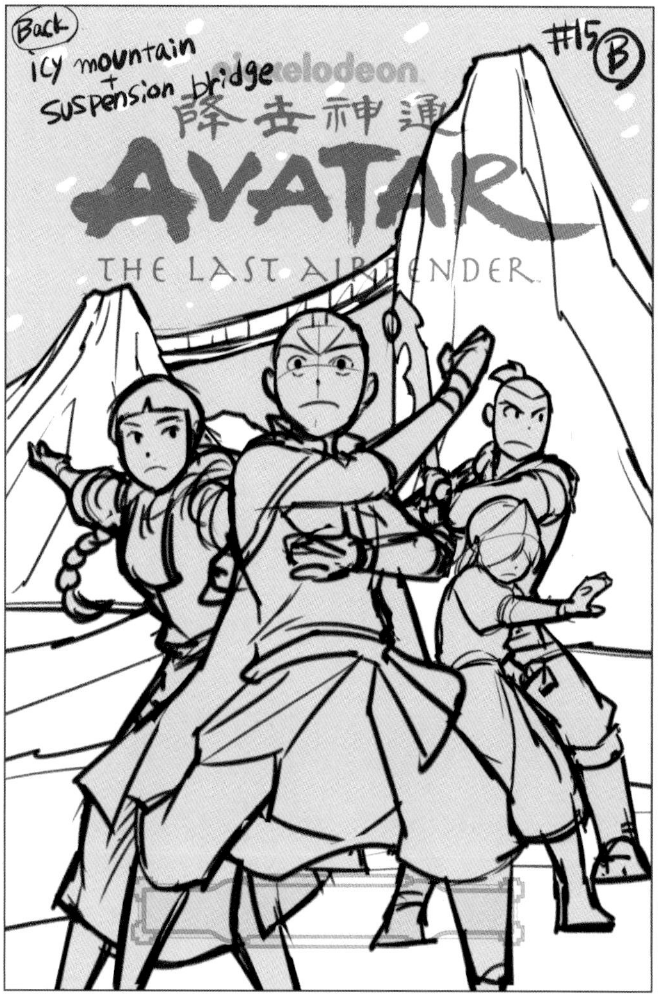
Back
icy mountain
+
suspension bridge
#15 B
nickelodeon
AVATAR
THE LAST AIRBENDER

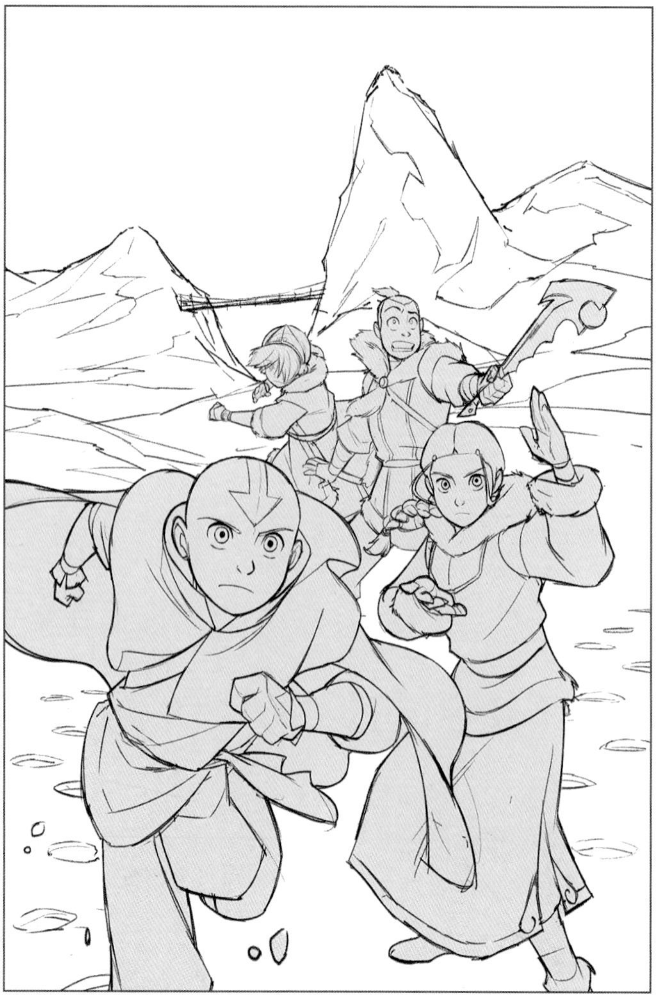

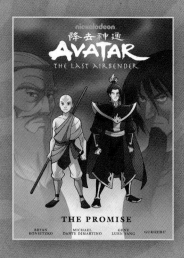

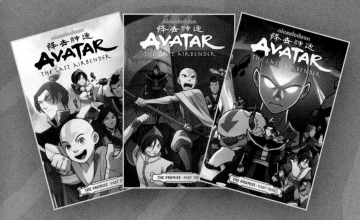

**Avatar: The Last Airbender—
The Promise Library Edition**
978-1-61655-074-5 $39.99

**Avatar: The Last Airbender—
The Promise Part 1**
978-1-59582-811-8 $12.99

**Avatar: The Last Airbender—
The Promise Part 2**
978-1-59582-875-0 $12.99

**Avatar: The Last Airbender—
The Promise Part 3**
978-1-59582-941-2 $12.99

**Avatar: The Last Airbender—
The Search Library Edition**
978-1-61655-226-8 $39.99

**Avatar: The Last Airbender—
The Search Part 1**
978-1-61655-054-7 $12.99

**Avatar: The Last Airbender—
The Search Part 2**
978-1-61655-190-2 $12.99

**Avatar: The Last Airbender—
The Search Part 3**
978-1-61655-184-1 $12.99

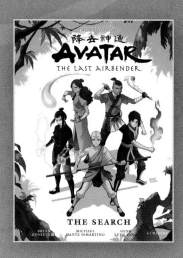

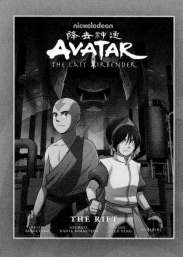

**Avatar: The Last Airbender—
The Rift Library Edition**
978-1-61655-550-4 $39.99

**Avatar: The Last Airbender—
The Rift Part 1**
978-1-61655-295-4 $12.99

**Avatar: The Last Airbender—
The Rift Part 2**
978-1-61655-296-1 $12.99

**Avatar: The Last Airbender—
The Rift Part 3**
978-1-61655-297-8 $10.99

**Avatar: The Last Airbender—
Smoke and Shadow Library
Edition**
978-1-50670-013-7 $39.99

**Avatar: The Last Airbender—
Smoke and Shadow Part 1**
978-1-61655-761-4 $12.99

**Avatar: The Last Airbender—
Smoke and Shadow Part 2**
978-1-61655-790-4 $12.99

**Avatar: The Last Airbender—
Smoke and Shadow Part 3**
978-1-61655-838-3 $12.99

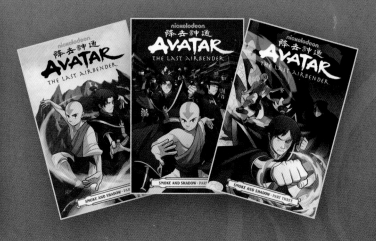

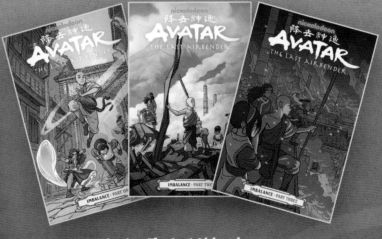